Railroads of America

THOMAS B. BREWER
General Editor

RICHARD C. OVERTON
Consulting Editor

HISTORY OF THE MISSOURI PACIFIC
by Thomas B. Brewer and Allen Dickes

HISTORY OF THE
ATCHISON, TOPEKA AND SANTA FE
by Keith Bryant

HISTORY OF THE BALTIMORE AND OHIO
by William Catton

HISTORY OF THE LOUISVILLE & NASHVILLE
by Maury Klein

HISTORY OF THE CANADIAN PACIFIC
by W. Kaye Lamb

HISTORY OF THE NORTHERN PACIFIC
by Robert L. Peterson

HISTORY OF THE CANADIAN NATIONAL
by G. R. Stevens

HISTORY OF THE ILLINOIS CENTRAL
by John F. Stover

History of the
Canadian Pacific Railway

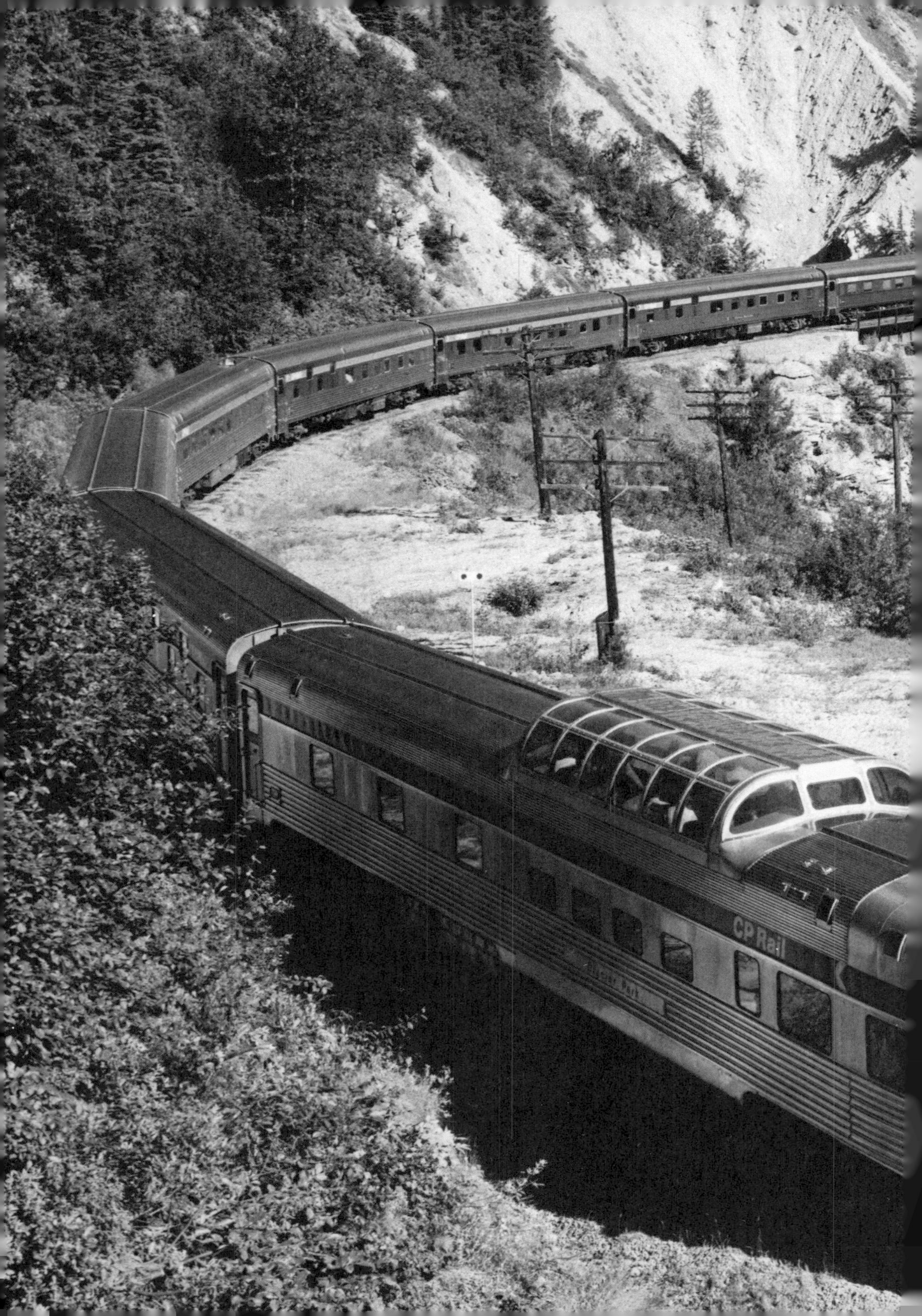
CP Rail

HISTORY OF THE CANADIAN PACIFIC RAILWAY

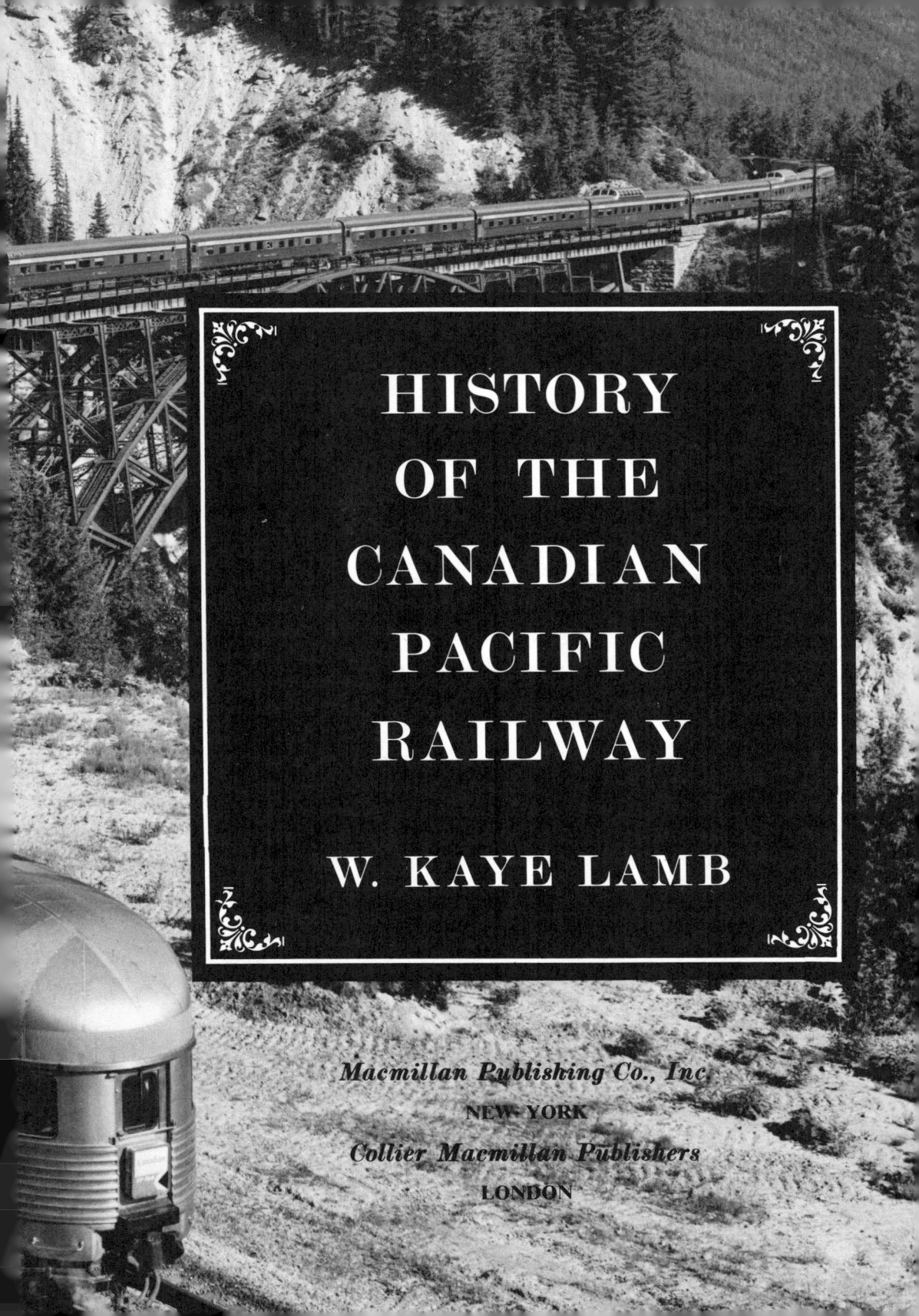

W. KAYE LAMB

Macmillan Publishing Co., Inc
NEW YORK
Collier Macmillan Publishers
LONDON

Copyright © 1977 by W. Kaye Lamb

All rights reserved. No part of this book may be reproduced or transmitted in any form or by any means, electronic or mechanical, including photocopying, recording or by any information storage and retrieval system, without permission in writing from the Publisher.

Macmillan Publishing Co., Inc.
866 Third Avenue, New York, N.Y. 10022
Collier Macmillan Canada, Ltd.

Library of Congress Cataloging in Publication Data

Lamb, William Kaye, 1904–
   History of the Canadian Pacific Railway.

   (Railroads of America)
   Bibliography: p.
   Includes index.
   1. Canadian Pacific Railway—History. I. Title.
II. Series: Railroads of America (New York)
TF27.C3L35   385'.0971   76-13593
ISBN 0-02-567660-1

First Printing 1977

Printed in the United States of America

For my wife

Contents

ILLUSTRATIONS	xiii
MAPS	xv
ACKNOWLEDGMENTS	xvii

1.
In the Beginning — 1

2.
The Pacific Scandal — 18

3.
The Tribulations of Alexander Mackenzie — 36

4.
A Vital Side Issue: The St. Paul and Pacific — 54

5.
The Main Issue: Syndicate and Contract — 64

6.
The C.P.R. Spans the Prairies — 77

7.
Conflict with the Grand Trunk: The Eastern Network — 94

8.
The Financial Crisis of 1884   104

9.
The Last Crisis and the Last Spike   116

10.
Equipping the Line   136

11.
Monopoly and Manitoba   155

12.
Expansion of the Eastern Network   165

13.
The Van Horne Years   176

14.
Van Horne versus Hill   195

15.
Land Grant Problems   214

16.
The End of Monopoly in the West   225

17.
Supremacy on Atlantic and Pacific   239

18.
The Growing Stake in Natural Resources   251

19.
The Golden Years   262

20.
The First World War   279

21.
The Specter of Nationalized Competition   288

CONTENTS

22.
Postwar Reconstruction — 300

23.
Beatty versus Thornton — 310

24.
Weathering the Depression — 328

25.
The Second World War — 345

26.
Crump and Dieselization — 360

27.
Wage Rates and Freight Rates — 376

28.
Diversification — 387

29.
On the Sea and in the Air — 401

30.
The Sixties and Seventies — 414

APPENDIX — 439

NOTES — 449

SELECTED BIBLIOGRAPHY — 467

INDEX — 477

Illustrations

NOTE: *Illustrations not otherwise credited appear through the courtesy of Canadian Pacific Limited.*

	PAGE
Sir John A. Macdonald.	9
Sir Hugh Allan.	21
Countess of Dufferin, the first locomotive in the Canadian West.	40
Sandford Fleming.	43
Alexander Mackenzie.	47
Donald A. Smith, later Lord Strathcona.	57
George Stephen, later Lord Mount Stephen.	69
Rock cut north of Lake Superior.	72
The temporary town at Rogers Pass.	120
A typical section of line in the Fraser Canyon.	123
Chinese workmen brought in by Andrew Onderdonk.	126
Troops leaving Winnipeg in April 1885.	129
Driving the last spike, November 7, 1885.	131
Construction workers driving their own last spike.	133
Snowsheds under construction in the Rockies.	138
Posters advertising the first transcontinental train.	141
Arrival of the first transcontinental train at Port Moody.	142
Arrival of the first train at Vancouver.	144
The first locomotive built by the Canadian Pacific.	147
Interior of a first-class sleeping car of 1886–90.	148
Interior of one of the first colonist cars.	150
A boiler explosion that blew a locomotive apart.	152
Empress of India, first of the famous *Empress* liners.	153

Athabasca, one of the first C.P.R. passenger ships on the Great Lakes.	162
William C. (later Sir William) Van Horne.	178
An early view of the Banff Springs Hotel.	181
The Banff Springs Hotel today.	181
Trestle replacement in progress.	184
Testing the second Stoney Creek bridge.	187
A lake and river service in British Columbia.	197
Immigrants on board the first *Empress of Britain*.	217
A first home and a first cash crop on the prairies.	220
Grain elevators along the C.P.R. line at Barons, Alberta.	221
Thomas G. Shaughnessy, later Lord Shaughnessy.	227
One of the three Atlantics built for the Montreal-Ottawa run.	229
One of the Canadian Pacific's huge fleet of ten-wheelers.	233
Lake Manitoba, largest ship of the first Atlantic fleet.	242
Canadian Pacific afloat in 1911.	243
Metagama, one of the first of the cabin-class liners.	244
Alsatian, last of the Allan Line fleet.	247
A passenger train struggling up the "Big Hill" near Field.	264
The spiral tunnels in the Rockies east of Field.	266
Winter conditions at their worst.	269
A unit grain train consisting of steel hopper cars.	273
Sicamous, last and largest of the Okanagan Lake steamers.	275
Empress of Russia in First World War camouflage.	283
Windsor Station, Montreal, headquarters of the Canadian Pacific.	284
Sir Edward Beatty.	303
One of the first of the famous Selkirk-class locomotives.	312
One of the later, streamlined Selkirks.	313
The *Trans-Canada Limited* leaving Montreal in 1929.	316
The superliner *Empress of Britain*, 42,000 tons.	317
Pier D, Vancouver, with units of the *Princess* and *Empress* fleets.	321
Canadian Pacific's remarkable multipressure No. 8000.	330
Locomotives being overhauled in Angus Shops, Montreal.	332
Locomotive No. 3100 in the Angus Shops.	335
The Hudson-class locomotive that hauled the Royal Train in 1939.	347
Locomotives and tanks mix at the Angus Shops.	349
The Northwest Staging Route to Alaska.	351
Grant McConachie.	353
One of the last locomotives built by the Canadian Pacific.	362
Norris R. Crump.	366
The *Canadian* on its inaugural run, April 24, 1955.	369

The *Canadian* dwarfed by the spectacular Rockies.	371
The *Canadian* crossing Stoney Creek bridge.	373
A piggyback train.	379
The Cominco smelter at Trail.	391
Canada Place, Montreal, a Marathon Realty project.	391
A Marathon Realty housing project in Vancouver.	393
Empress of Sydney, the aircraft that inaugurated service to Australia.	403
Empress of Asia, the first jumbo jet acquired by CP Air.	403
The Canadian Pacific's container dock at Wolfe's Cove, Quebec.	408
The third *Empress of Canada*, last of the *Empress* liners.	409
The *T. G. Shaughnessy*, giant unit of the CP (Bermuda) fleet.	409
Part of the Alyth freight classification yard at Calgary.	418
The Diesel Movement Control Center in Windsor Station, Montreal.	420
An 88-car unit train passing Columbia Lake.	420
Unloading continuous welded rail.	423
The road transport terminal at Lachine.	423
Corporate symbols of the Canadian Pacific over ninety years.	437

Maps

The bits and pieces from which the Canadian Pacific assembled the "Short Line" from Montreal to Saint John.	170
James J. Hill's invasion of southern British Columbia.	199
The Canadian Pacific system at its greatest extent, between 1933 and 1961.	315
Branch line construction in the Prairie Provinces by the Canadian Pacific and the Canadian National in the decade 1922–32.	318
CP Air Canadian and United States services.	406
CP Air International services.	407

Acknowledgments

This study could not have been prepared without the assistance of the Canadian Pacific, and I am happy to acknowledge my indebtedness to a number of the company's officials. Norris R. Crump, chairman of Canadian Pacific when work on the book began, granted me access to the invaluable letterbooks of Sir William Van Horne and Lord Shaughnessy. Mr. Crump, Keith Campbell, vice-president, and W. J. Stenason, formerly vice-president (administration) of Canadian Pacific Limited and now executive vice-president of Canadian Pacific Investments Limited, all discussed matters with me and arranged for me to have access to a number of relevant reports and papers.

I am especially indebted to Omer Lavallée, corporate archivist of Canadian Pacific Limited, and to his assistant, Denis Peters, who went to a great deal of trouble to provide me with photographs and with copies or facsimiles of rare reports and other items that otherwise would not have been available to me. In addition, Mr. Lavallée personally prepared several of the maps and diagrams that appear in this volume.

It is a pleasure to thank Mrs. William Van Horne and Lord Shaughnessy for information given to me orally and for access to correspondence and other family papers in their possession.

The staffs of the manuscript and picture divisions of the Public Archives of Canada and the British Columbia Provincial Archives were of great assistance, as was the staff of the Special Collections Division of the Library of the University of British Columbia.

Finally, I am grateful for the encouragement and helpful criticism given throughout the preparation of the book by Richard C. Overton, consulting editor of the Railroads of America series.

W. Kaye Lamb
Vancouver, British Columbia
January 1976

History of the
Canadian Pacific Railway

1

In the Beginning

The Canadian Pacific Railway was incorporated on February 16, 1881, but it fell heir to lines that were already built or building, as well as to a transcontinental project that had been talked about for a generation. Some of this prehistory, reflecting a surprising variety of motives and ambitions, is therefore an essential part of the Canadian Pacific story. It involves promoters and politicians seeking quick profits from the sale of charters, shares, and bonds; contractors looking for lucrative construction contracts; rival cities (notably Montreal and Toronto) anxious to divert tracks and traffic in their direction; railroads on both sides of the international border trying to gain control of the proposed Canadian transcontinental in order to shape it to suit their own purposes; international rivalries, when it became clear that the source from which the Canadian West was provided with transportation might well decide whether or not it would become part of the United States; and, finally, the determination of Sir John Macdonald, prime minister of Canada, to build and maintain a new nation that would extend from the Atlantic to the Pacific.

It is a far more complicated story than was implied by President Van Horne's blithe statement to a United States Senate committee in 1889 that "the Canadian Pacific was built for the purpose of making money for the share-holders and for no other purpose under the sun."[1]

Railroads were late in coming to Canada. By 1850 there were still only sixty-six miles of railway, made up of short portage and local lines, in the whole of what is now Canada. By contrast, rail mileage in the United States already exceeded 9,000. Canada's first railway boom came in the next decade, when some 2,000 miles of track were built. The line of prime importance then constructed was the Grand Trunk, which linked Montreal and Toronto in 1856. It had already absorbed lines that extended eastward from Montreal to Lévis, opposite Quebec City, and southward to Portland, Maine, the nearest ice-free Atlantic port. By 1859 it had pushed westward from Toronto to Sarnia, and a subsidiary had been built from Port Huron, across the St. Clair River from Sarnia, to Detroit, where connections were made with American lines to Chicago and other centers. Canada thus acquired a through east-west railway with connections to the American Middle West and a winter outlet on the Atlantic.

The Grand Trunk revived commercial hopes and ambitions that had long been cherished in Montreal. Both to the French and to the English who succeeded them, the St. Lawrence River and its vast system of tributary lakes seemed to be the natural and inevitable route that trade should follow between the interior of North America and the Atlantic seaboard. In the days of New France, Montreal had been the headquarters of a fur trade that extended throughout the Great Lakes area and far beyond it to the valleys of the Saskatchewan and Mississippi rivers. After the American Revolution this trade was cut off to the south, but by way of compensation the Montreal-based North West Company pushed right across the continent to the Pacific Coast. It was thus a blow to the city's trade and ambitions when, in 1821, the Hudson's Bay Company absorbed the North West Company, virtually abandoned Montreal, and shipped its supplies and furs to and from the West by its old established sea route through Hudson Bay.

When settlement spread westward, Montreal's hopes rose again. Before railroads appeared, water transportation was all-important, and Montreal expected the trade resulting from settlement to flow through the Great Lakes and their natural outlet, the St. Lawrence. Its merchants had visions of capturing the commerce, not merely of Upper Canada (the Ontario of today), but of a large part of the American Middle West as well. The Americans, on the other hand, looked upon the Hudson River and its tributary the Mohawk as their logical trade route, and as early as 1800 plans were afoot to strengthen its competitive position by building a canal that would connect the Mohawk with Lake Erie and Lake Ontario. This prompted Alexander Mackenzie, the explorer and fur trader, to warn the British government that the purpose of the project was "to make Albany what Montreal is intended by Nature to be, the Emporium of all the trade and Commerce of . . . the Great Lakes."[2] The Erie Canal duly materialized in 1825 and did in fact divert to New York much of the trade Montreal had hoped would come its way. Canada sought to counteract its effects by building a series of canals that would improve navigation on the Great Lakes and the St. Lawrence, but construction was slow and it was not until 1848 that canals with a water depth of nine feet were available all the way from Lakes Huron, Michigan, and Erie to the sea.

Unfortunately the new canals failed to live up to expectations. The rival Erie Canal, enlarged in 1851, continued to attract much more traffic than the St. Lawrence system. Even more important from the competitive point of view, Canada's preoccupation with canal building had delayed the construction of railways. Canadians were still inclined to think of them as being useful chiefly as portage lines or as feeders for waterways, and were slow to grasp the full significance of the rail network that was spreading rapidly through the American states south of the Great Lakes. Railways were becoming the major means of long-distance transportation; as someone has aptly remarked, "while the two great waterways were fighting it out, the railways ran off with the prize."

Only a railway could hope to compete with the American lines for the coveted trade of the Middle West, and thus the Grand Trunk came into being. At one time it was boldly conceived as a through line, 1,400 miles in length, extending all the way from Halifax to Sarnia and Windsor, and providing transportation between Nova Scotia and New Brunswick and Canada. In the face of various difficulties it was reduced to a 345-mile railroad between Montreal and Toronto. Even so, means to build it were lacking, and the English backers and contractors who finally launched it enlarged the project from a new point of view. They had perceived the great potential and strategic importance of Chicago, and their primary aim became a transit railway from Chicago to the ports of Montreal and Portland. Their interest in Canada was almost incidental. For the time being they were able to carry the line only as far as Detroit, and were dependent on American railways beyond that point; but the Grand Trunk clung tenaciously to its determination to reach Chicago by a track of its own, and this goal it finally achieved twenty years later.

Though built rapidly and in full operation by 1860, the Grand Trunk, like the St. Lawrence canals, failed to come up to expectations. As far as local traffic was concerned, most of its line paralleled the waterways and canals it was intended to supersede, and much less traffic moved from water to rail than had been anticipated. In competing for the export trade, it was handicapped by the inadequacies of its terminal ports. Montreal in summer and Portland in winter were no match for New York, from which cheaper and far more frequent shipping services were available to Europe and other markets overseas.

For these and other reasons, notably construction costs that had soared far above estimates, the Grand Trunk was soon in difficulties. In 1861 the London board sent Edward Watkin to Canada to see what could be done to remedy matters. Watkin had been in Canada before, and he had had considerable practical experience with railways in England. He managed to solve some of the Grand Trunk's immediate problems, but came to the conclusion that in the long run the company's best hope of prosperity lay in expansion. Eastward, he hoped to revive the original proposal to extend the main line to Halifax; but it was to the west that he saw the surest salvation. To work the Grand Trunk "so as to produce a great success in a few years" could in his opinion only be "done in one way. . . . That way . . . lies through the extension of railway communication to the Pacific."[3]

The idea was not new; the possibility of building a transcontinental railway through British North America had been discussed as early as 1834. A small library of books and pamphlets on the subject appeared during the next twenty years. Public figures began to refer to it in their speeches; thus in 1851 Joseph Howe, the most prominent politician in Nova Scotia, made his often-quoted prophecy that "many in this room will live to hear the whistle of the steam-engine in the passes of the Rocky Mountains and to make the journey from Halifax to the Pacific in five or six days."[4]

Both political and physical obstacles would have to be overcome before a railway could span British North America. Canada at that time consisted only of the southern parts of the present provinces of Ontario and Quebec; the prairie region to the west was under the control of the Hudson's Bay Company. Most of it was included in Rupert's Land, the vast domain granted to the company under its original charter in 1670; in the rest it held exclusive trading rights. The whole constituted an enormous game preserve kept in isolation for the benefit of the fur trade. No railway could cross it until the rights of the Hudson's Bay Company had been curtailed, if not canceled.

To this political problem there was added a formidable geological obstruction. Any line leading to the western plains by an all-British route would have to pass north of Lake Superior, and in so doing would have to force its way through the Laurentian Shield, which interposed a thousand miles of rocky wilderness between Canada and the prairies. It was this wilderness (which had no counterpart in the United States) that had enabled the fur traders to keep their preserve isolated. In the days of the North West Company canoe brigades had threaded their way regularly along its rivers and through its lakes from Montreal to the western posts, but, as already noted, the supplies and furs of the Hudson's Bay Company entered and left by Hudson Bay. Travel between Canada and the prairies had virtually ceased for a generation.

In spite of this, by the 1850s Canadians were becoming much concerned about the West and its future. This concern was felt chiefly in Upper Canada, and centered in Toronto, where George Brown, editor of the *Globe*, the most influential journal of the day, became its vigorous spokesman. The last good land in Upper Canada had been taken up about 1855. The expansion of settlement farther westward was blocked by the same thousand miles of barren and rocky country that troubled the railway planners. As a result, young people and immigrants alike were leaving Canada in large numbers to seek land in the Middle West of the United States. In the decade 1861–71 two people left Canada for every one that entered it. Brown and others contended that the only way to check this population drain was for Canada to acquire the Hudson's Bay Company's territory. "It is ours," the *Globe* declared, "and it is our duty to open it to civilization."[5]

The company's trading rights would expire in 1859, and in 1857 the British Parliament set up a committee of enquiry to consider their renewal, and, incidentally, the future of the territory. There would be little hope of diverting would-be settlers from the United States unless easy means of access to the West were available; therefore the matter of a railway naturally arose. Several witnesses expressed the opinion that a line could be built, and somewhat diffidently, W. H. Draper, chief justice of Upper Canada and spokesman for the Canadian government, echoed the faith expressed by Joseph Howe: "I hope you will not laugh at me as very visionary, but I hope to see the time, or that my children may live to see the time when there is a railway going all across that country and ending at the Pacific; and so far as individual opinion goes, I entertain no doubt that the time will arrive when that will be accomplished."[6]

The enquiry revealed how little was really known about the West, and even as Draper spoke, a British expedition led by Captain John Palliser was beginning the first exploration of the Canadian prairies and the Rocky Mountains made for purposes other than the fur trade. Its aim was to ascertain the general character of the country and to gauge its suitability for settlement. About the possibility of building a transcontinental railway entirely in British territory Palliser was discouraging. In his view the Laurentian Shield formed an insuperable obstacle and the choice of the 49th parallel as the international boundary made it impossible to bypass it to the south. Geography dictated that the natural point of entry to the prairie region was through the United States, by way of St. Paul and the Red River, and he expected a railway to follow that route.

Neither of the colonial secretaries to whom Palliser reported—Sir Edward Bulwer-Lytton and the Duke of Newcastle—relished the prospect of making an American railroad the chief means of access to the interior of

British North America. Here arose the clash between economics and politics that was later to characterize the planning and construction of the Canadian Pacific. It was undeniable that a railway from Canada to Red River, north of Lake Superior, would run through hundreds of miles of country that promised to be completely unproductive of local traffic, and that the cost of construction would be frightening. Lieutenant Colonel Lefroy of the Royal Artillery, who had spent years in Canada and was one of the few people who had some acquaintance with the Lake Superior country, had told the parliamentary committee investigating the Hudson's Bay Company that the "physical difficulties" involved in building a railway there would be "enormously great"—so great that he and many practical railroad men felt that the costs of construction and operation would make the financial success of an all-British line impossible.

This confirmed a view already widely held. In 1854, alarmed by a number of railway projects that promised to attract traffic to the rival city of Toronto, a Montreal group headed by the Hon. A. N. Morin had petitioned Parliament for an act incorporating a Northern Pacific railway company. Its line was to have extended from Portland and Montreal to the Pacific, but it would have made a long detour south of Lake Superior, through the United States. It would thus have been in effect an international line—a plan that was to be revived repeatedly in various guises during the next thirty years.

Edward Watkin, who became president of the Grand Trunk in 1862, was one of those who endorsed the scheme. He could do so very happily because it coincided neatly with the ambition of the Grand Trunk to reach Chicago, the rising center of the railway's main target area, the American Middle West. Spelling out his plan in 1863, he contended that the best route for a transcontinental from Nova Scotia to British Columbia would be a line from Halifax to Quebec, "then to follow the Grand Trunk system to Sarnia; to extend that system to Chicago; to use, under a treaty of neutralization, the United States lines from Chicago to St. Paul; to build a line from St. Paul to Fort Garry (Winnipeg) by English and American capital, and then to extend the line to the Tête Jaune [Yellowhead] Pass, there to meet a Railway through British Columbia starting from the Pacific."[7] To this view the Grand Trunk was to cling for forty years, with the result that it could have no part in the Canadian Pacific and was shut out of western Canada until it launched its disastrous Grand Trunk Pacific project after the turn of the century.

Shortly before Watkin outlined his proposal, a contrary view had been expressed. In 1857, the same year Palliser began his explorations, the government of Canada had sent an expedition of its own to examine the Lake Superior country and determine the best route for communication with Red River and the prairies. One of the leaders was Henry Youle Hind, a geologist of some note. He was much less pessimistic than Palliser about the possibility of railway construction through the Laurentian Shield and in 1862 published a pamphlet entitled *A Sketch of an Overland Route to British Columbia.* Today its chief interest lies in an appendix entitled "Practical Observations on the Construction of a continuous line of Railway from Canada to the Pacific Ocean on British Territory." This was contributed by Sandford Fleming, a Scot, who was to have much to do with planning the Canadian Pacific and who was to be one of its directors for the last thirty years of his long life. Fleming had a wide-ranging imagination and great perseverance, and over the years he was to see several projects dear to his heart carried to completion, including the Pacific railway, the establishment of a system of standard time, and the laying of a cable between Canada and Australia. He had been chief engineer of the Northern Railway of Canada for five years, and in 1858 had already published a pamphlet called *A Railway to the Pacific through British Territory.* His "Practical Observations" outlined in remarkable detail the steps by which he thought it could be brought into being. He was confident that a line could be built through the difficult country north of Lake Superior, but building costs and lack of traffic made immediate construction impracticable. He proposed that the initial step should be the building of "territorial roads," carefully routed and graded so that they could "in the course of time be converted, stage by stage, into railways" as settlement increased and traffic developed. Fleming, who was rarely in a hurry, expected the wait for a completed railway to be a long one; he seems to have had twenty years or more in mind. As it turned out, he was to be present at the driving of the last spike in the Canadian Pacific main line just twenty-three years later. Nor was his estimate of the cost of the line—$100 million—very wide of the mark.

Fleming was not dismissed as a visionary; he was already winning recognition as a highly competent railway engineer. Only a year after his "Practical Observations" was published, the government of Canada placed him in charge of the location surveys for the intercolonial railway that was to link Canada with New Brunswick and Nova Scotia, and only nine years later he would be appointed engineer in chief of the Pacific railway surveys.

These developments were the result of heightened anxiety regarding the future of the West and a realization that the scattered British colonies must get together if they were to survive. Uneasiness over the expansion of the United States, and the doctrine of Manifest Destiny to which it gave rise, had increased sharply. Texas, the whole of the Southwest, and Oregon had been added to the union relatively recently, and it was feared that American settlers would sweep north from Minnesota and engulf the Hudson's Bay territories. The British colonies were broken into three parts—the three maritime colonies on the eastern seaboard, the United Province of Canada in the St. Lawrence valley and north of the Great Lakes, and, far to the west, isolated on the Pacific Coast, the gold rush colony of British Columbia, huge in size but very small in population. All had much closer trading relations and much easier communications with the American states to the south of them than they had with one another.

Anxiety regarding the intentions of the United States increased during the Civil War, when the *Trent* incident and the depredations of the *Alabama* strained relations with Great Britain. As the war ended, some feared that the huge Northern army, having conquered the South, might next march northward. Thomas D'Arcy McGee, one of the strongest advocates of a union of the colonies, expressed an extreme view in a speech in 1865: "The acquisition of Canada was the first ambition of the American Confederacy, and never ceased to be so, when her troops were a handful and her navy scarce a squadron. Is it likely to be stopped now, when she counts her guns afloat by thousands and her troops by hundreds of thousands?"[8] That same year Congress gave notice of the abrogation of the reciprocal trade treaty that had been in effect between the United States and the British colonies since 1854. A strong economic motive was thereby added to the movement for confederation, since the colonies hoped that freer trade with one another would help compensate for the loss of American markets that soon would be closed to them.

The first definite steps toward union were taken by the maritime colonies, who called a conference at Charlottetown in 1864 to consider proposals that concerned themselves alone. This offered an opportunity that was seized upon by John A. Macdonald, leader of the confederation movement in Canada. Macdonald had a far wider union in mind, which he hoped would first embrace the maritime colonies and Canada, and would later include the Hudson's Bay territories and British Columbia. In short, he envisaged the Canada of today. To promote it he appeared in Charlottetown at the head of an uninvited Canadian delegation and succeeded in persuading the conference to consider the larger scheme. Details were hammered out at a second conference, held at Quebec later in 1864, and the British North America Act, passed by the British Parliament in 1867, brought the Dominion of Canada into being. It consisted at first only of Nova Scotia, New Brunswick, and the new provinces of Quebec and Ontario, into which the old United Province was divided, but the act provided for the later admission of Newfoundland, Prince Edward Island, the western territories, and British Columbia.

All concerned were well aware that a political union without easy and rapid communication would be largely pointless and almost certainly tem-

Sir John A. Macdonald, prime minister of Canada from 1867 to 1873 and from 1878 until his death in 1891. He deserves to rank as the most determined advocate of a Canadian transcontinental railway. This photograph was taken in 1883, when Macdonald was sixty-eight and construction of the Canadian Pacific was nearing the halfway mark. (COURTESY OF THE PUBLIC ARCHIVES OF CANADA)

porary. Indeed, Nova Scotia and New Brunswick would not have joined if specific provision had not been made for the building of a railway to connect existing lines in the maritimes with the Grand Trunk. Work was to begin within six months and was to continue "without intermission" thereafter.

Macdonald (now Sir John) lost no time in taking steps to add Rupert's Land, the territory of the Hudson's Bay Company, to the new dominion. Watkin, with his aspirations for the Grand Trunk in view, had helped prepare the way in 1863 by promoting the sale of the old Hudson's Bay Company to new proprietors who were willing to part with its ancient rights providing the price was right. Macdonald's negotiations, which involved both the new company and the British government, were concluded successfully in 1869. Under the terms of a deed of surrender the company, in return for a cash payment and generous land allotments, gave up its trading monopoly and proprietary rights in Rupert's Land, ownership of which was then conveyed to Canada by the imperial government.

Unfortunately the actual transfer of control of the territory was badly mishandled. In most of the vast area, the only inhabitants were fur traders and Indians, but there was one highly significant exception, the importance of which was not appreciated by Macdonald and his advisers. A substantial settlement with a population of about 11,000, consisting largely of Métis of mixed French and Indian blood, had grown up around Fort Garry (Winnipeg) in the Red River Valley. No one took steps to see that these people were properly informed of what was intended, and the sudden appearance of land surveyors, who seemed to be running their lines without any regard to the holdings of the Métis, alarmed them thoroughly. Led by Louis Riel, they seized Fort Garry and set up a provisional government. Their purpose was not rebellion, but simply resistance to a takeover by Canada that did not take their rights and properties into proper account. These matters were dealt with in due course, but in March 1870, just as Riel was achieving his objectives, and within a few months of the creation of the new province of Manitoba, his provisional government committed an incredible blunder by executing Thomas Scott, a defiant and troublesome young man from Ontario who had been imprisoned in Fort Garry. As a result, Riel was soon a fugitive, and it was considered prudent to send a military expedition to Red River to make it clear to all that Canada had taken possession of Rupert's Land. Because a military force could not travel through the United States, the troops had to struggle over the so-called Dawson Route, a makeshift combination of lakes, portages, and primitive roads between Lake Superior and Fort Garry, which had been opened to travel in 1858. It was fortunate they were not hurrying into battle, for it took them nearly three months to cover the 450 miles, and their journey demonstrated in a dramatic way how difficult it was to reach the prairies directly from Ontario.

As Palliser had pointed out, much the quickest and easiest way to approach Fort Garry was via the American railroads and St. Paul. A brisk trade had in fact grown up between St. Paul and the Red River settlement. This had begun largely because the Hudson's Bay Company was losing control of the colony. The company was admirably equipped by long experience to operate trading posts; to govern a substantial settled population that was growing rapidly and becoming increasingly restive under the restraints imposed by a trading monopoly was quite another matter. The settlers, seeking alternative markets where they could sell their furs at higher prices and purchase goods more cheaply than they could at Fort Garry, found them south of the border. It became more and more difficult to enforce the monopoly, and travel and trade increased steadily. Even the Hudson's Bay Company itself was forced to acknowledge the advantages of the St. Paul connection. With the advent of railways in the American West it became cheaper as well as very much quicker to import supplies by way of the United States rather than by the traditional Hudson Bay route, and as early as 1858 the company brought in a first shipment of goods by way of the Grand Trunk Railway, connecting American lines, and St. Paul.

Morin and Watkin were not alone in thinking that a transcontinental railway to serve Canada should be an international enterprise. The same idea soon took firm root in the United States. In 1864 Congress granted a charter to the Northern Pacific Railroad (a company entirely distinct from Morin's proposal of 1854) and authorized it to build from Lake Superior to Puget Sound. Duluth and Tacoma were later chosen as its terminals. The first group that controlled the Northern Pacific consisted mostly of New Englanders, and J. Gregory Smith, the president, was also president of the Central Vermont Railroad. He planned to link the Central Vermont to the Montreal-Detroit line of the Grand Trunk, and then seek connections between Detroit and the Northern Pacific at Duluth. Later the thought of using the Grand Trunk was abandoned, and a new Canadian link was envisaged that would run from Montreal to Sault Ste. Marie by way of the Ottawa Valley and Lake Nipissing —a line that would have followed part of the future route of the Canadian Pacific. A link from the Sault to Duluth would have completed the connection with the Northern Pacific.

Farther west the Northern Pacific had complementary ambitions. At the close of the Civil War, a movement to secure the annexation of western Canada sprang up in the United States. Feeling was particularly strong in Minnesota, and this meshed neatly with the Northern Pacific's aspirations. Its promoters hoped to block the construction of a Canadian transcontinental by preempting its field and diverting the commerce of the West to the United States. This they hoped to accomplish either by extending their railway to Fort Garry, and from there building west through British territory, or by placing their main line so close to the Canadian boundary that a series of short feeder lines, sprouting northward, could drain traffic to it.

Their motives were political as well as economic. Both railroaders and politicians were confident that transportation could determine the future of western Canada. If an American railway could penetrate quickly, they felt that annexation would follow. Conversely, if Canada succeeded in building a transcontinental line, prospects for annexation would be much poorer. Speed was therefore of the essence. In 1868, when Sir John Macdonald was opening negotiations for the acquisition of Rupert's Land, the essential preliminary to railroad building, the Northern Pacific issued a statement in which the urgency of the matter was stressed quite frankly: "Already the project of constructing a Pacific Railroad on British soil, north of our border, is a matter of serious consideration. . . . The construction of such a road would . . . preclude the idea of political relations between that people and our own."[9] The same view was echoed early in 1869 in a United States Senate *Report on Pacific Railroads*. "The opening by us first of a North Pacific Railroad," it declared, "seals the destiny of the British possessions west of the 91st meridian. They will become so Americanized in interests and feelings that they will be in effect severed from the new Dominion and the question of their annexation will be but a question of time."[10]

For the Northern Pacific, 1869 was a year full of promise. Although it had been given a large land grant, it had received no cash subsidy and had been unable to raise funds for construction. In 1869 Congress at last gave it authority to issue first mortgage bonds and thus cleared the way for the financing of the line. Later in the year Jay Cooke, the Philadelphia financier who had sold vast quantities of bonds for the United States government during the Civil War, agreed to become the Northern Pacific's financial agent and to promote the sale of its securities.

The political omens seemed equally propitious. General U. S. Grant was in the White House and Hamilton Fish was secretary of state; both were strongly in favor of annexation, though they were not prepared to go so far as to risk war with Great Britain to attain it. The resistance led by Riel seemed to indicate that the Red River people would not be averse to severing their new link with Canada. Finally, Jay Cooke himself looked forward to the acquisition of the Canadian West. Early in 1870 he would inform a correspondent in Red River that he was confident that annexation could be brought about "as a result of quiet emigration over the border of trustworthy men with families." He added, in words that recalled those of George Brown, "The country belongs to us naturally, and should be brought over without violence or bloodshed."[11]

Sir John Macdonald was aware of these developments, but they were brought home to him with special emphasis in January 1870, when he received a disturbing letter from C. J. Brydges, general manager of the Grand Trunk Railway. Brydges had just had a long talk with Gregory Smith, president of the Northern Pacific, and he explained to Macdonald, among other things, that that company hoped to locate its western lines "so near the boundary that drop lines into the [Hudson's Bay] territory may be constructed, and thus injure, if not prevent, the construction of an independent line in British territory." And he warned Macdonald that he was "quite satisfied . . . that there is some political action at the bottom of this, and that the United States Government . . . are anxious to take advantage of the organization of this Northern Pacific Railway to prevent your getting control for Canada of the Hudson's Bay Territory."[12]

Undoubtedly this letter convinced Macdonald that counteraction had to be taken with a minimum of delay. In a prompt reply to Brydges he showed that he was fully aware of the dangers involved: "It is quite evident to me not only from this conversation, but from advices from Washington, that the United States Government are resolved to do all they can short of war to get possession of the western territory, and we must take immediate and vigorous steps to counteract them. One of the first things to be done is to show unmistakably our resolve to build a Pacific Railway." The project would have to be undertaken by private enterprise, and Macdonald suggested that Brydges should take the lead. "The thing must not be allowed to sleep, and I want you to address yourself to it at once and work out a plan."[13]

Macdonald was already busy with a second essential preliminary—the extension of Canada from the Rocky Mountains to the Pacific. The military expedition to Red River was making its laborious way from Lake Superior to Fort Garry when a delegation of three arrived in Ottawa in June 1870 to negotiate the terms under which British Columbia would join Confederation. It was headed by J. W. Trutch, a civil engineer and the colony's chief commissioner of lands and works; the other members were Dr. J. S. Helmcken and W. W. (later Senator) Carrall. All three had been prominent in local politics. Macdonald had been critically ill since early in May, and his place as chief federal negotiator was taken by Sir George Etienne Cartier. He and Macdonald had headed the government of the United Province in 1858–62, and although the system of joint premiers, one English and one French, had been abandoned in 1867, he was still one of Macdonald's closest and most trusted associates.

It has often been said that British Columbia asked for a road to Red River and instead had a railroad thrust upon her. This is true in a sense, but nevertheless misrepresents the facts, for British Columbia was just as determined as the Maritime Provinces had been to have provision for a railway included in the terms of union. The lengthy debate that took place in the Legislative Council of British Columbia before the delegates left for Ottawa shows this clearly. In this discussion Helmcken was a key figure, and in the course of it he summed up the railway question in four short sentences: "This Colony would be just as much isolated as ever after a paper union, without a Railway as one of the conditions." "I consider this an essential condition. Without it Confederation must not take place." "We should be better off without Canada if we have no Railway."[14]

Privately, Helmcken was inclined to think that annexation was probably inevitable, especially since the purchase of Alaska in 1867. (Years later he recalled in his reminiscences that the Americans "boasted they had sandwiched British Columbia and could eat her up at any time!") He also had honest doubts about the practicability of building a railway through the mountains. Another legislative councillor doubted Canada's ability to finance a railway. "I consider the Railway the primary and essential condition of Confederation," he said, "and I think that Canada is too poor to guarantee such a work as this."[15] The British government, he suggested, should be asked to back the scheme in some way.

This and other remarks showed that the councillors realized that they were asking for something that would far exceed the Intercolonial Railway in scale and cost. Presumably it would also take much longer to build, and for this reason they asked for a road as a stopgap measure. These views were embodied in the railway clause of the draft terms of union that emerged from the debate: "Inasmuch as no real Union can subsist between this Colony and Canada without the speedy establishment of communication across the Rocky Mountains by Coach Road and Railway, the Dominion shall, within three years from the date of Union, construct and open for traffic such Coach Road . . . and shall further engage to use all means in her power to complete such Railway communication at the earliest practicable date. . . ."[16]

Helmcken's doubts as to whether the line could be built were cleared up on the way to Ottawa. "The journey from San Francisco by Railway opened our eyes not a little," he wrote later, "for a Railway had been built through a mountainous country quite as bad as that of British Columbia—if this one could be built so could one through British Columbia."[17] And to their surprise, the delegates found that Cartier and the cabinet committee with whom they negotiated had already made up their minds about the railway. In his diary Helmcken records that they "were enthusiastically in favour thereof. They do not consider that they can hold the country without it. It was a condition of union with the [Maritime] provinces and they could not see any reason why if agreed upon it should not be made a condition with us. They agreed that a railway was necessary to Red River, ours or that of B.C. would only be an extension of the Railway from Red River."[18] The proposal to build a wagon road was dropped; construction of the railway would make it unnecessary, and in any event travel over it would have been extremely slow at best and virtually impossible in winter.

The clause in the final terms of union relating to the railway read as follows: "The Government of the Dominion undertake to secure the commencement simultaneously, within two years from the date of the Union, of the construction of a Railway from the Pacific towards the Rocky Mountains, and from such point as may be selected, east of the Rocky Mountains, towards the Pacific, to connect the seaboard of British Columbia with the railway system of Canada, and further, to secure the completion of such Railway within ten years from the date of the Union."

To agree to the terms of union was one thing; to gain their approval by the Parliament of Canada was quite another. Macdonald and Cartier had no illusions about the struggle that lay ahead of them.

From the beginning, railways and politics in Canada had been inextricably intertwined. The power to grant railway charters rested with the various legislative assemblies, and assemblymen saw no impropriety in being associated with projected railways as directors, promoters, officials, and even as contractors. Sir Allan MacNab, joint premier of Canada in the middle 1850s, once remarked frankly, "Railways are my politics." He was president of the Great Western Railway and associated with half a dozen other lines over a period of twenty years. John Ross, first president of the Grand Trunk, was at the same time president of the Executive Council of United Canada; six of its first directors were members of Parliament. Cartier himself was for years solicitor for the Grand Trunk Railway.

To the rivalries, hopes, and fears aroused by any important railway proposal, there was added in 1871 a peculiar political situation, an aftermath of the struggle to bring about Confederation. The issue had cut across group and party lines; in each of the uniting provinces Confederation had been carried by a coalition government. In Canada, the coalition had consisted of Conservatives, led by Macdonald and Cartier, and Liberals headed by George Brown, an ardent reformer and editor of the influential Toronto *Globe*. Brown's support went far to bring about Confederation, but he had a deep antipathy for Macdonald personally and dropped out of the government as soon as union was assured. Macdonald, heading a Liberal-Conservative party, won the first Dominion election in 1867, but he was well aware that party lines were not yet drawn with any great firmness. The coalition had been based on the Confederation issue; now that it was settled, some members began to drift back to their old allegiances. George Brown helped to muster a Liberal party that became the official opposition in the new House of Commons. Though defeated himself in the 1867 election, thanks to the *Globe* he continued to be a powerful political figure. In the Commons the leading Liberals were two sharply contrasted figures, Alexander Mackenzie and Edward Blake. Mackenzie was a Scot who had started life as a stonemason, and had made his way in Canada both as a contractor and as a journalist; Blake, Canadian-born, was an immensely able lawyer, an impressive speaker, and a redoubtable adversary in debate. In combination, and in view of the uncertainty of party lines in the House, Mackenzie, Blake, and the *Globe* constituted a formidable opposition that was to level its guns at the Pacific railway for a decade.

It has been said that Macdonald's motive in sponsoring the railway was primarily political; that Confederation having been achieved, he seized upon it as a substitute major issue that promised to keep him and his supporters in power. Certainly he was aware of this aspect of the matter, but just as certainly it was not the basic consideration with him. Macdonald was one of the very few who had grasped the magnitude of the extraordinary opportunity offered suddenly to Canada in the 1860s—nothing less than the chance to secure control of half the continent of North America. To strengthen that control, as yet extremely tenuous west of Ontario, a railway was essential. It would bring British Columbia into the new union, would throw an unmistakable mark of ownership across the West, and would provide the means of settling and fully possessing it. And in view of the strength of annexationist sentiment in the United States, delay would be perilous. Cartier's promise to complete the railway within ten years, soon to be vehemently attacked as imprudent and impossible of fulfilment, gave notice of an intention to press forward with the project with the least possible delay and was a measure of the great urgency attached to its construction.[19]

The debate on the admission of British Columbia took place in March and April of 1871. The railway clause of the terms of union quickly became the chief target of the opposition. Outside Parliament the *Globe* thundered against it; in the Commons Blake denounced it as a "preposterous proposition" that would be fatal to Confederation.[20] Mackenzie pointed out that information needed to form a sound opinion was lacking; no route had been surveyed, nor had the cost of the line, which Blake believed would be ruinous, yet been calculated. He was willing to see surveys undertaken, but construction should go ahead only "at as early a period as the state of [the country's] finances" would justify. In his view, "a cheap narrow gauge railway with steamers on the smaller lakes" would meet the needs of the prairies for years to come.[21]

Not all Macdonald's own followers could be counted upon to support the railway clause. Few of the members from Nova Scotia and New Brunswick, which would derive little direct benefit from a Pacific railway, were enthusiastic, and some from Ontario wavered. Trutch, who was in Ottawa when the debate took place, described in a letter to Helmcken the final crisis that developed within the Conservative caucus:

The main point of attack by the Opposition was the Railroad engagement and they so worked this up that ruin and bankruptcy were made to appear the inevitable result of the admission of B.C. on the proposed terms, and so frightened were many of the ordinary Ontario supporters of Govt. that there appeared almost a certainty the day before the vote was taken that there would be a majority against the address. Some of the Cabinet urged that the Railway clause should be amended so as to read "within ten years if the financial ability of the Dominion would permit," or some words to that effect. To this of course I protested on behalf of B.C. whilst assuring them that of course we so understood the Engagement and were not likely to insist on ruining them and ourselves together by insisting on the literal fulfilment of the bargain in the sense the Opposition had construed it in.

Trutch credited Cartier, who in Macdonald's absence through illness had made the agreement with the delegates from British Columbia, with the final rallying of the government's supporters. If it had not been for his "pluck and determination," Trutch was convinced that "they would have given in, the measure would have been defeated and the Government broken up." To secure "fulfillment of the treaty he had made," Cartier declared that he would dissolve the House if need be, but "the Union with B.C. on the terms arranged should be carried and he would see it done."[22]

And done it was, but with overtones that were to echo through the years to come. The debate had been bitter and partisan—so bitter and so partisan that any calm and objective consideration of the merits of the case had been impossible. The Conservatives would admit to no fault in the railway proposal; the Liberals could see no merits. The Pacific railway thus became firmly identified with the Conservative party, a relationship that was to bring both advantages and disadvantages over a long period. A decade later, when the House of Commons debated the bill that granted a charter to the Canadian Pacific Railway and approved the contract for the construction of the line, the same bitter and partisan approach would mark the discussion.

In the end the government had been compelled to qualify in some degree the requirement that the railway must be completed within ten years. Mackenzie and Blake were able to exact an undertaking that construction must not entail any increase in taxation. A banquet was held in Ottawa at which Trutch repeated in public the assurances he had given the government caucus in private, that completion within a reasonable time would be satisfactory to British Columbia. In Parliament Cartier remarked that "no one could be compelled to perform an impossibility," if such it proved to be.[23] These qualifications of the time pledge were not welcomed in B.C., and delays in construction were to cause serious difficulties there.

But these, after all, were details. Macdonald and Cartier, utterly convinced that a transcontinental railway was essential to Canada's survival and future, had succeeded in committing the country to its construction.

2

The Pacific Scandal

So alluring a project as the building of a Canadian transcontinental railway naturally attracted promoters. Petitions for charters began to come in as early as 1869, but none was approved by Parliament. In the past, railway charters had been granted with rather gay abandon, and some had brought their sponsors handsome profits when they had had to be bought up to make way for larger projects. Thus the Grand Trunk had found that virtually the whole of its route had been preempted by earlier charters, and these had to be cleared away at considerable expense. Thanks to the government's refusal to act upon any of the early applications received, the main line of the Pacific railway encountered no such obstacles.

No one was more interested in the Pacific railway than Alfred Waddington, who had drafted a petition but realized that it was too early to submit it. Waddington deserves a small niche in the history of the C.P.R., both on his own account and because he helped unwittingly to set in motion the chain of events involving Sir Hugh Allan that resulted in the famous Pacific Scandal and very nearly ended the political career of Sir John Macdonald. Member of a well-known Anglo-French family (his nephew was prime minister of France), he had been attracted first to California and then to British Columbia by the gold discoveries. Transportation caught his interest in 1861, when rich new diggings in the Cariboo caused much excitement. The mines lay far inland, and the only way to get to them was through the formidable canyons of the Fraser River. Waddington believed they could be reached much more easily by traveling overland from the head of one of the inlets along the coast. His choice fell on Bute Inlet, and in the next several years he spent his personal fortune in an attempt to build a road from the inlet to the Cariboo. Trouble with the Indians finally forced him to abandon the project in 1864.

Before long outside events caused him to revise and greatly extend his plans and to think in terms of a railroad instead of the road he first had had in mind. Confederation, and the prospect that Rupert's Land and British Columbia would soon be included in it, made some means of east-west communication essential; in addition, Waddington feared that the railway being built overland through the United States to California would cost Britain much of her trade with the Orient unless it were countered by an all-British line across Canada. Remaining faithful to Bute Inlet, he proposed that the railway should run eastward from the inlet to the Yellowhead Pass and thence to Edmonton and Red River. Waddington pressed his proposals with considerable vigor, and his pamphlets, speeches, and newspaper articles did much to create interest in a Pacific railway. He knew more about the route he had in mind than anyone else, and his data relating to it were later purchased by the government on the recommendation of Sandford Fleming, the engineer in charge of railway surveys.

Waddington saw Sir John Macdonald in December 1870, but, as he no doubt expected, Macdonald told him that nothing could be done until the terms of union with British Columbia were approved by Parliament. For him and for most would-be Pacific railway promoters, 1870 was of necessity a year of waiting. Only one important point was settled—the location of the railway's eastern terminus. Montreal was the obvious and inevitable choice, but the susceptibilities of Toronto had to be taken into account. Private discussions between the governments of Canada and Ontario resulted in the selection of Callander (now Bonfield),[1] near the eastern end of Lake Nipissing. It was only a spot in the wilds, of no consequence whatever in itself, but it had the great merit of being near the point at which the Pacific railway could be expected to split into two lines, one leading to Montreal and the other to Toronto. In effect it thus dodged the touchy terminus issue. "We have been obliged to place the terminus far from your city," Cartier explained to a Montrealer, "and also from Toronto for political reasons on account of the [rival] ambition of Toronto and Montreal."[2]

There were significant developments in the new province of Manitoba. In September 1870, the Hon. Adams G. Archibald, the first lieutenant-governor, arrived in Winnipeg. A capable Nova Scotian, he calmed the aftermath of the Riel troubles and established civil institutions. The same month, James W. Taylor took up his duties as American consul in Winnipeg. A journalist by profession and a propagandist by temperament, Taylor had spent many years in St. Paul, where he had become an ardent annexationist, convinced that a railway to Winnipeg would help greatly to bring western Canada into the American fold. He had made the economic and political affairs of Minnesota and Manitoba his special study; Hamilton Fish, the American secretary of state, had employed him as a confidential investigator at the time of the Riel resistance, and the Northern Pacific subsidized him to promote its interests.

Archibald learned quickly that the thing Manitobans most desired was a rail connection with the outside world. While not unmindful of the importance of an all-Canadian line to the West, he regarded this as a distant prospect. Taylor had no difficulty in persuading him that a short, sixty-five-mile railway southward to the border, which could link Winnipeg with an American railroad, was a much more immediate possibility. And this American connection promised soon to be a reality. Work had begun on the Northern Pacific; Duluth and Tacoma had been chosen as its terminals; advances and bond sales by Jay Cooke were financing construction. As early as November, Taylor could report with obvious satisfaction that when referring to the proposed all-Canadian route, Archibald had made a "very emphatic" declaration "that the interests of his community must not remain isolated, for the sake of such a scheme. . . ."[3]

The Northern Pacific was most anxious to oblige by building a branch north to Manitoba, but found itself handicapped by the existence of a local railroad, the St. Paul and Pacific, which had a charter empowering it to build from St. Paul to the international border. This line had been built only as far as St. Cloud, about seventy miles from St. Paul, and there seemed little likelihood that the company would be able to extend it much farther in the near future. In December 1870, the Northern Pacific solved—or believed it had solved—this problem by gaining control of the St. Paul and Pacific. Only two months later Taylor, on behalf of Jay Cooke, was able to assure Archibald that the Northern Pacific itself would reach the Red River by August of 1871, and that the St. Paul and Pacific line to the border would be placed under contract within two years at the most. Meanwhile the Manitoba legislature, eager to promote this southern link, had passed a Taylor-inspired act that gave the lieutenant-governor authority to permit "any sufficient company" to build railways in the province—a measure Taylor hoped would clear the way for the extension of the St. Paul and Pacific to Winnipeg.

A few days before Taylor had given Cooke's assurances to Archibald, a new major figure strode onto the Pacific railway scene. On February 1, 1871, Sir Hugh Allan telegraphed to Sir John Macdonald inquiring what the government proposed to do about the formation of a company to build the road. A commanding, bewhiskered Victorian entrepreneur, Allan was probably the

Sir Hugh Allan, shipowner, financier, and industrialist, from a photograph taken not long after his maneuverings to secure the charter for the Canadian Pacific had resulted in the Pacific Scandal. (COURTESY OF THE PUBLIC ARCHIVES OF CANADA)

richest man in Canada. Best known to the public as head of the Allan Line, the leading steamship service of the day between Canada and Great Britain, he also had a great variety of other business interests, including banking, insurance, textiles, coal, and the major Canadian telegraph company. Recently he had become interested in the Northern Colonization Railway. This line was conceived originally merely as a means of bringing wood fuel cheaply to Montreal, but Allan saw that it might be made a vital link in the proposed Canadian transcontinental. It was already assumed that the line from the West would connect in the vicinity of Lake Nipissing with the Canada Central

Railway, whose charter empowered it to build from the lake to Ottawa. Allan planned to make his Colonization Railway the link between Ottawa and Montreal. "I saw at once," he later told a Royal Commission, "that if the Pacific Railway was built, the Northern Colonization Railway would become a necessity. Montreal especially could not do without . . . a direct connection with the Pacific." The Colonization Railway would carry "all the trade which the Pacific Road might bring across the continent for shipping by sea"[4]—most of it, he hoped, in Allan-owned ships.

Although from Macdonald's point of view Allan's wealth and position in the business world made him an ideal choice to head a syndicate to build the Pacific railway, he told Allan, as he had told Waddington, that no action could be taken until British Columbia became part of Canada. But in his letter he added a sentence that was clearly intended to encourage Allan, but which unfortunately in one highly important particular appears to have misled him. "The whole matter," Macdonald wrote on February 3, 1871, "will be brought before Parliament next session; meanwhile I see no objection to the capitalists of Canada or of England (or of the United States for that matter) joining together and making proposals for the construction of the road."[5] From the words in parentheses Allan undoubtedly gained the impression that Macdonald had no objection to American participation in the building of the railway—welcome news from his point of view, because he was convinced that Canadians by themselves could not possibly finance the road. Macdonald, on his part, had failed to make a distinction between American capital, which he was prepared to accept, and American control of the completed line, which he would on no account permit.

Macdonald was not aware at this time that Allan had no intention, in the first instance at least, of building an all-Canadian line north of Lake Superior. This meant that his ambitions and those of the Northern Pacific were converging so rapidly that it was certain they would soon be in touch with one another. The contact was made about the end of March. Allan had been making arrangements for a steamer service between Baltimore and Liverpool with a Mr. Garrett, and incidentally discussed the Northern Pacific with him. Garrett in turn mentioned Allan's interest to Henry Cooke, brother of Jay Cooke, who informed the latter on April 6 that Allan was "anxious that the Canadas should participate in the benefits of the N.P. by an extension of it from the eastern terminus [Duluth] eastward through Canada to Montreal and Quebec."[6] Allan of course expected the line from Montreal as far as Lake Nipissing to be provided by his own Northern Colonization Railway and the Canada Central Railway. Cooke planned to extend the Northern Pacific from Duluth to Sault Ste. Marie, and in the spring of 1871, through a Canadian intermediary, he secured a charter for a Sault Ste. Marie Railway and Bridge Company that was to build from the Sault to connect with the "projected railway near Lake Nipissing." The old international railroad project, intended to link the railways in eastern and western Canada by means of a line through the United States south of Lake Superior, thus seemed in a fair way to becoming a reality.

Cooke had an ulterior financial motive in his Canadian dealings. He had failed to sell Northern Pacific bonds in any quantity in London, where the market had become suspicious of American railway securities and in addition tended to regard the Northern Pacific (quite correctly) as a rival of the Canadian transcontinental project. Cooke hoped that a joint enterprise with Canadians would improve his financial prospects, and he was interested to hear through his brother Henry that Allan was confident that "if a unity of interests" could be established it would "remove all jealousy in England . . . and would enlist a powerful co-operation pecuniary and otherwise."[7]

A second important Canadian-American contact had been made in March, this time through Alfred Waddington. For a time Waddington thought that he had secured substantial financial backing in England for his Pacific railway proposals, but his hopes were disappointed and he began a search for American backers. In Ottawa he happened to meet George W. McMullen of Chicago, who was in the capital with a canal delegation. A Canadian by birth, McMullen was a restless soul with many interests, including canals, railways, and the Chicago *Post*. Allan's contacts were as yet confined to Jay Cooke and his financial associates; McMullen introduced Waddington to a group that included his broker associate, Charles M. Smith, and several influential directors of the Northern Pacific, notably General G. W. Cass and W. B. Ogden. All became interested in the Canadian transcontinental project, but with a motive that Waddington seems not to have suspected—a desire to shape the enterprise to accord with their own plans and ambitions. "This project," Ogden wrote to Jay Cooke in June, "seems to me so taking and strong and so clearly to belong to the Northern Pacific as a great auxiliary and strengthener" that he hoped it would be "prudent and proper to take the preliminary steps to cooperate with or control" it.[8]

The first move was made a month later when, at Waddington's request, Sir John Macdonald and his minister of finance, Sir Francis Hincks, received a delegation that included McMullen and Smith. W. B. Ogden and General Cass were represented by signature. The delegation was accompanied by James Beaty, a Toronto lawyer and adviser. "We said, as a matter of politeness," Macdonald recalled later, "that we were glad to see that American capitalists were looking for investments in Canada, but that we could not enter into any arrangement or receive any proposition from any body until after the next Session."[9]

In addition, Macdonald evidently made it clear that Canadians must be involved in the enterprise, for within days Beaty was asking Hincks for suitable names. He added that no money would be required, doubtless having in mind the time-honored device of a distribution of free stock. This prompted Hincks to retort that Beaty must see to it "that the Canadian promoters of any scheme are not only able, but willing to put money into it,—a most indispensable condition which you seem not to attach any importance to." The Americans would "find it expedient, if not absolutely necessary, to associate themselves with Canadians of equal position and means. . . ."[10]

Waddington obviously did not fall into this category, and Beaty soon informed Hincks that there was no longer any thought of including him on the board of the proposed Pacific railway company. This was the end of the line for Waddington, although, optimistic by nature, he seems to have continued to be hopeful until his death from smallpox the following February. On the other hand, Sir Hugh Allan met the specifications perfectly, and in the course of a visit to Montreal Hincks gave him the names and addresses of McMullen and Smith.

He did this without Macdonald's knowledge or authority, an indiscretion for which the prime minister later blamed him severely. No doubt Macdonald's resentment was due largely to the fact that the contact resulted in scandal and ultimately in the downfall of his government, but in addition Hincks seems to have made the introduction clumsily. There were misunderstandings from the beginning. Since Allan had been referred to them by the minister of finance, the Americans assumed that he had approached them at the behest of the government. When the negotiations with Allan finally collapsed, Smith contended, in an angry letter to Macdonald, that Allan had "stated that he came to us by direction of the ministry. . . ." From this they had assumed that the government could not be strongly opposed to Allan's plans.[11]

This was quite true, so far as Hincks was concerned. It was unfortunate that he happened to be the minister who was with Macdonald when he met the McMullen delegation, for he alone of all the cabinet had little or no nationalistic feeling about the ownership and control of the Pacific railway. Allan was equally indifferent, and the two also shared the view that although an all-Canadian route might be practicable and desirable at some time in the future, it was certainly not an immediate necessity. Early in August it became known that Allan was planning to build the projected railway between Lake Nipissing and Sault Ste. Marie that was intended to link the eastern Canadian lines with the Northern Pacific. Jay Cooke was delighted. "Canada will build to Sault

Ste. Marie to meet us," he wrote to his brother. "This is a grand thing for N. Pacific." And he added: "Hincks and Macdonald are cordially *with us*."[12] About Macdonald he was of course profoundly mistaken, but Hincks welcomed the news. He seems not to have realized the depth of Macdonald's feelings about an all-Canadian route and the firmness of his determination that the Pacific railway should follow it. Otherwise he could scarcely have written to Macdonald pointing out the advantages of the Sault Ste. Marie link as he saw them: "1st It would give us a line [to the prairies by way of St. Paul] that would answer for years. 2nd It would be, as it were, *forced* on us. I mean that *we would not* propose such a line, but being proposed to us [we] would accept it."[13]

1871 was a trying year for Macdonald. In January he had been appointed one of the five British members of the joint commission set up to try to settle the serious points at issue between Great Britain and the United States. The Treaty of Washington, signed in May, accomplished its main purpose, but in spite of Macdonald's best efforts the provisions on fisheries were unfair to Canada, and this inevitably increased his political difficulties at home. The negotiations kept him away from Ottawa for virtually the whole of the parliamentary session, and Cartier had had to pilot the terms of union with British Columbia through the House. So far as the railway was concerned, one practical step was taken. The organization of survey parties was authorized in March, and surveys actually began in British Columbia on July 20, the day union became effective. But action on the railway itself progressed no further than a resolution outlining policy in very general terms. The opposition was determined that the building of the line should not increase taxation, and this the resolution conceded. The railway, it declared, "should be constructed and worked by private enterprise and not by the Dominion Government" and public assistance to it "should consist of" (a phrase the opposition intended to mean "should be limited to") "such liberal grants of land, and such subsidy in money or other aid, not increasing the present rate of taxation, as the Parliament of Canada shall hereafter determine."[14]

No authority had been given to enter into contracts for the building of the line, but Sir Hugh Allan pressed on with his plans, evidently convinced that he could secure a private commitment from the government in advance of official action. In October he submitted his project to Macdonald in some detail. The company would expect to receive 50 million acres of land and a cash subsidy of $30 million. On paper the scheme seemed to provide an all-Canadian route; the main line was to extend from Lake Nipissing to the Pacific Coast by way of the Yellowhead Pass. But the true nature of the bid was not lost on the prime minister. "Allan has joined himself with a number of American capitalists," he wrote a few days later, "and they are applying to the Canadian government to be allowed to build our Pacific Railway. . . . You may depend upon it we will see that Canadian interests are fully protected, and that no American ring will be allowed to get control over it."[15]

Allan's proposal also presented political difficulties, since he was the only Canadian of real financial worth associated with it. By the autumn of 1871, in Macdonald's words, "a feeling of fear arose in Ontario, especially in Toronto, that the Pacific Railway might get into American hands and under American control, or might get into American and Montreal hands, and that in the construction of the Board the interests of Ontario might be forgotten or neglected."[16] To counter this, Macdonald encouraged the formation of an Ontario-based Pacific railway company that could compete for a charter with Allan's group; and it is probable that he already intended that the two should later amalgamate to form a single strong Canadian company from which Americans would be excluded. The leader of the Ontario movement was Senator David L. Macpherson, a close political associate of Macdonald, a man who had long had railway interests, and a partner in Macpherson, Gzowski and Company, railroad contractors.

In spite of these developments, Allan was still convinced that he could secure the Pacific railway contract and in anticipation he and his associates signed a formal agreement on December 23, 1871. Allan was the sole Canadian member; the Americans included Jay Cooke and Company, Ogden, Cass, and others prominent in the Northern Pacific, as well as McMullen and C. M. Smith. The capital of the company was to be $10 million, of which Allan was to subscribe $1,450,000. He seems to have been looking forward to a major new career in railroading, for at this time he was also trying to sell his Atlantic steamship line. However, the best offer received fell substantially below the asking price and no sale took place.[17]

A letter written by Cooke in mid-January 1872 shows how completely Allan had been taken into the American camp. There was need for secrecy, Cooke explained, "on account of the political jealousies in the Dominion, and there is no hint of the Northern Pacific connection, but the real plan is to cross the Sault Ste. Marie through Northern Michigan and Wisconsin to Duluth [where the line would connect with the Northern Pacific], then build from Pembina up to Fort Garry and by and by through the Saskatchewan to British Columbia." At the Sault, connections would be made with "roads now building from Montreal and Toronto." Lip service would be paid to the demand for an all-Canadian railway north of Lake Superior: "The Act will provide for building a North Shore Road to Fort Garry, merely to calm public opinion. . . ." Finally, the line from the Sault to Duluth was to be "blended with the Canadian Pacific and the bonds sold as such in London."[18]

Bonds were much in Cooke's mind at the moment, as his London house had just published a prospectus for a £4 million issue of Northern Pacific land grant bonds. In so doing they overstepped the mark and helped to doom their Canadian enterprise. In an earlier circular they had deprecated the building of a railway north of Lake Superior; "owing to insuperable difficulties of surface and climate" its construction would "not be seriously contemplated by practical people."[19] In the new prospectus the Northern Pacific was represented as being "in all essentials an international enterprise, whose early completion will strengthen the unity and promote the prosperity of the Dominion of Canada, and render accessible the vast and fertile portion of British America which extends from Winnipeg to the Rocky Mountains."[20] The day after the prospectus was issued, Sir John Rose, the Canadian government's unofficial representative in London, reported the gist of the statement to Ottawa. Macdonald's reaction was a prompt and emphatic cable to Rose: "Take steps to make known that Dominion is about to construct Pacific Railway through British Territory."[21]

At this point it dawned at last on Allan that his project had little chance of acceptance unless a significant group of Canadians were associated with it. Confident from practical experience in the power of money, he set about buying up the men he wanted with offers of complimentary stock, and drew up what may be fairly described as a price list. The dozen or so names included those of Senator Macpherson, C. J. Brydges, general manager of the Grand Trunk Railway, and Donald A. Smith, of the Hudson's Bay Company, who were each put down for $100,000; George Brown of the Toronto *Globe*, a longtime critic of railways, was to be offered $50,000. What actually happened is not clear. Allan reported to C. M. Smith that Macpherson—"rather an important person to gain over to our side"—had insisted on receiving $250,000 in stock; this Macpherson later denied flatly. George Brown denied that he was ever approached about the matter. Brydges seems to have been offered $200,000 but declined to join.

Neither Macpherson nor Brydges was under any illusions about the character of Allan's company. Macpherson told him that he was convinced Parliament would not approve "any scheme which, like it, would place our great Transcontinental Railway for ever under the absolute control of our rivals, our American neighbours."[22] Brydges commented to Macpherson that Allan was "the only Canadian in it, all the rest are Yankees."[23]

In spite of rebuffs, in February Allan was able to submit to the government the details of a proposed Canada Pacific Railway. He had managed to muster seven Canadian names to add to those of Jay Cooke and his Northern Pacific associates. They included Donald A. Smith, of the Hudson's Bay Company, whose primary interest was a rail outlet for Manitoba; Senator Asa B. Foster, a major shareholder and managing director of the Canada Central Railway; and J. J. C. Abbott, Allan's solicitor and a future prime minister of Canada.

A suggestion that the Canada Pacific intended to build a line from Montreal to Quebec that would compete with the Grand Trunk caused the latter to level its guns on the proposed company. Gregory Smith, president of the Northern Pacific, charged that its influence was "most bitterly arrayed" in opposition. In a letter to Jay Cooke that has been well described as a masterpiece of hypocrisy, he complained that Grand Trunk circulars alleged "that the friends of the Northern Pacific are at the bottom of the Canada Pacific and intend to gobble it up,—that Mr. Allan is but a figure head, and is put forward by our interest to get the Legislation giving large concessions in land and money which will all go into the hands and control of the Northern Pacific to enrich us"[24]—surely a simple statement of the truth.

In April Macdonald described to Sir John Rose the different groups that were interested in securing the Pacific railway charter. First there was "the Hugh Allan ring," with which Jay Cocke was associated; secondly, "the Montreal Ring proper," centering on Brydges; and thirdly, "the Ontario ring," headed by Macpherson. "There will, I have no doubt, be a coalition between numbers two and three," Macdonald wrote, "and Allan will, I think, be obliged to abandon his Yankee confreres. If so, we shall have a strong company of Canadian capitalists who will undertake and finish the Railway."[25]

To this end Macdonald inserted in the Railway Act of 1872 an astutely worded contingency clause. It empowered the government to enter into an agreement with any appropriate company, but if "no such company, with whom the Government deems it advisable to make an agreement" was found to exist, it could by charter incorporate one and make an agreement with it.

Contrary to Macdonald's hopes and expectations, the coalition between the Brydges and Macpherson groups did not take place. Macpherson was forming an Interoceanic Railway Company that was to be an all-Canadian concern with a line following an all-Canadian route. Brydges represented the Grand Trunk and envisaged a limited project that would not compete with it. Stating a view to which the Grand Trunk was to adhere for years, he told Macpherson that he had "no belief" in a line north of Lake Superior "for a long time to come." And it is also clear that he felt railway needs were being greatly exaggerated. A line from Winnipeg to Lake Superior and another from Winnipeg to an American railhead at Pembina would be "all that can possibly be wanted" for the next ten or fifteen years.[26]

Macdonald had also underestimated the tenacity with which Allan would adhere to his own plans. The power of money having failed him, Allan resorted to political pressure. The person upon whom he decided to exert it was Sir George Etienne Cartier, Macdonald's closest political associate. If concessions could be extracted from Cartier, Allan was confident that the government in turn would have to accept them.

The point of attack was shrewdly chosen. Cartier's health was failing; he was already suffering severely from the illness that was to cause his death within a year. A combination of local circumstances had lost him the solid support he had enjoyed for years in his Montreal constituency. Macdonald expressed the view later that only waning powers could have caused him to react as he did to Allan's tactics.

As early as June 12, Allan informed McMullen that he believed he had "the whole thing arranged through my French friends," and that he had "a pledge of Sir G. that we will have a majority [of the shares of the railway company], and other things satisfactory."[27] In an extraordinary letter written on July 1 to General Cass, soon to become president of the Northern Pacific, he described in detail his strategy and its success:

> On a calm review of the situation, I satisfied myself that the whole decision of the question must ultimately be in the hands of one man, and that man was Sir George E. Cartier, the leader and chief of the French party. This party has held the balance of power between the other factions. It has sustained and kept in office and existence the entire Government for the last five years. It consists of forty-five men, who have followed Cartier and voted in a solid phalanx for all his measures. The Government majority in Parliament being generally less than forty-five, it follows that the defection of one-half or two-thirds would at any time put the Government out of office. . . .
>
> A railroad from Montreal to Ottawa, through the French country north of the Ottawa river, has long been desired by the French inhabitants, but Cartier, who is the salaried solicitor of the Grand Trunk Railroad, to which this would be an opposition, has always interposed difficulties, and by his influence prevented its being built. . . . I saw, in this *French* railroad scheme, and in the near approach of the general elections, when Cartier as well as others had to go to their constituents for re-election, a sure means of attaining my object . . . I employed several young French lawyers to write it up for their own newspapers. I subscribed a controlling influence in the stock, and proceeded to subsidize the newspapers themselves, both editors and proprietors. I went to the country through which the road would pass, and called on many of the inhabitants. I visited the priests, and made friends of them, and I employed agents to go amongst the principal people and talk it up.
>
> I then began to hold public meetings, and attended them myself, making frequent speeches in French to them, showing them where their true interest lay. The scheme at once became popular, and I formed a committee to influence the members of the Legislature.

This succeeded so well that, in a short time, I had 27 out of the 45 on whom I could rely, and the electors of the ward in this city [Montreal], which Cartier himself represents, notified him that unless the contract for the Pacific Railway was given in the interests of Lower Canada, he need not present himself for re-election. He did not believe this, but when he came here and met his constituents, he found, to his surprise, that their determination was unchangeable.

He then agreed to give the contract, as required. . . .[28]

By this time the Canadian Pacific Act had become law, and in June the rival companies had been incorporated—Allan's Canada Pacific Railway Company and Macpherson's Interoceanic Railway Company. Their charters were virtually identical. This did not perturb Macdonald, because he had no intention of awarding the contract for the construction of the railway to either of them. When on July 3 the Canada Pacific made formal application for an agreement to build the line, Allan was informed, to his disappointment, that the government wished to see the two companies amalgamate. Negotiations began, and for a time made some progress. Most of the details were worked out satisfactorily by Macpherson and Abbott, representing Allan. But the attempt at union failed on two counts. Macpherson, quite correctly, did not believe that Allan was prepared to shed his American associates, and he refused to promise Allan the presidency of the new company in advance; the president, he insisted, should be chosen by the directors after the company had been formed.

But the presidency Allan was determined to have, and more besides. Macpherson having failed to accept his terms he turned again to Cartier and Macdonald, realizing full well that he had caught them at a highly vulnerable moment. Parliament had been dissolved, and for many reasons the outcome of the election was clearly in doubt. His lengthy illness in 1870 and the Treaty of Washington negotiations in 1871 had kept Macdonald off the Canadian political scene long enough to affect his position; the treaty itself was unpopular in Canada; the government's failure to bear down heavily on those responsible for the murder of Thomas Scott during the Riel troubles in Red River had roused the ire of many in Ontario. In addition there was violent disagreement on the railway issue. Macdonald and Cartier were convinced that unless it was built, the new Canada extending from ocean to ocean would not survive; the Liberal opposition had shown itself to be the project's declared and uncompromising enemy.

When Allan made his new move, the poll in Macdonald's Kingston constituency was only a fortnight away, but other polls, by the custom of the day, would be scattered through the following month—quite long enough for further trouble over the railway to influence the overall result of the election.

Amalgamation on his terms having failed, Allan now stated to Cartier the conditions upon which he would participate in the new Pacific railway company the government would be sponsoring. Not only were the directors to be pledged to elect him president, but he and his friends must be allotted a majority of the stock. Cartier, in desperate straits in his Montreal East constituency, was prepared to agree to this, but Macdonald was not. He wired Cartier authorizing him "to assure Allan that the influence of the Government will be exercised to secure him the position of President," but that was the utmost he was willing to concede. Undeterred, Allan now asked Cartier for a further undertaking that the railway contract would be given to his Canada Pacific company if a new company was not formed within two months. Cartier again felt compelled to agree; but when Macdonald heard of it, he at once repudiated Cartier's action and insisted that his own promise of support for the presidency was the only commitment that would be given. Settlement of all other points was to be left until after the election.

Cartier had raised the question of campaign funds with Allan, and although his demands had not been met, Allan nevertheless contributed heavily. Clearly, the fate of the government would also determine that of his Pacific railway ambitions; it was important in his own interest, as he later stated, "that those members of Parliament who had shown an interest in the Canada Pacific enterprise, and in other railway enterprises in which I was interested, and who were disposed to assist and further them, should be aided in their elections. . . ."[29] It is clear, moreover, that Allan still felt fairly confident that he could somehow bring the government to accept many, if not all, of his proposals.

The Kingston poll was held on August 1, and Macdonald retained his seat by a comfortable majority. The day before, he had received $25,000 from Allan, but none of the money was used in his own constituency, or to meet his personal expenses; Macdonald distributed it to other government candidates in the hard-fought battlefield of Ontario. The situation was critical, and twice he appealed for and received additional sums of $10,000—the second in response to a telegram sent on August 26 that was destined to become famous: "I must have another ten thousand. Will be the last time of calling. Do not fail me. Answer today." In addition to this total of $45,000, he knew that Cartier and others in Quebec had received substantial sums, but how substantial he was not to learn until later.

Late in the month it was clear that the government had been returned, though by a narrow majority, and Macdonald was able to resume his planning for the Pacific railway. Only frustration followed; two months of effort to bring about the amalgamation of the Canada Pacific and Interoceanic companies ended in failure. The stumbling blocks were the question of the presidency and Macpherson's well-based suspicion that Allan was still hand in glove with

American associates. A report issued by the executive committee of the Interoceanic Company pulled no punches on the implications of the latter issue:

> No more suicidal policy could be pursued by the people of Canada than to allow their [American] rivals to have such an interest in this national undertaking, as would virtually transfer to them the ownership and control of 50 million acres of Canadian territory, would invest them with the direction of the immigration policy, which must be inaugurated for the settlement of those lands; confer upon them the power to influence the construction and progress of the railway; and grant to them, in perpetuity, a monopoly of the traffic over the Canadian, which is the shortest and best trans-continental route.[30]

Allan was practicing deception on both the points in dispute. In August, when he told McMullen that Americans were to be excluded from the amalgamated company, he added: "But I fancy we can get over that one way or other."[31] To General Cass he explained that as foreigners could not be shareholders, "the shares taken by you and our other American friends, will therefore have to stand in my name for some time."[32] Macdonald had agreed to nothing except support to secure him the presidency, yet he told McMullen that he had been promised far more than this. "Yesterday," he wrote on August 6, "we entered into an agreement, by which the Government bound itself to form a company of Canadians only, according to my wishes. That the company will make me President, that I and my friends will get a majority of the stock, and that the contract for building the road will be given to this company in terms of the Act of Parliament." On this account he had the effrontery to expect the Americans to pay his political bills. He warned McMullen that the agreement had "not been obtained without large payments of money"; he had already paid out over $200,000 and there was more to come.[33] In mid-September, when the election was over and the bills had come in, he reported his total expenditure and presented a claim that staggered McMullen: "I have disbursed $343,000 in gold, which I want to get repaid. I have still to pay $13,500, which will close everything off."[34] In the spring the American group had set up an expense fund of $50,000 for Allan, which he had soon drawn upon to the extent of $40,000; but a grand total of $356,500 was quite another matter.

There is no evidence that Allan ever received anything beyond the $40,000; as it soon became clear that the Americans would receive nothing, they could scarcely be expected to reimburse him. Their association was, in fact, disintegrating. It had consisted of two groups, one (with which Allan first had contacts) in New York and Philadelphia, centering upon Jay Cooke and his financial house, and the other, including McMullen, Smith, Ogden, and Cass, in Chicago. The Northern Pacific was the link between them, and by the autumn of 1872 Jay Cooke and Company were more concerned about the financial state of that railway, which was spending money much faster than Cooke could raise it, than with the hypothetical future and profits of a C.P.R. But McMullen and Smith were storing up furious anger and resentment against Allan that were to have dire consequences for Macdonald and his government. For in October, at long last, Allan had realized that he must sever his relations with them. On October 24 he broke the news to McMullen: "The opposition of the Ontario party will, I think, have the effect of shutting out our American friends from any participation in the road, and I apprehend all that negotiation is at an end. . . . Public sentiment seems to be decided that the road shall be built by Canadians only."[35]

Unaware of most of Allan's activities, Macdonald continued to see in him the prospective president of the Pacific railway. He was even ready to find excuses for his dealings with the Americans. "Allan is not to blame for his connection with the Yankees," Macdonald wrote to Sir John Rose in October. "He opened negotiations with them at Hincks's suggestion." And he concluded: "Cartier and I promised Allan before the elections that we would see he was the first President, and this we must carry out."[36] By November it was clear that there was no hope of an amalgamation between the Canada Pacific and the Interoceanic; a completely new company was the only solution, and its character was decided upon by the cabinet in long and somewhat stormy sessions on December 2 and 3. Allan would be president, as promised; there would be thirteen directors, chosen initially by the government, five of whom would be from Ontario, four from Quebec, and one from each of the other four provinces. To reduce the political element, no senators or members of the House of Commons would be appointed to the board. The main line of the railway was to run north of Lake Superior, and it was to be completed, as required by the terms of union with British Columbia, by 1881. In February 1873, the Canadian Pacific Railway Company—the first corporation of the name—was duly incorporated, and in March Allan, having attained his ambition to be its president, left for London, accompanied by Abbott, to seek funds for its construction.

In the first days of the year, Macdonald had sent a cheerful letter to Cartier, who was in England, outlining the government's intentions. "Things are going on very quietly here," he wrote—clearly a remark intended to reassure a sick man searching vainly for relief from an illness that would soon prove fatal.[37] For the quiet was ominous from Macdonald's point of view. On New Year's Eve George McMullen had appeared in his office, armed with copies of Allan's correspondence, and Macdonald had learned for the first time the details of Allan's real plans and deceptions, and the full extent of his contributions to the Conservative campaign funds. Both McMullen and his associate C. M. Smith accused Allan of a flagrant breach of trust, contended that the government had been responsible for their contacts with him, and declared that they were determined to have substantial compensation. Macdonald denied that the government had any responsibility in the matter and contended that it was entirely Allan's affair. Strictly speaking, this was true, but the fact remained that Allan's letters would be most damaging if they were made public, both to the government and to Allan. Efforts were therefore made to ascertain whether McMullen would part with them, and late in February Hincks told Macdonald that Allan and McMullen had come to terms. But by this time McMullen was more interested in revenge than money; he failed to carry out the agreement and disposed of the correspondence to the Liberal opposition. Further revelations came to the Liberals from another source. Allan's campaign contributions had been paid out by J. J. C. Abbott, his solicitor; while Abbott was in England with Allan seeking funds for the railway, Abbott's confidential clerk was persuaded to rifle his safe and provide copies of letters and telegrams to and from Macdonald, Cartier, and others. Rumors about the Allan correspondence were soon circulating, and Macdonald was left in the highly uncomfortable position of having to wait and see how much the Liberals knew and what use they proposed to make of their knowledge.

The answer came on April 2, when L. C. Huntington, a Liberal member, proposed a resolution accusing the government of corrupt dealings with Allan and his American associates. The central charge was that "an understanding was come to between the Government and Sir Hugh Allan and Mr. Abbott, M.P.,—that Sir Hugh Allan and his friends should advance a large sum of money for the purpose of aiding the Elections of Ministers and their supporters at the ensuing General Election,—and that he and his friends should receive the contract for the construction of the Railway."

The resolution was promptly defeated by a vote on party lines, but Macdonald realized that an inquiry was essential. He therefore moved the appointment of a select committee of five; the redoubtable Edward Blake was to be one of the two Liberal members. Delays occurred, and the committee was just beginning its hearings, early in July, when most of the Allan-McMullen correspondence suddenly appeared in the Toronto *Globe* and the Montreal *Herald*. The letters and telegrams rifled from Abbott's safe appeared a fortnight later.

In August Macdonald substituted a Royal Commission for the select committee, but the move was unfortunate. The Liberals were displeased and chose to boycott its proceedings; material witnesses kept out of sight and failed to appear; there was no proper provision for the cross-examination of witnesses; the commissioners simply printed the evidence, unaccompanied by report, comment, verdict, or recommendation. Macdonald, Hincks, Allan, and Macpherson all appeared before it, and their evidence tells the story in all essentials. It was made clear that Macdonald had made no promises except with regard to the presidency, nor had he used any of Allan's money for his own election expenses. But he and others had distributed large sums to other constituencies, where they were used to influence voters in ways some of which were illegal. Such practices were almost universal, but in this instance the Conservatives had been caught red-handed.

As already noted, the government's majority was small, and as the debate on the Pacific Scandal, as it came to be known, continued, it began to dwindle away. As the debate drew to its close, Macdonald delivered one of the most remarkable speeches of his long career, to which Edward Blake replied in one of his immensely long and formidable orations. Convinced that he would be defeated on a division, Macdonald resigned on November 5.

The Canadian Pacific Railway Company was already dying if not dead. Huntington's charges were carefully noted in London, and in spite of the efforts of Sir John Rose, none of the leading financial houses would consider marketing a C.P.R. issue. The only offer received came from a firm that had recently sponsored a rather unusual stock transaction for the Grand Trunk. McEwen, Grant and Company proposed to purchase $25 million of Canadian Pacific bonds at $82\frac{1}{2}$, and to take a similar issue at the same or a higher price three years later; the railway's land grant of 50 million acres and $30 million cash subsidy would be held as security. This offer Allan accepted in June, but the government declined to approve the deal. It is doubtful if it would have become effective even if it had been accepted, for the financial crisis of 1873 was developing on both sides of the Atlantic. In September the proud firm of Jay Cooke and Company would close its doors, and the Northern Pacific would collapse with it.

Denied financial backing, the first Canadian Pacific Railway Company quietly disappeared. Sir Hugh Allan withdrew from the Pacific railway scene, and the threat of an American takeover ended.

By an odd turn of events, it was to be a Canadian takeover of the moribund St. Paul and Pacific a few years later that would make possible the organization of the Canadian Pacific of today.

3

The Tribulations of Alexander Mackenzie

Not a mile of the Canadian Pacific had been built when Alexander Mackenzie became prime minister in November 1873, but a good deal of progress had been made with the railway surveys. In April 1871, Sandford Fleming, engineer in chief of the Intercolonial Railway, had been appointed engineer in chief of the Pacific railway as well, and his survey parties had begun work in British Columbia in July, as soon as the colony had become a province of Canada.

The task Fleming faced was fantastic in scale. He was asked to locate the best route for the railway from the Ottawa Valley to the Pacific coast, a distance of over 2,500 miles. The prairie region between the Red River and the Rocky Mountains, roughly a thousand miles wide, posed no very serious problems, but the eastern and western sections were another matter. All but the last few miles of the track from the Ottawa River to the Red would be through the forbidding Laurentian Shield. Little of this thousand miles of wilderness had been explored, let alone mapped, except for the rivers and lakes followed by the fur traders, and their travel routes were quite unsuitable for a railway. In his history of surveying in Canada, Don W. Thomson pays tribute to the men who struggled through this territory: "The rugged land consisted of rock formations, uncounted lakes, unbridged streams and heavy forests cluttered with areas of formidable windfall. A wilderness of swamp and muskeg, insect pests, fierce summer heat and bitter cold all combined to test to the utmost the stamina and resourcefulness of the individual surveyor."[1]

In the West, the surveyors were faced with a hundred thousand square miles of mountains between the prairies and the Pacific. In this age of aerial surveys it is difficult to grasp what was involved in running surveys through a virtually unexplored mountainous area of this immensity, with no means of locomotion except a packhorse, a canoe, or the surveyor's own two feet.

The first essential was to decide which of the passes through the Rockies offered the best route for a railway, but in making a decision, what lay beyond the pass had to be taken into consideration; the best pass in the world would be useless unless it led to a practicable route to the coast. Quite early on, Fleming came to the conclusion that the Yellowhead Pass was the best available. His choice was approved officially by order in council in April 1872, and in September he visited the pass personally. G. M. Grant, his traveling companion, recorded their reaction in his well-known narrative entitled *Ocean to Ocean*: "We were all delighted with this our first view of the Yellow Head Pass. Instead of contracted canyon or savage torrent raging among beetling precipices as we had half feared, the Pass is really a pleasant open meadow. So easy an ingress into the heart of the Rocky Mountains as that of the Jasper Valley, and so favourable a pass as the Yellow Head could hardly have been hoped for."[2] The altitude was only 3,700 feet.

Traveling on westward, Fleming came to the upper waters of the Fraser River, then to those of the North Thompson, which he followed to Kamloops, whence he descended through the canyons of the Thompson and the Fraser to New Westminster and the adjacent magnificent harbor in Burrard Inlet. This became Fleming's own preferred route for the C.P.R., and it was his final recommendation to the government in 1879; but a great array of alternatives had been considered and reconsidered in the intervening seven years. Passes examined ranged from the Peace River and Pine River in the north to Howse Pass, 350 miles to the south, while possible terminal points on the coast ranged from Port Simpson, just south of the Alaska boundary, to Burrard Inlet, less than 20 miles from the state of Washington. It soon became apparent that Burrard Inlet offered great practical advantages, but for years it had a serious rival in Bute Inlet, to which Alfred Waddington had planned to build his railway. The mouth of Bute Inlet was near the point at which Vancouver Island pressed most closely to the mainland, and if the railway was to be carried to the island, it afforded the best approach. Some contended that the channels between island and mainland could be bridged; others were confident that train ferries could solve the transit problem satisfactorily. The forbidding character of the Homathko River canyon, leading to Bute Inlet, seemed to trouble them not at all.

Some of Fleming's engineers complicated matters by becoming fanatical advocates of one particular route or another in which they could see no blemish. Fleming himself became firmly wedded to the Yellowhead Pass, and, as already noted, soon developed a strong preference for Burrard Inlet as the western terminus. Walter Moberly, first engineer in charge of the surveys in British Columbia, agreed about the terminus but differed violently with Fleming about the pass. In 1865, while serving as surveyor general of the colony, he had discovered Eagle Pass, in the Monashee Mountains east of Kamloops, and had felt so certain that it was (as it proved to be) the future route of the transcontinental railway that he had blazed a tree and placed on it the inscription: "This is the Pass for the Overland Railway." The line, as he envisaged it, would continue eastward to the Columbia River, avoid the formidable Selkirk Mountains by following the Big Bend of the Columbia, which runs around the northern end of the range, and then breach the Rockies through Howse Pass. When given charge of the surveys, Moberly at once set about locating a line along this route, but just as he was preparing to explore Howse Pass he received the news—to him infuriating—that Fleming favored the Yellowhead and had instructed him to abandon the Howse Pass route and examine the Yellowhead in detail. Not surprisingly, this deep-seated difference of opinion led to a loss of confidence on both sides.

Marcus Smith, who succeeded Moberly in British Columbia, soon became a rabid advocate of a route through Pine Pass leading to Bute Inlet and a terminus on Vancouver Island. Smith was able but cantankerous, and relations with Fleming quickly became strained. Equally cantankerous but much less able was Charles Horetzky, who was not a trained engineer and is now remembered chiefly as a pioneer photographer. He contrived nevertheless for years to push his advocacy of a route that also used the Pine Pass but ended much farther north, at Port Simpson.

Fleming had to contend with many other problems in addition to these divisions within his ranks. Qualified and experienced surveyors were few and far between; men capable of enduring the exhausting physical work that the surveys involved were hard to find; political patronage burdened his work force with many who were unsuitable or downright useless. Much of the work was seasonal, and this was worrying to the men, who were left without employment in the winter months, and made it hard to retain the better-qualified workers. Where parties had to remain in the field throughout the winter, which happened frequently in the western mountains, they often suffered great hardships due to extreme cold and lack of proper food and shelter. Pack animals perished. Hazards from physical dangers were often great. By the time Fleming ended his trip along the projected route of the railway in 1872, fourteen men had already lost their lives—seven in forest fires and seven by drowning —and the toll would be nearly forty by the time the surveys were concluded.

In spite of the many difficulties, survey parties about a thousand strong were in the field season after season. Their efforts were concentrated in the western mountains, but good progress was made both on the much easier terrain of the prairies and in the rugged country between Lake Nipissing and Fort William. The choice of the Yellowhead Pass virtually dictated the route westward from Red River. To the great disappointment and anger of the people in the Winnipeg area, Fleming decided to bridge the Red at Selkirk, twenty miles north of the city, which meant that Winnipeg would not be on the main line. From Selkirk the line was to run northwest, cross Lake Manitoba at the narrows, continue on to the Swan River valley, and run thence to Battleford, Edmonton, and the pass. This route would have taken the railway through the so-called Fertile Belt, a name dating back to Palliser's explorations of the 1850s and designating a broad band of mixed prairie and woodland roughly following the valley of the North Saskatchewan River. Between Lake Nipissing and Fort William, a route that went north of Lake Nipigon had been sketched out by the end of the 1872 season; the following year an alternative route that seemed preferable had been located south of the lake. By the time Alexander Mackenzie assumed office, the surveys had thus proven that a practicable route for a railway to the Pacific could be found, and long sections of it had been examined in a preliminary way.

Mackenzie realized that the C.P.R. would be the most troublesome of his many problems, and he decided to take charge of it himself. In addition to being prime minister, he therefore took the portfolio of minister of public works, whose responsibilities then included railways. On the whole this was fortunate for the Pacific railway project, but it meant that from the beginning Mackenzie was badly overworked. His cabinet colleagues were not an impressive group. Five of them were being rewarded with office for having deserted Sir John Macdonald over the Pacific Scandal; a sixth, Richard Cartwright, his minister of finance, had joined the Liberals because he had not been given that portfolio in Macdonald's cabinet. By far the ablest and most impressive member was Edward Blake, but Blake, though a brilliant lawyer, was emotional and to some degree erratic. He was to prove this and embarrass Mackenzie considerably by resigning from the cabinet only three months after its formation.

The Liberals now found themselves responsible for the railway that they had been criticizing and denouncing for years. The two views on the project that mattered were those of Mackenzie and Blake. Mackenzie shared in a more limited way Macdonald's vision of a Canada extending from ocean to ocean, and he recognized that the pledge given to British Columbia, however irresponsible he might consider it, could not be ignored. It was the practical difficulty of building the line that troubled his frugal Scottish soul; he could not see how construction of the railway as a whole in the near future was financially feasible. But he approved the end in view; it was the means of attaining it

The *Countess of Dufferin*, first locomotive in the Canadian West, arriving at St. Boniface, across the river from Winnipeg, on October 9, 1877. She and the flatcars and van that accompanied her had come down the Red River by barge. They were brought in by Joseph Whitehead, contractor for the Pembina Branch. Although no railway company was yet in existence, the name Canadian Pacific was already in such common use that Whitehead painted it on his engine and cars. (COURTESY OF THE MANITOBA ARCHIVES)

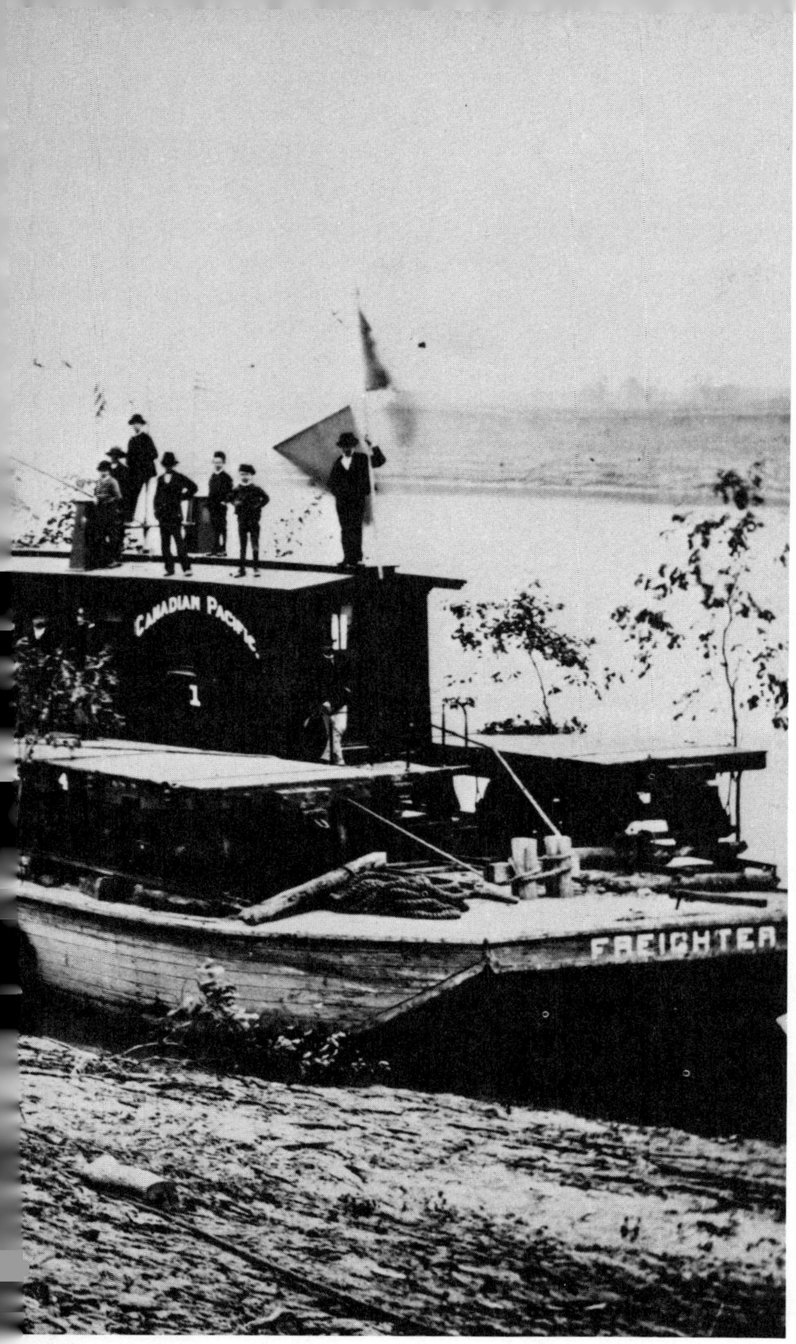
CANADIAN PACIFIC
1
FREIGHTER

that baffled him. Blake, by contrast, seems to have found little that was exciting, inspiring, or even politically necessary in the conception of a continent-wide Canada. As a consequence he did not view the railway as something essential; he saw in it merely a senseless or at best a premature project that would ruin the country if a serious attempt were made to build it in the near future. The one point upon which he and Mackenzie agreed completely was the folly that Cartier and Macdonald had committed when they promised British Columbia that construction would begin within two years and be completed within ten; "an outrageous bargain," "insane," and "a bargain made to be broken" are representative of the epithets that both hurled at the agreement year after year.

Mackenzie soon made known the considerations that he felt should govern policy on the railway. His two basic assumptions were, first, that as it was self-evident that the railway could not be completed by 1881, some modification of the agreement must be negotiated; and second, that economic conditions made it impracticable to tackle construction immediately other than in a modest way. The scale of the picture must be kept in mind. The financial resources of the federal government were slender at the best of times, and Mackenzie had the misfortune to hold office during a severe depression. Budgetary revenue was no more than $24.6 million in 1874; in 1875 it declined to $22.6 million and stayed at about that level for three years. Even then Blake considered the budget was burdensome; though Canada "had not reached the extreme of productive taxation," he considered that she "had gone a long way towards it."[3] Moreover, it is often forgotten that the government already had a railway project on its hands; it was still burdened with the contruction of the Intercolonial, which was not completed until 1876. Costs there had far exceeded expectations; total expenditure had been estimated at $20 million; the final bill would be more than $34 million—this for a line no more than 500 miles in length through country that was relatively easy compared with that north of Lake Superior and through the western mountains. No wonder the prospect of building a line five times as long gave Mackenzie pause.

As a stopgap, which he believed would meet actual needs for a good many years, he hoped to make use of the hundreds of miles of rivers and lakes between Fort William and the Rockies; short portage lines linking them should be sufficient for the time being. But so far as the section between Fort William and Winnipeg was concerned—the old Dawson road-and-water route—this plan was soon abandoned. If settlers were to flow freely into the Canadian West and if their produce was to find a market, it was obvious that better means of transportation would be essential. This Mackenzie proposed to pro-

Sandford Fleming (later Sir Sandford) in 1880, when he was about to leave his position as engineer-in-chief in charge of the Pacific Railway surveys. Later he was for thirty years a director of the Canadian Pacific. (COURTESY OF THE PUBLIC ARCHIVES OF CANADA)

vide, at least during the summer navigation season, by building lines from Red River to Lake Superior and from Georgian Bay to eastern centers. Steamers would provide a link between the two. No attempt was to be made to build the line north of Lake Superior. To give the Red River settlement its long-desired rail outlet to the south, a line would also be built from Winnipeg to the boundary, where it could connect with American railways to St. Paul and Chicago.

In the faint hope that private capitalists might be tempted to build the railway, the Canadian Pacific Railway Act of 1874 offered a subsidy of

$12,000 in cash and 20,000 acres of land per mile of main-line track, but there were no takers. It is doubtful if any large-scale bid could have been accepted, for the act repeated the proviso that the construction of the railway must not necessitate an increase in taxation.

The difficulty was that this program offered nothing to British Columbia, already restive because of the delay in building the railway. As the two-year period within which construction was to begin was drawing to a close, Macdonald had resorted hastily to the foolish expedient of arbitrarily selecting a terminus and arranging for the ceremonial turning of a first sod. An order in council passed on June 7, 1873, designated Esquimalt, adjacent to Victoria, as the terminus, and the sod was turned on July 19, just one day before the two-year period expired. This gave scant satisfaction, because no construction followed, and the choice of Esquimalt touched off a local battle that was to continue for years.

There had always been rivalry and some enmity between Victoria and Vancouver Island on the one hand and New Westminster and the mainland of British Columbia on the other. The difficulty in the present instance was that a railway that was to cross to the island, presumably from Bute Inlet, would be far to the north and of no service whatever to the mainland communities in the valleys of the Fraser and Thompson rivers. On the other hand, a line terminating at Burrard Inlet, which would serve the mainland settlements admirably, would leave Victoria and Vancouver Island dependent upon steamers for their link with the railway. It was a vital local issue over which friction became acute, in part because many of the substantial citizens both on the mainland and on the island were soon engaged in land speculation. Lord Dufferin, the governor-general, later noted that "the location of the Canadian Pacific Railway, and its terminus, along such a line, and on such a spot as may enhance the value of his own individual town lot, or in some other way put money into his pocket, by passing as near as possible to where he lives is the common preoccupation of every [British] Columbian citizen. In Victoria the one idea of every human being is to get the Railway to Esquimalt."[4]

Mackenzie was most anxious to work out some compromise with British Columbia, but the people of the province, particularly in Victoria, were not in a compromising mood. In February 1874, their eccentric premier, Amor de Cosmos, had suggested that some concessions be made on the railway issue in return for assistance with the construction of a badly needed dry dock at Esquimalt. He was almost literally thrown out of office by a mob of angry citizens who invaded the legislature, and was replaced by George A. Walkem, who was determined to hold the federal government to the provisions of the terms of union. It was with Walkem that J. D. Edgar, the emissary Mackenzie sent to Victoria in the spring of 1874, had to deal, and Edgar found him unyielding. Discussions dragged on from February to June, when Walkem found means of terminating them by suddenly questioning Edgar's credentials.

In the long controversy that followed, two outsiders caused difficulties and embarrassment for Mackenzie. The first was Lord Carnarvon, British secretary of state for the colonies; the other was the governor-general, Lord Dufferin.

Carnarvon came into the picture when Walkem decided to appeal to the Crown. Carnarvon felt that an arbitrator might be useful and offered his services. His action was highly questionable on constitutional grounds, since Canada had been recognized as fully self-governing since 1867 and the railway was a domestic issue. But in the hope of securing a settlement, Mackenzie finally agreed to accept Carnarvon's decision. The outcome was the so-called Carnarvon Terms. There were five provisions: a seventy-mile railway was to be built at once between Vancouver Island's two chief settlements, Victoria and Nanaimo (this would eventually become part of the main line of the C.P.R. if Esquimalt became the terminus); a wagon road and telegraph line were to be built immediately to link British Columbia with the eastern provinces; the railway surveys were to be "pushed on with the utmost vigor"; and as soon as it was feasible to begin railway construction in the province, at least $2 million would be expended annually in British Columbia. Finally, the date for the completion of the railway was advanced to December 31, 1890. This last provision, it is important to note, did not include the line north of Lake Superior; by the date specified the railway was to be "completed and open for traffic" only "from the Pacific seaboard to a point at the western end" of the lake. Carnarvon looked upon the line north of it "as postponed rather than abandoned" and hoped that the day when it could be built was "not very far distant."[5]

By and large these terms did not vary greatly from those that Mackenzie had authorized Edgar to offer, which Walkem had declined even to see, let alone consider. An increase in the rate of railway expenditure from $1.5 million to $2 million a year was the most significant material difference.

By the time Carnarvon submitted his terms in November 1874, Mackenzie had already awarded the first Canadian Pacific construction contracts. Something obviously had to be done about the railway, and he concluded that the government itself would have to build the parts that were most urgently needed. On August 30, 1874, a contract was awarded to Joseph Whitehead for the grading of a line from St. Boniface, across the Red River from Winnipeg, to the international boundary. The distance was sixty-three miles. Although invariably referred to as the Pembina branch, the line was on the east side of the Red River and would be linked at the border with St. Vincent, Minnesota, and not with Pembina, on the west bank. In keeping with tradition, Whitehead arranged for the turning of a first sod, but it may well have been the most modest ceremony of the kind on record. Mr. Peach, Whitehead's accountant, officiated on September 19 at a point about eight miles from Winnipeg. "There was no demonstration," the *Free Press* reported. "About half a dozen people were present, and a couple of wheelbarrows of earth constituted the work done."[6]

As was befitting, a much more elaborate sod turning, complete with speeches, followed the signing of a contract for the construction of a first segment of the main line. This was awarded in April 1875 to Sifton and Ward and covered forty-five miles of line (later reduced to thirty-two) from Fort William westward. At the time there was little at Fort William except the old Hudson's Bay trading post. The neighboring community of Prince Arthur's Landing, later Port Arthur, a few miles to the east, was the principal settlement. Hundreds of its citizens attended the sod-turning ceremony on June 1, at a spot about four miles west of Fort William.

Mackenzie was well aware that eastern connections would be essential, and in March Parliament had approved a subsidy of $12,000 a mile to assist the Canada Central Railway to extend its line from near Pembroke, in the Ottawa valley, to Lake Nipissing, a distance of about 120 miles. A contract had also been awarded for a connecting line that would in effect extend the Canada Central from Lake Nipissing to the head of navigation on the French River, which flows into Georgian Bay. A steamer service was planned between French River and Fort William.

This was a not unpromising beginning, but the unfortunate Mackenzie soon encountered fresh difficulties. A bill providing for the construction of the railway from Esquimalt to Nanaimo, in partial fulfilment of the Carnarvon Terms, passed the House of Commons but was defeated in the Senate—and defeated, it may be noted, by two defecting Liberal senators. Once again British Columbia was left with nothing to show for the railway clause of the terms of union.

To complicate the political situation further, it was evident that in spite of Edward Blake's highly critical attitude toward the railway, and in particular toward the obligation to British Columbia, Mackenzie had to devise ways and means of getting him back into his cabinet. In October 1874, in a famous speech delivered at Aurora, Ontario, Blake had expressed his opinions in no uncertain terms. Building the railway in the limited time specified would be a ruinous undertaking, and if failure to build it would result in British Columbia's secession, he was prepared to accept that consequence. Blake, in other

Alexander Mackenzie, prime minister of Canada from 1873 to 1878, whose political inheritance included the Pacific Railway project and a depression. (COURTESY OF THE PUBLIC ARCHIVES OF CANADA)

words, refused to regard the provision as a reasonable obligation; Mackenzie, on the other hand, recognized that a legal obligation existed that had to be dealt with, one way or another. Writing to Blake in April 1875, he made this clear: "I can only say . . . that I am bound in honour to do what we engaged to do unless we can make some other arrangement with the [British] Columbians, and that I am quite willing to try."[7]

As early as July 1874, in a report to Lord Dufferin, the governor-general, the government had contended that the railway terms were "directory rather than mandatory, and were to be interpreted by circumstances, the essence of the engagement being such diligence as was consistent with moderate expenditure, and no increase in the rate of taxation."[8] As evidence of the soundness of this view the report recalled the statement to that effect made both to the Conservative caucus and at a public banquet by J. W. Trutch, one of the three delegates from British Columbia who negotiated the terms of union. Later Senator W. W. Carrall, another of the delegates, would make a similar statement in the Senate.[9] But Walkem and the British Columbians would have none of it. "The terms and nothing but the terms" became their battle cry, and when Mackenzie tried to negotiate some modification of the Carnarvon Terms, following the defeat of the Esquimalt and Nanaimo railway bill, it was soon supplemented by a new cry, "Carnarvon Terms or Separation." Agreement seemed impossible. "My impression is that we will simply go on the even tenor of our way," Mackenzie wrote to George Brown, "begin as soon as we can, and go as fast as we can, and let them whistle."[10] This attitude had yielded one politically valuable dividend—Edward Blake had rejoined the cabinet in May 1875.

The controversy dragged on, and this occasioned a second incursion by an outsider. The governor-general decided that he could usefully intervene. Personally charming and an effective and fluent speaker, Lord Dufferin fancied himself in a diplomatic role. He decided to visit British Columbia and see what he could do to reduce the tension there. Mackenzie was not enthusiastic, but in the end he consented. Dufferin scored a distinct personal success on his tour and contrived to discuss both the Carnarvon Terms and the rival views about the railway terminus held on Vancouver Island and the mainland without giving offense to either side. His conclusions seem to have been that the province was entitled to greater compensation than Mackenzie was prepared to offer for the delay in construction and that Burrard Inlet was clearly preferable as the terminus. He said as much as he stepped off the train on his return to Ottawa, and only the deft confiscation of a reporter's notebook prevented a published statement that would have been extremely embarrassing to the government. In spite of this warning incident, Dufferin continued to press his views, and the result was an extraordinary interview at Government

House involving Mackenzie, Blake, and the governor-general in which everyone lost his temper and the speaking was very plain indeed. But all this, of course, was very much behind the scenes.[11]

Meanwhile Mackenzie did his best to push the railway forward in accordance with the Carnarvon Terms. In the fall of 1874 a telegraph line from Winnipeg to British Columbia was placed under contract, and early in 1875 provision was made for its extension eastward to Lake Superior. The railway surveys suffered a serious setback when much of the information that had been assembled with so much effort was destroyed by a fire in Ottawa in December 1873, but the work was pushed forward energetically. In the financial year 1873–74, when the government changed, expenditure on the surveys had fallen to $310,000; it climbed steeply thereafter to a maximum of $791,000 in 1876–77 and was almost as high the following year. Total expenditure from 1871 to 1878 was $3,734,000. Mackenzie thought little of the results achieved up to the time he took office in 1873. The government, he later told a Royal Commission, were not "in possession of opinions from the engineers, which would justify them in taking any decided action at that time."[12] But by 1876 he was most anxious that the surveys should have progressed sufficiently by the beginning of 1877 to make it possible to seek tenders for the building of the whole line. Tenders were duly invited through Sir John Rose, who had recently become the government's financial commissioner in London, but the depression still showed no great signs of lifting and the response was most disappointing; "notwithstanding all our efforts," Mackenzie later recalled, "we signally failed in obtaining one single offer (there was one imperfect offer made) for the construction of the railroad. . . ."[13]

This was doubly discouraging because the government's own experience of railroad building had been anything but happy. It had taken nearly four years to complete the grading of the sixty-three-mile Pembina branch from the international boundary to St. Boniface. Fortunately this did not matter greatly, as there was as yet no American railway with which the branch could make a connection. In May 1877, Joseph Whitehead, who had done the grading, was given a contract to extend it twenty miles northward to Selkirk, where the branch was to join the main line, and four contracts let in 1876–77 had provided for further grading and track laying on the main line itself. These were intended to complete it from Selkirk eastward to Keewatin and westward from Fort William to Eagle River.

This left a gap of 185 miles between Keewatin and Eagle River still unprovided for, and construction under the earlier contracts was lagging badly. The only encouraging and exciting events took place at St. Boniface, where track laying began at last in the autumn of 1877. The governor-general and Lady Dufferin graced the occasion and drove the first two spikes on September

29. Whitehead had purchased a locomotive and had named it *Countess of Dufferin* in the expectation that it would be delivered in time for the spike-driving ceremony, but a hitch occurred and it did not arrive until October 9, when it was brought down the Red River from Minnesota on a barge, accompanied by six flatcars and a van. A 4-4-0 American-type engine built by the Baldwin Locomotive Works, the *Countess* was the first railway engine in the Canadian West. Although no Canadian Pacific Railway existed at the time, the name was already coming into common use, and Whitehead painted "Canadian Pacific" and the numeral "1" on his locomotive. As it happened, the engine did pass to C.P.R. ownership in 1882. It was later acquired by the Columbia River Lumber Company, of Golden, British Columbia, and served them until it was taken to Winnipeg in 1910 for preservation. Restored to its original appearance in 1970, it now stands in a small park on Main Street, not far from where it was brought ashore nearly a century ago.

Slow as progress on the Pembina branch was, both the branch itself and an American line to connect with it were almost completed by the time Mackenzie left office in 1878. It was otherwise with the main line. Contractors for the various segments between Selkirk and Fort William had encountered many difficulties, and only about 150 miles of track had been completed. For one thing, Fleming's surveys often did not provide sufficient data upon which to judge with much accuracy the work that would be involved in construction. Thus the quantities of rock and earth that had to be moved frequently differed widely from the estimates, as the following example shows:

	ESTIMATED	ACTUAL
	(in cubic yards)	
Solid rock	260,000	76,800
Loose rock	10,000	110,000
Earth	1,000,000	1,970,000

Another problem, specially troublesome in building a line through the Laurentian Shield, was the unpredictable amount of material that might be required to build a firm foundation for the track through many of the swamps and muskegs. Such vast quantities of fill had to be dumped into one of the worst of the muskegs, near Barclay, about a hundred miles west of Fort William, that its depth was estimated at 200 feet. Faced with these and other difficulties, some contractors gave up; in other instances the contracts were canceled.

A Royal Commission that later investigated the whole building program of the Mackenzie government in great detail was highly critical of many things, including the tendering methods employed. Nominally the rule was that a contract was awarded to the lowest bidder, but in practice all manner of deals were concluded behind the scenes. No one questioned Mackenzie's personal integrity, but he was in power at a time when political patronage was rampant, and in practice he could be only as honest as the system made it possible for him to be. He described his dilemma to a colleague: "Friends expect to be benefited by offices they are unfit for, by contracts they are not entitled to, by advances not earned. Enemies ally themselves with friends and push their whims to the front. Some attempt to storm the office. Some dig trenches at a distance and approach in regular siege form. I feel like the besieged, lying on my arms night and day. I have offended at least 20 parliamentary friends by defence of the Citadel. A weak minister here would ruin the party in a month and the country very soon."[14]

The arrangements for the eastern lines were a case in point. The managing director of the Canada Central Railway, which had been given a cash subsidy to extend its line to Lake Nipissing, was Senator Asa B. Foster. By profession a railway contractor as well as a politician, Foster also received the contract to build the connecting branch from Lake Nipissing to Georgian Bay. It was generally accepted that it had been Foster who had secured from his friend George McMullen the copies of Sir Hugh Allan's correspondence, the publication of which had precipitated the Pacific Scandal and brought the Mackenzie government to power.

These rewards for services rendered were to bring no benefit either to Mackenzie or to Foster himself. The latter was soon in deep financial trouble; the Canada Central project made no progress and the Georgian Bay contract had to be canceled. Foster resigned from the Senate in 1875 and died a bankrupt in 1877.

Half a dozen of the contracts awarded in the West were given either to Joseph Whitehead or to a partnership that included J. W. Sifton. Whitehead had been a Liberal member of Parliament from 1867 to 1872, but he was at least qualified to undertake the work he proposed to do. He had been associated with railways and railway building most of his life, and was reputed to have acted as fireman on Robert Stephenson's pioneer locomotive on the Stockton and Darlington Railway. Sifton's associate in the first of his contracts was David Glass, a lawyer from London, Ontario, who had been the first follower of Sir John Macdonald to desert him over the Pacific Scandal.

In virtually every instance costs exceeded estimates, often by large margins. Part of Mackenzie's troubles undoubtedly arose because the government was facing the same problem in Ottawa that Fleming faced in the field—the lack of anything approaching an adequate number of qualified staff. The civil service was small and was composed in large part of political appointees. Able and reliable supervisors were sadly lacking. It is no wonder that Mackenzie looked forward to the day when it would be possible to hand over railway construction to private capitalists.

In spite of his lack of enthusiasm for the project and the very limited resources of the government, Mackenzie made adequate financial provision for the surveys and construction authorized while he was in office. Each year appropriations exceeded expenditure. During the four financial years ending June 30, 1878, $6,469,361 was spent on construction and $2,342,970 on railway surveys, a total of $8,812,331. The appropriations provided by Parliament in the same period totaled $14,889,900.

Since it was fairly certain that 1878 would be an election year, Mackenzie was most anxious to settle some points and to be able to report further progress before he appealed to the country. For a time Fleming's far-flung and continuing surveys had been a useful excuse for postponing construction; it was clearly impracticable to build the railway until its route had been determined. But by the spring of 1878 even Mackenzie was becoming impatient. In his last report Fleming had stated with obvious pride that "the length of the various lines surveyed and explored aggregate to close on 46,000 miles, of which no less than 11,500 miles have been laboriously measured, yard by yard, through mountains, prairies and forests, with the spirit level, chain and transit."[15] In spite of this, much remained uncertain. A firm decision seemed to have been made in favor of the Yellowhead Pass, but Fleming was still hesitating in choosing one of eleven different routes from the pass to the Pacific. If a decision had had to be made at once, he would undoubtedly have favored following the Fraser and Thompson rivers to a terminus at Burrard Inlet. But as luck would have it, when Mackenzie desperately needed a decision, Fleming was in England on leave, and his place had been taken by Marcus Smith, the archadvocate of the route to Esquimalt by way of Bute Inlet. In the end practical considerations prevailed. Carrying the railway from the mainland to Vancouver Island would be both costly and difficult; on the other hand, steamers could run up the Fraser as far as Yale, over a hundred miles inland, and a line from Yale to Kamloops, about 150 miles, could be put under contract without much delay. On July 12, 1878, the cabinet chose Burrard Inlet as the terminus and decided to call for tenders for the Yale line.

The reaction in British Columbia was immediate and vigorous. Just two weeks previously George Walkem, who to Mackenzie's relief had been out of office since early in 1876, had again become premier. As a strong partisan of Victoria and Vancouver Island he was unwilling to accept the choice of Burrard Inlet as a terminus and he had little faith in the performance of the Mackenzie government. On August 30 the British Columbia legislature resolved to take steps to withdraw from Confederation if construction of the railway within the province did not begin by May 1879.

This threat was not destined to trouble Mackenzie. No government that has the misfortune to be in office during a prolonged depression is likely to be popular, and inevitably it is blamed for conditions for which it has little or no responsibility. When Sir John Macdonald was crushingly defeated in the general election of 1874 as a result of the Pacific Scandal, many assumed that his career was ended. But after keeping very much in the background for a time, he began a quiet but effective campaign to rehabilitate himself and his party, one feature of which was a series of political picnics that were to become famous. He was a most astute, attractive, and beguiling politician, and it had never been thought that he personally had benefited from Allan's money. He emerged as the advocate of the National Policy—another name for a protective tariff that would encourage industries and agriculture in Canada and protect them against American imports, which had been dumped freely on the Canadian market during the depression years.

The election—the first in which the secret ballot was used—was held on September 17, 1878, and resulted in an overwhelming victory for Macdonald and the Conservatives. Mackenzie, who had expected to win, could scarcely credit the result; Macdonald, who had also expected to win, was astonished by the measure of his success. He was to be prime minister for the rest of his life. In failing health after five years of overwork and worry, Mackenzie at heart was probably not sorry to shift to someone else's shoulders the burdens of office, particularly the problem of dealing with the troublesome province on the Pacific and of finding ways and means to build the Canadian Pacific Railway.

4

A Vital Side Issue:
The St. Paul and Pacific

Prime minister once again in October 1878, Sir John Macdonald had the good fortune to find the railroad builders for whom Alexander Mackenzie had searched in vain. They were a remarkable group, brought together initially by a common interest in transportation in the Red River valley in Minnesota and Manitoba. When Macdonald returned to office, they were completing a complicated and controversial deal that gave them ownership of the St. Paul and Pacific Railroad. Bankrupt and decrepit at the time, the St. Paul and Pacific was destined to prosper amazingly and to make millionaires of them all. The history of the transaction is very much a part of the C.P.R. story, for it was this first successful venture into railroading that encouraged its promoters to undertake the construction and operation of the Canadian Pacific.

There were four members in the original group—Donald A. Smith, Norman W. Kittson, James J. Hill, and George Stephen. The first two were old fur traders. Donald Smith, the future Lord Strathcona, had come to Canada as a youth of eighteen and had entered the employ of the Hudson's Bay Company. After serving for a time at posts on the lower St. Lawrence, he had spent twenty years on the bleak coast of Labrador. This would have dulled the wits of many men, but Smith was confident that he would emerge some day from the wilderness and he prepared carefully for the event. He showed great enterprise in managing his unpromising district, read widely, and kept in touch with the outside world by correspondence. He invested his own modest funds shrewdly and was soon entrusted with the savings of others. As a result he was already a man of considerable means when he left Labrador in 1869, at the age of forty-nine, and was placed in charge of the Hudson's Bay Company's Montreal district.

Thereafter his rise to prominence was rapid. Late in 1869 Sir John Macdonald asked him to go to Red River as a special commissioner to try to negotiate with Louis Riel, who was leading the resistance to Canada's takeover of the western prairies. This difficult and hazardous mission he carried out with great courage and substantial success. As a result he became involved in politics, both in Manitoba and in Parliament, to which he was elected in 1871. The same year he was appointed chief commissioner for the Hudson's Bay Company in Canada, and in 1872 his prominence in business affairs was recognized when he was elected a director of the influential Bank of Montreal.

Traditionally the Hudson's Bay Company had been a determined enemy of settlement in the West, which it assumed would destroy the fur trade. A realist to the core, Smith took a different view. "You will understand," he had written as early as 1860, "that I, as a Labrador man, cannot be expected to sympathize altogether with the prejudice against settlers and railways entertained by many of the western commissioned officers."[1] Whether the company liked it or not, the West would certainly be settled eventually; the important thing, in Smith's view, would be to turn this to maximum account. Although as chief commissioner he was in charge of the fur trade, he was prepared to see it decline, and he felt that the company's prime asset lay in the seven million acres it was to receive under the terms of the deed of surrender that had ended its rule of Rupert's Land. Profits from land could arise only through settlement, and colonists would not come to the Canadian West in any numbers unless it were easily accessible. Hence his interest in transportation on the Red River and in the St. Paul and Pacific Railroad, whose charter provided for a line from St. Paul north to St. Vincent, just below the Manitoba boundary.

The other fur trader, Canadian-born Norman Kittson, had joined Astor's American Fur Company and had spent years in northern Minnesota, near the international border, where he had competed with the posts and traders of the Hudson's Bay Company. Later he settled in St. Paul, where he developed a flourishing general supply house, made a fortune in real estate, and was active in civic and territorial politics. He also acted as the St. Paul agent of the Hudson's Bay Company.

Kittson operated steamers and barges on the Red River, and this brought him into contact with James J. Hill. Later to become one of the towering figures in the history of American railroading, Hill was born in Ontario and had been in St. Paul since 1856. As a youth he had found work there as a shipping clerk, and by the 1860s he had a forwarding and transportation agency of his own as well as a flourishing fuel business. Concerned at first chiefly with the Mississippi trade, he had become more and more interested in the Red River valley to the north, which he expected would soon be filled with settlers. In his opinion, St. Paul was the logical point of entry not only to the valley itself, but to the vast expanses of the Canadian prairies that lay beyond.

Smith and Hill first met in March 1870, in somewhat dramatic circumstances. Smith was on his way back to Ottawa after his meeting with Riel; Hill was traveling north from St. Paul to gauge the effect the events in Red River were likely to have on trade and transportation. Both were traveling by dog team and they met by chance in the midst of a blizzard. The encounter led to a lifelong friendship and to close associations in business.

Transportation was already Hill's consuming interest, and his immediate ambition was to gain control of the traffic between St. Paul and Winnipeg. An opportunity to accomplish this came when steamers were introduced on the Red River. Those chiefly involved were the Hudson's Bay Company, Norman Kittson, and Hill himself. Kittson and Hill merged their operations, and after Hill and Donald Smith had met, the Hudson's Bay Company soon became a silent partner in the combine. The result was the Red River Transportation Company, which enjoyed a virtual monopoly of the trade and was inclined to deal roughly with would-be competitors.

It was clearly only a matter of time before the river steamers would be superseded by a railway, presumably the St. Paul and Pacific. Hill was well informed about its affairs because he had acted as its forwarding agent in St. Paul and his coal and wood business had supplied it with fuel. He longed to gain control of it, but there seemed little prospect that he would be able to do so. In spite of an unfortunate past that had been profitable only to promoters and speculators, it seemed to be on the verge of better days. The Northern Pacific had begun to build its main line westward from Duluth in 1870, and sharing Hill's conviction that the Red River valley would soon become a busy traffic artery, it had acquired control of the St. Paul and Pacific. A $15 million bond issue, sold mostly in the Netherlands in 1871, seemed to provide ample funds to complete and equip the line to the Canadian border. But the bulk of the money was never applied to the purposes for which it was nominally intended, and when hard times came the railroad ceased to pay interest on its bonds and fell into arrears in payments to its contractors. The collapse of its credit helped to pull down the Northern Pacific, and in 1873 both lines went into receivership.

In this collapse Hill thought he saw his opportunity. The Northern Pacific had lost control of the St. Paul and Pacific, and he was fascinated by the possibility of buying up the bonds in default at a heavy discount, foreclosing the mortgages they represented, and then purchasing the St. Paul and Pacific at foreclosure sales. Presently Donald Smith also became attracted by this pos-

Donald A. Smith (later Lord Strathcona) about the time he and James J. Hill succeeded in involving George Stephen in their efforts to gain control of the St. Paul and Pacific. (COURTESY OF THE PUBLIC ARCHIVES OF CANADA)

sibility. He had been interested for some years in promoting a railway or railways that would link Manitoba with the outside world and thereby open the Canadian West (including the lands of the Hudson's Bay Company) to settlement. Two lines to accomplish this were actually incorporated by the Canadian Parliament in 1872, and Smith had been a sponsor of both. The Manitoba Junction Railway was to run south to the international border, where it was expected to connect with the St. Paul and Pacific; the Lake Superior and Winnipeg was to build eastward to Thunder Bay, whence steamers would provide connections with the East. But the charters were to become effective by proclamation, and the Canadian government declined to proclaim either, for the very good reason that they would conflict with its own plans for a Pacific railway.

Today these stillborn companies are of interest because the sponsors of both included Donald Smith's cousin, George Stephen, the future Lord Mount Stephen, who would become the virtual founder and first president of the Canadian Pacific Railway. Stephen had come to Canada from Scotland in 1850. Shrewd, able, and hardworking, he had quickly made his way in the textile trade. Woollen and cotton mills and a wide variety of commercial and manufacturing enterprises were soon added to his interests. In 1871 he became a director of the Bank of Montreal, then the most important financial institution in Canada, and five years later became its president. The bank had taken an active but cautious interest in railway securities, in which its important New York branch specialized, and this continued under Stephen's guidance. Personally, however, his involvement in railway matters was still very marginal, consisting for the most part of shares in a number of firms—none very prosperous—that built locomotives and manufactured railway equipment. More interesting, in view of later events, was his reaction to an early effort to persuade him to join in a scheme to build the Pacific railway. The approach was made in 1874 by none other than Lucius Huntington, the Liberal member of Parliament who had moved the resolution in the House of Commons that touched off the Pacific Scandal. Stephen discussed the proposal with his friend Luther Holton, a railway contractor, and reported the gist of the conversation to Huntington: "I explained to him . . . that while nothing would induce me to take a pecuniary interest in any scheme that might be formed for building the road, I was quite willing to lend any assistance that might be within my power, towards aiding in the formation of an organisation such as the Govt. would be justified in entrusting with the work. . . ."[2] Here spoke the banker; the railroad builder had yet to appear.

That same year, 1874, the contract for the grading of the Pembina branch of the C.P.R. from Winnipeg to the Minnesota border was awarded by the Mackenzie government, a move that sharpened Donald Smith's interest in the St. Paul and Pacific. Settlement had just become his major concern, as he had been appointed land commissioner of the Hudson's Bay Company, and the Pembina branch would be of very limited assistance to colonization in the Canadian West until there was an American line with which it could connect at the boundary. Hitherto Smith had thought in terms of encouraging others to provide the connection; now he began to wonder if Hill's dream of gaining control of the St. Paul and Pacific might not offer a quicker and more profitable solution.

Meanwhile Hill had set about ascertaining every detail of the railway's condition, revenues, assets, and liabilities. He found that its income was derived almost wholly from a 207-mile main line from St. Paul westward to

Breckenridge, where connections were made with the steamers on the Red River, and a 76-mile branch that ran up the Mississippi to Sauk Rapids and St. Cloud. Two extension lines were partly built. Only a few miles of track had been laid on the first, which was to extend from Sauk Rapids north to Brainerd, on the main line of the Northern Pacific, and there were gaps totaling about 170 miles in the all-important 319-mile line from St. Cloud to St. Vincent and the Canadian border. As grading was well advanced, these lines could be completed fairly quickly, but in view of the prevailing depression early action was unlikely. Moreover, Minnesota was suffering from a plague of grasshoppers that devastated the whole countryside for four successive seasons and had brought settlement virtually to a standstill.

The physical condition of much of the track and equipment was deplorable, but in spite of everything the railway was earning something more than its operating expenses—indeed, its net revenues were actually higher than its reports indicated, for Hill noticed that items that should have been charged to capital account were being included in working expenses. Even so, revenue fell far short of the sum required to pay the interest on its bonds.

Many matters were complicated by the company's dual corporate structure. Some years earlier, its revenue-producing lines had been siphoned off to a First Division company, leaving only the partly built extension lines under the control of the St. Paul and Pacific proper. The latter was in the hands of a receiver; the First Division was being operated by a manager appointed by trustees. Fortunately the two posts were held by one man, Jesse P. Farley. Most of the mortgage bonds, which related to both divisions of the railway, were held in the Netherlands, and the Dutch bondholders had formed a committee to watch over their interests. Johan Carp of Utrecht made two visits to America on its behalf, and the committee was also represented by John S. Kennedy of New York, whose financial house specialized in railway securities. To secure complete control of the St. Paul and Pacific, it would be necessary not only to buy up the mortgage bonds but also to acquire a substantial block of First Division shares held by E. B. Litchfield, a Brooklyn financier.

In addition to its lines and equipment, the railroad possessed a valuable asset in its land grants. These totaled about 2.5 million acres, and it would be entitled to an additional 1.4 million acres when the extension lines were completed. But their value, from Hill's point of view, was uncertain, because under existing Minnesota law a bankrupt railway would forfeit its land grants if it passed to new ownership.

This hazard was removed in 1876, thanks to the efforts of Hill and a number of political associates, including Norman Kittson. Early in 1877, spurred on by this success, Hill and Kittson sent Carp an offer to purchase the

First Division company. They had no expectation that it would be accepted, but it enabled them to gain some idea of the valuation the Dutch themselves placed on their holdings. Bargaining then began in earnest, as time was becoming a vital factor. Already one attempt had been made by Litchfield to reorganize the railway, and the Northern Pacific, now itself reorganized, might soon be in a position to regain control of it—a move that would have been disastrous for the Dutch.

Money now became the prime necessity, and for help in financing the proposed purchase Hill turned to Donald Smith and, through him, to George Stephen. The three met in Montreal and placed tentative valuations on the five bond issues held in great part by the Dutch. The total price envisaged was about $4 million. In May Hill and Kittson again approached Carp and outlined a proposal based on this valuation. Carp did not consider it unreasonable —it was, in fact, over a million dollars more than the value assigned to the bonds recently on the New York exchange—and it became evident that an agreement was possible.

Stephen seems to have had lingering doubts, but these were stilled over the next few months. Hill prepared a detailed valuation of the entire St. Paul and Pacific property, which indicated that in his opinion, once the extension lines had been completed, the system would be worth nearly $13 million. This did not include the land grants, which would be worth at least another $6.5 million. He estimated that the cost of buying the mortgage bonds and completing the extension lines would be about $5.5 million. In August business took Stephen to Chicago; he traveled on to St. Paul and went over part of the railway with Hill. He was reassured by what he saw and decided that the railway was worth a gamble. In September he set out for London, where he expected to raise the funds required to make the purchase. To his surprise and mortification he met with complete failure. The financial woes of the Northern Pacific and numerous other companies had destroyed British confidence in American railroad securities.

It was characteristic of Stephen that he refused to admit defeat. While in Europe he had visited the Netherlands and discussed the whole transaction with the Dutch committee; he now went to New York, met John S. Kennedy, and with his help persuaded the committee to agree to a purchase on credit. Payment was to be made within six months of the foreclosure sales that would give Stephen and his associates ownership of the railway, and bondholders would be paid either in cash or (as most of them elected) in the bonds of a new company that would succeed the St. Paul and Pacific, plus a bonus of 25 percent in preferred stock.

In spite of this helpful arrangement, the cash sum needed immediately was substantial; the essential thing was to keep it down to a total the associates could hope to raise personally. A deposit of $100,000 was required as a guarantee of performance; interest at 7 percent on the purchase price of the bonds was to begin at once and continue until they were paid for in cash or new securities; the Dutch committee had to be reimbursed for various expenditures totaling about $280,000. The committee controlled only about 85 percent of the outstanding mortgage bonds; the rest would have to be bought in the open market. By pledging their own possessions as security, Stephen, Smith, Hill, and Kittson were able to borrow nearly $700,000 from the Bank of Montreal to meet these and other contingencies. By March 13, 1878, they were in control of the railroad.

Even so they were by no means out of the woods, for a deadline set by the Minnesota legislature for the closing of the first gap in the St. Vincent extension was little more than four months away. After an exasperating delay, the courts sanctioned the issuing of receiver's debentures to cover construction costs and the track was completed with one day to spare. Work was then pressed forward on the other gaps, and the through line from St. Paul and St. Cloud to St. Vincent was ready in November. It was extended over the boundary to Emerson, Manitoba, where it connected with the recently completed Pembina branch of the C.P.R. Winnipeg had at last secured the longed-for rail link with the outside world and on December 2 gave the first train from St. Paul a boisterous welcome at St. Boniface.

Donald Smith could now hope for a brisk sale of Hudson's Bay lands. As for Hill, convinced as he was that it would be many years before an all-Canadian railway battled its way through the rocky wilderness north of Lake Superior, he seemed to have achieved his ambition to control traffic to and from the Red River valley and, potentially, the Canadian West as well.

Stephen was still busy completing the last steps of the purchase. In January 1879, after difficult negotiations, he was able to buy Litchfield's First Division shares for $500,000. On May 23 the St. Paul, Minneapolis and Manitoba Railroad was organized to succeed the St. Paul and Pacific. Stephen became its president and Hill shared management with R. B. Angus, formerly general manager of the Bank of Montreal, whom Stephen had persuaded to move to St. Paul and watch over his new venture. Decrees of foreclosure had been granted in March, and in June the new company bought the various segments of the old at foreclosure sales for a reputed total of $6,780,000.

To pay the Dutch, to repay advances made by the Bank of Montreal and by the associates themselves, and to provide equipment and working capital, the St. Paul, Minneapolis and Manitoba issued some $16 million in mortgage bonds. In addition, common stock with a par value of $15 million was issued to the four partners. The actual value of the stock would depend, of course, upon whether the railway proved to be a profitable enterprise. This it did with surprising speed. Hill hoped that net revenue would soon reach $700,000 or $800,000 and would increase year by year as settlement spread. This proved to be a modest estimate, for net earnings in the new company's first fiscal year, ending June 30, 1880, totaled $1.58 million and rose to nearly $2 million the following year. The grasshoppers had vanished, the depression was lifting, and settlers were pouring into Minnesota. Traffic increased rapidly and the railway prospered.

The purchase of the St. Paul and Pacific has sometimes been represented as a swindle. For one, Gustavus Myers, who always assumed the worst about any capitalist, chronicled it in *A History of Canadian Wealth*, along with many other transactions that he considered dubious. The charge seemed to gain some support when Jesse Farley sued Hill and Kittson, alleging that they had promised him a substantial share in the St. Paul, Minneapolis and Manitoba. This could only be for services rendered, and the only services Farley could have rendered would have been to misrepresent the assets and prospects of the St. Paul and Pacific so that Hill and his associates could buy it up cheaply. It is clear that no such agreement existed, and, as pointed out in the courts, if it had existed it would have constituted a flagrant betrayal of Farley's trust as receiver and general manager. The case dragged on for twelve years until 1893, when it was dismissed by the Supreme Court of the United States. By that time Farley was dead.

An agreement did exist among Hill, Kittson, Smith, and Stephen. In March 1878, when they gained control of the railway, they agreed formally that two-fifths of "the profits and losses which may accrue from said enterprise" should be apportioned to Stephen, and one-fifth each to Hill, Kittson, and Smith, on the understanding that Stephen would use the extra one-fifth interest "for the purpose of securing the necessary means to carry out and complete our said agreement with said Dutch committee. . . ."[3] What Stephen did with the extra one-fifth was for many years a mystery, but Stephen's biographer recently discovered a letter written in 1908 that reveals that he gave it to John S. Kennedy, who had been "very useful" to him in negotiating the purchase of the St. Paul and Pacific. This must have been done some time after the event, as in November 1880 Stephen told Macdonald that Kennedy did not have "one dollar of interest" in the succeeding company, the St. Paul, Minneapolis and Manitoba.[4]

But the purchase was no clandestine affair. Hill had talked interminably to friends in St. Paul about his hopes of securing control of the railway. Stephen had failed to convince any London financial house that its purchase could be a highly profitable transaction. The only secret document involved was Hill's detailed valuation of the property, dated September 1, 1877, which placed the total at about $20 million.[5] It is interesting to note that in October Johan Carp, acting for the bondholders, estimated its value, including the land grants, at no more than $6,866,759.[6]

The risks taken were very great, for the legal and financial complications involved were formidable. Hill and his attorneys looked after the legal problems, but the key role was clearly played by George Stephen, without whose negotiating skill and financial planning the deal could not have been consummated.

Summary details of the purchase itself will be of interest. Bonds from three of the earlier issues were acquired at the market price; for a fourth series the price was increased from 45 to 75 cents on the dollar. Bonds in these four issues with a par value of $5,812,000 were purchased for $2,175,850. It was the notorious $15 million issue of 1871 that fared worst. It was quoted on the exchange at only 6⅝, but the associates agreed to more than double the price to 13¾. In all, bonds with a face value of $17,212,000 were acquired for $3,743,350.[7]

O. D. Skelton tells the story that when in 1880 Macdonald was looking about for railway builders, J. H. Pope, a future minister of railways, drew his attention to Stephen and his associates and remarked: "Catch them before they invest their profits."[8] But at the time those profits still lay mostly in the future. There is no foundation for Gustavus Myers's statement that immediately after the foreclosure sale the greater part of the land grant was sold for $13,068,887.[9] Nor is there any truth in the charge, to which he gave credence, that Stephen financed the transaction by taking $8 million from the Bank of Montreal (of which he was president) "without the consent or knowledge of the directors of that bank."[10] No doubt Stephen and his associates profited almost at once from the rise in the market value of their shares, but major returns did not materialize until a little later. No dividends were paid by the St. Paul, Minneapolis and Manitoba until 1882. By that time the Canadian Pacific was speeding across the prairies at the rate of several miles every working day.

5

The Main Issue:
Syndicate and Contract

Some months passed before the new Macdonald government made known its intentions regarding the Pacific railway. The prime minister had much else on his mind. The election had been won on a protectionist platform, and he was preoccupied with tariff changes and with securing parliamentary approval for them. He was anxious to open the negotiations with the British government that were to result in the appointment of a high commissioner for Canada in London. Nearer at hand, a highly unpopular lieutenant-governor was causing political complications in Quebec. Economic conditions had not improved, and for the time being it seemed impossible to do more than push forward construction of the fragments of the line that the Mackenzie government had placed under contract.

Railway policy was primarily the concern of Sir John Macdonald himself and of Sir Charles Tupper. Although devoted to his native province of Nova Scotia, Tupper shared Macdonald's broad ambitions for Canada. Briefly as minister of public works and subsequently as first incumbent of the new portfolio of railways and canals, he was responsible for railways in general and the Pacific railway in particular. A commanding political figure and a formidable debater, Tupper quickly became an ardent supporter of the project and he was to champion its cause with great vigor many times during the difficult years that lay ahead.

First decisions began to emerge in the spring of 1879. In April Tupper notified Sandford Fleming that two matters that had been regarded as settled —the choice of the Yellowhead Pass as the railway's route through the Rockies and of Burrard Inlet as its western terminus—were to be reconsidered. In spite of all the surveys that had been made, passes north of the Yellowhead were to be examined once again and another look was to be taken at Bute Inlet, with the possibility in mind of carrying the line to Vancouver Island and of having the terminus at Esquimalt, adjacent to Victoria. These appear to have been political moves, intended chiefly to provide a brief delay and to placate Victoria, which by a quirk of politics Macdonald now represented in Parliament. It is significant that Tupper announced in May that 125 miles of railway would be built in British Columbia—a proposal that was scarcely rational if the government really had no idea where the line was to be built.

Looking about for ways and means of financing the railway, the government explored the possibility of having it built by a board of commissioners. The necessary funds would be derived from the sale of bonds, which would be secured by 100 million acres of western lands. Macdonald was hopeful that the British government would help the scheme with loans or guarantees, and he and Tupper traveled to London to seek this assistance. Their mission was unsuccessful; the British were sympathetic, but the time was deemed to be inappropriate politically for any large new financial commitment.

Tupper made a popular decision when he rerouted the main line from Selkirk through Winnipeg and thence westward to Portage la Prairie, south of Lake Manitoba, instead of crossing the narrows of the lake as Fleming had intended. The change in route assured Winnipeg's future and, incidentally, made easier the much-discussed later adoption of a more southerly route across the whole prairie region.

In August the first hundred miles of line west of Winnipeg were placed under contract. By October the reports from the mountain surveys ordered in the spring had been received, and it was decided that they provided no justification for a major change of plan. The Yellowhead Pass was once again approved as the route through the Rockies, and the choice of Burrard Inlet as the terminus was confirmed. Tupper thereupon invited tenders for the construction of the line from Yale, the head of navigation on the Fraser, to Kamloops Lake, a distance of 127 miles. The route lay through the rugged canyons of the Fraser and Thompson rivers, and Tupper considered it "the heaviest and most difficult section" of the entire railway; its early construction would mean "the breaking of the backbone of the undertaking."[1] All four of the contracts involved were awarded to or taken over by Andrew Onderdonk, a young but experienced American engineer and contractor who had the backing of substantial capitalists including Ogden Mills of San Francisco and Levi Morton of New York. The total contract price was $9.1 million (just short of $72,000 a mile) and the line was to be completed by June 30, 1885.

These decisions and contracts represented significant progress, but prospects for building the railway as a whole remained uncertain. As late as April 1880 the government still believed that it would have to continue construction itself as best it could. "The policy of the Government," Tupper then informed Fleming, "is to construct a cheap railway . . . with any workable gradients that can be had, incurring no expenditure beyond that absolutely necessary to effect the rapid colonization of the country."[2] Within weeks there was a dramatic change in atmosphere and prospects—a surprising turnabout for which Tupper himself was largely responsible. Two considerations influenced him: clear evidence that the long depression of the 1870s was ending and some intimation that George Stephen might be prepared to take an interest in building the railway. The government was most anxious to turn construction over to private enterprise, and Tupper decided that the time had come to make a determined effort to do so.

Macdonald was recovering from his second serious illness within a year, so Tupper took the initiative. He asked his staff for cost estimates and was given figures that seemed to bring construction within the realm of practical politics. Having revised them downward to some extent, Tupper submitted a memorandum to the cabinet on June 15. He believed that the line could be completed from Lake Nipissing to the Pacific Coast for a cash subsidy of $45.5 million and a land grant of 25 million acres, and that the government could recover the subsidy (expected to be paid over a period of ten years) by sales from the 75 million acres that would remain out of the 100 million set aside by Parliament to finance the railway.

The money subsidy turned out to be much higher than the cabinet was prepared to approve, but the government did decide to offer a subsidy of $20 million, with 30 million acres of land. Quite as important, it approved Tupper's recommendation that "authority be given to negotiate with capitalists of undoubted means . . . who shall be required to give the most ample guarantees for the construction and operation of the line on such terms as will secure at the same time the rapid settlement of the public lands and the construction of the work."[3]

Specially significant was the reference to the *operation* of the line. Macdonald and Tupper were not looking for a contractor who would build the railway, pocket his profit, and disappear; they wanted to see a company formed that would both build and run the line and would therefore be vitally interested in sound construction and the railway's long-term prospects.

Also significant was the reference in Tupper's memorandum to "the great success which had attended the St. Paul, Minneapolis and Manitoba Railway Co." as being one of the factors that had encouraged him to prepare his submission. Although the first annual report of the railway had not yet been issued, word of the rapid increase in its revenues and land sales had reached Ottawa, and Tupper was hopeful that what had happened in Minnesota could be repeated in the Canadian West. Only four days after Tupper had spoken in cabinet, a confidential memorandum outlining the government's subsidy proposals was sent to Duncan McIntyre, and Macdonald and Tupper were well aware that it was in effect going to George Stephen. McIntyre controlled the Canada Central Railway, which would provide the C.P.R. with an extension eastward to Ottawa from its wilderness terminus near Lake Nipissing; he would have to be included in any transcontinental scheme, and the fact that he and Stephen had already been in touch was evidence of the latter's interest in the project.

McIntyre's response to the memorandum was a counteroffer to build the railway for a subsidy of $26.5 million and 35 million acres of land. Neither side would compromise, and on July 5 McIntyre informed Macdonald that he and his associates wished the subject to "be considered as being closed for the present."[4] The wording was encouraging; negotiations had been suspended but with an indication that they would probably be resumed.

The exchange had been most useful, for it had given Macdonald some idea of the probable maximum cost of the railway, which would be substantially less, in cash at least, than Tupper had estimated in June. Moreover, to Macdonald's surprise and satisfaction, other offers and inquiries were received. Onderdonk's backers were interested; Puleston, Brown and Company, a London financial house, sent a titled emissary to Ottawa to make inquiries; Brassey and Company, the famous English contractors who had built the Grand Trunk, were said to be anxious to build the Pacific railway. Macdonald decided that a visit to London would be appropriate. He sailed on July 10, accompanied by Tupper and another of his ministers, John Henry Pope, who had been a party to the negotiations with McIntyre and Stephen.

There was ample evidence that Stephen was still interested in the railway. McIntyre sailed with Macdonald, and when their ship picked up the mails at Rimouski, they included a remarkable letter from Stephen himself, written from a hideaway where he had gone to enjoy the fishing. He came to the heart of the matter in the second paragraph:

> There are two ways by which you can get a road built and operated: one by getting up a financial organization such as Allan contemplated and such as Jay Cooke & Co. got up for construction of the Northern Pacific Railway—with what result I need not remind you. A scheme of this nature involves the issue of a large amount of Bonds, just as large as an attractive prospectus will float . . . the outcome . . . is that the real responsibility is transferred from the Company to the people who may be induced to buy the Bonds, while the Company or the projectors pocket a big profit at the start out of the proceeds. . . . The other plan, and the one

I should have followed, had we been able to come to terms, would have been to limit the borrowing of money from the public to the smallest possible point, and . . . to have looked for the return of our own capital and a legitimate profit entirely to the growth of the country and the development of the property—after the work of construction had been fully accomplished. I could not be a party to a scheme involving a large issue of Bonds on a road which no one now can be sure will earn enough to pay working expenses. . . . No English or American organization could really do the work as advantageously and at so little cost as we could, nor could they so readily develop the earning power of the property; but, while we should wait for our profit and take the risk of its coming at all, they would inevitably pocket theirs at once.

Stephen explained that he had ended negotiations in order to leave Macdonald "perfectly free to make the best bargain you could on the other side." He continued:

Mr. Angus has been with me all the week, and we have done little else than discuss the matter, the salmon being few and far between. We are both satisfied of our ability to construct the road without much trouble, but we are not so sure by any means about its profitable operation; but in regard to this, if we cannot operate it successfully no one else can. . . . Our experience of settling lands in Minnesota would be a great help to us in the management of the lands granted to the Road. We are also clear on the point that the Canada Central and the Quebec roads would have to be incorporated. Nipissing is nowhere. Montreal or Quebec must be the starting point.

Although I am off the notion of the thing now, should anything occur on the other side to induce you to think that taking all things into consideration, our proposal is better upon the whole for the country than any offer you get in England, I might, on hearing from you, renew it and possibly in doing so reduce the land grant to some extent.[5]

Macdonald considered it expedient to make a gesture toward the Grand Trunk, and in London he and Tupper talked to Sir Henry Tyler, the Grand Trunk's president. Two versions of the interview have come down to us. Tupper stated in his *Recollections* that Tyler refused to consider an all-Canadian route for the railway and would not even submit the proposal to his board unless the line north of Lake Superior were omitted.[6] Tyler gave his version at a company meeting in 1891: "I never had the offer and I never refused it." He was certain the shareholders would have considered that he "had gone stark staring mad if I had in a brief conversation stated to Sir Charles Tupper my willingness to burden the Grand Trunk Company with such a contract, knowing nothing of the cost."[7] Whatever the truth may be, it is certain that in 1880 the Grand Trunk had little interest in the future of the Canadian Pacific other, perhaps, than a hope that it might acquire it cheaply later on, when it expected it to be in a bankrupt state. The Grand Trunk was just attaining its long-sought

George Stephen (later Lord Mount Stephen), the man chiefly responsible for the survival of the Canadian Pacific during the difficult construction period. This remarkable photograph was taken by William Notman, the famous Montreal photographer, in 1871. (COURTESY OF THE NOTMAN PHOTOGRAPHIC ARCHIVES, MCCORD MUSEUM OF MCGILL UNIVERSITY)

objective of a through line of its own to Chicago, and any approach it might make to the Canadian West would be by way of connecting lines from Chicago south of the Great Lakes.

When leaving Ottawa for London, Macdonald had stated that he had "three substantial offers for the C.P.R.—not only to build but to run it as a railway company, and to give satisfactory guarantees."[8] This was an exaggeration, as soon became apparent. Onderdonk's backers withdrew on the ground that there was insufficient time for them to prepare a detailed proposal. For a time Puleston, Brown and Company seemed to be serious bidders, but they too dropped out of the running. This left only Stephen and his associates, represented in London by Duncan McIntyre. Macdonald turned to him, and on August 12 an offer was received from Stephen to build the railway (excluding the portions already under construction by the government) for a cash subsidy of $25 million and a land grant of 25 million acres. Stephen had reduced the land requirement, as he had hinted he might do, and had slightly reduced the cash subsidy as well. Macdonald accepted these terms, and a preliminary agreement was signed on September 4, to Macdonald's immense satisfaction. Not only would the railway be built, but it would be controlled and operated by a strong and experienced Canadian-based group, headed by a man for whom he had the highest regard and respect. As president of the Bank of Montreal and in many other capacities, Stephen had won a commanding position in Canadian finance, and his association with the St. Paul, Minneapolis and Manitoba Railway was adding greatly to his wealth. He could afford to wait for a profit from the Canadian Pacific, as he had told Macdonald he was prepared to do.

September and October were busy and anxious months for both Macdonald and Stephen. The details of the formal contract had to be hammered out and arrangements made for initial financing. Negotiations began as soon as McIntyre returned to Canada with the preliminary agreement. "I have seen . . . the important document (which my *friends* and my *enemies* agree in affecting to think will be the ruin of us all) and I hope there will be no difficulty in our coming to terms upon all points," Stephen wrote to Macdonald. "I want whatever arrangement is made that it shall be *fair* and *creditable* to both the Government and ourselves, and that not a *day* should be lost in the preparation of the contract and the act of incorporation."[9]

Stephen was the heart and soul of the C.P.R. "syndicate," as the small closely knit group that launched the company came to be called, and in its critical first half-dozen years it was in great measure a personal enterprise. His was the determining voice in negotiations with the government and he had virtually complete charge of financial arrangements. For support he turned first to his associates in the St. Paul, Minneapolis and Manitoba Railway. Donald

Smith responded enthusiastically both because he believed the project had a great future and because of his heavy stake in western lands. James J. Hill joined because he felt he owed Stephen some assistance, and because he was confident that it would be found impracticable to build a line north of Lake Superior, to the immense benefit of the St. Paul and Manitoba. R. B. Angus was content to continue the close association with Stephen that dated back to his service as manager of the Bank of Montreal. Only Norman Kittson held aloof; one nerve-wracking venture into railroading had been enough. Duncan McIntyre joined the syndicate, since his Canada Central Railway would be an essential part of the Canadian Pacific system.

An initial stock issue of $5 million (50,000 shares) was planned, and half of this would be subscribed by the five associates—Stephen, Angus, Hill, Smith, and McIntyre—each of whom would take 5,000 shares. Stephen hoped to dispose of the rest in London, New York, and (at Macdonald's urging) Paris. In London he found that the old established houses of Baring Brothers and Glyn Mills, which had had many dealings with Canada, were not interested; Canadian railway securities were not popular at the moment, and in any event both firms were involved in the affairs of the Grand Trunk and viewed the new venture with some suspicion. Stephen turned to Sir John Rose, a close friend of Macdonald and a former Canadian minister of finance, who persuaded Morton, Rose and Company, from which he had recently retired, to lend some assistance. No London money was forthcoming, but the associated New York house of Morton, Bliss and Company (already involved indirectly in the Onderdonk contract) subscribed for 7,410 shares. Stephen also secured the support of J. S. Kennedy, who had represented the Dutch bondholders of the St. Paul and Pacific; his New York firm and associates took 5,000 shares.

In Paris the going proved to be difficult. A quick profit seemed to be the primary aim, but eventually Kohn, Reinach and Company took a longer view and joined the syndicate. Stephen had persevered because Macdonald felt that French participation would encourage French-Canadian support (which it failed to do to any marked degree), and also because he hoped that the association with Reinach and Company might encourage emigration to the Canadian West from France and Germany.

The formal contract between the government and the syndicate was signed in Ottawa on October 21, 1880, only four months and six days after Tupper had submitted his memorandum to the cabinet. Tupper signed on behalf of the government; Stephen, Hill, Angus, McIntyre, Kennedy, and Pasco du P. Grenfell (representing Morton, Rose and Company and Kohn, Reinach and Company) signed for the syndicate. To his intense annoyance and mortification, Donald Smith's name did not appear; Stephen told Macdonald that he was "excited almost to a craze" by the omission.[10] But Conservatives had not forgotten that Smith's refusal to support Macdonald in 1873, at the time of the Pacific Scandal, had precipitated the fall of the government, and the memory of a clash between Smith and Macdonald in 1878 that had shocked Parliament was still fresh in many minds. Macdonald was too good a politician to bear many grudges, but Smith's return to favor was gradual and Stephen judged it best to keep him in the background. Yet Smith, along with Angus, was to prove to be Stephen's surest source of support in the critical years to come; Hill, Kennedy, and McIntyre would all fall by the wayside, but Smith and Angus would not only complete the course, but would be associated with the C.P.R. for the rest of their very long lives.

The contract and its schedule,[11] remarkable documents that were to stand the test of time, were drafted by the same J. J. C. Abbott who had been Sir Hugh Allan's solicitor and was now to become counsel for the new Cana-

Rock cut north of Lake Superior. It was formidable terrain of this kind that convinced James J. Hill that it would be foolish and perhaps impracticable for the Canadian Pacific to follow an all-Canadian route. (COURTESY OF THE PUBLIC ARCHIVES OF CANADA)

dian Pacific. The railway was defined as a line extending "from the terminus of the Canada Central Railway near Lake Nipissing . . . to Port Moody," on Burrard Inlet. The government agreed to complete and hand over to the syndicate the Pembina branch line from Selkirk and Winnipeg to the international boundary and the portions of the main line between Lake Superior and Red River and between Lake Kamloops and Burrard Inlet, most of which were already under contract. The total mileage was about 710. The syndicate, for its part, undertook to complete the rest of the main line, totaling about 1,900 miles, within ten years. The standard of construction was to be equal to that of "the Union Pacific Railway of the United States as the same was when first constructed." As agreed upon, the government was to provide a cash subsidy of $25 million and a land grant of 25 million acres. In addition the company was granted valuable tax and customs concessions. When selected, its land grant properties were to be free of taxation for twenty years or until sold. Land required for the right of way, sidings, stations, and other installations was to be provided free and was to be exempt from taxation in perpetuity. Materials for construction, including rails, fishplates, and spikes, could be imported duty free.

One of the last provisions of the contract to be settled was intended to protect the main line against competition from the south. The C.P.R. was required to follow an all-Canadian route that called for the construction of an extremely costly line through the rocky wilderness north of Lake Superior, and Stephen feared that it would be orphaned of traffic by feeder lines in the West that would divert freight to the Northern Pacific. Just three days before the contract was signed, he stressed the point to Macdonald:

> Now what do you think would be the position of the C.P.R. or of the men bound to own and operate it if it were tapped at Winnipeg, or at any point west of that, by a line or lines running towards the U.S. boundary? What would, in such a case, be the value of the C.P.R. line from Winnipeg to Ottawa? No sane man would give a dollar for the whole line east of Winnipeg. I need not say more on this point, as it must be clear to you that *any and every line south* of the line of the C.P.R. running towards the boundary line, must be owned and controlled by the C.P.R. Otherwise the C.P.R. could be strangled. The fact is that if any doubt should exist in the minds of my friends on this point I could not carry them with me, and I need not say to you, that now I am into the thing I would not like to be forced to give it up.[12]

The solution was the notorious fifteenth clause—the "monopoly clause," as it was soon dubbed—which provided that for twenty years "no line of railway" was to "be authorized by the Dominion Parliament to be constructed South of the Canadian Pacific Railway, from any point at or near the Canadian Pacific Railway, except such line as shall run South West or to the Westward of South West; nor to within fifteen miles of Latitude 49" (the international boundary).

The contract gave the Canadian Pacific great freedom of action in several respects. It was given virtually unlimited power to build branch lines; it could acquire the Canada Central Railway, and it could similarly acquire, hold, and operate a line or lines from Ottawa (the eastern terminus of the Canada Central) "to any point at navigable water on the Atlantic seaboard or to any intermediate point." A Canadian Pacific extending from Atlantic to Pacific was thus already envisaged.

Some of the supplementary provisions were remarkably farsighted. For instance, the company was empowered not merely to build and operate telegraph and telephone lines, both for its own purposes and for "the transmission of messages for hire," but it could "use any improvement that may hereafter be invented (subject to the rights of patentees) for telegraphing or telephoning, and any other means of communication that may be deemed expedient by the Company at any time hereafter." It was almost as if Stephen had been able to foresee radio and space satellites.

Similarly he fully expected that Canadian Pacific ships would soon be plying rivers, lakes, and oceans, and the company was authorized "to acquire, own, hold, charter, work and run steam and other vessels for cargo and passengers upon any navigable water, which the Canadian Pacific Railway may reach or connect with." To serve its own and other ships it could build and maintain docks, dockyards, wharves, slips, piers, and grain elevators. The concept of the C.P.R. as a company interested broadly in transportation and communication and not merely in a railway was thus implicit in its charter from the beginning.

Throughout the negotiations the government had stressed that the railway must be operated, not just built, and the contract provided for financial guarantees covering the first ten years after its completion. In addition it stated in a single stark sentence that the basic obligation undertaken by the company in return for its subsidies, rights, and privileges was to "for ever efficiently maintain, work and run the Canadian Pacific Railway."

In order that work on the line might begin as early as possible in 1881, Parliament met early in December 1880, and the debate on the C.P.R. contract began on the thirteenth. Macdonald was expecting lively opposition from the Liberals, particularly from the formidable Edward Blake, who had succeeded Alexander Mackenzie as their leader, but he was scarcely prepared for the long and exhausting debate, lasting more than two months, that actually followed. Blake believed in all sincerity that to build the railway on the terms proposed was folly and financial madness. In the course of the debate it became apparent that what the Liberals really advocated was a line to Sault Ste. Marie, a railway across the prairies, and use of American lines south of Lake Superior to bridge the gap between. Macdonald, by contrast, was convinced that Canada could neither prosper nor even survive as a nation without a railway to the Pacific that followed an all-Canadian route. He had no illusions about the high price being paid, but he had accepted the best offer that had been submitted and he trusted George Stephen.

The Liberals were on shaky ground when they criticized the cash and land subsidies, for the Mackenzie government had offered more generous terms when it was in office, but the taxation and customs concessions and the monopoly clause were fairer game and more difficult to defend. On the monopoly clause, Macdonald encountered opposition within his own caucus. The Manitoba members, having experienced the high rates imposed by the Red River Transportation Company, felt that the C.P.R., in which Donald Smith and James J. Hill were again prominent, would be equally arbitrary in its policies. They would merely be substituting one monopoly for another. These suspicions and the enforcement of the restrictions on railway construction provided for in the clause were to engender bitterness against the company that endured for years and even lingers to this day.

Many of the Ontario members were restive because no Toronto men were included in the syndicate. They were further disturbed by the authority given to the C.P.R. to acquire the Canada Central Railway. Lake Nipissing had been selected as the eastern terminus of the Canadian Pacific because the choice favored neither Montreal nor Toronto. The Toronto Board of Trade complained that acquisition of the Canada Central "would destroy the neutral character of the Eastern terminus of the National Railway, and would practically transfer its terminus to Montreal."[13] As a concession to Toronto, the schedule to the contract was amended and the C.P.R. was required to "afford all reasonable facilities" to a projected Ontario and Pacific Junction Railway, which was intended to provide a link between Lake Nipissing and the existing railways leading to Toronto.

Largely because of this discontent and a feeling that Montreal had carried the day, the Liberals were able to induce a new syndicate, almost all from Ontario, to submit a last-minute counterproposal in mid-January 1881. On the face of it this appeared to be a better offer than Stephen's; the subsidy required was reduced to $22 million in cash and 22 million acres of land, no taxation or customs exemptions were requested, and the monopoly clause was omitted. But the proposal included options that would have permitted indefinite postponement of the construction north of Lake Superior and through the mountains in British Columbia, and Macdonald was able to show conclusively that the scheme was simply the Sault Ste. Marie diversion plan in a new guise.

Again in wretched health, Macdonald nevertheless defended the contract resolutely and refused to compromise; Tupper kept doubting party followers in line; a long series of proposed amendments were rejected one by one. The Pacific Railway bill passed its third reading on February 1 and received royal assent on February 15. The Canadian Pacific was incorporated the next day.

"At last the C.P.R. is a fixed fact," Macdonald wrote ten days later. "Royal assent given, royal charter under the act issued, company organized, and it now remains for Stephen and Company to show what metal they are made of."[14]

6

The C.P.R. Spans the Prairies

Stephen lost no time in organizing the company. The million dollars required to guarantee performance of the contract was deposited with the government on February 16, 1881, and the directors held their first meeting the next day. Stephen was elected president and Duncan McIntyre vice-president. Stephen, McIntyre, Hill, and Angus were named to the executive committee. An astute appointment was that of Charles Drinkwater as secretary and treasurer; he had been Sir John Macdonald's private secretary for nine years and was wise in the ways of politicians and governments. J. J. C. Abbott, destined to succeed Macdonald as prime minister of Canada, was appointed counsel.

The 1,900 miles of railway the company was to build consisted of two separate and distinct sections. One extended for 650 miles through difficult country north of Lake Huron and Lake Superior, between Callander and Thunder Bay. The other, spanning the 1,250 miles between Red River and Kamloops Lake, offered 850 miles of relatively easy going across the prairies, after which came some 400 mountainous miles through the Rockies, the Selkirks, and lesser ranges beyond.

Callander as an eastern terminus was merely a polite fiction. Stephen had insisted that the C.P.R. be given statutory authority to acquire the Canada Central Railway, whose charter empowered it to build from Callander to Ottawa. The purchase was arranged in March 1881, and the line was merged with the Canadian Pacific in June. At that time the Canada Central extended only from Brockville, on the St. Lawrence River, to Ottawa and thence to the vicinity of Pembroke; there was a gap of about 120 miles between Pembroke and Callander. Work to fill this began immediately, but construction required two seasons and was not completed until the autumn of 1882. The Canada Central was an essential purchase for two reasons. It would extend the main line of the C.P.R. to Ottawa, which was no great distance from Montreal, the eastern terminus Stephen always had in mind, and it would provide a means of getting supplies and materials into the country west of Callander, through which the Canadian Pacific would be building the eastern section of its main line.

Construction headquarters for the western lines were established in Winnipeg. It was the obvious location, because it lay at the end of the supply line from the United States provided by the St. Paul, Minneapolis and Manitoba Railway and the Pembina branch. Moreover, it would continue to be the main base of supplies, because the long line westward would be built through a country completely without roads, let alone railroads, or other means of bringing in materials. This meant that the line would have to be built entirely from the Winnipeg end and from this single supply source. It also meant that as soon as one mile of track was completed, it would become a busy working railroad, carrying the materials required to build the miles beyond.

Alpheus B. Stickney, who had held a similar position on the St. Paul, Minneapolis and Manitoba, was appointed superintendent of construction in the West, and Thomas L. Rosser, who had risen to the rank of major general in the Confederate Army, was named chief engineer. Hill was much the most experienced railroader in the syndicate, so these and many other appointments were in effect made by him. Then and later there was an outcry because Americans received the better jobs, but to a considerable extent this was inevitable. Canada was building her first western railroad, and Canadians with the kind of experience required were few and far between. Hill naturally favored the men he knew, and the close proximity of Minnesota to Winnipeg was another factor.

The contract stipulated that work on the prairie section was to begin not later than May 1, and on May 2 (a Monday) General Rosser turned a first sod. The same day the government handed over to the Canadian Pacific the Pembina branch and its extension to Selkirk, together with 162 miles of the government-built main line extending eastward from Selkirk to Cross Lake. The C.P.R. had already taken over the shakily built track from Winnipeg to Portage la Prairie, the only legacy of the contract for 100 miles of railway awarded in 1879, and of a second contract for a further 100 miles awarded in 1880. Most of this line was later relocated, but such as it was, it enabled the Canadian Pacific to begin work at once from Portage westward. Men, teams, plows, scrapers, timber, poles, ties, rails, and all manner of materials and supplies had been piling up in Winnipeg and Portage for weeks, and the work began with a promising rush.

But one very basic matter had still to be decided—the route the main line was to follow beyond the western boundary of Manitoba. The first important departure from the route blocked out by Sandford Fleming had been the diversion of the main line from Selkirk southward to Winnipeg and thence westward to Portage la Prairie. The city of Winnipeg had taken prompt action to ward off the possibility of a reversion to the original plan by making generous concessions to the railway. It built the Louisa Bridge across the Red River, completed in July 1881; provided free land for right-of-way, station, and yards; and exempted the railway's property from municipal taxation. Now the question was whether the line should swing northwestward, to rejoin Fleming's route leading to the Yellowhead Pass, or continue on across the prairies, sixty or seventy miles north of the international border.

It is clear that Stephen and his associates had had a change of route in mind for some time. When McIntyre reopened negotiations with Sir John Macdonald in London in August 1880, he had stated that "we should expect to be allowed to locate the line as we would think proper."[1] In November, R. B. Angus made inquiries in Winnipeg about the feasibility of a more southern route than Fleming had recommended. Angus was then living in St. Paul, working with Hill, who certainly favored a southern line. Within days of the incorporation of the C.P.R., Hill engaged Major A. B. Rogers, a railway locating engineer whose work had attracted his attention, and instructed him to search for a practicable pass in the Rockies south of the Yellowhead. Hill may even have had the Kicking Horse Pass, the route ultimately chosen for the Canadian Pacific, already in mind.

There were two obstacles to the adoption of a southern route. One could be considered a technicality: the Yellowhead Pass was mentioned specifically in the contract and could not be abandoned without the consent of Parliament. The other was the belief, dating back to the explorations of Captain Palliser, that beyond the future site of Moose Jaw a southern line would encounter hundreds of miles of near desert, where the rainfall was so scanty and uncertain that the country was unsuitable for settlement. The strongest voice opposing this view was that of John Macoun, Canada's most noted exploring botanist, who contended, on the basis of personal visits made in 1879 and 1880, that rainfall was adequate and the area well suited for agriculture. In mid-May of 1881, Hill asked Macoun to come to St. Paul, and at a meeting there with Stephen, Angus, and Hill himself, Macoun's assessment of the country was accepted, and the decision was taken to build the Canadian Pacific along a southern route and to gamble on the existence of suitable passes through the mountains. It was a momentous decision that altered substantially the future pattern of settlement in the Canadian West, and whether the change was for better or worse is still a matter of debate.

Similarly, the reasons that prompted the switch to a southern route are still much discussed, as none of the key figures seems to have put them on record. It was hoped that Hill's papers would throw light on the decision, but they leave the mystery unsolved.[2] Two reasons were mentioned in Parliament —the line would be shorter, and being much nearer the border would afford better protection against encroachments by American railways. The long prairie section would also be quicker and easier to build, for in great part it would parallel rather than cross water courses. (There are only two large bridges on the 832 miles of the Canadian Pacific line between Winnipeg and Calgary.) Speed was important, because it would mean that the railway would begin to receive revenue from through traffic at an earlier date.

These were the considerations that probably carried most weight with Stephen and Hill; others have been suggested. The shorter growing season in the north may have raised doubts as to whether grain would ripen there; the early-ripening varieties of today had not yet been developed. Ever since his early activities in the fuel business, Hill had taken a great interest in coal. Murray Gibbon states that he "had reports on coal-bearing areas in the southern prairies and British Columbia, which convinced him that it would be more profitable to locate the Canadian transcontinental nearer the international boundary, so as to secure paying local traffic from the very first."[3] Donald Smith, deeply involved in the affairs of the Hudson's Bay Company, is said to have favored the southern route because it would interfere less with the fur trade. Finally, it has been pointed out that Fleming's recommended route was well known and that land speculators had been busy acquiring likely townsites and the best farming land along it; the southern route would be through unsettled areas where the railway could control townsites more easily and benefit by so doing. This latter motive is highly questionable. The railway's revenue from prairie townsites was never very substantial—certainly it was quite insufficient, even in prospect, to cause a drastic change in the location of the line.

Despite formidable physical difficulties, Major Rogers made remarkable progress in his search for practicable passes in the western mountains. By the end of the 1881 surveying season he was reasonably certain that the Bow River Valley and the Kicking Horse Pass would provide a route through the Rockies, and his nephew, Albert Rogers, exploring from the west, had glimpsed what appeared to be a pass through the Selkirk Mountains. If the worst came to the worst, the Selkirks could be avoided by following the big bend of the Columbia River, which skirted them to the north, and on December 20, 1881, the Canadian Pacific requested legislation that would allow it to use a pass south of the Yellowhead. To this the government agreed, provided the pass was not less than 100 miles from the international boundary, a proviso the Kicking Horse met with about 75 miles to spare.[4]

Adoption of the southern line involved the total discard of the vast array of surveys that Sandford Fleming had carried out between Red River and Kamloops Lake. A second change in route soon discarded most of those that had been made between Callander and Thunder Bay. In sum, the C.P.R. chose a completely new location for almost all the 1,900 miles of railway that it constructed itself.

Hill never made any secret of the fact that he considered it would be folly, at least for many years to come, to build a railway through the barren Laurentian Shield north of Lake Superior. Angus had consulted him about the whole C.P.R. project early in July 1880, when negotiations with the government were first in progress, and Hill had made his views clear. The government, he felt, should be persuaded "to postpone the Nipissing line for the present at least." He "would be very sorry to have the time and money spent in building a line that, when completed, would be of no use to anybody and would be a source of heavy loss to whoever operated it." "Would it not be a much better arrangement," he continued, "for the Government to have the all-rail line run via Sault Ste. Marie where it would have a local timber and mineral business both sides of the line?"[5] Hill, of course, envisaged a line that would consist of the Pembina branch, his own St. Paul, Minneapolis and Manitoba Railroad, and a Hill-controlled connecting line between St. Paul and the Sault.

His biographer contends that Hill joined the Canadian Pacific syndicate only to help it along and get it off to a good start. In a measure his motive undoubtedly was to help Stephen, but the conclusion is inescapable that he also joined because he hoped and expected that the economic absurdity and high cost of building the line north of Lake Superior would in the end force the abandonment of the all-Canadian route. In that event his St. Paul line and its connections would become indispensable links between the C.P.R. systems in the East and the West, with immense benefits to himself.

At one time Stephen had shared Hill's opinion; he confessed later to Macdonald that he had once looked upon the proposal to build a line north of Lake Superior as "great folly."[6] By the summer of 1881, he had come round completely to Macdonald's point of view: "all [the] misgivings I had last year" had disappeared, he told Macdonald. Without an all-Canadian line the Canadian Pacific "never could become the property it is certain to be having its own rails running from sea to sea. I am sure you will be glad to hear this from me because I do not think but for your *own* tenacity on that point, would the line North of the Lake *ever* have been built; events have shown you were right and all the rest wrong."[7]

Fleming had surveyed a line that would run through relatively easy country well to the north of Lake Superior. By November 1881, Stephen had all but decided to adopt instead a southern route by way of Sault Ste. Marie that would skirt the shore of Lake Superior from the Sault to Thunder Bay. A line along the lakeshore could be built much more quickly, because supplies and materials could be brought to it easily by water; for this reason Stephen was confident that it could be completed within five years.[8] But this decision was not in fact final. Within a year a compromise route had been adopted. This ran inland in great part (though not nearly as far inland as Fleming had intended), shortened the line considerably, and reached the shore of the lake at Heron Bay, about 200 miles from Thunder Bay.

In spite of Stephen's efforts, 1881 was a disappointing season for the Canadian Pacific. A little token work had been done west of Callander, but uncertainties about the route and difficulties of access had prevented anything more. In the West, Stickney and Rosser had built the track only as far as Oak Lake, then known as Flat Creek, no more than 110 miles from Portage la Prairie. Their interest seems to have been diverted to the spectacular real estate boom that the start of construction had touched off in Winnipeg, and which had spread rapidly to prospective townsites along the railway. Both were soon in disfavor with the company as it became apparent that they were turning their inside knowledge of location surveys and construction plans to personal account.

Hill became restive and in October he asked William Cornelius Van Horne, the thirty-eight-year-old general superintendent of the Chicago, Milwaukee and St. Paul Railroad to visit Winnipeg with him and take a look at the C.P.R. Van Horne already had a considerable and well-deserved reputation as perhaps the ablest of the younger railroaders in America. Born in Illinois of Dutch ancestry, he had had to earn his own living from the age of fourteen. He began his career as a telegrapher, but railroads quickly became his passion and he set about learning every detail about their construction, equipment, and operation. His curiosity was boundless, as his keen and expert interest in such varied subjects as painting, ceramics, fossils, gardening, and cattle breeding was to demonstrate. His energy and physical strength were alike prodigious, and his capacity for work astounded his colleagues. On the lighter side, he enjoyed convivial company and a game of poker, and a mischievous streak frequently found an outlet in practical jokes.

By the time he was twenty-seven he was superintendent of the Chicago and Alton Railroad, and at thirty-one was given an omnibus post as president, general manager, and superintendent of the Southern Minnesota. This position was a challenge because the line was both in wretched physical condition and in deep water financially, but the complete authority to be given to him attracted Van Horne and he was confident that he could resuscitate the company. This he succeeded in doing, and it was his performance there that had led to his appointment to the Milwaukee road.

Whether Hill had it in mind from the first to offer Van Horne a position with the Canadian Pacific we do not know, but he realized quickly that he was precisely the kind of general manager the company required. "You need a man of great mental and physical power to carry this line through," he wrote at the time. "Van Horne can do it." Fortunately the far-ranging nature of the project and the challenge it offered to management appealed to Van Horne and within a few weeks he had agreed to join the Canadian Pacific.

To his recommendation of Van Horne Hill had added a word of warning: "He will take all the authority he gets and more, so define how much you want him to have."[9] Once satisfied about Van Horne's ability and integrity, Stephen asked for nothing better than an opportunity to delegate virtually complete authority over the construction and operation of the railway. He had hoped and expected that he would need to concern himself only with general policy and finance; Van Horne's advent made this possible. The partnership between the two, one of the most remarkable in railroad history, was to last a decade.

Van Horne took charge in Winnipeg on January 2, 1882. Next to the signing of the contract in October 1880, it was the most important date in the early history of the Canadian Pacific.

Van Horne's arrival was soon followed by the departure of Stickney and Rosser and, inevitably, by a further influx of Americans—men Van Horne knew and whose capacities he trusted. One of the first was John Egan, who had worked with Van Horne on both the Minnesota Southern and the Milwaukee lines and who became the new general superintendent in the West. Egan quickly acquired the reputation of firing Canadians and hiring Americans, and this propensity, coupled with his strong Fenian sympathies, helped to generate the unpopularity from which the C.P.R. soon suffered in Manitoba.[10] But Egan was a highly competent superintendent, and in spite of complaints Van Horne refused to part with him until after the completion of the main line to the coast.

Van Horne's most notable recruit was Thomas George Shaughnessy, general storekeeper of the Chicago, Milwaukee and St. Paul, the railway Van

Horne had left to join the Canadian Pacific. He first approached Shaughnessy early in 1882, but without success; Shaughnessy was active in local politics and at the time was president of Milwaukee's board of aldermen. In November, however, he yielded to Van Horne's blandishments and became general purchasing agent of the Canadian Pacific. It was an appointment second in importance only to that of Van Horne himself, for Shaughnessy quickly displayed two talents that were of the highest importance to the C.P.R. in construction days—an extraordinary ability to secure value for every dollar expended and an equal ability to ward off creditors and persuade them to wait for payment in times of financial stringency.

These qualities were not outwardly apparent, for Shaughnessy was only twenty-nine and something of a dandy. E. N. Bender, one of the clerks in the purchasing office, later described his arrival:

On a dull, overcast morning in November, 1882, Bender looked up to see a young man of striking appearance enter the room. He had clean-cut features, sharp Irish eyes and, according to the fashion of the Western United States in those days, his face was adorned with a moustache and an Imperial. He wore a black felt hat, a soft-flowing black tie, a morning coat and light striped trousers.

He announced in a few words that he was T. G. Shaughnessy, that Mr. Van Horne had appointed him General Purchasing Agent, and ten minutes later he was at work.[11]

Suppliers quickly discovered that the only things Shaughnessy cared about were "price, quality, and rapidity of delivery." Not long after his arrival, one of the directors of the Canadian Pacific resigned because he found that friends dealing with the company no longer received favored treatment.

To begin with, Van Horne was no more friendly to the British than Egan. In some manuscript reminiscences J. H. E. Secretan, an Englishman who was serving as a surveyor, has recorded his impressions:

We did not like Van Horne when he first came up to Winnipeg as General Boss of Everybody and Everything. His ways were not our ways and he did not hesitate to let us know what he thought of the bunch in a general way. At first he had no use for Englishmen or Canadians especially Engineers and told me once "if he could only teach a Section Man to run a transit he wouldn't have a single d——d Engineer about the place."

I was one of the few who got to know him and to know him was to like him and then to admire his extraordinary *versatility*. He seemed to know *everything* and in spite of being a very busy man with awful responsibilities, he always had lots of time to talk on any conceivable subject, would sit in his office and smoke a cigar a foot long while he talked and at the same time make a splendid etching on the blotting pad in front of him, all the time apparently thinking of something else, and probably gazing at a map on the wall. He was a great big man with a gigantic intellect, a generous soul with an enormous capacity both for food and work.[12]

In addition to an American general manager and an American western superintendent, the Canadian Pacific was about to turn over construction of the western line to American contractors; the job was too big and complicated for the company to undertake itself. Tenders were invited in January 1882, and in February a contract was awarded to the firm of Langdon and Shepard, of St. Paul. D. C. Shepard, well known to Hill, was an experienced and capable engineer and contractor, as the performance of his company was to demonstrate. The contract covered the line from Oak Lake, near the western boundary of Manitoba, to the end of the prairie section at the crossing of the Bow River, at Calgary. The distance was approximately 675 miles.

Van Horne and Shepard between them quickly brought into being a vast construction assembly line that soon extended many miles across the prairies. The route the railway was to take was first located and staked by C.P.R. engineers and surveyors; the contractor's grading crews then took over and prepared the roadbed. The earth work was unusually heavy for prairie country, averaging about 16,300 cubic yards to the mile, or over 10 million cubic yards in all, because Van Horne wanted the grade line raised well above ground level to reduce the risk of trouble with snow in winter.

Van Horne described the supply system as it existed in 1882 and 1883:

During the rapid construction, material yards were established at intervals of 100 miles where all materials and supplies were assorted and forwarded to the front in train lots, each train taking an accurately adjusted lot of rails, ties, fastenings, telegraph material and all other necessary items so that no material was scattered along the line. At these material yards were the head-quarters of the construction department, the offices and houses making quite a village, but all the houses were portable and of such a size as to be readily moved on flat cars; and as the track advanced each 100 miles, [and] it became necessary to move on to a new point the change could be made in a day and without delay to the work.

The thousands of tons of steel rails required were imported from England and Germany; the hundreds of thousands of ties, almost all tamarack, came from the forests around the Lake of the Woods. Van Horne emphasized the incredible smoothness with which the assembly line functioned:

The transportation department was charged with the delivery of all materials and supplies at the end of the track and, when the quantity of these and the great distances they had to be transported are considered, it will be thought no small feat to have moved them to the front day after day and month after month with such regularity that the greatest delay experienced by the tracklayers during the two seasons work was less than three hours.[13]

Van Horne made no mention of the "end of track"—the scene of vast activity where the track was actually being laid. Here again there was a portable village, but in this case it centered about a row of supply and office cars, and tall three-storey boarding and dormitory cars that fed and lodged the working crews, all of which could be moved forward at any time and so keep up with the men.

Stations were located about eight miles apart; all had a 2,000-foot passing track, and in addition alternate stations had a depot, a section house, a water tank, and a 1,000-foot business track. Divisional points were established at intervals of about 125 miles—the distance a locomotive of the day could steam comfortably without refueling. Each had a train yard, an engine shed, and a coal shed, and every other divisional point had a repair shop.

The C.P.R. had a follow-up force of its own, soon dubbed "the Flying Wing," that followed on the heels of the contractors, checking, making good small deficiencies, and making sure that all was ready for the traffic that would begin to roll over the line the moment it was completed.

Van Horne had told the Canadian Pacific directors that he would build 500 miles of the western main line in 1882. He was defeated at the very beginning by floods in the Red River valley, the worst in many years. Coming in April, just when construction was about to resume, they washed out sections of the Pembina branch and thus blocked the flow of materials to Winnipeg. The trouble lasted for weeks, and Van Horne's critics pointed out with glee that he had laid no more than 70 miles of track by the end of June. But thereafter he and Shepard hit their stride, and 349 miles were laid in the next six months. Frost stopped the grading crews on November 13, but the tracklaying season continued until the end of the year. In all, 419.86 miles of the main line had been built, and if 28 miles of sidings and a 100-mile branch in Manitoba were included, Van Horne had added well over 500 miles to the C.P.R. system. The peak achievement had come in August and September, when on forty-two consecutive working days the crews had laid an average of 3.14 miles of track per day.[14]

At the end of the season the track extended some distance beyond Swift Current, about 575 miles west of Winnipeg, and since early October trains had been operating over 350 miles of the line to the new settlement of Regina, soon to become the capital of the Northwest Territories.

Grading was resumed late in March 1883, and the tracklayers were back at work on April 18. In July and August they exceeded the record established the previous season when on forty-eight consecutive working days they laid an average of 3.46 miles of track per day, and on two incredible occasions—July 7 and 28—laid 6.02 miles and 6.38 miles respectively. *Engineering* noted that the latter feat involved the laying of 2,120 rails, weighing 604 tons, which called for 16,000 ties, 4,240 plates, 8,480 bolts, and 63,000 spikes.[15]

Steel reached Calgary on August 13; Langdon and Shepard had completed their contract in fifteen months. But there was no slackening in the work. The track was pushed on up the Bow River valley and thence to the Kicking Horse Pass. By November 27, it had neared the summit and there paused for the winter—almost a mile above sea level and 962 miles from Winnipeg. The two seasons had witnessed a prodigious construction feat that had never been equaled in railway history.

The crossing of the prairies had been accomplished with remarkably little disturbance. There was trouble occasionally with the Indians, and the surprising thing is that there was not considerably more. The railway came at a particularly difficult time for the native population; the great buffalo herds, upon which their age-old way of life depended and which had provided them with virtually every necessity, including food, clothing, fuel, and shelter, were suddenly disappearing. The government was trying to hive the Indians onto reserves, where it was hoped they could be persuaded to take up a fixed and agricultural existence, but the transition was difficult and distressing. To many of the Indians steel rails and telegraph wires were just another limitation to their freedom of movement, and at times, in anger and exasperation, they took action against them. Long lines of surveyors' pegs were pulled up; on one occasion tepees were set up on the track; in the eastern forested areas, logs were piled on the right-of-way and efforts were made to derail locomotives. Workmen unfamiliar with Indians were fearful of them and upset by their habit of squatting in rows near the line and stolidly observing all that went on.

The North-West Mounted Police, a federal force organized in 1873 to preserve law and order in the West, handled the difficulties well, and in many instances with some understanding of the Indians' dilemma and point of view. The most serious dangers threatened when the railway entered the area long occupied by the proud and aggressive Blackfoot Indians, in what is now southern Alberta. The fur trade had not been extensive there, and the Blackfoot had had relatively little contact with white men. Insufficient preparation had been made for the advent of the railway, and difficulties were avoided in great part thanks to Father Lacombe, a devoted Oblate missionary whom the Indians knew and trusted. The pleasant story that Father Lacombe was made president of the C.P.R. for an hour in recognition of his intervention may or may not be true, but Van Horne was keenly aware of the company's obligation to him. Both he and Chief Crowfoot of the Blackfoot were given life passes on the railway, and supplies for the Oblate mission were carried free of charge.

Financial problems caused the Mounted Police some trouble. Langdon and Shepard employed about 300 subcontractors; not all of them paid their workmen regularly, and discontented employees turned to the police for help. The work camps inevitably harbored some bad characters and attracted crooks and prostitutes. But it was whisky peddlers who caused the most trouble. By law, in the interests of the Indians, liquor had been prohibited in the Northwest Territories, in which the western prairies were then included, but thousands of laborers engaged in hard, monotonous work and living under rough conditions offered the bootlegger a tempting and lucrative market.

The overall picture seems to have been remarkably orderly. On January 1, 1883, Van Horne paid tribute to the police in a letter to Commissioner Irvine: "On no great work within my knowledge where so many men have been employed has such perfect order prevailed."[16] A year later John Egan wrote in a similar vein.

In accordance with the division of labor agreed upon between Stephen and Van Horne, Stephen had been absorbed in the task of financing the railway. Van Horne felt that he had much the better of the bargain. "My part was easy," he recalled later. "I had only to spend the money, but Stephen had to find it when nobody in the world believed [in the C.P.R.] but ourselves."[17]

To begin with, Stephen seems to have thought that the line could be built for $45 million, Sir Charles Tupper's official estimate. He explained to a correspondent that $30 million of this was already in sight—the $5 million that the directors and a few others had paid for 50,000 shares issued at par, and the $25 million cash subsidy. "We can provide the remaining $15,000,000 from our own resources," he wrote, "if we deem it necessary, or expedient, to do so."[18]

On paper the company appeared to have ample means of raising funds. It had authority to issue common stock, preferred stock, land grant bonds, and mortgage bonds to a combined total of $90 million, to which could be added the $25 million cash subsidy. Nevertheless Stephen proceeded very cautiously. A total of $6.1 million in common shares had been sold at par by early March, but the bulk of them had been purchased by the syndicate members to meet the stipulation that $5 million in stock had to be subscribed for and 30 percent paid up before the contract with the government would become effective. The sale was therefore no test of the market, and Stephen deemed it wise to delay a public offering until the railway had in a measure proved itself and could show some revenue from land sales and perhaps from completed sections of the line. The C.P.R. was still under frequent attack in the press, led by the Toronto *Globe* in Canada and abetted by the *Times* and other papers in London. Canada as well as the railway was a target in England, where a famous and often-quoted tirade appeared in the September 1 issue of *Truth*. Among other things, it represented British Columbia as being "a barren, cold, mountainous country, that is not worth keeping," alleged that in Manitoba men and cattle were "frozen to death in numbers that would rather astonish the intending settler if he knew," and contended that Canada as a whole was "one of the most over-rated colonies we have."

Mortgage bonds were a popular method of financing railways, but Stephen was determined not to burden the Canadian Pacific with fixed charges. His hope, as he explained in a memorandum on the "position and prospects" of the company issued late in 1881, was to place it in "the exceptionally advantageous position of being free from bonded debt." In spite of the many financial difficulties he was to face in the ensuing four years, he nearly succeeded in doing so.

In June of 1881, Stephen resigned as president of the Bank of Montreal. This was partly because he was becoming more and more absorbed in the C.P.R. (years later he was to remark that he "seemed to have been born utterly without the faculty of doing more than one thing at a time"),[19] and partly because the bank and the railway would be having many dealings with one another, and some conflict of interest would be inevitable. The first important transaction came in August. Land sales had been promising—some 300,000 acres had been sold in England in the spring—and Stephen decided that the time was propitious to offer the $25 million in land grant bonds authorized by the charter. The Bank of Montreal, in association with J. S. Kennedy and Company of New York, agreed to take $10 million of the issue at a net price of 92, payment to be made over a period of thirteen months, and took options on two further lots of $5 million each at 95 and 97½. This was an encouraging beginning, but arrangements for the sale, as set by the contract, were cumbersome. One fifth of the issue had to be deposited with the government as a guarantee of performance; the proceeds of the sale of the other four fifths had to be paid to the government, and the money could be released to the C.P.R. (at the rate of one dollar per acre) only as construction of the line proceeded and the subsidy lands the bonds represented were earned. As a result, funds would be a long time in reaching the coffers of the company.

Van Horne had no greater admirer than Stephen, but the pace at which the western line was being pushed toward the mountains in 1882 caused Stephen concern as well as pleasure. Construction costs were soaring in a frightening manner, and it was becoming evident that Tupper's estimate of costs had been far wide of the mark. "The so-called Prairie Section," Stephen explained to Macdonald, "is not prairie at all in the sense that the Red River Valley is a prairie. The country west of Portage la Prairie is a broken rolling country and the amount of work on our road bed is more than double what it would have been had it run along the valley. In short, the road as we are building it, both as regards its physique and its rapidity of construction, is costing us a great deal more than the subsidy and a great deal more than we expected."[20]

To complicate matters, 1882 proved to be an election year. When the vote came on June 20, Macdonald's Conservative party won handily and fully maintained its large majority. This was a matter of great importance to the Canadian Pacific, for the Liberals and much of the press were as hostile as ever to the railway. Two charges in particular were made repeatedly against the C.P.R.: it was alleged that the company had no real intention of building the line north of Lake Superior, and it was accused of spending funds derived from its cash and land subsidies for purposes other than building the railway to the Pacific Coast. The latter charge was usually made or inspired by the Grand Trunk, which was doing its best to prevent the Canadian Pacific from spreading eastward. It had objected to the purchase of the Canada Central and returned to the charge in March 1882, when the C.P.R. bought the Montreal-Ottawa line of the Quebec, Montreal, Ottawa and Occidental Railway from the government of Quebec. Coming shortly before the election, the purchase caused Macdonald some worry, because the political support of the Grand Trunk was important to him, but it settled a troublesome party legacy. The railway had long been a financial burden to Quebec, and about a decade earlier Sir George Cartier had promised that the federal government would find some way of taking it off the province's hands. When the C.P.R. contract was before Parliament, the Quebec Conservatives virtually made their support of the measure contingent upon its purchase, and Macdonald was now carrying out the bargain. He had an additional motive, because the Northern Pacific, already scheming schemes in Manitoba, was taking an interest in the Quebec line. Macdonald was therefore relieved to see it safely in Canadian hands, and of course the Canadian Pacific was delighted to secure an entry into Montreal.

Neither of these purchases really provided much justification for criticism on financial grounds. The Canada Central had been acquired by assuming its net mortgage, which totaled only about $1.8 million; the cost of the Quebec takeover was $4 million, for a railway that was said to have cost the province $14 million, and only $500,000 of the purchase price had to be paid in cash.

The slow progress made on the line between Callander and Thunder Bay offered the railway's critics a better target. James J. Hill, who opposed its construction, may have used his considerable influence to delay the work, but Stephen was determined to build it and he had a staunch ally in Van Horne. Without it the C.P.R. would be dependent on other railways for its connections between east and west, and quite apart from political considerations this was abhorrent to both men. Work was held up by uncertainty over the route to be followed and difficulty of access; the Canada Central—the essential supply line from the East—was not completed until after the election. As for the route to be followed, Stephen reminded Macdonald that a complete change had been deemed necessary. "You will not forget," he wrote in August 1882, "that we had to begin *de novo*. The locations and surveys of the Government were useless to us." He hoped that by the end of the season the whole of the new line would have been located except for the very difficult section along the shore of Lake Superior between Heron Bay and Nipigon. "No clamor will induce us to put a spade into that section till we are sure we are right in our location of the line." A mistake "might cost us millions."[21]

The deliberate and frequently unpredictable ways of governments always baffled and exasperated Stephen. Macdonald was consistently friendly, but the Canadian Pacific was encountering two problems that were making the promised subsidies less helpful than Stephen had expected. There was frequently a long time lag between the completion of a twenty-mile segment of the main line and payment of the subsidy to which this entitled the railway, and similarly there were long delays in designating the precise sections of land that were to form part of the land grant.

Even at this relatively early stage, Stephen and to a lesser extent several of his associates had found it necessary to assist the company. In March 1882, the C.P.R. had had to ask the Bank of Montreal for a short-term loan of $1.5 million; this was secured by the deposit of St. Paul, Minneapolis and Manitoba shares owned personally by Stephen, Angus, and Donald Smith. Writing to Macdonald in September, Stephen had remarked: "We are just about even with the world at the moment, but to reach this position we have had to find 5 million more dollars from our own resources. To enable me to make up my quota I had to sell my Montreal Bank Stock."[22] The money had been raised by selling $20 million in capital stock to a few shareholders at about twenty-five cents on the dollar, which produced $4,974,475. Earlier in the year Stephen had asked Sir Leonard Tilley, the minister of finance, to assist the C.P.R. by releasing the million dollars deposited when the company was incorporated and allowing it to substitute £339,800 in Credit Valley Railway debentures—securities that were Stephen's own property. To his surprise and annoyance,

Tilley demurred, but the exchange was finally permitted late in the year. In November Stephen told Macdonald that by the end of 1882 he and his associates would have "at least 14 millions" of their own money invested in the property.[23]

One further effort to raise funds was made at this time. The Canadian Pacific had done its best to avoid selling large tracts of land to speculators. The railway's primary interest was in settlement and not merely in sales; unoccupied land being held for a capital gain generated no traffic. But the need for money was pressing, and in the summer of 1882 Stephen compromised by encouraging the formation of the Canada Northwest Land Company. This was an Anglo-Canadian corporation which brought together an English group interested in purchasing western lands and some close associates of the C.P.R. in Canada. E. B. Osler of Toronto, a banker and broker who, as we shall see, helped Stephen build up eastern lines, was a key figure. The land company undertook to purchase 5 million acres of land at three dollars per acre and intended to pay for them by buying $13.5 million in C.P.R. land grant bonds, which could be acquired at a discount and applied to land purchases at a premium of 10 percent.

All seemed well at first, but the company soon found that it could not operate on the scale anticipated. The total land to be purchased had to be reduced to 2.2 million acres and the bond purchase cut to $6 million. All the land was paid for, but the assistance given to the C.P.R. was much below expectations. The same was true of the bond issue as a whole. Sales were discouraging, and only $10 million in bonds were sold instead of the anticipated $20 million.

The way construction costs had mounted during the year had been frightening. It has been estimated that the Canadian Pacific spent almost $22 million in 1882. There were a few encouraging signs, including the fact that the gross earnings of the railway, despite its fragmentary state, had totaled $2,484,760, not including freight on construction or other materials carried for the company. But Stephen realized that financial needs in 1883 would be enormous. Determined as ever not to issue mortgage bonds, he turned once more to the sale of additional common stock. In December, the authorized capital of the Canadian Pacific was increased from $25 million to $100 million, and armed with $75 million in new shares Stephen departed for New York.

Two transactions of major importance were concluded there. The first was a contract with the North American Railway Contracting Company, a new corporation that represented a blending of Canadian Pacific and American interests. The company undertook to complete the main line and accept payment partly in cash and partly in shares. In round numbers, the cost of the Lake Superior section was to be $14 million in cash and $20 million in stock, while the western section, including the line through the mountains to Kamloops Lake, was to cost $17.9 million in cash and $25 million in stock. The railway retained full supervisory powers and was otherwise well protected, but the terms were sufficiently attractive to gain the participation of such important New York houses as Kuhn, Loeb and Company and Drexel, Morgan and Company.

Having thus allocated $45 million of the new stock, Stephen proceeded to sell the remaining $30 million. A syndicate headed by J. S. Kennedy agreed to purchase the shares in three instalments of $10 million each at an average price of 52½, which by the summer of 1883 would yield the Canadian Pacific a net return of $15,463,178. Stephen was jubilant. "I start with a light heart," he wrote to Macdonald as he left for London, "having added greatly to our *achieving power* since I came here. . . . The C.P.R. will be built without a dollar of money from London."[24]

Stephen was referring to the London money market, not to individual investors. While in Britain he was able to persuade friends and others to subscribe for over $3 million of the new shares. He then went to Amsterdam, where J. L. Pierson, of Adolph Boissevain and Company, formed a syndicate that sold some $4 million of the shares, mostly in the Netherlands, Germany, and Belgium. Years later Stephen recalled the circumstances: "No one in England would take a shilling in the company and I could not get a stock exchange quotation for the shares except by a round about expedient. No one in London believed in the success of the company. My Amsterdam friends were the first Europeans to invest in C.P.R. shares. . . ." The assistance given at this critical time was not forgotten; R. V. Martinson of Amsterdam was elected to the board of directors of the Canadian Pacific in 1883, and Allard Jiskoot, a grandson of J. L. Pierson, is a director at the present time.[25]

So far as the main line was concerned, Stephen now felt that all was well. But he had come to London in the hope of securing funds to help finance the expansion of a network of eastern lines that he was assembling, to some account of which we must now turn.

7

Conflict with the Grand Trunk: The Eastern Network

In the course of its first half-century the Canadian Pacific fought long defending actions against three rivals—the Grand Trunk, James J. Hill and his Great Northern Railroad, and the Canadian National. It was faced with the first of the three even as it came into existence.

George Stephen realized that to survive, let alone prosper, the C.P.R. would have to have eastern outlets and be able to tap Canada's main market for transportation, which lay in Ontario and Quebec. In 1881, over 70 percent of the country's total population lived along the St. Lawrence and the Great Lakes between Quebec City and the Detroit River. By contrast, most of the C.P.R.'s main line would be built through virtually uninhabited territory, and the white population of its western destination, British Columbia, was little more than 15,000. Settlement would generate traffic eventually, but it would take years to develop, and in the interval the railway could face bankruptcy. Quite apart from this, the C.P.R. wanted to be able to pick up and deliver passengers and freight in the heavily populated area and to secure a share of the traffic in it. "Just imagine," Stephen wrote to Sir John Macdonald in 1888, "what a fiasco the C.P.R. would have been without its ramifications in Ontario and the eastern provinces—a mere trunk line away in the 'air' without the power of drawing over it a lb. of freight except from the city of Montreal. It would have been a monumental folly and a reproach to you and me for all time."[1]

The charter implied as much, for, as already noted, it empowered the Canadian Pacific to acquire the Canada Central Railway, which would extend its main line from the nominal terminus at Lake Nipissing to Ottawa, and gave it authority to lease or acquire lines from Ottawa "to any point at navigable water on the Atlantic seaboard." But it made no specific reference to that vital area, southern Ontario.

Inevitably any invasion there would result in conflict with the existing railways, notably with the giant among them, the Grand Trunk, whose main line from Montreal to Toronto and Sarnia was the spinal column of the existing Canadian railway system. Stephen felt that eastern lines that would compete with the Grand Trunk were part of the "legitimate and necessary development" of the Canadian Pacific; naturally Sir Henry Tyler and Joseph Hickson, president and general manager of the Grand Trunk, thought otherwise. In their view the C.P.R. in the East should have consisted of the main line and nothing more, and if it had ended at Lake Nipissing it would have been so much the better, for the Grand Trunk could have linked up with it there, by means of a line running north from Toronto. This had been the Grand Trunk's attitude ever since the Pacific railway had become a serious possibility. Sir Hugh Allan had encountered it in 1873, when trying to raise funds in London. When taken to task for opposing Allan's efforts, Richard Potter, the president of the Grand Trunk, replied (in Macdonald's words) "that the G.T.R. would cordially assist in the project" but that this would not "extend to the rival lines east of Nipissing, which they felt themselves at liberty to oppose."[2]

Only a few days after the signing of the C.P.R. contract, Hickson warned Sir John Macdonald that the building of lines "apart altogether from the Pacific line proper" would undoubtedly result in "a collision of interests and some friction" between the two companies.[3] On Christmas Eve he wrote again, expressing the fear that Stephen was entering upon a course that would "render friendly relations with the Grand Trunk impossible." Stephen, he said, had been buying up the bonds of the Credit Valley Railway, a line running southwestward for 121 miles from Toronto to St. Thomas, and was believed to be interested in a scheme to build a railway from Toronto to Ottawa.[4] Actually, Stephen had bought debentures, not bonds, and the purchase had nothing to do with the C.P.R.; it was made before the syndicate was formed and was a rescue operation in aid of his friend George Laidlaw, a railroad contractor, who was deeply involved in the affairs of the Credit Valley. Stephen took over most of his holdings and arranged financing for the completion and equipment of the line.

Once the C.P.R. was incorporated, Stephen undoubtedly saw in the Credit Valley the nucleus of a rail system in southern Ontario, but his immediate concern was to gain possession of the Canada Central Railway, which extended from Brockville, on the St. Lawrence, north to Ottawa and thence for a hundred miles up the Ottawa valley. Its only interesting feature was the oldest railway tunnel in Canada, opened in 1860, which pierced a high bluff at Brockville and gave trains access to the river. Its importance lay in its charter, which empowered it to build to Lake Nipissing. Its purchase was approved only six weeks after the C.P.R. came into existence, and it was merged with the Canadian Pacific on June 1. Work on an extension began promptly, and by the middle of October the track had been laid for ninety-four miles, to Mattawa. It reached Callander in August 1882. The Canada Central was a broad-gauge line, and in order to avoid delay and be able to make immediate use of available locomotives in construction work, the extension to Callander was also broad-gauge to begin with, and was converted to the Canadian Pacific's standard gauge after its completion.

Hickson's suspicion that Stephen had an Ottawa-Toronto link in mind was well founded. The same Parliament that chartered the C.P.R. also revived the dormant charter of the Ontario and Quebec Railway, incorporated originally in 1871 to build from Ottawa to Toronto via Peterborough. The new charter was much more flexible than the old, and in particular made liberal provision for leasing, acquiring, or amalgamating with other railways. It had no corporate connection with the Canadian Pacific, but E. B. Osler, a Toronto financier who worked closely with the C.P.R., became its president, and in July of 1881 George Stephen and Duncan McIntyre joined its board. Stephen's friend George Laidlaw, president of the Credit Valley, next brought the Toronto, Grey and Bruce Railway into the C.P.R. orbit. It was of interest because its line from Toronto to Owen Sound gave access to a port on Georgian Bay, which would enable the Canadian Pacific to share in the western and Great Lakes trade. In addition it would provide a route by which supplies could be shipped to the part of the main C.P.R. line to be built along or near the north shore of Lake Superior.

Stephen also had his eye on the Great Western Railway, extending from Niagara Falls to Windsor, by way of Hamilton and London. Built in the early 1850s, it was the earliest of the "bridge" lines that provided a shortcut through Canada between Michigan and New York State. It had aspired originally to be the western section of the Canadian "main line" route, but the Grand Trunk had chosen to construct a line of its own, and the two had been competitors for a generation. Osler has recorded that the Canadian Pacific opened negotiations with the Great Western with a view to having it build the Ontario and Quebec line and become the C.P.R.'s Ontario partner.[5]

This plan, if consummated, would have constituted a formidable invasion of areas highly productive of traffic that the Grand Trunk had long dominated, and it was quick to take defensive measures. One obvious method was to secure the cooperation or control of independent railways, like the Great Western, that might fall under the influence of the Canadian Pacific. A very early reaction came in February 1881, when Joseph Hickson concluded a confidential agreement (later succeeded by a lease and ultimately by outright ownership) with the Midland group, eight short lines in the country north of Lake Ontario. Tyler and Hickson then set their sights on the much more vital Great Western. To counter the Canadian Pacific proposal, they made an offer of amalgamation and engineered its approval at a meeting of Great Western shareholders late in June 1882. By August the merger was complete.

This acquisition gave the Grand Trunk control of all lines in Ontario that had connections westward to Chicago except one—the Canada Southern. Extending from Niagara Falls to Windsor, it was part of the Vanderbilt railroad empire and provided a shortcut across Ontario between the Michigan Central lines in the West and those of the New York Central in the East. By good fortune the Canada Southern ran through St. Thomas, the terminus of the Credit Valley Railway, and Stephen intended to turn this to good account. In times past, traffic had been exchanged between the Vanderbilt lines and the Grand Trunk, but this had ceased when the latter (in spite of Vanderbilt's opposition) had secured a line of its own to Chicago. Stephen proposed to offer the Credit Valley as a substitute, and, incidentally, secure connections for his Ontario lines with Detroit and Chicago. Late in 1882, presumably while he was in New York, he was successful in arranging with Vanderbilt for a traffic exchange between the Credit Valley and the Canada Southern.

An eastern network controlled by a group associated with the Canadian Pacific and linking St. Thomas, Owen Sound, Toronto, Ottawa, and Montreal was thus coming into existence. Nor was this all that Stephen had in mind. Looking to the east and south, he was interested in the charter of the Atlantic and North-West Railway, primarily because it had authority to bridge the St. Lawrence at Lachine, near Montreal, and in the South Eastern Railway. The latter was a small system in southern Quebec, important because it could provide a through line to Newport, Vermont, where existing railways would provide connections with Portland and Boston. Osler and Laidlaw were soon busy devising ways and means of bringing both under the control of the Canadian Pacific.

Shortly before Stephen went to New York and London, an effort had been made to persuade the Canadian Pacific and the Grand Trunk to come to terms. The prime mover was Sir John Rose, who had become alarmed by the hostility being shown by both sides. Using a memorandum prepared by Rose as a basis for discussion, Stephen and Hickson had met in September 1882 and talked about the relations between the two railways. Weighed down momentarily by the C.P.R.'s financial problems, Stephen seemed to have been ready to make concessions. Hickson thought that most of the differences had been disposed of, but on October 5 Stephen wrote to inform him "that after very full discussion with such of his colleagues as he had been able to reach they had come to the conclusion that no such radical change of policy as was talked of at our conference was at the present moment practicable."[6] This drama was to be repeated in London, as we shall see.

Major responsibility for financing the Ontario network inevitably fell upon Stephen. Funds were needed to complete the main line of the Ontario and Quebec, to erect the bridge over the St. Lawrence at Lachine, and to build the fifteen miles of track required to connect the bridge with the South Eastern Railway. The Atlantic and North-West was little more than a company on paper, but the Ontario and Quebec had a paid-up capital of $2 million and had entered into a contract for £750,000, covering the completion of its line. Stephen decided that the best plan would be to form a new holding corporation, and a copy of a confidential proof of the prospectus for a Great Central of Canada Company is preserved in the Macdonald Papers. Its purpose was "to acquire and hold the Bonds, Securities and Stocks of the Credit Valley, Ontario and Quebec, and Atlantic and North West Railway Companies, and to exercise all powers of nomination of Directors, voting and otherwise, incidental to the ownership thereof. . . ."[7] Stephen hoped to float an issue of £1 million of 5-percent debenture stock in London, the yield from which he was confident would be sufficient to complete the bridge and lines he had in mind.

Fresh from his success in disposing of $30 million of Canadian Pacific common shares, Stephen was in high spirits and full of confidence. "The G.T.R. people here are in a blue fright about the Ontario and Quebec and Credit V[alley] connection with the Vanderbilt systems," he told Macdonald on March 22, and added that "a *whisper* has got abroad and the consequence is a very dull weak market for G.T.R. securities."[8]

A week later, at the semiannual meeting of Grand Trunk shareholders, held in London, Sir Henry Tyler made a spirited attack on the Canadian Pacific. It is probable that he knew the substance of the Great Central prospectus; Sir John Rose states that it had been "judiciously communicated beforehand" to Grand Trunk interests.[9] The prospectus specifically disclaimed "all feeling of hostility to the Grand Trunk Railway," but the intention to compete vigorously was clear. "The C.P.R.," Sir Henry said, "is a gigantic undertaking, and possibly those who are carrying it out have hardly realized the task which they have undertaken; and I say so because from what I know of their proceedings, they do not seem to have found it enough for them. They have come into our territory in different directions, and have acquired lines of railway, and entered upon schemes of aggression. . . . The last thing we hear is that they are going to make a connection with Mr. Vanderbilt, and . . . compete with us for traffic between Montreal and the West." To the charge that the Grand Trunk had done its best to keep the C.P.R. out of the money markets in London and elsewhere, he replied that the directors "as a board" had never taken any steps of the kind, but he emphasized the "very important influence" exercised by the Grand Trunk's 20,000 shareholders, and implied that he expected it to be brought to bear against the C.P.R. if it endeavored to raise money in London that would be used to compete against the Grand Trunk in Canada.[10]

Stephen took the unusual step of replying to these charges by addressing an open letter to the Grand Trunk shareholders. Briefly, his contentions were three in number. First, the Grand Trunk, still under the "illusion that they must monopolise railway enterprise in Canada," were out to stifle the construction of rival lines, as they had done in the past. Secondly, there was room for competition; the Grand Trunk's single-track line between Montreal and Toronto was hopelessly congested; it had "to serve the traffic coming from the Western American States, in addition to the through Canadian traffic proper, and its carrying capacity is notoriously entirely inadequate to these purposes." Thirdly, Tyler's contention that the Grand Trunk board as such had not opposed the C.P.R. was meaningless; he could "scarcely pretend to say that individual members of his board, and gentlemen high in the confidence of himself and his colleagues, have not done all in their power to discredit and damage the C.P.R. Company in the eyes of the British public."[11]

This letter was dated April 5. What took place between Tyler and Stephen in the next six days is a mystery, for on April 11 they sent a joint cable to their respective general managers in Canada, Joseph Hickson and W. C. Van Horne, that represented a complete C.P.R. surrender to the demands of the Grand Trunk. Hickson and Van Horne were instructed to prepare an agreement between the two railways embodying the following terms:

Grand Trunk undertaking to afford full and liberal facilities for Canadian Pacific traffic by all Grand Trunk lines and connections to and from Canadian Pacific. . . . The Canadian Pacific undertaking to cede on terms to Grand Trunk Credit Valley, Ontario and Quebec Railway, Atlantic Northwest and Southeast [railways]. Ontario and Quebec to be completed and the Lachine Bridge [across the St. Lawrence] to be built unless other satisfactory accommodation provided. Canadian Pacific to give their traffic to Grand Trunk Railway and the two companies to avoid competition and work together in all respects for mutual benefit.

Sir John Rose's letters to Sir John Macdonald give some indication of the sequence of events. The Great Central proposal, and the intense competition that it portended, evidently upset the financial houses in London that were deeply involved in the none too prosperous affairs of the Grand Trunk. The result, Rose reported, "was an appeal to myself personally that I would meet Tyler and discuss possible terms. I thought it better that this business should be handed over to Stephen. . . . The truth is Tyler is completely under Stock Exchange influences, and they saw what a serious blow these new arrangements [the Great Central project and the Vanderbilt connection] could be if promoted in a hostile spirit."[12] In a word, the market closed ranks against Stephen and he was made to realize that there was no possibility of selling Great Central debentures in London. Even Morton, Rose and Company, which with its sister house in New York was the largest shareholder in the Canadian Pacific itself, declined to participate. "Strictly Entre nous," Rose told Macdonald, Stephen "had to be told that he had got to the limit of Financial support; the load that M[orton] R[ose] Co and their friends have on them both on C.P.R. and affiliated schemes is as heavy as they will assume and neither the *public* here—nor on the continent—nor in the U.S. look with favour on it yet."[13]

It was probably significant that Stephen faced this predicament at a time when he sensed that some of the members of the original C.P.R. syndicate were beginning to falter in their support. In particular, he must have known that James J. Hill would be leaving the Canadian Pacific board in May, and he doubtless suspected that John Kennedy would be following him shortly. Though courageous, stubborn, and persevering, Stephen was also impulsive and mercurial; his letters occasionally reflected a rapid change from a state of near elation to one of pessimism and depression. Van Horne was to remark at a later date that while Stephen was an optimist when in Canada, he was apt to become fearful when abroad.[14] If the weight of his C.P.R. responsibilities, his Ontario and Quebec difficulties, and his own personal financial involvements suddenly bore down upon him, it is comprehensible that he could react by coming to terms with Tyler and the Grand Trunk.

But the agreement between the two lines was never concluded; Stephen's colleagues in Montreal, repeating their performance in October, refused to accept it. On April 16, he informed Tyler that he feared that their "united attempts to harmonise the interests" of the railways were impracticable. "It would serve no good purpose," he wrote, "to enter into the details of all the objections which have been encountered, beyond stating that the control of the Ontario and Quebec, contrary to my expectations, cannot be surrendered to the Grand Trunk Railway."[15]

Who led the opposition we do not know; Stephen's letters are silent on the subject. Sir Charles Tupper, the minister of railways, has been suggested, and he would certainly have favored rejection. But the chief objector was probably Van Horne. Already a power within the company, he was by far the most experienced railwayman in its management, and would realize how important the Ontario lines would be, initially as a source of badly needed revenue and later as part of the comprehensive rail system the Canadian Pacific already had in mind. Combative by nature, he would certainly not have been put in an accommodating mood by the action of the Grand Trunk, a few weeks earlier, in purchasing the eastern section of the North Shore Line (the Quebec, Montreal, Ottawa and Occidental Railway) extending from Montreal to Quebec. This was a distinctly provocative purchase, for the Grand Trunk already had a line along the south shore of the St. Lawrence, and it was clearly intended to keep the Canadian Pacific out of Quebec City. G. R. Stevens, official historian of the Canadian National Railways, considers that the proposed agreement was "a far-reaching and sensible solution" to the battle that had developed between the two lines, that responsibility for its rejection "rests squarely upon the Canadian Pacific," and that the latter "therefore must accept most of the blame for the long and bitter controversy that followed."[16] But it is a moot point whether the C.P.R. could have survived financially in the next decade without its eastern lines.

Once negotiations had ended, the Canadian Pacific moved quickly to secure firm control of its affiliates. The Great Central scheme was abandoned, and on April 20 it petitioned Parliament for authority to lease the Credit Valley, the Ontario and Quebec, and the Atlantic and North-West railways. The necessary legislation became law in May, but later it was decided to make use of the convenient powers in the Ontario and Quebec charter to bring the various lines together. On July 26, the Toronto, Grey and Bruce Railway was leased to the Ontario and Quebec, the Credit Valley Railway was added by amalgamation on November 30, and the Atlantic and North-West by purchase on December 3. Then, on January 4, 1884, the Ontario and Quebec itself, and these subsidiary lines, were leased in perpetuity to the Canadian Pacific. The C.P.R. had already secured control of the South Eastern Railway by a mortgage foreclosure, and the considerable network that Stephen had in immediate view was thus completed.

In April, in conjunction with the Michigan Central, the Canadian Pacific began operating "a new palace sleeping car" in an overnight daily service between Toronto and Chicago. Advertising posters emphasized the point that this was "the only line of through cars" between the cities. The start of the service had been delayed for a time because Van Horne had insisted that none but the finest equipment should be used.

Work was pushed forward on the main line of the Ontario and Quebec, and it was completed from Perth (where it connected with the Canada Central) to West Toronto—193.8 miles—in August 1884. A "sink-hole" that developed suddenly at Kaladar disrupted traffic temporarily, but freight and passenger services were soon in regular operation. At the end of October, Van Horne sent an optimistic report to Stephen: "I think we are now carrying considerably more than half the passengers between Toronto and Montreal originating at those points. We have all the business between Ottawa and Toronto and between Peterboro and Toronto." Both through and local freight were "also very satisfactory."[17]

The Grand Trunk had not accepted these developments passively. In February, when, as will be related, the Canadian Pacific was in deep financial trouble and a relief bill was before Parliament, the Grand Trunk directors protested vigorously to Macdonald "against legislation embracing assistance to lines acquired by the Syndicate outside of the objects of the Canadian Pacific charter, thus using public money for competition against private enterprise."[18] Hickson apparently suggested that the government should require the C.P.R. to exchange its Ontario lines for the North Shore Line from Montreal to Quebec, which the Grand Trunk had purchased in 1883. A joint lease of the Ontario and Quebec was also proposed. Van Horne saw the correspondence and replied in characteristic fashion to this latter suggestion: "The Ontario and Quebec Railway has been leased and firmly bound to the Canadian Pacific for the term of 999 years, and we will be unable to treat for its sale until the end of that time. . . ."[19]

It is clear that there was actually little substance in the Grand Trunk's charge that the C.P.R. was using subsidy funds to acquire the Ontario lines. Stephen's personal involvement in the Credit Valley Railway has been noted, and he, Donald Smith, and others participated in many other transactions. The finances of the Ontario and Quebec had been kept quite distinct from those of the Canadian Pacific, and Stephen told the C.P.R. shareholders in June 1885 that "the Ontario and Quebec system was acquired and constructed by individuals, independent of assistance from any portion of the funds of this Company."[20] Official returns to the government provide some details. The share capital of the Credit Valley Railway was $500,000, fully paid up; in addition it sold debenture stock to a total of $4,567,000, and received a cash bonus of $531,000 from the government of Ontario and a further total of $1,085,000 from various municipalities along its route. In June 1884, the paid-up capital of the Ontario and Quebec Railway was $2 million, and outstanding 5-percent debentures totaled $4,979,750.

In December 1884, after the amalgamation of the two lines, Morton, Rose and Company sponsored a debenture issue of $9,590,000, interest on which was guaranteed by the Canadian Pacific. This was the first direct financial connection between the Ontario and Quebec and the C.P.R., and also the first occasion upon which a security connected with the C.P.R. had been offered in London. The Canadian Pacific was in dire straits at the time, and the issue was a complete failure, but this embarrassed the Ontario and Quebec only temporarily. Once the C.P.R. was itself out of the woods, it was able to dispose of debentures without difficulty.

By June 1885, Stephen could report that the acquired or leased lines south and east of Callander (in other words, the eastern network) were showing "a net revenue exceeding by 25 per cent. the fixed charges upon them, and exceeding by 10 per cent. the interest upon the entire cost of those extensions and leased lines, including such fixed charges."[21]

He must have wished that the long main line to the Pacific Coast was completed and in an equally satisfactory financial position.

8

The Financial Crisis of 1884

As we have seen, Van Horne continued to push the main line westward at a furious pace in 1883. The sheer volume of construction made expenditure mount alarmingly, and it was certain to increase further, because work would soon be concentrated on the most difficult and expensive sections of the railway. By the middle of the year it was clear that the utmost economy was essential, and Van Horne looked about for ways and means of saving money. Among other things, the line from Calgary to the summit of the Rockies was reexamined and revisions were made that promised to cut costs by $500,000. The track was rerouted so as to eliminate a long tunnel—a change that Van Horne found particularly welcome because it would save time as well as money, since the tunnel would have taken up to a year to bore.

As a result of one economy measure, the Canadian Pacific experienced its first serious strike. In April 1882, the company (in the words of Van Horne's circular) "not unmindful of the high cost of living" in the West, "resulting from various more or less temporary causes," had granted its engine drivers and firemen bonuses of twelve dollars and six dollars per month. In December 1883, Van Horne decided that the bonuses would have to be cut in half, and John Egan, the able but unpopular western superintendent, issued an order carrying the reduction into effect. The Brotherhood of Locomotive Engineers thereupon held a meeting and countered with a demand that the bonus be increased, not decreased. This roused Egan's Irish temper, and he announced that the reduction must be accepted within twenty-four hours and that the men must sign an acceptance before going to work. The engineers then went on strike, and the company closed its shops and roundhouses, alleging that they feared they might be damaged. The Winnipeg *Free Press* estimated that as many as 3,500 men were involved in the work stoppage.[1]

The shops were reopened in a week, but the dispute with the engineers, settled largely on the company's terms, lasted a fortnight. Train service of a sort was maintained by officials and others on the Pembina branch and later from Winnipeg westward. Some outside engineers were brought in, and the bitterness this caused was increased when the North-West Mounted Police not only took steps to protect Canadian Pacific property and trains, but in some instances operated locomotives as well.[2]

In the East the line north of Lake Superior still hung fire. In February 1883, only forty miles of track had been laid west of Callander. In July Van Horne explained that contracts were being delayed because efforts were being made to improve the location of the line. He estimated that the changes made would save $2 million or more.[3] The volume of work that would have to be done was frightening; some 4.6 million cubic yards of rock excavation would be required in one stretch of a hundred miles.[4] He believed that it should be possible to go over some obstructions instead of through them: "I hope," he wrote to one of his construction chiefs, "careful attention will be given to the suggestion I made as to raising the grade line and shortening the rock cuttings, using temporary trestles wherever suitable material cannot be readily borrowed for the embankments. . . . One yard of rock excavation will pay for a great many yards of earth. . . . By raising the grade line and reducing the width of the cuttings the cost of construction can be enormously decreased and also the time of completion."[5]

In May 1883, the nearly completed line from Winnipeg to Thunder Bay, which had been built by the government, was turned over to the Canadian Pacific. Very early on the morning of July 8, the first through train from Winnipeg was welcomed at Port Arthur by a cheering crowd, a bonfire on the esplanade, and an Indian war dance.

That same summer the C.P.R. completed a branch line from Sudbury to Algoma Mills, on the North Channel of Lake Huron, and also gained control of the Toronto, Grey and Bruce Railway, which terminated at Owen Sound, on Georgian Bay. This made possible the establishment of several all-Canadian supply routes. Steamers based at Collingwood and Owen Sound sailed to Port Arthur, and the North-West Transportation Company, known as the Beatty Line, ran from Sarnia both to Thunder Bay and to railway construction camps along the north shore of Lake Superior. Henry Beatty, manager of the company and father of a future president of the Canadian Pacific, had been invited to join the C.P.R. syndicate but had limited his participation to the purchase of a thousand shares. Later Van Horne was able to persuade him to take charge of the Great Lakes fleet that he and

Stephen were planning for the C.P.R. One of his first duties was to go to the Clyde and there watch over the construction of three 2,300-ton steel passenger and cargo steamers, the *Athabasca, Alberta,* and *Algoma*. All were launched in July 1883 and crossed the Atlantic to Montreal in October. There they were cut in two to enable them to pass through the St. Lawrence canals and towed to Buffalo, where the halves were rejoined and they were prepared to enter service when navigation opened in 1884. It was first intended that they should operate from Algoma, where the Canadian Pacific also planned to build a summer tourist hotel, but it was decided to base them instead on Owen Sound, which offered a convenient connection with Toronto and (after the completion of the Ontario and Quebec line in August) with Ottawa and Montreal as well. With their arrival the Canadian Pacific was able, during the summer season, to offer first-class and immigrant services all the way from Montreal to the Rocky Mountains.

In 1883, the C.P.R. had bought the small side-wheeler *Champion No. 2* to help carry men and supplies to the north shore construction sites. She and several other small craft acquired for the same purpose were the first of over 250 ships of all shapes and sizes, varying from tugs and river craft to a deluxe Atlantic express liner and giant bulk freighters, that the company was to own over the next ninety years.

The establishment of these services and the certainty that the line north of Lake Superior would be built prompted James J. Hill's withdrawal from the Canadian Pacific. They meant the end of his hopes that his St. Paul line might form the permanent link between the C.P.R.'s eastern and western systems. ("Hill has never forgiven me for building the line north of the Lake," Stephen remarked to Macdonald in 1887.)[6] Moreover, even the Canadian Pacific's temporary dependence on the St. Paul, Minneapolis and Manitoba was coming to an end. For three seasons it had controlled the only supply route to Winnipeg and the Canadian West and had enjoyed what Hill himself described as "a very comfortable monopoly" of the heavy traffic arising from C.P.R. construction across the prairies. In 1882–83 this had amounted to between 35 and 45 percent of the line's entire traffic.[7] By coincidence, it was the day after Hill's term as a director expired that the Canadian Pacific took over the government-built line to Thunder Bay.

The ascendancy Van Horne was gaining in the Canadian Pacific was probably another factor in Hill's decision. His own influence in the company had declined steadily since Van Horne—his own choice for the post of general manager—had taken over. Finally, Hill foresaw that a clash of interest was in prospect. He was already envisaging the Great Northern Railroad of the future, which would be an expansion of the St. Paul, Minneapolis and Manitoba westward to the Pacific Coast. Competition with the Canadian Pacific would be inevitable, and between two rivals as able and aggressive as Van Horne and himself, he knew that few holds would be barred. Some years later, before a Senate committee, Hill summed up the matter in a dozen words: "I saw that conflict was coming, and I said, 'We will part friends.' "[8]

As a reciprocal gesture Stephen, Donald Smith, and R. B. Angus resigned from the board of the St. Paul, Minneapolis and Manitoba, but both Stephen and Smith retained very substantial holdings in the company and in the Great Northern that succeeded it. Indeed, in 1889, shortly after Stephen retired as president of the Canadian Pacific, he and Smith rejoined Hill's board and both were still large shareholders in his railways when they died, many years later.

Van Horne had moved his office from Winnipeg to Montreal at the beginning of 1883, and with Hill's departure the Canadian Pacific administration was more than ever centered there. Hitherto the directors had all been paid only $1,000 a year, but in June the shareholders authorized modest increases for the officers. The president's salary was fixed at $6,000, and those of the vice-president and members of the executive committee at $5,000.[9]

Stephen had been confident that the sale of $30 million of stock in December 1882 had solved his financial problems, but instead it afforded him only a relatively brief respite. By the autumn of 1883, the Canadian Pacific was again critically short of funds. His only consolation lay in the railway's earnings, which already were sufficient to support his contention that it would pay its way if only the line could be completed. Gross revenues would be $5.4 million in 1883, and the net operating profit $561,143. The latter figure would be doubled in 1884.

Still determined not to resort to the sale of mortgage bonds, Stephen once more looked for relief to a further sale of common shares. Who suggested the proposal that he presented to Macdonald late in October 1883 is not clear. Some think it was suggested by English and French bankers; others feel that he found a precedent in the guarantees of interest on railway bonds that had been given by the government from time to time. From the beginning the Canadian Pacific had paid regular semiannual dividends of 5 or 6 percent, and by August 1883, its shareholders had already received $2,128,000—payments Stephen hoped would make the shares attractive to investors, and which he felt were justified by the company's long-term prospects. He now proposed that the C.P.R. should guarantee 3-percent dividends on its stock for a period of ten years by depositing with the government the sum required to make the payments. In addition, he intended to pay another 2 percent from other sources, thus maintaining a total dividend of 5 percent. His hope was that this prospect would cause a sharp rise in the price of the stock and the demand for it, and that the issue of additional shares would bring in the money required to complete the main line.

Initially Stephen proposed to guarantee dividends on the entire authorized capital of $100 million, but this was quickly amended to limit the guarantee to the $65 million that had actually been issued. The remaining $35 million would be deposited with the government, to be released in whole or in part upon receipt of a payment sufficient to include it within the guaranteed income scheme. The guarantee fund would total somewhat less than $16 million, and the plan called for an immediate payment of $8.56 million, which would be sufficient to cover the dividends for the first five years.

The government approved the proposal by order in council on November 7, and Stephen thereupon left for New York to borrow the money required for the immediate deposit. Of the $65 million of issued stock, $55 million was in the hands of the shareholders. The $10 million still in the company's treasury was pledged as security for a $5 million loan from J. S. Kennedy and Company. Another $2.5 million was borrowed from Unger and Company, the security in this case being C.P.R. stock and St. Paul, Minneapolis and Manitoba shares, all the property of Donald Smith, R. B. Angus, and Stephen himself—a further instance of the way in which these three repeatedly risked their personal fortunes to support the Canadian Pacific.

The dividend guarantee involved a further complication, for in the previous December all stock over and above that held by shareholders had been earmarked as part payment to the North American Railway Contracting Company, which had undertaken to complete the main line. To release the stock for deposit with the government, the contract had to be canceled. Fortunately this could be done without much difficulty, as none of the shares had actually been handed over. Supervision of construction had been in Canadian hands throughout, and full and direct responsibility for it now devolved upon the Canadian Pacific.

All these arrangements had scarcely been completed, and the immediate cash payment deposited, when Stephen made the shattering discovery that it had all been done in vain. After rising some ten points on the market, C.P.R. stock began to decline, and it became clear that any attempt to sell shares in quantity would simply depress the price still further.

There were a number of reasons for this disheartening result. The western land boom had collapsed and in September a severe frost had done great damage on the prairies. This combination of circumstances caused many to take a dim view of the future of the Canadian West and the railway that would serve it. Manitoba was in a ferment; freight rates were felt to be too high, and the monopoly clause, which restricted the building of competing railroads, had aroused deep resentment. Press attacks on the C.P.R. persisted in London and New York. In November the *Wall Street Daily News* noted that the Canadian Pacific was "masquerading around as a five per cent security" and declared that it was "a dead skin, and every investor who buys the stock on the humbugging pretences made for it will lose every cent. The road itself is not called for by commercial necessity."[10] Even the simple, straightforward character of Stephen's guaranteed dividends plan aroused suspicion; some thought it might not be as simple as it seemed. Finally, a depression was developing. At the annual meeting of the Bank of Montreal in June, C. F. Smithers, who had succeeded Stephen as president, gave a discouraging report on conditions: "As regards general business, as far as I can learn from diligent inquiry, extreme dullness is the great feature of the day."[11] To top it all off, the Northern Pacific again went into receivership, an event that naturally depressed the market for railway securities. But it is possible that this was a blessing in disguise. Rumors were afloat that Sir Henry Tyler was considering ways of extending the Grand Trunk from Chicago to Duluth, and of pushing on toward Manitoba by means of an agreement with the Northern Pacific—a menacing possibility removed by the receivership.

Writing to Sir Charles Tupper on November 22, Sir John Macdonald remarked that "Geo. Stephen—for the first time—seemed depressed notwithstanding his enormous pluck. . . ." Macdonald still professed to believe that with the dividend guarantee C.P.R. stock "ought to find ready sale at 70 or more on the English market,"[12] but Stephen knew better. The simple truth was that the Canadian Pacific was millions of dollars worse off than it had been in October, and its plight was worsening, day by day.

There is a story, attributed by O. D. Skelton to Van Horne, to the effect that when Stephen approached Macdonald and expressed the conviction that only direct government assistance could tide the company over its difficulties, Macdonald refused abruptly to entertain the idea. John Henry Pope, acting minister of railways and throughout the construction period a staunch supporter of the C.P.R., then intervened and pointed out to Macdonald how closely the life of his administration was bound up with that of the railway: "The day the Canadian Pacific busts the Conservative party busts the day after."[13] Quite apart from party considerations, the failure of the C.P.R., coming at the beginning of a depression, would have had immense repercussions in financial and business circles in Canada. But Macdonald's problem was not an easy one, for although he had a comfortable majority in Parliament, neither his supporters nor his cabinet were by any means unanimous in favoring relief measures for the railway.

For help in the battle he foresaw would ensue, both within the Conservative caucus and in the House of Commons, Macdonald turned at once to the most redoubtable of the Canadian Pacific's champions, Sir Charles Tupper. Although still officially minister of railways, Tupper had been acting high commissioner for Canada in London since the spring. On December 1, Macdonald addressed a cable to him that has become famous: "Pacific in trouble. You should be here." To which Tupper replied at once: "Sailing on Thursday."

Six weeks passed before the details of the assistance to be given to the railway were finally worked out—six dreadful weeks for Stephen, who saw the company's debts increasing by millions and its critics rejoicing over its difficulties. "Things have now reached a pass," he wrote to Macdonald on December 15, "when we must either stop or find the means of going on. Our enemies here and elsewhere think they can now break us down and finish the C.P.R. for ever."[14] For temporary help he turned to the Bank of Montreal, to which the C.P.R. already owed nearly $2 million, and in spite of fears and opposition within the board of directors, the bank saw him through the crisis—proof, one may assume, that the bank was convinced that Macdonald would not permit the Canadian Pacific to collapse. By the time the crisis was over, the C.P.R.'s indebtedness had increased to nearly $7 million, and part of the advances had been made at Tupper's urgent request and upon his assurance that assistance for the railway would be forthcoming from the government.

This was not brought about without a hard struggle. The aid agreed upon had been set forth by Stephen in a letter to Macdonald dated January 15, 1884. Essentially it consisted of a loan of $22.5 million, of which $7.5 million was to be made available immediately. The remaining $15 million would be paid along with the balance of the original cash subsidy, but subsidy (and loan) payments would not be paid on a mileage basis, as heretofore, but would be calculated upon the proportion of the work done to that which remained to be done. There were a number of other provisions, including the return of the bonds deposited to guarantee performance; since the railway was already earning substantial revenues, the C.P.R. was able to insist that the deposit was no longer necessary. As security for the loan the Canadian Pacific was required to give a blanket mortgage on all its railway properties and its land and to assign certain revenues to the government. Stephen also undertook to complete the main line by May 1886, in only half of the time stipulated in the original contract.

It was a high price to pay—a dangerous price, since it encumbered the total assets of the company and left it with no basis upon which to secure further credit, should this be necessary. But once again Stephen was confident that the loan and the subsidy would be adequate to meet all requirements. In November the cost of completing the railway had been estimated to be $25.1

million; this Stephen now raised to $27 million. The immediate loan of $7.5 million and the performance deposit would pay off the floating debt, which exceeded $8 million; the balance of the loan, $15 million, and the $12.7 million of cash subsidy still to be earned would meet construction costs.

The bitterness and, as he considered it, the meanness of the opponents of the relief bill in Parliament appalled Stephen, but he was even more upset by the length of the debate in the House. He never became reconciled to the delays inseparable from contentious parliamentary proceedings, and he found the waiting and suspense almost unbearable. "I am going down [to Montreal] in the morning," he wrote to Macdonald on January 22, "and you may be sure I will do all I can to keep things moving, and in life, till relief arrives, but you must not blame me if I fail. . . . If I find we cannot go on, I suppose the only thing to do will be to put in a Receiver. If that has to be done, the quicker it is done the better. . . . I am getting so wearied and worn out with this business that almost any change will be a relief to me."[15] At that time not even the loan bill resolutions had been introduced in the House, and Stephen was greatly disturbed when Tupper told him that he expected the measure would not become law for another five weeks. "Had I supposed it would take to March 1 before help could reach us," he told Tupper, "I would not have made the attempt to carry on."[16] Tupper's forecast proved to be surprisingly accurate. The bill passed the Commons on February 28, and after passing the Senate became law on March 6. The Bank of Montreal debt was cleared on the thirteenth.

Macdonald and Tupper had had their troubles. The Conservative members from the Maritime Provinces, with the exception of Tupper, were not greatly concerned about a railway to the West, but they were interested in a line from Montreal to Saint John and Halifax that would be shorter than the roundabout route provided by the Intercolonial Railway. If largesse was to be distributed, the Quebec members were determined that their province should also receive its share. The Manitoba members were angry and rebellious. It seemed almost as if the railway that was intended to bind all Canada together were splitting it asunder instead.

Manitoba received no immediate concession, doubtless because it had only five members in the House, but the support of the fifty-two Quebec Conservatives and those from the Maritimes was essential, and they were able to extract bounties from Macdonald. Tupper announced in April that the C.P.R. would be extended to Quebec City, if necessary with the taxpayers' money, and that a subsidy would be provided for a more direct line from Montreal to the Maritimes. In addition, Quebec was awarded a retrospective cash subsidy of $2.4 million "in consideration of having constructed the railway from Quebec [City] to Ottawa . . . a work of national and not merely provincial utility"—this despite the fact that the line had already been sold by the province. The section between Ottawa and Montreal had been purchased by the C.P.R. and the Montreal–Quebec portion had been acquired by the Grand Trunk.

It is easy to gain the impression that the Canadian Pacific had subsisted chiefly on government subsidies and loans, but this is not so. With his request for a loan, Stephen had submitted a summary financial statement that is revealing. Total expenditure to December 31, 1883, had been $58,695,377. Only $12,289,211 of the cash subsidy of $25 million had been earned, and the land subsidy had produced about $9 million. The balance of $37,377,155 had been found by the company itself. In 1882, the highly suspicious Liberal opposition in Parliament had insisted that the C.P.R. should submit each year immensely detailed returns and accounts, and these were printed in the official *Sessional Papers*. From this source it can be ascertained that actual cash expenditure on engineering, construction, subsidiary lines, and rolling stock had been $10.1 million in 1881 and just under $22 million in each of the succeeding years, or a total of $54.1 million in all.

Stephen carried on with his accustomed energy and with undiminished faith in the Canadian Pacific, but he was faced with the fact that his original team was breaking up. In a letter written in 1909, he listed the nine original directors, placed an X opposite the names of James J. Hill, Duncan McIntyre, J. S. Kennedy, and Baron J. de Reinach, and added: "The four marked X deserted and I had to buy them out."[17]

The circumstances in each case were different. Hill's resignation in May 1883 has been mentioned. In January and February he had sold 14,509 of his Canadian Pacific shares, but the transfer books show that they were mostly acquired by the New York financial houses belonging to the syndicate that had made the $30 million stock purchase the previous December. Kennedy also began selling his stock, but he and Hill each retained 10,000 shares as token support for Stephen.[18] Kennedy had become a close associate of Hill, so it was not surprising that when one left the other followed. McIntyre seems simply to have lost his nerve and become convinced that the C.P.R. was headed for bankruptcy. He later had contacts with the Grand Trunk and tried to persuade them to move their headquarters to Montreal—sound advice that they would have done well to follow. Baron de Reinach, representing French interests, resigned in December 1884.

Of the five original North American directors, only Stephen and R. B. Angus were left, but they had the backing of Donald Smith, who had joined the board in 1882. To Stephen's pleasure and relief, the unwavering support Smith had given him throughout the company's financial difficulties had made it possible for him to bring about a reconciliation between Smith and Sir John Macdonald. The two had been estranged since the Pacific Scandal a decade before. Stephen arranged a meeting and later wrote to Macdonald to thank him for the "kind and cordial reception" he had given Smith. His letter continued:

The pluck with which he has stood by me in my efforts to sustain the credit of the C.P.R. made it almost a duty on my part to try and restore friendly relations between one who has stood so courageously by the company in its time of trouble and you, to whom alone the C.P.R. owes its existence as a real Canadian railway. I hope some day this fact will become more generally known than it is now. But for you, the C.P.R. would undoubtedly have terminated at Port Arthur in summer, and the line for six months of the year would have been simply an extension of the American line running up from St. Paul to the international boundary line, in short not a *Canadian* Pacific Railway at all—and the destiny of Canada politically and commercially something very different to that which is now a matter of certainty—unless our people from sheer want of faith throw away their grand inheritance.[19]

It is a measure of the value the Canadian Pacific had come to place on the ability of its general manager that Van Horne succeeded McIntyre in May 1884, both as a director and as vice-president. Thereafter the executive committee consisted of George Stephen, Donald Smith, R. B. Angus, and Van Horne—a tightly knit and determined group, sharing the conviction that the company must not and would not fail.

Work was at last in full swing on the line north of Lake Superior, soon to become notorious as the unprofitable but essential "bridge" line that spanned the rocky wilderness separating the productive areas of eastern and western Canada. For a hundred miles or more, where it skirted the lake, construction involved almost continuous heavy rock work. Men and supplies could be brought to this section by water, but long segments of the route had to be reached by supply roads pushed inland from the shore. Thus, for example, the mouth of the Michipicoten River became a supply base and the starting point of a forty-eight-mile road that led north to Dog Lake and the Canadian Pacific right-of-way.

Here, incidentally, Van Horne met the demon rum in a particularly dangerous way. He did his best to counter its attractions by seeing that the construction crews (who usually paid four dollars a week for their board) were well fed, but life was rough and liquor vendors found a ready market. In the West, which was under federal jurisdiction, the sale of liquor was forbidden, but this was not so in Ontario. To his annoyance, Van Horne discovered that the authorities at Sault Ste. Marie, eager for revenue, had issued licenses for the sale of liquor at the Michipicoten River supply base. He wrote at once to the minister of railways, explaining that the road was the means whereby supplies reached a hundred miles of the line and that "an enormous quantity of high explosives" was carried over it. The least carelessness could therefore result disastrously and he hoped (vainly as it proved) that the licenses would be canceled.[20]

Stephen remained confident for some time that sufficient funds were in hand to complete the main line, but even in the spring of 1884 Van Horne was less sanguine and realized that once again the utmost economy would be essential. John Ross, superintendent of construction north of the lake, proved to be a stumbling block, for he was inclined to build a better railway than the Canadian Pacific could afford, complete with extensive masonry work and iron bridges. Van Horne, on the other hand, felt compelled to negotiate with the government's chief engineer, Collingwood Schreiber, to secure some modifications in specifications, always providing they were consistent with safety. The free use of timber bridges and trestles would result in substantial savings, and in April Van Horne notified Ross that Schreiber had agreed "to accept such structures as permanent work." Money, he explained, was a crucial consideration: "It will be infinitely better to come out a million ahead with a large number of timber structures to replace later on than to come out a million dollars behind with more permanent work."[21]

In letter after letter during the summer, Van Horne urged upon Ross the absolute necessity of keeping expenditures down to the essential minimum. Rock cuts were to be reduced to sixteen feet in width where the line was straight and to eighteen feet on curves; they could be widened later. Timber trestles could take the place of large earth fills. Gradients and curvature were to be sacrificed last, but even they could be improved later if need be. Masonry continued to be a sore point. Van Horne complained that "more than twice as much was expended on the Port Arthur and Nipigon Section [completed early in 1884] than on all the rest of our work together and this contributed largely to our [financial] difficulties and compelled us to discard masonry in many places of infinitely greater importance. . . ."[22]

Work had continued on the Lake Superior section all through the winter of 1883–84; at Christmastime slightly more than 9,500 men were employed there. And in spite of constant harping on the need for economy, Van Horne appreciated what Ross had accomplished by the fall of 1884. "You have made a splendid foundation for the railway," he wrote, "and we can take our time to put on the polish, we cannot possibly raise the money to do it now. . . . The work remaining must be limited to making the roadway safe for the passage of trains at a moderate rate of speed. . . . We will finish the ballasting in one, two or ten years, as the resources of the Company may permit."[23]

At the time Van Horne wrote, the gaps in the line between Sudbury and Thunder Bay still totaled nearly 400 miles, but by the end of the year they had been reduced to 254 miles. If fortune smiled, the whole difficult line might well be completed in another six or seven months.

9

The Last Crisis and the Last Spike

In 1884 construction in the West centered on the immensely difficult section of the line beyond the summit of the Rockies. In contrast to the two previous seasons, when the railway had raced across the prairies at breakneck speed, here it required a whole season to advance the track no more than eighty miles.

The Canadian Pacific line through the Rockies and the Selkirks followed watercourses; it found its way where rivers and creeks had already found theirs. In the fall of 1883, it had followed the Bow River and a small tributary up the eastern slope of the Rocky Mountains. After reaching the Great Divide at the summit (5,337 feet), where the station was appropriately named Stephen, it would transit the Kicking Horse Pass and descend the western slope, following the Kicking Horse River to its junction with the Columbia at Golden. For the next twenty-eight miles it would parallel the Columbia, crossing it at Donald and running on to Beavermouth, where the Columbia is joined by the Beaver River. The line would then ascend the eastern slope of the Selkirks to Rogers Pass (altitude 4,275 feet) by following the Beaver and its tributary, Bear Creek, and run down the western slope in the valley of the Illecillewaet River to the site of Revelstoke and a second crossing of the Columbia, which in the interval had made a great swing around the northern end of the Selkirks.

Major Rogers had announced the discovery of the pass that bears his name in August 1882. Stephen was relieved and delighted. "I felt sure from what Major Rogers had told me last year, that we should succeed," he told Macdonald, "but was very glad to have my impression confirmed. This secures us a direct short through line, and adds greatly to the commercial value of the line as a transcontinental line."[1] In September the C.P.R. asked the government to approve the Rogers Pass route, and in the spring of 1883 this was agreed to, but with certain reservations. The government wanted to be quite sure that the southern passes offered the advantages claimed for them, and until this was ascertained no subsidy would be paid on construction beyond a point 404 miles west of Winnipeg. This meant the vicinity of Moose Jaw, from which it would still be possible to swing the line northwestward to the Yellowhead, if this should be deemed advisable. To secure an independent opinion, Sandford Fleming was asked to go over the ground, and this he did in August and September. From Kamloops he wired the directors, telling them (in Stephen's words) that he had found "the Rogers pass quite practicable and highly satisfactory"[2]—a remarkable endorsement to come from the champion of the Yellowhead.

Privately, Van Horne also seems to have wished for some reassurance, mostly because of Rogers's personal eccentricities. J. H. E. Secretan, an English engineer who worked with both Fleming and Rogers, described him as a "short, sharp, snappy little chap with long Dundreary whiskers . . . a master of picturesque profanity, who continually chewed tobacco and was an artist in expectoration."[3] Rogers was given to starting off into the wilds with the scantiest of provisions, and to feeding his survey crews on meager rations that consisted mostly of beans—a practice Van Horne, who relished good food and plenty of it, did his best to correct. "It is exceedingly important," he wrote to Rogers on one occasion, "that an ample supply of good food be provided and that the quantity be beyond the possibility of doubt."[4] He had considerable faith in Rogers, but so much was at stake that he took the precaution of sending "two competent and disinterested engineers over his work . . . in order to make sure of it."[5]

The line would drop over 3,800 feet—almost three quarters of a mile—in the 150 miles between Stephen and Revelstoke, with the Selkirks forming a vast barrier in between that would have to be climbed. The trains would be climbing up or running down almost continuously; there were few near-level stretches of any length. The western slopes were long and in places steep. The first part of the descent from Stephen, soon to become famous as the "Big Hill," proved to be a railroader's veritable nightmare. Between Hector, near Stephen, and Field, a distance of only about seven miles as the crow flies, the line dropped 1,141 feet. Worse still, the greater part of the drop occurred in the first few miles west of Hector.

The maximum gradient permissible on the Canadian Pacific main line had been fixed at 2.2 percent, or 116 feet per mile. Rogers had worked out a route down the Kicking Horse River that did not exceed this, but as construction approached it was seen to have two serious faults: the stability (and safety) of some of the proposed roadbed was doubtful, in part because of the close proximity of a glacier, and it would necessitate the boring of a 1,400-foot tunnel through solid rock. This could well delay the completion of the line by as much as a year. Sandford Fleming is credited with having suggested that the C.P.R. should seek permission to build a temporary and considerably steeper line, and to this the government agreed at the end of May.

On the "Big Hill," as it was originally completed, a westbound train first encountered a four-mile stretch on which the gradient was 4.4 percent—twice the official maximum—and after a relatively level interlude ran down a second descent almost as steep and almost as long. Fortunately, as Van Horne explained to the minister of railways, these grades were "on a section of the railway where the traffic must be very light for many years, where there will be no local traffic whatever and three or at the most four trains each way per day will carry all the business to be done. . . ."[6] There was the further point that westbound freight traffic, which would be coming down the hill, was expected to be heavier than the eastbound that would have to be hauled up it—which is still very much the case today.

All this was true enough, but the line, like many temporary structures, had a far longer life than intended, and the eight miles of track from Hector to Field were for over twenty years perhaps the most difficult and expensive to operate in the whole Canadian Pacific system.

Taking a train up the hill was primarily a matter of motive power. Consolidation-type locomotives were provided from the first, and as train weights increased, so of necessity did the number and power of the engines used. Four locomotives were required in the early days for even a relatively short freight train. When the Duke and Duchess of York (the future King George V and Queen Mary) visited Canada in 1901, the C.P.R. took no chances with the royal train; the nine-car special was taken up the "Big Hill" by five locomotives.

Bringing a train down called for the utmost care and caution. Three safety switches were installed, so that a train that threatened to run away could be diverted to an uphill spur that (in theory at least) would bring it to a halt. Brakes were checked before a descent, and passenger trains came to a full stop before each safety switch to make sure that all was in order. Even so, trains would arrive at Field with brake shoes smoking at every wheel.

Lurid stories have been told about runaway trains on the "Big Hill," but most of them seem to have had little foundation in fact. Pensioners are apt to embellish their reminiscences, and gullible travelers were told tall tales. One of them, Prof. G. G. Ramsay, came to Canada to attend the meetings of the

British Association for the Advancement of Science and went down the "Big Hill" on a work train in September 1884, soon after the rails were laid. In his account of the experience he describes a runaway:

Once a train, with 270 men going down for their day's work, broke loose. One by one, all the men jumped off. Scarce had the last man leapt, when the train, rushing at forty or fifty miles an hour down the new-laid track, and scorning a side line up the hill turned open to intercept the runaway, "jumped" the rails at the curve close to the second crossing of the river, and dashed straight on into a precipitous face of rock. "There was just enough old iron left," said the pointsman who saw the crash, "to fill a moderate sized wheelbarrow."[7]

The difficulty with this and other similar stories is that they do not accord with the facts. The records show that the Canadian Pacific emerged from the construction period with the full complement of locomotives that had been assigned to work in the mountains, and that every one of them continued in service for a dozen years or more.

The track reached the Columbia in October. A temporary pile bridge across the river had been built at Donald, which was to be a divisional point, and in November steel was laid to Beavermouth.

The following season the construction crews tackled the Selkirks. The line up the eastern slope from Beavermouth, twenty-two miles in length, climbed 1,867 feet to Rogers Pass and the summit; on the western descent to Revelstoke, forty-six miles, it dropped just over 2,900 feet. The grades, though steep, nowhere exceeded the official maximum of 2.2 percent. But the Selkirks presented formidable problems of both construction and operation that were peculiar to them alone.

As the line came up the valley of the Beaver River, it encountered tributaries that had cut deep gorges in the hillside. Huge timber bridges were required to span them, the most notable being at Mountain Creek, Surprise Creek, and Stoney Creek. This last, said to have been the highest structure of the kind on the continent, carried the track 295 feet above the water.

Snowfall in the Rockies is relatively light; in the Selkirks, particularly on the western slope, it is extremely heavy. The seasonal total can be thirty-five feet or even more; on one occasion eight and a half feet fell in six days. This resulted in two problems for the railway. Establishing a solid roadbed was frequently extremely difficult, because the sandy loam in the region took on the characteristics of quicksand when wet; parts of the line had to be stabilized by driving double rows of piles along either side. Much more serious was the almost constant danger from slides. Mountains towered over the Rogers Pass and the track for miles on either side of it, and avalanches, and the accompanying hurricanelike winds peculiar to them, came hurtling down on the line with frightening force and frequency. Miles of snow sheds afforded a partial solution, but as long as Rogers Pass remained in use slides were a major hazard and displayed a disconcerting ability to occur suddenly and in unexpected places. Near Glacier station, just west of the summit, the track twisted back and forth across the Illecillewaet valley in a fantastic series of immense timber trestles that soon became known as "The Loop." This was primarily to reduce grades but had the important added advantage of keeping most of the track beyond the reach of avalanches.

Another Ross—James Ross—was in charge of construction in the mountains. The son of a Scottish shipowner, he had been building railways in the United States and Canada ever since he had come to America in 1868. He had built the Credit Valley Railway and had been a consulting engineer on the Ontario and Quebec. His assistant superintendent was Herbert S. Holt, who had worked with him on both these projects. In addition to Holt, Ross had attracted a remarkable group of engineers and contractors, several of whom

The temporary town (typical of many) that sprang up at Rogers Pass in construction days. (COURTESY OF THE BRITISH COLUMBIA PROVINCIAL ARCHIVES)

were to make their mark in the business world. Among them were William Mackenzie and Donald Mann. Holt, Mackenzie, and Mann would all be knighted, and along with Ross himself would figure largely in railway, tramway, industrial, and power developments and in banking, not only in Canada but in Mexico and South America as well. Later Mackenzie and Mann would reenter the Canadian Pacific story in a very different capacity—as creators of a rival system, the Canadian Northern Railway.

Meanwhile Andrew Onderdonk had been engaged in building the line from Yale to Kamloops Lake, which had been put under contract by the government in 1879. The route, which followed first the Fraser and then the Thompson River, was virtually one continuous canyon. The contracts stipulated that curves must not exceed 4 degrees, but location work had no more than started when the government began to impress upon Onderdonk the need for the utmost economy. The only way to make major savings was by going around the obstructions instead of through them, and by reducing the size of the tunnels and rock cuts that were found to be unavoidable.

The result was a poorly constructed line with hardly a mile of straight track in its whole length, and with innumerable curves that exceeded official specifications.[8] Who was actually responsible for this substandard work is difficult to determine; the likelihood appears to be that Onderdonk, whose ability was beyond question, felt that he had official blessing for cheaper construction. He had found that thirteen tunnels were required in the first twenty miles beyond Yale, and this may well have made him welcome a lowering of standards. In any event, the deficiencies of the line were to give rise to an unhappy dispute between the government and the Canadian Pacific.

Onderdonk's supply base was at Yale, the head of navigation on the Fraser, and here he built himself a comfortable residence that was a local landmark for over half a century. W. H. Holmes, who was responsible for checking, loading, and timekeeping at Yale, has left a vivid impression of the scene there in the early days of the contract:

> Men coming in from everywhere by the hundreds—all kinds of good men—as well as rough-necks from San Francisco—Barbary Coast hoodlums. The streets were crowded—saloons doing a roaring business, and fights a daily occurrence; steamboats arriving daily loaded with freight, and no place to put it, for although all available teams had been hired—there were not half enough of them to haul it all away. Men of all kinds had to be sorted out; stewards, cooks, flunkeys, drillers, carpenters, teamsters, stablemen and blacksmiths;—in fact, men of all trades, besides the office staff, timekeepers, and checkers.
>
> In these days everything was done by hand; bridges had to be built, and tunnels driven by hand-drilling; grades had to be cut through solid rock, as well as open cuts, all by hand. It was hammers and drills, picks and shovels, blasting night and day, and work for everybody who wanted it.[9]

In spite of every effort, Onderdonk found it impossible to recruit an adequate work force in British Columbia and California, and he is remembered chiefly because he brought in thousands of Chinese, a move greatly resented locally. At the height of building activity, the work force consisted of about 2,500 whites and 6,500 Chinese. Holmes remarks upon the "incredible carelessness" with which explosives were handled. This applied also to the construction crews on the parts of the line north of Lake Superior, where much rock work was encountered, and as a result accidents were frequent in both areas.

Onderdonk was awarded two additional contracts, one by the government and the other by the Canadian Pacific. The first covered the ninety miles from Yale to Port Moody, the official terminus on Burrard Inlet. The first dozen

A typical section of the line built by Andrew Onderdonk through the canyon of the Fraser River. (COURTESY OF THE BRITISH COLUMBIA PROVINCIAL ARCHIVES)

miles were in the lower canyon of the Fraser, but the rest of the route was an easy run down the river's widening delta. The C.P.R. contract extended from Savona, at the western end of Kamloops Lake, 125 miles eastward to Eagle Pass, a remarkably easy route through the Monashee Mountains, the range west of the Selkirks. Here rails from the West were expected to meet those being laid from the East. This was actually the last part of the main line to be located. The initial survey was made by Major Rogers in 1884, but once again Van Horne had another engineer check his work. Onderdonk was delighted with the survey and reported to Stephen: "The grades and allignments [sic] are easy, and the character of the work the cheapest mountain work I have ever seen."[10] In all, Onderdonk constructed 338 miles of the main line, from Eagle Pass to Port Moody.

In the summer of 1884, Van Horne visited the West with two purposes in mind. The time had come when decisions had to be made about terminal facilities on Burrard Inlet—a matter of special interest, since it conditioned the rise of what has become the third-largest city and the greatest port in Canada—and he was anxious to see for himself the main line, built and building, between Port Moody and Rogers Pass.

In 1871 British Columbia had transferred to the federal government a land reserve forty miles wide (soon to be known as the "railway belt") along the route of the Canadian Pacific within the province. This was to begin at "English Bay or Burrard Inlet"—an ambiguous description, as the point chosen could vary by the length of the inlet, about twelve miles. Port Moody had been declared the official terminus (which it continues to be to this day) simply because it was at the eastern end of the inlet, and the government considered that it would have done its duty when it had brought the railway to the nearest tidewater. But the suitability of Port Moody either for a rail terminus or for the site of a major new city and seaport remained open to question.

Stephen, who already had a trans-Pacific steamer service in mind, had long had doubts about Port Moody. He was much alarmed when he heard, in 1883, that British Columbia intended to lift the reserve on the railway belt west of Port Moody, on the logical grounds that the C.P.R. would not extend beyond the town. "This is of enormous importance to us," Stephen wrote to Macdonald, "and I trust you will permit nothing to be done . . . until we have had an opportunity of inquiring into the fitness of the harbour of Port Moody for the business we have reason to expect at our Pacific terminus."[11] In spite of this protest the reserve was lifted in May 1884, but British Columbia qualified the cancellation by giving notice that the land would not be available immediately for purchase or preemption.

In Victoria, Van Horne discussed the terminus problem briefly with Premier William Smithe and then went to see Burrard Inlet for himself. A glance was sufficient to convince him that Port Moody was quite inadequate for the railway's purposes, and it was equally obvious that the best location would be a dozen miles to the west, on the peninsula between the inlet proper and English Bay. When he returned to Montreal, the directors agreed with this opinion, and by early September Van Horne was negotiating with Premier Smithe for a terminus there.

He was extremely anxious to secure the site in question, but the Canadian Pacific was desperately short of money. The government loan and subsidy would all be required to build the main line; additional funds to provide such essentials as rolling stock, stations, yards, wharves, and grain elevators were extremely difficult to muster. About $5 million had to be found for such purposes in 1884, and the budget could be stretched no further. Van Horne made this clear in a letter to Smithe. He pointed out that "a comprehensive plan for a terminus providing reasonably for the future as well as for the present" would "involve a large immediate outlay of money," and that the directors did not "see their way clear to the extension of their line of railway beyond Port Moody and the provision of the necessary docks and other facilities at a new point unless they can acquire sufficient property so situated as to be made immediately saleable for a sufficient amount to recoup the outlay mentioned." On behalf of the directors, he then stated their claim for special consideration:

> They feel that as the lands west of Port Moody recently relinquished by the Dominion Government were originally intended and set apart to aid in the construction of the Canadian Pacific Railway to English Bay and as the lands would have been so applied had the Dominion Government fixed upon English Bay instead of Port Moody as the western terminus, all of these lands should, in fairness, be granted to the Company in the event of their taking up the work where the Dominion Government has left it and continuing the line to English Bay.
> But our Directors wish to meet your Government in a liberal spirit and to ask for no more than they believe to be necessary to cover their outlay within the near future in making their terminus all it should be in the interest of the country.[12]

Van Horne drove a hard bargain, and the formal agreement with the province was not signed until February 25, 1885. It gave the railway a long segment of waterfront on the inlet, where it built its terminals and docks; some 480 acres on the peninsula; thirty-nine lots in the little townsite of Granville, which had existed on the inlet for nearly twenty years; and a tract of land on False Creek (an extension of English Bay), where yards, shops, and a roundhouse were built. The agreement was subject to the rights of third parties, but owners of property within the grants were required to hand over one third of their holdings to the railway.

These concessions met the Canadian Pacific's terminal needs handsomely, but in addition Van Horne secured a large tract of nearly 5,800 acres south of English Bay and False Creek, a large part of which is now the high-class residential district of Shaughnessy Heights. Nevertheless, lavish as the total grant was, the C.P.R. made no great profits from it in early years; times were difficult and property values low.

It seems certain that it was Van Horne who chose the name Vancouver for the terminal city. Murray Gibbon has pointed out that his favorite reading dealt with explorers and adventurers, and Captain George Vancouver had

Some of the thousands of Chinese workmen brought in by Andrew Onderdonk to work on the line between the Coast and Kamloops Lake. (COURTESY OF THE BRITISH COLUMBIA PROVINCIAL ARCHIVES)

named both Burrard Inlet and English Bay in the course of his visit to the region in 1792. To someone who questioned the choice, he wrote in November 1884: "The fact that there is an insignificant place in Washington Territory named Fort Vancouver should not in my opinion weigh in the matter. The name Vancouver strikes everybody in Ottawa and elsewhere most favourably as approximately locating the point at once" (a reference to nearby, widely known Vancouver Island).[13]

From Port Moody Van Horne headed eastward over Onderdonk's line to Kamloops Lake. Later it became clear that he was not pleased with what he saw, but in his brief report to the directors he avoided the issue: "Wishing to give all the time possible to our own work, I did not examine in detail that of the Government. . . ."[14] The railhead was then about seventy-five miles from Yale. The next 180 miles were covered fairly comfortably by roads, rivers, and lakes that closely paralleled the route of the C.P.R., but from Sicamous to the end of steel beyond the Selkirks was another matter. Some parts could be traveled on horseback; others had to be covered on foot. The going was rugged; heavy rain produced seas of mud; snow, three feet deep in places, dissolved into slush. At one time the party was without food, possibly because the frugal Major Rogers had made the arrangements for the journey. In spite of his phenomenal strength and stamina, Van Horne confessed later to Onderdonk that the trail from Eagle Pass to the East Columbia, nearly a hundred miles, had been "a terrible one."[15]

Through the mountains Van Horne had been accompanied by S. B. Reed, who had been in charge of mountain construction for the Union Pacific. He reported favorably on the new Canadian Pacific line, including the temporary track at the "Big Hill" on the Kicking Horse. As for Van Horne, he submitted a report to the directors that was so enthusiastic that one suspects it was intended to keep their spirits up. But he had clearly been impressed with the resources in timber, coal, and fisheries that he had seen in British Columbia and by the vast extent of agricultural land on the prairies. He was convinced that the Canadian Pacific had "more good agricultural land, more coal and more timber between Winnipeg and the Pacific Coast than all the other Pacific Railways combined, and that every part of the line from Montreal to the Pacific *will pay.*"[16]

It would pay provided it was completed—and there was to be one last and nearly fatal financial crisis before this was assured. As early as January 1884, Van Horne was again emphasizing the urgent necessity for economy. Staffs were to be reduced to an absolute minimum; salaries were to be trimmed wherever possible. Van Horne and other senior staff cut their own salaries by 20 percent. John Ross (never as satisfactory a construction chief as his namesake James) and the Lake Superior line were again worrying Van Horne. "By cutting every corner and cheapening the work in every practicable way," he told Ross late in August, "we may be able to build the line for the money available. . . . If we cannot do that, we must stop the work."[17] Two months later the lake line costs were still causing him acute anxiety: "The money saved on the Mountain Section is being rapidly absorbed on the Lake Superior Section," he warned Ross, "and we are again very near our *danger line.*"[18]

The difficulty arose in part because of the quite unavoidable necessity of making expenditures for essential facilities and equipment that could not be financed from the government loan. The $5 million being expended on such items in 1884 would have to be followed by an equal sum in 1885, and Stephen could see no available source from which the money could come. He and Donald Smith and the few others who had stood by the company were coming to the end of their personal credit, and the whole of the Canadian Pacific was mortgaged to the government.

Macdonald had told Stephen that he could not expect any further help from him. "You must not look for any more legislative assistance for the C.P.R.," he wrote to Stephen in July, "& must 'work out your own salvation' by your own means."[19] But the government was the only possible source of assistance, and by the end of the year it was clear that Stephen must once again appeal to Macdonald. Nearing the end of his tether, Stephen turned to the one possibility he had always avoided because of his determination not to burden the Canadian Pacific with a bonded debt—the issue of first-mortgage bonds. The $35,000,000 of unissued stock held by the government would be of no help, because an attempt to sell it would only further depress the market, on which C.P.R. shares had fallen below 40, but if mortgage bonds could somehow be substituted for the stock, sufficient funds might be raised to see the company out of the woods.

Early in January 1885, Stephen proposed this solution to Macdonald. The result was discouraging, for it was so strongly opposed in cabinet that Macdonald doubted if he could muster sufficient support among his own followers to secure the passage of another C.P.R. relief measure through Parliament. Unfortunately Tupper was back in London and had ceased to be a member of the cabinet. To him Macdonald wrote on January 24: "I myself fear that *The Week* is right when it says that however docile our majority, we dare not ask for another loan."[20] To this the redoubtable Tupper answered in no uncertain terms: "I have been greatly concerned by your letter . . . and for the first time I regret that I left Parliament. I like the position [of high commissioner] here . . . but I look upon the success of the C.P.R. as so vital to the progress and greatness of Canada, that I have no hesitation in placing myself unreservedly in your hands. . . . If you let the C.P.R. down, you will sacrifice both the country and the party, and throw all back again for ten years. I do not believe that either Parliament or the country will consent to this."[21]

Still Macdonald hesitated. The Canadian Pacific had a good friend in J. H. Pope, Tupper's successor as minister of railways, and he did his best to secure some relief for the company through the Bank of Montreal. Before the end of February, the bank agreed to grant a loan of a million dollars, guaranteed by Macdonald, Pope, and Sir Leonard Tilley, the minister of finance. Meanwhile Stephen and Donald Smith had between them raised $650,000 to pay the semiannual 2-percent supplementary dividend that the C.P.R. was paying over and above the 3 percent provided by the guarantee fund on deposit with the government, and they endorsed a million-dollar note to tide the company over for a few weeks. "What Smith and I have done and are doing individually," Stephen wrote to Macdonald, "is simply absurd on any

THE LAST CRISIS AND THE LAST SPIKE

kind of business grounds. . . . But as long as we are able to save and protect the Company against its enemies who seem bent on its destruction, we shall not grudge any risk or loss that may occur. Personal interests have become quite a secondary affair with either of us."[22]

In the middle of March, in an effort to bring matters to a head, Stephen presented a formal proposal to the government. Essentially it was the plan of assistance that was ultimately adopted. The $35 million of unissued shares held by the government were to be canceled, and in their place the Canadian Pacific would issue first-mortgage bonds to an equal par value. The government was asked to make an immediate loan of $5 million to tide the company over until proceeds of the bond sale began to come in, to cancel the blanket mortgage on the railway, and to accept instead deposit of the new bonds.

This plan the cabinet rejected, and Stephen felt that the end of the C.P.R. was very near. Before he left Ottawa for Montreal, where he expected to wind up its affairs, he sent a sad little note to Macdonald that read in part: "I need not repeat how sorry I am that this should be the result of all our efforts to give Canada a railway to the Pacific Ocean. But I am supported by the conviction that I have done all that could be done to obtain it."[23]

Troops leaving Winnipeg on a Canadian Pacific train in April 1885 on their way to assist in the suppression of the Northwest Rebellion. (COURTESY OF THE PUBLIC ARCHIVES OF CANADA)

At this eleventh hour help came from two quite different quarters. The first was political. Senator Frank Smith, a minister without portfolio and a highly influential figure in the Conservative party in the key province of Ontario, intercepted Stephen as he was about to leave Ottawa and then championed his cause with Macdonald and the cabinet. He told the hostile ministers what J. H. Pope had told them a year before—that the government and the party would sink with the C.P.R., and he added that he would do his best to see that any of them who opposed its relief were defeated if they sought reelection. He failed to secure approval of Stephen's plan, but he warded off its outright rejection, and the cabinet agreed to give it further consideration.

Secondly, on March 26, the day Stephen wrote the note to Macdonald, armed insurrection broke out at Duck Lake, thirty-five miles from Prince Albert, in Saskatchewan. Many of the Métis who had taken part in the Red River resistance of 1869–70, led by Louis Riel, had moved to lands along the Saskatchewan River. In 1884, nursing new grievances, they had asked Riel to rejoin them there, and after an uneasy interval, what is known as the Northwest Rebellion followed.

Riel had overlooked the telegraph and the railway and the speed with which they could carry news of the outbreak to the East and bring troops to the West to control it. The minister of militia, anticipating trouble, had already been in touch with the Canadian Pacific, and Van Horne undertook to move troops from Montreal to Fort Qu'Appelle, west of Winnipeg, in eleven days. Actually the first contingent, which was on its way in little more than forty-eight hours, reached Winnipeg in only seven days, but the trip had been a severe ordeal for the troops. The weather was wintry and the line north of Lake Superior was still incomplete. Gaps in it totaled eighty-nine miles. In other sections, even though the track had been laid, only flatcars were available, and these gave little or no protection from wind and weather. Sleighs bridged some of the gaps, but two twenty-mile marches had to be made across the frozen lake. In all more than 3,000 men traveled to the prairies by way of the railway. The breaks in the line were being filled in rapidly, and the train carrying the final contingent arrived at the last of them just as the rails between East and West were about to be joined near the Blackbird River, west of Jackfish. The honor of driving the last spike was therefore accorded to the commanding officer of the troops, Lt. Col. W. R. Oswald, of the Montreal Garrison Artillery.

Publicity was certainly not Van Horne's chief motive when he offered the services of the railway, but he realized fully the value of so dramatic a demonstration of its usefulness at the very time that the company's survival was in doubt.

The driving of the last spike at Craigellachie, in Eagle Pass, on November 7, 1885, probably the most famous of all Canadian historical photographs. Donald Smith is driving the spike; behind him (with the white beard and top hat) stands Sandford Fleming. Van Horne is next on the left.

From Stephen's point of view, the action of the government continued to be maddeningly deliberate. But if he had his troubles, so had Macdonald. Some of his followers were still wavering; others were demanding a price for their support of a relief measure. "The Quebec M.P.'s," Macdonald told Tupper in March, "have the line to Quebec up again. The Maritimes are clamorous for the Short Line, and we have blackmailing all round. How it will end, God knows!"[24] The government was soon under heavy fire regarding the rebellion, and it was the middle of May before news of military success came from the West. Less understandable as a cause of delay was a curious infatuation Macdonald developed for a bill designed to substitute a uniform nationwide franchise qualification for the varying provincial franchises that had been used hitherto in federal elections. Later he would tell Tupper that he considered the passage of the bill the greatest triumph of his life. Meanwhile it occasioned a long debate that dragged on for weeks to the exclusion of other matters.

On the first day of May, Macdonald finally gave notice that he would propose measures to assist the Canadian Pacific. Details had not been settled at that time, and another six weeks passed before the bill was introduced. But the notice meant that Macdonald had once again contrived to bring his followers into line, and in that event passage of the bill was certain. In spite of this, the Opposition had much to say; Edward Blake, the railway's most formidable opponent in Parliament, contributed a speech (characterized by Stephen as "the *meanest* thing of the kind that has ever come to my notice")[25] that lasted more than six hours. But the bill finally passed the House on July 10 and received the Royal Assent on July 20—six months after Stephen had first laid the plight of the company and his plan of assistance before Macdonald.

For Stephen it had been a shattering experience; time after time he had told Macdonald that he did not see how the company could carry on. Shaughnessy helped with his almost incredible ability to buy shrewdly, keep supplies flowing, and cajole impatient creditors into waiting for their money. On several occasions the pay car could not be sent out, and the resourceful Van Horne sought to reduce discontent among the construction crews by making sure that whatever else was lacking, the food was abundant and good. But one serious riot did develop in the approach to Rogers Pass, where the men downed tools and demanded their money, and it required the armed intervention of the North-West Mounted Police to restore order.

The financial crisis ended swiftly once the necessary legislation had been passed. The day the measure became law, the Canadian Pacific shareholders approved the issue of £7,191,500 ($35 million) of 5-percent sterling first-mortgage bonds. Stephen was already in London arranging for their sale, and within a week he was able to report that Baring Brothers, who had long held aloof from the C.P.R., had taken £3 million at 95. Later the balance of the issue was disposed of at 104—proof that the financial future of the Canadian Pacific was regarded as assured once the main line was completed and in operation.

Up to the last the Grand Trunk seems to have expected the C.P.R. to collapse, with a takeover by the government to follow. In that event, Sir Henry Tyler had made it known that he would be ready to "assist." He was in Ottawa in June, and when the introduction of the relief legislation made it evident that the Canadian Pacific would survive, he took a trip to the West over the line to see the property that was now beyond his grasp.

Two months later the C.P.R. was able to extend its eastern network at the expense of the Grand Trunk. It will be recalled that in 1883 the latter had

A group of construction workers holding a "last spike" ceremony of their own. (COURTESY OF THE BRITISH COLUMBIA PROVINCIAL ARCHIVES)

purchased the North Shore line from Montreal to Quebec (the eastern section of the Quebec, Montreal, Ottawa and Occidental Railway). This was obviously done to keep the line out of the hands of the Canadian Pacific, which had bought the western section, from Ottawa to Montreal, in 1882. The Grand Trunk had no real need for it, as it already had a line on the south shore of the St. Lawrence. Politicians in both Quebec City and Ottawa soon rallied to the support of the Canadian Pacific. Railway monopolies are seldom popular, and the people of Quebec were not happy to have both lines to Montreal in the hands of the Grand Trunk. In Ottawa, Sir Charles Tupper, then minister of railways and an ardent C.P.R. expansionist, announced in 1884 that the Canadian Pacific would be extended to Quebec. In the summer of 1885, legislation was passed granting the C.P.R. a subsidy of $1.5 million to build to Quebec unless the Grand Trunk surrendered the North Shore line within two months of the date when the measure became law. Under this threat the Grand Trunk turned the line over to the government on September 19, and the same day it passed into the possession of the Canadian Pacific.

This acquisition included the oldest track in the whole Canadian Pacific system, a little line six and a half miles in length extending from Lanoraie, on the St. Lawrence River, to the town of Joliette. The third railway in Canada, it had been built in 1849–50 by La Compagnie du Chemin à Rails du Saint-Laurent et du village d'Industrie (as Joliette was originally named). The North Shore Line had absorbed it in 1881.[26]

Another pioneer railway, the St. Lawrence and Ottawa, originally the Bytown and Prescott Railway, was acquired in 1884. Its fifty-four-mile line from Prescott to Ottawa, first to reach the capital, had been completed in 1854.

But in 1885 all eyes were upon the West, where the last gaps in the line to the Pacific were being filled in. On July 29 Andrew Onderdonk completed the line to Savona, on Kamloops Lake, covered by his original government contracts, and on September 26 he issued a flyer announcing the completion of the additional work he had undertaken for the C.P.R. It said in part: "As our last rail from the Pacific has been laid in Eagle Pass to-day, and the balance of work undertaken by the Canadian Pacific Railway Company between Savona and point of junction in Eagle Pass will be completed for the season on Wednesday, all employees will be discharged on the evening of September thirtieth."[27] It was a happy coincidence that the "point of junction" happened to be in Eagle Pass, for Walter Moberly, who had discovered it in 1865, had even then declared that the transcontinental railway of the future would run through it. Van Horne had decided beforehand that the spot where the rails would meet, which turned out to be 28.3 miles west of Revelstoke, should be named Craigellachie, after a famous mustering place of the Clan Grant, to which both George Stephen and Donald Smith were related. It had been their rallying cry in their darkest hour, and Van Horne decided that it should commemorate their triumph.

Although the line had been completed in the incredibly short period of fifty-three months, this seems to have been some two months longer than Van Horne expected. In the fall of 1884, perhaps out of bravado, he had told Professor Ramsay that on August 22, 1885, a train would "start from Montreal at twelve o'clock noon to carry the directors and a distinguished party all the way from the Atlantic to the Pacific—a distance of 2,900 miles—all over their own lines."[28] As it turned out, ceremony was reduced to a minimum. Bad weather had delayed the work, and the exact time of completion was difficult to gauge in advance. Bringing any number of special guests to such a remote spot would have been a major undertaking, and expense was a consideration. Perhaps Van Horne recalled the experience of the president of the Northern Pacific, who in 1883 had spent $250,000 to bring "332 of the most influential men in the United States, England and Germany, riding in forty-three private cars in four trains" to a last-spike ceremony in Montana, only to have to resign four months later because the railway was in financial difficulties.[29] "The last spike," Van Horne announced, "will be just as good an iron one as there is between Montreal and Vancouver, and anyone who wants to see it driven will have to pay full fare."[30] It might well have been a silver spike, as Lord Lansdowne, the governor-general, had expected to be asked to officiate and had had one prepared. He had traveled westward over the incomplete railway in August, but had been obliged to return to Ottawa in October, when there was still a gap of twenty-eight miles in the line.

Although ceremony was reduced to a minimum, the moment when the last spike was driven was a dramatic and moving one. The group that assembled at Craigellachie on the morning of November 7, 1885, was a family party. Stephen could not attend, but Donald Smith, Sandford Fleming, and Van Horne had come from Montreal; Major Rogers, John Egan, James Ross, and others who had surveyed the route and superintended construction were there, and behind them crowded some of the men whose labor had built the line. Rogers, we are told, "held the ends of the two ties connecting the roadbed from the east and from the west" while Donald Smith drove the last spike. When called upon for a speech, Van Horne responded with fifteen words that have become famous: "All I can say is that the work has been well done in every way."[31] A silence fell. "It seemed as if the act now performed had worked a spell on all present," Sandford Fleming wrote later. "Each one appeared absorbed in his own reflections."[32] The immensity of the achievement that the last spike symbolized, and its significance, were in all minds in varying degrees. Then cheers broke out, the official party climbed aboard the cars that were to carry them to the Pacific, and after their departure the men had a last-spike ceremony of their own.

10

Equipping the Line

The ready sale of $35 million in first-mortgage bonds enabled Stephen to bring stability to the Canadian Pacific's finances in remarkably short order. At the end of 1885 the company's indebtedness to the government totaled $29,031,612. Under the terms of an agreement signed on March 30, 1886, the government reduced this by $9,880,912, by accepting the return of 6,793,014 acres of the original land grant at a valuation of $1.50 per acre. Stephen undertook to pay off the balance left outstanding—$19,150,700—in two instalments. The first, amounting to $9,987,347, was paid on May 1, and the debt was cleared by a second payment of $9,163,353 on July 1.

Inevitably there were some minor disputes and complications. Among other things, arrangements had to be made regarding the land grant bonds still in the hands of the government, and the company was anxious to receive the $460,000 of the cash subsidy that had been withheld when the temporary line with substandard grades was built in the Kicking Horse Pass. But these were details; the railway was at last its own master, and in November, in a second agreement, the government acknowledged formally that the Canadian Pacific had fulfilled its contract.

At the same time, all the government-built parts of the system were formally transferred to the C.P.R., subject to a settlement of alleged deficiencies in the road built by Onderdonk between Yale and Kamloops Lake. The cost of the lines handed over had been $37,785,320—far more, in Van Horne's opinion, than they should have cost. Indeed, in 1889 he went so far as to tell a United States Senate committee that they were not worth "over $10,000,000, for this reason: The company would have gone an entirely different route, and would have saved a great deal of money on the rest of the line that they built if it had not been for the necessity of making use of these pieces [between Thunder Bay and Winnipeg and Kamloops Lake and Port Moody]. That is especially true of the line in British Columbia."[1] Unfortunately there seems to be no record of the alternative routes he had in mind.

As of December 31, 1886, Stephen placed the total cost of the Canadian Pacific system, including acquired and branch lines and those built by the government, at $164,454,322. At the same date, $10,520,959 had been spent on equipment.

By 1887 gross earnings had begun to rise substantially. That year and again in 1888, net earnings were sufficient to meet fixed charges, which had jumped with the sale of the mortgage bonds and in 1888 amounted to $3.5 million. All through its financial troubles, Stephen had held stubbornly to the policy of paying an extra 2-percent dividend over and above the 3 percent paid from the guarantee fund deposited with the government. The cost was $1.3 million a year, and on at least one occasion the entire half-yearly payment had been provided by Stephen himself and Donald Smith.[2] Relief finally came in 1889, when for the first time net earnings were sufficient to pay both fixed charges and the extra dividend.

Through Lord Lansdowne, the governor-general, Queen Victoria had sent her congratulations upon the completion of the main line, and in January 1886 a baronetcy was conferred on Stephen. Donald Smith was knighted not long after. Both were destined to be raised later to the peerage. But their most enduring monuments may well be the peaks in the Rockies and the Selkirks that bear their names. Mount Stephen stands in splendor, towering over Field, while Mount Sir Donald looks down on Rogers Pass. Macdonald, Tupper, Fleming, and Shaughnessy all have mountains named after them in the same vicinity. Van Horne is commemorated by the Van Horne Range, whose nearer peaks come into view not long after a westbound train leaves Field.

In a burst of enthusiasm and optimism, Stephen had told the Canadian Pacific shareholders in June 1885 that by early in 1886 the main line would "be finished and in perfect condition, thoroughly equipped, possessing every requisite facility for doing its work economically and efficiently, and at least equal to the best of its competitors in all respects; particularly as to curves and gradients, permanent way and rolling stock. . . ."[3] Van Horne would scarcely have made such a statement. As a practical railroad man he knew how much had still to be done to bring the line up to the standards Stephen was claiming for it. For hundreds of miles it consisted of little more than the ties and the two rails that rested upon them, with a row of telegraph poles along one side carrying two wires on a single stubby crosstree. Divisional points had been given the essential minimum of equipment, but most of the system cried out

Snowsheds under construction in 1886 near the summit of the Rockies. (COURTESY OF THE BRITISH COLUMBIA PROVINCIAL ARCHIVES)

for more loading platforms, warehouses, and a hundred other items. There was little or no ballast on the line across the prairies, except where it had been provided on the spot when the track passed through a cut. In more rugged country, notably in the western mountains, in order to save time and money the line had gone around many minor obstructions instead of battling through them. The result in places was a wondrously crooked line with a plethora of curves. It is a characteristic of pioneer railways that having been built, they must forthwith be rebuilt, and much of the main line of the Canadian Pacific was no exception. Solvent, but nevertheless chronically short of money, the C.P.R. had to begin this task immediately after its nominal completion.

In 1886 alone, $6.2 million was spent on additions and improvements. On the line north of Lake Superior cuts needed to be widened, bridges and culverts improved, and ballast added. Between Callander and Thunder Bay, expenditure on such work totaled $1,783,000. Both there and in the mountains wooden trestles had been used very freely; for the most part they were temporary structures that had to be replaced as soon as possible by embankments or by masonry or iron bridges. The trestle problem would be tackled in earnest somewhat later. In the four-year period 1890-93, in a rising crescendo, no fewer than 1,525 timber bridges were eliminated. The 537 replaced in the fourth year had a combined length of slightly over nine miles.

Between Canmore, west of Calgary, and the Pacific Coast, $3.6 million was expended. No attempt had been made to keep the railway open in the winter of 1885-86, but engineers were stationed in the mountains to observe snow conditions and to try to ascertain where the line would have to be protected by snowsheds from slides and avalanches. The winter's experience was scarcely reassuring. Forest fires, most of them due to the carelessness of construction crews, had swept many of the mountainsides, and the trees that would normally have held back much of the snow had been destroyed. Slides were therefore numerous; the worst of the avalanches covered 1,300 feet of track, some of it to a depth of 50 feet. It was found that no sheds were required in the Rockies, where the snowfall was relatively light; the danger was concentrated in Rogers Pass and its approaches, though some sheds were needed in and near Eagle Pass as well.

To counter the slide hazard, thirty-five massive snowsheds were built in 1886, at a cost of $1,477,000. Changes and additions were found to be necessary, as slides occurred in unforeseen places, and a further sum of $691,000 was expended in 1887. Even so, protection could not be absolute; six men were killed in 1887 as they worked to clear the track, and the same season traffic was interrupted for thirty-three days. By 1888 the number of sheds had increased to fifty-three. Of these, forty-three were in the Rogers Pass area, and for more than twenty miles, one mile in four of the line was inside a shed. Later both summer and winter tracks were provided in many places, the latter inside the sheds and the former running along outside them. This had the advantage of allowing summer tourists to have a much better view of the magnificent scenery, but the chief purpose was to reduce fire hazard in the dry season. Sparks and live coals were always a danger, and elaborate fire-fighting arrangements were made as soon as funds permitted.

The reduction in costs that could accrue from reconstruction was demonstrated by the work done on the older part of the Canada Central Railway. Many curves were eliminated, and by 1890 the maximum gradients between Montreal and Chalk River, 246 miles, had been reduced to forty feet to the mile for westbound trains and thirty-five for eastbound. This increased by about 150 tons the weight of a train that could be hauled by a typical locomotive.

But the part of the line that caused Stephen most anxiety was the section from Yale to Kamloops Lake, built for the government by Andrew Onderdonk. Early in 1885, Edward Blake, the ever suspicious and watchful leader of the Opposition, inquired in the House of Commons about the condition of that part of the line. It was extremely important, he said, "that there should be such an efficient oversight of the work" that there would be no difficulty about "the acceptance by the railway company of the work when completed." J. H. Pope, who had succeeded Tupper as minister of railways, replied that his engineers were satisfied with the work, and added that his chief engineer had been over the line personally.[4] The line was, in fact, considerably below the standard expected, but once having taken a stand, Pope felt compelled to hold to the view he had expressed in the House. He and Van Horne were soon at loggerheads, and Stephen, who shared Van Horne's opinion of the road but remembered gratefully the solid support Pope had given the railway in construction days, had the difficult task of working out some solution with Sir John Macdonald.

The Canadian Pacific contended that it was up to the government to bring the line up to standard, and it was thought that the cost might be as much as $12 million. For political reasons the government could not countenance such a payment, which the Liberals would have considered to be simply a further subsidy to the C.P.R., but Macdonald's letters show that he realized some compensation would have to be forthcoming. In an effort to prod the government into action, Van Horne had as little work done on the line as possible and constantly drew attention to its deficiencies. Thus in March 1887, near the end of a winter that had been a very difficult one for rail traffic in the West, he told Macdonald that he had just been informed of "three extensive breaks in the embankments, three bridges gone and four heavy rock slides" on the Onderdonk section; it would be exceedingly dangerous, he added, to delay work on it.[5] Arbitration was decided upon, and at the hearings in 1888 Van Horne gave an unvarnished account of the condition of the road. There is no doubt about his sincerity; in a private letter to Stephen he emphasized the risks the directors were taking in working the section, even with passenger trains running at only between four and fifteen miles per hour in many places. There were "more than a hundred *imminently dangerous* places, where a large amount of work should be done without delay."[6]

Pope died in April 1889, to Stephen's great sorrow, and still the matter was not settled. The government in effect contended that it had the right to build any sort of railway it liked—a claim that reflected so gravely on Macdonald and Tupper, his minister of railways until 1884, that Stephen declined to take it seriously.[7] A decision was reached finally in 1891; the amount of the award to the Canadian Pacific was only $579,225, which the company deemed it best to accept without protest and then forget the matter.

Stephen and Van Horne had something in common with Sir George Simpson, who for a generation and more had managed the fur trade of the Hudson's Bay Company with conspicuous efficiency. When someone questioned whether farming should be any part of the company's activities, he replied: "I consider that every pursuit tending to lighten the Expence of the Trade is a branch thereof." Similarly, the Canadian Pacific from the beginning provided for itself a number of services that most companies left to others or paid for on a rental basis.

The posters that announced the departure of the first transcontinental train from Montreal on June 28, 1886, and that of the regular train leaving on the same day fifty years later.

The first of these was the telegraph, which was regarded as essential for the railway itself, quite apart from its importance as a service to the public. The charter gave full authority to "construct, maintain and work a continuous telegraph line and telephone lines throughout and along the whole line" and to "undertake the transmission of messages for the public." Commercial telegrams were first accepted in the summer of 1882, when they could be transmitted from Winnipeg westward to the end of steel. In 1884, Western Union tried to purchase the telegraph franchise, but Van Horne protested vigorously and the offer was turned down.

It was also upon his insistence that the Canadian Pacific went into the express business. In other hands this service, in Van Horne's view, would skim off the cream and leave the skim milk for the railway. He arranged for the purchase of control of the dormant Dominion Express Company, which had been in nominal existence since 1873, and in 1882 service began over the 291 miles of line between Rat Portage (now Kenora) and Oak Lake. By 1884 it

The arrival of the first Canadian Pacific transcontinental train at Port Moody on July 4, 1886.

had reached Port Arthur, and in conjunction with the Canadian Pacific steamers sailing between Port Arthur and Owen Sound, and the Vickers Express Company beyond that point, provided the first all-Canadian service between eastern and western Canada.

The social importance of the establishment of this express service must not be overlooked. It antedated by many years the introduction of parcel post and provided a quick and safe means of forwarding small packages to distant and otherwise isolated communities. The express service given over the Canadian Pacific lines first made practicable what later became known as mail-order merchandising; it enabled the prairie farmer and his wife to select and obtain items described in the catalogs of such houses as the T. Eaton Company and the Robert Simpson Company.

While serving with the Chicago and Alton Railroad, Van Horne had set a precedent by purchasing and operating dining cars, instead of following the usual practice of using equipment secured from the Pullman Company. If profits were to be made, he wanted the Chicago and Alton to make them. When he came to the Canadian Pacific, he extended the principle to sleeping cars and parlor cars as well as diners—to all the special passenger equipment, in fact, that would be used on the transcontinental and other long-distance trains. To a young railway desperate for traffic, long-distance passengers were highly important, and Van Horne sought to attract them by making its first-class cars elaborate as well as particularly comfortable. The sleepers, a contemporary description states, were "of unusual strength and size," and those on the transcontinental trains were provided with bathrooms. "The exteriors are of polished red mahogany and the interiors are of white mahogany and satinwood elaborately carved; while all useful and decorative pieces of metal work are of old brass of antique design."[8] Van Horne engaged special artists to decorate the interiors and supervised every detail. He stipulated, for example, that the berths should be somewhat longer and wider than was usual—a personal reaction to the difficulty he had experienced in fitting his own considerable bulk into the smaller berths in American pullmans.

The Canadian Pacific hotel system came into existence partly because dining cars were heavy and Van Horne wished to avoid the necessity of hauling them up the steep grades in the western mountains. Meal stops were substituted, and as the three locations chosen all had spectacular settings, the restaurants developed quickly into small hotels. Mount Stephen House at Field, Glacier House near Rogers Pass, and Fraser Canyon House at North Bend were the result. In addition, with an eye to future travel to and from the Orient, it was considered essential that the new terminal city of Vancouver should from the beginning have a first-class hotel, and the original Hotel Vancouver was completed in 1887. Van Horne was interested in scenery as a saleable commodity, and hot springs at Banff, in the heart of the Rockies, were selected as the site for a large summer tourist hotel that was also opened in 1887. Three years later a primitive little chalet claiming to provide nothing more elaborate than good plain meals and a resting place for travelers was built at a second spot that was to become equally famous—Lake Louise. But of these and other hotels, more later.

In April 1886, with winter ending, work began on the considerable task of preparing the track in the mountains for use by regular passenger trains. Service did not begin quite as soon as expected, but on June 28, at 8:00 P.M, the first through passenger train left the old Dalhousie Square Station in Montreal. It arrived at Port Moody sharp on time at noon on July 4. The scheduled running time was 139 hours (5 days 19 hours) and the average speed, including all stops, was 20.86 miles per hour. The train had been christened the Pacific Express, and it became the Atlantic Express on the eastward journey.

Edward Wragge, a Toronto civil engineer, has left an account of a trip to the Coast made in September 1886, which includes interesting remarks about the condition of various parts of the line. The train was delayed by "a slight land slide" near Jackfish, on the north shore of Lake Superior (where the track had "many sharp curves and steep grades"), and by trouble with a trestle near Kenora, but, like the pioneer, it arrived at Port Moody on time.[9] Traffic was light in the first year or two; a traveler who left Vancouver in June

1887 remarked that the train "was *unusually* long, having *two* sleepers instead of one sleeper usually operated." This had been made necessary by the arrival of the pioneer liner *Abyssinia*, with passengers from China and Japan.

A special effort was made to provide for emergencies that might arise owing to the severe winter weather. Rotary plows were still a thing of the future, but heavy wing pilot snowplows were available, and snow trains stood by, ready to take a plow and a work crew to any point where the track had been blocked. Van Horne was much concerned about the safety and comfort of passengers. "In view of the possibility of trains being snowed in where food cannot be had," he wrote late in 1883 to John Egan, his western superintendent, "it is exceedingly important that every train should be sufficiently provisioned. A few barrels, or boxes, of provisions of a character that can be kept without injury should be carried on every train where passengers are taken,

The arrival of the first train from Montreal at Vancouver on May 23, 1887. The elaborate decorations on the locomotive included a portrait of Queen Victoria, whose birthday was on May 24 and who was about to celebrate her Golden Jubilee. (COURTESY OF THE BRITISH COLUMBIA PROVINCIAL ARCHIVES)

either east or west of Winnipeg."[10] When the line through the mountains was opened, "provision magazines" were established at intervals of ten or a dozen miles, and coal and oil supplies for the passenger cars were likewise cached. Emergency fuel supplies for locomotives and material for repairing tracks and bridges were kept loaded on cars, ready to respond to an emergency.[11]

In 1879, when Sandford Fleming was still in charge of the government's Pacific railway project, he sought advice about the motive power that should be acquired. Charles Blackwell, an experienced engineer, was of the opinion that to begin with, passenger and freight traffic could be handled quite satisfactorily by one class of engine—a 4–4–0 American-type locomotive, similar to the standard passenger engines then in use on the Pennsylvania Railroad. He added that if all the engines were alike, it would simplify and cheapen servicing.[12] This was sound advice, as the 4–4–0 locomotive was by far the most popular type of the day, with an excellent reputation for reliability and economy. Quite as important, it had a three-point suspension that put considerable weight on its leading four-wheel bogie truck, and was noted for its remarkable ability to stay on a track, however uneven, and to negotiate sharp curves without derailing.

The C.P.R. soon possessed a large fleet of 4–4–0 type engines, but they were not of the uniform design that Blackwell had had in mind. Some had been purchased from contractors, others had been taken over from the government, while the several railways that were leased or otherwise absorbed each contributed to the motley collection. Some were new and some were old, the most notable of the antiques being one of the locomotives acquired with the North Shore Railway in 1885. This was its engine No. 1, formerly the *Jason C. Pierce*, built in 1837 and owned originally by the Champlain and St. Lawrence, the first railway in Canada.

Most of the new engines the Canadian Pacific purchased closely resembled the Pennsylvania prototype that Blackwell had had in mind. Of the eighty or so bought in 1881–82, all but a few were the 4–4–0 type, with cylinders measuring 17 by 24 inches and 62-inch driving wheels. This came to be considered the standard C.P.R. engine, and the same dimensions were followed when the company began to build locomotives in its own shops. It was typical of Van Horne that within a year of joining the Canadian Pacific he should be ready to plunge into something as venturesome as engine building.

The Grand Trunk had brought to Canada Francis R. F. Brown, an able young engineer who had had experience with railways in Britain, India, and the United States. Early in 1883 Van Horne lured him away, and he became the first mechanical superintendent of the Canadian Pacific. About the same time, the company opened new shops on Delorimier Avenue in Montreal. There in November, Brown completed engine No. 285—the first of over a thousand locomotives that would be built by the Canadian Pacific. Fourteen others followed in the next few months, and Stephen referred to them approvingly in his annual report: "The extensive workshops of the Company at Montreal are now in full operation, and locomotives are being built at a price considerably less than hitherto paid by the Company. Fifteen heavy freight engines have just been turned out at a cost of a little over $7,000 each." One of Brown's later engines, No. 371, brought the first transcontinental passenger train into Port Moody in July 1886, and in May 1887 another of them, No. 374, hauled the first through train into Vancouver, where it is now preserved in a city park.

Then, as throughout its history, the Canadian Pacific preferred general-purpose engines to specialized types, the objective being to have versatile motive power that could meet a variety of needs almost anywhere in the

The first locomotive built by the Canadian Pacific in its own shops. It emerged from the new Delorimier Avenue shops in Montreal in 1883. The C.P.R. built and bought many more of this same type, and the 4–4–0 engine with cylinders 17 × 24 inches was for some time the standard Canadian Pacific locomotive.

system. There were exceptions, of course, the most obvious being the need for extra power on the "Big Hill" at Field and the climb to the summit of the Selkirks. To provide it, four Consolidation-type 2–8–0 engines with 48-inch drivers were ordered from the famous Baldwin Locomotive Works, and Francis Brown built seven more in the company's own Delorimier Avenue shops.

The Canadian Pacific had appeared on the scene very late in the long reign of the 4–4–0 locomotives. Trains were becoming heavier, and larger engines were soon required. Brown's American-type engines would continue in service for many years (one actually served from 1887 to 1960), but he built his last 4–4–0 in 1888. His first replacement was a 2–6–0 type that proved to be too light for the traffic that was developing, and in 1889 production shifted to the 4–6–0 ten-wheeler, destined to be the most numerous of all Canadian Pacific engine types. About a thousand of them were acquired over the next twenty-four years. Like the 4–4–0, they were general-purpose engines that could handle both passenger and freight trains. They had a greater tendency to leave the rails, but this was largely countered by improved roadbeds.

Francis Brown resigned in the fall of 1889, but he left an indelible mark on Canadian Pacific's motive power. He had an eye for appearance, and the engines he built had features that came to be regarded as characteristic of the C.P.R. Omer Lavallée, the authority on C.P.R. locomotives, considers that Brown's first ten-wheeler, No. 456, was "the most handsome 4–6–0" he had ever come across.[13] It was one of two with 75-inch drivers—among the largest in Canada up to that time. Others had 69-inch drivers, and those of engines for freight service measured 57 inches. Brown's last engines had the steel cabs with smoothly rounded corners that came to be typical of the Canadian Pacific.

Van Horne's conception of comfort and elegance: a Canadian Pacific first-class sleeping car of the 1886–90 period.

In 1883, Brown's first year with the company, the C.P.R. had 236 locomotives; by the end of 1889, the number had risen to 413. There had been corresponding increases in other rolling stock. Passenger coaches and baggage cars numbered 154 in 1883 and 362 in 1889. Sleeping, parlor, and dining cars (with which were lumped official cars) increased from 22 to 78. Freight cars of all kinds totaled 6,121 in 1883 and 11,318 in 1889. In 1887 the number of passengers and the tons of freight carried both passed the two-million mark, and by an extraordinary coincidence both rose in 1889 to precisely the same figure—2,638,690.

From the beginning Stephen had envisaged the Canadian Pacific as part of an all-British through route from Europe to the Orient. In his first report, issued in November 1881, he pointed out that the railway would be "in a position to command a full share of the traffic from China and Japan, which is now carried by the Union and Central Pacific. . . ."[14] A map of the railway and its connections issued a year later already included a projected steamer line from British Columbia to Yokohama and Hong Kong.

In October 1885, just before the last spike was driven, the British postmaster general invited tenders for a mail service across the North Pacific, a route not yet served by any British shipping company. The Canadian Pacific responded by offering to provide a fortnightly service, maintained by steamers capable of thirteen or fourteen knots, for an annual subsidy of £100,000. Nothing came of this, partly because of a change of government in Britain and partly owing to effective opposition from the old established P. & O. Line, which naturally wished to retain its subsidy for carrying mails to the Far East by way of Suez.

For a time Stephen thought of encouraging the newly formed Nippon Yusen Kaisha or the Norddeutscher Lloyd to provide a service, but he dropped the idea, probably because he doubted if they would have ships available that would meet the somewhat exacting standards he had in mind. The competition to be faced would come from the services based in San Francisco. Stephen had investigated these with care—ships, schedules, passenger traffic, and freight manifests had all been scrutinized in detail.[15] His conclusion was that to be successful, a service from Vancouver would have to be appreciably faster and offer superior passenger accommodations. On the practical side, he realized that the £100,000 subsidy for which he had asked originally was too high, and that chances of an agreement would be greatly enhanced if Canada would contribute to any subsidy granted. Negotiations with the British government were reopened in 1887, and in December it was agreed that the Canadian Pacific would provide a monthly service to the Orient for an annual subsidy of £60,000, of which Canada would contribute £15,000.

To Stephen's disappointment, a new obstacle delayed the actual signing of the contract. The existing steamer lines from Britain to Canada were too slow to form a satisfactory part of a fast all-British route to the Orient, and the British government was unwilling to subsidize the Pacific service until a faster Atlantic service to complement it was assured. The long and complicated story of the efforts to secure a fast Atlantic service to Canada need not be detailed here; it is sufficient to recall that in July 1889 Anderson, Anderson and Company, managers of the Orient Line, had undertaken to provide a twenty-knot service to Quebec in summer and to Halifax in winter. This being so, the contract with the Canadian Pacific for the trans-Pacific service was signed on July 15. Three days later, it is interesting to note, Stephen offered to assign this contract to the Andersons if they would add a service from Vancouver to Australia to that between Britain and Canada. Instead of accepting this expansion of the scheme, the Andersons decided in October to withdraw altogether.

Worse still, in a cable to Sir John Macdonald in which they notified him that they were surrendering their Atlantic contract, they said they were doing so because they could "no longer reckon on the cordial cooperation of [the] Canadian Pacific Railway, Sir George Stephen having intimated that he has ceased to take [an] interest in the scheme."[16] This was untrue; Stephen and Sir Donald Smith had indicated that each would contribute £50,000 to the capital required to finance the Atlantic line, but their participation was based on the assumption that the Canadian Pacific would be given access to Halifax, its winter terminus, over the Canadian government's Intercolonial Railway. This had not yet been granted, but once it was arranged, they would be quite prepared to assist the Andersons.

One of the first colonist-class cars, designed to give immigrants reasonable comfort and sleeping accommodation at minimum cost.

Meanwhile a temporary service had been established on the Pacific. In 1886 seven chartered sailing ships brought some 7,770,000 pounds of tea to Port Moody, the first being the bark *W. B. Flint*, which arrived on July 27. Three days later a special ten-car tea train left for Montreal, where it arrived on August 6 to make the quickest delivery of goods from Japan on record.

At this point G. E. Dodwell, shipping manager of Adamson, Bell and Company, China merchants, happened to visit Canada. He saw that the Canadian Pacific badly needed a much better service than sailing ships could offer and he happened to know that Sir William Pearce, proprietor of the Fairfield yard on the Clyde, had on hand three small retired Cunarders that he had accepted as part payment for new liners. The result was a traffic agreement

Like all railways, the C.P.R. suffered occasionally in its earlier days from locomotive boiler explosions. This engine was blown completely apart. (COURTESY OF THE BRITISH COLUMBIA PROVINCIAL ARCHIVES)

between Pearce and the Canadian Pacific, with Adamson, Bell and Company acting as agent for both parties. The service was inaugurated by the 3,651-ton *Abyssinia*, which arrived at Vancouver for the first time on August 14, 1887. By that time the railway had been extended from Port Moody to Vancouver, a dock had been built there, and Hotel Vancouver was ready to offer comfortable rooms and good food to travelers.

Stephen referred to the service as being "poor and transient," but it was not unimportant to the railway. In the three-year period 1888–90, the three old liners, supplemented occasionally by other steamers, landed over 100,000 tons measurement of cargo at Vancouver. Most of it was consigned to distant destinations and made a substantial contribution to rail revenues during those depression years. A considerable volume of United States imports from Japan and China was carried by the steamers—sufficient to catch the attention of a Senate committee appointed to investigate competition from Canadian transportation lines. Van Horne gave evidence and contended that the traffic had been taken almost wholly from the Suez Canal route; it had not been secured at the expense of the San Francisco services.

In October 1889, three months after the mail contract was signed, the Canadian Pacific ordered in England the three liners needed to maintain the monthly service. Named *Empress of India, Empress of Japan,* and *Empress of China,* they were the first of the famous *Empress* steamers that were to sail the seas for eighty years. Graceful, clipper-bowed vessels 485 feet long and of 5,940 tons gross, they were the largest and finest ships yet built for the Pacific and also the first to have twin screws—an important safety feature on what was then a very lonely ocean. The contract covered the carriage of mails across Canada as well as across the Pacific. The time in transit from Halifax or Quebec to Hong Kong was not to exceed twenty-eight and a half days in summer and thirty days in winter. The ships on the run were to be capable of a sustained sea speed of sixteen knots. In service it was found that an average of fourteen to fifteen knots was sufficient to maintain the schedule. The *Empresses* quickly gained a reputation for reliability; sixteen years passed before any of them incurred a penalty for the late arrival of the mails at Hong Kong. Even then the fault did not lie with the ship. The mails were four days late in reaching Vancouver, and she could not sail until they were received.

The *Empress of India,* first of the three sisters to be completed, sailed from Liverpool for the Pacific by way of Suez on February 8, 1891. For months the Canadian Pacific had been advertising world tours in connection with the maiden voyages of the *Empresses,* and undertook to carry passengers "around the world in 80 days for $600." More than a hundred first-class passengers were on the *India* when she sailed on what was the nearest approach to a world cruise that had yet been offered.

The *Empress of India,* first of the famous *Empress* liners that sailed the seas for eighty years. She and her two sisters, completed in 1891, were built for service between Vancouver and the Orient. (COURTESY OF THE BRITISH COLUMBIA PROVINCIAL ARCHIVES)

She docked in Vancouver on April 28. Van Horne (by this time president of the Canadian Pacific) and some of the directors were on hand to welcome her. A grand banquet and ball was held in the evening in the Hotel Vancouver, but Van Horne, who disliked such functions, left for Montreal in the afternoon. Ironically, the Hon. Edward Blake, who had been one of the severest critics of the C.P.R. in construction days, happened to be in town and was asked to assume the role of guest of honor.

The *Empress of India* was the first ship to fly the famous red and white checkerboard house flag that was flown by all Canadian Pacific ships for eighty years. In 1913 Van Horne (whose addiction to poker has been mentioned) was asked about its design. He replied: "Yes, I designed the house flag—partly to differ from any in use and partly that it might be easily recognized when hanging loose. It has no historical or heraldic significance. Somebody has suggested that it meant 'three of a kind' but that would not be a big enough hand for the C.P.R. for which a 'straight flush' only would be appropriate."[17]

By 1891 the Canadian Pacific thus spanned both Canada and the Pacific. In 1886, reiterating his ambition to see the railway as part of a continuous Imperial route from Europe to the Orient, Stephen had mentioned to Sir John Macdonald the need "to perfect the Liverpool end of the C.P.R." But its own spanning of the Atlantic was still nearly two decades in the future.

11

Monopoly and Manitoba

One of the misdeeds of which Edward Blake accused the Canadian Pacific in 1883 was the building of 135 miles of branch lines—a strange charge, for upon such lines would depend in considerable measure the spread of settlement and the growth of traffic, without which the railway could not prosper. Prairie settlement was then virtually confined to Manitoba, which was demanding more branches, and the C.P.R., pressed to the limit by construction costs of the main line, was finding it difficult to provide them. Through an oversight, as Stephen pointed out to Sir John Macdonald, there was "no provision under the charter for providing capital to build branch lines. We have no right to put a bond on a branch nor can we issue common stock to cover the cost."[1] This was one reason why the Canadian Pacific was glad to gain control of connecting local railways that had received cash subsidies or land grants to help meet the cost of their construction.

Manitoba and the C.P.R. agreed that more branches were desirable; they locked horns over lines southward to the American border that would connect with roads in the United States. On the face of it, the Pembina branch from Winnipeg to Emerson seemed to meet the need adequately; it was certainly capable of handling all the traffic that offered. But it had got off to a bad start and to Manitobans had highly unpopular associations. Before being handed over to the Canadian Pacific, it had been operated for over a year by the government of Canada, and the freight rates charged had roused bitter resentment. In October 1880, just after the Canadian Pacific contract was signed, C. J. Brydges, formerly general manager of the Grand Trunk and then in charge of the Hudson's Bay Company's land department at Winnipeg, wrote privately to Macdonald on the subject. Rates on grain were his special concern: "The lowest rate that can be obtained, and that as a special favor, is $176 a car [of 400 bushels] from Portage la Prairie (71 miles west of here) through St. Paul and Chicago to Toronto." This was forty-four cents a bushel —a prohibitive rate that Brydges considered "simply destructive of the rapid settlement of our North West." And he summed up the point at issue very well in one sentence: "You cannot settle this country unless you can arrange transportation charges so as to allow the farmer to get a profit on what he grows."[2]

Brydges pointed out that a "great proportion" of the forty-four-cent rate was charged between Portage la Prairie and St. Paul—in other words, by the government line to the border and by the St. Paul, Minneapolis and Manitoba beyond it. To the people of Manitoba the railway seemed to be a reincarnation of the transportation monopoly that had been held previously by the Red River Transportation Company, and they were aware that the three principal figures in that company, James J. Hill, Norman Kittson, and Donald Smith, were major shareholders in the railway and that two of them promised to be influential figures in the Canadian Pacific as well. To counter this monopoly, many Manitobans were determined to secure a second line to the boundary that would provide competition and thereby reduce freight rates.

Other people had other fears. John Norquay, premier of Manitoba, told Macdonald that there were "very grave apprehensions" that the Canadian Pacific syndicate intended to make the railway simply a feeder for their American lines, and that they would build the main line as near to the border as possible in order to connect "with their own system" in the United States.[3] Alexander Morris, the former lieutenant-governor of Manitoba, voiced much the same opinion. A branch line running to the border could "create a most effectual cut off, making the whole trade of the Canada Pacific of the west tributary to the St. Paul and Manitoba."[4]

In his negotiations with Macdonald, George Stephen had, of course, taken a stand directly contrary to that anticipated by Norquay and Morris. He kept his Canadian and American railroad interests quite distinct from one another, and insisted on having power to isolate the Canadian Pacific from all contact with American lines in the West except over its own branches. The result was the notorious Clause 15—the monopoly clause—included in the contract because, as Macdonald had told Norquay, Stephen and his associates would otherwise have refused to sign it.

The clause raised difficult legal problems. Manitoba clearly had authority to charter railways that would be wholly within its borders, but Ottawa questioned its right to allow them to make connections with foreign lines. The federal government had to protect the interests of the country as a whole, and it contended that it would be detrimental to Canada to allow traffic to be diverted from the Canadian Pacific's main line to alternative routes through the United States. If necessary it would have to use its power of disallowance to annul provincial acts that incorporated railways with that end in view.[5] Macdonald hoped that Premier Norquay would be able to discourage such legislation, but feeling against the Canadian Pacific became so strong and political circumstances were such that he was unable to do so. Charter after charter was granted, only to have the laws disallowed by the federal government. Macdonald complained to Norquay about his "reckless Railway Legislation," but the stream of new charters continued and tension over disallowance mounted steadily during the 1880s.

Meanwhile the Canadian Pacific had begun to build branches in Manitoba. It found at once that it had to reckon with the doubtful intentions of an independent company, the Manitoba South Western Colonization Railway, which had been chartered in 1879. Ostensibly its plans were unobjectionable; its announced intention was to build southwest from Winnipeg for thirty miles or so and thence westward to the Souris coal deposits. But in the summer of 1881 the Northern Pacific, ever anxious to find a way into the Canadian West, secured control of the Manitoba South Western in the hope that it might be twisted southward and made to connect with its lines in North Dakota. To counter this, the Canadian Pacific gave first priority to a Pembina Mountain branch, carefully located with both traffic and strategic considerations in mind. The original Pembina branch was on the east side of the Red River; the mountain branch ran south from Winnipeg down the west side to within thirteen miles of the border, then turned and ran westward, roughly paralleling the boundary and forming a guard line between it and the Manitoba South Western. By 1883 this branch had been built as far as Manitou, 101 miles, and a thirteen-mile link had also been added to connect it with a new line the St. Paul, Minneapolis and Manitoba had built to the border west of the Red River.

When it became clear that no swing to the south by the South Western would be permitted, the Northern Pacific turned to the Winnipeg South Eastern Railway, which had visions of building to Duluth, but this prospect faded when its charter was disallowed in 1882, and for the moment the Northern Pacific lost interest in Manitoba.

Some fifty-two miles of the Manitoba South Western had been built, and both because it was a badly needed line and because it might again prove threatening in unfriendly hands, the Canadian Pacific moved to gain possession of it. The cost was over a million dollars—an expenditure the C.P.R. could ill afford at the time—but control was secured by a lease that became effective June 1, 1884.[6]

The South Western brought with it a valuable land grant. It had been given the usual federal subsidy of 6,400 acres per mile available to railways deemed to be "for the general advantage of Canada," and when Van Horne pointed out that the Canadian Pacific had no funds with which to extend it, the government agreed to support further construction with a similar subsidy. The C.P.R. subsequently used the line's charter to extend both the South Western itself and the Pembina Mountain branch, and the land grant eventually reached the handsome total of nearly 1.4 million acres. But at the time the country was in a depression and the company was land poor. Sales from the Manitoba South Western lands averaged less than 18,000 acres a year during the next decade.

Because funds available were very limited, the Canadian Pacific concentrated on branches south of its main line. A Souris branch, running southwest from near Brandon, linked up with both of the South Western lines and produced something approaching a system in southern Manitoba; by 1887 nearly all the settlements there were within reach of railway facilities. North of the main line the Manitoba and North Western Railway, based on Portage la Prairie, had built nearly 80 miles of line by 1883, and this was increased to 130 miles in 1885 and to 207 miles in 1886. Although it would have no corporate connection with the Canadian Pacific until 1900, it brought considerable traffic to the main line.

In spite of this substantial construction, Manitoba was still far from satisfied, and in 1887 and 1888 resentment and agitation against the C.P.R., especially against the monopoly clause, reached a climax. Some of the causes had little to do with the railway. A severe depression had set in, destined to last the better part of a decade. Four successive abnormally dry seasons had resulted in as many poor harvests. In 1883 the duty on agricultural implements, at the best of times a source of complaint to western farmers, had been increased 10 percent. But the chief bone of contention was freight rates, which the Winnipeg Board of Trade claimed had been raised an average of 59 percent by a new tariff introduced in March 1883. The C.P.R. contended that rates had to be raised because costs of operation were high and traffic was relatively light; the Manitobans contended that the railway had been heavily subsidized in order that rates could be low, and that it should be operated at a loss if necessary. The Canadian Pacific pointed out that its freight revenue per ton mile had declined from 1.45 cents in 1884 to 1.20 cents in 1885 and to 1.10 cents in 1886—figures substantially below those earned by the Northern Pacific and the St. Paul, Minneapolis and Manitoba. The critics replied that rates in the East, where the C.P.R. had to meet competition from other lines and from water transportation, were much lower than in the West, where it enjoyed a monopoly position.

Some reductions had been made in the rates on grain, which was already being carried in considerable volume. In 1882 the Canadian Pacific carried 3.9 million bushels; even with poor harvest years, the total had risen to 7.8 million in 1885 and to 10.9 million in 1886. When the through line from Winnipeg to Thunder Bay opened in 1883, the rate on grain from Brandon to the lakehead had been 41 cents per 100 pounds, the equivalent of 24.6 cents per bushel; special eastbound rates introduced in January 1884 reduced this to 33 cents per 100 pounds, or 19.8 cents per bushel. Even so, when it is remembered that a bushel of No. 1 hard wheat sold in Brandon in 1886 for as little as 53 cents, the concern of the growers can be appreciated. A strong, militant Farmers' Protective Union sprang up, and the Canadian Pacific was one of its chief targets. It insisted that the railway's equipment was inadequate, that its rates were exorbitant, and that the monopoly clause was being used to prevent competition that would force the C.P.R. to reduce them.

These charges were given special point in 1887, when a good growing season produced a bumper crop that swamped the railway's grain-handling facilities. The C.P.R. had tripled its number of freight cars from 3,072 in 1885 to 9,296 in 1887, but enough of them could not be mustered in the West to meet the unprecedented demand. And Van Horne's insistence that elevators must be erected at stations, instead of warehouses, which were cheaper but much less efficient, contributed to the railway's difficulties. Time vindicated his policy, but in the short run it tended to limit the number of shipping points.

Van Horne had made his decision in favor of elevators advisedly and in the light of experience, his own and other people's. All the American frontier railways, he explained to George Stephen in 1884, had been "obliged to meet the same question and have met it successfully in the same way that we have started out." He recalled his years with the Minnesota Southern: "Ten years ago I took charge of a railway in Minnesota, the only railway in that country that permitted flat warehouses on its depot grounds, and as a consequence the only railway that had not a single elevator from one end of it to the other . . . and it was not until we were able to drive out or buy out the flat warehouses and give the necessary protection to elevators that we were able to secure anything like the grain traffic naturally tributary to the line, and to remove all cause of complaint on the part of the farmers who had been robbed for years by a horde of small buyers." Warehouses would be "a curse to the country as well as to the railway" if they were permitted.[7]

The elevator network Van Horne envisaged was planned most carefully. The probable volume of grain shipments from each station in grain-growing areas was estimated and an appropriate capacity, usually 10,000, 20,000, or 30,000 bushels, was assigned to it. "As many persons as like may erect elevators at any of our stations," Van Horne explained in a memorandum, "provided that they are suitable structures and are of a capacity required at the particular station." The operator would be "required to handle and store grain for all persons without preference or discrimination at fair and reasonable rates."[8] He did not agree that elevators were expensive. The railway would provide a site practically rent free and would transport construction materials at half rate; the cost of a building with a capacity of 10,000 bushels, complete with cleaning equipment, would be about $3,000.[9] The only warehouses allowed on station property were to be those erected by persons who had contracted to build elevators within a reasonable time.

The first country elevator in the Canadian West was a round structure built at Niverville, twenty-two miles south of Winnipeg, in 1879. The second, erected at Gretna in 1881, was a square building that set the pattern for those that were to follow. In 1882 there were six elevators; by 1888 there were forty-four, and their silhouettes were becoming a familiar feature of the prairie landscape.

The Canadian Pacific owned no country elevators; it felt their provision could be left to the enterprise of others. Its own efforts were concentrated on the highly important task of providing terminal facilities on the Great Lakes and at Montreal. Its first elevator, with a capacity of 300,000 bushels, was built at Port Arthur in the fall of 1883. The C.P.R. had recently taken over the line from Winnipeg to Thunder Bay, and Van Horne was anxious to have the elevator ready as soon as possible. "Don't stand up on any little difference in expense, but *rush the work*," were his uncharacteristic instructions to John Egan, his western superintendent.[10] He wanted to be sure that it would be in operation for the 1884 navigation season, when the Canadian Pacific's own steamers would begin to run between Thunder Bay and Owen Sound.

The following year work was pressed forward on an extensive elevator-building program. A second unit was built at Port Arthur, and storage capacity at the lakehead jumped to 2 million bushels when a much larger elevator was completed at Fort William. A 250,000-bushel elevator was built at the steamer terminus at Owen Sound. Van Horne had been highly critical of grain-handling facilities in Montreal, and to improve them the C.P.R. erected elevators there with a capacity of 1.2 million bushels. By the end of 1885 the company's elevator chain, added to many times in the years to come, thus extended from Thunder Bay to tidewater.

The Canadian Pacific got little credit for this when it failed to handle the 1887 harvest satisfactorily. It moved over 15 million bushels, but in spite of its best efforts grain piled up along the tracks and discontent flourished in Manitoba.

Stephen still insisted upon the protection of the monopoly clause as essential. "Had there been any doubt on this point," he wrote to Macdonald in May 1887, "I never should have undertaken the work, and I am equally sure no one would have risked a cent of capital in the enterprise."[11] Two days later he received a telegram from James J. Hill warning him that the Northern Pacific had agreed to build a line north to the Canadian border if Winnipeg interests would build south to meet it. Those concerned were trying to persuade the government of Manitoba to build the line itself, and Stephen's instant reaction was a long and emphatic telegram of protest to Premier Norquay. He denounced the proposal as "an act of undeserved hostility" and a breach of faith, and stated that if the Canadian Pacific continued "to be treated as a public enemy by the people of Winnipeg," the railway would take steps at once to establish its main shops at Fort William and reduce Winnipeg to the status of an ordinary divisional point.[12]

But agitation had reached such a pitch that Norquay could not draw back. In June the legislature authorized the construction of a line from Winnipeg to the border, to be known as the Red River Valley Railway. It was to be the property of the province and a million dollars was appropriated toward the cost of construction. In addition, and in a further move to assert its independence of the Canadian Pacific, the legislature passed an act that guaranteed interest on $4.5 million for the construction of a railway to a port on Hudson Bay. Macdonald described a Hudson Bay railway as the "most hopeless of all enterprises," but it was attractive to Manitobans because it would provide an outlet far to the north, indisputably beyond the reach of the monopoly clause.

It was a foregone conclusion that the legislation providing for the Red River Valley Railway would be disallowed, but its passing was nevertheless highly detrimental to the C.P.R. Its shares had fallen to a low of 49½ and the company was finding it impossible to borrow the funds without which it could not expand and improve its facilities. The continual attacks upon it, coupled with the depression and the succession of poor crops, had discredited the Canadian West and discouraged immigration, settlement, and investment. In view of this Stephen began to wonder if the monopoly clause was not doing the railway more harm than good. He suggested to Macdonald that when the legislation was disallowed, he should state that the government intended to discuss cancellation of the clause with the Canadian Pacific; but this Macdonald was unwilling to do, and Stephen was compelled for a time to keep his doubts to himself.

In a letter to shareholders in September, he insisted that the Canadian Pacific had not failed Manitoba: "almost simultaneously with the commencement of work on its main line," it had begun work "on a system of branch

The *Athabasca*, one of the first steamers built by the railway for service on the Great Lakes, tied up at the first grain elevator on Thunder Bay. Both ship and elevator were built by the C.P.R. in 1883. (COURTESY OF THE PUBLIC ARCHIVES OF CANADA)

lines extending south and south-west of Winnipeg" and had expended more than $5.7 million of its own funds upon them. All the 433 miles of branch lines operated by the company in the northwest were in Manitoba, and all but 65 miles (the original Pembina branch, built by the government) had been paid for by the company. Moreover, "many miles were made prematurely at the urgent solicitation of the provincial Government and without expectation of immediate profit." The attempt of the Norquay government to divert traffic from the C.P.R. by building a railway to the boundary was "unfair, unjust, and a breach of faith with the company."[13]

Nevertheless Stephen became more and more convinced that the monopoly rights must be given up. Just when he began to think in terms of compensation for the surrender we do not know, but his reasoning is clear. The Canadian Pacific's capital needs were immediate and pressing, and additional funds would be required to equip the railway to meet the competition to which cancellation must certainly give rise. If compensation could be secured in the form of a government guarantee of a substantial issue of Canadian Pacific securities, the whole problem might be turned to good account.

On the morning of October 19, 1887, Stephen discussed this possibility with Sir John Macdonald. Later in the day, in a hurriedly written confidential letter, he set down his plan on paper. Capital expenditures in the current year would require $5 million; he estimated that in 1888 rolling stock, shops, terminals, and the like would require $10 million, or a total of $15 million in all. "The 'monopoly' clause of the contract," he wrote, "must in the interests of the Coy, as well as in the interests of the *peace* of the North West, be cancelled and given up. And I see no way of settling the question and saving the Coy from the wreck to the verge of which this disallowance agitation has brot it, except for the Coy to cancel the monopoly clause of the contract, and in consideration therefor the Govt to guarantee the 4% Land Grant bonds of the Coy to an amount not exceeding $1.50 per acre on the 15,000,000 acres unsold lands of the Coy. This would restore the credit of the Compy. and enable it to perfect the line and put it in a thoroughly efficient state for conducting its business properly and economically, so as to hold its own against the competition of the American transcontinental lines. . . . The Govt will in this way get clear of the monopoly of the C.P.R. without costing the country one cent, and the Company will be placed in a position to protect the traffic of the New West from falling into American channels."[14]

For some reason Macdonald was still reluctant to drop the policy of disallowance, but a provisional agreement to end it enabled Stephen to arrange with Barings in London to market the proposed new land grant bonds. Details were not settled until March 1888. Macdonald insisted that the issue should not exceed $15 million and that the rate of interest should be reduced to $3\frac{1}{2}$ percent. At the end of May Barings offered the whole issue at 95, and the net proceeds to the Canadian Pacific were about 91.

Clause 15 had disappeared, but it left in western Canada an antagonism to the C.P.R. that persisted for many years and a suspicion and dislike of railway monopoly that has been an important factor in Canadian railroad history ever since.

Cancellation was followed quickly by the competition in Manitoba that Stephen anticipated. In January 1888 a change in government had occurred; Norquay was succeeded by Thomas Greenway, who headed a Liberal administration. In determining his railway policy, his chief consultant was his volatile and belligerent attorney general, Joseph Martin, who also became the province's commissioner of railways. They came to the conclusion that it was impracticable for the government itself to build and operate the Red River Valley Railway, and decided to lease it to a private company. To the fury of the Canadian Pacific, their choice was the Northern Pacific, and a subsidiary, the Northern Pacific and Manitoba, was incorporated in the province. Rather than see a third line built between Winnipeg and the border, the C.P.R. offered to lease the new company one of its two lines, but the latter preferred to go its own way and completed its track to the border in the fall of 1888.

Feeder lines were essential if the Northern Pacific and Manitoba was to compete at all effectively for the grain trade; its next project, therefore, was a line from Winnipeg to Portage la Prairie. About fifteen miles from Winnipeg, it had to cross the Manitoba South Western, and this gave rise to the fracas known to history as the Battle of Fort Whyte. The Northern Pacific had failed to complete certain preliminary formalities; the Canadian Pacific, not averse to being difficult, secured an injunction to block the move. Joseph Martin decided he had the right to ignore the injunction, and the Northern Pacific proceeded to install a diamond. Acting upon instructions from Van Horne, William Whyte, the C.P.R.'s western superintendent, had the diamond torn out, brought up a locomotive (promptly dubbed Fort Whyte) to obstruct the crossing, and mustered a defense force from the company's Winnipeg shops. Martin countered by swearing in scores of special constables and calling out the militia. In spite of this considerable display of force no clash occurred, though tension lasted for a fortnight. The C.P.R. had to give way in the end, but Van Horne was happy just to have held up the Northern Pacific, however temporarily, although this was scarcely worth the increased unpopularity suffered by the Canadian Pacific.

The Northern Pacific and Manitoba proved to be a disappointment both to its sponsors and to the province. A 145-mile branch extending from Morris, on the Red River, to Brandon was completed in 1889, but thereafter it languished and began to share the financial troubles of its parent line. The agreement with Manitoba had provided for some control over maximum freight rates, but this failed to work satisfactorily in practice. Reductions were much less than anticipated, and before long the rates differed little from those charged by the Canadian Pacific.

A private railway venture much farther west, in what is now Alberta, should also be mentioned. This was the 109-mile narrow gauge railway from Dunmore, on the Canadian Pacific's main line near Medicine Hat, to Lethbridge, where coal had been noticed in 1879 by Elliot Galt, son of Sir Alexander Galt. With English associates, the family organized the North Western Coal and Navigation Company, which completed the line in September 1885. The Lethbridge mines became an important source of fuel for the C.P.R., which by 1890 was taking their entire production of several hundred tons per day. The Dunmore-Lethbridge line would be leased by the Canadian Pacific in 1893 and purchased in 1897. Converted to standard gauge, it would become the first segment of a second through route to the Pacific Coast, by way of the Crowsnest Pass.[15]

12

Expansion of the Eastern Network

While Stephen and Van Horne were encountering criticism and competition in Manitoba, they were busy with plans for expansion in the East. Within five years of the completion of the main line to the West, they had extended the Canadian Pacific system to the Maritime Provinces, had built a line to Windsor and Detroit, and had gained control of two American railways that gave them access to Duluth and St. Paul.

Priority was given to the improvement and extension of their line from Montreal to Toronto, which would enable them to compete more effectively with the Grand Trunk. In 1887 a new direct line was opened from Montreal to Smiths Falls that speeded traffic and cut costs by making it unnecessary for trains to and from Toronto to follow the longer roundabout route via Ottawa. The same year the line was extended twenty-seven miles westward, from Woodstock to London. Windsor and Detroit were clearly the objectives the Canadian Pacific had in view, and Van Horne said later that before building the London-Windsor link, the C.P.R. had made "earnest efforts" to lease what he termed one of the Grand Trunk's "spare lines." But Sir Henry Tyler would grant running rights only if the Canadian Pacific would in return give similar rights over its new branch from Sudbury to Sault Ste. Marie. This, for reasons that will appear, the C.P.R. declined to do, and it completed its own line to Windsor in 1890. Two large steel train ferries provided the connection with Detroit, where for a quarter of a century traffic to and from Chicago and other points west was exchanged with the Wabash Railway.

Sundry branches were added later, notably one from Sudbury to Toronto that freed the C.P.R. from the necessity of depending upon running rights over a Grand Trunk track, but the through line from Quebec and Montreal to Windsor may be said to have completed the basic grid of the Canadian Pacific in the all-important transportation market of southern Ontario. While it was being assembled the Grand Trunk, in self-defense, had felt compelled to absorb many small railways, whether it really wanted them or not, to prevent them from becoming feeders of the C.P.R. "They say a great deal about the aggressiveness of the Canadian Pacific," Van Horne told his shareholders in 1889, "about its extensions and acquisitions in Ontario, regardless of the fact that since the Canadian Pacific came into existence, the Grand Trunk has absorbed in that province more than two miles of railway for every one made or acquired by the Canadian Pacific, aside from its main line."[1] The result was that in 1890, with the exception of the Vanderbilt-controlled Canada Southern, virtually all the railways in Ontario belonged either to the Grand Trunk or the C.P.R.

At a recent meeting Sir Henry Tyler had once again denounced the expansionist policy of the Canadian Pacific. Van Horne's comment to the shareholders was: "Had you stopped at the completion of your main line across the continent your enterprise would have come to ruin long ago, or at best it would have existed only as a sickly appendage of the Grand Trunk. Like a body without arms it would have been dependent upon charity—upon the charity of a neighbor whose interest would be to starve it."[2]

As the Grand Trunk's wish to secure running rights to Sault Ste. Marie suggests, its ambitions and those of the Canadian Pacific had clashed in a new area. When the C.P.R. charter was being granted, Ontario interests had attached great importance to a direct rail connection between the main line and Toronto. They soon became anxious to add an extension westward to Sault Ste. Marie, toward which American roads were building. A railway already existed as far north as Gravenhurst, 112 miles from Toronto and about halfway to Callander, and in 1881 two railways were chartered that proposed to build from Gravenhurst all the way to Sault Ste. Marie. One built nothing, but the Northern, Northwestern and Sault Ste. Marie had important political connections, secured a cash subsidy, changed its name to the Northern and Pacific Junction Railway, and completed a line to Callander in January 1886. Joseph Hickson, the general manager of the Grand Trunk, had kept a watchful eye on this enterprise, and early in 1888 the Grand Trunk absorbed not only the Northern and Pacific Junction Railway, but the tangle of lines that connected Toronto with Gravenhurst as well.

The Canadian Pacific thus found the Grand Trunk on its doorstep in northern Ontario and in possession of a through line from Callander to Toronto. However, in any race to reach Sault Ste. Marie the C.P.R. had two important advantages. Its branch to the Sault could be much shorter, since it would leave the main line at Sudbury, ninety miles west of Callander, and the line was already built as far as Algoma, leaving only eighty-four miles to be constructed. The Grand Trunk made an effort to prevent its completion, alleging that it infringed the rights of the other two lines chartered to build to Saulte Ste. Marie, but the move was unsuccessful. The dispute went to arbitration, but even in the face of an unfavorable verdict the C.P.R. pressed on, and the Sault branch opened for traffic late in 1888.

Recent events had made it highly important to the Canadian Pacific that the Grand Trunk should be blocked in its effort to reach Sault Ste. Marie. The American lines building toward it were the Minneapolis, St. Paul and Sault Ste. Marie (the Soo Line), based on the twin cities, and the Duluth, South Shore and Atlantic Railway, running from Duluth along the south shore of Lake Superior. Through St. Paul and Duluth they would provide connections with Winnipeg and American ports on the Pacific Coast, and if the Grand Trunk succeeded in establishing a link with them, it could offer most damaging competition to the main Canadian Pacific line north of Lake Superior.

Stephen was acutely aware of this, and to his fears there was now added a further anxiety. Both the American lines were in financial difficulties, and it seemed possible that Vanderbilt might secure control of the Soo Line. Writing in great distress to Sir John Macdonald in January 1888, Stephen pointed out that in Vanderbilt's hands the line would be "a most potential instrument for diverting traffic from the Canadian channels and drawing it forever into U.S. channels. The supreme importance of the 'Soo' line to Canada . . . though felt in a languid sort of way by most Canadians is to me so clear that the bare idea of its being turned against us oppresses me almost beyond endurance."[3] Painfully short of money, the Canadian Pacific itself could do nothing, but in April, with the help of Donald Smith, Stephen warded off the danger by personally gaining control of the Soo Line. "What Smith and I have done," he told Macdonald, "is simply at our own *cost*, and individual *risk*, to secure such control over the Sault route as to prevent it ever being used against the C.P.R. and the Canadian route to the seaboard."[4]

Stephen expected that the Soo Line would soon be taken over by James J. Hill and associated with his St. Paul, Minneapolis and Manitoba (the future Great Northern), but for some reason Hill decided against this. By 1890 both the Soo Line and the Duluth, South Shore and Atlantic were about to default on their bonds, and by that time the Canadian Pacific was able to come to their rescue. When Stephen and Smith had first intervened, the Soo Line had agreed to an exclusive interchange of traffic at Sault Ste. Marie; in 1890 both lines (in the words of the Canadian Pacific's annual report) made C.P.R.

control of their traffic "secure and permanent" in return for a guarantee of the principal and interest of their funded debt. The terms, the report noted with undue optimism, were "so favorable that no loss or expense to your Company is to be feared."

Physical contact between the Canadian and American lines had already been established at Sault Ste. Marie by joint construction of a bridge over the St. Marys River. On June 3, 1889, a through train left Boston bound for St. Paul by way of Montreal and the Sault—the precise route envisaged in the Northern Pacific's international railway dream of forty years before.

The same day, by coincidence, the first Canadian Pacific train to arrive in Saint John, New Brunswick, received a spectacular welcome that celebrated the opening of a new "Short Line" between Montreal and the Maritime Provinces.

Its charter empowered the C.P.R. to acquire and operate "a line or lines . . . to any point at navigable water on the Atlantic seaboard," but for a time no steps were taken to exercise these rights. Indeed, in December 1881, Duncan McIntyre, then vice-president, told Sir John Macdonald that the directors had "quite made up their minds that our terminal point is here in Montreal, and that we will take no part in any movement beyond this city."[5] But this was close to dissembling and true in only the narrowest sense, for just as Stephen, George Laidlaw, and E. B. Osler had brought together a network of lines in Ontario that the Canadian Pacific eventually absorbed, so Stephen and McIntyre were beginning to assemble a network that would extend eastward from Montreal. Atlantic steamship connections loomed large in Stephen's conception of the Canadian Pacific, both as part of a new all-British route from Britain to the Orient and as a source of traffic and revenue for the railway. Ships and trains could meet in Montreal and Quebec in summer, but if direct contact was to continue in winter, the C.P.R. must reach an ice-free port.

Portland, Maine, attracted Stephen, as it had the Grand Trunk a generation earlier, because it was much the nearest port available, and the city of Portland saw in the Canadian Pacific a likely purchaser for the partly built Portland and Ogdensburg Railroad, of which the city was the major shareholder. Stephen went so far as to visit Portland in October 1883 and discuss the matter with civic officials, but no deal resulted. By that time, in fact, he had opted for an alternative route, the first part of which would be provided by the Atlantic and North-West Railway, whose wide-ranging charter Stephen and McIntyre had helped to secure in 1879. It was empowered to build from the Atlantic Coast to Lake Superior, but the point of immediate importance was that it had authority to bridge the St. Lawrence in the vicinity of Montreal. In the spring of 1883, legislation had been passed authorizing the Atlantic and North-West to lease to the C.P.R. "such portion of the line as may be necessary to carry the Canadian Pacific to the Atlantic Coast." Later in the year, by a foreclosure sale, the C.P.R. gained control of the South Eastern Railway, a small system in southern Quebec that included a valuable link with Newport, Vermont, where existing railways provided connections with both Portland and Boston.

Politics, as happened so frequently, now became a determining factor. Stephen's dalliance with Portland had aroused a storm of protest in Nova Scotia and New Brunswick. Politically it was obviously preferable that the winter port should be in Canada, at Saint John or Halifax; the difficulty was one of distance. Both ports were much farther from Montreal than Portland, especially by an all-Canadian line, which had to run north of Maine. The Maritimes pointed out that the distance could be reduced considerably by building a railway directly eastward across the central part of the state—hence the designation "Short Line" which was applied to the route. The idea was not new; a charter for the part of the line that would be in the province of Quebec had been granted as long ago as 1870 to the International Railway Company of Canada. More recently the charter of the Atlantic and North-West had gone even further and had given it power to build or acquire lines across the state of Maine, insofar as the laws of the United States permitted.

Sir Charles Tupper, a Nova Scotian and stalwart champion of the Canadian Pacific, was an ardent supporter of the Short Line project, and it also had the strong backing of John Henry Pope, his successor as minister of railways. In 1884 Parliament approved a cash subsidy to aid the construction of the Short Line, and pressure on the Canadian Pacific to take over the project increased sharply. New inducements were added to the subsidy already offered. In particular, Sir John Macdonald evidently assured Stephen that if the C.P.R. acquired a line to Saint John, it would be granted running rights over the government-owned Intercolonial Railway from Saint John to Halifax. Not only this, but through traffic between Montreal and Nova Scotia and New Brunswick would be routed over the Short Line, and the longer Intercolonial would be operated primarily as a local railway. There was the additional attraction that the government was preparing to offer a substantial subsidy for a much faster Atlantic steamer service that would be based at Halifax in winter, a project in which Stephen was deeply interested, and which he was most anxious to see operated on a year-round basis in conjunction with the Canadian Pacific.

Nevertheless Stephen and Van Horne always contended that it was only with the greatest reluctance that they concluded a Short Line agreement with the government. The deciding factor seems to have been a threat by the

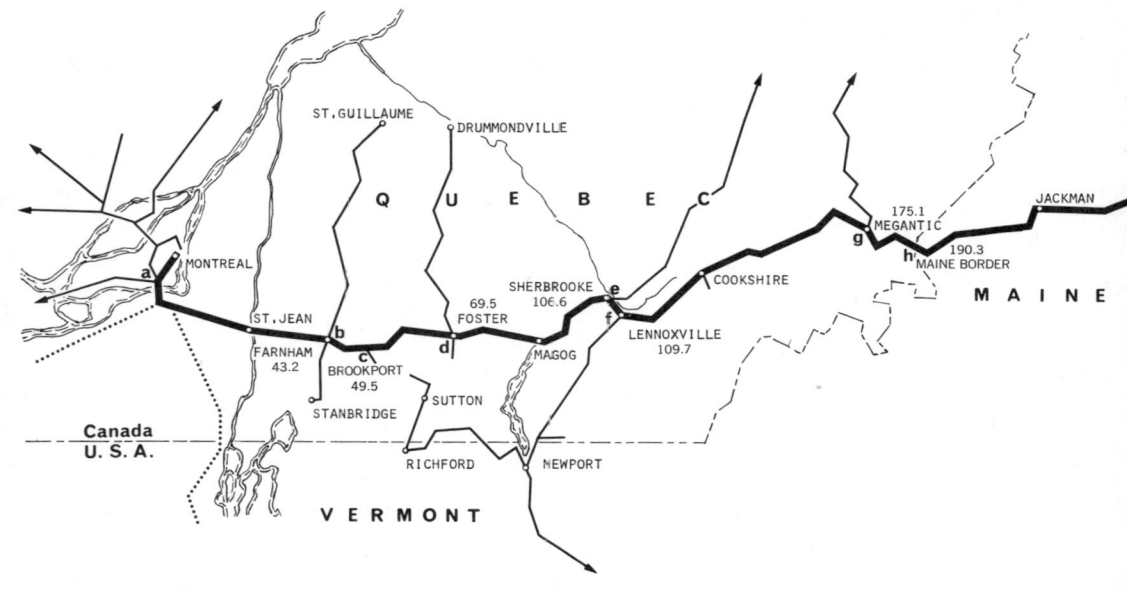

The great array of bits and pieces from which the Canadian Pacific assembled the "Short Line" from Montreal to Saint John. The figures indicate the mileage from Montreal. The line was made up as follows:

a (Montreal) to **b** (Farnham). Built by the Canadian Pacific in 1887 under the charter of the Atlantic and North West Railway, which had been incorporated in 1879 and had come under direct C.P.R. control in 1884.

b to **c** (Brookport). Built in 1871 by the South Eastern Railway, which came under the control of the Canadian Pacific in 1884.

c to **d** (Foster). Same as **a** to **b**.

d to **e** (Sherbrooke). Built by the Waterloo and Magog Railway, 1877–84. Leased in 1887 to the Atlantic and North West Railway (C.P.R.), which relocated the line almost completely.

e to **f** (Lennoxville). Same as **a** to **b**.

---

members of Parliament from the Maritimes to oppose the financial assistance that the C.P.R. needed desperately to complete its main line. Stephen seems also to have been swayed by a personal consideration. He had a high regard for John Henry Pope, both as a friend and because of the unflinching support he had given the Canadian Pacific during the trials and tribulations of the construction years. Pope was president of the International Railway and deeply involved in its affairs. A takeover by the Canadian Pacific would extricate him from his difficulties as well as give the C.P.R. an important segment of the Short Line.

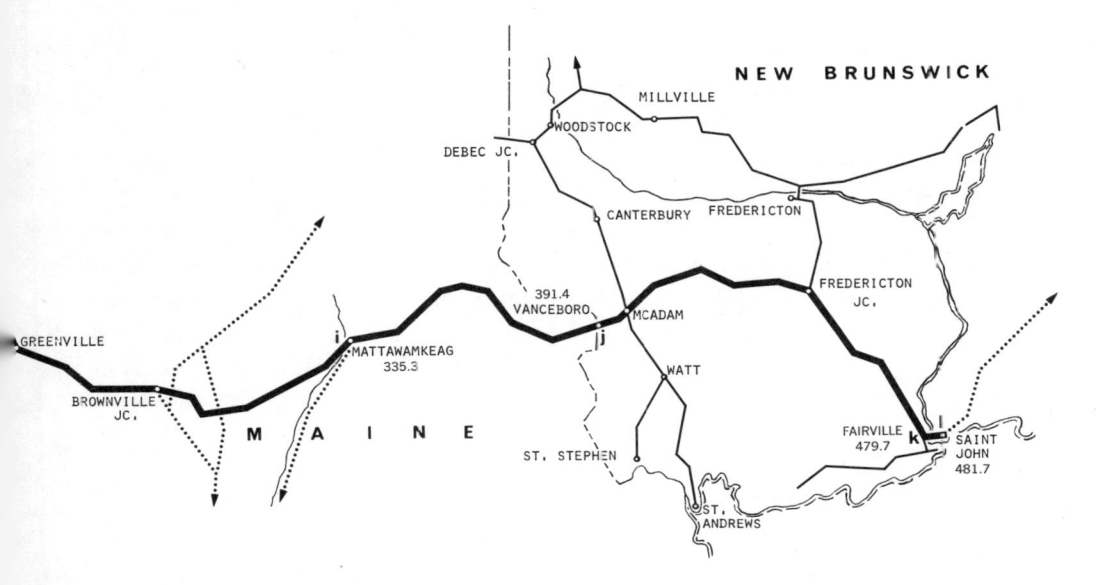

f to g (Megantic). Built by the International Railway Company (Canada), 1875–79. Leased to the Atlantic and North West Railway (C.P.R.) in 1887.

g to h (Maine border). Same as **f to g**, but built in 1884.

h to i (Mattawamkeag). Built by the Canadian Pacific, 1887–89, under the charter of the International Railway of Maine.

i to j (Vanceboro). Built in 1873 by the European and North American Railway. Leased to the Maine Central Railroad, from which the Canadian Pacific secured running rights. Purchased by the C.P.R. in 1974.

j to k (Fairville). Built in 1871 by the Saint John and Maine Railway, which operated for a time as the Canadian section of the European and North American Railway. Leased to the New Brunswick Railway in 1883, which in turn was leased by the Canadian Pacific in 1890.

k to l (Saint John). Built in 1885 by the Saint John Bridge and Railway Extension Company. Leased to the New Brunswick Railway, and with it to the Canadian Pacific in 1890.

A few days after the last spike was driven at Craigellachie, the contract for the Short Line was awarded by the government to the International Railway. A year later the railway was purchased by the Atlantic and North-West (which meant in effect the Canadian Pacific), and the contract was transferred with the ownership.

The various pieces of the Short Line soon began to fall into place. In 1887 the Atlantic and North-West completed its bridge across the St. Lawrence and opened a line to Farnham, where it connected with the South Eastern Railway. In 1888 purchase of the short Waterloo and Magog Railway and rerouting of its lines provided a link between the South Eastern and the International Railway.[6] This carried the track to the Maine border. Beyond it the Atlantic and North-West and the Canadian Pacific together formed the International Railway of Maine to build 145 miles of line across the state to Mattawamkeag. This was completed in 1888. It is interesting to note that fifty-three of those miles were built by William Mackenzie and Donald Mann, the astonishing railway builders who later created the Canadian Northern Railway. Both, it will be recalled, had worked on the Canadian Pacific's main line, but this was their first venture in partnership. Years later Mann recalled that they lost heavily and decided to appeal to the C.P.R. for some redress. They first saw Sir George Stephen: "He said he did not know earth from hardpan, and [told us to] go and see Van Horne, and Van Horne would not talk to us and we went to Shaughnessy, and he . . . struck a compromise and let us out even; we did not lose anything or make anything out of that contract."[7]

For the rest of the way through Maine the Short Line made use of the Maine Central Railway, which granted running rights (replaced by C.P.R. ownership as recently as 1974) over the fifty-six miles of its road to Vanceboro, near the New Brunswick border. There contact was made with New Brunswick lines that extended to Saint John.

It was over this variegated system that the first Short Line through passenger train made its way in June 1889. Canadian Pacific control of the Montreal–Saint John route was completed in 1890, when it leased the New Brunswick Railways (in which Stephen had long had a personal interest) for 999 years. They included a 155-mile line running north through the province to Edmundston, a link with Fredericton, and half a dozen local branches.

Even before its completion, the Short Line was causing Stephen and Van Horne acute distress. Van Horne told Macdonald in December 1888, that it had "proved a terrible load for us." The following August he outlined a financial tale of woe in a memorandum prepared for Stephen: "We are losing more than $400 a day in working the 'Short Line' and adding interest our daily loss is more than $1,000 including Sundays; and this in addition to $500 per day of interest paid by the Government."[8] The latter reference was to the twenty-year annual subsidy of $186,000 that had been granted by the government and was intended to meet interest charges on construction costs.

In his frequently outspoken letters to Macdonald, Stephen lamented the decision to build the line, especially after the first of a long and unsuccessful sequence of negotiations to secure the fast Atlantic service to Halifax had fallen through. "It is a criminal waste of money building that line unless Halifax became the winter Port of a Fast Atlantic line," he wrote in November 1888; "there is nothing for a railway to do in the absence of that."[9] Quite as serious, Macdonald was either unwilling or unable to give the Canadian Pacific access to the Intercolonial Railway on the terms Stephen had been led to expect. The Intercolonial's loyal employees and many friends fought successfully against the proposal to reduce it to the status of a local line, and even though Canadian Pacific trains did secure running rights to Halifax, the C.P.R. charged that they were so discriminated against by the Intercolonial in time schedules and at ticket offices that the rights were of little value. "If you have resolved on keeping the C.P.R. out of Halifax," Stephen wrote angrily to Macdonald in September 1889, "I hope you will lose no time in saying so, and let Van Horne take such steps as may be open to him to avoid the daily loss which is now incurred by his fruitless efforts to do business in Halifax. . . . How deeply I repent the confidence and credulity through which I was cajoled by Tupper and Pope to undertake the building of the Short Line."[10] In September 1890 an agreement was at last worked out, but it still fell far short of expectations.

By 1890 the Canadian Pacific's entire eastern network was approaching completion. Extending from Saint John, Quebec, Montreal, and Ottawa to Toronto, Windsor, and Detroit, and from Sault Ste. Marie over affiliated lines to Duluth and St. Paul, it exceeded considerably in span the system of its great rival, the Grand Trunk. To have built the main line to the Pacific and acquired this network in only nine years was indeed a remarkable accomplishment.

Seven years of almost constant struggle and anxiety had taken such a toll of Sir George Stephen's health and spirits that he had resigned the presidency of the Canadian Pacific in 1888. Van Horne, vice-president since 1884, succeeded him on August 7. His withdrawal, Stephen assured Sir John Macdonald, did not "in any sense mean *desertion*"; he was simply relieving himself "of what had become to me an irksome and unendurable responsibility because of my want of *practical* railway experience. . . ."[11]

He can scarcely have been unaware of the magnitude of his achievement. It is customary to say that no man is indispensable, but it is difficult to see how the Canadian Pacific could have survived through the construction period without Stephen. He was the key figure who assembled the original syndicate, and the steadying influence through all its financial vicissitudes. Time after time, usually with the help of his cousin Donald Smith, he provided funds from personal resources to assist the C.P.R. at critical moments. A recent instance had been the purchase of control of the Soo Line; after his resignation he advanced money to the hard-pressed company to enable it to build a sixteen-mile addition to the Souris branch in Manitoba.

Stephen's close personal relationship with Macdonald had been of immense importance. Often they were in touch daily; hundreds of private letters passed between them, and they had few secrets from one another. Macdonald's trust in and respect for Stephen and the latter's courage and persuasive powers had more than once determined his decisions to push through relief measures for the railway, even when some of his cabinet and many of his followers were wavering in their support.

Stephen wished to withdraw completely, but Van Horne was able to persuade him to continue to serve as a director and a member of the executive committee. He still wrote to Macdonald much as before, but his letters show an increasing exasperation with the attitude of Macdonald and the government toward the company and its problems. The arbitration over the shortcomings of the Onderdonk contract was dragging on; there was no sign that through traffic would be diverted from the Intercolonial Railway to the Canadian Pacific's Short Line, as had been promised; negotiations for a fast Atlantic steamer line to connect with the Short Line had come to nothing; difficulties and delays had arisen in the selection of the lands the C.P.R. was to receive as part of its land grant subsidy. A letter dated June 4, 1889, is revealing:

Tomorrow I begin my 61st year and looking back ten years, I am far from being the free man I then was (It was on 23 May 1879 that the St. Paul, Minneapolis and Manitoba was born). When I think of the misery I have suffered in these ten years, I cannot help thinking what a fool I was not to have taken advantage of the opportunity I then had to end my work and enjoy the leisure which I had earned by 40 years of hard work.[12]

Two months later he allowed his feelings to explode in another private letter to Macdonald:

It is simply heartbreaking to me to see the indifference with which the govt. seem to regard everything affecting the interests of the C.P.R. Co. and in justice to myself I have made up my mind to sever my connection with the Company and so relieve myself from all responsibility in connection with it. I feel keenly the humiliation of being forced to terminate my connection with the C.P.R. Co. because of the attitude of the Govt towards the Company on every matter that comes up for settlement but my present position has become unendurable.[13]

As has been pointed out, Stephen had no patience with politics and little appreciation of the conflicting interests and difficulties that Macdonald encountered at every turn. In a good-tempered reply, Macdonald pointed out by implication that he was not indifferent to the C.P.R., for the life of the government was closely related to the success of the railway; he and Stephen were in much the same boat: "I am glad to believe that there is such a community of interest between the Govt. and the C.P.R. that nothing can separate them. My own position as a public man is as intimately connected with the prosperity of the C.P.R. as yours is as a Railway Man."[14]

Once again Van Horne was able to persuade Stephen to postpone his complete retirement, though he made his home in England in the fall of 1890, and finally left the board in May 1893. In the interval he had been raised to the peerage as Baron Mount Stephen. Feeling far from well, he seems to have feared in 1889 that his days were probably numbered, but he was destined to live for thirty more years, to the venerable age of ninety-two. In this pleasant autumn of his life he became an intimate friend of royalty and made his home in Hertfordshire, at Brocket Hall, the historic old mansion that had been the residence of two famous British prime ministers, Lord Melbourne and Lord Palmerston.

13

The Van Horne Years

When Van Horne joined the Canadian Pacific, he signed a five-year contract that would expire at the end of 1886. The first of several offers submitted in the hope that he could be lured back to the United States reached him shortly after the driving of the last spike at Craigellachie. They were tempting, but he had decided to throw in his lot permanently with the C.P.R. Perhaps his decision was influenced by his knowledge that Stephen did not intend to retain the presidency indefinitely and that he would be the obvious person to succeed him.

Stephen was right in thinking that sound practical management had become the Canadian Pacific's prime need. Although it would have financial problems owing to the prevailing depression, it would never be in serious danger of bankruptcy, and it was certain to prosper as soon as economic conditions improved. In the meantime it required sound and prudent management, and this it received from Van Horne and from Thomas Shaughnessy, who in 1889 was promoted from assistant general manager to assistant to the president.

Except for the last two years, the whole of Van Horne's term as president was a period of prolonged depression which, after a brief and partial recovery in 1892, plunged to its worst depth in 1894. In spite of this he contrived to make innumerable improvements in the system and to expand it appreciably. In 1888 it totaled 5,186 miles; by the end of 1899 mileage had increased to 7,000, and if the controlled American lines are included, the increase exceeded 3,500 miles, or 65 percent.

Some of this expansion was due to the rivalry that developed quickly between Van Horne and James J. Hill, which will be described in the next chapter. By the time Hill withdrew from the Canadian Pacific, it was known that he had a line of his own to the Pacific Coast in mind, and the Great Northern Railway, to which the properties of the St. Paul, Minneapolis and Manitoba had been transferred, was completed to Seattle in 1893. It was not by coincidence that the same year the Canadian Pacific built a link between the Soo Line and Pasqua, on its main line near Moose Jaw, and leased the narrow-gauge railway that the Galt interests had been operating between the main line and Lethbridge. The latter was to become part of a Crowsnest Pass southern route to the Pacific, nearly half of which was in operation before Van Horne left office. It was also in 1893 that Van Horne secured control of the Duluth and Winnipeg Railway, which to his sorrow he would be compelled to relinquish to Hill in 1897.

In its first years, for defensive reasons, the Canadian Pacific had limited its activities in the West to the area south of its main line, but it was obvious that Regina and Calgary were points from which railways were certain to push northward. In 1883 the Qu'Appelle, Long Lake and Saskatchewan Railroad and Steamboat Company had been chartered to build from Regina to the North Saskatchewan River, but by 1886 it had completed only twenty-five miles of track. There it tarried until 1889, when it was leased to the C.P.R. The next year the Canadian Pacific also leased the recently chartered Calgary and Edmonton Railway. The terms of both leases were unusual—no rental for six years with an option to purchase at the end of the period.

James Ross, who had been a tower of strength to Van Horne in mountain construction days, undertook to build both lines, and with him were associated three men who had worked with him on earlier contracts—Herbert Holt and the partnership of William Mackenzie and Donald Mann. Steel reached Prince Albert, 255 miles from Regina, in 1890, and the line from Calgary to Strathcona, across the river from Edmonton, 192 miles, was completed in August 1891. The following year the Calgary and Edmonton Railway was extended south 103 miles to Fort Macleod. In addition to local traffic, Van Horne hoped that these lines would stimulate settlement and land sales. "Both of these railways," he told his shareholders in May 1890, "are of especial importance to your Company, from the fact that they will make easily accessible large areas of your lands now too far away from railways to be available."[1]

In the East, a branch running north from Mattawa, in the upper Ottawa valley, gave access to what was then considered the most important timber country in eastern Canada, and a new line from Vaudreuil to Ottawa provided a much better and shorter route from Montreal to the capital. Farther east an

William C. Van Horne (later Sir William) about the time he completed building the transcontinental main line. He was later president of the Canadian Pacific from 1888 to 1899 and chairman from 1899 to 1910. (COURTESY OF THE PUBLIC ARCHIVES OF CANADA)

interesting possibility arose in 1892, when for a time there was some likelihood that the Canadian Pacific would gain control of the government-owned Intercolonial Railway connecting Quebec, Saint John, and Halifax. The Intercolonial was producing deficits and the C.P.R. was still anxious to secure free access to Halifax. Sir John Macdonald had died in 1891 and had been succeeded as prime minister by the Hon. J. J. C. Abbott, first general counsel of the C.P.R. and later one of its directors. Abbott was not averse to some arrangement by which the Canadian Pacific could use the Intercolonial, and various proposals were discussed. These varied from complete absorption by the C.P.R. to a plan for cooperation with the Grand Trunk. The latter would take over the line from Quebec to Moncton, the Canadian Pacific would absorb the Saint John–Moncton line, and the two railways would operate the Moncton–Halifax line jointly. A considerable body of opinion seemed to favor some such move, but at the critical moment ill health forced Abbott to resign. His successor, Sir John Thompson, a Nova Scotian, was strongly opposed to any such scheme, and negotiations were abandoned forthwith.[2]

Innumerable small improvements were made in roadbeds and equipment. Most of the timber bridges and trestles that had been built in the interests of speedy construction and low first cost were coming to the end of their lives, and reference has already been made to the comprehensive effort to replace them with embankments or with masonry or steel bridges. Some, such as the spectacular trestles in the famous Loop near Rogers Pass, had to be retained, but in the six-year period 1890–95 no fewer than 2,178 were eliminated. It soon became apparent that substantial economies could be secured by using larger locomotives that could haul longer and heavier trains—the same train crew could handle twenty-five cars as readily as twelve. But stronger bridges and improvements in tracks were essential before heavier engines could be operated safely. As funds permitted, gradients and curvatures were reduced, and over a period of a decade the fifty-six-pound rails laid originally on most of the main line were replaced by seventy-two-pound steel. In 1897 the eighty-pound rail became the standard renewal on all the principal lines.

It was in Van Horne's time that the faithful 4–4–0 American-type locomotives were superseded by heavier 4–6–0 ten-wheelers, which the Canadian Pacific ordered in quantity. Although they were excellent general-purpose engines, within a few years more powerful locomotives were needed for freight service. In the last years of the century, when the depression had lifted and track conditions permitted, the C.P.R. chose the very successful 2–8–0 Consolidation-type for its standard freight engine. A few had been in use since early days on the "Big Hill" at Field, but over 200 were acquired between 1895 and 1900. Engine weights had increased sharply. The first 4–4–0 built in the Canadian Pacific's own shops in 1883 had weighed forty-five tons; the largest Consolidation in service in 1900 tipped the scales at over ninety-eight tons.

The C.P.R.'s approach to motive power has always been conservative, with reliability the prime requirement. But economy is also important, and when compound locomotives appeared, which saved fuel by using steam twice over, it was willing to give the new system a trial. Fourteen compound ten-wheelers were purchased in 1891, and over half the Consolidations acquired at the end of the decade were compounds. The most interesting engine of the kind was one of three 4–4–2 Atlantics—the only engines of the type ever owned by the Canadian Pacific—that were built in the Montreal shops in 1899. Famous in their day, they had immense, eighty-four-inch drivers and were designed specially for a high-speed passenger service between Montreal and Ottawa, a route on which the C.P.R. was being challenged by the Atlantics of the Canada Atlantic Railway.

New and better equipment was as important as more powerful locomotives. In 1888 the Canadian Pacific had 11,020 freight and cattle cars. The number rose to 14,077 in 1891, but increased very little thereafter until 1898, when the total jumped to 16,942 and rose steeply again to 19,005 in 1899.

Carrying capacity increased in still greater proportion, because the new cars were larger than the old. All through the depression passenger equipment consisted of about 575 coaches and, in the later years, just under 100 sleeping and dining cars.

It was during Van Horne's regime that two highly important safety devices became mandatory—air brakes and automatic couplers, to replace the dangerous link and pin that had cost many a brakeman life or limb. The Canadian Pacific had long been interested in air brakes; as early as 1886 it had conducted a series of test runs that proved conclusively the superiority of the new system over the old. By law all cars in interstate service in the United States were required to have automatic couplers and air brakes by the end of 1897, and as many Canadian cars found their way across the boundary, the law virtually applied to Canada as well.

On June 18, 1899, a new and faster transcontinental train went into service between Montreal and Vancouver. Christened the *Imperial Limited* (a name reflecting the conception of the Canadian Pacific as an all-British Imperial route to the Orient) it reduced the running time across the continent from 136 hours to 100½ and raised the average speed from 20.86 to 28.8 miles per hour. Two years previously three observation cars, the first acquired by the Canadian Pacific, had gone into service through the mountains as part of an effort to increase the attractiveness of the trip for tourists.

Van Horne was a man with immensely wide and varied interests; someone who knew him well once remarked that he seemed to know everything about everything. Among other things he was an enthusiastic amateur architect and from the beginning he took a particular interest in the designs of the railway's innumerable buildings. Often the smallest details would catch his attention. A letter written in 1883, when the station at Port Arthur was being designed, is typical. Along with a sketch went this directive: "The upper story is intended to be battened vertically, using horizontal siding on the lower story, except the dado, which will be vertical matched strips."[3]

The Canadian Pacific's hotel chain owes its transcontinental scope to Van Horne, and the last two hotels for which he was responsible influenced architecture in Canada profoundly for half a century. Both were designed by Bruce Price, an American architect (and, incidentally, the father of Emily Post) who had been engaged by the C.P.R. in 1886 to design the Windsor Street Station in Montreal—many times enlarged and altered in later years, but still the headquarters of the railway. Price's original proposal for the station proved to be too elaborate, but after some delay Van Horne pushed ahead with a simplified design in 1888 and the massive stone building was completed early in 1889.[4]

An early view of the Banff Springs Hotel. As first built it consisted only of the structure to the left.

The Banff Springs Hotel, one of the continent's great mountain resorts, as it appears today. Originally open for only a few months in summer, it now operates all year to cater to conventions and winter sports enthusiasts.

The origin of the hotel system has been noted—three modest structures in the western mountains at Field, Glacier, and North Bend, intended initially to provide meal stops for the trains and make it unnecessary to haul heavy dining cars up the steep grades. The agreement concerning the land grants in the new city of Vancouver included an undertaking to build both the first Hotel Vancouver and, it is interesting to note, an opera house. The hotel was built quickly and opened in May 1887, but the opera house was not ready until February 1891. Many of the most celebrated singers, actors, and actresses of the time appeared on its stage during the next twenty years.

The sale of lots in the Vancouver townsite paid for the hotel and other terminal facilities and provided a surplus that enabled Van Horne to undertake another hotel venture. Hot springs had been discovered in a spectacular setting in the Rockies at a spot that Donald Smith named Banff, after the Scottish county in which Sir George Stephen was born, and there Van Horne built the first Banff Springs Hotel, completed in 1888.

For its design he turned to Bruce Price. A five-storey frame structure, it provided very comfortable accommodation for 280 guests. Its dormers, corner turrets, and oriels show that the intention was to suggest a château or castle, perhaps with Banffshire and the Scottish Highlands in mind. The general effect was picturesque, though it now seems somewhat nondescript. The building survived one major blunder during construction. By mistake the contractor faced the building the wrong way, giving the best view to the kitchens. Van Horne, furious but practical, sketched out a rotunda pavilion, ordered it added to the building, and thereby rescued the view for the guests.

Whatever its merits or defects, the Banff hotel initiated the château style that was to characterize a succession of hotels built by the Canadian Pacific and other railways, as well as railroad stations, apartment blocks, and several large government buildings in Ottawa. How much Van Horne had to do with the Banff design we do not know, but he was certainly influential when Bruce Price was planning the building that was to bring the style resoundingly to public attention—the Château Frontenac in Quebec City.

Various projects for a luxury hotel in Quebec had been afoot since 1880. One progressed to the stage of inviting tenders in 1891 before it collapsed. The next year the Château Frontenac Company was formed by eight associates, seven of whom, including Van Horne, Donald Smith, R. B. Angus, and T. G. Shaughnessy, were directors of the Canadian Pacific. Van Horne was its president. At first the company was not a C.P.R. subsidiary—the capital was subscribed privately—but the hotel was built as part of an arrangement with the government of Quebec, which canceled a contingent liability relating to the provincially owned North Shore Railway, which the Canadian Pacific had taken over in 1885.

The magnificent site, acquired by lease, had been occupied originally by the Château St. Louis, the residence of intendants and governors in the days of New France. Price's design, which Van Horne watched over at every stage, was clearly derived from the French Renaissance châteaux in the Loire valley. Horseshoe-shaped, the original building had as its central feature an imposing round tower overlooking Dufferin Terrace and the St. Lawrence River. (Van Horne is said to have taken Price out on the river in a small boat one day to make sure that the elevation was "sufficiently majestic.")[5] Opened in December 1893, the Château soon became what Van Horne hoped it would be, the most talked-about hotel on the continent. Price had made particularly lavish provision for public rooms, and it became apparent that additional bedrooms were needed; a new wing was built in 1897-98. By that time the Canadian Pacific had acquired all the capital stock of the original company, which totaled $280,000.

Windsor Street Station served lines entering Montreal from the west, but the C.P.R. wished to build a new eastern terminal as well, to replace the old Dalhousie Square station. Windsor Street was a combined station and office building; at Place Viger the railway built a combined station and hotel. Although adapted for a quite different setting, Price's design for the Place Viger building was once again in the château style and quite clearly derived from the Château Frontenac, with a lesser tower, turrets, and dormers in the Loire style. Though it still exists, the building is now forgotten. The hotel flourished for a time, but the social center of Montreal moved westward and it gradually declined to such a degree that it was closed in 1933.

Place Viger was completed in 1898. The same year a combined station and office building was erected in Vancouver, where the railway had hitherto been accommodated in rather makeshift quarters. Once again the château motif was adopted; though the work of a different architect, its towers, pointed dormers, and high pitched roofs obviously echoed the Château Frontenac.

So far as operations were concerned, Van Horne, with increasing help from Shaughnessy, was in complete control of the railway, but since he had had relatively little experience in finance, he continued to rely heavily on Stephen and, for day-to-day advice, on R. B. Angus. Stephen continued to oppose bond issues, and instead the Canadian Pacific secured authority from Parliament in 1889 to issue perpetual 4-percent consolidated debenture stock. This found a ready market (the initial offering was subscribed five times over) and the proceeds were used both for new capital expenditures, such as the construction of the three Pacific liners, and the reduction of fixed charges by buying up outstanding securities upon which a higher rate of interest was being paid. The amount issued increased quickly from $12 million in 1890 to almost $40 million in 1893 and had risen to over $54 million by 1899. Debenture stock continued to be an important source of capital for many years. The total outstanding exceeded $100 million in 1906, passed the $200 million mark in 1918, and reached its maximum of $295 million in 1937. In 1893, in a further move to raise capital, 4-percent noncumulative preference shares were offered for the first time. Sales were moderate during the depression years but nearly $27 million had been sold by 1899.

In spite of hard times the Canadian Pacific gradually improved its financial position. Gross revenues rose steadily from $13,195,000 in 1888 to $21,409,000 in 1892, and net earnings increased from $3,870,000 to $8,420,000. In 1889 the railway earned its first substantial surplus after the payment of fixed charges—$2,226,000. Encouraged by this the directors (in the words of the annual report) "felt warranted in increasing the dividends on the shares of the Company to five per cent per annum, 3 per cent being payable

Trestle replacement in progress: masonry piers rising to support the new bridge that replaced one of the timber structures in the famous "Loop" near Glacier, west of Rogers Pass. (COURTESY OF THE BRITISH COLUMBIA PROVINCIAL ARCHIVES)

from the Guaranty fund deposited with the Dominion Government and 2 per cent from surplus earnings." They also expressed confidence that "a very small increase in earnings" would make it possible to maintain the 5-percent rate after the guarantee fund was exhausted in 1893.

The first supplementary dividend payments were made in February and August of 1890. No doubt the shareholders were pleased, but to Sir George Stephen, disillusioned with the government and much else, the payments served only to remind him of how far the Canadian Pacific still fell short of his hopes and expectations for it. In October, the tenth anniversary of the signing of the C.P.R. contract, he was prompted to write to Sir John Macdonald, commenting on the history of the enterprise. He first recalled the hostility of the Grand Trunk and noted with obvious satisfaction the change in its fortunes since 1883, when Sir Henry Tyler and Joseph Hickson had launched their most determined attack on the Canadian Pacific: "At that time, G.T.R. 1st Preference shares were selling here [in London] at 109, last week they were selling at 61. The common shares were 27 they are now about 9½. C.P.R. shares were selling in a small way in New York and Amsterdam about 60/62. They are now about 80." But Stephen insisted that this was nothing to boast about: "Success—commercially—is still in the future, but with reasonably fair treatment at the hands of the Govt. and people of Canada it is certain to come, to the extent at least, indicated in the last annual report. . . . But there is nothing in that that can be called a great success. So far, as you know, the net earnings of the railway have yielded the shareholders just two dividends of 1% each, that is, 2% in ten years out of *net earnings*. The 3% dividend is nothing but a return of the shareholders' own capital, though the scheme of providing a guaranteed dividend really saved the Company. . . . It was a wonderful thing that the future was hidden from us. . . . [The C.P.R.] has avoided a collapse or a failure and that is about all, speaking of course in a financial sense. Yet Canada is full of people who ought to know better, who believe it to have been a great 'bonanza' to all connected with it."[6]

One of Stephen's major disappointments had been the failure of any number of Canadian investors to support the Canadian Pacific in its early days. "There is nothing I am so anxious about, as to the C.P.R.," he had written to Macdonald in 1887, "as its Canadianisation paid in the coinage. I am bound if I can to have it managed and controlled by Canadians, and not only that, but I hope to see it become a favorite investment with our own people."[7] Two years later he told the governor-general, the Marquis of Lorne, "that there were less than 100 people in the whole Dominion who had any pecuniary interest in the enterprise though the amount of Canadian money in it was greater than the capital of the Bank of Montreal"[8]—which at the time was $12 million.

Stephen's ambition would be fulfilled eventually, but not until our own day.

In 1893, for the first time in its history, the revenues of the Canadian Pacific declined and net earnings fell by nearly $700,000. This was worrying because fixed charges were rising and the exhaustion of the guarantee fund would make the company's current income the only source of dividends. The year had been one of financial chaos in the United States, where railroads by the score had passed into the hands of receivers. Canada and the C.P.R. had escaped relatively lightly, and Van Horne was hopeful that things would improve in 1894. Instead, the Canadian Pacific found itself facing the worst crisis it would experience in nearly forty years.

In 1894 the Canadian Pacific was able to replace the immensely high wooden bridge over Stoney Creek with a steel structure. Here six locomotives are testing it for strength. The old bridge is still standing, intertwined with the new. The much heavier present bridge, third on the site, was completed in 1929.

Its troubles were not all in Canada or of its own making. Both its American subsidiaries, the Soo Line and the Duluth, South Shore and Atlantic, had been very hard hit by the virtual collapse of the timber, iron, and other industries upon which they depended for revenue. At the time the C.P.R. had secured control and had guaranteed many of their fixed charges, the possibility that the guarantee might have to be made good seemed remote; but in 1894 the Canadian Pacific was called upon to advance $1,150,000 to meet their interest payments and an additional $704,000 for certain essential capital expenditures.

Considering conditions, freight traffic on the Canadian Pacific's own lines held up surprisingly well. Measured in ton-miles, it declined nearly 10 percent in 1894 but revenue from it fell by less than 8 percent. Earnings were derived chiefly from grain, flour, livestock, lumber, and manufactured goods, and it is interesting to note that the lowest carryings in grain and livestock were in 1893, while the low points for flour, lumber, and manufactured goods were in 1894. The decline in revenue was curiously uniform over the whole rail system, with the low price of wheat the main cause in the West. Grain continued to flow to market, but the farmers received so little for it that westbound shipments of manufactured goods, upon which the railway made most of its profit, were sharply curtailed.

Outside circumstances dealt the Canadian Pacific two financial blows in Canada. Hitherto the interest on land grant bonds had been paid out of funds derived from land sales. In 1894 immigration had dwindled to such a point that sales virtually ceased, and the railway had to provide $656,618 for bond interest from its general revenue. And in British Columbia unprecedented floods in the lower valley of the Fraser River washed out tracks, forced the suspension of transcontinental traffic for forty-one days, and cost the C.P.R. an estimated $550,000 in track repairs and lost revenue. In the whole gloomy picture there were only two small bright spots, separated by the width of the continent. In the East the Château Frontenac was paying handsomely and in the West the Pacific *Empresses*, which had made a profit each year thay had been in operation, increased it by over $80,000 and brought the railway long-distance passenger and freight traffic that contributed significantly to its revenues.

Fixed charges exceeded net earnings in 1894, and instead of the usual surplus there was a deficit of $526,000. To this had to be added a dividend on the first issue of the new 4-percent preferred shares. In addition, believing that conditions must soon take a turn for the better, the directors declared a dividend of 2½ percent on the common stock. Although net earnings increased and the American subsidiaries required relatively little assistance in

1895, the dividend had to be reduced that year to 1½ percent, with the result that Canadian Pacific shares fell to a low of 33. Greatly upset and evidently fearful for the future, Lord Mount Stephen advised friends to sell their holdings while they still had some value. When the stock began to recover, he is said to have sold his own shares to avoid profiting from his failure to follow the advice he had given to others.[9]

This apparent loss of faith in the Canadian Pacific is puzzling, for the company's assets far exceeded its liabilities, and when times improved it was certain to prosper. Loss of confidence in Van Horne may have been the reason; there is some evidence that differences on policy had developed between them. In spite of this, Van Horne still wrote freely and frankly to Mount Stephen (though in a formal style that seems odd in view of their long and close association) and kept him informed about company affairs. Although distressed and disappointed by the financial crisis, he himself never became discouraged and never doubted the future of the enterprise. Late in 1894 he had an opportunity to compare the Canadian Pacific's operating expenses with those of the Great Northern and other comparable American lines and was much encouraged by the result. "I find," he told Mount Stephen, "that notwithstanding our higher cost of coal, our expenses were less in our most extravagant year than had been those of any of the other lines during the period of impending receivership when they resorted to every expedient to save expenses. The figures bear out the statement I made to Your Lordship some years ago to the effect that no important railway in the world was ever operated so cheaply as the Canadian Pacific in its most extravagant year." And in explanation he added: "When the Canadian Pacific was built we had the advantage of the experience of all the railways in North America, and were able to lay out the entire system with a view to the greatest possible economy and convenience in working, and I do not believe that any important railway in the United States can possibly get down to our figures."[10]

By the spring of 1895 Van Horne was feeling cheerful, and by the autumn business had recovered in a way that justified his optimism. Westbound traffic was picking up; livestock shipments were higher; the harvest had been plentiful; the Soo Line was "doing splendidly." "Indeed," he wrote to a Dutch friend in October, "all the clouds in our sky seem to have disappeared. We are in very good shape for business although we are likely to be very short of freight cars and Locomotives."[11] Little rolling stock had been purchased for some years, and the demands from new business were great. The increase in the lumber trade on the Short Line through Maine, he told Mount Stephen, required 500 cars a day to meet its needs.

Gross and net earnings in 1896 were almost back to the 1892 level, but the common share dividend was held to a prudent 2 percent. In 1897 both set new records—gross revenues exceeded $24 million and net earnings were $10.3 million—and the dividend rose to 4 percent. In 1899, the year Van Horne retired as president, revenues rose still further, to $29.2 million, and the 5-percent dividend was at last resumed.

There were two disappointments in these last years. One was the surrender (as Van Horne regarded it) of the Duluth and Winnipeg to Hill, a matter that will be discussed in the next chapter; the other was the failure of the Canadian Pacific and Vancouver to compete successfully with the American lines and Seattle for the rush of business arising from the Klondike gold discoveries in the Yukon. The C.P.R. purchased two liners for a service from Vancouver to Skagway, but they were too large and arrived too late; and it acquired a fleet of river steamers to connect with a projected railway from the Stikine River to the Yukon that was never built. But in spite of these setbacks, it was obvious that a period of great prosperity had begun, and the company moved quickly to take advantage of it.

Van Horne outlasted both his antagonists in the Grand Trunk, Joseph Hickson, the general manager, and Sir Henry Tyler, the president. Hickson, able and valiant servant of the Grand Trunk as well as doughty opponent of the Canadian Pacific, retired in December 1890. To the end Van Horne was convinced that he had "staked everything on the chance, which he regarded as a certainty, of his being able to bust the C.P.R."[12] In January 1890, upon the recommendation of Sir John Macdonald, who as an accomplished politician could appreciate an opponent and rarely bore a grudge for long, he had been knighted. About the same time Macdonald offered a knighthood to Van Horne, but for personal and political reasons the title was not conferred until 1894.

With Hickson's successor, Lewis Seargeant, Van Horne was on better terms, and the two railways settled down to more friendly rivalry. Tiffs developed between them occasionally, as in 1898, when in response to charges by the Canadian Pacific that it was violating an agreement on rates, the Grand Trunk for several months canceled the running rights it had granted the C.P.R. over its lines from North Bay to Toronto, but such open clashes were few. In part this was because it was clearly beyond the Grand Trunk's power to halt the progress of the C.P.R.; the latter was a presence that had to be lived with. In 1892 its gross revenues were 50 percent greater and its net earnings 75 percent higher than those of the Grand Trunk. True, the Canadian Pacific carried much less freight, but it carried it a much longer distance and at higher average rates. Much of the Grand Trunk's traffic was on relatively short hauls and on lines where cheap water transportation could compete during the navigation season.

Without Hickson's capable support, Sir Henry Tyler was soon in difficulties. Some of the Grand Trunk shareholders turned to Lord Mount Stephen, seeking his help and advice. Van Horne even suggested that Mount Stephen should take over the presidency of the Grand Trunk and lead it out of the wilderness. Mount Stephen countered with the proposal, apparently made with some support in London, that Van Horne should become its president. The idea attracted and intrigued Van Horne, but he turned it down because he feared that in the long run it would injure the C.P.R. "It would be a matter of the most intense gratification to me," he wrote to Mount Stephen. "It would be a fitting termination to the war they have waged on us from the beginning. Our victory would be absolute—but profits, not pride, should govern us."[13] In view of what happened in later years, it is interesting to note that some sort of merger of the two railways was also discussed, but rejected as impracticable because it was felt that the Canadian public would be unalterably opposed to a railway monopoly.

When in the last years of the old century the depression lifted and the Canadian Pacific was prospering, those close to Van Horne seem to have felt that he was beginning to lose interest in the company. This is not apparent in his letters to Mount Stephen, but more and more of the day-to-day administration was being turned over to the meticulous and untiring Thomas Shaughnessy, who as his successor in the presidency would develop the C.P.R. on an unimagined scale. Van Horne was a pioneer in spirit who most enjoyed building something new, and although he would continue to be chairman of the board of the Canadian Pacific until 1911, his attention would shift largely to new enterprises, notably to railway construction in Cuba.

But his contribution to the Canadian Pacific had been immense. He had superintended the construction of most of it and as president had brought it through the great depression of the 1890s. In part his success had been built upon an interest in and attention to detail, both important and unimportant, that continually astonished and frequently amused his colleagues and employees. Endless examples of this could be cited, but a few will suffice. Although the Grand Trunk and the C.P.R. were at loggerheads in 1883, he nevertheless sent Lewis Seargeant a shrewd tip about new freight cars: "An ordinary [wooden] box car will dry out from 600 to 900 lbs. during the first fifteen months after it is built, and if the tare is marked when the car is new and green, it will result in our carrying a very considerable amount of freight for nothing until the tare is corrected."[14] When in 1884 he sailed in the new steamer *Alberta* from Port Arthur to Owen Sound, he found the ship "very satisfactory indeed" but offered two small criticisms: the passengers were called needlessly early in the morning and the coffee served was weak and contained "a considerable percentage of burnt peas."[15]

Later the same year Alexander Mackenzie, the former prime minister, was to travel in one of the Great Lakes steamers. Although in his heyday Mackenzie had fought the Canadian Pacific project with all the power he could muster, Van Horne sent detailed instructions and suggestions to ensure his comfort on shipboard. He noted that Mackenzie was "a man of plain habits; he likes porridge with good milk for his breakfast, and his food plain but well cooked. As to liquors, he is generally abstemious though not a teetotaller."[16] Nor did Van Horne's interest in detail end when he ceased to be president. In 1904 he visited the West Coast and en route had a meal in the company's hotel at Field. This, he told Shaughnessy, was anything but satisfactory. The wine in particular annoyed him: "I ordered a bottle of Chambertin at $3.50, as I remember, and it certainly had never been nearer France than Hochelaga and would have been dear at 25¢." He suggested that when occasion offered, Shaughnessy should stop off and see for himself, keeping the option open to return to dine in his private car: "I advise you to keep a string on the dinner in your own car, for I imagine you will have need of it."[17] Every detail of new passenger equipment received close personal attention. The names of new sleeping cars were all submitted to him for approval, and when the first of them were under construction he worried about the monogram *CP* which was to be carved into the woodwork, lest it be taken to mean "Pullman Company," and advised that *CPR* be substituted.

Although the ties between the Canadian Pacific and Sir John Macdonald's Conservative party were close and clear, the company was reluctant to intervene publicly in politics. For this Macdonald occasionally took both Stephen and Van Horne to task. When the agitation in Manitoba over the monopoly clause was reaching its climax, Macdonald felt that the Canadian Pacific could have countered it by political means and was disappointed when it made little attempt to do so.

The general election of 1891, fought by Macdonald only a few months before his death, proved to be an exception. The Liberals were advocating reciprocity with the United States, and Van Horne could not restrain his strong opposition to it. Impulsively he sent a lengthy letter to Senator G. A. Drummond, chairman of the Conservative party in Montreal, in which he denounced the proposal in no uncertain terms. "I am well enough acquainted with the trade and industries of Canada," he wrote, "to know that unrestricted reciprocity would bring prostration and ruin." He added that he realized he might be "accused of meddling in politics, but with me this is a business question and not a political one, and it so vitally affects the interests that have been intrusted to me that I feel justified in expressing my opinion plainly; indeed, since the opposite views have been attributed to me, I feel bound to do so."[18]

Despite this disclaimer the Canadian Pacific was tarred with a political brush, and this being so, Van Horne threw the weight of the company and its employees behind the Conservative cause. Some later contended that this support was an important factor in Macdonald's victory.

In spite of his views on reciprocity, Van Horne was attracted to young Wilfrid Laurier, who had succeeded Edward Blake as leader of the Liberal party. The two were soon on friendly terms. When a general election was called in 1896, Van Horne resolved to stand aloof. "I am doing my best to keep on the fence," he told Laurier, "although it turns out to be a barbed wire one."[19] And to Mount Stephen he wrote: "We are keeping clear of the fight and I don't think we have anything to fear from the Grits [Liberals] if they get in. . . ."[20] How much of this attitude was owing to Van Horne's personal conviction that the Conservatives would be badly defeated, as they were, does not appear.

Between these two elections, in May 1894, Van Horne had been knighted. The honor had been offered to him by Macdonald in 1890 and again in 1891, but had been declined primarily because Van Horne thought the timing was inopportune; in 1891, just after the election, it could have been construed as being a political reward. Van Horne's retention of American citizenship was a further obstacle. This was finally overcome by creating him an Honorary Knight Commander of the Order of St. Michael and St. George (K.C.M.G.).

The significance of three events that took place in the later years of Van Horne's presidency was hidden at the time he retired in 1899.

The first was a change in the management of the Grand Trunk Railway. Sir Henry Tyler resigned in 1895. One of the early changes made by his successor, Sir Charles Rivers Wilson, was to recruit Charles M. Hays, an able and energetic American, as general manager. Within a few years Hays's ambitions for the Grand Trunk were to spread beyond Quebec and Ontario into western Canada.

A second development of great importance was the Crow's Nest Pass Agreement, concluded between the government of Canada and the Canadian Pacific in September 1897. At the time its most important provisions seemed to be those that provided a subsidy to assist the construction of a railway through the Crowsnest Pass. Of far greater long-term import was the Canadian Pacific's undertaking to reduce rates on grain shipped to Thunder Bay and, by inference, to maintain the new rates in perpetuity.

The third event was the emergence of William Mackenzie and Donald Mann as railway proprietors in western Canada. Both men, as has been noted, singly and in partnership, had been contractors for parts of the Canadian

Pacific's main line and other segments of the system, and Van Horne had been associated personally with Mackenzie in a number of profitable ventures involving urban street railways. In 1896 Mackenzie and Mann bought the Lake Manitoba Railway and Canal Company, chartered in 1889. It had never built a mile of track, but it was entitled to a federal land grant of 6,400 acres per mile, and, in what became a characteristic move, Mackenzie and Mann persuaded the government of Manitoba to give them a cash subsidy of $8,000 a mile as well. As a result the 125-mile line from Gladstone to Lake Winnipegosis was in operation by 1897, and running rights between Gladstone and Portage la Prairie provided a link with the C.P.R. The next move of the enterprising partners was to secure control of the Winnipeg, Great Northern Railway, and in January 1899 they threw their holdings together and incorporated the Canadian Northern Railway.

Many of Shaughnessy's problems in the years to come were to spring from these three events.

14

Van Horne versus Hill

About the time that relations between the Canadian Pacific and the Grand Trunk began to improve, tension mounted in another quarter. In 1889 James J. Hill created the Great Northern Railway to assume control of the St. Paul, Minneapolis and Manitoba and other lesser lines in which he was interested, and rivalry developed quickly between the Great Northern and the C.P.R.

In great measure this soon became a personal struggle, first between Hill and Van Horne and later between Hill and Shaughnessy. Hill had the great advantage of having for most purposes complete control of his railway. Van Horne's position was much more complicated. He had succeeded Sir George Stephen as president of the Canadian Pacific in 1888, but Stephen continued to be a member of the four-man executive committee until 1892 and a director until 1893. Stephen's authority within the C.P.R. had been virtually absolute, and Van Horne's final and unsuccessful appeal to him to remain a member of the board reveals how great it continued to be even after he ceased to be president. "You have been, as nearly as possible, President and Board of Directors combined right up to the present time," Van Horne wrote, "for we have been substantially governed by your views in all cases, however much everyone here may have opposed them. Your withdrawal would not be the withdrawal of a Director, but of the soul of the enterprise."[1]

There was an element of exaggeration in this tribute, but not a great deal. Van Horne had an immense respect for Stephen's ability and judgment, and the latter had continued to be a director at Van Horne's personal request. So far as the internal affairs of the Canadian Pacific were concerned, this somewhat unusual relationship between a past president and his successor rarely caused much difficulty. Stephen was interested primarily in finance and matters of high policy; Van Horne, the practical railroader, was absorbed in the actual operations. But where the interests of the C.P.R. and the St. Paul, Minneapolis and Manitoba (and later the Great Northern) clashed, problems arose. Until 1892 the executive committee of the Canadian Pacific consisted of Van Horne, Stephen, Donald Smith, and R. B. Angus. The last three were substantial shareholders in Hill's railway; indeed, for some years the combined holdings of Stephen and Smith exceeded Hill's own. Although they had resigned from the St. Paul board in 1883, both had rejoined it in 1889. Smith served as vice-president for a time and was a director until 1895. Stephen dropped off the board in 1892, but his close relationship with Hill continued for many years. To expect an executive committee with this membership to see things exclusively from the Canadian Pacific's point of view, as Van Horne naturally saw them, would be to expect the impossible.

Stephen felt that the two railways could be on friendly terms, but Van Horne had his doubts. Relations began amicably enough, while Stephen was still president of the Canadian Pacific. By 1886 Hill had in view a line of his own to Puget Sound, and in order to participate in the traffic to the coast immediately, he made arrangements with the C.P.R. to ship through freight from St. Paul to Winnipeg and thence over its main line to Vancouver. In 1887 a new steamer built by the Canadian Pacific Navigation Company (unrelated to the C.P.R., despite its name, except by contract) provided the final link between Vancouver and Puget Sound.

It was understood that these arrangements would terminate when Hill's own line to the coast was completed, and it became evident that this would not be long delayed. After creeping slowly westward to Minot, North Dakota, the St. Paul, Minneapolis and Manitoba made a sudden leap forward in 1887 to Havre, in Montana. There it paused for a time, but it was clear that the halt would be very temporary. Hill had insinuated his line into the territory between the Northern Pacific and the international boundary, which would make it easy to build spur lines northward into Canada, and Van Horne was sure that this was his intention. In 1890 Stephen urged Van Horne to talk to Hill and try to work out some arrangements for the future. This he did, but Hill was noncommittal, and Van Horne came away convinced that trouble lay ahead. At the same time his own ambitious and aggressive temperament, so like Hill's in many respects, enabled him to appreciate his adversary. "I never admired him so much as on this occasion," Van Horne wrote to Stephen. "He is, of course, entitled to all the advantage he can get out of the situation. His course in the matter is precisely that which I should take if I were in his place; so I don't complain of it at all."[2]

An example of the north-south services established by the C.P.R. in the 1890s on the interior lakes and rivers of British Columbia. The train has just arrived at Arrowhead from Revelstoke, on the main line; passengers are transferring to the stern-wheeler *Nakusp*, which will take them 125 miles down the Columbia River to Robson. There the Columbia and Kootenay Railway will provide connections with Nelson and other points.

Van Horne's fears were soon confirmed. Hill showed little inclination to use the Soo Line, which the Canadian Pacific had controlled since 1888, as an eastern connection. Rumors were current that branches extending into Canada would soon materialize. Hill was said to be seeking a connection with the Calgary and Edmonton Railway, which had been leased by the C.P.R., and he was becoming actively interested in southern British Columbia. He was in the habit of screening his intentions by working through local subsidiaries, and early in 1891 one of them, the New Westminster Southern, completed a line from the border north to the Fraser River opposite New Westminster. Lack of a bridge prevented it from building on to Vancouver, but Hill's intention was clear. "He is not building a line down the Sound to New Westminster because he loves us," was Van Horne's acid comment to Stephen. He countered Hill's move by bridging the Fraser at Mission, thirty-four miles east of New Westminster, and running a branch of his own to the boundary. There it met the Bellingham Bay and British Columbia Railway, a local line connecting at New Whatcom (now Bellingham) with railways to Seattle and other points south. The first Canadian Pacific train arrived at New Whatcom on May 28, 1891, and through passenger trains ran for a time to Seattle. The arrival of the first of them at New Whatcom was somewhat marred when hoses intended to provide graceful water arches over the train were misdirected and thoroughly drenched the special guests, who were in coaches with open windows.

By 1891 interest had shifted from the coast to the Kootenay region in southeastern British Columbia, where mining was developing on a considerable scale. Mining is an industry peculiarly dependent on transportation, and the approach of a railway that promises to provide it fairly cheaply always sends prospectors swarming into the hills. They appeared in large numbers during and after the construction of the Canadian Pacific through the western mountains and roamed over much of the area between the railway and the international boundary.

Few discoveries of any promise were made near the main line, but it was otherwise further south in the Kootenay. In 1886 the Silver King mine, a rich silver-copper deposit, was found on Toad Mountain, and this and other mines near Kootenay Lake resulted in the founding of Nelson, on the west arm of the lake, in 1888. Two years later Rossland came into existence as a result of the discovery of gold and copper deposits, including the famous War Eagle and Le Roi mines, on Red Mountain, a few miles west of the Columbia River. In 1891 additional important discoveries were made in two other areas—in the Slocan country, between Kootenay Lake and the Columbia, and in what became known as the boundary country, near the American border thirty or forty miles west of the Columbia, where the new towns of Grand Forks and Greenwood soon sprang into being. Copper was the chief mineral in the boundary country; silver, lead, and zinc were found in the Slocan.

Coal was also discovered, and as early as 1887 Colonel James Baker, who had attained some prominence in provincial politics, called on Sir George Stephen in the hope of persuading the Canadian Pacific to build a branch line that would reach extensive deposits he had located in the Crowsnest Pass area. At that time the nearest Canadian railway, the narrow-gauge line to Lethbridge, was a hundred miles and more away and was controlled by the Galts, who had coal of their own to sell. Stephen was not encouraging. "I have seen Col. Baker," he wrote to Sir John Macdonald, "and have convinced him that his coal mine is beyond the reach of the C.P.R. If the coal is all that he thinks it is, he ought to be able to sell it to some of the great mining coys in Montana just south of it, which use enormous quantities of coal for smelting purposes."[3]

This was an open invitation to the Americans to move in, and by the time Van Horne had settled in as president, this was about to happen. It was a natural development, for geographically the Kootenay was clearly part of the "inland empire" in eastern Washington, of which Spokane was the natural

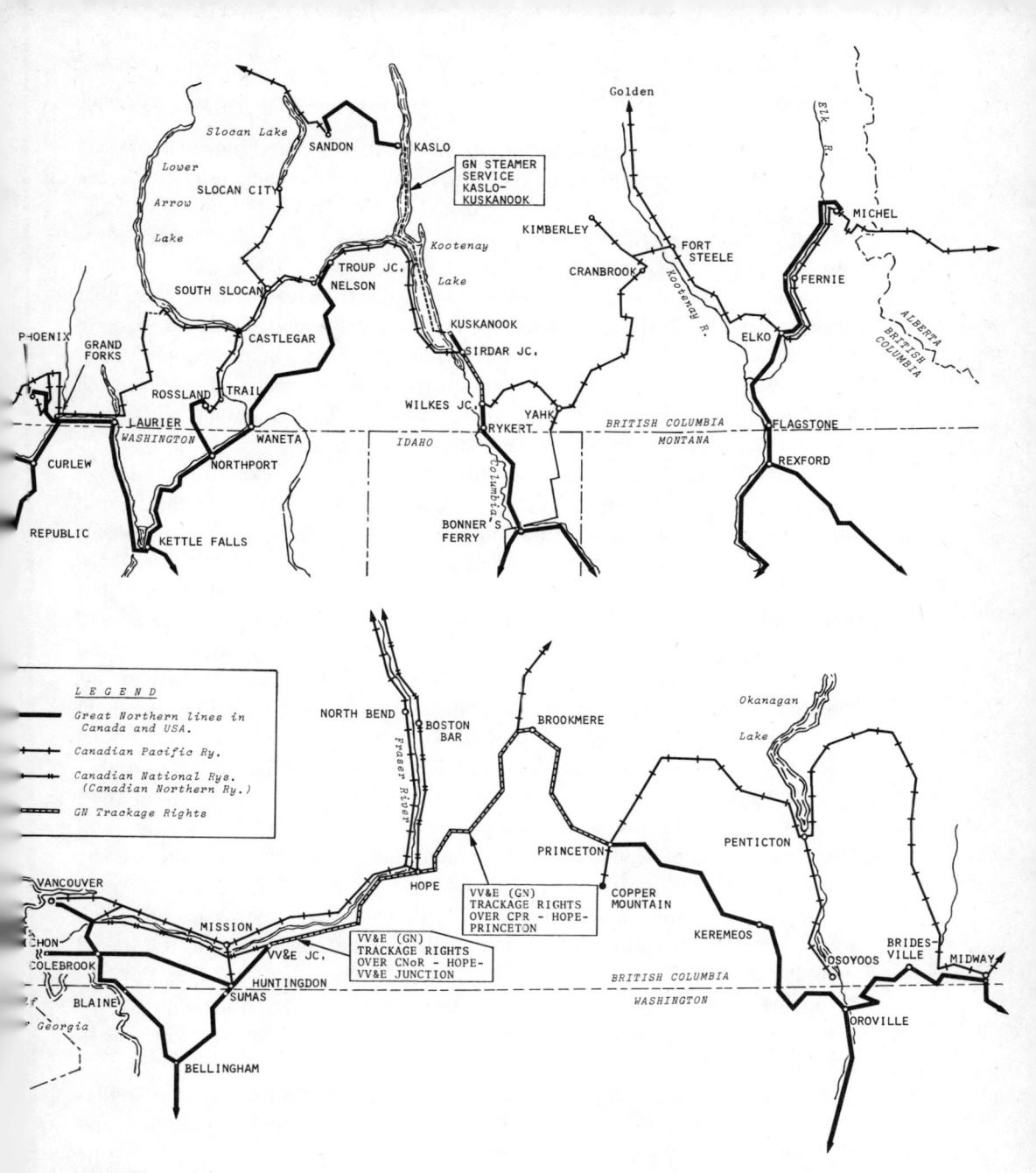

James J. Hill's invasion of southern British Columbia. At one time the Great Northern crossed the Canadian border at eleven points between Vancouver and the Alberta boundary.

supply center. It was much easier of access from the south than from the north, and the vast majority of the miners and mining companies that were flocking into the country were American. In 1889 D. C. Corbin, a Spokane railwayman, sensing this, incorporated the Spokane Falls and Northern Railway to build north to the border and, he hoped, into Canada. Rebuffed by Stephen, Colonel Baker had secured a charter from the British Columbia legislature for a Crow's Nest and Kootenay Lake Railway, intended to serve his coal deposits. Unable to raise funds to build the line, he turned to Corbin. Baker and Corbin soon proposed two projects—an extension of the Spokane Falls and Northern to Nelson, and an east-west line running right across British Columbia from the Crowsnest Pass to the coast.

Both charters, as amended by the B.C. legislature, included conditions and time limits that Corbin would not accept, and in any event the federal approval required was not forthcoming from Ottawa. But Corbin's proposals had alarmed Van Horne, who had long-range plans of his own for a southern through line to the coast. As an interim measure he felt that short branches and steamer services connecting with the Canadian Pacific's main line should serve the area south of it reasonably well. In providing these, advantage would be taken of the region's distinctive terrain, which was characterized by mountain ranges running north and south, with long narrow valleys between them occupied by navigable rivers and lakes. Thus in West Kootenay, part of the Kootenay River and Kootenay Lake lay in one valley, while the Arrow Lakes and the Columbia River (of which they are enlargements) occupied another. While Corbin's charters were being discussed, Van Horne informed Sir John Macdonald that the Canadian Pacific would build a twenty-eight-mile railway between Nelson, on Kootenay Lake, and Robson, on the Columbia. Working in conjunction with steamer services on both waterways, this would provide a somewhat primitive but fairly comprehensive transportation system, linked with the rest of Canada through Revelstoke, where the Canadian Pacific's main line crossed the Columbia. To carry out this undertaking, the C.P.R. used the charter of the Columbia and Kootenay Railway, and the line was in operation by April 1892.

Farther west, in the Okanagan valley, Van Horne employed a similar strategy. In 1890 the Canadian Pacific agreed to lease the Shuswap and Okanagan Railway, which had been chartered to build southward from the main line of the C.P.R. to the north end of Okanagan Lake, a distance of fifty-one miles. Some delays occurred, but the branch was completed in May 1893. Here the Canadian Pacific itself provided a connecting service along a hundred miles of the lake with the stern-wheeler *Aberdeen*, the first of the many steamers the company would operate on the lakes and rivers of British Columbia over a period of half a century.

Hill had not yet appeared on the Kootenay scene, but Van Horne was well aware that he had long had an eye on the Crowsnest Pass. "I know that Mr. Hill has looked upon it for many years as of enormous importance," he told Macdonald in 1891. "I can hardly imagine anything more dangerous to the interests of the Dominion in the West than the granting of a charter through the Crow's Nest Pass to any company that may by any possibility fall under American control."[4] Macdonald would have liked the Canadian Pacific to stake out its claim immediately by announcing its intention to build through the pass, but Van Horne felt that a railway there would be premature: "I do not see what possible use there can be for a railway through the Crow's Nest Pass for a good while to come, although in the course of ten or fifteen years I have no doubt that the possession of the Pass will be enormously important. . . . There is nothing whatever outside Col. Baker's vivid imagination to justify a railway there at the present time."[5]

When Van Horne undertook to build the line from Nelson to Robson, he understood that the government of British Columbia had agreed not to charter competing railways that would be under the control of American interests. He therefore felt betrayed when the province promptly chartered the Nelson and Fort Sheppard Railway. This was controlled by Corbin and enabled him to complete his projected line from Spokane to Nelson in December 1893. Strictly speaking, it extended only to the outskirts of Nelson, as the Canadian Pacific had received a land grant that blocked its entry and Van Horne was in no mood to make concessions to a rival.

It was a frustrating end to a difficult and significant year. In January the Great Northern had been completed to Everett, on Puget Sound, and Van Horne was certain that difficulties with Hill lay ahead. Since he had assumed the presidency of the C.P.R. he had been losing faith in Hill, whom he accused of "concealing his poison in friendly words," and in 1891 he had said so quite frankly to Sir George Stephen: "I have passed the stage of distrust and feel sure now that he has neither good will nor good intentions toward the Canadian Pacific, whatever his inside feelings toward yourself and Sir Donald [Smith] may be." "I only hope you will not think me captious if I refuse to believe anything he tells me in the future, and if I shape my plans on the assumption that he is the most dangerous enemy of the Canadian Pacific."[6]

Hill had been annoying in petty ways (for a time the Great Northern refused to honor the tickets of passengers booked to sail on the Canadian Pacific's trans-Pacific steamers), and he had initiated a rate war that did the C.P.R. relatively little harm but forced the Northern Pacific into receivership. Later this enabled Hill and some associates (including Stephen) to gain control of it, and thereafter it became simply a second line for the Great Northern. But the collapse of the Northern Pacific precipitated a depression that swept the continent and kept the Canadian Pacific desperately short of capital funds for several years.

Before the worst of the depression, Van Horne was able to take two steps to protect the C.P.R.'s position. Once the Great Northern was completed, it could not expect to share any longer in the traffic from the Twin Cities to the west coast unless it could be carried over its own lines. To make this possible, the Soo Line was hastily extended in 1893 to the Canadian border at Portal, where it met a branch that linked it with the main line of the C.P.R. near Moose Jaw. This gave the Canadian Pacific a through route to St. Paul independent of the Great Northern.

Some of Hill's actions may have been in retaliation for a second defensive move Van Horne had made late in 1892. Some time previously he had learned that the Duluth and Winnipeg Railway was in financial difficulties. At first he was not inclined to assist, but later reports suggested that the line had considerable potential. It consisted of 108 miles of completed road built northwestward from Duluth and it owned 18,420 acres of iron lands in the Mesabi and Vermilion ranges, with as much more under lease—properties later to prove fabulously rich in iron ore. If completed, the Duluth and Winnipeg would be a very useful addition to the struggling Duluth, South Shore and Atlantic, which the C.P.R. already controlled, and in conjunction with it would provide a through line south of Lake Superior from Sault Ste. Marie to Emerson and Winnipeg. This was a pleasing prospect in itself, but a clear invasion of what Hill considered to be his territory.

What Van Horne did not know was that the loan that the Duluth and Winnipeg was trying desperately to pay off had been advanced by Hill himself, and that he expected by means of it to gain possession of the company. Hill wanted it because it could provide a much shorter route from Lake Superior to the Red River and the West than the Great Northern's own line, and because he was convinced of the richness of the Mesabi iron deposits. His wrath can be imagined when he learned that the Canadian Pacific had advanced $1,316,924 to the Duluth, South Shore and Atlantic to enable it to acquire control.

The purchase marked the beginning of four trying and frustrating years for Van Horne. Hill wanted the Duluth and Winnipeg; Van Horne was determined to keep it. He realized that in order to become a paying proposition it would have to be extended, and he worked out a plan that included completion of the line to the Canadian border and spur lines to the iron mines. This he submitted to Lord Mount Stephen, whose reaction was not encouraging. The cost would be between two and three million dollars, and the depression soon became so acute that an immediate expenditure on that scale was out of the question.

Two aspects of the matter are of particular interest—Hill's negotiating techniques and the influence Mount Stephen continued to wield in the Canadian Pacific's affairs even after he had ceased to be a director.

Van Horne attempted several times to reach some sort of understanding with Hill, but he found this impossible. Hill consistently avoided serious discussion by talking interminably about other matters. After a typical encounter in 1894, Van Horne sent an account of it to Mount Stephen. The session had begun at lunch and had continued until the approach of train time in the evening.

Up to that time nothing was said about any business matter. I reminded him then that we had only an hour left for the discussion of the Duluth and Winnipeg matter, and we started out fairly well on that question for a few minutes. . . . [But] he soon wandered away from the subject . . . [and] . . . we did not get back to the D. & W. until he had to start for his train. Then he said he would think it over, and if I would try to think out some scheme, we could discuss it at St. Paul on my way back from the Pacific Coast. I promised to do so; and then, taking me affectionately by the arm, he said: "Van, it is a very nice thing that although we may disagree about business matters, our personal relations are so pleasant. We would do anything for each other." (The skunk.)[7]

Strangely enough, there appears to have been a considerable measure of truth in Hill's last remark; mutual regard between Van Horne and him seems to have survived their differences. Van Horne inferred as much in a letter to one of Hill's henchmen: "I have some very decided opinions about matters that have occurred between the two companies . . . but I would like it to be distinctly understood that whatever personal feeling I have is against the actions of your company and not against Mr. Hill or anybody else. . . . When I damn you or him for your numerous sins as, unhappily, you give me frequent occasion to do, I beg to assure you that you are damned in a strictly official sense."[8]

When Van Horne acquired the Duluth and Winnipeg, Mount Stephen had at first approved the move and considered it "a very wise thing," but as his reaction to Van Horne's plans to extend the line indicated, he soon began to have doubts. Although Mount Stephen had taken up permanent residence in England, Van Horne continued to write to him frequently, giving him details of the company's problems and activities. Indeed, if one did not know to the contrary, it could easily be assumed that they were still letters of a general manager to his superior. Only very occasionally does any criticism of Mount Stephen's views or of the validity of the basis upon which they were formed appear in the correspondence. It is perhaps significant that the strongest remarks of the kind were made in July 1894, when the difference of opinion over the Duluth and Winnipeg had become pronounced. Van Horne in effect told Mount Stephen in a diplomatic way that he felt that the man on the spot was the best judge of a situation: "Difficulties and dangers always look greater to everybody at a distance and I think I have noticed or thought I noticed a good many times in the history of the company that where you were full of belief here you were more or less of a pessimist in London. . . . I believe it to be impossible for anybody in London to make a correct diagnosis of the conditions in Canada, however familiar he may have been with the country two years ago. . . ."[9]

Unfortunately, within a week the C.P.R. was unable to pay the half-yearly dividend on its common shares, and this had a much greater effect on Mount Stephen's opinions than Van Horne's letter. The depression deepened thereafter, total annual dividends dwindled from the 5 percent of 1893 to only 1½ percent in 1895, and under the circumstances already related Mount Stephen sold out his Canadian Pacific holdings. His confidence in Van Horne's judgment and management had been shaken, and he had come to the conclusion that the C.P.R. would be well advised to relinquish the Duluth and Winnipeg to Hill. Unconsciously, perhaps, he was influenced by his heavy financial involvement in the Great Northern.[10] True, he did not entirely desert the C.P.R.; he was quick to come to its defense when Hill tried to have a bonding privilege important to it canceled, and instigated attacks on it in a New York newspaper. Mount Stephen found this "so inconceivably senseless" that he warned Hill that it would compel him and his friends "to withdraw all connection with the Great Northern Railway."[11] But he felt strongly about the Duluth and Winnipeg, and his views were reflected in the executive committee through Sir Donald Smith and R. B. Angus. Van Horne fought a good fight. "The D. &. W. is the best property we have and this year will demonstrate that," he wrote to Thomas Skinner, one of his directors, as late as April 1896. "It is moreover our *only* weapon of defence against the Great Northern and Northern Pacific and we must keep it."[12] But the contrary view prevailed and a few months later the railway passed into Hill's possession. The only reference to the transaction in the annual report of the Canadian Pacific was a note stating that the advance made to the Duluth, South Shore and Atlantic to acquire it had been repaid.

In the hope of salvaging some advantage, Van Horne had secured an undertaking that Hill would give the Duluth, South Shore and Atlantic his eastbound traffic. But Hill chose not to observe this agreement, and it was not enforceable by law.

Meanwhile, in spite of the depression, mining had developed rapidly in the Kootenay, and Van Horne had taken the first important step toward his projected railway across southern British Columbia. Late in 1893 the Canadian Pacific leased the narrow-gauge line that the Galt interests had built from Dunmore, near Medicine Hat, westward to Lethbridge. The terms provided for its conversion to standard gauge and included an option to purchase. This carried the C.P.R. halfway to the Crowsnest Pass, but there the depression caused it to tarry for a time.

Within the Kootenay itself, only minor improvements were possible. Chief of these was the Nakusp and Slocan Railway, which by arrangement with the government of British Columbia the Canadian Pacific leased and completed in 1894. This thirty-seven-mile line from the Upper Arrow Lake (a widening of the Columbia River) reached the Slocan mining areas. There it encountered the Kaslo and Slocan Railway, which provided a competing outlet for the mines to Kootenay Lake and to steamer services that connected with the Great Northern at Bonner's Ferry, in Idaho. From the first Van Horne suspected correctly that the Kaslo and Slocan was the Great Northern in disguise, but as late as 1898 Hill, who was much given to moving in mysterious ways through local subsidiaries, characteristically assured Van Horne that this was not so. Feeling between the rival railways in Slocan ran high at times. When the C.P.R. built a new depot in the town of Sandon, employees of the Kaslo and Slocan arrived in the night, threw a cable around it, hitched it to a locomotive, hauled it from its foundations, and dumped it into nearby Carpenter Creek.

The Kaslo and Slocan was Hill's first thrust into southeastern British Columbia. Others would soon follow, but for the moment the next American initiatives came from other interests.

Smelters had become the crying need in Kootenay. Soon after the completion of the Canadian Pacific's main line, small smelters had been built at Vancouver, Revelstoke, and Golden, but all had languished for lack of ore. In the South, by contrast, the mines were now flourishing and there was an abundance of ore, but no smelter. Ore had to be freighted out to smelters at Butte or Helena in Montana, or to Tacoma, on Puget Sound, and costs were so high that this could be done only selectively. Even medium-grade ores could not be moved at all.

The earliest smelters in the region were on Kootenay Lake—one at Pilot Bay, which began operations in 1895, and the other, blown in a year later, at Nelson. By that time the gold-copper mines near Rossland had been discovered, and almost simultaneously two Americans, interested in both railways and mining, took steps to meet the need for smelters there.

One was F. Augustus Heinze, a colorful and volatile character who had made a fortune in Montana and was looking for new worlds to conquer. He signed a contract to treat 75,000 tons of ore from the famous Le Roi mine at Red Mountain, and decided that the best location for a smelter would be at

Trail Creek (as Trail was then called), on the Columbia River. Construction began in September 1895 and the Trail smelter began operation the following February. To bring the ore from the mine to the smelter, Heinze secured a charter for the Columbia and Western Railway, and in the summer of 1896 completed a narrow-gauge line from Trail to Rossland. The difference in altitude was over 2,000 feet, and as the little thirteen-mile railway squirmed up the mountainside, its steep grades, sharp curves, trestles, and switchbacks made it an operational nightmare. Indeed, operation was possible only because the heavy ore traffic was carried on the downhill run.

Much the same was true of a competing railway built by D. C. Corbin. Although the owners of the Le Roi mine had entered into a contract with Heinze, they decided that it might be as well to have a smelter of their own. The site they chose was at Northport, Washington, on Corbin's Spokane Falls and Northern Railway, a few miles from the Canadian border. The project required a seventeen-mile branch line to Rossland, of which nine and a half miles were in British Columbia. Because the line straddled the border, two corporations were necessary—the Columbia and Red Mountain Railway in the United States and the Red Mountain Railway in Canada. The latter was chartered in 1895 and the line was completed in December 1896. Work then proceeded on a railway bridge across the Columbia at Northport and on construction of the smelter itself. The whole scheme came into operation when the smelter was blown in on January 1, 1898.

Though apparently solidly established in Kootenay, both Heinze and Corbin were to disappear within a matter of months, the one permanently, the other temporarily. Their passing would increase the friction between Van Horne and Hill, for Heinze's interests would be acquired by the Canadian Pacific while those of Corbin would pass into the possession of the Great Northern.

Heinze had great ambitions for his Columbia and Western Railway. In 1897 he had built a standard-gauge branch up the Columbia from Trail to Robson and from there he planned to build westward to Penticton, on Okanagan Lake. This prospect disturbed Van Horne greatly, as the line would occupy a large part of the route the Canadian Pacific itself hoped to follow to the west coast. Heinze's methods were as unpopular as his plans, for he had financed a press campaign to blacken the name of the C.P.R. When Shaughnessy complained of this to the city editor of the Rossland *Miner*, the latter replied: "If you hired a painter to paint your house white he would paint it white, and if you hired him to paint it black he would paint it black. I was hired to paint you black."[13] Fortunately for the Canadian Pacific, Heinze's fortunes declined just as its own were definitely improving. He failed to raise funds in England to finance the western extension of the Columbia and Western, and when he returned, found himself involved in such serious legal and financial difficulties in Montana that he decided to dispose of his Canadian holdings.

He first set a price of $2 million on his railway and smelter and let it be known that he would not sell one without the other. The Canadian Pacific had no great wish to enter the smelter business, but it did attach considerable importance to getting rid of Heinze. Van Horne felt that some expert counsel was required and on the advice of a friend engaged Walter Aldridge, an able and astute young mining engineer. It was a fortunate choice, for Aldridge had been a classmate of Heinze's at the Columbia School of Mines and knew something of him and his ways.

Aldridge inspected the smelter, saw at once that Heinze's price was far too high, and countered it by ostensibly going ahead with plans to build a rival plant. Heinze attempted to go behind Aldridge's back by offering a lower price to C.P.R. headquarters in Montreal; this Shaughnessy accepted tentatively, but Aldridge pointed out important omissions in the proposal and the deal was suspended. Forced to negotiate directly with Aldridge, Heinze is said to have suggested that they should play poker for his holdings; Aldridge declined and suggested they seek an arbitrator. Heinze agreed to this, and the manager of the Bank of Montreal in Rossland was roused from his bed in the dead of night to fulfil this role without delay. By morning a price had been agreed upon, and almost all the Heinze properties passed to the Canadian Pacific.[14] For the Columbia and Western Railway the C.P.R. paid $600,000, plus half the land grant the company had earned to date. The smelter was acquired for $200,000, and an additional $5,980.16 covered materials and supplies on hand, making a grand total of just under $806,000. The sale was concluded on February 11, 1898.

From this small beginning were to develop the vast operations of Cominco, first known as the Canadian Smelting Works and later for many years as the Consolidated Mining and Smelting Company.

Heinze was gone, but Van Horne had other causes for worry, because interest in a southern line to the coast was not confined to Heinze. In 1897 the British Columbia legislature had chartered the Vancouver, Victoria and Eastern Railway and Navigation Company, with powers to build from Vancouver to Rossland. No construction was undertaken for some time, but the charter was to fall into Hill's clutches and cause the Canadian Pacific much trouble a few years later. Meanwhile D. C. Corbin had revived his hopes of building a line from the Kootenay westward. He had incorporated the Kettle Valley Railway in Washington State and in 1898 tried to secure a federal charter in Canada. At first all seemed to go fairly well; his application was approved in

March, though by a narrow margin, by the railway committee of the House of Commons. But opposition then developed in the British Columbia legislature, which urged the government to deny the charter because the proposed railway would divert Canadian business to the United States. The Canadian Pacific also brought to bear all the influence it could muster, and was said to have lured members of Parliament back to Ottawa from their Easter vacations on free special trains if they would promise to vote against Corbin's project.[15] To Van Horne's relief the House rejected the charter by a vote of 64 to 44.

This was in April 1898. By the time Corbin returned to Spokane, he was aware that someone was attempting to secure control of his Spokane Falls and Northern Railway. It proved to be a curious mix-up, for unknown to one another, both the Northern Pacific and the Great Northern were involved; the price of shares was pushed up and some purchasing was done at cross purposes. In the end the Northern Pacific secured a majority interest, but by an agreement that became effective on July 1, 1898, it relinquished control to the Great Northern. Hill had made his second thrust into Kootenay, and this had given him direct access to Nelson and Rossland.

Corbin's charter had undoubtedly been denied partly because the Canadian Pacific was ready at last to push through the Crowsnest Pass and in other ways strengthen its position in southeastern British Columbia. The first steps were mentioned in the annual report for 1896. The company had found itself "at a great disadvantage in reaching the traffic of the mining districts . . . in having to depend upon steamboat connections controlled by other parties." Rates were excessive and services inadequate. The C.P.R. had therefore purchased the Columbia and Kootenay Navigation Company, much the largest shipping enterprise on both the Columbia River and Kootenay Lake, and had already ordered additions to its fleet of steamers and barges. Even more essential for the Canadian Pacific were direct rail connections of its own. "Until then," the report continued, "the greater part of the mining traffic will be beyond its reach, and will continue to be . . . carried by the American lines southward." The directors could not "too strongly urge the immediate construction of a line from Lethbridge to . . . Nelson, a distance of 325 miles," and anticipating the approval of shareholders, had "already taken steps towards commencement of the work" in the spring.[16]

Those steps had included surveys west of Lethbridge, upon which about $100,000 had been spent. Their purpose was to make it possible for construction to begin promptly as soon as financial conditions permitted. A second sum of $100,000, spent discreetly through a Montreal broker, had enabled Van Horne to acquire the capital stock of the British Columbia Southern Railway, which was Colonel Baker's original line under the new name it received in

1891. Its charter would be useful, since it had been authorized to build from a somewhat indefinite point near the Crowsnest Pass to Hope and Burrard Inlet, and the purchase warded off the danger that it might fall into the wrong hands. In order to safeguard its entitlement to provincial land grants at the rate of 20,000 acres for each completed mile of line, it was not absorbed immediately by the Canadian Pacific; the shares were held on behalf of the C.P.R. by nine individuals, seven of whom were prominent in the company. Van Horne, Shaughnessy, Angus, and E. B. Osler were among the number.

It had been recognized for some time that a Crowsnest Pass line was unlikely to be built unless it was subsidized. Four times in the five-year period 1891–95 British Columbia had asked the federal government to provide assistance. In 1893 Van Horne had proposed a cash subsidy of $5,000 a mile, supplemented by a loan from the government of $20,000 a mile. Later a cash subsidy of $10,000 without the loan was discussed, but no agreement resulted. The cabinet assembled by Wilfrid Laurier when he became prime minister in 1896 included Clifford Sifton, minister of the interior, a man dedicated to the settlement and development of the Canadian West, and A. G. Blair, minister of railways. Both hoped that the C.P.R.'s anxiety to secure a subsidy could be turned to good account, and they were the key figures in the behind-the-scenes negotiations between the government and the Canadian Pacific that began within a few weeks of the election. The outcome was the much-discussed Crow's Nest Pass Agreement, confirmed in a federal statute that became law on June 29, 1897, and destined to be a factor in the Canadian economy and in railway finances far beyond the lifetime of any of the men who drafted it.

The essential provisions were two. The government granted the Canadian Pacific a cash subsidy of $11,000 a mile, up to a total not exceeding $3,630,-000, to aid in building a railway from Lethbridge to Nelson. The C.P.R., for its part, agreed to make certain reductions in freight rates, all for the benefit of settlers and farmers on the prairies. Westbound rates from central Canada on a considerable variety of items, including building materials, furniture, agricultural implements, and livestock, were to be reduced by 10 percent; the rate on coal oil (essential for lighting before the days of rural electrification) was to be cut 20 percent, and that on fresh fruits by one third. Most important of all, however, was the reduction of the eastbound rate on grain between points on the prairies and Thunder Bay by 3 cents per 100 pounds. To cite examples, this cut the rate to Thunder Bay from Winnipeg (420 miles) to 14 cents per 100 pounds, from Regina (776 miles) to 20 cents, and from Calgary (1,242 miles) to 26 cents.

At the time these reductions inflicted no great hardship on the railway; the lower rates yielded a modest profit and continued to do so until the First

World War. The difficulty was that the statute stated specifically and without qualification "that no higher rates than such rates or tolls shall be hereafter charged by the Company between the points aforesaid"—a provision interpreted as meaning that the rates were to remain in force in perpetuity, regardless of future cost and price levels.

Shortly before his death in 1929, Sir Clifford Sifton wrote an open letter to the press on railway matters that has been quoted in his biography and other studies. In it Sifton stated that Van Horne and Shaughnessy came to see him regarding the Crowsnest Pass line, "said that they had to build the line and wanted a large bonus for doing it, that the C.P.R. was on the verge of bankruptcy." "The subsidy," he continued, "saved the C.P.R. and saved a good many other things in Canada."[17] This simply does not accord with the facts. By 1897 the Canadian Pacific was in no danger of bankruptcy, and the subsidy, which was expected to meet about half the cost of building the Crowsnest line, actually met little more than one third of it. Construction costs totaled $9,898,392, and the C.P.R. received $3,404,720 in subsidy payments.

The importance the C.P.R. attached at this time to coal is frequently overlooked. Coal was important both as a potential source of traffic for the new Crowsnest line and as a commodity that the smelters in Kootenay needed desperately at a reasonable price. Hitherto they had been under the necessity of importing it from the coast by a ruinously expensive route that required repeated transfers and handling. There was an abundance of coal in the Crowsnest region, but there had been no point in mining it until a railway was available to move it to market. Now that the railway was being provided, the Canadian Pacific was anxious to make sure that mining would begin without delay, and was prepared to make substantial concessions to bring this about.

From the British Columbia border westward to Kootenay Lake, the Crowsnest railway was to be built under the charter of the British Columbia Southern. Its subsidy lands would include a large part of the known coal-bearing areas in the region; indeed, the only other important holding was a block of some 10,000 acres held by the Kootenay Coal Company. The Canadian Pacific proposed to turn over most of the coal lands to the latter if it would undertake to begin mining operations promptly. At this point the federal government intervened in the public interest and required the British Columbia Southern to allow it to select 50,000 acres from the coal-bearing lands, the purpose being to provide a contingency reserve that could be developed if coal prices charged by the company were deemed to be excessive.

These arrangements were confirmed in a tripartite agreement concluded on July 30, 1897, by the Canadian Pacific, the British Columbia Southern, and the Kootenay Coal Company (soon to be renamed the Crow's Nest Pass Coal

Company). So far as the first and third parties were concerned, the terms were simple: the C.P.R. undertook to build the Crowsnest railway and the coal company agreed to develop the coal mines and to sell coal at a reasonable price. The impact of the agreement on the British Columbia Southern was far greater. It was required to convey to the Kootenay Coal Company all coal-bearing lands that it would receive in its subsidy except the 50,000 acres to be selected by the government of Canada and 3,840 acres (six square miles) that were to be conveyed to the Canadian Pacific. The precise area the coal company received over the years is difficult to calculate, but it seems to have been about 240,000 acres.

Location surveys for the Crowsnest line, following up the preliminary work done earlier, began in April 1897 and grading began in July.[18] The route from Lethbridge to the pass was straightforward and the pass itself, with an altitude of 4,450 feet, offered no great difficulties. West of the pass the objective was to reach Kootenay Landing, at the south end of Kootenay Lake, and over the route the line twisted and turned, roughly in the form of a gigantic S. As the crow flies, the distance from the pass to Kootenay Landing is about 90 miles; by rail it is 182 miles. Most of the twists were due to the mountains, but the veer northward to Cranbrook was not unconnected with the fact that the ubiquitous Colonel Baker had large land holdings there and gave the Canadian Pacific a generous part of the townsite in return for bringing the railway in his direction. Later this diversion proved convenient for an unforeseen reason; a short, nineteen-mile-branch line from Cranbrook could reach the fabulous Sullivan mine at Kimberley.

Grades on the line exceeded 1 percent in only two places, and in neither of these did they reach 2 percent. Nevertheless there were a few problems for the builders. The first was encountered at its very beginning, as the line left Lethbridge. Here it had to cross the valley of the Oldman River, a vast gully a mile wide and 300 feet deep. Years later an immense steel viaduct would carry the railway directly across, but as first constructed it ran south for over seven miles along the east bank of the river, dropping steadily as it went, crossed the floor of the valley on a trestle, and then began a long climb up the west bank. Cuts were numerous and trestles so frequent that they totaled three miles in all.

A few miles west of the Crowsnest Pass, the line twisted deeply into a valley and out again in order to keep grades as low as possible, forming what became known as the Michel Loop. And on the Kootenay River flats, where the river enters Kootenay Lake through a broad delta, four and a quarter miles of trestles were necessary, as well as a steel bridge with a swing span to accommodate the river traffic. Finally, because of the very heavy and costly work that would be involved, it was decided to postpone construction of the fifty-five miles of line along the lakeshore from Kootenay Landing to Nelson. Passengers were carried across this gap in lake steamers while tugs and barges handled freight traffic. This water link was shortened by twenty miles in 1902, when a track was built from Nelson to Proctor, but it was not extended to Kootenay Landing (at a cost of about $3 million) until 1930.

As chief of construction Van Horne had chosen Michael Haney, a fiery and capable Irishman who had worked on the main line between Winnipeg and Thunder Bay and later was a superintendent for Onderdonk in the canyons of the Fraser and the Thompson. Faced with the necessity of building the great number of timber trestles required, he used again a technique he had developed for Onderdonk. At Macleod trestles were prefabricated; timbers were sawn and shaped there to the exact dimensions required and then shipped to construction sites where they were quickly assembled.

Haney was a great driver of contractors and construction crews, but he was rough and ready and had to learn that times had changed since the building of the main line. Complaints reached Ottawa, and in January 1898 Clifford Sifton appointed a commission to inquire into the treatment of laborers in the Crowsnest construction crews. Its report, submitted in April, told a tale of poor accommodation, bad sanitary conditions, and low wages. In part the bad living conditions were almost inevitable because of the temporary nature of most of the camps; they were abandoned as the track moved forward. More surprising were the wages, which at times were as low as a dollar a day, and seem never to have been over $1.75 a day—rates below those paid on the main line twelve or fifteen years before. To a considerable extent contractors were responsible for these conditions, but the Canadian Pacific had to shoulder its share of the blame.

The North-West Mounted Police were responsible for law and order east of the Rockies, and by arrangement with the government of British Columbia their jurisdiction was extended to the whole of the line. Cases of desertion and of nonpayment of wages by contractors were fairly frequent; there was some violence in the camps and occasionally a murder. But most of the problems of the police were caused by those seeking to relieve the workmen of the little they could save after paying their board—"illicit whisky vendors, gamblers, thieves and prostitutes, all bent upon fleecing the poor railway man of his hard earned gains."[19] Owing to the Klondike gold rush, the Mounted Police were shorthanded, and there were never more than a dozen officers on duty along the line. All expenses of the force while it acted in British Columbia were met by the Canadian Pacific.

Poor weather delayed construction somewhat, but the line was completed in remarkably quick time. The last rail was laid, without ceremony, on October 7, 1898, only fifteen months after grading had begun. Within a year coal mines and sawmills were in operation in several localities, and the traffic for which Van Horne had hoped began to develop.

Before the Crowsnest Pass line was in operation, the Canadian Pacific had begun construction of another segment of its line through to the coast. British Columbia had agreed to give Heinze's Columbia and Western Railway the usual provincial subsidy of 20,000 acres of land per mile, and in May 1898 the government agreed to extend the time limit within which the subsidy could be earned. Using the Columbia and Western charter, the C.P.R. then began to build from Robson to Midway, a distance of about a hundred miles. Here the chief construction problems were a high-level bridge over the Kettle River and a 3,000-foot tunnel through the summit of the Monashee Mountains. The tunnel took the better part of a year to bore, but the line was completed in November 1899.

Mining activity was moving westward, and this Columbia and Western extension took the railway to Grand Forks and Greenwood, in the heart of this new activity. There, in the boundary country, Hill and the Canadian Pacific would clash anew in the first decade of the new century.

15

Land Grant Problems

Prompt settlement of the Canadian West was vital to the Canadian Pacific; its financial success would depend upon the traffic that settlement would generate. Sir Alexander Campbell, Sir John Macdonald's law partner, who had some doubts about the C.P.R., emphasized this point when the contract with the company was debated in the Senate. "I should rather be disposed to consider that the construction of the railway was not the greatest part of their undertaking," he said. "They have undertaken, in addition to constructing the railway, to people a continent. If they do not send settlers in very large numbers into the Northwest, it is impossible that the [subsidy] lands could be of any value, and the railway would be less than valueless: it would be an insupportable burden."[1]

No one was more aware of this than George Stephen. At the time the contract was approved, he was already in England making the first of several attempts to persuade the British government to embark upon an assisted emigration scheme, with the Irish especially in mind. He even entertained some hope that migration might be linked to a loan that would help finance the building of the railway. He still expected construction costs to be no more than about $45 million, $30 million of which had been provided by the cash subsidy and an initial sale of stock. Writing to W. E. Forster, secretary of state for Ireland, he suggested that if the British government would advance the £3 million "which the C.P.R. Co. have still to provide for the completion and equipment of their line, the Coy might undertake to spend a sum of £150,000 or more annually during the next ten years in building houses for emigrants, cultivating portions of the soil, so as to have the land ready for sowing on the settlers' arrival, and selling the freehold to him at a nominal price. . . ."[2] But neither then nor later did the British government agree to participate in an emigration scheme.

When it gave the land grant of 25 million acres to the Canadian Pacific, the government was following an American precedent that the United States was just abandoning. Federal grants totaling over 131 million acres had been allocated to American railways, the largest of which, some 46 million acres, had been made to the Canadian Pacific's erstwhile rival, the Northern Pacific.[3] But the Canadian grant differed in several important respects from American practice. It was not given on a mileage basis; it provided a fixed acreage, regardless of the length of the line, and is said to have been unique on the continent in this respect. When the directors decided to adopt a shorter southern route, the company therefore suffered no loss of land. Much more important, the company was not obliged to accept any areas that consisted "in a material degree of land not fairly fit for settlement." This proviso, which attracted little attention at the time but was much criticized later, did not originate with the C.P.R. The charter given in 1873 to the company headed by Sir Hugh Allan had stipulated that it would "not be bound to receive any lands . . . not of the fair average quality of the lands in the sections of the country best adapted to settlement." This clause was simply reworded and carried forward into the Canadian Pacific contract. It would appear to have been suggested in the first instance by the American associates with whom Allan had been in touch earlier, and who had had extensive experience with land grants. In the United States these had usually been limited to areas along the railways and had included all land, good, bad, and indifferent. It was to avoid the loss this entailed that the fitness provision had been insinuated into the Allan contract.

The lands selected by the Canadian Pacific had to be on the prairies, because the federal government did not control land in either Ontario or British Columbia. True, British Columbia agreed to reserve a "railway belt" forty miles wide along the route of the railway from the summit of the Rocky Mountains to tidewater, an area of over 10 million acres, but the C.P.R. declined to select any of its subsidy lands in this generally mountainous region. Much of the grant was expected to be along the main line and was to consist of "alternate sections of 640 acres each, extending back 24 miles deep, on either side of the railway" from Winnipeg to the Rockies. But even if all the land in this vast reserve had been available and acceptable, it would have yielded only about 10 million acres. As it happened, some of the land had already been alienated, some could be claimed by the Hudson's Bay Company, and some would be included in school reserves. When the Canadian Pacific had exercised its right to pick and choose and had rejected land judged not to be "fairly fit for settlement," it was thus certain that the greater part of the C.P.R. lands would have to be found elsewhere. Many acceptable extra sections could be selected along branch lines, but the deficiency would still be very substantial.

The contract provided for this contingency. The company could "with the consent of the Government, select . . . any tract or tracts of land [owned by the government] . . . as a means of supplying or partially supplying such deficiency," but at first no one suspected the extent to which this provision would have to be invoked. Nor is it likely that Stephen and his associates realized for a time how profoundly it would affect the Canadian Pacific's land activities, which they expected (except in certain townsites) to be relatively short-term. Stephen looked to the land grant for immediate help to meet the C.P.R.'s two most pressing needs—money to build the railway and settlers whose produce and requirements would provide it with traffic and revenue. The money he would secure by mortgaging the grant and issuing land grant bonds, which would be deposited with the government and redeemed by land sales to the colonists Stephen expected to flock into the Canadian West. The subsidy lands were to be exempt from taxation until sold or for twenty years, and this probably reflects Stephen's opinion as to how long the company was likely to have a substantial interest in them. But if land had to be selected in huge tracts far away from any line the Canadian Pacific expected to build for many years, this time schedule would obviously be upset. Quite unexpectedly, land was to become a permanent preoccupation of the railway.

Both Stephen and the government remembered the brisk land sales the St. Paul, Minneapolis and Manitoba Railway had enjoyed in Minnesota, and they were hopeful that comparable sales could be secured in Canada. Policy was framed with traffic in mind, not a quick profit. The objective was to populate the prairies—to attract the individual settler and farmer and encourage him to develop his holding and stay on it. "It is *settling*, not *selling* that we must aim at . . . if our lands won't sell we will give them away to settlers," Stephen wrote in May 1881.[4] Initially land was offered at a flat rate of $2.50 per acre, payable over five years, with a rebate of half the purchase price if the property was under cultivation within four years. The Canadian Pacific hoped to avoid selling acreage to land companies that intended to hold it in expectation that it would appreciate in value; vacant property being held for someone else's profit brought no traffic to the railway.

The start of construction had touched off a spectacular real estate boom in Winnipeg and nearby regions, and to begin with land sales were encouraging. But complications soon developed. One was due to the great amount of government-owned land, which included most of the alternate sections in the railway belt. This was available under the terms of the Homestead Act of

Some of the two million immigrants who flocked to Canada in the seven years preceding the First World War amusing themselves on the foredeck of the first *Empress of Britain*. (COURTESY OF THE PUBLIC ARCHIVES OF CANADA)

1872, and settlers were not likely to buy land from the Canadian Pacific, even on easy terms at $2.50 per acre, if they could take up a homestead of 160 acres free of charge. On this prospect the C.P.R. had mixed feelings. Settlers on government land were as likely to produce traffic as any others, and as the government lands filled up those of the railway would increase in value; but this was small comfort to the Canadian Pacific's hard-pressed treasury. In spite of this, the railway promoted and advertised the government's lands along with its own and never disguised the fact that the homesteads were free.

Although applications for land from "private settlers" had totaled about 360,000 acres by November 1881, Stephen soon felt obliged to negotiate with several land companies. A $10 million issue of land grant bonds for which he had high hopes had not sold sufficiently well to encourage the offering of further issues. In 1882, to bolster both bond and land sales, the Canadian Pacific encouraged the organization of the Canada Northwest Land Company, an Anglo-Canadian corporation that proposed to purchase 5 million acres of land in the main line reserve at the price of three dollars per acre and to pay for them with land grant bonds; the latter were available at a discount and could be applied to land purchases at 110. But it soon became apparent that the scheme was overly ambitious, and within a year or so the Canada Northwest land purchase had to be scaled down to 2.2 million acres.

Governments move slowly, and it took time to survey and allocate specific sections in the land reserve. Until this was done the railway could not know precisely what it had to sell. By January 1882, however, the Canadian Pacific was already satisfied that it would not find more than 6 million acres of acceptable land in the main line reserve. (In the end the total turned out to be no more than 5,255,870 acres.) Later in the year, as the government had begun to dispose of large tracts to land companies and was beginning to make land grants with some freedom to other railways, the Canadian Pacific felt that it had to safeguard its interests and asked that reserves be established within which the balance of the 25 million acres to which it was entitled could be selected. The government agreed, and in October and November two reserves were set aside. One, the so-called first northern reserve, was an immense tract between latitudes 52 and 54, extending roughly from Saskatoon to the Rockies. The other, known as the southern reserve, lay between the international boundary and the main line and extended from the western boundary of Manitoba to the Coteau hills, a distance of about 150 miles.

The Canadian Pacific had lost no time in launching a vigorous campaign to encourage immigration and land sales. John McTavish, who had been in the service of the Hudson's Bay Company and was familiar with the country, was appointed land commissioner, and a little later Alexander Begg became the C.P.R.'s general emigration agent in Great Britain. Advertisements, press releases, pamphlets, posters, and maps were distributed widely and were supplemented with lectures and exhibitions. Here again, little or no distinction was made between the railway's lands and those owned by the government.

In 1883 Stephen was still endeavoring to interest the British government in an assisted emigration scheme, with a migration from Ireland to Canada the immediate objective. First contacts were promising, but Gladstone, the prime minister, was opposed to such schemes on principle and the negotiations came to nothing. Before they were concluded Stephen's enthusiasm seems to have waned somewhat. Memories of the Fenian troubles were still fresh; Sir John Macdonald had not forgotten the murder of D'Arcy McGee, a member of his first cabinet, in 1868. In a letter to Macdonald, Stephen remarked that the Irish were "a doubtful lot at best,"[5] and Macdonald was still more outspoken: "*Entre nous*, we don't want the Western Irish emigration. They are bad settlers and thoroughly disloyal. It won't do to have a little Ireland in the North West. I look forward with considerable apprehension to Fenian intrigues between our Irish and Yankee Irish. . . ."[6]

The promotional effort was not confined to Europe. Many of the newcomers in the West were from the old provinces of Canada and a considerable number came from the United States. At the end of three years, results appeared to be fairly promising. By the end of 1883, 794,240 acres had been sold to individual settlers and 2,837,400 (including the 2.2 million acres sold to the Canada Northwest Land Company) to corporations, a total of 3,631,640 acres. The average selling price had been $2.85 an acre. Including $178,864 from townsites (of which more later), sales had totaled $10,378,900. After deducting deferred payments and expenses, the net revenue, devoted to the redemption and cancellation of land grant bonds, was $6,667,000.

It was a return the like of which the Canadian Pacific was not to look upon again for a considerable time. Beginning in 1884 a succession of crop failures afflicted the prairies. The climate entered a dry cycle, and drought caused much of the damage. A severe August frost in 1885 ruined the crop that year. Immigration fell off sharply, and until the last years of the century more people left Canada than came to it. A depression developed that seemed to be lifting in 1892, but became worse than ever following the acute financial crisis in the United States in 1893. The cumulative effect of these conditions on land sales and western settlement was devastating. In the seven years from 1889 to 1895 the Canadian Pacific's net receipts from land averaged less than $50,000, and in 1891 they fell to just over $14,000. Cancellations were numerous, and in spite of the company's efforts, net sales in the main line reserve to December 31, 1896, totaled only 3,623,066 acres, or slightly less than they had been thirteen years before. Moreover, the transfer of 2.2 million acres to the Canada Northwest Land Company accounted for 60 percent of this total. Some comfort could be drawn from the fact that almost all the rest of the land had been sold to individual settlers, 5,770 of whom had been placed on company land.[7]

Townsites had offered special problems because they promised to be particularly profitable to land speculators. A. B. Stickney, the C.P.R.'s first superintendent of western lines, and General Rosser, the first chief engineer, had been dropped by the company because they had become involved personally in land deals. Van Horne's first act when he took over as general manager was to let it be known that in future, townsites would be chosen by the railway, by it alone, and "without regard to any private interest whatever."[8]

Two months later the government lent its assistance by temporarily with-

A first home and a first cash crop on the prairies at the beginning of the century: a house built of sods and the buffalo bones that Van Horne encouraged the settlers to gather. The price varied from five to eight dollars a ton. (COURTESY OF THE PUBLIC ARCHIVES OF CANADA)

drawing from sale or homesteading its alternate sections in the first mile on either side of the Canadian Pacific's right-of-way. This created a reserve two miles wide within which townsites could be located without interference from speculators. Cooperation between company and government was soon carried a step further. When the Canada Northwest Land Company was formed, the C.P.R. agreed to turn over to it townsites between Manitoba and the Rockies, on the understanding that the railway would receive half the net revenue from sales. The government followed suit by turning over the management of its alternate sections to the same group, as trustees.

Forty-seven townsites were involved in this transaction. Generally speaking, the smaller towns were located on the railway's sections, but those expected to become larger centers were usually on both C.P.R. and government lands. This was true, for example, of Regina and Moose Jaw. Lauchlan A. Hamilton, the Canadian Pacific's assistant land commissioner, was responsible for the surveys of these larger towns, and the first plans of Regina, Moose Jaw, Swift Current, and Medicine Hat were all prepared under his direction. The first Calgary subdivision was the work of A. W. McVittie, a dominion land surveyor. Although the C.P.R. was anxious to secure revenue from townsite sales, there is little to suggest that prices were unreasonable. Turner Bone, who attended the first sale in Calgary, noted that corner lots sold for $450 and inside lots for $300. Terms were one-third down with the balance payable in two annual instalments. A rebate of 50 percent was allowed if a building was erected on the property and occupied by a specified date.[9]

Vancouver, the new terminal city that the Canadian Pacific was virtually creating on Burrard Inlet, proved to be the most profitable of all the townsites. The C.P.R. land grant included most of what is now the main business district of the city, on the peninsula between the harbor and False Creek. L. A. Hamilton carried out the first survey of the area in 1885. It was heavily forested, and clearing operations began early in 1886. By June parts of the townsite were dotted with pyramids of logs, stumps, and roots, but many of the trees lay where they had fallen, "tumbled, one upon another . . . in a vast tinderous mass, twenty feet thick of branches, moss, punk, pitch, and leaves drying in the hot summer sun; an ideal setting for a gigantic fire."[10] On June 13 a clearing fire got out of control and within an hour had wiped out the beginnings of the new city and the adjoining older townsite of Granville.

Grain elevators standing in line along the Canadian Pacific track at Barons, Alberta, a typical scene on the Canadian prairies. (COURTESY OF THE CANADIAN DEPARTMENT OF AGRICULTURE)

Fortunately for the railway, only a beginning had been made on its terminal facilities and the loss was slight. The city recovered with amazing rapidity; within three years its population was approaching 10,000.

The agreement with the government of British Columbia for the land grant had been made early in 1885, when the Canadian Pacific was desperate for ready money, and Van Horne had made it clear that funds to develop the terminus would have to come from the sale of lots. And come it did, in surprising quantity. Total townsite sales in the West to the end of 1888 totaled $1,399,327. Of this, $868,059 was derived from sales in Vancouver. From the proceeds Van Horne was able to build not only the first Hotel Vancouver, a makeshift rail terminal, and a wharf for the trans-Pacific steamers, but also the Banff Springs Hotel.

The huge task of selecting the lands to which the company was entitled continued to trouble both the Canadian Pacific and the government. It had been complicated in 1886, when the C.P.R. arranged to reduce its indebtedness to the government by scaling down the land grant by 6,793,014 acres, at a valuation of $1.50 an acre. The railway assumed that the unlocated portion of the land grant of 25 million acres would simply be reduced by that amount, but the government contended that the acreage to be returned must be found in C.P.R. reserves that had already been set aside. In the end the latter view prevailed and a substantial part of the first northern reserve, which included a large amount of excellent land, reverted to the government.

This reduced the basic land grant to 18,206,986 acres, but it was supplemented from other sources. Mention has already been made of the subsidy lands totaling nearly 1.4 million acres that were received through the leasing and extension of the Manitoba South Western Railway. The Souris branch, running southwest from near Brandon and reaching the Souris coal fields, which became an important source of fuel for Winnipeg, brought the railway land grants of just over 1.6 million acres. Far to the west, the Columbia and Kootenay Railway, which the C.P.R. leased in 1891, was entitled to a provincial grant of 190,000 acres, while the British Columbia Southern and the Columbia and Western, both parts of the Crowsnest Pass route to the coast, were between them entitled to over 5 million acres in British Columbia.

The difference of opinion over the reduction of the grant arranged in 1886 took some years to resolve. It had worried George Stephen and it caused Van Horne much concern after he became president. "I am anxious beyond expression about this question," he wrote to Sir John Macdonald in January 1890, a few months before the matter was settled.[11]

In his annual report, Van Horne stated that "all questions relating to the original grant, and to the grants subsequently made to the various branch lines have been fully and satisfactorily disposed of, and the Company is now in a position to select in favourable localities the remainder of its lands." But this statement proved to be far too optimistic. The grants to the Manitoba South Western and the Souris branch had accentuated the selection problem because, as in the case of the main line, much of the acreage to which they entitled the Canadian Pacific could not be found along or near their rights-of-way.

This caused the railway to take another look at the area in the western prairies between Swift Current and the Rockies in which it had as yet accepted no land. This was the region about which John Macoun had given enthusiastic reports when the switch to a southern route was under consideration, but it had become evident that his impressions had been based on visits that happened to be made during seasons when rainfall had been abnormally heavy. Van Horne had serious doubts about the suitability of the area for raising grain, and in 1883–84 the Canadian Pacific had established ten experimental farms along 350 miles of its line west of Moose Jaw to test its capabilities. On the whole the results were not reassuring. In subsequent years, however, various private interests, including the Mormon colony in what is now southern Alberta, had experimented to some extent with irrigation, and results were sufficiently promising to prompt the government to pass the North-West Irrigation Act in 1894. They also encouraged the C.P.R. to consider the possibility of diverting water from the Bow River to irrigate lands along its line east of Calgary. Irrigation would obviously be feasible only in a compact block of land, not in a scattered grant consisting of alternate sections, and Parliament duly authorized this change in the subsidy conditions.

Van Horne thereupon agreed to accept a block west of Medicine Hat in the expectation that irrigation could be provided eventually. Later, as part of the final settlement of the main line land grant that was arrived at in 1903, twenty-two years after it had been sanctioned by Parliament, this block was relocated and enlarged to nearly 3 million acres. The Canadian Pacific then undertook an expensive and extensive irrigation scheme that was to bring the company much credit but little profit.

The search for sufficient land "fairly fit for settlement" led to the designation of two additional, relatively small reserves in 1895. One was west of Lake Dauphin, in Manitoba; the other, a second northern reserve, was east and northeast of Edmonton. Each comprised about 400,000 acres. At one time Van Horne hoped to build branch lines that would reach some at least of the northern areas where the company was coming into possession of extensive land holdings, but the depression of the 1890s made construction out of the question.

Through all the ups and downs of its land dealings in its first decades, the

Canadian Pacific never lost sight of its prime objective—to see individual settlers established on properties along its main and branch lines. When financial considerations compelled it to revise its land prices and deal with land companies, it still kept the individual carefully in mind. The price advanced to $5.00 an acre, but the down payment of $1.25 became the full price if the land was under cultivation within five years. In effect the price to the speculator, who intended to hold the land for a capital gain, was thus four times that charged to the settler who developed his holding. And when hard times came, the company did everything possible by means of postponed payments and canceled interest to enable the prairie settler to remain on his property.

Thus far the land grant had failed to fulfil to any degree the hopes and expectations of Stephen and his associates, as regards either revenue or settlement. James Hedges, whose detailed study of Canadian Pacific land policies must be anyone's prime source of information, points out that "in the main, the period which closed in 1896 was void of results at all commensurate with the effort and means employed. It was a discouraging business, this settling of a frontier country." But the railway would "stand or fall, prosper or decline with the settlement and development of its country, and there could be no turning back."[12]

Fortunately, better times were coming. Late in 1896 it became evident that the depression was lifting. Land sales doubled in 1897; by 1899 they were almost five times the 1896 figure.

16

The End of Monopoly in the West

In June 1899 Van Horne retired as president of the Canadian Pacific and assumed the newly created position of chairman. Over the years the relative influence of the chairman and the president of the C.P.R. has been a matter of inclination and personality. Van Horne chose to defer to Thomas Shaughnessy, his successor as president. For a time he was still the leading figure in the company in the eyes of the public, but Shaughnessy quickly became the power within the corporation, as Van Horne intended. Van Horne himself gradually diverted much of his attention to other interests, notably the building of railways in Cuba. He had the highest regard for the new president, and when he retired from the chairmanship in 1910, he told the shareholders that he felt his greatest service to the Canadian Pacific "was in being instrumental in inducing Sir Thomas Shaughnessy to come to Canada."[1]

Some mystery surrounds Van Horne's decision to step down. He was only fifty-six and as vigorous as ever. D. C. Coleman, one of his successors as president, suggested in later years that Lord Mount Stephen and James J. Hill, business associates in the Great Northern Railway, were in part responsible. Stephen, he thought, had lost confidence to some degree in Van Horne. Hill, "who always preserved friendly personal relations with those in exalted positions, did not hesitate to undermine the position of one who had thwarted some of his cherished plans."[2] Sensing the change in atmosphere, Van Horne was big enough to retire, because he felt that it would be in the best interests of the Canadian Pacific if Shaughnessy took over.

Temperament was probably the deciding factor. Van Horne was a pioneer and a builder. He enjoyed battling against difficulties; if the odds were heavily against him, his gambling instincts strengthened his determination to struggle on. He had built the main line in an incredibly short time and with Shaughnessy's help had brought the company safely through a major depression that many feared would cause it to collapse financially. (O. D. Skelton suggested that "it was a greater achievement to operate the Canadian Pacific successfully than to build it.")[3] By 1899 the country and the company were flourishing. The new kind of challenge this presented was one that appealed to Shaughnessy more than it did to Van Horne.

Shaughnessy's approach to business matters was shrewd, logical, and realistic. Boundlessly ambitious for the Canadian Pacific, he nevertheless saw to it that contingency plans were always in readiness to meet any setback that might occur. There was a touch of the martinet in his makeup, though stories that suggest this are often capable of other explanations. One of them contends that he would not allow an employee to ride with him in an elevator. This was true, but the reason sprang from the precision with which he planned his movements; an elevator was expected to be standing by when he entered the lobby of Windsor Station, ready to take him instantly to his office on the second floor. Though kind and generous, as countless actions showed, his highly strung nature and quick Irish temper prompted biting remarks and harsh criticisms that were not readily forgotten. To quote D. C. Coleman a second time: "He sometimes appeared to feel that railway officers responded best to rough treatment. Occasionally he rebuked them in scolding terms in the presence of their own subordinates and their friends, forgetting that a wound so administered is one that heals slowly."[4]

Van Horne was gregarious; Shaughnessy kept much more to himself. Murray Gibbon remarked upon a small point that illustrates how the two men differed: "Van Horne was a poker player; Shaughnessy preferred Napoleon's favourite card game of solitaire, on which he spent many an evening, thinking out incidentally the problems that came before him day after day in connection with the Canadian Pacific enterprise."[5]

Van Horne regarded the legacy that he turned over to Shaughnessy with justified pride and satisfaction. He had said as much to the shareholders at the annual meeting in the spring of 1898: "An analysis of the traffic of the various sections of the main line, the branch lines, and the auxiliary services on the sea, lakes and rivers, shows that practically no mistakes have been made in the development of the system so far as we have gone. Some things have had to be done ahead of time in order to protect our future, and we have had to wait for a good many vacant spaces on our lines to become productive, but nearly all these spaces are now yielding revenue and practically all of our branch lines are self-supporting."[6]

Thomas G. Shaughnessy (later Lord Shaughnessy) in 1903, when he had already been president of the Canadian Pacific for four years. He held the office from 1899 to 1918 and was chairman from 1918 to 1923. (COURTESY OF THE PUBLIC ARCHIVES OF CANADA)

In the next fifteen years Shaughnessy was to expand the system beyond Van Horne's imagining, for he took over in the early stages of a boom that was to develop into one of the longest periods of sustained economic expansion ever known. With a single break in 1907—much more severe in the United States than in Canada—it was to last until 1913. During these years the migration from Europe to North America that had been building up for several decades reached its climax and immigrants crossed the Atlantic literally by the millions. For many new arrivals, Canada had hitherto been merely a staging point on the way to the United States; after 1898 those who stayed were substantially more numerous than those who left the country. Tens of thousands of them found their way to western Canada. There they were joined by other thousands who came from the United States, where good land was becoming scarce, and by still other thousands who came from central and eastern Canada. Two new provinces—Saskatchewan and Alberta—were created in 1905, between Manitoba and the Rocky Mountains. The population of the whole prairie region, only 419,000 in 1901, tripled in the next ten years, and by 1921 there would be over 2.5 million people in Canada west of Ontario.

This great influx had been encouraged by the Hon. Clifford Sifton, the able and immensely energetic minister of the interior in the Laurier cabinet, who was responsible for immigration, but the Canadian Pacific contributed substantially to the effort to attract settlers to the West. Over a long period of years it spent more than the government of Canada on the promotion of immigration and settlement and it had a more active staff of agents in both Europe and the United States.

Traffic, of course, was the objective the railway had in view, and to promote and sustain settlement it was prepared to build branch lines. "Railways," as W. A. Mackintosh aptly expressed it, "and continually improving transportation were as essential as rain and sun to progressive settlement on the Canadian prairie."[7] Sometimes the railway would be first on the scene; at other times the settlers would take up land in an area through which they were reasonably certain that a branch line would soon be built. Over the years a rough-and-ready rule grew up that governed the spacing of many branches. Through dire necessity farmers sometimes hauled grain fifty miles or more to a railway, but in horse and wagon days it had not usually been economically feasible to haul it much more than ten miles, or fifteen at the most. As a consequence the complicated grid of lines that sprang up in the grain-growing areas in the first third of the century consisted in great part of branches that were seldom more than twenty miles apart. Conversely, the grain-growing areas were of necessity near the railways. Settlers on more distant farms might grow grain, but they used it to feed cattle and hogs; in Mackintosh's words, this was "a means of condensing field crops to transportable bulk."[8] The sharp increase in livestock shipments on the Canadian Pacific, which grew at the rate of about 100,000 head a year, shows that it was widely practised.

Another factor that influenced railway construction was the development of new strains of wheat that were better suited to climatic conditions on the prairies. The short growing season demanded a wheat that ripened early; in addition one was required that was resistant to disease, notably to rust. Red Fife had been the favored variety at the turn of the century, but it was succeeded by the famous Marquis wheat, first grown in quantity in 1909. Marquis ripened a week or more earlier than Red Fife, and this made it possible to extend the wheat-growing region considerably farther north—so far, in fact, as

In 1899 the C.P.R. built three high-speed Atlantics—the only engines of the type ever owned by the company—to compete on the Montreal-Ottawa run with Atlantics operated by the Canada Atlantic Railway. Note the immense 84-inch drivers.

to be beyond the reach of the Canadian Pacific's main line and the branches that would normally spring from it. This offered an opportunity that the infant Canadian Northern Railway was quick to exploit.

The Canadian Northern was able to take advantage of another circumstance—the great unpopularity of the Canadian Pacific on the prairies, particularly in Manitoba and among the farmers. Van Horne's insistence that storage and shipping facilities for grain should be provided by elevators was undoubtedly wise, but the rigidity with which the policy was applied quickly gave rise to resentment and opposition. Many of the elevator operators conveniently forgot the "fair and reasonable rates" they were expected to charge; where only one elevator existed at a station they were in a position to force down prices, to their own profit. The railway in effect supported their monopoly by its ban on the construction of flat warehouses and its refusal to allow grain to be loaded directly from wagons to cars.

By 1899 discontent had reached such a pitch that the federal government appointed a Royal Commission to study and report upon the grain trade. Its findings led to the passing of the Manitoba Grain Act, which defined weight and grade standards and gave farmers the right to load grain into freight cars through flat warehouses or directly from wagons if they so chose. But cars could not be loaded unless they were available, and the railway was accused of favoring the elevators by so arranging matters that cars for direct loading were few and far between.

To make matters worse, the grain crop was increasing faster than the Canadian Pacific's ability to handle it; 1901 is remembered as a year in which there was an acute shortage of cars. For this the C.P.R. was not really to blame. It had added over 3,000 freight and cattle cars to its rolling stock since the end of 1898 and had as many more on order as manufacturers could deliver. But this was small comfort to farmers who had difficulty in disposing of their crops. It was in this critical year of 1901 that the Territorial Grain Growers' Association came into being, the first successful effort to organize the farmers with a view to making their influence felt in the sale and handling of grain. Cooperative marketing and cooperative ownership of elevators soon became features of the prairie scene.

The Canadian Pacific handled its relations with the farmers badly; it enjoyed a monopoly over vast areas and its agents were apt to be arrogant. Many of them were from other parts of the country and had little understanding of the region and its problems. In 1904, when Shaughnessy became fully aware of the state of affairs, he sent William Whyte—popular, able, and intimately acquainted with the prairies—back to Winnipeg as western superintendent. Matters soon began to improve, but immense damage had been done. The hostility generated against the company has never entirely disappeared and has influenced public policy on railway matters on many occasions.[9]

It had an immediate effect upon the building of new railways on the prairies. The great influx of new settlers made the construction of additional lines essential, and there was a widespread desire that they should not all be built by the Canadian Pacific. At the federal level, the C.P.R. had always been associated in the public mind with the Conservative party; Sir Wilfrid Laurier and his Liberal followers welcomed the prospect of promoting railways that they could call their own. In Manitoba the government and people were eager to see the Canadian Pacific faced with strong competition.

Mackenzie and Mann and their fledgling Canadian Northern Railway were quick to take advantage of this situation. At first their activities had not caused the C.P.R. much concern; it had even lent its young rival a helping hand from time to time. But Mackenzie and Mann had much more in mind than a few lines forming a feeder system for the Canadian Pacific.

Their first major objective was a track to Thunder Bay that would breach the monopoly of the C.P.R. and enable them to participate independently in the movement of western grain to the Great Lakes. The government of Manitoba aided this project in several important ways. It facilitated the taking over of the Manitoba South Eastern Railway, between Winnipeg and the Lake of the Woods. It went so far as to help finance the part of the extension of this line to Thunder Bay that was in the province of Ontario. It also leased the Northern Pacific and Manitoba Railway, which the parent Northern Pacific was glad to shed, and immediately turned it over to Mackenzie and Mann, thus enabling the Canadian Northern to gain control of over 300 miles of branch lines in southern Manitoba. It had declined to lease the railway on more favorable terms to the Canadian Pacific—clear evidence that the end in view was competition with the C.P.R.

By the last days of 1902, the Canadian Northern had a through line to Port Arthur in operation. Its completion was a shock to the Canadian Pacific but delighted the farmers. The Canadian Northern increased its popularity further by reducing freight rates, including the rates on grain that had been set in the Crow's Nest Pass Agreement between the Canadian Pacific and the federal government. These reductions the C.P.R. had no alternative but to match.

The second objective Mackenzie and Mann had in mind was nothing less than a transcontinental railroad. As early as 1901 they had applied for charters that would empower them to extend their lines eastward to Quebec and westward to the Pacific Coast. Nor were they alone in this ambition. The new century had no more than begun when it became apparent that the Grand Trunk wanted to expand into western Canada. Charles M. Hays, general manager of the Grand Trunk since 1896, had pulled the railway out of the doldrums and had become convinced, like Edward Watkin forty years earlier, that the way to greater prosperity lay in expansion. Hays's first proposal was to build a line from the Grand Trunk's existing terminus at North Bay, in northern Ontario, to the Pacific Coast. A much less expensive plan would have been to link the Grand Trunk system in eastern Canada with the Canadian Northern lines in the West, and an effort was made to bring this about. Some preliminary sparring took place between Hays and William Mackenzie, but each was too much wrapped up in his own ambitions to be willing to agree to a joint enterprise. Laurier tried to bring them together but without success.

In retrospect it is clear that Laurier should have insisted on a merger of some kind; had he done so, it is probable that the combined enterprise would still be in existence today as a privately owned railway. But the matter was bedeviled by politics. Support in Quebec was vital to Laurier, and the Hays plan would have involved no construction in that province. A totally new far northern line from Quebec City westward to Winnipeg was therefore envisaged, and when New Brunswick made it clear that it was unhappy at being left out of the scheme, it was expanded to include a line from Quebec to Moncton. From the tangle of negotiations there emerged finally a two-fold plan: the Grand Trunk Pacific, a subsidiary of the Grand Trunk, would build westward from Winnipeg; the government itself would build a National Transcontinental Railway extending from Moncton to Winnipeg, which the Grand Trunk Pacific would operate upon completion. Independently, the Canadian Northern would pursue its own plans to expand to the Atlantic and the Pacific. Canada was enjoying unprecedented prosperity; confidence and optimism were at a high pitch; it was easy to assume that there was a viable future for two new transcontinental railways

These projects did not win unanimous approval. A. G. Blair, Laurier's minister of railways, resigned, and Clifford Sifton objected strenuously to the building of the National Transcontinental. Robert L. Borden, leader of the Conservative party, also opposed the agreement with the Grand Trunk. He turned to Shaughnessy for advice. One proposal that emerged from their discussion was that the government of Canada should purchase the Canadian Pacific line between North Bay and Thunder Bay and grant running rights over it to other railroads, a plan that would have avoided the necessity of building two new tracks through the wilderness north of Lake Superior. Borden advocated this plan in a notable speech in the House of Commons on August 18, 1903. Borden would have gone further and given competing railways running rights over the Canadian Pacific's line from Thunder Bay to Winnipeg as well. It seems very unlikely that Shaughnessy would have been willing to share the use of this highly lucrative line with the rival railways; he certainly cannot have approved Borden's additional suggestion that the government-owned Intercolonial Railway should be extended from Montreal to North Bay, whence running rights over the C.P.R. would carry it to Winnipeg. This, Borden contended, would "give the people control over rates." It would also "place the people in a position to own and operate their own line through the west to the coast, in case of oppressive rates. . . ."[10] Here we see the beginnings of Borden's advocacy of a publicly owned transcontinental railway, a proposal to which Shaughnessy was strongly opposed.

The Grand Trunk Pacific and the government were soon busy building the thousands of miles of railway provided for in their agreement. The Canadian Northern, by contrast, advanced piecemeal, using a considerable number of individual charters, each of which seemed to promise some local advantages. In the end, however, the two lines were completed within a few months of one another. The first through train to travel over the Grand Trunk Pacific from Winnipeg to its Pacific terminus at Prince Rupert completed its journey on April 9, 1914. The National Transcontinental line between Quebec and Winnipeg was opened on June 1. The last spike in the Canadian Northern's

This handsome example of the Canadian Pacific's huge fleet of ten-wheeler locomotives was built by the railway in its own shops in 1902. About a thousand of the type were acquired between 1889 and 1911. Note the steel cab with smoothly rounded corners that was characteristic of C.P.R. locomotives.

transcontinental line to Vancouver was driven in January 1915. By that time the boom had broken, the First World War was raging, and conditions were far different from those expected when the projects had been undertaken.

It was against this background that Shaughnessy carried through a vast program designed to expand and improve the Canadian Pacific. Some aspects of it—the purchase of steamers to provide a coastal service in British Columbia, the inauguration of the trans-Atlantic steamship service, land transactions, the irrigation project undertaken in southern Alberta, and the company's developing interest in mines and smelters—will be dealt with in subsequent chapters. Here we are concerned with the expansion of the rail system itself and with the second round of the C.P.R.'s bout with James J. Hill and the Great Northern Railway.

Major attention was devoted to the prairies, in response both to need and to competition, actual and prospective. The rapid spread of settlement required the construction of scores of branch lines, many of which served areas in which the C.P.R. had land for sale. When Shaughnessy became president in 1899, the Canadian Pacific had an even 7,000 miles of track in Canada. By 1913 the total had risen to 11,366 miles, and more than half of this mileage was in Manitoba, Saskatchewan, and Alberta. Some of the branches, in addition to serving local purposes, joined up with others to relieve the main line, on which traffic at times was very heavy. In this way alternative routes became available for most of the way between Calgary and Swift Current and from

Regina to Winnipeg. By the end of 1909 a through line from Winnipeg to Saskatoon and on to Wetaskiwin and Edmonton had been assembled in much the same fashion.

It was Shaughnessy who pushed the system northward. In addition to building branches, the C.P.R. leased several existing lines that it feared might fall into "unfriendly hands"—meaning those of Mackenzie and Mann. In 1900 the Manitoba North Western and Great North West Central railways, which had become important contributors of traffic, were acquired. In 1903 the Canadian Pacific leased the Calgary and Edmonton Railway, which it had operated since its completion, and to make possession doubly sure the C.P.R. soon purchased its capital stock. This was another defensive move against the Canadian Northern, which was making two great leaps westward and would complete lines to Edmonton in 1905 and to Prince Albert in 1906. In a surprising move, the Canadian Northern then acquired the line from Prince Albert and Saskatoon to Regina which the C.P.R. had been operating for English bondholders since 1890. Why the C.P.R. relinquished it is a mystery; it was just beginning to pay and its location gave it considerable potential. A good many years were to pass before Canadian Pacific trains would again run to Prince Albert.

Outside the prairie region, the most important new construction was in Ontario. Since 1888 Toronto-bound trains had left the C.P.R. main line at North Bay and had traveled south over a track owned by the Grand Trunk. The Canadian Pacific had always intended to build a line of its own, and accordingly a 226-mile branch south from Romford, near Sudbury, was completed in 1908. A few years later, pressure of traffic on the Toronto–Montreal line was relieved by the construction of the Agincourt–Glen Tay branch, which skirted the north shore of Lake Ontario and in addition to providing an alternative route brought Oshawa, Trenton, Belleville, and other cities within the C.P.R. orbit.

Throughout Shaughnessy's presidency, the C.P.R. was constantly leasing or otherwise acquiring local or regional railways that either promised to be useful as feeders or might prove troublesome if they fell under the control of the Canadian Northern or the Grand Trunk. As a rule they were leased for 99 or 999 years, with the annual rental fixed at a sum sufficient to pay the interest on the funded debt. In most instances the C.P.R. then proceeded, as opportunity offered, to buy the common shares and the securities it had guaranteed and in this way convert the lease into ownership. It also continued to acquire and use other charters to build branches when this was convenient. Thus the Agincourt–Glen Tay line, to which reference has just been made, was built nominally by the Campbellford, Lake Ontario and Western Railway and then leased to the Canadian Pacific.

Two important purchases a continent apart extended the system to Vancouver Island and Nova Scotia. In 1905 the Canadian Pacific bought the Esquimalt and Nanaimo Railway for a million dollars. Vancouver Islanders had hoped at one time that it would form part of a Canadian Pacific transcontinental line terminating at Esquimalt or Victoria. Instead it became the only railway enterprise in Canada to attract the support of Charles Crocker, Leland Stanford, and Collis P. Huntington, of Central Pacific fame. Robert Dunsmuir, owner of coal mines on the island, headed the company that the Americans helped to finance. The railway was completed to Nanaimo in 1886, and on August 13 Sir John Macdonald, who had just traveled westward from Ottawa over the Canadian Pacific, drove the last spike. By 1902 James Dunsmuir, son of Robert, was sole proprietor of the railway, and it was from him that it was purchased by the C.P.R.

In a separate transaction that was to prove highly profitable the Canadian Pacific bought the 1.4 million unsold acres of the land grant that the Dunsmuir road had received from the province of British Columbia. The railway itself was extended north and west; mileage increased from 78 to about 200. A general refurbishing included improved rolling stock and the replacement of a number of spectacular but aging timber trestles with embankments or steel bridges. The line carried large quantities of coal and forest products, and until bus services became well established, passenger traffic was heavy.

In 1910 the Canadian Pacific took steps to gain control of the Dominion Atlantic Railway in Nova Scotia. Its main line extended from Yarmouth, at the southern tip of the province, to Halifax by way of Digby.[11] The purchase included the Digby–Saint John steamer service across the Bay of Fundy that linked the Dominion Atlantic with the C.P.R.'s Short Line from Montreal. Here again, a refurbishing was in order, with better rolling stock and new bridges among the requirements. Both these railways, separated by water from the main Canadian Pacific system, continued to operate under their own names.

A third purchase, this time by a subsidiary in the United States, gave the C.P.R. an entry into Chicago from the West. The Soo Line had been expanding steadily in the area south and west of Lake Superior. In 1909 it acquired a majority of the common stock of the Wisconsin Central Railway and leased it for ninety-nine years. This in effect extended the Soo Line to Milwaukee and Chicago and complemented the eastern Chicago entry that Van Horne had secured earlier by cooperative arrangements with the Wabash and Michigan

Central. The Soo Line had already linked up at the Canadian border with the Pembina branch to Winnipeg, and the Wisconsin Central lease thus completed an alternative route from Winnipeg to eastern Canada south of the Great Lakes—the specter that George Stephen had feared so greatly in construction days—but under the Canadian Pacific's own auspices.

The expansion of the Soo Line did not please James J. Hill. After its first track to the Canadian border had been completed in 1893, he had built what became known as the "spite line" between Fargo and Minot, in North Dakota, which paralleled it much of the way. He reacted to the building of the link with the Pembina branch, which his own trains had been using to reach Winnipeg since 1879, by transferring them to the line on the other side of the Red River, which had come under the control of the Canadian Northern. This was not surprising, for at the time the Great Northern and the Canadian Pacific were once again battling one another in southern British Columbia.

By the turn of the century Hill had already pushed across the border at four points, with his own lines to Kootenay Lake and New Westminster and with those built by Corbin to Nelson and Rossland. He was now determined to secure a substantial share of the traffic generated by new mining developments in the southeastern part of the province. To accomplish this he was prepared to participate in mining itself. His first step was to secure control of the Crow's Nest Pass Coal Company, to which the Canadian Pacific had surrendered extensive coal lands under the tripartite agreement of 1897. To reach the mines he pushed a branch line north from Rexford, in Montana, that reached Morissey in 1903 and was subsequently extended to Fernie and other centers.

Nearly 200 miles farther west, in the boundary country, where rich copper mines were being developed, Hill purchased a substantial interest in the Granby Company, owner of much the largest of the three smelters in the region. All were served by the westward extension of the Canadian Pacific's Crowsnest Pass line. The C.P.R. did its best to check the spread of Hill's feeder lines but succeeded only in delaying them; for some years the Great Northern hauled great quantities of ore to the Granby smelter both from Canadian mines and from others in Washington State. A particularly long battle was fought over the traffic from the mines around Phoenix, high in the mountains northwest of Grand Forks. Here the C.P.R. succeeded in blocking the Great Northern's competing line for five full years, but as soon as it was completed, Hill was able to demand two thirds of the traffic and halved the freight rate for good measure.

Farther west again, Hill built still another branch up the Similkameen valley to tap new mines in the vicinity of Princeton. At the coast, since the Fraser River had been bridged at New Westminster, he took steps to extend his branch from New Westminster to Vancouver. This he succeeded in doing in 1908, in spite of strenuous, but rather pointless, opposition from the Canadian Pacific.

In one sector Shaughnessy planned a counter invasion of Hill's territory. D. C. Corbin had reappeared on the Kootenay scene, and in 1905 Shaughnessy reached an agreement with him for the construction of the Spokane International Railway, extending from Spokane to a junction with the C.P.R.'s Crowsnest Pass line. It was completed in 1906. Later the Canadian Pacific increased its interest in the company and in 1916 purchased it outright.

To facilitate north-south communication in the Kootenay, the C.P.R. used the charter of the Kootenay Central Railway to build a branch south from Golden, on its main line, to the Crowsnest Pass line, a distance of 260 miles. Completed in 1914, it was a useful addition, but no one could then have foreseen that it would in time become one of the most heavily traveled lines in the whole system, carrying millions of tons of coal each year for export to Japan.

Shaughnessy attached considerable importance to the completion of the projected southern line to the West Coast, which by 1899 had been built as far as Midway, west of Grand Forks. For this purpose he used the charter of the Kettle Valley Railway. Here again Hill contrived to get in the way of the C.P.R., for he had extended his Princeton branch some thirty-eight miles westward. Having built from Midway to Princeton, the Canadian Pacific was loath to duplicate this line. An exchange of running rights was arranged finally, and the C.P.R. filled in the fifty-two-mile gap between the end of Hill's branch and a junction with its own main line at Hope, on the Fraser River. This last section, through the Coquihalla Pass, completed in 1915, was the most difficult and costly part of the entire southern route. There are said to have been twenty-seven tunnels and trestles in a single mile. Though the scenery was spectacular, many people found the trip through the pass daunting. It may not have been entirely by chance that passenger trains were usually scheduled to go through it at night.

At one time Hill seems to have toyed with the idea of building a railway in Canada all the way from Manitoba to the West Coast. In 1905, in an address to the Canadian Club of Winnipeg, he announced that a line westward from the Crowsnest Pass would be completed within eighteen months. Nothing came of this, and his activity was confined to the branches tapping mines and smelters in British Columbia and a few that he pushed up to or across the border of Manitoba.

In course of time many of the mines that had attracted Hill to British Columbia became depleted, and as traffic fell off his interest declined with it.

He was always ready to cut losses and withdraw promptly from any unprofitable enterprise. The history of the Kaslo and Slocan Railway is interesting in this regard. Always a makeshift, narrow-gauge affair, within a few years it was not considered worth the cost of upkeep. It was devastated by slides and a forest fire in 1909-10 and was reduced to such a sorry state that the Great Northern sold the right-of-way and rolling stock for $25,000. Eventually the Canadian Pacific was persuaded to lend a hand. This it did by linking the least damaged, eastern part of the Kaslo and Slocan to its own Nakusp and Slocan Railway, converting it to standard gauge and refurbishing it generally. The result was a through line from Nakusp to Kaslo.

The Great Northern's duel with the Canadian Pacific was to a considerable extent Hill's personal affair. After his death in 1916 tempers cooled, and within a few years much of the Great Northern trackage in British Columbia, as well as lines leading to Brandon and Portage la Prairie in Manitoba, were being abandoned and torn up. Today all that survives in the West is the line to Nelson, part of the line to Princeton, and—much the most important of the three—the line to Vancouver.

The old captains of the transportation world were departing. Lord Strathcona, who as plain Donald Smith had played so important a role in supporting Stephen in construction days, died in January 1914 at the age of ninety-three —still in office as governor of the Hudson's Bay Company and as high commissioner for Canada in London. He had been a director of the Canadian Pacific since 1882, but for a good many years had been too much occupied with his duties in England to take any part in its affairs. In July 1915 Sir Sandford Fleming, who as the government's chief engineer had been responsible for the original Canadian Pacific surveys, and who had been a director since 1885, died at the age of eighty-eight. Two months later he was followed by Hill's doughty adversary, Sir William Van Horne, who had supervised the building of the main line and had nursed the railway through the critical years that followed its completion. With Hill's passing, only two survived of the little group that had taken over the St. Paul and Pacific in 1878 and had later become key figures in the Canadian Pacific syndicate—Lord Mount Stephen, living in retirement in England, and R. B. Angus, still active as a director and a member of the railway's executive committee.

17

Supremacy on Atlantic and Pacific

Many railroads have had shipping interests, but no other railway company ever developed services comparable in scope and scale to those of the Canadian Pacific. In spite of their number and diversity, each in its day was a logical and carefully integrated segment of the company's transportation system. The C.P.R.'s first shipping venture, already mentioned, was a good example of this. In the spring of 1884 three Clyde-built steamers, the best of their type then in service on the Great Lakes, were placed on the run between Owen Sound and Port Arthur. Initially they were intended to provide a link between eastern and western Canada pending the completion of the railway line north of Lake Superior, but they continued for many years to maintain a service that proved to be both profitable and popular with tourists. Its long years of success were marred by only one serious accident. On November 7, 1885, the day Donald Smith drove the last spike at Craigellachie, the *Algoma*, groping her way through heavy fog and off course, was wrecked on Ile Royale with the loss of forty-eight lives. She was replaced by the *Manitoba*, and in 1907, in Shaughnessy's day, two substantially larger steamers, the *Assiniboia* and the *Keewatin*, joined the fleet. The five ships must surely have set a record of some sort, for among them they maintained the service for no fewer than eighty-four seasons, until 1967, and all had individual and virtually blameless careers that lasted from sixty to sixty-three years.

The establishment of the *Empress* line from Vancouver to the Orient in 1891 gave Stephen and Van Horne great satisfaction. Stephen remarked to Sir John Macdonald that the *Empresses* would be "quite enough 'Navy' to begin with," but it was not in his nature to rest content with things accomplished. He was deeply concerned about the failure of the Andersons to provide the fast Atlantic service that had seemed assured at the time the *Empresses* were ordered in 1889, and he kept urging Macdonald to take steps to revive the project. Frequent and fast services from Canadian ports on both the Atlantic and Pacific were in his view essential for purposes of trade as well as for communication, and he wanted to see steamers plying between Vancouver and Australia as well as more frequent *Empress* sailings to the Orient.

Speed was a paramount consideration to Stephen; Van Horne viewed the shipping problem somewhat differently. Fast services were concerned primarily with the carriage of passengers and mail; Van Horne was more interested in better arrangements for freight. In October 1890, he reviewed the problem at some length in a private and confidential letter to Sir John Macdonald. The leading steamship services between Canada and Europe were then provided by the Allan and Dominion lines. Both were operating ships that Van Horne considered completely obsolete, but neither seemed anxious to rebuild its fleet. Both had traffic agreements with the Grand Trunk, and because of Stephen's advocacy of a fast Atlantic line, which neither favored, the C.P.R. had "not found it easy to secure a fair share of the traffic controlled by them." If, Van Horne wrote, they learned that the C.P.R. was also advocating a much better freight service, "they would probably go in exclusively with the Grand Trunk and deny us any part of their traffic." He continued:

> But a first class Canadian Atlantic freight line is of the greatest possible importance to the Dominion of Canada and to its railways—a line of the largest carriers, fitted for carrying water ballast when necessary, provided with the very best and most economical engines and steaming 11 or 12 knots—vessels such as will take across the Atlantic a given amount of freight at the least possible cost and such as will be able to make every day in the year at least as low rates across the Atlantic as prevail at the same time from and to New York, Boston, Philadelphia or Baltimore. We are enormously handicapped now. Our Canadian Atlantic rates are regulated from day to day not by the prevailing rates from New York but by the amount of freight offering here and at the very time when we are most in need of low ocean rates we usually find them the highest. Only for a comparatively few days in the year are our export rates as low as from New York or Boston and we have at times been compelled to send Canadian freight through Montreal to Boston or New York because of the high rates asked from Montreal. The difference in ocean rates puts the great bulk of the export freight from the western and northwestern States beyond our reach and a great part of that of Ontario as well. . . . Another disadvantage under which we labour is uncertainty as to cargo space at all times and as an illustration of this I may point to the situation at Montreal on the 5th of October last year when all the cargo space was taken up to the close of navigation putting us out of the export trade for nearly two months of the season of navigation.

It is necessary to the full development of our export trade that we should be able to count with certainty on cargo space and much more necessary that we should be able to count on practicable ocean rates at all times and as low rates as enjoyed by our American competitors.[1]

We see here principles and problems closely akin to those that led to the purchase of an Atlantic fleet in 1903, to the building of the *Beaver*-class freighters in 1928, and to the Canadian Pacific container ship service of the 1970s.

In 1893 a service to Australia materialized unexpectedly. James Huddart, general manager of Huddart, Parker and Company, an Australian shipping firm, had decided to branch out on his own and had built two 3,500-ton steamers for the intercolonial run between Australia and New Zealand. Owing to severe competition and the depression of the 1890s, the venture failed. Huddart thereupon negotiated a traffic agreement with the C.P.R. and operated the ships between Sydney and Vancouver. Subsidies to support the service were given by the governments of Canada and New South Wales. The first ship of this Canadian-Australian Line, the *Miowera* (soon to be dubbed the "Weary Mary"), arrived at Vancouver on June 9, 1893, and sailings were monthly thereafter. Small as the steamers were, they were more than adequate to handle the existing traffic, and Huddart's efforts to add a third steamer involved the line in financial difficulties. Its future was uncertain until 1901, when it was taken over by the Union Steam Ship Company of New Zealand. The service was always closely associated with the C.P.R., and the railway shared ownership with the Union Company for the last twenty-two of the sixty years the line existed.[2]

It was also in 1893 that the Canadian Pacific built the first of the many steamers, tugs, and car barges that it operated on the lakes and rivers in the southern interior of British Columbia; the useful way in which they supplemented rail lines has already been noted. The railway next became interested in services on the Pacific Coast. Soon after the transcontinental line was completed, Stephen was planning to run steamers from Vancouver and Victoria south to San Francisco, but funds were scarce and the necessary ships could not be acquired. He had to be content with services connecting Vancouver, Victoria, and Puget Sound, provided by the Canadian Pacific Navigation Company, the local concern that dominated the trade. The first coastal service operated by the C.P.R. itself came in 1898, when Van Horne hastily assembled a fleet in an effort to capture a share of the traffic arising from the Klondike gold rush, most of which was flowing through Seattle, to the profit of the Great Northern and the Northern Pacific. Two elderly liners that had spent

The *Lake Manitoba*, largest of the fifteen ships purchased by the Canadian Pacific when it entered the transatlantic trade in 1903.

their best years running between England and South Africa—the *Tartar* and the *Athenian*—were purchased to provide a service between Vancouver and Skagway, and a dozen wooden stern-wheelers were built to run from Wrangell, Alaska, up the Stikine River to Glenora, the starting point of a railway that Mackenzie and Mann proposed to push northward to Teslin Lake, in the Yukon. Neither venture succeeded. The liners were too large for existing traffic and they arrived too late; they were laid up after each had made only six trips to Skagway, and were later used on the Pacific, where they supplemented the service provided by the *Empresses*. The railway to Teslin Lake was never built and the stern-wheelers, most of which never saw the Stikine, were quietly disposed of during the next few years.

Despite this failure the C.P.R. continued to take a keen interest in the British Columbia coast. It had long been dissatisfied with the connecting services provided by the Canadian Pacific Navigation Company, and in 1894 had gone so far as to invest $221,000 in the construction of a fast steel paddle steamer, the *Prince Rupert*, for service between Vancouver and Victoria. But the friends of the C.P.N. (as it was known locally) objected to her coming with such vigor that she was not brought to the coast. Within a few years circumstances changed. The public that had risen to the defense of local enterprise in 1894 had by 1900 become highly critical of the services it was providing. New steamers were becoming essential, but no one showed any inclination to spend the money to build them. In January 1901, the C.P.R.

solved the problem by purchasing control of the C.P.N. It was an interesting acquisition, for the navigation company was the successor of the earliest shipping enterprise in the region. It was owned in part by the Hudson's Bay Company, which had employed sailing vessels in the coastal trade as early as 1827, and had brought the *Beaver*, the first steamer on the North Pacific Ocean, to the coast in 1836.

The C.P.N. was soon reconstituted as the British Columbia Coast Service of the Canadian Pacific Railway, and Captain J. W. Troup, who had built up the C.P.R.'s lake and river services, became manager. Under his guidance the coast service expanded rapidly. The fourteen-ship fleet of the C.P.N. consisted of a curious assortment of vessels, large and small; many were old and only a few relatively modern. Troup discarded most of them as opportunity offered and replaced them with the famous *Princess* steamers. (One of the oldest and best known of the C.P.N. fleet was the *Princess Louise*, and this suggested the substitution of the *Princess* prefix for the *Prince* the C.P.R. had used in 1894.) Most notable of the earlier steamers was the *Princess Victoria*, completed in 1903, and in her day the fastest ship on the Pacific Coast. Troup was ambitious, the C.P.R. was prospering, and Shaughnessy backed his plans for fleet

The amazing extent of the Canadian Pacific's stake in shipping is suggested by this advertising montage published about 1911. It includes all the ships then engaged in the company's ocean, coastal, lake, and river services. In 1911 the C.P.R. also owned the fifteen-ship Atlantic fleet of the Allan Line, not included in the picture.

The *Metagama*, one of the first of the eleven cabin-class liners built for the Atlantic service between 1914 and 1929.

expansion. The purchase price of the C.P.N. had been $531,000; by 1914 Troup had persuaded the company to invest ten times that sum in new coastal steamers. Eleven *Princesses* had been built and two purchased; services blanketed the coast and served scores of centers, large and small, all the way from Seattle to Skagway.

When the First World War broke out, two 6,000-ton, 23-knot steamers were being completed on the Clyde; they were larger and much faster than the original Pacific *Empresses* and may well have been the finest ships of their type afloat. Unfortunately, neither was ever to see the Pacific Coast. Both were requisitioned by the British Admiralty and converted into the Royal Navy's most efficient minelayers. One, full to the brim with mines, was totally demolished by an internal explosion; the other was bought by the Admiralty.[3]

Soon after the purchase of the Canadian Pacific Navigation Company, the matter of an Atlantic service came to a head. Shaughnessy was as concerned about freight as Van Horne had been, but he was also interested in better passenger and mail steamers. Several additional proposals for a faster service had been put forward, the latest in 1897, but nothing had come of them. By 1902 the C.P.R. was in a flourishing state, and Shaughnessy decided that the time had come when the company must have a service of its own. On July 24 he announced that the C.P.R. had offered to build four twenty-knot liners that would provide weekly sailings for an annual subsidy of £265,000 (about

$1,288,000), and that it was also prepared to build a fleet of cargo ships with a speed of twelve or thirteen knots. This was in effect Van Horne's 1890 freighter plan with a fast passenger and mail service superimposed upon it. No decision having been made by October, Shaughnessy informed his shareholders that, regardless of the outcome, the C.P.R. must take action: "The rapid growth of your export tonnage and the necessity for being in a position to meet the rates of any competitors, make it imperative that your Company be so situated on the Atlantic that it can quote through rates of freight and give through bills of lading without being compelled to negotiate for space and rates with independent steamship lines."[4]

He hoped to begin the service by purchasing one of the existing steamer lines, in order to avoid increasing competition in the Canadian trade, but his inquiries were not always taken seriously. Sir Alfred Jones, of the Elder Dempster Company, was ready to consider a sale, but Henry Allan, of the Allan Line, advised him not to let Shaughnessy "humbug" him; Shaughnessy, he wrote, "made similar overtures to us on several occasions, and it seems practically certain that he does not mean business."[5] But Shaughnessy did mean business. The C.P.R.'s bid for a fast service was not accepted, but in March 1903 the company bought the Canadian services of Elder Dempster and fourteen of the ships engaged in them for £1,417,500 (about $6,890,000); a fifteenth ship was added soon after. Shaughnessy had driven a hard bargain, as he recounted with obvious satisfaction to one of his directors: "It was like pulling teeth, but I finally got them down £250,000 below the price demanded at the time the Board gave authority to purchase. At the figure I think we have an excellent bargain and I shall be much disappointed if our Atlantic Service fail to be a link of very great value indeed in our system."[6]

Shaughnessy had made a shrewd purchase, and it is said that Sir Alfred Jones later deeply regretted the sale. None of the steamers acquired was more than a few years old, as Elder Dempster had just completed an extensive building program. Eleven of the fifteen ships were freighters, all but one with a carrying capacity of up to 10,000 tons, and they formed an outstanding cargo-liner fleet. The other four ships, basically similar, had been redesigned as passenger liners to maintain the old-established Beaver Line service, which Elder Dempster had taken over in 1899. Named *Lake Champlain, Lake Erie, Lake Michigan,* and *Lake Manitoba,* in accordance with Beaver Line nomenclature, they had accommodation for from 680 to 750 passengers, 100 or more of them in first class; their gross tonnage varied from 7,400 to 9,600. Freighters and *Lake* steamers alike had a speed of twelve to thirteen knots, but this had been sufficient to enable Elder Dempster to secure the Canadian mail contract in 1899.

Three services were soon established, one from Liverpool, maintained mostly by the *Lake* steamers, a second (soon discontinued) from Avonmouth, devoted mostly to cargo, and a third from London and Antwerp. On the Antwerp run the emigrant trade was important, and to cater to it some of the freighters were fitted with steerage accommodation. The first Canadian Pacific trans-Atlantic sailing was made by the *Lake Champlain*, which sailed from Liverpool painted in C.P.R. colors and flying the company's checkerboard house flag on April 14, 1903.

Faced with the prospect of severe competition from the new Elder Dempster ships, the Allan Line had been reorganized in 1899 and had set about rebuilding its antiquated fleet. Seven new ships were completed in only three years; two of them exceeded 10,000 tons, had a maximum speed of sixteen knots, and were the largest and fastest steamers yet built for service to Canada. Only weeks after the C.P.R. purchase, the Allans ordered two additional 10,000-ton liners, this time with a speed of eighteen knots, and they caused a sensation a few months later by announcing that they would be propelled by steam turbines—the first on the Atlantic.

These orders were prompted by the conviction that the Canadian Pacific would not be content for long with a passenger service offering nothing better than the rather Spartan accommodation and thirteen-knot speed of the *Lake*-class steamers. In so thinking, the Allans were quite correct. Late in 1904, while the Allan turbiners *Victorian* and *Virginian* were still fitting out, the C.P.R. ordered two first-class passenger ships, the *Empress of Britain* and the *Empress of Ireland*, which were intended to outstrip them in size, standards of accommodation, and, to a modest extent, speed. The *Empresses* were 550 feet in length, of 14,190 tons gross, and had a sea speed of eighteen to nineteen knots. They were not adventurous in design; seaworthiness and reliability that would enable them to maintain a schedule were the qualities the C.P.R. had chiefly in mind. This accounted for their heavy construction, high freeboard, and reciprocating engines—turbines had still to be tested in service. They were the largest and fastest ships sailing to Canada and the first steamers in the trade to be fully equal to all but the largest of the intermediate liners on the New York run. They were also the fastest ships that Shaughnessy felt could hope to make a profit without a substantial subsidy. They could carry a payload of 4,900 tons, yet were fast enough to capitalize on the fact that the distance from Liverpool to Quebec is appreciably shorter than that from Liverpool or Southampton to New York. A slower ship, much less costly to build and operate, could therefore match, or nearly match, the passage time of considerably faster vessels on the southern run. Through the years the Canadian Pacific traded consistently upon the advantage afforded by its shorter sea

The *Alsatian*, last of the Allan Line fleet, shown here after the First World War, when she had been renamed *Empress of France*. (COURTESY OF THE BRITISH COLUMBIA PROVINCIAL ARCHIVES)

route, and in 1931 a new twenty-four-knot *Empress of Britain* would rival the time of the twenty-seven-knot *Europa* and *Bremen*, sailing to New York.

From the beginning the C.P.R. gave special attention to third-class passengers. At a time when many companies still provided neither bedding nor dishes in steerage, the C.P.R. (in the words of an early advertisement) "supplied . . . all necessaries for the voyage free of charge. The Outfit consists of Bed, Pillow, Blanket, Plate, Drinking Cup, Knife, Fork and Spoon. . . ."[7] The *Empresses* set new standards that few other ships of the day could rival. Two thirds of their third-class passengers were accommodated in cabins instead of the more usual large dormitories, china tableware replaced metal pannikins, and meals were served in a large midship dining saloon with individual chairs instead of benches.

The steps by which the Allan Line and the C.P.R. drew together over the next few years are reasonably clear. Rumors soon went the rounds that the Allans intended to build two much larger and faster turbine liners, which would outclass the *Empresses*, but this proved to be beyond their financial means. This meant that the terms of their mail contract, which would require four eighteen-knot steamers to be in service by August 1907, could be met only by a subcontract with the C.P.R.; thereafter the *Empresses* shared a sailing schedule with the *Victorian* and *Virginian*. In 1908 the White Star Line and the Dominion Line, both of which had been taken over by the powerful New York-based International Mercantile Marine (the "Morgan Combine"), set about building two liners for the Canadian trade that would be a little larger, though slower, than the *Empresses*. The time seemed to have come when Canadian interests should draw together, and in secrecy that was remarkably well maintained for five or six years, the Allans and the Canadian Pacific negotiated a merger of their shipping interests. F. E. Meredith, a Montreal lawyer, acted for the C.P.R., and a formal agreement was signed on September 8, 1909, providing for the transfer of all shares owned by the Allan family. The purchase price was £1,709,000 ($8,305,000). By the following July the C.P.R. had picked up the rest of the stock and had complete control of the company.

Since Shaughnessy placed a high valuation on the popularity and good will of the Allan Line, it continued to operate under its own name and, so far as the general public was concerned, as a separate entity. Shipping men noted a few outward signs of amalgamation, notably the establishment of joint catering and maintenance staffs at Liverpool. The only break in official silence came in a statement by Shaughnessy at the meeting of the C.P.R. shareholders held in October 1913: "Your Atlantic fleet has, in recent years, been supplemented by the acquisition of eighteen steamships with a gross tonnage of 146,361. The earnings of these steamships have been utilized in reducing their cost to the Company, which now stands at about $2,750,000."[8] It will be noted that even here no mention was made of the Allan Line by name.

More remarkable still, the Allan identity was preserved when the C.P.R. embarked on the first large-scale expansion of its passenger fleet. This was in the last year before the First World War, the outbreak of which somewhat obscured the fact that by 1914 the Canadian Pacific had taken the leading position in ocean services to Canada on both the Atlantic and the Pacific.

Increased competition made new ships necessary on both oceans. In 1910 Mackenzie and Mann, anxious to rival the C.P.R. on every front, purchased two 11,000-ton liners that could rival the *Empresses* in speed and placed them in service between Montreal and Bristol. The following year the Cunard Line entered the Canadian trade. On the Pacific, the original *Empress* liners were badly outclassed by American and Japanese competitors, and the need for new tonnage was increased when the *Empress of China* struck a reef near Yokohama and was so badly damaged that she was abandoned to the underwriters.

The first step taken was the purchase of two liners to strengthen the secondary services of the Allan Line. The next was the construction of two new *Empresses* for the Pacific. Of nearly 17,000 tons, the *Empress of Asia* and *Empress of Russia* were the fastest and best-equipped ships on the Pacific when completed in 1913. They were followed by two liners for the Atlantic; of about 18,000 tons, they were the largest yet built for the Canadian trade. Because they were financed by the C.P.R., one would have expected them to be *Empresses*, but instead they were added to the Allan fleet and entered service as the *Alsatian* and *Calgarian*. These four new liners represented an investment of over $10 million. They will be remembered in maritime history as the first large merchant ships to have cruiser sterns.

Two smaller steamers of a different type were being built for the Atlantic run when war was declared. The 12,400-ton *Metagama* and *Missanabie* carried passengers in two classes instead of three—cabin class, at fares approximating those charged for second class in three-class ships, and third class. Shaughnessy surmised correctly that this type of carrier, in which the best accommodation was comfortable but less elaborate than in the larger and faster liners, had an important future in the Canadian trade, and he took his manager sharply to task when he referred to the cabin accommodation as second class: "It is not in any sense 'second' class, but 'single' class, and in the matter of food, service, etc. we should approach close to the standard on the *Alsatian* or the *Empress of Britain*. A very large number of most excellent people would be glad to take advantage of this one-class accommodation who would sooner stay home than travel second-class."[9] The C.P.R. is often credited with having originated the cabin-class liner, but this is not so. A modest prototype had appeared as early as 1906, and the *Metagama* and her sister were built to compete with somewhat larger cabin liners that the Cunard Line had completed for its new Canadian service in 1913.

By 1914 the Canadian Pacific had become one of the world's major shipowners. Its ocean, coastal, lake, and river fleets consisted of about a hundred ships, over thirty of them on the Atlantic. The book value of the ocean and coastal fleets, plus the steamship replacement fund, totaled nearly $31 million. Contrary to expectations, the Atlantic freighters had yielded only a small margin of profit, but when times were good the passenger ships had done well. Traffic and rates fluctuated, but Shaughnessy felt that the company could, "with safety, anticipate an annual revenue of $2 million from the trans-Atlantic and trans-Pacific lines after making due provision for interest on their cost and for depreciation."[10]

A great tragedy and what appears in retrospect to be a touch of comedy remain to be noted.

The loss of the *Empress of China* in 1911 had occasioned no loss of life, but it was far otherwise with the *Empress of Ireland*. Late on the night of May 29, 1914, while creeping down the St. Lawrence in foggy weather, she was rammed by the heavily laden collier *Storstad* and was so badly holed that she sank within a few minutes, with the loss of over a thousand lives. The only consolation was the finding of the official inquiry, which found the collier to blame for the disaster.

In 1912 the C.P.R. had been brought into touch with the Austrian State Railways, which were anxious to promote both tourist trade and the port of Trieste. To attract tourists, the C.P.R. suggested that observation cars of the type included in its transcontinental trains should be used on some of the scenic routes in Austria. The proposal was accepted, and the C.P.R. agreed to provide the cars and operate them on a percentage basis. Built in Europe to Canadian designs at a cost of over $185,000, they were ready for service in the late summer of 1912 and were operated by the C.P.R. until the outbreak of war. They were then seized as enemy property and were used during the war years by the Austrian Red Cross. After the war, still in excellent condition, they were repossessed by the C.P.R. and sold to the Italian State Railways, which used them between Rome and Naples.

The C.P.R. also agreed to establish a steamer service between Trieste and Montreal. Emigrants were flowing through the port in substantial numbers, and it hoped to divert some of them to Canada. Early in 1913 the *Lake Champlain* and *Lake Erie* were given the appropriate new names of *Ruthenia* and *Tyrolia* and placed on the Trieste run. But the service never paid, and it roused the ire of the German shipping lines, which wanted to confine the Austrian emigrant traffic to ships they owned or controlled. The final outcome was the arrest of the staff of the C.P.R. office in Vienna on a trumped-up charge and a bizarre battle in the courts that has been described by Murray Gibbon. Among other things, the C.P.R. was accused of having persuaded 600,000 Austrians of military age to emigrate to Canada, with the promise of free land and two buffalo to work each farm. The actual number of emigrants carried by the Canadian ships was only 13,000, but it took so long to establish these and other pertinent facts that the case was still in progress when war broke out and proceedings lapsed.[11]

18

The Growing Stake in Natural Resources

The Canadian Pacific expected its Atlantic steamer service to be of considerable help in promoting immigration and settlement in western Canada. For one thing, it enabled the company to offer through rates to inland destinations; this had been difficult to arrange with independent lines. The agents for its steamers could assist with advertising, and they would be anxious to see that Europeans traveled in C.P.R. ships directly to Canada—an important point, since immigrants who landed at American ports were apt to succumb to the lure of the United States. By equipping some of its big freighters with steerage accommodation, the C.P.R. expanded facilities on the Canadian route, and when the *Empress* liners entered service, they markedly increased its attractions for travelers in all classes.

By a coincidence the Canadian Pacific entered the Atlantic trade in the same year, 1903, that the company and the government of Canada finally agreed upon the last parcels of land that were to be included in the historic grant of 25 million acres, made twenty-two years before. Settlement was spreading rapidly, and it had become essential for all concerned that uncertainty about the location of railway lands should end.

Looking back over the Canadian Pacific's colonization efforts, Shaughnessy remarked in 1918 that the land grant had been for long "a great drag on the Company."[1] Land grant bonds, expected to provide a substantial part of the funds required to build the main line, had in fact yielded only about $9 million. After an initial flurry, the land itself had sold much more slowly than had been anticipated, and prices were so low that the net return was no more than $1.50 to $2.50 an acre. A second bond issue of $15 million, sold in

1888, had provided funds urgently needed for equipment, but the bonds became a burden on the railway when revenue from land sales became insufficient to meet interest charges. In 1894 net sales less cancellations totaled only 9,482 acres, and in the following two years cancellations exceeded sales by 212,000 acres. The limited acreage "fairly fit for settlement" found to be available in the southern part of the prairies made it necessary to accept land in northern reserves, where it was unlikely to be saleable for many years to come. The railway accordingly found itself in the land business on a long-term basis, which was quite contrary to its plans and expectations.

Fortunately, a change in its fortunes had occurred shortly before Shaughnessy became president. The turning point came in 1897, and sales soon increased dramatically. In the year ending June 30, 1902, the Canadian Pacific sold 1,362,852 acres from the main line and Souris branch reserves, and the following year sales reached the all-time high of 2,260,731 acres. These proved to be quite exceptional years, but in the following decade, when settlers were pouring into the West, sales averaged 638,000 acres.

A striking feature in the 1902–12 decade was the heavy influx of immigrants from the United States. In the earlier years, much of the impetus behind this migration was provided by American land companies that purchased large blocks of land which they proceeded to sell by means of energetic campaigns. The high sales figures of 1902 and 1903 reflect their activities. The first substantial purchase was made late in 1901; the 170,000 acres transferred were all sold to settlers from the United States within five months. In 1902, the largest purchaser, the Northwest Colonization Company, bought 337,000 acres of Canadian Pacific and Manitoba South Western lands and later increased its holdings to about 750,000 acres. All had been sold to American settlers by the spring of 1905. By July 1906 colonization companies had bought a total of 2.3 million acres of the railway's land.[2]

By that time most of the subsidy lands in Manitoba and southeastern Saskatchewan had been sold, and the Canadian Pacific turned its attention to the reserves in Alberta. Here it undertook the largest irrigation project yet attempted in North America—a venture from which it was to emerge with much more honor than profit.

The scheme grew out of Van Horne's act of faith in 1894, when he agreed to accept as land "fairly fit for settlement" a large tract in southern Alberta between Medicine Hat and Calgary. The rainfall was known to be scanty and crops could not be grown with certainty without irrigation, but whatever its faults, the land at least had the advantage of being adjacent to the C.P.R.'s main line. When the final settlement with the government was made in 1903, the area to be accepted was moved somewhat farther west and greatly enlarged to 2.9 million acres. It comprised a solid block, and in order to secure the complete ownership desirable for irrigation, the Canadian Pacific bought from the Hudson's Bay Company the 102,000 acres within it to which the company was entitled under the terms of the Rupert's Land purchase of 1869.

Shaughnessy and his board decided to go ahead immediately with the irrigation project. Some guidance was provided by preliminary investigations that had been made by the federal government, and the Canadian Pacific took into its service the man chiefly responsible for them, J. S. Dennis, Jr. The company had also watched with interest and had subsidized an irrigation scheme being carried out farther south in Alberta by the Alberta Railway and Coal Company. This had encountered difficulties, but the results were promising. Because working irrigated land entailed much more labor than ordinary farming, individual holdings were expected to be relatively small (the C.P.R. had 160 acres in mind), and Dennis and Shaughnessy envisaged a populous and highly productive area that would provide much traffic for the railway.

The source of water was to be the Bow River, and for development purposes Dennis divided the reserve into western, central, and eastern blocks. Each consisted of about a million acres, but because of land levels and other considerations, only parts of them were irrigable.

Work began in the western block in 1904. Here the objective was to irrigate about 220,000 acres. The Bow River was tapped on the outskirts of Calgary, and over a period of five years, 1,600 miles of canals and ditches were dug to distribute the water. In 1910 work began on the much more extensive and costly system in the eastern block, in which 400,000 acres (later scaled down to 250,000 acres) were to be irrigated. Water was provided by a huge dam on the Horseshoe Bend of the Bow, near Bassano, completed late in 1913. The network of canals and ditches leading from it had a combined length of 2,500 miles. The initial cost of the two systems was more than $15 million, and estimates of the expenditure that would be required to extend irrigation to the central block were so high that plans to do so were abandoned.

By 1906 land in the western block was being offered for sale, but the response was disappointing. Only 23,000 acres of irrigated and 14,000 acres of nonirrigated land were sold in fifteen months. The price of the irrigated land was relatively high, and, in the words of J. B. Hedges, men preferred "to gamble on the vagaries of the weather rather than assume the arduous and exacting duties of irrigation."[3] To confuse the issue, the climate had entered a wet cycle that seemed to indicate that rainfall was adequate and raised doubts as to whether irrigation had been necessary.

For two years or more, sales were managed by an outside agency, the

Canadian Pacific Irrigation Colonization Company, but at the beginning of 1908 the C.P.R. took over this company and it became a subsidiary, with headquarters in Calgary. The United States was the most promising market, and relations were quickly established with a large number of active selling agencies there. Sales increased sharply. By the end of 1909, over 400,000 acres had been sold, over half of them irrigated land.

In a circular sent in answer to inquiries, the railway's objective had been made quite clear: "Ours is neither a land nor a water-selling scheme. . . . The C.P.R. is spending millions of dollars on this project purely and simply to build up the most prosperous agricultural community in America. This sounds like philanthropy but it isn't. The railway wants a prosperous community in order to create the greatest possible volume of traffic."[4] Unfortunately the company had neglected to make occupancy a condition of sale. The large amount of land left vacant by absentee owners threatened to defeat the purpose of the whole operation. To counter this, the Canadian Pacific mounted a campaign with two objectives—to try to get rid of purchasers who had bought land for purely speculative purposes and to persuade and assist others either to develop their properties or to surrender them.

In addition the C.P.R. promoted resident farming by introducing two new purchasing plans. Under the first of these, a purchaser paid a small down payment and thereafter turned over half of his crop each year until his land was fully paid for. This plan, designed to appeal especially to prospective buyers in the United States, made it possible for an immigrant with some capital to devote most of it to equipping and improving his property. The second plan, intended to attract British farmers, offered ready-made farms, on which a house, barn, and fences were provided and an initial acreage had been plowed and sometimes even seeded as well. Here selection of the immigrants who would take over the farms was all-important, and unfortunately the company's agents in the United Kingdom did not always display the best of judgment.

By the end of 1909 most of the irrigated land in the western block had been sold, if not occupied. In order to keep its sales force, the Canadian Pacific decided to sell other reserves through the Calgary office—the first step in a shift that would make Calgary the center of its colonization efforts in place of Winnipeg. The railway had just built two branches running eastward from the Calgary-Edmonton line that made a large acreage of subsidy lands accessible, and 200,000 acres in the area were sold by the summer of 1910. The following year the C.P.R. turned its attention to the large northern reserves in Alberta and Saskatchewan. It had hoped to push branches through them, but had been forestalled by the Canadian Northern and the Grand

Trunk Pacific. Since settlement would bring it no benefit and the lands were still free of taxation, the C.P.R. was inclined to hold them for future speculation, but it decided instead to put some of them on the market. Here for once profit, not traffic, was the end in view; sales were ordinary real estate transactions, with a good price the objective, and no occupancy requirement—the necessity for which the C.P.R. was learning the hard way—was attached to contracts.

On paper the results of this vigorous selling effort were impressive. In the three years ending June 30, 1912, sales totaled $34.7 million. But there was another side to the coin. Expenses and irrigation costs had been so high that net proceeds were only $7.9 million, and a careful review of all outstanding contracts showed that, in spite of the generous instalment terms offered, large numbers of purchasers were badly in arrears in their payments. Equally disturbing was the proportion of holdings that were still unoccupied.

It was clear that many contracts would have to be canceled, but every effort was made to assist and protect the genuine settler, then and always the Canadian Pacific's prime concern. Dennis and Shaughnessy had authorized land agents to assure applicants that the C.P.R. "had never dispossessed a farmer on its land because of failure to pay the deferred payments, as long as he actually occupied the farm," and this was reflected in the policy governing cancellations. This may be summarized as follows: If a purchaser was living on his farm and doing his best to work it, the company pressed him for neither principal nor interest. If he hoped to occupy the property soon, it asked only for an interest payment. But if payments were badly in arrears and the property was both unoccupied and unimproved, it insisted upon cancellation. What happened in the irrigation blocks illustrates the extent of the problem. Up to the end of April 1914, sales of irrigated and unirrigated land had totaled 1,577,459 acres. More than one third, 577,922 acres, were found to be held under contracts that had to be canceled.

Speculative buying had crept in to an unsuspected extent, and in the autumn of 1912 the Canadian Pacific decided that in future it would sell farmland only to individual settlers. The down payment required was reduced to one twentieth of the purchase price, and as the average selling price of C.P.R. lands in 1912 was $15.20 an acre, this meant that a quarter section of 160 acres could be secured for an immediate outlay of as little as $121.60.

For the most part the annual reports published during Shaughnessy's presidency are brief, and apart from statistical tables consisted of only a few pages; the text of one runs to only two. At the annual meetings, however, he was more expansive. In May 1918, on the eve of his retirement as president, he delivered a remarkable valedictory address in which he reviewed the history of the company with which he had been associated intimately since the second year of its existence. He described the Canadian Pacific's experience with the original land grant. In round numbers, over the period of thirty-seven years, 14 million acres had been sold for $94 million at an average price of $6.72 an acre, irrigated land included. From this revenue there had to be deducted approximately $17 million, which the company had spent encouraging immigration and otherwise promoting sales and settlement. More than $15 million had been expended on the Alberta irrigation blocks. The net return was thus about $62 million, or $4.50 an acre. Profits from land sales had provided most of the funds required to redeem $17.8 million of land grant bonds; after redemption was completed, in 1906, a supplementary dividend of 1 percent was paid from land revenues to holders of C.P.R. common shares. The substantial balance still remaining was used for capital expenditures by the railway, which in this way was partly reimbursed for the cost of the many branch lines that had had to be built to make the land accessible. This was a particularly welcome source of capital, since it provided funds without increasing fixed charges.

The accompanying table gives details of the grand total of 36.3 million acres of land which, from a considerable variety of sources and over a period of almost half a century, came into the possession of the Canadian Pacific. One or two of the items call for comment. The Alberta Railway and Irrigation Company was the successor to the Alberta Railway and Coal Company, whose irrigation project has been mentioned. The C.P.R. secured control of it in 1908. The purchase included the irrigation project and the residue of its million-acre land grant.

As this illustrates, the Canadian Pacific was by no means the only railway to be given land subsidies, though it received much the largest share of them.

The Calgary and Edmonton Railway's grant, one of the last given by the federal government, serves to emphasize again that the Canadian Pacific was interested in encouraging settlement in general in the regions it served, not merely the colonization of its own holdings. Although it had operated the Calgary and Edmonton line since its completion, the land grant was marketed largely through Osler, Hammond and Nanton, brokers and promoters in Winnipeg. Sales could bring no profit to the Canadian Pacific, but the agents were authorized to advertise that settlers bound for the properties could secure "all special rates, stop-over privileges, etc., granted by the C.P.R. Co. to intending settlers on their own lands."[5] The part of the Calgary and Edmonton grant received by the Canadian Pacific had been held as security against an obligation to the government. Its transfer in 1912 prompted the organization of a Department of Natural Resources, which superseded both the Canadian

CANADIAN PACIFIC LANDS

Lands in the Prairie Provinces	ACREAGE ACQUIRED	UNSOLD AT DEC. 31, 1958
Main line grant (the initial land subsidy)	25,000,000	581,126

[In 1885, 6,793,014 acres of the subsidy lands were returned to the Crown in partial settlement of the company's debt to the government of Canada, leaving a net total of 18,206,986 acres.]

Grants to branches and acquired lines		
Souris Branch and Pipestone Ext.	1,609,024	278,593
Manitoba South Western	1,396,800	5,141
Great North West Central	320,000	10,539
Manitoba and North Western	3,153	—
Saskatchewan and Western	98,880	—
Calgary and Edmonton	407,402	5,249
Alberta Railway and Irrigation Co.	181,249	4,899
Interprovincial and James Bay	306,760	—
Northern Colonization Railway	96,000	—
Townsites	85,626	926
Land in the Alberta irrigation block purchased from the Hudson's Bay Co.	102,174	416
	29,607,068	886,889
Lands in British Columbia		
Grants to acquired lines		
British Columbia Southern	3,755,733	—
Columbia and Kootenay	188,593	—
Columbia and Western	1,315,273	—
Vancouver townsite	6,272	520
Esquimalt and Nanaimo Railway		
Estimated acreage bought in 1905	1,440,495	366,372
	6,706,366	366,892
Grand Totals	36,313,434	1,253,781

Source: Acreage figures are from a memorandum prepared for the president of the Canadian Pacific in April 1959.

Pacific Irrigation Colonization Company and the land office in Winnipeg and concentrated control over all land interests in Calgary.

Of the grants in British Columbia, the important items were the acreage in the Vancouver townsite and the subsidy lands that the Canadian Pacific purchased for $1,330,000 when it acquired the Esquimalt and Nanaimo Railway in 1905. Within seven years, 250,000 acres of the Esquimalt and Nanaimo lands had been sold for $3,364,000, and the million and more acres remaining included vast stands of timber. By contrast, the three grants in the Kootenay were far less valuable than their great size suggests. Over a period of years 434,000 acres were sold, but the price they fetched was only $1.77 an acre. In 1912 the bulk of the land was sold back to the government of British Columbia for about sixty cents an acre; 543,000 acres were retained for a time as a possible source of timber and ties for the railway's own use.

Welcome and substantial as the profits from land sales had been in the prosperous first decade of the century, they were never an important factor in the financing of the Canadian Pacific. Far more significant, as George Stephen had foreseen from the beginning, was the peopling of the prairies and the traffic that crops and the needs of the population would provide for the railway, year after year.

When addressing the shareholders in 1913, Sir Thomas Shaughnessy pointed out that American railways had been required to segregate their accounts relating to the railway proper from those recording other operations and income. No similar requirement had yet been made in Canada, but the Canadian Pacific nevertheless judged it best to make somewhat similar changes in its reports. From the beginning the company had operated its own express and telegraph services; to these, hotels and ocean, coastal, lake, and river steamers were soon added. The company had become much more than a railway; it was interested in the whole broad field of transportation and communication. And even this definition did not cover the whole of its activities, as Shaughnessy reminded the shareholders: "Legacies that came to you with acquired lines, the utilization of your coal lands, and other circumstances have involved you in a number of enterprises that do not ordinarily come within the province of a railway company."[6]

At the time Shaughnessy spoke, the Canadian Pacific was directly involved in coal mining in three locations. At Bankhead, not far from Banff, it had developed a subanthracite mine that promised well at first but got into difficulties when the proportion of large-sized lump coal decreased; at times only about a quarter of the output was of merchantable size. An even greater disappointment was encountered at Hosmer, in the Kootenay. The tripartite agreement of 1897 had given the C.P.R. six square miles of coal lands, but it had agreed not to market coal from them for ten years. Production began late in 1908, but irregularities and faults in the seams soon caused serious trouble. By 1912 Shaughnessy was out of patience with both the Bankhead and Hosmer operations, which between them had entailed a capital expenditure of about $4.5 million. He thought there had been "most disgraceful miscalculation" in connection with both of them, and if they could not be operated profitably, they must be shut down.[7] Accordingly, the Hosmer mine was closed in July 1914, after producing 984,000 tons of coal and coke. Bankhead survived until 1923, by which time it had produced over 4 million tons of coal and briquettes.

The third and much more satisfactory operation was the mine at Lethbridge, developed originally by the Galts. It came to the C.P.R. in 1912, when the Alberta Railway and Irrigation Company was taken over. Eventually it was merged in Lethbridge Collieries Limited, in which the Canadian Pacific holds a majority interest.

Although it controlled extensive timberlands, activity was still confined to a small sawmill at Bull River in the Kootenay, which produced ties and lumber; "a doubtful commercial enterprise," Shaughnessy noted, "excepting in so far as it serves to keep prices within reasonable bounds."[8] Much more interesting was the first unobtrusive appearance in the Canadian Pacific's annual reports of details of its shareholdings in the Consolidated Mining and Smelting Company, which owned the smelter at Trail. In 1914 these amounted to 26,190 shares. By 1917 they had increased to 177,025, valued at $4,425,625. One of the great success stories of the mining industry was in the making.

The smelter, it will be recalled, had been acquired in 1898, almost by accident; the Canadian Pacific bought the Columbia and Western Railway from Augustus Heinze who insisted that the smelter be included in the deal. W. H. Aldridge, who had negotiated the purchase, was put in charge of the smelter and immediately set about modernizing and expanding it. He saw that the first essential was to broaden its output. Heinze had built it with the gold-copper ores of the Rossland region in mind, but there were signs that those mines had passed their peak. Aldridge added a lead furnace and presently installed equipment to refine lead by the new Betts electrolytic process. This was one of the first installations of its kind and, as Lorne McDougall has pointed out, was a landmark both in the technology of the industry and in the history of the Consolidated: "If one wants to date the very beginning of the modern Cominco [as the company was renamed officially in 1966], it is here in the transition from a gold-copper base to a wider range of metals, and in a receptiveness to new inventions. Here was a first step towards technical excellence and away from a plodding use of techniques known and used elsewhere. The year was 1901."[9]

Aldridge next turned his attention to the problem of ore supply. The ore that was flowing to the smelter was coming mostly from three mines, two in Rossland and one in East Kootenay, that were neither owned nor controlled by the smelter company or the Canadian Pacific; it was conceivable that their output might be directed elsewhere. If large expenditures on the smelter were to be justified, it was essential that an adequate supply of ore be assured for a long period. As a first step Aldridge recommended the purchase of the three mines in question, and this was done. As the Canadian Pacific had provided most of the purchase money, it found itself with a controlling interest of some 54 percent in the combined enterprise that assumed ownership of both the mines and the smelter.

The link with the Canadian Pacific was to be of immense importance to both companies. For the Consolidated it meant financial security and access to funds in case of need. Shaughnessy grumbled, but in the end money for research and development was forthcoming. From the point of view of the C.P.R., the venture represented a gamble that was to pay off beyond its wildest expectations, largely because it could afford to wait for results.

For five years, from 1907 to 1912, the Consolidated paid no dividends; its profits were used to build up reserves and finance improvements. In 1910 it first leased and then purchased the Sullivan Mine at Kimberley, destined soon to be world famous. Discovered in 1892, the mine was known to have immense deposits of lead-zinc ore, but four successive ownerships, including the Guggenheims, had been defeated by the problem of separating its components. By carefully selecting ore, the Consolidated managed to make the Sullivan return a modest profit; by 1914 it had become the largest producer of lead in Canada. Presently the company was ready to tackle the separation problem. Wartime shortages of zinc made a solution urgent, the C.P.R. saw to it that research funds were available, and a breakthrough became a matter of time.

Meanwhile a marriage of convenience had been arranged between the Consolidated and the West Kootenay Power and Light Company. The smelter required great quantities of electricity, which it secured from the West Kootenay hydro plants on the Kootenay River. The Consolidated and the power company soon became so important to one another that a merger was clearly desirable, and this was achieved in 1916, when West Kootenay common shares were exchanged for Consolidated stock.

One resource remains to be noted—petroleum. All mineral rights were included in the transfer of subsidy lands from the government to the railway, but for a time it took no steps to reserve any of them when the properties were sold. Presently coal rights were reserved, and in 1905 the reserve was extended to include all coal, petroleum, and valuable stone. When the Department of National Resources was established in 1912, it acquired a full-time solicitor in the person of George A. Walker, a future chairman of the Canadian Pacific. Upon his insistence the reserve was extended to all mines and minerals. The latter provision was imposed in time to apply to 9.6 million acres of C.P.R. lands in the Prairie Provinces, and the company held partial rights in an additional 3.2 million acres.

For some years revenue from mineral rights was negligible; by 1915 it had totaled no more than $5,654. But Shaughnessy was on the watch. In April 1914 he had read with close attention a report on oil-producing areas in the United States and immediately wrote to J. S. Dennis, of the Department of National Resources, telling him that he was convinced "that we cannot be too careful about the regulations that we may put in force with reference to oil leases on our lands. . . ."[10] The same year the first important discovery of oil in western Canada was made in the Turner valley, south of Calgary, on C.P.R. land; the most profitable well there would bring the company $8,000 a month in royalties.

A generation was to pass before the Canadian Pacific would begin to develop its nonrail resources on a large scale, but their potential was becoming evident, and Walker and others were taking steps to safeguard them for the future.

19

The Golden Years

In spite of the attention they devoted to shipping, settlement, and smelters, Shaughnessy and his directors never for a moment neglected the railway, which continued to be far and away the most important interest and activity of the Canadian Pacific. The rapid expansion of the system has been described, but the mileage increase by itself does not give a proper idea of what was accomplished.

Soon after 1900 it became evident that considerable double tracking would be essential. The need became particularly pressing between Winnipeg and Thunder Bay. For seventeen years after its completion, this line had been the sole rail link between western Canada and the Canadian ports at the head of Lake Superior. Long after the rival Canadian Northern line to Port Arthur was opened, at the beginning of 1902, it continued to be the main outlet for grain shipments from the prairies. As settlement spread and wheat production mounted, traffic on the single line increased at times to the saturation point. Work on a second track began late in 1904 and was completed in 1908—just in time, for the area under grain in the West had more than tripled in ten years and was approaching 10 million acres. Thereafter each year's budget included a substantial appropriation for additional double tracking, much of it on the main line west of Winnipeg.

Grade reduction was another means by which efficiency was increased and operating costs were reduced. "The line between Moosejaw and Swift Current is being practically rebuilt on a new location," Shaughnessy wrote to John Egan in July 1903, "and we are cutting down grades over the whole main line between North Bay and the mountains."[1] Later in the year he told share-

THE GOLDEN YEARS   263

holders that grade reductions that had been or soon would be made would have the effect of increasing the capacity of locomotives by 50 to 100 percent over 1,200 miles of the main line.

Many of the improvements were relatively small projects, but by 1907 the Canadian Pacific was ready to undertake two spectacular engineering feats that were to set records. Both were planned by John E. Schwitzer, who had just become senior engineer on the western lines. The purpose of the first was to modify the famous "Big Hill" in the Kicking Horse Canyon, between the summit of the Rockies and Field. It had always been recognized that the original line, with its 4.4-percent grades, officially described as "temporary" and built by special permission of the government, would have to be replaced. It was difficult and extremely costly to operate; the problem of bringing heavy trains down safely was matched only by that of mustering sufficient motive power to haul them up. A short freight train required four engines and an eight-car passenger train, three. Over a period of twenty-four years, 30,000 passenger trains passed over the line without accident, but freight and work trains occasionally came to grief. The three safety switches intended to divert runaway trains up steep spur tracks proved their worth, though one old railroader remarked sardonically that the chief result was that "wrecks could take place without hindering traffic on the main line."[2]

It was impossible to improve matters during the depression years, but prosperity and the increased traffic in which it resulted made action both possible and imperative. To reduce the grade by half, it would be necessary to double the length of the line, and the problem was how to do this in the narrow canyon without constructing a perfect labyrinth of bridges, embankments, and tunnels. Schwitzer knew that spiral tunnels had been used successfully in Europe, notably near Wassen, on the famous St. Gotthard line, and he found that they could solve his Kicking Horse dilemma. Two tunnels were built, one within Cathedral Mountain and the other, across the canyon, inside Mount Ogden. The first (or upper) tunnel has a length of 3,255 feet, a curvature of 288 degrees, and a difference of 56 feet between the upper and lower portals. The second is 2,922 feet long and has a curvature of 226 degrees and a difference of 50 feet between entrances. These tunnels and the three long approaches to and between them reduced the notorious "Big Hill" to a maximum of 2.2 percent and thereby doubled the hauling capacity of the locomotives that handled trains over the summit. Traffic first passed through the tunnels on September 1, 1909. They are still the only tunnels of the kind in North America.

Schwitzer's second project was quite different. It called for the construction of the highest railway bridge in Canada—a vast viaduct over a mile

Three locomotives struggling up the "Big Hill" near Field with an eight-car passenger train, about 1906. Within a few years the heaviest grades had been eliminated by the completion of the famous spiral tunnels.

(5,328 feet) in length and 314 feet high, supported by thirty-three steel towers, that carried the Crowsnest Pass line across the deep valley of the Oldman River, at Lethbridge. It eliminated the original long, steep, roundabout track that had taken trains down one side of the valley and enabled them to climb laboriously up the other. Trains first crossed the viaduct on November 3, 1909, just two months after the opening of the spiral tunnels.

Unfortunately Schwitzer's brilliant career was soon to be cut short. He was appointed chief engineer of the Canadian Pacific in January 1911, but died of pneumonia the same month.

It soon became evident that Shaughnessy's aim was nothing less than the double tracking of the main line all the way from Thunder Bay to Vancouver —a stupendous proposal when the physical obstacles to be overcome in the western mountains and canyons are taken into account. Work proceeded year by year on the prairie section between Port Arthur and Calgary, and by 1913 about 850 of the 1,255 miles had been completed. Survey crews had been busy for a year in the Rockies and Selkirks, and Shaughnessy told a correspondent, who was under the illusion that the cost of doubling the Calgary-Vancouver line would be no more than $12 million, that it would be nearer $75 million.[3] He informed the annual meeting that it was not the intention "to proceed with the second track in the more difficult sections along the Thompson and Fraser Rivers until your Kettle Valley Line is ready . . . in 1915, so that you may have an alternative route available between Medicine Hat and Vancouver via the Crow's Nest Pass if anything unforeseen should occur during the prosecution of the double track work to obstruct traffic on the main line."[4]

It would be interesting to know where the C.P.R. proposed to locate the second track, particularly in the narrow gorges of the Fraser canyon. The opposite side would have been the obvious place, but this had been preempted by the Canadian Northern, whose line from Kamloops to the coast was approaching completion in 1913.

The First World War brought Shaughnessy's double-tracking program to a halt, and it was never resumed on any scale. However, by 1915 it had made substantial progress and had increased greatly both the capacity and the efficiency of the railway in the prairie region. Double track was continuous for 600 miles west of Thunder Bay, and after two short breaks it continued for another 200 miles to Swift Current, while loop lines that provided alternative routes for freight carried it in effect as far as Calgary.

No work had been completed in the mountains except at Rogers Pass. The company had long been worried by the hazards and heavy costs, both in lives and money, of railroading through the pass. Slides and avalanches were a constant threat, especially in the early spring. Miles of snowsheds and trestles safeguarded the traffic to a great extent, but there were tragic exceptions. Two accidents in particular are well remembered. The first occurred in 1899, when a slide suddenly overwhelmed the original Rogers Pass station and took eight lives. Clearing slides became almost a matter of routine; their number and severity varied with the season. The winter of 1909–10 was a particularly dangerous one, and in March, the month when hazards were likely to be greatest, it brought the worst disaster in the history of the pass. While a locomotive, rotary snowplow, and large work force were busy clearing an earlier slide, a stupendous avalanche suddenly overwhelmed them, rolling the engine over and over, smashing the snowplow to fragments, covering a quarter of a mile of track, and taking the horrifying toll of sixty-two lives. When the seasons of 1911 and 1912 showed that slide hazards continued to be high, the railway decided that drastic action was essential.

This took the form of the Connaught Tunnel, five miles long through the heart of Mount Macdonald. At one stroke it eliminated the old line through Rogers Pass, with its trestles and nearly five miles of snowsheds, reduced track curvature by over 2,300 degrees (more than six complete circles), and lowered the summit of the line by 540 feet. The gain in both safety and economy of operation was immense.

The tunnel, a remarkable accomplishment, was completed in December 1916, but owing to the war received little notice. Inevitably there were difficulties at first: ventilation was inadequate; wet rails sometimes caused driving

The locomotive has just emerged from one of the famous spiral tunnels near Field. The cars above are about to enter the upper entrance. Taken some time ago, this was a posed photograph, inasmuch as the train had to be broken because it was not as long as the 2,900-foot tunnel; but the mile-long unit trains that now pass through them daily far exceed the tunnel lengths.

wheels to slip, stalling trains traveling upgrade; loose rocks were a danger and a nuisance. Ventilation was improved and a costly concrete lining disposed of the other problems. Originally the tunnel was double-tracked, but in recent years it has been reduced to a single track, a change that has increased clearance and made the work of maintenance much easier and safer.

In view of present electrification proposals, it is interesting to find that Shaughnessy planned to use electric locomotives in the tunnel. Later he suggested that they should be used over the whole distance from the summit of the Rockies through the Selkirks to Revelstoke. The Kootenay River was considered as a source of power, but it was thought that loss in transmission over the type of lines then available would be too high. Shaughnessy wondered if the unmarketable coal that was piling up at the Bankhead mine near Banff might not provide fuel for a steam plant, but like many other projects, electrification plans were dropped when it became clear that the war was developing into a lengthy conflict.

The wisdom or folly of deciding to build the Canadian Pacific through the Kicking Horse and Rogers passes instead of the Yellowhead is still argued; a whole book entitled *The Great Kicking Horse Blunder* appeared in 1973. The spiral tunnels and the Connaught Tunnel reduced greatly their original disadvantages, and today the shorter southern route has much in its favor.

THE GOLDEN YEARS

Traffic increased by leaps and bounds in the first dozen years of the century; at times the Canadian Pacific found it impossible to muster sufficient rolling stock to meet the demand. The critical shortage of cars to handle grain in 1901 has been noted. At first the railway had reacted cautiously to prosperity and was obviously fearful that the greatly improved state of the economy might not last. But traffic figures were reassuring; except for one minor faltering in 1908, reflecting the threatened recession of that year, freight tonnage increased steadily from 7,155,813 tons in 1901 to 29,741,814 tons in 1913, and in the same period the number of passengers rose from 4,337,799 to 15,480,934.

Shaughnessy soon became confident and more venturesome. In 1901 the Canadian Pacific had 20,083 freight and cattle cars. By 1904 the number had risen by 40 percent to 28,066, and by 1906 by 70 percent to 34,152. Yet in October of the latter year there was still a serious shortage: "Although neither effort nor money is spared," Shaughnessy told the shareholders, "we find it almost impossible to provide cars and locomotives rapidly enough to meet the requirements of the business developed along your lines in such a manner as to satisfy, with desirable promptness, the demands of your patrons."[5] Huge orders for rolling stock were placed in the following years, and by the fall of 1912 the C.P.R. had 65,241 freight cars; although 49,118 of them were boxcars, 23,890 additional boxcars were on order. By 1914 these were in service, and the freight car inventory rose to 88,090.

Rolling stock did not merely increase in numbers; thousands of older cars were replaced by new cars with greater carrying capacity. At one time a 20-ton wooden boxcar had been standard equipment; these were soon being superseded by larger cars, and after 1905 by cars in which the structure was steel and only the siding and floor were of wood. Trains were getting longer and locomotives heavier, and stronger cars had become essential; larger cars were also more economical, because capacity increased much more, proportionately, than car weight. In the seven years between 1908 and 1915, the number of 30-ton cars in service on Canadian railroads increased from 69,416 to 116,541, the number of 40-ton cars increased from 9,790 to 64,191, and 50-ton cars began to appear in substantial numbers. By 1916 the average capacity of all cars was 41 tons.[6] Thus while the number of Canadian Pacific freight cars more than quadrupled between 1901 and 1914, their carrying capacity probably increased nearly tenfold.

Freight cars clearly received top priority when rolling stock was ordered, but new passenger equipment was also required in quantity. Day coaches proliferated, for mixed trains trundled along most of the numerous new branch lines two or three times a week, and each required a coach or combination car of some sort. For the intercity runs between such points as Saint John, Quebec, Montreal, Ottawa, and Toronto, more and more first-class coaches, sleeping cars, dining cars, and parlor cars were needed as the traffic grew. The same was true of the transcontinental trains; in addition to standard sleepers of the Pullman type, the Canadian Pacific developed for them two special kinds of sleeping car. The colonist car, a Spartan type, was intended to give the cheapest possible night accommodation, with immigrants especially in mind. It had the usual upper and lower berths, but was not upholstered and passengers provided their own bedding.[7] The tourist sleeper, completely but simply equipped, provided berths at about half the rate charged in the first-class or standard sleeper. Colonist cars were a feature of the transcontinental service for over seventy years and did not disappear until 1956. The tourist sleeper survived until 1965.

The different types of passenger equipment are not tabulated clearly or consistently in the Canadian Pacific's annual reports, but in 1901 there were about 800 cars in all—115 first-class sleeping cars and diners, a few parlor cars, and 662 first- and second-class passenger cars. (This last seems to have been an omnibus category that included colonist cars and also baggage, express, and mail cars.) Shaughnessy informed a correspondent in October 1912 that the company then owned 403 parlor, sleeping, and dining cars, 95 tourist cars, 690 first-class coaches, and 597 second-class and combination cars, or a total of 1,785. To make a proper comparison with 1901, 505 baggage, express, and mail cars should be added, making a grand total of 2,290.[8] An additional 239 cars were on order (and this figure was soon increased substantially) as existing equipment was proving woefully inadequate. "We are deplorably short of passenger equipment to meet the demands of our passenger traffic this summer," Shaughnessy had written in August. "Indeed, we are put to our wits' ends to keep our trains properly equipped until we receive additional sleeping cars that are on order."[9]

Van Horne had taken the keenest interest in every detail of the design and decoration of the Canadian Pacific's sleeping cars and seemed always to regard them with pride and satisfaction. Shaughnessy's opinion of them was far different. "There is a lack of taste and comfort about our sleeping cars that is absolutely disgusting," he wrote in 1913.[10] Even the compartments and drawing rooms in the later cars failed to please. "Some day," he commented to the president of the Soo Line, "somebody will devise a sleeping car that will be an improvement on the present abomination without involving the use of compartments, which we find unprofitable and unsatisfactory."[11] Later he returned to the attack: "The present sleeping car is, to my mind, a relic of barbarism. Less progress has been made in providing improved sleeping ac-

Winter conditions at their worst: two views of a rotary plow and a work crew battling to reopen the line in Rogers Pass in March 1910, after it had been overwhelmed by one of the worst slides on record. (BOTH COURTESY OF THE BRITISH COLUMBIA PROVINCIAL ARCHIVES)

commodation at reasonable cost, for first-class passengers, than in any other branch of the service."[12] Little came of these outbursts; the standard Canadian Pacific sleeper, as good as most of its kind, went its way virtually unchanged for a good many years. Innovations were made mostly in compartment cars, with which Shaughnessy found fault, and in observation cars, which appeared in considerable variety. In 1909 observation sleeping cars were introduced, as well as buffet-parlor-observation cars. In 1906 three cars with a glass roof and cupolas at either end—an early hint of the vista-dome—were built for use through the western mountains, and open-top observation cars were introduced in 1915.

Conservatism was characteristic of the company, and this extended to its locomotives, which some found lacking in originality. Thus E. S. Cox in *World Steam in the Twentieth Century* made only brief reference to any Canadian engines, because he felt that they all followed American practice completely and "displayed no feature worthy of additional mention."[13] But the C.P.R. was not interested in novelty for its own sake; it wanted reliable, economical, and versatile locomotives that were well adapted to meet the extremely varied needs of its exceptionally far-flung system. It secured them by concentrating on a few well-proven types, details of which were varied and refined in the light of experience and changing needs.

For many years the workhorse of the fleet was the 4-6-0 ten-wheeler. First acquired in 1889, it was still being built in 1913. The improved D-10 class, the first of which emerged from the company's own shops in 1905, became the most numerous locomotive class in Canada; they were placed in service by the hundreds during the next seven or eight years. "If there was such a thing as a 'typical' Canadian Pacific steam locomotive, familiar throughout Canada from Atlantic to Pacific," Omer Lavallée, the authority on C.P.R. steam, has written, "that title, surely, was attributable to the 502 units of the D-10 class." Even when heavier engines appeared in the 1920s, the D-10s "never really became secondary engines. Capable of a multitude of tasks complementary to main line operation, at home alike on freight, mixed and passenger trains, in yard, pusher and work service, they could be found in just about every enginehouse from Nova Scotia to Vancouver Island."[14]

The men responsible for the design of the D-10 class were H. H. Vaughan, superintendent of motive power, and A. W. Horsey, whose primary interest was in the steaming qualities of locomotives. They had watched with interest the development of the new 4-6-2 Pacific-type engines, so named because the prototype, built by the Baldwin works in 1901, had been ordered for the New Zealand railways. The Pacifics were a logical development of the ten-wheeler. Their purpose was to increase train speeds, and because this required more steam, a larger boiler had to be provided, which in turn called for a larger firebox. Because engines had to be designed within strict limits of height and width, the boiler could be larger only if it were longer, and a larger firebox could be accommodated only by moving it back beyond the cramped space available between the driving wheels. In the Pacifics the longer boiler occupied all the space over the six drivers, and the enlarged firebox was supported by a trailing truck.

Vaughan and Horsey built the first Pacifics for the C.P.R. in 1906. It soon became apparent that they had found in them another versatile engine that could serve many purposes all over the system. Tractive effort in the earlier engines was little different from that of the D-10, but the higher speed desired was provided by the increased steam supply and larger driving wheels—70 inches as compared with 63 inches in the Pacifics intended for general purposes, and 75 inches in those built expressly for passenger service.

The Pacifics were handsome as well as successful engines, unmistakably Canadian Pacific in appearance. The railway continued to use them to the end of steam. The last engines built by the C.P.R. in its own shops were two Pacifics produced in 1944, and the last of the 498 locomotives of the type bought by the Canadian Pacific was acquired as late as 1948.

For the first dozen years of the century, the Consolidation 2–8–0 continued to be the company's standard heavy freight locomotive. Then in 1912 a successor put in an appearance in the form of Mikado-type engines (said to have been so named because they were first ordered by the Imperial Japanese Railways) with a 2–8–2 wheel arrangement. Their relationship with the Consolidations was similar to that of the Pacifics with the ten-wheelers—a trailing truck was added to provide the extra length required for a larger boiler and larger firebox. There was no difference in tractive effort or driving wheels between the later Consolidations and the first Mikados, but the increased steam they generated produced the higher speeds that were the end in view.

In some respects the Canadian Pacific was more venturesome than Cox's disparaging remark suggests. The railway had compound locomotives as early as 1890, and in 1901 Horsey equipped an engine with a Schmidt-type superheater—the first installation of the kind in North America. Later Schmidt superheaters became virtually standard equipment on American locomotives. Horsey and Vaughan also developed a superheater of their own design, which was installed on many C.P.R. engines. Superheaters, incidentally, resulted in greater economies than compounding, so many of the Canadian Pacific's compound engines were converted to single expansion and equipped with them.

The C.P.R. twice experimented with special types of locomotives that it hoped would simplify operations on the "Big Hill" in the Rockies, but neither proved satisfactory. In 1900 it acquired the first of three Shay-type engines. Their gearing and smaller driving wheels greatly increased tractive effort, but their maximum speed was only fifteen miles an hour. In 1909–11 the company tried again, this time building six Mallet-type articulated compound locomotives, with an 0–6–6–0 wheel arrangement. The two sets of cylinders were back to back, which was unusual. They were intended to act as pushers, but maintenance was found to be expensive and they were rebuilt as conventional 2–10–0 engines in 1917.

Year by year the locomotive roster expanded. In 1901 engines numbered 708. The total had more than doubled, to 1,478, by 1909. That year the average age of Canadian Pacific engines was only about 10.5 years, and by 1912 it was less than 10 years—a very low figure when the long life of a steam locomotive is taken into account. The number of engines continued to rise until 1915, when 2,255 were in service—a figure that was to remain constant until some time after the end of the First World War.

The Canadian Pacific spent $130 million on rolling stock in the years 1902–14, nearly $50 million of it in the two years ending June 30, 1914. These were vast sums at the time, and the price levels then prevailing must be remembered. A steel-framed boxcar of the kind the C.P.R. ordered by the thousand cost about $1,150; a colonist sleeping car could be secured for about $14,000 and a dining car for about $23,000. One of the new Mikado-type freight locomotives could be purchased for $22,000.

During the same thirteen years, Canadian Pacific facilities of every kind were replaced or expanded; $206.3 million was spent on double tracking, reduction of gradients, strengthening and rebuilding of bridges, terminals, freight yards, shops, and a great variety of other improvements. A few deserve mention.

New and greatly enlarged shops had become a prime necessity. The C.P.R. started life with small shops in Montreal, Perth, and Carleton Place that it had inherited from acquired lines. In 1883 it opened the Delorimier Street shops in Montreal, where the first company-built locomotives were produced. Shops were soon needed at Winnipeg for the western lines, and the tremendous expansion that took place after the turn of the century called for much more. In 1904 the huge Angus Shops opened on a 200-acre site in the east end of Montreal. Here, in addition to locomotives, both passenger and freight cars could be built. In 1912, the peak year of prewar traffic and prosperity, Shaughnessy was expecting it to produce 10,000 freight cars at the rate of thirty a day.[15] In 1907 the Weston Shops were opened in Winnipeg; the Ogden Shops in Calgary followed in 1914. Both had large-scale facilities

A unit grain train, consisting of steel hopper cars each with a capacity of 3,000 bushels, crossing the great mile-long viaduct across the valley of the Oldman River at Lethbridge, Alberta.

for every kind of maintenance and repair work. The three shops between them had a work force of over 11,000.

Stations, terminals, and yards were added or enlarged all along the line. The Windsor Station and headquarters building in Montreal was more than doubled in size. Large new passenger depots were built in Winnipeg and Vancouver. A new yard of spectacular size was developed at North Transcona, six miles east of Winnipeg. It was specially designed to handle the many thousands of cars that were pressed into service when heavy grain movements were in progress. Partly completed in 1914, the Transcona yard could then accommodate 7,500 cars; later the number was increased to 13,000.

The hotel system shared generously in the expansion program. Major new hotels were added to the chain in Winnipeg, Calgary, and Victoria; extensive additions were made to the Château Frontenac in Quebec, and Hotel Vancouver was completely rebuilt. At Banff and Lake Louise, fireproof wings began the progressive replacement of the earlier frame structures. Smaller resort hotels were acquired in the Maritimes; chalets and camps were added in the Rockies. It is interesting to note that although the château style which Van Horne had introduced in the Château Frontenac was adopted for the Empress Hotel in Victoria, with a setting that included sea and mountains, the C.P.R. felt it was unsuitable for the prairie cities.

Some statistics illustrating the growth in rail traffic and revenues between 1902 and 1913 are given in the table. The tonnage of freight carried increased 336 percent, but freight train milage increased only 234 percent. Improved

RAILWAY REVENUES AND REVENUE FREIGHT CARRIED

	THOUSANDS OF DOLLARS	THOUSANDS OF TONS
1902	$ 37,503	8,770
1903	43,957	10,181
1904	46,469	11,136
1905	50,482	11,892
1906	61,670	13,934
1907	72,218	15,733
1908	71,384	15,040
1909	76,313	16,550
1910	94,989	20,551
1911	104,168	22,536
1912	123,320	25,940
1913	139,396	29,472

tracks, larger cars, and heavier engines were producing economies, and the average train load, 275.4 tons in 1902, rose to 415.3 tons in 1913 and continued to rise sharply thereafter. Nevertheless, except in the exceptional wartime year of 1916, the operating ratio never again reached the low point of 62.44 set in 1902; but even the high of 69.92 to which it rose in 1909 before declining to 66.92 in 1913 would make any modern railroader green with envy.

Passenger earnings made an important contribution to total revenue, rising from $9.3 million in 1902 to $35.5 million in 1913. A railway was still the best, and in most instances the only, means of traveling any considerable distance. Passenger traffic helped to make 1912 and 1913 the most prosperous years in the history of the Canadian Pacific. With the exception of a small setback in 1908, gross earnings had risen steadily since 1902, reaching $123.3 million in 1912 and $139.3 million in 1913. Net earnings were $43.2 million and $46.2 million in these years.

The *Sicamous*, one of the last and largest of the many stern-wheelers built by the C.P.R. for service in British Columbia. She sailed the waters of Okanagan Lake from 1914 to 1942 and is now preserved as a museum at Penticton. (COURTESY OF THE BRITISH COLUMBIA PROVINCIAL ARCHIVES)

Shaughnessy showed great astuteness in the means used to finance the railway's capital expenditures, which totaled $336.3 million between 1902 and 1914. Like George Stephen, with whom he had worked closely in the early years of the company, he was determined to avoid bond issues that would burden the railway with fixed charges. In the Stephen tradition, he set out to finance expansion chiefly by the sale of additional common shares.

This was made possible by the great and visible improvement in the fortunes of the company. In the worst days of the depression of the 1890s, the stock had fallen as low as 33, but by 1901 it was being quoted at slightly above 100. The next year an issue of $19.5 million of common shares was authorized, followed by a second of $25.5 million in 1904. Both were sold without difficulty, mostly to shareholders. By the latter date shares were being quoted at a premium, and they soon began the dizzy climb that was to carry them to an all-time high of 283 in 1912. Shaughnessy felt that the C.P.R. was entitled to benefit from this and decided that subsequent issues should be priced well above par. Shareholders, who bought nearly all of them, were accordingly offered additional stock at 125 in 1909, at 150 in 1912, and at 175 in 1913, prices that were much below the average market quotations of the day.[16] In all, between 1902 and 1914, common shares with a par value of $195 million were sold, and thanks to the prices fetched by the later issues, they brought $262.1 million to the Canadian Pacific treasury.

Part of the handsome premium of $67.1 million was used to retire the $35 million issue of first-mortgage bonds that had saved the day for the C.P.R. in 1885, most of which were still outstanding. A further sum of $26.1 million paid for railways and steamships not included in Shaughnessy's total of $336.3 million of capital expenditures. After these deductions, $202,150,000 was still available from the sale of common shares to be applied against that total. Of the $134,150,000 still required, $56,500,000 was secured by the sale of preference shares and equipment certificates and $77,650,000 came from surplus earnings. This appropriation from surplus and the premium from the common shares between them gave the company $111 million of capital funds upon which no interest need be paid, and at the same time fixed charges were reduced by the redemption of the mortgage bonds. Thanks to this and other circumstances, the Canadian Pacific's funded debt continued to be remarkably low. In spite of the tremendous expansion that took place between 1902 and 1914, fixed charges increased only from $7,334,825 to $10,227,311 and the charges per mile decreased appreciably.

Other capital transactions in the period included the sale of nearly $110 million of 4-percent consolidated debenture stock. The proceeds were used to retire or acquire bonds of subsidiary lines that bore a higher rate of interest and for capital expenditures on such nonrail activities as the British Columbia coast steamers and the trans-Atlantic service.

The company's prosperity was reflected in its dividends. Payment of 5 percent on the common stock had been resumed in 1899, and the rate had been increased to 5½ percent in 1903, to 6 percent in 1904, and to 7 percent in 1910. In 1910 an additional 1 percent was paid from the proceeds of land sales. Later, as revenue from this and other nonrail sources grew, it was accumulated in a "special income" account (referred to in later years as "other income"). By 1912 dividends had been increased to a total of 10 percent, 7 percent of which was derived from rail earnings and 3 percent from special income. This rate was to be maintained for nearly twenty years.

For a time revenues would have permitted still higher dividends, but having experienced the depression of the 1890s, Shaughnessy preferred to build up contingency funds. In 1910, when he had announced that the rail dividend would be increased to 7 percent, he had acknowledged that some shareholders might consider the increase "scarcely sufficient," but he pointed out that conditions might not always be so favorable. "We may have lean years," he said, and in that event cash reserves would be "a source of convenience and strength."[17]

That time came sooner than expected. In the spring of 1913, when it became clear that the boom was faltering, he acted swiftly to reduce future commitments. Branch line building, to cite one example, was soon reduced to the completion of projects already under construction. But Shaughnessy had built a corporation of immense financial strength and it was to weather without difficulty the troubled decade that lay ahead.

By 1918, the year he retired from the presidency, the railway, not including the lines taken over from the government, represented an expenditure of $818 million. Shaughnessy's habit of devoting a substantial part of surplus earnings and "other income" to debt reduction or current capital expenditure had in effect written off $131 million. Outstanding capital totaled $623 million, all but a small portion in common shares, preference shares, or consolidated debenture stock. Fixed charges were low, and substantial reserves had been built up in depreciation funds and other accounts.

Shaughnessy was in office until the last weeks of the First World War, but the vast program of expansion he had initiated had attained many of its objectives by the time hostilities broke out in August 1914. Major projects still in progress, which in themselves illustrate the scale and variety of the company's activities, included the Alberta irrigation scheme, the Kettle Valley line, the Connaught Tunnel, the rebuilding of Hotel Vancouver, and construction of two liners of a new type for the Atlantic service.

In fifteen short years the railway had almost doubled in mileage, its facilities and equipment had been improved immeasurably, it had played a major role in the peopling of the Canadian West, and it had taken the first steps in developing the natural resources acquired with its land holdings. Steamer services had been established on the Atlantic and along the coast of British Columbia, and these and the older Pacific service had won commanding positions in their respective trades. Financially the results had been spectacular: net earnings in 1914 were over 45 percent higher than gross earnings had been in 1899.

Quite appropriately, this period in the Canadian Pacific's history has been referred to as the golden years.

20

The First World War

When hostilities began between Great Britain and Germany on August 4, 1914, Canadians had had no experience of modern warfare; they had no conception of what was in store for them. Most people, Shaughnessy included, assumed that the war would be short; it would be merely a tragic interruption that would soon be followed by the return of prosperity and normal times. This was implied in the wording of the Canadian Pacific's announcement that it would allow full pay to all permanent staff members who joined the armed forces for six months "or for any shorter time during which the men are engaged in the military service of the Empire."[1] Shaughnessy was doubtful for a time that hostilities would last through the winter, and in the spring of 1915 he was still expecting an early end to the war. "I am convinced that it cannot last long now," he wrote to James Dunsmuir in March.[2] Only later in the year did it become apparent that the struggle for an Allied victory would be long and costly.

Shaughnessy had at once put the facilities of the company at the disposal of the prime minister, and it is interesting to note that his first anxiety was about arrangements to secure and forward foodstuffs to Great Britain. Within a week a senior staff member, A. H. (later Sir Arthur) Harris, had been given responsibility for flour shipments, with instructions from Shaughnessy to "use the routes and the steamers that would most effectively carry out the Government's policy" and to be "absolutely impartial" when dealing with the C.P.R. and other companies.[3] Later Harris and a staff of thirty C.P.R. men were placed in full charge of ship chartering and services. In the course of the war they arranged a total of 2,146 sailings from Canadian ports.

The Canadian Pacific felt the impact of the war immediately in its own shipping operations. The *Empress of Asia* was requisitioned at Hong Kong the day before war was declared; by the end of August all the largest and fastest ships in both the Atlantic and Pacific fleets had been taken over for service as transports or auxiliary cruisers. Early in October, when the first Canadian contingent sailed for England, thirteen of the thirty-one liners in the convoy were Allan or Canadian Pacific ships.

Some of the freighters continued to operate much as usual, but Canadian export trade was badly disrupted and the war cut off many European markets. Thus the service to Antwerp ceased when the German army overran Belgium. Two C.P.R. ships, the *Montrose* and the *Montreal*, in harbor at the time, had a narrow escape when the Germans besieged the port. The *Montrose* had no fuel and the *Montreal*'s engines were under repair. Coal was hastily transferred from one ship to the other, the *Montrose* took the *Montreal* in tow, and both reached England safely. It was a first skirmish with an enemy that was to destroy more than a dozen of the company's ships during the next four years.

The first economic effect of the war in Canada was to deepen the depression that had begun in 1913. Export difficulties; a great reduction in immigration (from a record 400,870 in 1913 to only 36,665 in 1915); army enlistments, which exceeded 218,000 by the end of 1915; and the beginning of a rapid rise in prices—all were disturbing factors. It took time to ascertain wartime needs and for Canada, still not a heavily industrialized country, to adapt, mobilize, and expand her industries to meet them.

The result was a marked falling off in rail traffic and revenues. Freight carried by Canadian Pacific trains declined from 29.4 million tons in 1912–13 to 21.4 million in 1914–15, while gross earnings fell from $139.3 million to $99.8 million—a reduction of almost $40 million, or about 30 percent, in only two years. Then war production began to build up, and traffic bounced back to 29.2 million tons in 1915–16; it continued at that level or above until the end of the war. For a time revenues increased more rapidly than costs, and net earnings reached a record high of $49.2 million in 1915–16; but thereafter, as we shall see, it was another story.

As the war progressed, demands on rail services became greater and greater, but the Canadian railways managed to meet them remarkably well. In January 1918, when traffic conditions were very serious in the United States, Shaughnessy commented upon this in a letter to the president of the Soo Line: "In Canada, notwithstanding the work that the transportation companies have been called upon to perform during the past three and a half years, we have escaped anything like serious congestion, and, barring occasional interruptions due to severe storms or intense cold, everything is running along smoothly."[4] A war control board was talked about but never became necessary.

Many senior C.P.R. staff members in addition to Arthur Harris undertook special war duties. George Bury, a vice-president and former superintendent of western lines, went to Russia in 1917 to assist with railway problems there. He was later knighted for helping to reorganize the railways behind the western front in France. George McL. Brown, European general manager, became assistant director-general of railways in the British War Office and was also knighted. Edward Fitzgerald handled vast purchases in Canada for the governments of South Africa and Russia, the India Office, and the Imperial Munitions Board. J. S. Dennis headed an effort to persuade Britons and Canadians residing in the United States to enlist in the Allied forces and reaped a harvest of 47,000 voluntary recruits.

Within weeks of the outbreak of war, Shaughnessy had discussed with Sir Robert Borden, the prime minister, the possibility of manufacturing munitions in the Angus Shops in Montreal.[5] This was found to be feasible, and in January 1915 the C.P.R. received a large order for 18-pounder shells and brass shell cases. Locomotive building virtually ceased, and shell production was under way by March. Production continued twenty-four hours a day seven days a week for over two years and a half. Meanwhile the Weston Shops in Winnipeg had also been equipped to manufacture shells, and large numbers were turned out there. Shell making ceased about the end of 1917, for special munitions factories were then ready to take over the task. During these busy years, it should be noted, the Angus Shops became the first Canadian industrial enterprise to compensate for a shortage of manpower by employing women on a large scale.

Some unusual chores came to the Angus Shops. Two pile drivers were reconditioned and shipped abroad for use in rebuilding French railways; as if to illustrate both the fortunes and the cost of war, one was destroyed by German shellfire the first day it was in operation. The shops also manufactured fourteen hay presses for use on the Montreal docks—a reminder that in the First World War horses and mules were used extensively, and that baled hay was included in the war supplies exported from Canada.

The Canadian Pacific was also directly involved in some aspects of the financing of the war. By 1916 shortage of dollars to purchase essential materials in the United States had become a critical problem for Great Britain. To assist in its solution, a massive transaction was planned that involved the Canadian Pacific's debenture stock and the debenture stock and mortgage bonds of some of its subsidiaries, all of which had been issued in pounds sterling. A large proportion of them were held in Great Britain, and the British government proposed to "take over or acquire . . . from all persons ordinarily resident in the United Kingdom" all their holdings of these securities and to lodge them with the Canadian Pacific. In return the company would issue 5-percent collateral trust bonds in dollar denominations, principal and interest to be payable in gold in New York or Montreal. The rate of exchange was to be £21 to $100, which was only slightly below the official prewar rate.

Had the conversion been carried out as planned, the C.P.R. would have been called upon to issue bonds to the value of $198,979,580, but the entry of the United States into the war made this unnecessary. A much smaller transaction was then substituted. Debenture stock to the value of $40 million in sterling was issued and sold to the British government at 80 percent of its face value. The dollar equivalent of the proceeds ($32 million) was then loaned to the government and became available for its operations on the American market.

By 1916 wage levels had become a matter of serious dispute. Railwaymen had been unhappy before 1914 because wages in other trades had risen more than theirs, but sharing the general opinion that the war would be short, they had tacitly agreed to postpone pressing their case until it was over. As the war dragged on and prices soared, their attitude naturally changed. In 1916 the cost of living was 24 percent higher than in 1913, and in 1917 it would be 47 percent higher. The Canadian Pacific granted wage increases in 1916, but they were insufficient to match the rise in living costs. Its rail employees, especially the more highly skilled workers, were discontented both on this account and because the gap between their incomes and many of those in other trades had continued to widen. The C.P.R., in common with other Canadian railways, held firmly to the position that it could afford to do no more unless the Board of Railway Commissioners authorized an increase in freight rates. This the board showed no sign of doing. Sir Henry Drayton, its influential chairman, seems to have felt that as long as the C.P.R., thanks to its low fixed charges, was managing to make ends meet and pay dividends, no action was necessary. The plight of the less happily situated new western railways moved him not at all.

In the end, events in the United States forced adjustments in wages and freight rates in Canada. By the last months of 1917 wartime traffic, particularly to the crowded eastern seaports, had reduced vital parts of the American rail system to near chaos, and it was clear that centralized control had become essential. President Wilson issued a proclamation providing for operation of all railroads by the government, and William G. McAdoo was appointed director-general of railways. As in Canada, living costs had risen some 40 percent in two years, and finding that wages were a burning issue, McAdoo appointed

The *Empress of Russia*, one of the transpacific fleet, camouflaged when carrying American troops across the Atlantic in 1918.

a commission headed by F. K. Lane to investigate and make recommendations.

This was clearly a preliminary to wage concessions, and the move could not be ignored in Canada. Canadian railways operated lines in the United States, working conditions in the two countries were in many respects similar, and many railway employees in both belonged to the same international unions. If wage increases were granted in the United States but not in Canada, the repercussions would be immediate and severe. Even before any awards were made, the government of Canada took the extraordinary step of requiring Canadian railways to agree to accept and implement the McAdoo Award (as it became known) without amendment. For its part, the government undertook to permit an increase in rates.

Windsor Station, Montreal, headquarters of the Canadian Pacific as it appeared after substantial additions had been completed in 1915. The original building, opened in 1889, extended only as far as the first dormer to the left of the smaller tower.

The new McAdoo wage rates became effective in the United States in May, and in Canada in July, 1918. Although they raised the average wage of Canadian railwaymen to 58 percent above the 1913 level, they did not attain this by an across-the-board percentage increase. The Lane Commission had been especially concerned about the plight of the many lower-paid railway workers, and these received proportionally much more than the more highly skilled men. When the wages of the time were taken into account, this is understandable. In 1914 a sectionman on a Canadian railway was paid only $10.80 a week; after the McAdoo Award took effect, his weekly wage was $19.20, an increase of 78 percent. By contrast, the wage of an engineer, which had been $27.53 a week in 1914, rose by only 21 percent to $38.40, a figure with which he could scarcely be expected to be content.

The McAdoo Award included increases in freight rates as well as wages, for it was obvious that the railways could not pay the one without receiving more revenue from the other. The same was true in Canada. On March 15, 1918, three years and seven months after the outbreak of war, the Board of Railway Commissioners had at last granted an initial rate increase of 10 to 15 percent, and in August, in keeping with the McAdoo Award and the government's undertaking, this was raised to fractionally less than 30 percent.

In Canada freight rates were complicated by the Crow's Nest Pass Agreement of 1897, by which the Canadian Pacific had bound itself to carry western grain to Thunder Bay at special low rates. These rates, detailed in the statute that approved the agreement and assumed to be perpetual, were unaffected by the McAdoo or any other rate revision. The basic rate prescribed was 14 cents per 100 pounds from Winnipeg to Fort William for grain in carload lots. This had been reduced by the C.P.R. in 1903 to 12 cents to meet the competition of the Canadian Northern, which had agreed to lower its charges in return for financial and other assistance received from the province of Manitoba. In spite of this reduction, the Canadian Pacific lived with the rate fairly happily until the rapid rise in costs that followed the outbreak of war. Even then an exceptional harvest in 1915 resulted in such heavy traffic that its sheer volume compensated in large degree for the low grain rates. In 1915-16 the C.P.R. carried over 256 million bushels—nearly twice the volume moved the previous year. Although the Crow's Nest rates contributed to a reduction in average revenue per ton mile from .76 cents to .64 cents, net earnings for the year, as already noted, reached a record level, and the operating ratio fell to 59.75 percent, a figure never since approached.

Thereafter soaring costs and the low Crow's Nest Pass rates began to cut heavily into the railway's net earnings. The operating ratio jumped to 69.46 in 1916-17, to 78.10 in 1917-18, and to 81.39 in 1918-19. By then revenues had risen to $176.9 million, as compared with $129.4 million in 1915-16, but net earnings had declined by one third, and the surplus, after payment of fixed charges and the usual dividends, was no more than $844,249.

In spite of this, the Canadian Pacific was popularly regarded as a wealthy corporation that was profiting handsomely from the wartime boom in business, and its consistent payment of a 7-percent dividend on its common stock, supplemented by a further 3 percent derived from special income, reinforced this impression. So much was this the case that when the first increase in freight rates was granted in March 1918, the Canadian government, under the War Measures Act, considered it necessary to impose special taxation on the C.P.R. to avoid the criticism that the new rates would simply increase its surplus. Lord Shaughnessy (who had been raised to the peerage at the end of 1915) accepted this with a good grace: "The amount," he told the shareholders, "whatever it may be, will be paid without protest or embarrassment to your finances," and he went on to emphasize that the government had not been "actuated by any spirit of hostility to the Company," but by the enormous wartime demands on the national treasury.[6]

The desperate need of the new western railways for revenue that would cover operating expenses finally persuaded the government to allow some modification of the Crow's Nest grain rates, which in effect applied to them as well as to the C.P.R. Parliament in 1919 authorized their suspension for a period of three years. By then the war was over, but there was still no sign of a decline in the prosperity or price levels arising from it. By 1920 the cost of living was twice what it had been in 1913, and the railways were having to pay ever-increasing prices for fuel, materials, and all manner of supplies. Circumstances were similar in the United States, and a second American wage and rate settlement set the pattern for increases in Canada. Known as the Chicago Award, it was handed down in July. The new wage levels were on the average 121 percent above those prevailing in Canada in 1914. Ostensibly freight rates were raised by 40 percent in the East and in most cases by 35 percent in the West, and passenger fares went up 15 percent, but the C.P.R. contended later that in practice freight rates rose only 30 percent and the passenger tariff 10 percent.

These increases marked the peak of rates, wages, prices, and the cost of living occasioned by the war. Within months they were beginning to fall almost as quickly as they had risen.

Besides contributing skilled personnel to the war effort, the Canadian Pacific added significant numbers to the armed forces. Enlistments from all its services totaled 11,340, of whom 1,116 lost their lives. The company had undertaken to provide the same or equivalent positions for returning veterans, and 7,573 were reemployed. In addition 13,112 other former service personnel were taken on, making a total of 20,685 in all.

In a material sense, the Canadian Pacific suffered its most serious losses at sea, an inevitable result of the scale upon which its ships were involved in the auxiliary naval and transport services or in trading through the various war zones. Thirteen of its ships were sunk, including the new Atlantic passenger liners *Calgarian* and *Missanabie*. Two others were lost by accident, and eight were purchased by the British Admiralty, which employed them for a wide variety of purposes. Some masqueraded for a time as dummy battleships; the oldest of them was sunk as a block ship to protect a harbor entrance. The Admiralty also took over the *Princess Margaret* and *Princess Irene*, which were being completed on the Clyde for the British Columbia coast service, and converted them into minelayers for which their speed and handiness made them admirably suited. The *Princess Irene*, full of mines, was shattered by an internal explosion in 1915, but the *Margaret* survived. The elderly *Empress of India*, which had been plying the Pacific since 1891, was purchased by the Maharajah of Gwalior, renamed *Loyalty*, and converted into a hospital ship.

The new *Empress of Asia* and *Empress of Russia* of the Pacific fleet served in many capacities. Both were requisitioned in August 1914 and fitted out as auxiliary cruisers. Within a few weeks they were in the Indian Ocean, aiding in the search for the elusive German cruiser *Emden*. When she was finally found and destroyed, the *Empress of Russia* carried the surviving crew members to Colombo. Later the sister *Empresses* maintained patrols in the Gulf of Aden and the Red Sea. Back on the trans-Pacific run for a time, they carried thousands of Chinese coolies who were to form labor battalions in France, and the rice that was the mainstay of their diet. Finally, they spent the last six months of the war ferrying American troops across the Atlantic.

No ship in the fleet rendered greater service than the *Alsatian*, sister of the *Calgarian* and largest of the Allan liners. She was commissioned as an auxiliary cruiser in August 1914 and in December became flagship of the Tenth Cruiser Squadron, a force that spent weary years patrolling the dark and stormy waters between the Shetland Islands and Iceland. Originally the squadron had been composed of old cruisers, but these proved quite incapable of the sustained steaming that the patrol required, and liners were substituted. The *Alsatian* was ideal for the purpose—large enough to ride out the northern storms, able to stay at sea for six weeks at a time, and fast enough to overtake almost any merchant ship she might encounter. The older *Virginian* and *Victorian* both served with the *Alsatian* for extended periods. The purpose of the patrol was to stop and examine all steamers bound for the Continent that might be carrying contraband of war destined for Germany. By the time her long tour of duty ended, late in 1917, the *Alsatian* and her consorts had intercepted nearly 9,000 ships.

The *Empress of Britain* served chiefly as a transport. Together, she and other Canadian Pacific ships carried 810,000 Allied troops, while passenger ships and freighters between them transported 4 million tons of munitions and supplies. It was a record matched by very few other merchant fleets.

21

The Specter of Nationalized Competition

The war produced many problems for the Canadian Pacific, but during the years of conflict Shaughnessy's main preoccupation may well have been the predicament of the other principal railroads in Canada. Certainly he came to consider railway policy the most important question facing the country, next to the war itself. The issue was crucial for the C.P.R., for the likelihood grew that it would have to meet the competition of a publicly owned rival transcontinental railway system.

The roads immediately concerned were the Canadian Northern, the Grand Trunk, and the new line from Winnipeg westward that the latter had sponsored, the Grand Trunk Pacific. All three were heading for financial trouble by 1914, the Canadian Northern and the Grand Trunk Pacific on their own account, and the Grand Trunk because of guarantees and advances it had given to its subsidiary.

The new western lines were the result of the railway policy of the Laurier government, which was based on the dual conviction that it was desirable to break the monopoly of the Canadian Pacific on the prairies and that additional railways were needed in the vast area north of the region it served. The federal government had ceased to give land grants, though most of the provinces continued to do so, but it was prepared to assist construction by giving cash subsidies and, in particular, by guaranteeing securities. The latter seemed an easy and cost-free way of enabling the new railways to borrow money at reasonable rates; in the heady atmosphere of the boom years, the possibility of default entered into no one's calculations.

In this setting the Canadian Northern, the creation of William Mackenzie and Donald Mann, grew up with a financial structure diametrically different from that which George Stephen had insisted upon for the Canadian Pacific. Stephen kept fixed charges to a minimum and raised as much capital as possible by the sale of common shares. In case of need, the C.P.R. could reduce or pass dividends, as it had been forced to do once and would be compelled to do again. The Canadian Northern made no provision for such a contingency. Mackenzie and Mann sold no common stock; they retained virtually the whole of it personally. Except for a relatively small sum derived from the sale of land, their system of nearly 10,000 miles had been financed entirely by cash subsidies or by borrowing. Roughly half the securities issued had been guaranteed by the government of Canada or by one of the provinces. By 1916 cash subsidies and guaranteed securities would total nearly $300 million, and almost $200 million more would be owed to the investing public.

Subsidies and guarantees to the Grand Trunk Pacific had been somewhat less lavish but they nevertheless totaled over $125 million. In addition, the federal government itself had built the National Transcontinental, extending 1,800 miles from Winnipeg to Moncton, in New Brunswick. This was intended to be the eastern section of the Grand Trunk Pacific, which had agreed to lease it upon completion.

A Conservative government headed by Robert Borden succeeded Laurier's Liberal administration in September 1911. The change came just as good fortune was beginning to desert the western railways. Within a month of the election, the Canadian Northern found itself unable to pay the interest due upon a small issue of debenture stock and the government had to make good its guarantee. The sum involved was trifling, but it was a portent of the future. As long as settlers were pouring into the Canadian West by the tens of thousands and the Canadian Northern was building cheap branches on the prairies, where traffic existed or developed quickly, it earned its operating expenses and contributed to its fixed charges. But construction costs had doubled in ten years, and when it started to build into the mountains and around Lake Superior, it found, as the Canadian Pacific had found a generation earlier, that costs were frightening and that traffic was scanty or nonexistent. The Grand Trunk Pacific, built to much more exacting standards and with many fewer profitable branch lines, was in an even worse position. By 1913 neither of the lines had been completed and neither company had the funds to continue construction.

Borden and his minister of railways, Francis Cochrane, soon realized that they were facing railroad problems of the first magnitude. One concerned the

National Transcontinental. Its cost had been estimated originally at $61 million; Borden found that this had been exceeded by over $100 million. As the annual rental was to be 3 percent of cost, the Grand Trunk Pacific was anxious to get free of its obligation to lease it. This was no surprise to Shaughnessy, who had expected as much when the original agreement was entered into between the Grand Trunk and the Laurier government in 1903. He felt certain, he wrote to a friend at the time, that the Grand Trunk would "ultimately leave the Government portion of the line on the hands of the Government to lie idle or to be operated at enormous loss for a good many years."[1] In 1915 operating losses and fixed charges of the National Transcontinental between them totaled $6 million.

Subsidies, loans, and guarantees had involved the government so deeply in the affairs of the Canadian Northern and Grand Trunk Pacific that Borden and his able and uncompromising minister of finance, Thomas White, concluded that they were entitled to some return for the further assistance that had become imperative. When the Canadian Northern asked for additional subsidies of over $15 million, they were therefore given on condition that $7 million of the common shares so jealously guarded by Mackenzie and Mann should be assigned to the government. In the spring of 1914, when the partners asked the government to guarantee a bond issue of $45 million, which they professed to believe would enable them to complete the transcontinental line, they were required to hand over an additional $33 million in shares, which increased the government's holdings to 40 percent of the total. Similarly, when the Grand Trunk Pacific applied for a loan of $15 million, the government asked for a first mortgage on the line as security.

The outbreak of war complicated railway matters for all concerned. Most of the Canadian Northern securities had been sold in Great Britain; that market was suddenly closed to it, and it was able to secure only a small fraction of the $45 million it had expected to raise. New York would lend, if at all, only on a short-term basis. Fixed charges of both the Canadian Northern and the Grand Trunk Pacific had become crushing, and it was clear that both were bankrupt in all but name. Furthermore, it was becoming evident that the Grand Trunk itself had become so entangled in the affairs of the Grand Trunk Pacific that the failure of the latter would imperil its own solvency.

Shaughnessy had watched with mounting anxiety as this situation developed. He was already worried about the Canadian Northern before the boom broke. "I cannot help feeling," he wrote in March 1912, "that day by day they are getting into a financial corner that it will not be easy to escape."[2] By the time matters had progressed to the point where the government owned 40 percent of the stock, he was thoroughly alarmed. The specter he saw ahead was a nationalized transcontinental railway, which, if the government so chose, could compete with the Canadian Pacific on terms that no private company that had to pay its way could possibly meet.

The solution he proposed was to let the two railways go into receivership, as countless other lines had done, and work out their salvation through the familiar, if painful, process of reorganization. But for several reasons the government found this course impracticable. The war in Europe was at a desperate stage; Borden and White were convinced that such large-scale failures would have a devastating effect on Canadian credit. One of the major banks was deeply enmeshed in the Canadian Northern, and Borden had given assurances privately that he would protect its interests. Pending a decision regarding longer-term policy, the government postponed a crisis by making loans to both railways. The Grand Trunk, trying to stave off disaster, deepened its involvement in the troubles of the Grand Trunk Pacific by making substantial cash advances to it.

Borden had never been frightened of nationalization, which was very much in the air by the spring of 1915. The railway problem was by then arousing public concern, and in March Sir William Mackenzie, doubtless seeing in nationalization the best hope of salvaging something from the Canadian Northern, urged Borden to call an election on the issue. This proposal White firmly opposed. The same month Borden consulted Shaughnessy. Their discussion was friendly, though Shaughnessy made his opposition to nationalization clear; but the same could not be said of a meeting between the minister of railways and E. W. Beatty, vice-president and general counsel of the C.P.R. Cochrane made what were construed to be threats, and Borden felt it necessary to assure Shaughnessy that he would be "the last to entertain any intention of a policy which would be attended with injustice" to the Canadian Pacific.[3]

Shaughnessy suggested that the whole railway problem should be looked into by a nonpartisan inquiry, a proposal Borden considered for a time but finally postponed. Advice poured in to the prime minister from every side, and Shaughnessy would have been deeply disturbed by a letter Borden received in June. It came from Sir Joseph Flavelle, a prominent industrialist and financier who would be created a baronet in 1917 for his services as chairman of the Imperial Munitions Board, the organization responsible for the procurement of war materials in Canada for Great Britain. Flavelle's recommendations justified Shaughnessy's worst fears and, indeed, foreshadowed the creation of the Canadian National Railways:

> If to meet the situation arising out of the embarrassment of the Grand Trunk Pacific and Canadian Northern Railway Companies, the Government were to

adopt a broad constructive measure, might it not command the imagination of the country and at the same time efficiently meet a situation which has assumed grave proportions?

If you were to create a "National Railway System of Canada" and acquire the Grand Trunk Railway System, the Grand Trunk Pacific, the Canadian Northern Railway, and add to them the Intercolonial Railway, would you not present a constructive policy of commanding importance and to the permanent advantage of Canada?

Do not the very difficulties of the situation create an opportunity for the establishment of a state-controlled national railway system under circumstances of exceptional advantages, in which the country out of its necessities owing to various guarantees, and out of the crippled position of the railway corporations, can enter into possession of great properties and for all time control the railway policy of Canada?[4]

Borden was about to leave for Europe when Flavelle wrote. His enormous preoccupation with a war that was not going well must always be borne in mind; the time and thought he could give to railway matters were often very limited. No doubt this was one of the reasons why the policy of stopgap loans to the faltering railways was followed for another year and more.

In this interval, Shaughnessy's views had changed radically. Reluctantly he had come to the conclusion that nationalization of the bankrupt lines was probably inevitable. His opposition had always been based on fears that publicly owned competition would damage the Canadian Pacific financially and on a conviction that political influences would bedevil the management of nationalized railways. He now had a plan in mind that he thought might avoid both dangers. If the interests of the C.P.R. shareholders could be protected adequately by means of a guaranteed annual dividend, it might be best for all concerned if the rail lines of the Canadian Pacific were included in any broad nationalization scheme; and the management dilemma could be solved by making the Canadian Pacific responsible for operating the entire nationalized system.

These proposals Shaughnessy embodied in a memorandum that he sent to Borden in the middle of May 1916. In a paragraph reminiscent of Flavelle's letter, he wrote: "To an onlooker who thinks that he understands the situation thoroughly, there would appear to be but one course for the Government to adopt, and that is the nationalization of most railway systems of the country. The public mind in almost every Country in the world where private ownership exists, has been gradually centring on the nationalization of these essential arteries of commerce, and nowhere else is there such an opportunity or are there so many good reasons for adopting that policy as in Canada to-day. With the exception of the Canadian Pacific, the share capital of no Canadian railway company is worth a penny."

The Grand Trunk, Shaughnessy considered, might be left out of the scheme, because it was an international line extending from Chicago to Portland, Maine, and with other branches in the United States; he was thinking primarily of the bankrupt Canadian Northern and Grand Trunk Pacific: "By combining the Canadian Pacific, with its large earning power, with these other lines, for the advantage of the Canadian people, the annual deficit would be substantially reduced, and, in time, the whole property might be put on a profitable basis."

"But," Shaughnessy hastened to add, rounding out his proposal, "Government management of the combined railway system would be ruinous, and beyond all thought. Management by Commission is little better, because it is so difficult to establish a public Commission that would be free of political influence, if not control. It might be feasible for the Government to enter into an Agreement with the Canadian Pacific shareholders by which that Company would undertake the management and operation, not only of their own property, but of the other Canadian railway lines excepting the Grand Trunk, for the benefit and advantage of the Country, receiving in return an agreed annual dividend on their shares, to be guaranteed in perpetuity by the Dominion Government." Later he added that although "the Express, Telegraph, and probably some other services intimately associated with the railway operations, would go with the railway system, the shareholders would wish to retain as their own property the steamship lines, lands, investments and other assets from which they would get some return"—in other words, the sources of the "special income" from which the C.P.R. had been paying a supplementary 3-percent annual dividend on its common shares.[5]

By coincidence, the *Grain Growers' Guide*, a voice of the prairie farmers, had advocated a substantially similar scheme a week before Shaughnessy submitted his memorandum. "If the government is going into public ownership of railways," its editorial read, "obviously the only sensible thing to do is to take over the profit making railway along with the two losing railways. . . . A capable management for this great government scheme of railways could easily be secured from the present management of the C.P.R."[6]

But for several reasons official ears were deaf to Shaughnessy's proposal. Sir Thomas White had just reviewed the railway problem in detail in Parliament and had stated that in view of the military situation, emergency grants to the Canadian Northern and Grand Trunk Pacific were still the wisest policy to pursue. In his memorandum, Shaughnessy had denounced such advances as "shameful and indefensible raids . . . on the public Treasury," a remark that was not likely to gain him favor. Borden, who had a high opinion of Shaughnessy, characterized his memorandum as "somewhat impertinent."[7] Recently Shaughnessy had further displeased the government by delivering an address in

Montreal that was highly critical of the proposal to increase the strength of the Canadian armed forces to 500,000; far too many men, he contended, were being recruited months before they could be used effectively. But the basic objection to his plan was that it would create a railway monopoly in the West. Notwithstanding the views of the *Grain Growers' Guide*, anything of the kind, particularly if it were to be under the management of the Canadian Pacific, would be anathema there.

In July Borden decided to proceed with the inquiry that Shaughnessy had suggested the year before. A three-man Royal Commission was appointed consisting of A. H. Smith, president of the New York Central Railroad; Sir Henry Drayton, chief commissioner of the Board of Transport Commissioners of Canada; and W. M. Ackworth, an English authority on railroads. It would be interesting to know if Sir Robert Borden was aware that two of the three men were friendly to public ownership. Drayton had had practical experience of it in Ontario, and Ackworth was a great admirer of the Prussian State Railways.

The commission was urged to report with all convenient speed, and its findings were tabled in May 1917. It had been instructed to look at the Canadian Pacific as well as the faltering systems, and its views on the C.P.R. may be noted first. The Canadian Pacific it found to be "one of the wealthiest and financially strongest railway companies in the world; fully able to raise, on its own credit and on most favourable terms, all the new capital which will be required to meet the demands for new development that the future will bring."[8] Admittedly it had received substantial cash subsidies and land grants from the government, but the commission held that "the fact that it received large help from public sources in its early days, is not any reason why the existing status of the company should now be disturbed. This company has carried out its bargain. . . . We believe that Canada has had good value for what it has given."[9]

Although so favorably impressed by the C.P.R., the commission firmly rejected Shaughnessy's plan for Canadian Pacific management of a unified railway system. The Canadian people had "spent or guaranteed . . . hundreds of millions of dollars, largely with the object of breaking a private monopoly, [and they] would never consent to the re-establishment of a still greater monopoly, even if the Government were a partner in the concern."[10]

Drayton and Ackworth were equally uncompromising in their verdict on the Canadian Northern, the Grand Trunk, and the Grand Trunk Pacific: "These companies have broken down. We see no way to organize new companies to take their place. Their only possible successor is in our view a public authority. We are confronted with a condition and not a theory."[11]

On the nature of the public authority they were less clear. Political control or interference was the bugbear to be avoided; the best suggestion they could offer was a self-perpetuating board of trustees appointed in the first instance by the government.

A. H. Smith disagreed with these recommendations and presented a minority report of considerable interest. "The Grand Trunk," he wrote, "succeeded in the East and failed in the West. The Canadian Northern succeeded in the West and was jeopardized by its eastern expansion." Regional unification and the elimination of duplicate lines could effect great economies and produce two viable rail systems: "Let the Canadian Pacific alone; let the Grand Trunk operate the eastern lines now held by that company and the Canadian Northern; let the Canadian Northern operate the western lines, now held by that company and the Grand Trunk Pacific system; let the Government operate the connections or procure their operation by private companies; all of which should be done under arrangements that are equitable and yet look to the not distant day when the country will have survived the war and resumed its prosperous growth."[12]

To Borden, Smith's proposals must have had a familiar ring, for in essentials they were those that he himself had advocated in Parliament (with Shaughnessy's knowledge and approval, it will be remembered) in August 1903.

Shaughnessy had some foreknowledge that the commission's majority report would recommend nationalization. His immediate reaction was to consider ways and means of reducing the impact that competition from nationalized lines would have on the C.P.R.; his conclusion was that the best defensive move would be to purchase the Canadian Northern. This was being discussed in March, and Shaughnessy drafted a memorandum that reviewed the proposal in some detail. The Canadian Northern was not a burden to be assumed lightly. Its liabilities totaled $376 million, and Shaughnessy estimated that it would require an immediate outlay of another $90 million to complete lines and secure essential equipment. On the other hand, in several respects it could be made to mesh advantageously with the C.P.R. system. Some 1,350 miles of its lines could be used as a substitute for double tracking that the C.P.R. expected it would have to build at a probable cost of $78 million. It was doubtful if the lines in eastern Canada could pay their way for some time to come, but the C.P.R. could "in many cases, practically abandon [them], or so couple them with our own lines that the cost of maintenance and operation would be reduced to a very low figure, without in any important degree affecting the public interest." The duplicated line from Sudbury to Toronto was cited as a case in point.

To counter the deeply rooted Western opposition to a railway monopoly, Shaughnessy contended that "if the Dominion Government will take over the Grand Trunk Pacific line and operate it as a portion of the Canadian Government Railway System . . . the people of the Country will have no grounds for complaint upon a lack of competition, as they will have their own railway system from Coast to Coast."[13]

By May Shaughnessy was discussing possible terms of a takeover with Sir Joseph Flavelle, who had assumed the role of honest broker. The terms Flavelle suggested were onerous enough, but Shaughnessy was prepared to accept them. The C.P.R. was to repay the loans made to the Canadian Northern by the government since the beginning of the war, it was to assume the bond guarantees made by the federal and provincial governments, and it was to pay not less than $15 million for the $60 million of common stock still in private hands. The government for its part was to turn over the $40 million in common stock that it had held since 1914.[14]

The proposal was most attractive financially to the government, but because of Western feeling it was politically hazardous. Yet for a moment Borden evidently felt that it might be turned to important political account. He had returned recently from France, where the state of the war had convinced him that although over 400,000 Canadians had enlisted voluntarily, military needs were such that compulsory service had become necessary. He was extremely anxious to have Sir Wilfrid Laurier, the Liberal leader, join in a coalition administration to deal with the conscription issue on a nonpartisan basis, and he was hopeful that Lord Shaughnessy, who was on close terms with Laurier, might help to persuade him to cooperate. There seems to have been some suggestion that if Shaughnessy succeeded in this mission, Borden might look with favor on the purchase of the Canadian Northern by the C.P.R. But Shaughnessy's efforts were unsuccessful, and on June 22 Borden informed him that the Canadian Northern would be nationalized. Some further correspondence took place, but in reality the purchase proposal was a dead issue. To his credit, it should be noted that Shaughnessy did not on this account abandon his efforts to be helpful to Borden; he was one of a small group that met with the governor-general in Ottawa early in August in a last futile effort to persuade Laurier to join a union government.

Shaughnessy's fear of competition from a government-owned, nationwide system was fully appreciated by Borden. In July he described it well in a letter to J. W. Dafoe, the influential editor of the *Winnipeg Free Press*. The C.P.R. management, he wrote, were convinced that the formation of such a system, "not at first but eventually . . . would gradually undermine the strength and destroy the prestige of the Canadian Pacific Ry." Their fear was that in the end political pressure would "force a reduction of rates which will not take into account capital expenditure; that as the roads nationalized gain increasing strength the Canadian Pacific, obliged to meet rates which take no account of invested capital, will be practically driven to the wall."[15]

The further progress of railway nationalization need be noted only briefly. The government blocked any sale of the Canadian Northern by refusing to part with the 40 percent of the common stock in its possession, and it acquired the railway by legislation that became law in September 1917. Three months later the Canadian Northern, the National Transcontinental, the Intercolonial, and other smaller government lines were united as the Canadian National Railways.

The Grand Trunk Pacific was placed in receivership in March 1919, with the minister of railways as receiver, and was taken over subsequently and added to the Canadian National Railways. The parent Grand Trunk, ruined by advances and guarantees given to the Grand Trunk Pacific, was nationalized later in the year, but prolonged litigation delayed for some time its final integration into the government system. By 1922, however, the Canadian Pacific was faced with the rival that Shaughnessy had feared—a publicly owned system considerably more extensive than the C.P.R. and with lines in every province, from coast to coast.

He had not given up easily. In January 1918 he had sent Sir Robert Borden a draft paper in which his plan for a nationalized system that would include the Canadian Pacific but exclude the Grand Trunk was again outlined. And in 1921, when the Hon. Arthur Meighen had succeeded Sir Robert Borden as prime minister, Shaughnessy again put forward his proposal in the vain hope that it would meet with favor.[16]

In the interval the Canadian Pacific had been accused of making a last effort to reduce competition by gaining control of the Grand Trunk. The minister of railways was convinced that some plan of the sort was afloat, but E. W. Beatty of the C.P.R. denied it in the most explicit terms: "The acquisition of the Grand Trunk, or any portion of it, has never been suggested to the Canadian Pacific or by the Canadian Pacific, and has never been considered or contemplated in any way or by any means direct or indirect."[17] There is no doubt, however, that the C.P.R. would have much preferred to see the Grand Trunk retain its independence. To counter this view, Arthur Meighen turned to the Canadian Pacific's own experience and recalled a statement by Van Horne:

In constructing a great railway system you must never consider a part as separate from the whole. When we first completed the main line of the C.P.R. it ran through unsettled country and, while we made every effort to settle the country through which our main line ran, we would have become bankrupt if we had not acquired lines in well-settled districts of Ontario. . . . Our enterprise would have been a failure if we had not stretched out in Ontario and Quebec.

Similarly, Meighen contended, the recently built Canadian National lines in the West must have the support of the Grand Trunk lines in the East: "Our problem can be solved in no other way than in the same direction given by Sir William Van Horne."[18]

When Meighen spoke, Shaughnessy had retired as president of the Canadian Pacific but continued to serve as its chairman. He had worked for a time under the severe handicap of partial blindness, and for a year had been unable to read or write. His sight restored by surgery, he emerged to deliver a remarkable review of the history of the company to its shareholders in May 1918. A few months later, on October 10, he resigned the presidency—four days after his sixty-fifth birthday and six days before the forty-first birthday of his successor, Edward Wentworth Beatty.

Shaughnessy's reign of nineteen years had seen an astonishing development in the Canadian Pacific: rail mileage had virtually doubled; equipment of all kinds had been vastly improved; the company owned the finest fleets plying to Canada on both the Atlantic and the Pacific; the various enterprises that contributed to its special income were almost all flourishing. Issued common stock had increased from $65 million to $260 million; preferred stock from $26.7 million to $80 million; and consolidated debenture stock from $54.2 million to $216 million. But this vast expansion had been so skilfully managed that fixed charges had risen only from $6.8 million to $10.1 million, and the company was paying dividends at the rate of 10 percent per annum. "I would be lacking in candour," Shaughnessy told the next annual meeting, at which compliments were showered upon him, "if I failed to admit great pride in the progress of the Company during my Presidency and in its present splendid position, physically and financially. . . ."[19]

E. W. Beatty, fourth president of the Canadian Pacific, was the first Canadian-born and also the first who had not been with the railway since the early days of its existence. The son of Henry Beatty, first manager of the company's Great Lake steamers, he graduated from the University of Toronto, studied law, and joined the C.P.R.'s legal staff in 1901. His rapid rise to prominence began in 1913, when he was named general counsel. In December 1914 he became a vice-president and in January 1916 was elected a director. In the fall of the year he became a member of the executive committee, and the presidency followed two years later. Beatty was not a railroader in the sense that Van Horne and Shaughnessy were, but he brought to the C.P.R. the same complete devotion. He was a bachelor, and the company became for him an almost totally consuming interest and preoccupation. Indeed, he may be said to have personified its pride, energy, and ambition.

Beatty had worked very closely with Shaughnessy throughout the war and during the period when the nationalization issue was to the fore. It would be interesting to know the extent to which he contributed to Shaughnessy's rather unexpected advocacy of a nationalized rail system that would have included the C.P.R. The basic proposal may well have been his, as it bore a striking similarity to the railway unification scheme that he was to press with such persistence in the depression days of the 1930s. Certainly one was derived from the other.

The three last survivors of the remarkable group that had nursed the Canadian Pacific into existence all died in the early postwar years. Lord Mount Stephen, to whom the company in great measure owed its existence, died in November 1921, aged ninety-two. He was followed less than a year later by R. B. Angus, at the age of ninety-one. Angus had been first associated with Stephen in the Bank of Montreal, then in the St. Paul, Minneapolis and Manitoba Railway, and later in the Canadian Pacific. He had been a director since the railway's inception, a period of forty-one years. Finally, in December 1923 Lord Shaughnessy died, at the relatively early age of seventy. His term of devoted duty to the railway had been comparable in length to that of Angus, including as it did thirty-two years as a director, nineteen years as president, and five years as chairman of the company.

22

Postwar Reconstruction

Beatty took over at a difficult moment. The war was within a month of its end; severe industrial and commercial adjustments were sure to follow. The first result of peace was a rush of business, as supplies of all sorts were sent to a devastated and exhausted Europe. For a time this brought increased traffic to the railway. Gross rail revenues of the Canadian Pacific rose by over $59 million, from $157.5 million in 1918 to a record high of $216.6 million in 1920. But in the same period higher wages and soaring prices for supplies and materials increased working expenses by over $60 million to $183.4 million, a figure not to be exceeded for over twenty years.

The brief postwar boom broke late in 1920; 1921 was a year of sudden and severe depression. By 1922 earnings had fallen $30 million below the 1920 level, but working expenses had also fallen by a like amount. Shaughnessy was a firm believer in keeping the property in first-class condition, and by and large he had succeeded in doing this, even in wartime. As a result it was possible to postpone or temporarily cut back on many maintenance items with safety and without reducing efficiency. The company's surplus, after the payment of fixed charges and the usual dividends, actually increased from $4.4 million in 1921 to $4.8 million in 1922.

Good luck as well as good management contributed to this result, for the first postwar years were a time of great uncertainty. Wages, freight rates, prices, and the cost of living had not yet been stabilized, and it was too early to gauge what might be involved in competition with a nationalized rail system. Setting about the complicated task of putting the Canadian Pacific's house in order, Beatty gave early attention to one of his own special interests, its ocean and steamer services. These were in a measure removed from immediate problems in Canada, and something could be done about them fairly quickly. The railway itself would call for a longer-term, more complicated, and much more expensive program.

Beatty was determined that the C.P.R. should maintain the leading position in the services to Canada on both oceans that it had attained by 1914. His aim was twofold: to provide the finest first-class ships on both the Pacific and the Atlantic and to supplement those on the Atlantic with a fleet of superior cabin-class liners. In addition, ten freighters bought during or just after the war would provide cargo services.

As early as 1916, building berths had been reserved in Clyde shipyards, and four new passenger liners were put in hand as promptly as circumstances permitted. Three were for the Atlantic and the fourth for the Pacific. Because rival lines were concentrating on cabin-class tonnage, all three of the ships for the Atlantic were of this type. The C.P.R.'s prototype *Metagama* had survived the war, and two somewhat larger ships being built in Great Britain for German owners had been purchased. The three new liners, larger still, thus increased the modern cabin-class fleet to six ships. On the Pacific severe American and Japanese competition was expected, and the *Empress of Canada*, of 21,500 tons, was designed to be the largest and finest ship on that ocean.

Shipbuilding immediately after the war proved to be costly and trouble-plagued, and the Canadian Pacific decided to postpone further construction, especially since former German liners could be purchased from the Reparations Commission at bargain prices. Four of these were acquired in 1921. Two were misfits, but the other two were notable ships. The 25,000-ton *Kaiserin Auguste Victoria* had been the largest liner afloat when she was completed in 1906; refitted and renamed *Empress of Scotland*, she replaced the lost *Calgarian* and gave the Atlantic fleet a luxurious flagship and much the largest vessel engaged in the Canadian trade. The new and even more luxurious *Tirpitz* became the *Empress of Australia*, was assigned to the Pacific, and was by a small margin the largest liner plying that ocean.

In the course of the war, the Allan and Canadian Pacific fleets had been taken over by a single management, Canadian Pacific Ocean Services, a name changed to Canadian Pacific Steamships Limited in 1921. The Allan identity was fast disappearing; the *Alsatian* had already been renamed *Empress of France* when she returned to civilian life, and in 1922 the older Allan ships that were considered worth retaining for a time were converted to cabin class and, like the Canadian Pacific's own ships of the type, were given names beginning with the letter *M*.

All this very considerable shipping expansion and reorganization had been accomplished by 1922. The Atlantic fleet was then headed by the *Empress of Scotland*, the *Empress of France*, and the *Empress of Britain,* providing what soon became the only first-class service between Canada and Europe. Early in 1922 the *Empress of Scotland* carried out the first cruise by a Canadian Pacific liner—the first of more than five hundred that would be made by C.P.R. liners over a period of fifty years. On the Pacific, the new *Empress of Canada* and *Empress of Australia* joined the *Empress of Asia* and *Empress of Russia* in the finest and fastest service across that ocean.

Canadian Pacific ocean shipping had become big business. The eight passenger liners built or purchased in 1919–22 and two ships acquired to augment the freighter service represented the expenditure of almost $50 million, of which nearly $22 million had been provided from the steamship replacement fund and other reserves.

Meanwhile Beatty had been wrestling with the problems of the railway. Costs, as always, were the chief concern. When the postwar boom broke late in 1920, prices and the cost of living began to fall and the Board of Railway Commissioners decided that freight rates should fall with them. The first reductions were made at the beginning of 1921 and others followed on December 1. The overall result was to reduce rates to only 56 percent above the prewar level, whereas operating expenses per train mile were still twice what they had been in 1913.

In 1922 the prime question was whether or not the Crow's Nest grain rates, suspended by Parliament for three years in 1919, would be reinstated. A backward glance is needed to make the position clear. As mentioned earlier, the basic rate to which the C.P.R. had agreed was 14 cents per hundred pounds from Winnipeg to Fort William. This the railway had reduced in 1903 to 12 cents to meet competition from the Canadian Northern. For a decade the rapid increase in the volume of grain handled and such economy measures as the use of larger cars kept these low rates remunerative. During the war years, however, as operating costs soared, all the railways, particularly the new western lines, suffered heavy deficits on their grain trade. As a first step, the C.P.R. raised its rates to the permissible maximum of 14 cents. This was clearly not sufficient, and in 1918 the government authorized an increase to 18 cents as part of the adjustments following the McAdoo Award. Justifying this concession in Parliament, Sir Robert Borden said: "We had our choice between the bankruptcy and cessation of the railways and taking that step. There was absolutely no alternative."[1] Finally in 1919, Parliament agreed to the suspension of the Crow's Nest rates for a period of three years.

Sir Edward Beatty, president of the Canadian Pacific from 1918 until 1942 and chairman from 1924 until 1943.

The changes in the rates on grain from Regina to Thunder Bay will illustrate the fluctuations that followed. The Crow's Nest charge was 20 cents per hundred pounds. This had been increased to 24 cents in 1918, and after the Chicago Award rose to a maximum of 32.5 cents in September 1920. The rate reductions ordered in 1921 had cut this to 29 cents by December, and on July 7, 1922, when Parliament allowed the suspension of the Crow's Nest rates to lapse, the original 20-cent maximum was restored.

Parliament's action is understandable. The whole purpose of the Crow's Nest agreement from the government's point of view had been to secure low and stable freight rates that would ensure that the grain harvest, the chief source of revenue on the prairies, could move to market even when wheat prices were relatively low. This was the case in 1922; grain prices had fallen far below the wartime levels and would fall still further in 1923.

It was and is a complicated matter. Movement of the crop to market was of vital interest to the railway as well as to the farmer, for much of its revenue from westbound freight was derived from goods that would be bought by prairie farmers whose purchasing power depended in very large measure upon grain sales. Eastern Canada was also affected, because most of the manufactured items brought into the West were produced there. The basic grain rate thus became of great importance to a large part of the country—so important, indeed, that regulation of it has never been delegated to the Board of Railway Commissioners or their successors, but has been retained by Parliament itself. But it has been tacitly assumed that if the railways find the rate unremunerative, they will have to recoup their losses by raising other tariffs.

Many of these points were illustrated in the three years of confusion that followed the reinstatement of the Crow's Nest rates. In a move that seems in retrospect to have been ill-advised, but was presumably taken in the hope that it might give the Canadian Pacific a bargaining position, the railway contended that the rates applied only to lines that had been in existence on January 1, 1898, when the original agreement became effective. Naturally there was a storm of protest. The *Winnipeg Free Press*, the voice of Manitoba, described the railway's action as a "conspiracy to break the law, rob the people and bulldoze Parliament." Beatty in return protested against the reimposition of "special statutory rates made under conditions which do not now obtain and which have no relation to present day costs and operating conditions. . . ."[2] The Board of Railway Commissioners next complicated matters by holding hearings and issuing an order that restored the rates that had been in effect before July 7, 1922. This meant in effect that the board agreed with Beatty that the Crow's Nest rates were no longer fair and reasonable, and the ruling also indicated that the commissioners believed that they had the power to alter them.

This claim the government would not accept. The Crow's Nest rates were reimposed by order in council, and the whole matter was referred to the Supreme Court of Canada. The judgment of the court, brought down in 1925, ruled that the railway commissioners had no authority to alter the rates, but agreed with the C.P.R. that they were applicable only to lines in operation on January 1, 1898. It was obvious that however sound this latter decision was in law, the inequalities in which it resulted could not be allowed to continue, and the rates question was settled by statute later in the year. The Crow's Nest rates were confirmed and made applicable not only to all rail lines in existence, but to any that might be added to the systems in future. The law made no reference to the reduced rates on westbound commodities to which the C.P.R. had also agreed in 1897; these would in future be subject to the jurisdiction of the Board of Railway Commissioners.

By the time this law took effect, a further grain problem had arisen. The opening of the Panama Canal in 1914 made transport by water from the

Pacific Coast to Europe so much quicker and cheaper that ports in British Columbia could hope to participate in the export trade in grain. Long before the canal was completed, the question was raised as to whether the C.P.R. planned to erect grain terminals in Vancouver, as it had done at Montreal and elsewhere. Shaughnessy had considerable doubts about the future of the Panama route, as he explained to the minister of trade and commerce in 1913; in his view, much would depend upon the volume of inward cargoes. "The grain traffic by itself would not be remunerative, except as a return cargo for vessels that would otherwise be compelled to return home light. . . ." In a major miscalculation he declared that it could "be taken as an accepted fact" that no vessels would come to British Columbia "merely for the purpose of getting a load of grain."[3] The C.P.R. had always intended to erect a transfer elevator at or near Vancouver, but before going ahead with construction it wanted reliable information about the quantity of grain that was likely to be handled.

The transfer elevator never materialized, but H. H. Stevens, Member of Parliament for Vancouver, persuaded the federal government to build a million-bushel elevator, which was completed in 1915. Inevitably the war prevented it for a time from serving its purpose effectively. The first major grain shipment to Europe—100,000 bushels—was not made until late in 1917; but after the war, trade grew rapidly. The first large-scale shipments were made in the crop year 1921–22. Only four years later, nearly 53 million bushels of wheat—37.2 percent of all wheat exported through Canadian seaports—were shipped from Vancouver. Freight rates on grain traveling from the prairies to Pacific Coast ports were obviously a vital factor in this trade, and after 1925 the Board of Railway Commissioners applied to it rates comparable to the Crow's Nest scale.

This gave rise to what may be termed a grain watershed on the prairies—the point at which freight rates determine whether it is more economical to ship grain eastward or westward. This was found to be in Saskatchewan, about fifty miles east of the Alberta border.

One other special case affected freight rates in the 1920s. The Maritime Provinces had long considered that union with Canada had not brought them the economic advantages they had been led to expect. In particular, freight rates on the railways to central Canada were held to be so high that Maritime ports and industries could not compete effectively in the main markets in Quebec and Ontario. A Royal Commission agreed with this view, and in 1927 Parliament passed the Maritime Freight Rates Act, which provided a 20-percent subsidy for certain "preferred movements" by rail. Roughly, these included local traffic within the Maritime region, traffic from it destined for points elsewhere in Canada, and export freight to be shipped overseas through ports in the Maritimes. The matter was of greater concern to the Canadian National than to the Canadian Pacific, as the former handled much more of the traffic in the region. Beatty was glad to receive the subsidy instead of having the new regional rates established at the expense of rail revenues, which he felt had been done in the case of the grain rates, but he opposed the plan in principle. In his view, some regional disparities were inevitable, especially in a very large country, and he was opposed to attempts to correct them by means of subsidies paid for by taxation. Had he known it, this was merely an early application of a policy that Canada was later to adopt on a massive scale.

The decision to restore the Crow's Nest grain rates was a severe blow to the revenue prospects of the Canadian Pacific, especially as it became evident that there would be no compensating increase in the general freight tariff. Nevertheless, it became clear that Shaughnessy's worst fears regarding competition from a nationalized system would not be realized; the government clearly had no intention of using reduction in rates as a major weapon with which to humble the C.P.R. In October 1920 it instructed the Board of Railway Commissioners to try to determine what would constitute "a fair and reasonable rate, without taking into account the requirements of the Canadian National Railway system." This meant in effect that the C.P.R. would be used as a yardstick and that rates would be set at a level that would enable it to survive and prosper; if the nationalized lines could not make ends meet with the tariff authorized, they would have to be subsidized from tax revenues. The commissioners came to the conclusion that the rates already in force were adequate for the purpose in view, and as it turned out, no increases were to be authorized for the incredible period of twenty-six years.

Since rates were not going up, Beatty strove to secure increased economy and efficiency that would safeguard and improve the railway's financial position. The two major items that he hoped to reduce were the wage bill and operating expenses.

The cost of living and American precedents were the chief factors that influenced wage changes in the early postwar years. Living costs began to decline late in 1920 and had fallen over 20 percent by 1922. Thereafter they changed only slightly for eight years. When freight rates were cut in 1921, it was obvious that wage reductions must follow, but remembering the McAdoo and Chicago awards, which had been made applicable to Canada, the Canadian railways waited to see what would happen in the United States. Action there came in May 1921, when the Railroad Labor Board ordered wage reductions varying from 5 to 18 percent and averaging 12 percent. In July, acting on the precedent of earlier awards, and without either government sanction or negotiations with the unions, the Canadian railways applied the new American wage scales. Trouble promptly arose on two scores. The government pointed out that their action violated Canadian labor laws, and the unions, though recognizing that wage cuts were inevitable and justified, objected that the specific reductions made were unfair to lower-paid workers. A long wrangle followed before matters were finally settled.

The wage question was next raised in 1924, when action in the United States once more spilled over into Canada. Since the McAdoo Award, there had been virtual parity in the wages of railwaymen in the two countries. In 1924 those employed by the American lines secured an increase of 5 to 6 percent, and the unions asked for a similar increase in Canada. This the railways refused on the grounds that the cost of living had not gone up and that conditions in the United States and Canada were no longer comparable. Actually, in spite of the postwar reductions, the railwaymen were still better off than formerly. Real wages had risen by 10 percent since 1920, and the paycheck of 1924 had appreciably greater purchasing power than the larger one of 1920.

Two years later American railwaymen received a further increase, and the disparity between American and Canadian wage rates rose to between 12 and 13 percent. The Canadian workers again asked for parity, and when this was refused by a board of conciliation, a strike was called. The presidents of the Canadian Pacific and the Canadian National then sat down with the union leaders and worked out an agreement that provided for wage increases averaging about 6 percent. But Beatty made it quite clear that henceforth he would not be willing to be governed by events in the United States. "We have not been able to convince ourselves," he told his shareholders in May 1927, "that wage scales fixed in a foreign country, either through negotiation or otherwise, and under conditions that do not obtain in Canada, should be accepted as reasonable on Canadian roads."[4]

Beatty had tackled the problem of operating expenses the moment the war was over. The most effective way of reducing them, as he explained some years later, "was by providing means for moving the largest possible tonnage of traffic with the fewest possible train miles and car miles."[5] Generally speaking, car miles can be reduced by using larger cars of greater capacity, and train miles can be cut if more powerful engines are available that can haul longer and heavier trains.

Beatty acted at once to secure the required engines. W. H. Winterrowd had recently become chief mechanical engineer, and under his guidance a new generation of locomotive types emerged from the Angus Shops in Montreal in

1919. First came No. 5300, prototype of a new 2–8–2 Mikado class of heavier freight engines with a tractive effort of 56,000 pounds. Ten came from the Angus Shops, and during the next decade ninety-five were supplied by other builders. Then followed two new classes of Pacific-type 4–6–2 engines, more powerful than the earlier Pacifics and designed to handle both passenger and fast freight trains. Finally, late in the year, came No. 5800, a 2–10–2 Santa Fe engine, the largest yet built by the C.P.R., with a tractive effort of 66,000 pounds. Nearly 200 of these four types were acquired by 1928, fifty-three of which the company built itself. As it happened, this was virtually the swan song of the Angus Shops as locomotive builders. Over a thousand engines had been produced by the company since 1883, but owing to a change in policy, it built only five more after 1921.

The drive for operating economy was aided greatly by the heavy purchases of rolling stock that had been made in the years just before the war. Beatty estimated that the engines and cars then acquired would have cost an additional $96 million at 1918 prices.

To this backlog he added thousands of new and larger freight cars. This policy was not peculiar to the C.P.R.; the total rolling stock of the country was transformed during the next fifteen years. In 1920, cars with a capacity of 30 and 40 tons were much more numerous than any others; 229,175 were in service on Canadian railways. By 1935 their number had fallen to 81,726. By contrast, in 1920 there were only 265 cars in service with a capacity of from 45 to 60 tons, whereas in 1935 they numbered 104,854. Over the fifteen years, the average capacity of all Canadian Pacific boxcars increased by nearly five tons, or over 12 percent, while the average capacity of flatcars increased by more than seven tons, or over 22 percent.[6] By 1932 the company had spent $72.5 million on this concerted effort to equip itself with larger-capacity engines and cars. Its reward was a substantial decrease in freight train operating costs that was sometimes as great as 40 percent.

Heavier trains required stronger tracks and bridges, and the C.P.R. undertook an improvement program almost comparable to that carried out by Shaughnessy in the dozen years before the First World War. Since 1908 the 85-pound rail had been the standard on main lines; in 1921 the 100-pound rail was adopted, and by 1937 it had been laid on 4,000 miles of track. Between Revelstoke and Field, in the Selkirks, where wear and tear was particularly severe, rail weight was increased to 130 pounds.

To gain access to the heart of Montreal, the Canadian Northern bored a tunnel under Mount Royal, and in 1916 this prompted the Canadian Pacific to begin ballasting certain of its busiest lines with rock spoil from the excavations.[7] Rock ballast offers the triple advantages of strength, good drainage, and freedom from dust, and it was first applied to the near sections of the main lines leading out of Montreal. After the war additional rock was obtained from other sources, including the nickel mine dumps near Sudbury. Over 2,500 miles of track had been rock ballasted by 1938, including the through line from Quebec and Montreal to Toronto and Windsor and the heavily traveled double track from Winnipeg to Fort William, which carried the eastbound grain traffic.

Heavier trains gave ties a severe beating, and with over 60 million in the system, replacement was an expensive maintenance item. Originally the C.P.R. used cedar ties whenever possible because of their resistance to decay, but in time the supply became exhausted. Substitute woods usually had a short life, so as early as 1906 the company was taking an interest in experiments with ties treated with creosote oil or zinc chloride. The first of a number of treatment plants was opened at Transcona, near Winnipeg, in 1911, but large-scale adoption of treated ties came in the Beatty period. Though considerably more expensive than untreated ties, they are also stronger, and more than pay for themselves by their much longer life. Today they are used throughout the Canadian Pacific system except where the life of a track is expected to be very short.

The first half-dozen years after the First World War were a period of uncertainty, but the Canadian Pacific, by equipping itself to do its work more economically and efficiently, managed to maintain its dividends and earn a modest surplus besides. Fortune varied from season to season: 1923 was a promising year when freight tonnage rose to 30.8 million tons, a figure exceeded only in the busiest of the wartime years, and the surplus rose to $5.7 million. But 1924 was disappointing: tonnage fell to 28.7 million and the surplus to just under $2.6 million. A recession began in late 1924 that lasted into the first part of 1925, but within months it became evident that a new stir was in the air, and the economy began the feverish buildup that was to lead to a climax in 1928 and to disaster in 1929.

By 1925 the Canadian National Railways had shaken themselves down into the semblance of a system, and under a dynamic leader were preparing to give the Canadian Pacific a run for its money. The famous duel between E. W. Beatty and Sir Henry Thornton was about to begin in earnest.

23

Beatty versus Thornton

In October 1922, Sir Henry Thornton became president and chairman of the Canadian National Railways. It was to prove an important date in the history of both national rail systems.

Thornton, fifty-one years of age, had been born in Indiana and educated at the University of Pennsylvania. He began his career with the Pennsylvania Railroad and was later general superintendent of the Long Island Railroad. In 1914 he went to England to become general manager of the Great Eastern Railway. The Great Eastern's main concern was with passengers rather than freight, and Thornton succeeded in making its patrons both numerous and well content with its services. He also succeeded in establishing happy relations with his railwaymen, as he was later to do with the labor force of the Canadian National. In 1917 the British government sent him to France, where he did outstanding work in managing military transport behind the battle lines. For this he was knighted in 1919.

A huge man physically, with a striking and attractive personality and a flair for publicity, Thornton was a marked contrast to his predecessor, D. B. Hanna. A shrewd and capable Scot, Hanna had been with the Canadian Northern Railway since its infancy. He had been the practical railroader who kept the trains running and earning their operating expenses while Mackenzie and Mann raised capital and built new lines. He had accomplished a great deal in most difficult circumstances since the government had taken over the Canadian Northern, created the Canadian National, and placed him in charge of it. He had struggled through repeated reorganizations as one railway after another was added to the system, and had managed to bring a measure of order out of chaos. The government had been generous in its support; an initial appropriation of $50 million in the spring of 1918 had enabled him to place substantial orders for new engines and rolling stock, and some $200 million had been made available for capital expenditures in the four years 1919–22. As a result, the physical state of the nationalized lines in the West had improved greatly.

Hanna would have been content to build up a sound but unspectacular system, devoted mainly to freight, that would eventually have paid its way. Thornton's approach was quite different. It became his frank ambition to make the Canadian National a railway that could compete energetically with the Canadian Pacific on almost every front, and he saw in the public purse a bountiful source for the funds this program would require. He was especially interested in the passenger business, and being very conscious of the power of publicity, believed that the handsome trains, hotels, and ships that would be needed for a first-class service would catch the eye and interest of the public and thereby gain both patronage and popular support for the railway.

Incidentally, this ambition was immensely helpful in building up staff morale and creating a new loyalty to the Canadian National that would supersede that to the particular company the individual worker happened to have served previously. Not a little of Thornton's success in creating a remarkable esprit de corps was due to the excitement of serving under a chief who was out to do battle with the Canadian Pacific. Conversely, the staff of the C.P.R. rallied to their company's support when it was faced with an aggressive rival. Neither railway was particularly generous to its workers during the Thornton decade, and a cynic might wonder if labor relations might have been more difficult if this sense of battle between the two railways had not tended to divert the attention of their staffs from such mundane matters as rates of pay and working conditions.

No doubt the rivalry between them and the prodigal expenditures it occasioned will long continue to be a matter of controversy. In 1932, when the Depression had ended the duel between Beatty and Thornton, Beatty remarked to a Royal Commission: "I do not know anything that taxes the judgment and the courage of a business executive more than an attempt to compete strongly and yet not unwisely."[1] It was a sentiment that might have been expressed just as appropriately by Thornton.

Both railways promptly set about expanding their systems, with the emphasis heavily upon new branches in the Prairie Provinces.[2] Indeed, all but 145 miles of the 2,266 miles of new lines built by the Canadian Pacific between 1923 and 1931 were located there. The old stamping ground in the South was not neglected, but more than half the new mileage was the result of

One of the first of the mighty Selkirks, built in 1929. The first of the class were the heaviest; they tipped the scales at 453,000 pounds.

a thrust farther north than the C.P.R. had yet penetrated. Before the war it had had no branches north of the main line of the Canadian Northern in Saskatchewan and Alberta; after 1923 it pushed hundreds of miles of track beyond it.

There were several reasons for this. Improved varieties of wheat that ripened earlier and had greater resistance to frost had extended the grain-growing belt considerably to the north; traffic that would support branches there appeared to be in prospect. Some of the new lines were through the northern reserve land grant area, in which the Canadian Pacific still had a large acreage of unsold land; it was only natural that it should wish to secure some of the traffic that would result from settlement, rather than allow all of it to be absorbed by the Canadian National. Mineral discoveries were being made in the north country, and there were other stirrings of life there in which the C.P.R. wished to share. Finally, Beatty was not averse to invading territory that the Canadian National regarded as exclusively its own.

These considerations affected different lines to different degrees. The 250-mile Willingdon branch, perhaps the most controversial of all, ran from Cutknife to Edmonton, for the most part through the land reserve area. There was no such justification for the network built farther east in Saskatchewan, more or less centering on Prince Albert, where the C.P.R. had no land but was simply setting out to compete with its rival for traffic. This spirit showed up most clearly in 1928, when Beatty announced a new branch building program that totaled 1,200 miles. Thornton countered with proposed new lines totaling 700 miles. The minister of railways tried to bring Beatty and Thornton together but their talks led to little change in the plans of either. "I decline to acknowledge the right of the Canadian National to claim any part of Canada as a special preserve," Beatty declared, "and I intend to proceed with my programme."[3]

His plans called for a thrust still farther to the north, with lines that would have reached the Churchill River and the Foster Lakes, but the Depression came and they were never built. The Canadian Pacific's northern limit on its own lines became Meadow Lake, just beyond the 54th parallel, but a purchase carried it beyond this point. In 1929 the C.P.R. and the Canadian National jointly bought from the government of Alberta 900 miles of regional lines that they reorganized as the Northern Alberta Railways. Based on Edmonton, they had been built originally by private interests but had later been taken over by the province. One of the two principal lines ran north to Waterways, adjacent to the Athabasca River, and the other northwest 500 miles to the Peace River country. A fifty-mile extension completed late in 1930 carried the latter over the border to Dawson Creek, in British Columbia.

The later Selkirks were streamlined, after the fashion first set by the light Jubilees and then followed in the later Hudsons. Selkirk 5921 was outshopped in 1938.

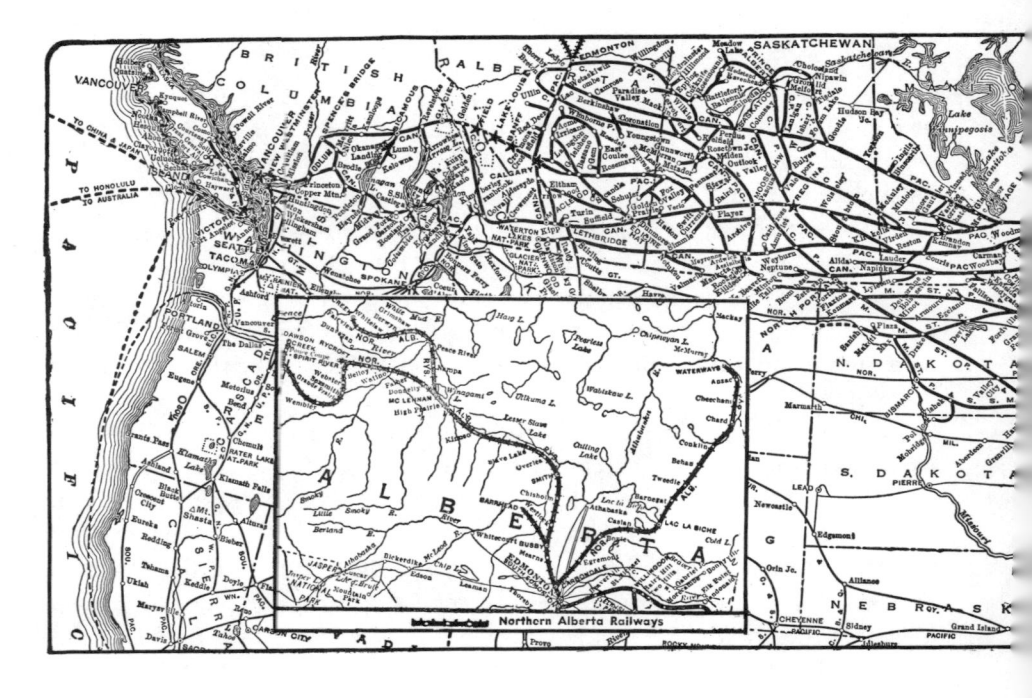

The Canadian Pacific system at its greatest extent, between 1933 and 1961. Mileage in Canada was then slightly more than 17,000. Lines in

    Between them the two companies added 4,161 miles to their systems in the nine-year period from 1923 to 1931, not including the Northern Alberta Railways and other lesser acquisitions. Canadian Pacific branches totaled 2,266 miles; those of the Canadian National 1,895 miles. Cost figures show the great extent to which construction centered in the Prairie Provinces. Almost exactly half of the $138 million spent by the two companies represented lines in Saskatchewan, and expenditure on the prairies as a whole exceeded $106 million—over three quarters of the total.

    When hard times came, the railways were freely accused of reckless spending and needless duplication of lines. On the score of costs, the C.P.R. made much the better showing. The average cost of its branches had been $32,000 per mile, and the figure had dropped steadily over the nine-year period. By contrast, the cost of the Canadian National branches had risen steadily and had averaged half as much again as that of the C.P.R.[4]

    Duplication of lines was actually much less extensive than critics of the

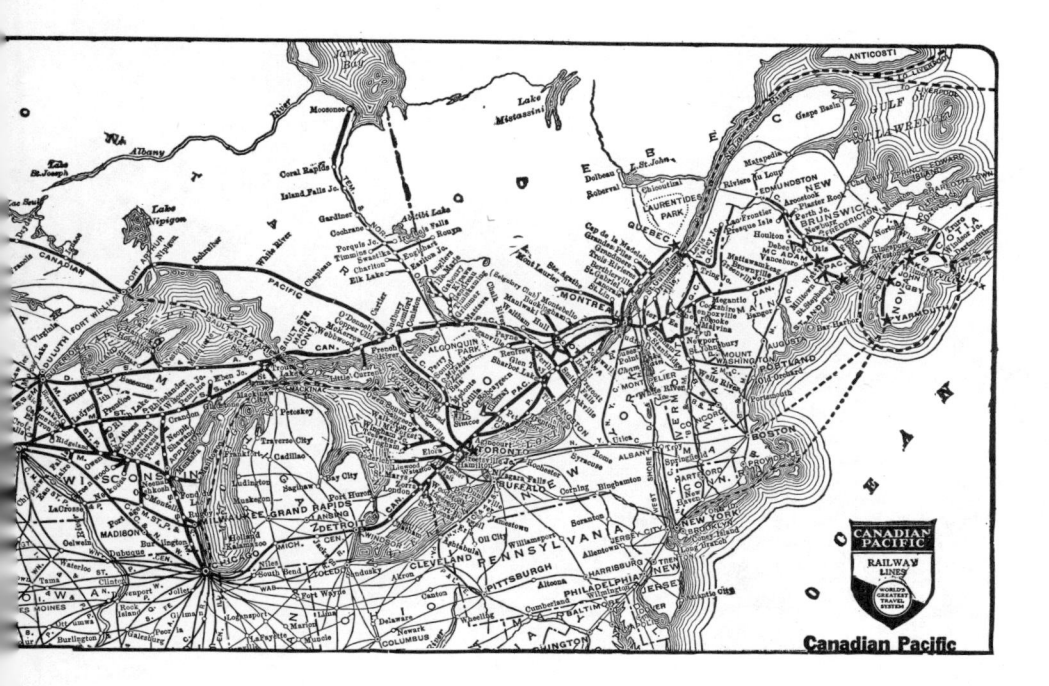

e United States totaled
out 4,700, making a total of
proximately 21,700 miles in

railways contended. A glance at the map will show that few of the rival lines paralleled one another closely. Much more important is the question of whether the new branches were needed and had some prospect of justifying their existence within a reasonable time. Competition or expectation of it undoubtedly prompted much construction; each railway invaded the other's territory, and both built branches into promising areas adjacent to their lines to protect them against such invasion, regardless of immediate traffic prospects. But the spirit of the times must be taken into account; the railways were building for a future that looked secure. The peak of their branch planning came during a brief period of great optimism and prosperity that seemed to suggest that Canada was well launched on another decade or more of rapid expansion similar to that which had ended in 1913.

There was still failure or reluctance to recognize that the First World War had caused fundamental and permanent changes. The stress Beatty placed on immigration is a case in point. Large-scale immigration had been responsible

The *Trans-Canada Limited* pulls out of Windsor Station in 1929, hauled by a heavy Pacific. This train represented the peak of Canadian Pacific passenger equipment before the introduction of air conditioning.

in great part for the earlier boom in the West, and Beatty repeatedly urged the government to adopt an energetic policy that would stimulate its resumption on the prewar scale. The C.P.R. manned and equipped its own land and colonization department and its Atlantic ships with this end in view. Canada, Beatty assured his shareholders in 1927, could "readily absorb 300,000 people per annum"—a figure that had been exceeded only three times in the palmiest days of the past. But the massive exodus from Europe to North America was over; in only three of the eleven years between the First World War and the Depression were immigrants from all sources even half as numerous as Beatty hoped they might be.

"In its early stages," Beatty told an audience in 1934, "the policy of the Canadian National was to co-ordinate its railway lines and its activities, to avoid capital expenditures which would add to the enormous financial burden, and to refrain from challenging the position of the Canadian Pacific in fields where that company pioneered." This was the Canadian National of Hanna's presidency; it was very different in Thornton's day. "In 1923, following a change of directorate and of management, that policy was discarded. It became the object of those in charge to establish a position of primacy at all costs, to duplicate or surpass every facility furnished by the Canadian Pacific and . . . to reduce the privately-owned railway to a condition of inferiority."[5]

This charge was true in great measure. Thornton believed that as long as the Canadian National was visibly inferior to the Canadian Pacific, it could neither prosper nor engage fully the loyalty and enthusiasm of its employees. Parity or, if possible, superiority therefore became his objective.

Beatty's reaction was to fight back on every front, and he had the major advantage of heading a system that had been planned as an entity from the beginning, whereas the Canadian National suffered from the handicap of being a conglomeration of lines that were never intended to be unified. In great part Beatty simply expanded and strengthened the system he had inherited from Shaughnessy; there were changes in scale but few in fundamental policies.

In typical fashion, the Canadian Pacific concentrated on the improvement rather than the expansion of its rolling stock. For the most part, new locomotives were refinements of the types introduced in 1919; engines increased in power but became somewhat fewer in number (2,130 in 1931 compared with 2,345 in 1922). Average tractive effort rose nearly 4,000 pounds, and freight train speeds increased. Changes in freight cars reflected a similar trend toward

The 42,000-ton superliner *Empress of Britain* nearing her dock at Wolfe's Cove, with Quebec City and the Château Frontenac in the background. This great vessel, largest ship lost in the Second World War, was destroyed by bombs and torpedoes in 1940.

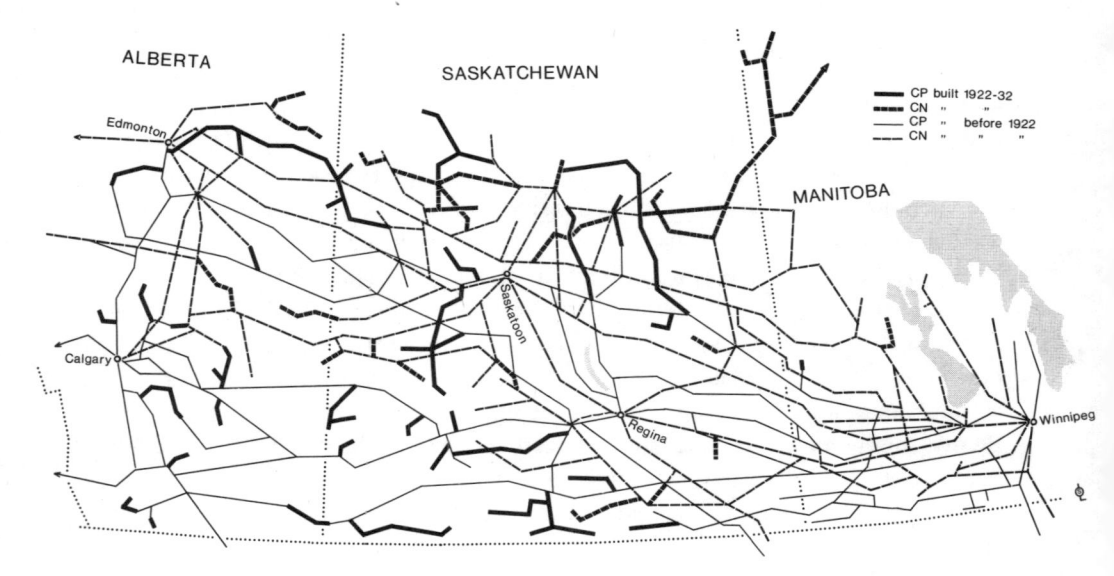

Branch line construction in the Prairie Provinces by the Canadian Pacific and the Canadian National in the decade 1922–32. This reflected the intense rivalry between Sir Edward Beatty and Sir Henry Thornton. It should be noted that the C.P.R. made extensive incursions into the country north of the C.N.R. Winnipeg-Saskatoon-Edmonton main line.

larger and fewer units. Thousands of old cars were retired and replaced; in a single year the C.P.R. ordered 7,500 sixty-ton boxcars. Though the total number of freight cars declined from 92,716 in 1922 to 89,406 in 1931, their average capacity increased from 37.1 to 40.8 tons. If it had been possible to bring them all together, they would have formed a continuous train over 650 miles long capable of carrying 3,647,765 tons of freight.

The freight-handling capacity of the Canadian Pacific was put to a sudden test in 1928, when it was called upon to move over 395 million bushels of grain—over 100 million more than it had ever handled previously in a single season. Traffic was heaviest between Winnipeg and Thunder Bay, and it reached a climax between September 15 and November 30. In seventy-seven working days, 111,475 carloads of grain left the yards at Winnipeg, an average of 1,447 cars carrying over 2.5 million bushels of grain every twenty-four hours. This was the equivalent of a sixty-car train every hour throughout the entire period.

But records of this kind aroused little attention. Passenger trains, hotels, and coastal steamers were the things that caught the public eye, and by them the rival railways were apt to be judged. Hanna had been relatively indifferent to passenger traffic and had made no attempt to match the Canadian Pacific's transcontinental services. Thornton, on the other hand, with his personal interest in passengers, set about equaling or surpassing the C.P.R.'s standards. Within a few months of the armistice, the Canadian Pacific had fortified its position by putting its first all-sleeping-car train on the run between Montreal and Vancouver, but its consist was made up of existing cars. Thornton soon began to counter its attractions by acquiring new and more luxurious sleepers, diners, and parlor cars. By 1929, not to be outdone, the C.P.R. had completely reequipped its transcontinental trains and had added the all-sleeping-car Mountaineer, operating between Vancouver and Chicago. Critics contended later that the new passenger cars upon which the rival systems lavished nearly $61 million were an extravagance quite unjustified by public needs or demands, but to a great extent the Canadian lines were only keeping in step with other major railroads on the continent. The period between the wars was the last great age of steam railroading, when numerous new name trains blossomed everywhere. Even if the Canadian National had offered no serious challenge, the Canadian Pacific would certainly have acquired equipment to keep its principal passenger trains competitive with those operated by neighboring American lines.

In the annals of Canadian Pacific steam, 1929 was a year comparable to 1919, which had seen the advent of heavier Mikados and Pacifics and the first of the huge Santa Fe–type locomotives. In September 1928, H. B. Bowen became chief of motive power. He designed two striking new engines that would deserve a place in any locomotive hall of fame—the 4–6–4 Hudson and the 2–10–4 Selkirk. They were, respectively, developments of the heavy Pacifics and the Santa Fes. Just as the 4–6–2 Pacific was a ten-wheeler with a two-wheeled trailing truck added to support a larger firebox, so the Hudson was a Pacific with a four-wheeled trailing truck to accommodate and carry a still larger boiler and firebox. The Selkirk was derived similarly from the 2–10–2 Santa Fe. The Hudson type had been used extensively by the New York Central and was named after the river that paralleled its line between New York and Albany. In the United States, the wheel arrangement of the Selkirk was known as the Texas type; its Canadian name, recalling the mountains through which many of the engines operated, was chosen after a competition among Canadian Pacific employees.

Twenty Hudsons and twenty Selkirks were built in 1929 and 1930. Both were remarkable engine types, handsome in appearance and fine performers. The Hudsons were intended primarily for heavy passenger service and had a tractive effort of 45,300 pounds. The Selkirks—at the time the largest and heaviest steam locomotives in the British Commonwealth—were used primarily in the mountains between Calgary and Revelstoke and were employed in both freight and passenger service. Their tractive effort was 78,000 pounds and the locomotive weight about 220 tons.

In the period 1923–31, the Canadian Pacific spent $14.5 million on locomotives; the Canadian National purchases were $20 million higher. Thornton had a larger system (22,277 miles in Canada in 1928 as compared with the 15,819 miles of the C.P.R.) and he had inherited a good deal of motive power that had to be discarded as soon as possible. Even so, the contrast between the two figures is striking. By and large, Parliament gave Thornton whatever funds he requested, and in 1923–31 capital expenditures of the Canadian National on rail and inland water lines totaled $394.2 million, while in the same period the Canadian Pacific spent $220.8 million. Neither total includes expenditures on hotels and coastal steamships—both items that were severely criticized in subsequent years.

Little exception could be taken to the Canadian Pacific's first postwar hotel projects. In July 1924 the old wooden wing of the Château Lake Louise, one of its two large resort hotels in the Rockies, was destroyed by fire. It was promptly replaced by a concrete structure that was ready in time for the succeeding tourist season. Six months later, fire heavily damaged the oldest part of the Château Frontenac in Quebec; here again rebuilding was prompt, and in 1926 the Château enjoyed the busiest year it had yet experienced. Meanwhile, it had been decided to complete the rebuilding of the Banff Springs Hotel, part of which still dated from 1887. This extensive project, completed in 1928, resulted in a huge, 600-room, brown limestone structure in what has been described as "a Scottish Baronial derivation of the château style."[6]

For a dozen years Regina had been the only major city on the main line between Montreal and Vancouver that did not have a Canadian Pacific hotel. This omission was made good by the completion of the Hotel Saskatchewan in 1927. The same year, the C.P.R. became involved in a complicated hotel tangle that developed in Halifax. The original proposal was for the construction of the Lord Nelson Hotel by a private company in which both the Canadian Pacific and Canadian National would purchase shares. The C.P.R. was to provide $100,000 and the Canadian National was to recommend to the government that it participate to the extent of $250,000. What happened subsequently is a controversial story that need not be detailed here; the Canadian National withdrew from the scheme and built a combined hotel and terminus at a cost of about $2.5 million, while in order to complete the Lord Nelson, the C.P.R. increased its subscription to $350,000.

Substantial additions were made to the Canadian Pacific hotels in Victoria, Vancouver, and Calgary, and three small hotels in the Maritimes were financed wholly or in part by the company. But what roused most criticism

Pacific Coast shipping in its heyday: three units of the *Princess* coastal fleet and the transpacific liner *Empress of Canada* tied up at Pier D in Vancouver about 1926. (COURTESY OF THE VANCOUVER PUBLIC LIBRARY)

later were two major projects in Toronto and London, England. In Toronto the Canadian Pacific built the Royal York, opened in June 1929. Its first season was so promising that an addition was built that increased its size to 1,156 rooms and made it the largest hotel in the British Commonwealth. Its cost was just under $16.5 million. By the time it was completed, the C.P.R. had determined to extend its chain overseas to London. A large property on Berkeley Square was acquired at a cost of nearly $5.5 million, but owing to the Depression and the Second World War, the project did not progress further.

The Canadian Pacific did not expect its hotel chain to make large profits. It was looked upon as an attraction and convenience that would cause tourists and other travelers to patronize C.P.R. trains and ships. If the company could offer comfortable accommodation as well as transportation, there was less likelihood that travelers would stray into the hands of rival companies. But there was always the additional consideration that a Canadian Pacific hotel that became the social center of a city was an excellent advertisement for the entire system and its services.

Lord Shaughnessy stated the case in 1918, in wartime prohibition days, in answer to an inquiry from H. D. Reid, of the Reid Newfoundland Company: "As a commercial venture I would not commend to you the erection, equipment and maintenance of expensive hostelries. The direct profit, even in our case, represented but a small return on the investment before prohibition became general. In present conditions all profit has disappeared, but even so the contingent advantages to the Company and to the localities served by the Company's lines, are such that we would not be without the hotels even though they were operated at a substantial loss."[7]

The loss was indeed substantial if the capital invested is taken into account. Even in the four very prosperous years from 1926 to 1929, the entire hotel chain, representing an investment of over $70 million, earned an average operating profit of only $1.1 million a year. Additions and improvements were financed from annual capital appropriations, and no provision was made for obsolescence until 1937, when a first transfer of $620,000 established a hotel depreciation reserve.

The Canadian National had fallen heir to three first-class hotels, the widely known Château Laurier in Ottawa, built by the Grand Trunk, and others in Winnipeg and Edmonton erected by the Grand Trunk Pacific. Thornton greatly enlarged the Château, added new hotels in Halifax, Charlottetown, and Saskatoon, and began building a $10 million hotel in Vancouver. Only the last competed with the C.P.R. chain, and this was not of Thornton's choosing. Mackenzie and Mann and the Canadian Northern had made lavish promises to the city of Vancouver that were legally binding on the Canadian National, and the city agreed to accept construction of the hotel as a settlement of all its claims—a point conveniently overlooked by Thornton's critics.

Thornton's least successful venture was an attempt to outclass the Canadian Pacific's British Columbia coast service. The C.P.R. had dominated the trade since 1901 and had built a succession of *Princess* steamers well adapted for the various routes served. By the time the First World War ended, half the fleet was past its prime, and eight new passenger ships were built between 1922 and 1931. Finest of them were the *Princess Kathleen* and *Princess Marguerite*, 22-knot steamers of 5,875 tons, completed in 1925. They were designed for the fast "triangle" run connecting Vancouver, Victoria, and Seattle.

Thornton had inherited a coastal service established by the Grand Trunk Pacific, engaged mainly in the trade north from Vancouver to Prince Rupert and Skagway. The service did not pay its way, but a link between the two Canadian National terminals at Vancouver and Prince Rupert was clearly desirable. The steamers employed dated from 1910, so a new ship to supplement them was fully justified. But instead of building a suitable steamer of moderate speed, the Canadian National ordered three ships that were larger, faster, and more luxurious than the best of the *Princesses*, and used two of them to inaugurate a rival service on the "triangle" route. It is doubtful if it could have cleared expenses in the best of times; launched as it was in 1930, at the beginning of the Depression, the results were disastrous. Deficits forced its abandonment within a year.

Comparison of the capital costs incurred by the two railways is interesting. C.P.R. investment in the British Columbia coast fleet increased by $8.7 million between 1923 and 1931. For this it secured eight new passenger ships, a freighter, a tug, and miscellaneous equipment. The three new Canadian National steamers alone cost almost $6.5 million. Here, as in many other instances, the Canadian Pacific secured much better value for its money.

One field in which the Canadian National made no attempt to emulate the C.P.R. was ocean shipping. This was an activity in which Beatty took a great personal interest, which no doubt explains in part the very large expenditures made on the company's fleet between 1926 and 1931. The purpose was to make still more dominant the position it had held on both the Atlantic and the Pacific since before the First World War.

On paper that position looked secure in 1925, but actually the company was in trouble. Many of its ships had passed their prime, and the machinery in all four of the new passenger liners that had entered service in 1922 was proving unsatisfactory. In addition, the luxurious *Empress of Australia*, the former *Tirpitz*, had turned out to be a problem child. The Germans had equipped her with experimental hydraulic gearing that failed in service, and as a result she was both expensive to run and too slow to maintain a satisfactory schedule.

In London Beatty met John Johnson, a brilliant marine engineer who believed that substantial economies could be achieved by the use of water-tube boilers, higher pressures, superheated steam, and single reduction-geared turbines. Johnson recommended that the *Empress of Australia* be given new machinery; Beatty agreed, and in the spring of 1927 the *Empress* emerged from the shipyards four knots faster and the most economical liner of her speed and size afloat. Reengining of all four of the unsatisfactory postwar ships followed. Meanwhile Beatty and Johnson had mapped out a building program that was to add 200,000 tons of new steamers to the fleet.

The company's Atlantic operations consisted of three distinct services—the first-class passenger service maintained by ships of the *Empress* class, the cabin-class passenger services provided by the *M* class steamers, and a freighter service. Beatty and Johnson set about making great improvements in all three, tackling them in the reverse order of that in which they have just been named.

During and just after the war, the Canadian Pacific had purchased a dozen general-purpose freighters, two of which had become war casualties. The survivors and three old Allan liners, demoted to freighter status, comprised the first postwar freighter fleet. Within a few years it was clear that better and more economical ships were needed, but circumstances caused delays in acquiring them. The standard ships mass-produced in emergency war programs were flooding the freight markets, and the situation was complicated further by a proposal that the government of Canada should sponsor a subsidized Atlantic service. This project was abandoned in 1925, which cleared the way for the building of the new ships Beatty had in mind.

Orders were placed for five new freighters that would be among the largest and fastest afloat. Of 10,000 tons gross, they had a nominal service speed of fourteen knots, sometimes exceeded sufficiently to allow them to overhaul the passenger ships of rival lines. They enabled the C.P.R. to maintain a fast weekly service between Canada and London and the Continent; sailing from Montreal on a Friday, they could be depended upon to begin unloading in London only nine days later—a great step forward in freighter schedules. Their names recalled the Beaver Line that the Canadian Pacific had purchased in 1903. The first of them, the *Beaverburn*, entered service in December 1927, and all five were on the run by the middle of March.

Plans for the new passenger liners had to reckon with a fundamental change in trans-Atlantic traffic. Like other companies, the Canadian Pacific had expected a postwar boom in immigration and had given each of its new ships accommodation for 1,200 or more third-class passengers. Owing to changed circumstances in Europe and drastic restrictions on entry into the United States, this traffic failed to develop on any scale. To make good the serious loss in revenue this involved, shipping lines began to upgrade sections of their third-class quarters in the hope of attracting students and other travelers who avoided the steerage but could not afford a cabin-class fare. The move was highly successful, and from it evolved the new intermediate class known at first as tourist third cabin and later simply as tourist. Its introduction meant that many ships intended to carry passengers in two classes were called upon to carry them in three, and in most of them tourist differed from third class chiefly in the food and service offered rather than in the actual accommodation.

In 1926 and 1927, the Canadian Pacific ordered four new liners that were among the first to take full account of these changes. They offered the best cabin-class accommodation in ships sailing to Canada, spacious and comfortable tourist-class quarters especially designed for the purpose, and a relatively small third class. Of 20,000 tons, with a speed of eighteen knots, they were the first liners in which Johnson's ideas were given full scope in the engine room. They were regarded as sufficiently outstanding to deserve distinctive names and went to sea as *Duchesses*. The first two entered service in 1928; the others followed in 1929. The advent of the *Beavers* and the *Duchesses* resulted in a wholesale retirement of older ships; of the former Allan liners, only the *Empress of France* was retained, and all the old freighters disappeared.

There remained the first-class service. The *Empress of Scotland* and *Empress of Britain* were both over twenty years old; replacements had become imperative. Here Beatty's plans were spectacular. Like Lord Shaughnessy before him, he intended to take advantage of the fact that Quebec is considerably nearer to Southampton than is New York. In 1907, when Shaughnessy was being urged to support a plan to build 24-knot ships, his reply was: "I believe in a boat of about 21 knots, one that will come from Liverpool to Quebec or Montreal as quickly as a 25-knot [steamer] can go from Liverpool to New York."[8] Shaughnessy never built faster ships than the 18½-knot *Alsatian*, but Beatty applied the concept on a grand scale. He planned a ship with the speed of 24 knots or better, which could match the passage times of the 27-knot liners that were about to be placed on the New York run, and increased its size to 42,000 tons, in order that its accommodation could compare with that of any ship afloat. The result was the second *Empress of Britain*, the only superliner ever built for service to Canada. Completed in 1931, she was capable of making a round trip across the Atlantic every fortnight. She was designed as a dual-purpose ship, with off-season cruises around the world in mind, and she had circled the globe eight times before the Second World War broke out in 1939.

The reengined *Empress of Australia* had been transferred to the Atlantic, and to replace her on the Pacific the C.P.R. built the second *Empress of Japan*. She was in many respects a scaled-down, 26,000-ton version of the *Empress of Britain* and once again gave the Canadian Pacific the finest and fastest ship on that ocean.

All this construction and renovation cost money. The C.P.R. spent $59,309,000 on ocean and coastal steamships between 1927 and 1931. In the latter year, the book value of the fleet was $116,398,000 and the steamship replacement fund stood at just under $27 million. The building program had reached an astonishing climax in 1928–29, when eleven ships had been launched for the company in only 366 days—nine for the ocean services and two for the coastal fleet.

Progress at sea had been matched by the development of rail traffic, which was building up to new peaks. Rail revenues had declined to $182.5 million in 1924, but they rose steadily thereafter to a record high of $229 million in 1928, when net operating revenues soared to $51.7 million. It was an intoxicating year, the climax of the pre-Depression boom. Even the debt-ridden Canadian National managed for once to pay the whole of the interest on its securities in the hands of the public.

In 1929 gross earnings declined $20 million, but other income was up and the net was still $43.1 million. The drop in revenue was due almost entirely to a poor harvest and the late movement of grain; the volume handled dropped by nearly 120 million bushels. The Wall Street crash in October came too late to affect the year's traffic and returns. In spite of the huge reduction in grain, the freight tonnage fell only from 40.3 million tons in 1928 to 38.2 million in 1929. It was in 1930 that the Depression first struck with some force, yet in May Beatty assured the shareholders that there was "no general or widespread depression in Canada" and that there was nothing "of a fundamental character which should prevent the return of normal business conditions within the next few months."[9] But by the end of the year rail revenues had fallen another $20 million and they would plummet a further $38 million, to $142.3 million, in 1931, a drop of 38 percent in only three years. The preference dividend was paid as usual, but in 1931 the return on common shares was cut from the 10 percent that had been distributed since 1911 to 5 percent. Even this amount was not earned; still hopeful that an upturn was coming, the company drew on reserves to make the payment; but it was to be the last dividend on common shares for eleven years.

It is not easy to pass judgment on the rivalry between the Canadian Pacific and the Canadian National, which was to a considerable degree a personal rivalry between Beatty and Sir Henry Thornton. Thornton worked wonders for the Canadian National and brought it up to standards that at many points compared well with the C.P.R. Thornton was a superb showman and a popular figure; his activities early produced the impression that he was humbling his rival. One observer wrote in 1925: "The C.P.R. no longer bestrides Canada like a colossus. It is almost impossible to realize fully the greatness of the change. Yesterday it was the only transcontinental, unchallenged ruler of the West. . . . To-day all that is changed; the country is more fully developed, and another great railway system has been built up, largely on the strength of Government contributions, to curb the giant's power."[10] But in truth neither system gained appreciably on the other; the proportion of the total freight traffic that each captured remained remarkably stable.

As the Depression deepened, the financial position of the Canadian National worsened rapidly; inevitably but unfairly, Thornton's popularity waned, and appreciation of his accomplishments declined with it. In 1929 net income fell short of interest due the public by $13.4 million; in 1931 the deficiency increased to $60.8 million.

The Liberal administration of W. L. Mackenzie King, which had appointed Thornton in 1922, had supported him generously. Political interference in the affairs of the railway had been surprisingly limited. In the critical years between 1926 and 1929, he had had the support of a minister of railways, C. A. Dunning, who was popularly supposed to have C.P.R. sympathies but was nevertheless fair to the Canadian National. After a general election in 1930, the King government was succeeded by a Conservative administration headed by R. B. Bennett, which took a dim view of Thornton and his works. The new minister of railways, R. J. Manion, was particularly critical.

Just as Lord Shaughnessy had been deeply concerned about the difficulties of the Canadian Northern and the Grand Trunk Pacific during the war years, so Beatty was profoundly worried by the state of the Canadian National in 1931. Convinced that a thorough airing of the whole Canadian railway problem was an essential preliminary to any solution, he suggested privately to Thornton that he should ask for such an inquiry. Thornton did so, the government agreed, and a Royal Commission was appointed in November 1931. It may be taken as marking the end of the Thornton era.

24

Weathering the Depression

The Royal Commission on Railways and Transportation appointed in November 1931 consisted of seven members. The chairman was Lyman P. Duff, a justice of the Supreme Court and soon to be named chief justice of Canada. The other members included Sir Joseph Flavelle, who had long been concerned with railway matters and had served as interim president of the Grand Trunk when the government first assumed control; Lord Ashfield, chairman of the London Underground Railways; and L. F. Loree, president of the Delaware and Hudson Railroad.

The preamble to the commission's sweeping terms of reference both censured the railways and showed awareness of some of their difficulties: "Having regard to the vital importance of transportation to the trade and commerce of Canada, the serious and continuing deficits of the Canadian National Railways System, and the diminished revenues of the Canadian Pacific Railway System, conditions which have been brought about in part by duplication of tracks, facilities and services of every kind and in part by competition by other modes of transportation, particularly motor vehicles operating on highways," the commissioners were directed to "inquire into the whole problem of transportation in Canada, particularly in relation to railways, shipping and communication facilities therein, having regard to present conditions and the probable future developments of the country. . . ."[1] Public hearings were held all across the country from Halifax to Victoria, and the commission submitted its report in September 1932.

It roundly charged the railways with needless expansion of lines and with providing unnecessary and expensive services. It alleged, for example, that they had established "a standard of passenger travel quite beyond the requirements of the country,"[2] and had invested "very large sums . . . in hotels which were not justified from any point of view. . . ."[3] Capital expenditures since 1923 were analyzed and investments in new branch lines, rolling stock, hotels, and coastal steamers set forth in detail.

When the commission was appointed, friends of Sir Henry Thornton and the Canadian National felt that it would reflect the Conservative government's prejudice against the system, and so it proved. Both railways shared its displeasure, but it bore down much more heavily on the Canadian National. Thornton's work received scant recognition, although the report did admit that the National system had been "energetically administered" and had "deservedly won approval by its success in welding together the various working forces of the separate companies in the consolidated system." But in a frequently quoted sentence it added that "running through its administrative practices" there had been "the red thread of extravagance." The fault lay in its ready access to public funds. "The disciplinary check upon undue expenditure, inherent in private corporations because of their limited financial resources, has not been in evidence. Requisitions of the management have been endorsed by governments, and successive parliaments have voted money freely, if not lavishly."[4] As a result the Canadian National had indulged in "costly adventures in competitive railways out of proportion to the needs of the country."

As the Depression deepened, Beatty had been more and more drawn to the conclusion Lord Shaughnessy had reached during the First World War, when the Canadian Northern and the Grand Trunk Pacific were sinking into bankruptcy. Unification of administration, if not outright amalgamation of the two railway systems, preferably under Canadian Pacific management, with a proviso that would give the C.P.R. shareholders a guaranteed dividend, seemed to Beatty to be the only solution to the Canadian railway problem— meaning thereby some arrangement that promised to relieve the government and therefore the taxpayer of having to provide tens of millions of dollars every year to meet the deficits of the Canadian National Railways.

It seems that for a time Thornton had been forced to a very similar conclusion. Government interference in the affairs of the Canadian National had become so marked that he felt that unification might be the only way in which to protect the system from the politicians. But by the time he appeared before the commission, he had come to the conclusion that unification was politically impossible. Beatty refused to recognize this and insisted that common management was the only solution in sight. But the commission would have none of it.

"Whatever merits or demerits this proposal may have," its report read, "the time is not opportune for giving serious consideration to this particular

The remarkable multipressure experimental locomotive built by the Canadian Pacific in the Angus Shops in 1931. It is said to have been the largest steam locomotive ever operated in Canada; its weight was 495,000 pounds.

remedy; neither complete public nor complete private ownership is possible." The old fear of monopoly, however hedged about with safeguards, was as strong as ever. "To establish a monopoly of such magnitude and importance would place in the hands of those responsible for the administration of the system powers that would, if not properly exercised, prejudice the interests of the Dominion as a whole."[5]

Thornton's counter suggestion was close cooperation between the two systems, watched over by a tribunal with power to enforce economy measures if need be. Neither his defense of the Canadian National nor the case for compulsory cooperation was presented to the commission with the effectiveness we would have expected from Thornton. Perhaps the cancer that was to claim his life within a year was already sapping his vitality. The fire seemed to have gone out of the man; feeling that his usefulness to the Canadian National had ended and that the politicians were determined to have their day, he resigned before the commission had submitted its report. But the idea of compulsory cooperation had caught the interest of the commissioners, and they recommended it as the best available solution to the country's railway problem.

In October 1932, when the government announced that it would introduce legislation to implement the recommendation, Beatty sent a spirited defense of the Canadian Pacific and a vigorous protest against compulsion to Prime Minister Bennett. Confronted with an ambitious competitor supported generously by Parliament, the C.P.R. had been "compelled to choose between meeting the competition, or, accepting a secondary position, face a gradual decline from the encroachments of its rival." The course pursued by the Canadian Pacific, Beatty insisted, had been "defensive and not aggressive." With the various proposals for cooperation the company was in entire accord, but it was strongly opposed to their enforcement by compulsory arbitration. This would "take away from the owners of the Canadian Pacific the power of deciding what is in their own interest, and vesting it in persons over whom they have no control. The company cannot allow this to become law without protest. It is regarded as an invasion of its rights, secured by its charter and by its fifty years of public service."[6]

Beneath Beatty's signature as chairman and president appeared the words: "By Order of the Board of Directors." It is perhaps significant that the letter made no reference to unification or common management as an alternative policy. Many within the Canadian Pacific, including some of Beatty's closest associates, believed that, however great its economic merits, political considerations ruled out unification, and the board was reluctant to be identified with it. But Beatty, convinced and adamant, soon launched a one-man campaign in an effort to bring it about. The chief means employed was a series of addresses in the principal Canadian cities, the first of which was delivered before the Canadian Club of Toronto in January 1933. His basic contention was that the creation of one system with one management was the only way in which really effective economies could be obtained. "By no other means," he said, "can we secure a sound business administration for our railway undertakings and relief to the taxpayers of Canada."[7] The federal income tax paid by individuals afforded a measuring stick with which to gauge the problem. In the ten preceding fiscal years it had yielded a total of $249 million, "or less than half the deficits of the Government railways."[8]

Over and over again, in succeeding years, Beatty would tell the same story. A barrage of pamphlets supplemented the speaking effort. His biographer states that some forty stenographers were added to the public relations staff "who sent out hundreds of thousands of pieces of unification literature."[9] Predictably, in view of the political circumstances, it all produced no practical effect whatsoever.

Beatty's hopes rose briefly in 1938, when the Senate, which had looked with favor upon the proposal for unified management in 1925, decided to consider it a second time.[10] Each of the railways was asked to estimate the annual savings in which the plan might result. The Canadian Pacific's estimate was $75.3 million at 1930 traffic levels; the Canadian National figure was $56.2 million. Beatty suggested that the matter should be studied by indepen-

Locomotives being overhauled in the Angus Shops, Montreal, in the days when steam still reigned supreme.

dent experts in engineering and accounting, but Parliament prorogued without any action having been taken.

The Canadian National–Canadian Pacific Railway Act, providing for cooperation between the railways and including provision for an arbitral tribunal, had become law in May 1933. The results it achieved were very limited. Chief among them was the pooling of passenger services on the heavily traveled routes between Montreal and Quebec, Montreal and Toronto, and Ottawa and Toronto. At the end of 1934, the C.P.R. estimated that the annual savings of the two systems attributable to cooperation was $1,220,510. By 1937 the total had crept up to $1,756,000. Numerous proposals were discussed, but few were agreed upon; as Beatty had remarked to a Senate committee, it would "tax the ingenuity of any board of trustees or board of directors to reconcile competition and co-operation."

The arbitral tribunal to which the Canadian Pacific had objected so strenuously never materialized. The statute stated that the chief commissioner of the Board of Railway Commissioners was to be its chairman, but since the government left the position of chief commissioner vacant, the tribunal was never constituted.

The Depression induced one other instance of significant cooperation between the two railways. Work on the new Canadian National hotel in Vancouver had slowed to a crawl; it never actually ceased, though at one time the work force was said to consist of only two or three plumbers installing fixtures in 560 bathrooms. By 1938 it was approaching completion, but it was obvious that under existing conditions neither it nor the Canadian Pacific's Hotel Vancouver could possibly meet expenses if they competed with one another. To solve the problem, the C.P.R. undertook to close its hotel, and the Canadian National agreed to the operation of the new building as a joint enterprise. The Royal Tour of 1939 afforded an occasion for the changeover. In May, as the King and Queen were arriving in Canada, historic old Hotel Vancouver closed its doors after fifty-two years, and its name and staff migrated to Thornton's much-maligned castle a block away.

Meanwhile Beatty had been piloting the Canadian Pacific through the most difficult years it had experienced since construction days. Like other major carriers on the continent, the C.P.R. faced (in Beatty's words) "an economic storm of unparalleled violence" and saw its revenues fall alarmingly year by year. By 1933 they were less than half the 1928 total. Thanks to high maintenance standards and other circumstances that made temporary substantial reductions in costs possible, working expenses could be cut back almost to a like degree. Nevertheless, in the seven years from 1932 to 1938 net rail earnings were insufficient, though sometimes only by a narrow margin, to meet fixed charges. It was the additional income from nonrail sources—ocean and coastal steamships, hotels, communications, and miscellaneous investments—that enabled the company to meet its obligations. To Beatty's distress, for the first time since its inception the company paid no dividend on its common shares in 1932, and the preference dividend had to be passed as well in 1933. This was a shock to investors, especially those of modest means, for both dividends had been paid with such regularity that they had come to be looked upon as an unfailing source of income.

Yet it was the ability to pass dividends when necessary that helped the Canadian Pacific to weather the storm. The lavish capital expenditures of 1926–31 had increased the total of outstanding securities to $951.5 million, but almost exactly half of this ($472.2 million) represented common and preference stock. Beatty had added $133 million to the funded debt, which had increased fixed charges by 50 percent, or $7.3 million, to $22 million, but when it was hard pressed, the company could compensate for this more than five times over by passing dividends, which in 1930 had still totaled a generous $38 million.

Two special financial difficulties added to Beatty's problems. The first was the virtual impossibility of arranging for refinancing on any scale during the worst years of the Depression. Securities totaling $38 million would mature in 1933, and others that would push the total to well over $50 million would fall due in 1934. Default, which could well have a devastating effect on the whole Canadian financial structure, had to be avoided at all cost, so Beatty turned to Prime Minister Bennett for help. In response the government guaranteed a loan of $60 million at 5 percent by a syndicate of Canadian banks. As collateral, the company deposited $100 million of 4-percent consolidated debenture stock. Grave though the crisis had been, it proved to be of relatively short duration. In 1934 the Canadian Pacific was able to reduce the notes outstanding to $48 million, and the entire issue had been retired by 1936.

The second special problem concerned the company's American subsidiaries, which were particularly hard hit by the Depression. Chief of these was the Soo Line—the Minneapolis, St. Paul and Sault Ste. Marie Railway—with lines totaling over 4,000 miles. Much of its expansion had been financed by the sale of securities, the interest on which had been guaranteed by the C.P.R., and as its fortunes declined, this guarantee had to be made good. A first advance of $1.4 million was required in 1931; in succeeding years the sums needed were much greater, and in 1934 and again in 1935 approached $5 million.

In 1932 the Wisconsin Central, controlled by the Soo Line, failed to earn even its operating expenses. Unable to help, the Soo Line had no alternative but to let it go into receivership. The same year, in the Far West, the small Spokane International Railway was taken over by a trustee. Sorely pressed as it was by its own problems, the C.P.R. deemed it prudent to set aside $4 million as the nucleus of a reserve to provide for the probable writing down of its investments in American lines, and this was added to annually thereafter.

In the East, the Duluth, South Shore and Atlantic was also in trouble. It was compelled finally to file a petition in bankruptcy at the end of 1936, when an issue of mortgage bonds was about to mature and it found itself without funds to redeem them. A year later the Soo Line filed a similar petition; to remain solvent, it would have required a substantial advance over and above that called for to meet the interest charges the Canadian Pacific had guaranteed, and the C.P.R. did not feel justified in providing it.

No. 3100, shown here in the Angus Shops lifted clear of its running gear, was of the only two Northern 4-8-4 type locomotives ever acquired by the Canad Pacific.

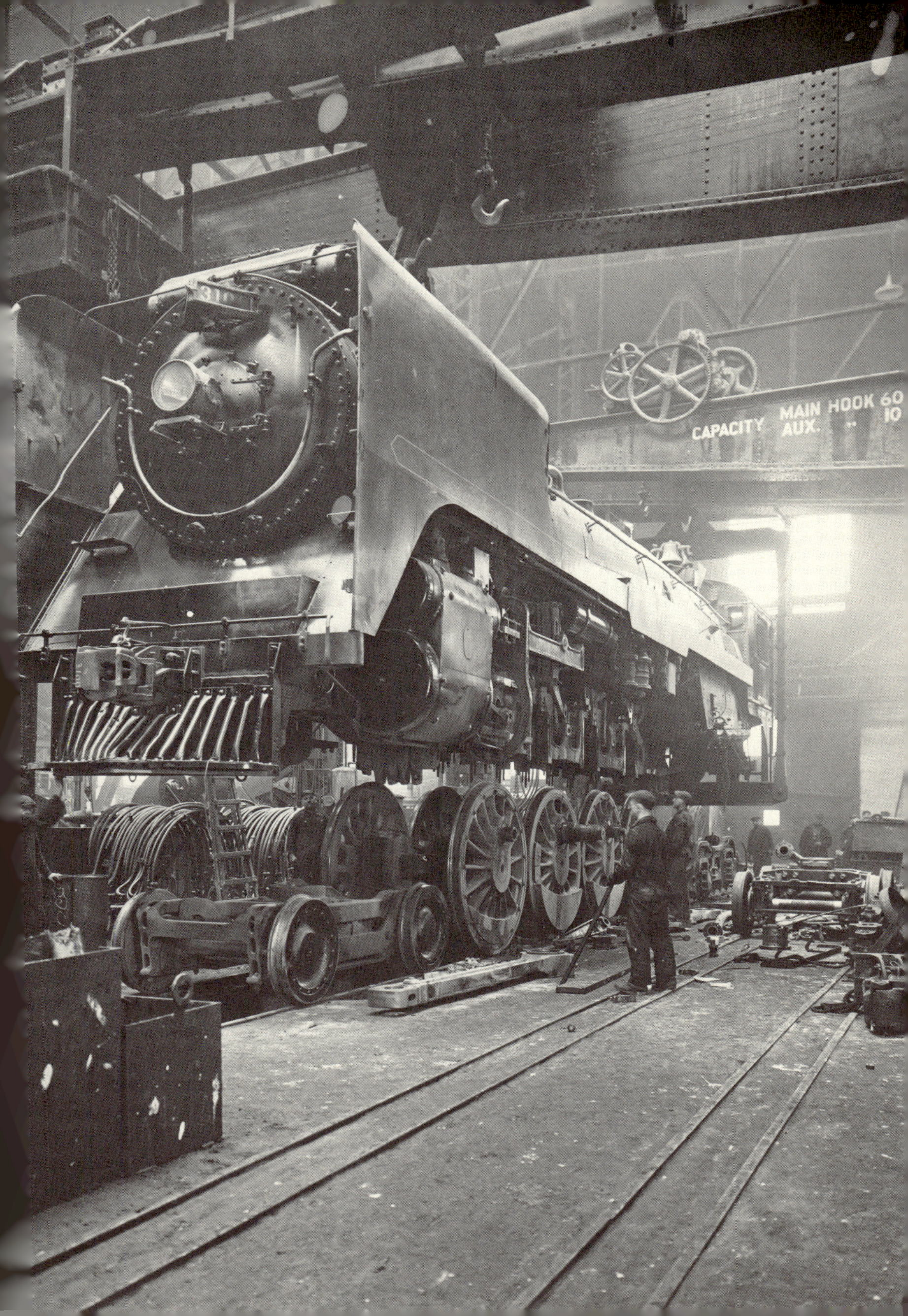
CAPACITY MAIN HOOK 60
AUX. " 10

Over the next year it was able to cut its Soo Line liabilities substantially. Two issues of first-mortgage bonds, totaling nearly $65 million and constituting about two thirds of the securities upon which the C.P.R. had guaranteed the interest, matured in 1938. The Canadian Pacific took the view that its guarantee expired when the maturity date was reached, whether or not the principal had been repaid, and this view was sustained by the courts.

In May 1938, Beatty summarized the financial story of the controlled lines in the United States as follows: total investment, including advances, had been $61,162,000; interest and dividends received over the years had totaled $33,657,000; the reserve built up against capital loss had reached $23,508,000.[11] A year later, $15,650,021 of this reserve was used to write off the Canadian Pacific's holdings of Soo Line, Duluth South Shore, and Spokane International stock. As it turned out, the year 1938, in which it failed to earn its operating expenses, was the lowest point in the Soo Line's fortunes. Much better days lay ahead, but reorganization was not completed until 1944.

Drought, rust, and early frosts in the grain-growing area it served had been a major cause of the Soo Line's difficulties. In 1928 it had carried 58 million bushels of grain; in the years 1931–35 the average dropped to 19 million and in 1936 fell to only 11 million. The Canadian Pacific had a similar experience. Agricultural income in Canada dropped from $856 million in 1928 to only $233 million in 1932. Contributing substantially to this decline was a dry period in the prairie weather cycle, which produced drought conditions over a large area in southern Saskatchewan and Alberta that was served principally by the C.P.R. Grain traffic had reached a sudden and dramatic peak in the golden year of 1928, when the C.P.R. carried 370 million bushels; the average figure of 241 million for the years 1925–30 gives a better idea of what had come to be looked upon as normal traffic. The average fell to 164 million bushels in 1931–33. For most industries in Canada, the turning point in the Depression came late in 1932 or early in 1933, but grain was an exception and this boded ill for the C.P.R.

In spite of the low rates imposed by the Crow's Nest Pass Agreement, grain traffic was of vital importance to the railway, both for its own sake and for the purchasing power grain sales provided in prairie communities. "In a very peculiar sense," Beatty told his shareholders in May 1934, "the prosperity of the Company depends upon the prosperity of agriculture, and, therefore, of Western Canada, from which territory about 60% of its freight earnings are normally derived."[12] While other traffic began to pick up, grain continued to lag. In 1934–36 average carryings were 141 million bushels, and in 1937 they plummeted to only 94 million. Thereafter, at long last, the drought cycle began to moderate; rail revenues from grain and grain products rose by over $15 million in the next two years.

At this difficult time, "other income," derived from hotels, ocean and coastal steamships, communications, and miscellaneous investments, though much reduced, was of key importance; added to rail net earnings, it enabled the company to pay its fixed charges and have a small surplus as well.

In 1932, for the first time, the hotel chain failed by a narrow margin to earn its operating expenses. Far from being the cause of this deficit, the Royal York in Toronto, which critics had assailed as the very symbol of reckless extravagance, had contributed substantially to income and had helped to carry those hotels that had slipped into the red. In spite of having been opened in 1929, on the eve of the Depression, it had earned $1.5 million in net revenue by the end of 1932. However, plans to build the projected counterpart in London were abandoned. The Berkeley Square site was leased in 1936, and the large office building erected on it was used during the war by the British Air Ministry. In 1944 the site was sold.

That other alleged symbol of extravagance, the superliner *Empress of Britain*, was doing as well as the Royal York. In the difficult year of 1931, when she entered service, her Atlantic voyages earned an operating profit of nearly $400,000. The number of passengers she attracted increased each year, and her annual cruise around the world became a great event of the winter season. Some alleged that her revenues were gained at the expense of the other ships of the fleet. No doubt this was true to some degree, but all Canadian Pacific ships benefited from the prestige won by the fast and luxurious *Empress*. Proof of this came in 1933, when C.P.R. liners carried 60 percent of the passengers traveling between Canada and Europe, although they made only a third of the sailings. Naturally, Beatty the ship enthusiast was gratified by the success of the *Empress*. "The service afforded by this ship," he said with justice in 1935, "has enabled the Company, in the face of the most severe competition, to maintain a position in the shipping world which otherwise would not have been possible."[13]

Nevertheless, the Atlantic fleet felt the full force of the Depression. Just as the railway reduced working expenses by making the greatest possible use of its most efficient locomotives and rolling stock, so the ocean services laid up older liners and maintained curtailed schedules with the newest and most economical ships. The *Beaver* freighters sailed each week as usual, but at the lowest ebb, only the *Empress of Britain* and four of the dozen other passenger liners were in regular transatlantic service. To give ships and crews some employment, the C.P.R. turned to low-cost cruises. These proved highly popular, and the *M* class cabin liners made over 200 cruises from British ports at fares of about a pound per day. Eventually four of the older steamers were sold, including the *Empress of France*, the former *Alsatian*. She was the last survivor of the famous Allan Line fleet, which had been plying the Atlantic since 1819.

The Pacific *Empresses* fared somewhat better; the addition of Honolulu as a regular port of call resulted in a welcome increase in patronage. Harder hit was the service from Vancouver to Australia, maintained for many years by the Union Steam Ship Company of New Zealand, which was facing damaging competition from heavily subsidized new American liners based at San Francisco. To bolster the Canadian service, the C.P.R. became half owner of a new company, the Canadian Australasian Line Limited, which took over the liners *Niagara* and *Aorangi* and planned to replace them with new ships as soon as conditions permitted. The link connecting Canada, New Zealand, and Australia was regarded as highly important to the Commonwealth; for that reason it had received subsidies at various times from the British, Canadian, New Zealand, and Australian governments. It was hoped that these would be increased sufficiently to cover the higher operating costs of much larger and faster new liners.

The C.P.R. would also soon be faced with the necessity of replacing the two older transpacific liners, which had been in service since 1913, and on the Atlantic a sister ship for the *Empress of Britain* was required to make possible a weekly deluxe express service. With the two proposed Australian ships, a building program to include five liners totaling about 150,000 tons was thus in prospect. Beatty was hopeful that the five could be secured for about $45 million. As the Depression began to lift, plans for the new ships were prepared, and in July 1938 he arrived in Britain expecting to place the first orders. Instead, he found that the British rearmament program had pushed up shipbuilding prices, and the bids he received were so high that he decided to defer construction. The Second World War then intervened, and none of the five liners envisaged was ever built.

Developments at the Trail smelter will be described later, but it is relevant to note here that dividends from the Consolidated Mining and Smelting Company were substantial and important to the Canadian Pacific in the worst Depression years. Payments rose steadily from just over a million dollars in 1934 to $5.8 million in 1937. In 1936 and again in 1937 they amounted to half the total of the "other income" that made it possible for the C.P.R. to meet all fixed charges from revenue. Nor did these dividends represent the whole of the contribution made by the smelter; business related to it made a substantial contribution to freight revenue.

Its lands were of no assistance to the C.P.R. at this time; quite the contrary. High grain prices during the later years of the war had cushioned for a time the effects of the collapse of the boom in 1913, but the 1920s were a disappointing period on the prairies. Grain prices were low and the farmers shared only to a limited extent in the hectic prosperity of 1926-29. Although land sales were substantial, in the years from 1921 to 1929 new contracts exceeded cancellations only in 1928 and 1929; sales totaled $31.5 million and cancellations $36.4 million. In the Depression years from 1930 to 1937, the negative balance was greater still; sales totaled $10 million and cancellations $17.7 million.[14]

In keeping with its usual policy, the Canadian Pacific did its utmost to help the genuine settlers to remain on their properties, almost regardless of how much their payments might be in arrears; cancellation was a last resort. In 1932 the company began to grant rebates on interest payments, and adjustments on principal followed. By 1936 these and other concessions had totaled over $9.5 million. They continued to be granted year by year until after the Second World War, and by 1948 had reached an aggregate of over $28 million.

To the Canadian Pacific's disappointment, the Alberta irrigation project, upon which it had spent millions, was less successful than it had expected. There were a number of reasons for this. Some difficulties developed in the irrigation system itself; the demand for water varied from season to season with the rainfall; and many of the farmers preferred to take a chance on raising a crop without irrigation in order to avoid the expense and labor involved. The C.P.R. established demonstration farms to show the variety of crops that could be grown advantageously and profitably by irrigation, but many of the farmers still raised little besides grain. The greatest problem of all was to secure the type of settlers who would take up the irrigated land and exploit it successfully.

The Canadian Pacific came at last to the conclusion that the whole enterprise might have a better chance of success if it were managed by some sort of local authority that would represent the landowners themselves. In 1935 the eastern block of the irrigation project was turned over to the trustees of an Eastern Irrigation District; the transfer included 1,233,000 acres of unsold land, the deferred payments still due on land under contract, and a cash payment of $300,000 to assist the new district during the transition period. A decade later the western section would be transferred to a similar body, and the Lethbridge system would be turned over to the province of Alberta. It was not the future the C.P.R. had envisaged for a project upon which it had expended $32.9 million by 1937.

As traffic declined, employment declined with it, and at the depth of the Depression the working force of the railroads had been reduced drastically. In 1928 the Canadian Pacific had 75,709 employees and the annual payroll was $117.4 million. By 1933 there were only 49,412 employees, a reduction of 26,297, and the payroll had fallen to $63 million. The peak of employment by the Canadian National came a little later, in 1929, when its work force totaled 109,096, but by 1933 only 70,625 were employed. Between them, the two systems thus laid off nearly 65,000 workers, and their combined payrolls were reduced by $131.8 million. This by itself constituted a very substantial contribution to unemployment and a serious reduction of purchasing power in Canada.[15]

Inevitably, wage cuts were another characteristic of the Depression years. In May 1931 Beatty announced that the salaries of office staffs had been cut by 10 percent and that all executive officers had accepted a similar reduction. When dealing with the railway unions, the Canadian Pacific and the Canadian National acted in concert, and in September both gave notice that wages would be reduced by 10 percent in October. The move can scarcely have been unexpected, but it was nevertheless arbitrary and contrary to the procedures prescribed by law; it was therefore rejected immediately by the unions. A board of conciliation found in favor of the railways, and the 10-percent reduction was made effective until the end of January 1933.

In this and later discussions, the railways based their case primarily upon two considerations: inability to pay, owing to the drastic fall in their revenues, and the sharp fall in the cost of living. The first argument the unions refused to recognize then or subsequently, but the decline in the cost of living was a difficult point to counter. By the end of 1931 the index had fallen over 11 percent as compared with 1930, and a year later the drop was nearly 20 percent. In spite of the wage cut, therefore, real wages had increased rather than decreased.

In 1931 both parties hoped, and probably expected, that the Depression would be relatively short. Neither had any such expectation when the next round of discussions took place, in 1933. The railways proposed wage cuts of 20 percent; the board of conciliation agreed, but the unions refused to accept the reduction and called a strike vote, which was supported overwhelmingly. The prime minister then intervened, and a compromise settlement providing for a 15-percent cut became effective November 1, 1933. The salaries of all senior officials were also reduced by 15 percent, directors' fees by 20 percent, and Beatty's own salary by 35 percent.

While a third round of wage discussions was in progress in the fall of 1934, events in the United States had repercussions in Canada, just as they had had in 1917 and 1918. Wages there had been reduced by 10 percent, but an agreement was reached for the elimination of the cut in three stages: full wage rates were to become effective again on April 1, 1935. In the light of this, the Canadian railways agreed to reduce deductions to 12 percent at the beginning of 1935 and to 10 percent on April 1. All concerned knew that this was merely a preliminary settlement, and in the autumn twenty-one unions made a joint approach to the companies. The railroads pleaded inability to pay; this argument the unions again refused to accept, and a second strike call went out. As before, the government intervened. The outcome was an agreement under which the wage deductions were to be removed in eight stages, with full rates to be restored on April 1, 1938. Throughout the period when the wage cuts were in effect, the decline in the cost of living had always been greater than the cuts, and real wages had thus been higher than in 1930.

These prolonged wage disputes put a severe strain on employer-employee relations, but in spite of this, loyalty to the Canadian Pacific continued at a high level. When things were at their worst, the search for economies extended to the smallest items, and employees did their best to make do with what was available. Former President Crump tells a story of a shop foreman who ordered some black paint. The requisition was promptly questioned, and he was asked why the paint was required. "To brighten up the place" was the classic reply!

Various measures were taken by the Canadian Pacific in cooperation with the government to ease the impact of unemployment during the Depression. By 1933 the company's shops were working only ten or twelve days a month. Early in 1934 this was increased to fourteen days. Later, advances made by the government, to be repaid over a period of years, made it possible to undertake maintenance work that would otherwise have had to be postponed. In 1936, maintenance projects gave employment to some 5,000 men from relief camps that were being closed. The government paid the men's wages and certain incidental expenses, while the C.P.R. supplied materials, supervision, work trains, and overhead expenses. The whole project cost $3 million, of which the company absorbed $1.6 million.

In 1936 another government project enabled both the Canadian Pacific and the Canadian National to acquire some new rolling stock. Locomotives and cars were built to specifications supplied by the companies; the government paid for them and sold them to the railways, which undertook to repay the cost in thirteen instalments beginning in 1938. The Canadian Pacific's share, amounting to $5,730,000, included 5 engines, 16 passenger cars, 1,120 freight cars, and—an item of special interest—its first diesel-electric locomotive.

In spite of the Depression, the 1930s had seen great advances made in the railway world, with the development of faster passenger trains—lighter in weight, air-conditioned, streamlined in design, and diesel-powered—an outstanding feature. The first of the famous Burlington *Zephyrs* had entered service in 1934, and a Union Pacific streamliner had come hard on its heels. Lighter high-speed steam locomotives seemed to offer a viable alternative for motive power, and the five engines ordered by the C.P.R. through the government were of a striking new 4–4–4 type designed with fast passenger service in view. Named the Jubilee class in honor of the fiftieth anniversary of the start of transcontinental service, they were characterized by higher boiler pressure, huge eighty-inch driving wheels, and roller bearings. Given a good roadbed, they were capable of speeds well over 100 miles per hour. They were intended to power fast day services between Toronto and Detroit, Montreal and Quebec, and Calgary and Edmonton.

The sixteen lightweight coaches built to operate with the Jubilees were both a new type and the first air-conditioned cars ordered by the Canadian Pacific. But they were not its only air-conditioned equipment. The company had been keeping a watchful eye on air-conditioning experiments for some years: the first appropriation to equip existing cars was included in the estimates for 1936. A few were fitted with mechanical compressor systems for comparative purposes, but in Canada, where the period during which cooling would be needed is comparatively short, the simpler ice-activated system was found to be more economical. Ice boxes under the cars, capable of carrying from three to five thousand pounds of ice, which could be replenished at specially equipped divisional points, solved the problem quite satisfactorily. The Angus Shops in Montreal were soon working busily on the conversions, and 129 cars were equipped in 1936—no small feat. In 1937 an additional 141 cars were converted, and in 1938 another 90. By the end of 1938 more than 400 new or converted air-conditioned coaches, sleepers, and diners were in service.

The lone diesel-electric locomotive acquired in 1937 was a small switcher whose electrical equipment came from England and whose 600-horsepower diesel engine was supplied by Harland and Wolff of Belfast. It was assembled by the National Steel Car Company of Hamilton. Like most pioneers it had its troubles, but in the seven years it was owned by the C.P.R. it demonstrated the advantages of diesel switchers, which the railway was acquiring in some numbers by the time it was retired. Sold and reengined, it served a pulp mill for a quarter of a century and is now preserved in the Canadian Railway Museum at Delson, near Montreal.

WEATHERING THE DEPRESSION

More new rolling stock was becoming essential, as many engines and cars had been retired during the worst Depression years and few had been replaced. The prevailing low prices eased the financial problem involved, and the Canadian Pacific began to place fairly substantial orders for new equipment. Including those secured through the government, 90 new steam locomotives and over 7,500 freight cars were added in the three-year period 1936–38.

Of the engines, 25 were Jubilees, 40 were 4–6–4 Hudsons, 10 were heavy 2–10–4 Selkirks, and 15 were additions to the Canadian Pacific's huge fleet of Pacifics. The Hudsons and Selkirks, though basically similar to the earlier locomotives of their classes, were streamlined after the manner of the Jubilees. In the opinion of many train buffs, they represented the acme of steam power and were as handsome as any engines ever put in service on the continent.

Beatty gave some interesting details of the railway's rolling stock as it existed at the end of 1937. Steam locomotives then numbered 1,955. Of these, 123 were less than ten years old, 199 were between ten and twenty, 1,159 were between twenty and thirty, and 474 were over thirty years old. The average age was 25.7 years—a figure that would be reduced slightly when 35 new engines arrived in 1938. Beatty noted that high average age was "not peculiar to the Canadian Pacific"; the steam locomotive was a long-lived machine, and for many services it was cheaper to keep an elderly engine in repair than to purchase a new one. They had been well maintained; 84.1 percent were in serviceable condition. Many had been modernized; 1,791 were equipped with superheaters, 405 had feedwater heaters, and 233 had automatic stokers. A substantial number, including those operating through the western mountains, burned oil fuel.[16]

For a decade the roster had included a remarkable locomotive that deserves to be remembered, particularly since the Canadian Pacific is usually regarded as having been highly conservative and unadventurous in its engineering. The diesel challenge was on the horizon (the Canadian National Railways had pioneered with a heavy experimental diesel in 1929), but many were reluctant to abandon the steam engine, which had served so long and faithfully. The problem was to increase its thermal efficiency—in other words, to enable it to produce more power per unit of fuel burned. Compound engines were developed and met with some success, but a simple engine equipped with a superheater gave as good or better results. H. B. Bowen, the chief of motive power who had produced the Hudsons and Selkirks, decided to build an experimental engine to test more fully the capabilities of steam. The result was No. 8000, a 2–10–4 that was a Selkirk in wheel arrangement but unique in almost every other respect. Omer Lavallée, historian of Canadian Pacific steam, has described this remarkable engine and its brief career:

> No. 8000 had three pressure chambers. One, a closed circuit, which was really only an elaborate heating unit, carried pressures up to 1,750 lb. p.s.i. A high-pressure boiler, producing steam for a high-pressure cylinder located between the engine frames, carried steam at 850 lb. p.s.i., while a normal pressure boiler produced 300 lb. p.s.i. steam for the regular cylinders.
>
> No. 8000 was outshopped in March, 1931. It was subjected to exhaustive tests on Eastern Lines, notably from Montreal to Smiths Falls, Ontario, before being sent to western Canada. According to contemporary accounts, the performance of No. 8000 was nothing short of sensational, but its Achilles heel was its mechanical complexity. It is said that No. 8000 never left the shops in charge of an engine crew alone—there was always a motive power department engineer along, to take care of contingencies. Even in an era when other railways were designing high-pressure engines, No. 8000 stood apart. The tests of this interesting unit lasted until about 1935, when it was finally put away for good. . . . After giving up many of its standard parts to keep other 2-10-4s in repair, No. 8000 was finally dismantled at Angus Shops, its birthplace, in December, 1940.[17]

At the end of 1937, freight cars of all types numbered 79,966, with an average capacity of forty-two tons; 81 percent of them were all-steel or had steel underframes, and over 93 percent were serviceable. They were kept well painted in the Tuscan red that was a familiar sight across Canada. Passenger cars, in the same livery, numbered 3,025; work cars of all sorts, 5,786. Most of the latter had been retired from passenger or freight service; it was the end of the line, where old cars worked out their last days of usefulness.

25

The Second World War

By the spring of 1939 everyone feared that the days of peace were numbered, but the spirits of Canadians were lifted briefly by the visit of Their Majesties King George VI and Queen Elizabeth. It was the first time a reigning British monarch had set foot in Canada, and circumstances made it an occasion both for elaborate celebration and a remarkable display of loyalty to the Crown.

Because of the threat of war, it was judged best to keep all major British warships in home waters; instead of traveling in a battle cruiser, as intended, the King and Queen crossed the Atlantic in Canadian Pacific *Empresses*. The voyage to Canada in the *Empress of Australia* was marred by heavy fog, which caused a late arrival at Quebec, but the return trip from Halifax in the *Empress of Britain* was all that could be desired.

Between these voyages the royal couple crossed Canada by rail. The train was provided jointly by the Canadian Pacific and the Canadian National; westbound it traveled over C.P.R. lines, while the return trip was made over the Canadian National. Hudson-type locomotive 2850, specially refinished in royal blue and aluminum, with a golden crown at the front of each running board, hauled the train from Quebec to Vancouver. It covered the 3,224 miles without a hitch of any kind, and a second Hudson performed equally well on the pilot train. After the visit, when the standard Tuscan red livery was restored, No. 2850 retained the golden crowns on its running boards, and they were soon carried by all forty-five of the streamlined Hudsons, which thereafter were designated "Royal Hudsons."

When war broke out in the first days of September, many suspected that the struggle would be long and bitter. Sir Edward Beatty (who had been knighted in 1935) had become president of the Canadian Pacific shortly before the end of the First World War, and many of the senior staff also had wartime memories and experience. Beatty's own participation in the second conflict was to be limited by ill health, which was becoming serious by the end of 1940. Many of the president's duties were taken over by the vice-president, D'Alton C. Coleman. In May 1942 Coleman became the Canadian Pacific's fifth president, but Beatty continued to serve as chairman until his death in March 1943.

Coleman was a railwayman of long experience; he had been with the company for over forty years. His most notable service had been in Winnipeg, where he had been vice-president in charge of western lines from 1918 to 1934. The great branch-building program of the 1920s on the prairies, which had added over 2,200 miles to the C.P.R. system, had been carried out under his supervision. In 1934 he had moved to Montreal as vice-president of the company and had been elected a director and a member of the executive committee. He was admirably equipped to direct the efforts of the Canadian Pacific to meet the unprecedented demands that developed during the four and a half years that he was its president.

Apart from the conquest of Poland, little seemed to happen on land during the first seven months of the war, but as in 1914, the C.P.R. felt its impact immediately in ocean shipping. Four of the Atlantic passenger liners were requisitioned at once and a fifth followed within a few weeks. The *Montcalm* and her two sisters were promptly fitted out as auxiliary cruisers. The *Empress of Britain*, pride of the fleet, which had been tied up at Quebec since September, was taken over in November; and halfway across the world, the *Empress of Japan* and *Empress of Canada*, largest units of the Pacific fleet, were also requisitioned. By the spring of 1940 eighteen of the company's twenty ocean liners and freighters had been taken over, and one had been lost. The *Beaverburn*, which had opened the highly successful fast freighter service to London in 1928, was torpedoed and sunk in the North Atlantic in February 1940. The loss was the first of many, for few shipping companies were to suffer as high a proportion of fleet casualties as the Canadian Pacific.

All Atlantic shipping services were disrupted, which naturally affected the export trade. Grain was a notable example. There had been a fair harvest in 1938, but in 1939 the crop totaled 494 million bushels, the second highest on record. Even the drought areas in southern Saskatchewan were getting back into production, and faith in the future of the prairies was fully restored. But shipping difficulties necessitated an embargo on grain shipments for all of

The streamlined Hudson-class locomotive that hauled the Royal Train from Quebec to Vancouver in 1939, shown here in the special livery it was given for the occasion. When the engine returned to regular service, the golden crowns on the running boards were retained and similar crowns were placed on all locomotives of the same class, which were known thereafter as Royal Hudsons.

October and half of November, so instead of a bonanza, the heavy crop produced a storage problem. Both terminal and country elevators were jammed to capacity, and since grain could not be moved, the revenue of the railways suffered.

On the whole, however, freight traffic increased, and it was to climb steadily and steeply throughout the war. A variety of circumstances contributed to this growth. Some freight that would normally have traveled by sea was diverted to the railways. Thus a shortage of ships on the Pacific soon made it necessary to send large quantities of lumber from British Columbia overland to the East instead of by the sea route via Panama. After Pearl Harbor, shortages of gasoline and rubber reduced the services that could be offered by trucking firms, and the scarcity of new trucks soon added to their problems. Shippers turned to rail transport as an alternative. Much export freight that would normally have been consigned to Montreal or Quebec was sent on to Saint John or Halifax. Submarines made navigation in the Gulf of St. Lawrence hazardous, and in any event the shorter sea passages from the Atlantic ports made better use of ships, which were soon in desperately short supply. Finally, there was a gradual, but eventually tremendous, increase in industrial activity in Canada.

The accompanying table shows the growth of traffic between 1938, the last year of peace, and 1945. Freight tonnage rose from 30.5 million tons in

1938 to 44.7 million in 1941 and to 55.7 million in 1944. Not only was much more freight handled, but it was carried, on the average, a considerably longer distance. The average had been 398 miles in 1938; by 1944 it had risen to 497 miles. Traffic measured in ton-miles thus rose even more rapidly than by ton weight. In 1938 the total had been 12,135 million ton-miles; by 1944, the peak year, it had soared to 27,376 million, and despite the end of the war, it declined only slightly in 1945.

As usual, grain traffic fluctuated. In 1942 the Canadian Pacific carried 181 million bushels. In 1943 both Canada and the United States made more ships available for grain, and the total rose to 257 million bushels. In 1944 it jumped to a record 377 million, exceeding the old record of 370 million set in 1928.

RAILWAY REVENUES AND REVENUE FREIGHT CARRIED

	THOUSANDS OF DOLLARS	THOUSANDS OF TONS	MILLIONS OF TON-MILES
1938	$ 142,259	30,471	12,135
1939	151,281	33,030	14,037
1940	170,965	36,746	16,028
1941	221,446	44,710	22,376
1942	256,864	47,972	22,600
1943	297,108	52,552	24,951
1944	318,871	55,679	27,376
1945	316,109	54,822	27,252

Traffic in this volume put an immense strain on employees and on equipment. "Motive power and other rolling stock were utilized to a degree never before reached in the history of your Company," Beatty told the shareholders in the annual report for 1941. During the First World War traffic had reached its peak in 1917. In 1942 the Canadian Pacific handled 50 percent more freight, although it had 10,000 fewer freight cars and 600 fewer locomotives than in 1917; larger cars, heavier engines, and longer trains had greatly increased efficiency. The next year, as freight tonnage rose by another 10 percent, the railway surprised itself: "The volume of traffic handled in 1943 surpassed what might have been thought possible a year ago. Freight, passenger, mail and express traffic all reached levels never before attained."[1]

A ruling by the transport controller requiring all cars to be loaded to capacity helped the railway to make the best possible use of rolling stock; car utilization increased by 98 percent over the period 1938–45. Motive power was employed intensively; engine mileage went up by 54 percent. One Hudson

A Hudson-class locomotive moves out of the Angus Shops past some of the 1,400 Valentine tanks that were produced there during the Second World War.

covered 19,053 miles in a month, an average of about 635 miles per day.[2] Maximum use was highly important, because only limited quantities of new equipment could be procured during the war. No more than 151 locomotives could be acquired—mostly in 1943 and 1944—and only a few thousand freight cars could be added. Fifteen diesel switchers were purchased; this was the Canadian Pacific's first venture into diesel-electric power with the exception of the experimental locomotive acquired in 1937. They do not seem to have been greeted with any great enthusiasm, but they proved to be the forerunners of a complete changeover in motive power that would come in the postwar years.

The war saw the last and greatest surge of passenger traffic on the Canadian railways. In recent years, so much use had been made of road transport that the growth in population had not been reflected in traffic figures. In 1939 the C.P.R. carried only 7.2 million passengers, a figure that had varied little for a decade. By 1944 the total had risen to 18.4 million, the highest ever achieved by the system. Military traffic contributed substantially, and gasoline rationing, which reduced the use of private automobiles, caused many to travel by rail instead of road. The capacity of equipment was strained to the limit, and changes had to be made in many services. Parlor cars disappeared from the trains connecting Montreal, Ottawa, and Toronto, and a score were converted into coaches. To meet military needs, ten compartment-observation cars were rebuilt as hospital cars and twelve commissary cars were placed in service. Reduced fares on holidays and weekends were canceled, and there were few extra sections. The average passenger, like the average ton of freight, traveled a longer distance. In 1940 his journey had averaged 119 miles; by 1945 it had risen by more than a third, to 162 miles.

Inevitably, the war resulted in serious staff problems. The number of employees was at a low level when it began; the total had fallen from over 75,000 in 1928 to only 48,689 in 1939. By 1945 it had risen again to 70,775, and the increase had not been achieved without great effort and severe growing pains.

Recruiting staff was difficult, especially when industrial expansion increased and alternative employment became readily available. New employees usually lacked training and were inexperienced; instructional programs had to be provided for them. Where possible, retired employees were persuaded to return to work, but they were relatively few in number. Some staff members disliked or could not withstand the pressure under which the railway was soon working. The war itself took a heavy toll of experienced staff; many in senior positions were assigned to special duties, and as the conflict progressed, more and more employees joined the armed forces. By the time it ended, 20,742 men and women had enlisted, the equivalent of 45 percent of the entire work force in 1939. It is not surprising that labor turnover was three times higher than normal.

The prevailing wage rates contributed to the Canadian Pacific's labor problems, most of which it shared with the Canadian National. The record is not greatly to the credit of either of them. Deductions made during the Depression had been fully restored in 1938, but no wage increases were granted during the next three years. Then and later, the Canadian Pacific contended that since freight rates had remained unchanged, wages should be unchanged also; one increase should not be made without the other. Both the C.P.R. and the Canadian National, which usually acted in concert in wage matters, tried to limit the application of a government order providing for a cost-of-living bonus, but it was made effective for all workers in 1941.

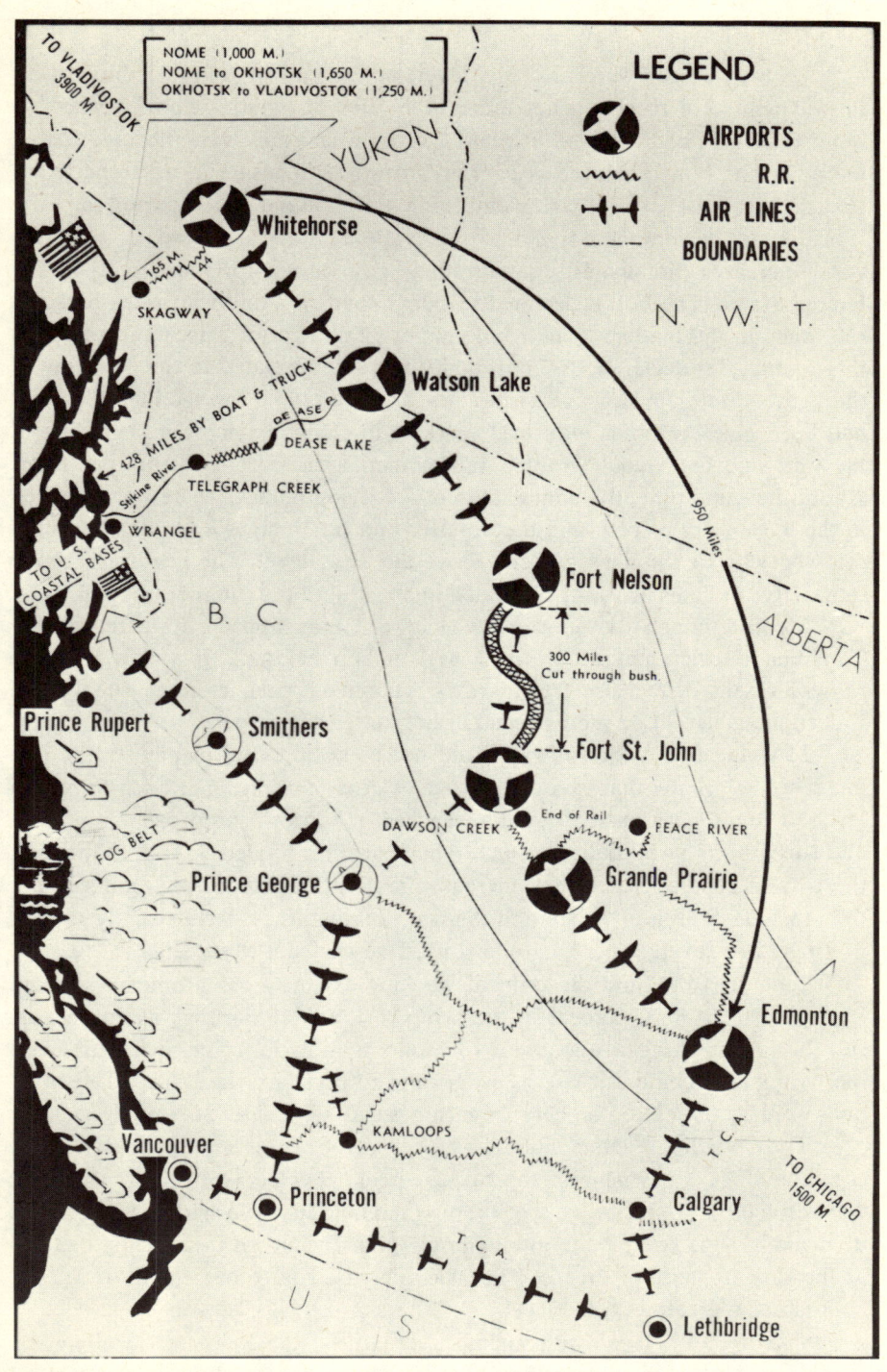

Map of the Northwest Staging Route, over which supplies and planes were flown to Alaska and Russia during the Second World War. Canadian Pacific Air Lines played an important part in these operations.

Railway wages were at a low level; at the end of 1939, a third of all railwaymen were receiving not more than $100 a month. Many workers in other industries had received increases before wage rates were officially frozen in 1941. The bonus secured that year did not compensate in all respects for the rise in the cost of living. Remembering what had happened during the First World War, the unions applied to the National Labour Board in 1944 for wage increases that would equalize their pay rates with those paid in the United States. The board declined to admit that the American rates had any relevance in the matter: "The whole policy of control of wages and prices in this country," it declared, "is entirely distinct and unrelated to the economy of the United States."[3] However, it undertook to survey the wage increases that had been given to other industrial workers in Canada since the beginning of the war, and as a result granted railwaymen a raise of six cents per hour. About the same time, the cumulated cost-of-living bonuses were incorporated in the basic rates of pay, and the bonuses and pay increases together brought rail wages up to about 25 percent above the 1941 level. The new rates, made retroactive to dates in 1943, continued in effect until the summer of 1946.

Modest though the six-cent wage award may appear, it increased the Canadian Pacific's payroll by over $10 million in 1944. It was a levy the railway resented, because freight rates remained frozen at their 1941 level. Indeed, no general rate increase had been granted since 1920.

In spite of this, the railway could not plead inability to pay; traffic had increased so greatly that even at 1944 rates gross earnings had risen to record levels. The old peak of $229 million reached in 1928 was approached in 1941 and surpassed substantially in 1942, when earnings totaled $256.8 million. In the two succeeding years they increased still further, to $297.1 million and then to $318.8 million. In spite of the war's ending, they declined only slightly in 1945. But revenue per ton-mile drifted down from .876 cents in 1943 to .838 cents in 1945, and the ratio of working expenses to earnings rose from 83.4 percent to 88.6 percent in the same period. Net earnings again became substantial, reaching a maximum of $49.2 million in 1943, but with costs increasing they could not rise in proportion to revenues. In 1944, when revenues were $21.7 million higher, net earnings actually fell by $6.1 million.

The Canadian Pacific could not be accused of cosseting the holders of its common shares. Payment of the full 4-percent dividend on preference stock was resumed in 1940, but the common shareholders, who had last received a dividend in 1931, were paid nothing until 1943. Even then the distribution was at the rate of only 2 percent. This was increased to 5 percent in 1944 and maintained thereafter at that level.

The directors, faced with various alternatives, had characteristically given first place to the long-term welfare of the company, which they were convinced

Grant McConachie (1909–65), to whose drive and enthusiasm the rise of Canadian Pacific Air Lines (now CP Air) was largely due.

was also the policy in the best interests of the common shareholders. In 1940 they were faced with the fact that $150 million in bonds, notes, and certificates would mature before the end of 1946. No one could foretell the state of the money market or the effect that war financing by the government might have upon it. The prudent course, therefore, seemed to be to make every effort to reduce the debt from the company's own resources. In this way very substantial blocks of securities were retired without refunding. They totaled $29.9 million in 1940, nearly $29.5 million in 1941, and $35.4 million in 1942, or an aggregate of $94.8 million in the three years. Further reductions were made in the succeeding years, and by 1945 the Canadian Pacific's bonded indebtedness, which had been $237.9 million in 1939, had fallen to only $93.6 million. The welcome concomitant was a $6 million drop in fixed charges. It was only after this debt reduction program had passed the $100 million mark that payment of dividends on common shares was resumed.

Virtually every facility and service of the Canadian Pacific felt the impact of the war. The huge Angus Shops in Montreal turned to the production of munitions, as they had done during the First World War. Their initial assignment was the building of Valentine tanks. In 1941 the shops reached their objective of three tanks per day, and 1,420 had been turned out by the time production ceased late in 1943. Many of them were sent to Russia, where they were highly regarded. The Angus Shops then turned to the manufacture of marine engines for corvettes, frigates, and heavy landing craft.

Late in 1941, the Ogden Shops at Calgary began to turn out naval guns and gun mountings. In all, 3,000 guns and 1,650 mountings were manufactured. In addition to these major items, the C.P.R. shops produced thousands of components for antisubmarine devices, range finders, and gunnery control equipment. Total value of the munitions exceeded $135 million.

For some of the Canadian Pacific hotels the war brought enforced idleness; for others, an unprecedented press of business. The great mountain resorts in the Rockies at Banff and Lake Louise were closed, but hotels in the major cities had a busy time. The Château Frontenac was the setting for the Quebec Conferences of 1943 and 1944, the sixth and eighth meetings of President Roosevelt and Prime Minister Churchill, at which Prime Minister Mackenzie King of Canada acted as host. The entire hotel was taken over for these occasions, both for security reasons and to provide accommodation for the large number in attendance; over 700 were present in 1943 in a wide variety of capacities. By a happy coincidence, top-level arrangements for the conference between the railway and the government were simplified because they were made between two brothers—D. C. Coleman, president of the Canadian Pacific, and E. H. Coleman, under-secretary of state for Canada.

Reference has been made to the company's shipping losses. In the grim autumn of 1940, three Canadian Pacific ships were sunk within the short space of thirty-six days. First to go was the pride of the fleet, the 42,000-ton *Empress of Britain*, which was serving as a transport. On October 26 German aircraft attacked her off the northwest coast of Ireland and set her ablaze. The Polish destroyer *Burza* reached her and took her in tow, but progress was painfully slow and on October 28 she was torpedoed and sunk.

Eight days later the pocket battleship *Admiral Scheer* attacked a convoy of thirty-six ships that was being escorted by the auxiliary cruiser *Jervis Bay*. Ordering the convoy to scatter, the *Jervis Bay* engaged the *Admiral Scheer* in the hopeless half-hour action for which her gallant commander and crew are justly famous. It is seldom remembered that after the *Jervis Bay* sank, the Canadian Pacific freighter *Beaverford*, armed only with one four-inch and one three-inch gun, also engaged the *Admiral Scheer* and fought her for five long hours before going down with all hands. The *Beaverford* therefore shares with the *Jervis Bay* credit for having enabled all but five of the ships in the convoy to make good their escape.

The third ship lost was the liner *Montrose*, which was torpedoed on December 2 while serving as H.M.S. *Forfar* in the highly vulnerable role of auxiliary cruiser. She and her two sisters were among the score of liners that had established a patrol north of the Orkney and Shetland islands not unlike that maintained by the *Alsatian* and the 10th Cruiser Squadron during the First World War. The *Montcalm* and *Wolfe* (ex-*Montclare*) survived this dangerous service but were purchased by the Admiralty and converted into depot ships.

The monetary loss inflicted on merchant shipping is seldom mentioned, but it may be noted that the three ships lost in just over a month had cost the Canadian Pacific over $20 million. Loss of another kind had been caused on the other side of the world in June, when the Canadian-Australasian liner *Niagara*, in which the C.P.R. had a half interest, was mined and sunk off the coast of New Zealand. All on board were saved, but the *Niagara* took to the bottom gold bars valued at about £2.5 million. An epic salvage operation followed. The wreck was located in February 1941, and although it lay in 438 feet of water, a heavily reinforced diving bell enabled divers to examine it. Explosives smashed a way to the ship's strong room, from which grapples recovered 555 of the 590 gold bars. By coincidence the last of them were delivered to the Bank of New Zealand the day the Japanese attacked Pearl Harbor. After the war, most of the gold still left in the wreck was recovered.[4]

George Musk, who has compiled a record of the Canadian Pacific's shipping activities, summarizes the varied duties the fleet performed during the war:

> The passenger liners, whether from Atlantic or Pacific services, moved about the face of the seas at the direction of the Admiralty and became equally at home in tropical as well as Northern ports. They served as troopships, armed merchant cruisers, prisoners of war carriers, as passenger liners or on special missions such as the expedition to Spitzbergen with a demolition force to destroy the coal mines, the Madagascar landing, the removal of freed prisoners from Odessa, the evacuation of Narvik and Brest. They carried troops from Australia and New Zealand to Suez, from North American ports to North Africa; they saw the hell that was Salerno, were bombed at Oran, took reinforcements to Singapore, rescued Dutch from Batavia, ferried Canadian contingents from Canada to Britain, shipped landing craft in place of lifeboats for service in the Mediterranean and carried more than 6,000 unescorted children from Britain to Canada.[5]

The 26,000-ton *Empress of Japan*, renamed *Empress of Scotland* after Pearl Harbor, proved to be the ideal troopship—large but not too large, fast and designed for relatively long voyages. Her record of service was truly remarkable. In the course of the war she steamed 607,783 miles, carried 258,292 troops and other passengers, and ranged over most of the globe. Her narrowest escape came early in November 1940, a few days after the loss of the *Empress of Britain*. German bombers found her off Ireland, as they had found the *Britain*; near misses damaged her machinery, but she was able to reach the Clyde. Six weeks later, once more in excellent condition, she was ready to resume service.

Six *Empresses*, four *Duchesses*, and five *Beavers* steamed a total of 3,617,000 miles and carried over a million military and civilian passengers and about a million tons of cargo. The cost was high; by the end of the war eleven of the fifteen ships had been lost, nine by enemy action and two by marine accident.

This total includes neither the *Niagara* nor the *Princess Marguerite* of the British Columbia coastal fleet. She and the *Princess Kathleen* had been requisitioned and sent to the Mediterranean, where their speed and handiness made them invaluable auxiliaries. The *Marguerite* was torpedoed in 1942, but the *Kathleen* survived. She was the first troopship to reach Greece as hostilities were ending and was also the first to arrive in Rhodes, where she took the German commander and his staff on board as prisoners of war.

It was during the war that the Canadian Pacific's growing air interests and activities resulted in the organization of Canadian Pacific Air Lines Limited (now CP Air) in 1942.

As early as 1919 the C.P.R. had secured authority to own and operate aircraft commercially, but no practical steps were taken until 1930, when the Canadian Pacific and the Canadian National each invested $250,000 in Canadian Airways Limited. Controlled by James Richardson of Winnipeg, a director of the C.P.R., this was a consolidation of a number of local airlines. Canadian Airways was soon operating regional services in several of the provinces, and it seemed likely that it would become a nationwide system in which the two railways would have a growing equity. However, in 1936 a federal department of transport was organized and given jurisdiction over civil aviation. Its able and forceful minister, the Hon. C. D. Howe, created Trans-Canada Airlines (now Air Canada) and made it clear that only this government-sponsored corporation would be permitted to provide a transcontinental air service. At one time it was proposed that the Canadian Pacific and the Canadian National should each subscribe half of Trans-Canada's capital, but the C.P.R. would have had only minority representation on the board and it declined to participate on that basis.

Sir Edward Beatty was determined nevertheless that the Canadian Pacific should take to the air. Even in its earliest days, the C.P.R. had never intended to confine its activities to the railway; it took the view that its mandate was to provide transportation and communication in whatever forms might be practical and appropriate.

Beatty turned to the privately owned local and regional airlines that were maintaining somewhat chaotic but highly important services, particularly in western Canada and the North. Few of them were much beyond the bush pilot stage, and a survey carried out in 1939 suggested that integration and development of a group of them would be a worthwhile project. The end in view would be greatly improved services, mostly north-south, that would not compete with Trans-Canada Airlines but would act as feeders both for it and for the Canadian Pacific's own rail lines.

In 1941 the C.P.R. set about buying control of the companies it planned to include in the scheme. By the end of the year, ten had been acquired. They included Canadian Airways, in which the railway had made its first aviation investment, and Yukon Southern Air Transport Limited, whose remarkable young president, Grant McConachie, was to do much to shape the future of the railway's air activities.

Integration of the ten was not easy. Their routes were a tangle; their seventy-seven aircraft were of many shapes and sizes. The C.P.R. took them over executives and all, and they included a good many strong and independently minded personalities who did not relish the idea of serving under one another.

Early in 1942 Canadian Pacific Air Lines, a subsidiary of the railway, came into being, and the assets of the acquired companies were transferred to it. By present-day standards the whole operation had been a modest one. Up to the end of 1942, the Canadian Pacific expended $4,725,917 and received in return $4 million in Canadian Pacific Air Lines capital stock and $725,917 in notes. To watch over its investment, the C.P.R. appointed its treasurer, L. B. Unwin, president of the airlines. C. H. ("Punch") Dickins of Canadian Airways, famous for his exploits in the First World War and his remarkable flights as a pioneer bush pilot, became general manager.

Financial control lay in Montreal, with Unwin and Dickins, both of whom were inclined to pinch pennies, but so far as the West was concerned, policy matters were dealt with by W. M. Neal, the railway's vice-president in Winnipeg. Neal had been much attracted by Grant McConachie's enthusiasm and ambition, and he appointed him general manager of western airlines.

Since, in the words of a close associate, McConachie "defined success as expanding the airline rather than making money,"[6] some friction with Montreal was inevitable.

The C.P.R. had already carried out one important air assignment in which Dickins played a major part. The idea seems to have originated with Sir Edward Beatty. By the summer of 1940 the prompt delivery to Britain of military aircraft manufactured in North America had become a matter of vital importance. Ferrying planes across the Atlantic by air had not yet been tried, but Beatty was prepared to have the C.P.R. make the attempt. A Canadian Pacific Air Services Department was organized, and in November an initial flight of seven Lockheed Hudsons crossed safely from Newfoundland to Britain. Thereafter, there was a steady flow of aircraft across the Atlantic. The C.P.R. was responsible for the ferry service until July 1941, when its contract expired and the Royal Air Force Ferry Command took over.

Meanwhile the company had become involved in the British Commonwealth Air Training Plan, a large-scale program organized to train air crews in Canada. Six of the plan's air observer schools were operated on a nonprofit basis by the C.P.R.; in 1944 alone, the aircraft attached to them flew over 56 million miles. The railway also operated five overhaul plants which serviced aircraft of the Royal Canadian Air Force.

After Pearl Harbor, the defenseless state of Alaska caused much anxiety and gave sudden new importance to air services and facilities in the Yukon and Northwest Territories. Canada had been developing what became known as the North West Air Staging Route, a succession of airfields between Edmonton and Whitehorse, in the Yukon. This now became of enormous importance both in the defense of Alaska and as a means of ferrying aircraft to Russia. Its improvement, the building of the Alaska Highway, and other, lesser projects developed traffic that taxed the facilities of the infant Canadian Pacific Air Lines to the limit. Much of this activity took place in the area served formerly by Yukon Southern Air Transport, and McConachie was in his element superintending it.

By 1943 C.P. Air Lines were operating services based on Vancouver, Edmonton, Regina, and Winnipeg that extended far to the north. In the East, a service paralleling the St. Lawrence ran from Montreal and Quebec to the Strait of Belle Isle. That year Canadian Pacific transport planes flew 6.1 million miles and carried 9.5 million pounds of cargo.

McConachie was full of peacetime plans, including international services. In 1940 Yukon Southern, with very limited resources, had had the temerity to announce a service to Siberia in cooperation with Pan American Airways. It failed to materialize, but with the resources of the Canadian Pacific behind him, McConachie thought that much ought to be possible. Unfortunately the outlook was anything but promising. About 90 percent of the existing traffic was related to the war effort; how much traffic there would be to take its place when the war ended remained to be seen. Price controls were holding rates at uneconomic levels, and to Montreal's annoyance the airlines, though working to capacity, were operating at a loss.

In April 1943 an air policy statement by Prime Minister King seemed to set severe limits to the future of the enterprise. Transcontinental air services were to be strictly reserved for Trans-Canada Airlines, which were also to be "the sole agency which may operate Canadian international services." Unwin and Dickins protested vigorously and, as it turned out, somewhat unwisely. They had a strong case; the Canadian Pacific had been providing international services by sea for half a century—surely it was logical to allow it to employ aircraft as well as ships. But the wording of their protest was provocative: "If equity and justice have any place in the Canadian Government plan," they wrote, "Canadian Pacific should be allowed to carry traffic in the air to supplement its long-established sea routes."[7]

The key minister concerned, C.D. Howe, was not pleased; he responded in March 1944 with a government order announcing that transport by air was to be rigorously separated from surface transportation, and that railways would be required to divest themselves of all air activities within a year of the end of the war.

The C.P.R. already had problems enough that would be awaiting it when peace returned. The railway itself had taken a beating, for its tracks and trains had handled unprecedented traffic for years under limitations of labor and materials that made maintenance to the usual standards impossible. Only three of its ocean fleet would come back to it in a state that would make reconditioning feasible, and now its airlines were under a sentence from which it seemed probable there would be no reprieve.

But the future was to be less grim than this state of affairs suggested. Problems there would be in plenty, but on land, on sea, and in the air, Canadian Pacific would rebuild, modify, and expand its vast system.

26

Crump and Dieselization

When the war ended, the government of Canada feared that a depression would develop. To cushion the expected slump, it increased the money supply; inflation and higher prices were preferable to unemployment. For this and other reasons, instead of a depression Canada enjoyed an almost unbroken period of prosperity between 1946 and 1954. In some respects the railways benefited, as traffic reached record levels; the difficulty was that freight rates were not permitted to increase nearly as much nor as quickly as the cost of labor and materials. As a result, net rail revenues fell sharply. In 1945 the Canadian Pacific's net return from rail operations had been $36 million; in 1948 it was only $18.4 million, the lowest in forty-three years.

Even when rate increases were granted, they came so long after the application for revision had been submitted by the railways that further increases had become essential by the time the changes went into effect. The Board of Transport Commissioners held hearings on applications, and parties opposing an increase, often including a number of provincial governments, were given ample time in which to prepare their cases. In October 1946 the railways asked for a general freight rate increase of 30 percent; procedural routines delayed the verdict of the board for nineteen months. In April 1948 an increase of 21 percent was authorized, but while the application had been under consideration, the wholesale price index in Canada had risen almost 46 points.

In this difficult period, income from its nonrail activities came to the rescue of the Canadian Pacific. In 1946–49, when net revenue from railway operations was at its lowest, other income was substantially higher than it had been during the war years. As a result, total net income was relatively stable at about $44 million a year. This was sufficient to meet fixed charges, pay dividends of 4 percent on preference stock and 5 percent on common shares, and leave a modest surplus. But the low rate of the return on the railway itself was evident to all and made it hard to interest investors in providing the additional capital sorely needed to rehabilitate the system.

The railway's position was complicated by the advantages enjoyed by competing means of transportation. Both road and air transport had benefited greatly from experience gained during the war. Heavy trucks and diesel engines developed for military purposes were the immediate ancestors of the trucks and tractor-trailers that would soon be rumbling along Canadian highways. The big bomber was likewise the ancestor of the postwar airliner. Moreover, it was clear that the government of Canada had in mind massive expenditures that would subsidize these and other competitors. A Trans-Canada Highway built to high standards was being planned; many millions were to be spent on airports. It also seemed fairly certain that Canada and the United States would build the St. Lawrence Seaway, which would permit large ocean-going ships to reach ports on the Great Lakes.

It was under these conditions that the Canadian Pacific doggedly set about the vast task of reconditioning its fleets and rail system.

Some preliminary planning had been done quite early in the war. Even when he was forced by illness to curtail his activities, Sir Edward Beatty continued to take a special interest in Canadian Pacific's ocean shipping. To him the sinking of the great flagship *Empress of Britain* had seemed almost a personal tragedy. By the end of 1941, four of the five *Beaver*-class freighters had gone to the bottom, and complete rebuilding would be necessary if the fast cargo service that had been so successful were to be revived. John Johnson, who had had much to do with the designing of the prewar *Empresses, Duchesses,* and *Beavers,* had left the Canadian Pacific in 1936, but in response to a cable from Beatty he came to Montreal, where together they planned the revival of the Atlantic fleet.

First priority was given to the freighter service, which was of major importance to the railway. Four new *Beavers* of about 10,000 tons were projected; their higher speed of sixteen knots would enable them to maintain the service that formerly required five ships. It was found possible to place orders before hostilities ceased, and the first of the new *Beavers* was launched in August 1945. All four were afloat within a year.

The next step was to restore the passenger service. As an interim measure, Beatty and Johnson concluded that the best plan would be to reconstruct the 20,000-ton cabin-class *Duchess* liners, upgrade them to something ap-

This Pacific and its twin, No. 1200, turned out in 1944, were the last locomotives built by the Canadian Pacific in its own shops. A hundred others of the same class were purchased from other builders from 1945 to 1948.

proaching *Empress* standards, and have them provide a first-class service until such time as new ships could be built.[1] By the time this plan could be carried into effect, only two of the *Duchesses* survived. Since three ships were required to maintain a weekly service, the 26,000-ton *Empress of Scotland*, the only unit of the Pacific fleet that had come safely through the war, was diverted to the Atlantic. Except for a few public rooms, the accommodation in all three liners was completely rebuilt and devoted entirely to first and tourist classes; third class was eliminated. Before the war the *Duchesses* could each carry 1,570 passengers; as *Empresses* they accommodated only 700. The *Empress of Scotland* carried only 663.

The best-laid plans can meet with delays; efforts to reestablish the passenger service met with many obstacles. The ships were retained on government requisition much longer than expected; the extensive reconditioning they underwent took time. It was not until May 1950, five years after the war in Europe had ended, that the third ship returned to peacetime service and the traditional weekly *Empress* sailings could be resumed.

In 1946, with the resumption of trading on the Pacific in mind, the Canadian Pacific purchased two ships very similar to the new *Beavers*, but fitted with accommodation for thirty-five passengers. However, in 1952, when two steamers were assigned to the Pacific, the service was confined to freight and two of the Atlantic *Beavers* were sent instead. Traffic failed to come up to expectations and the ships returned to the Atlantic in 1954. Because of the difficulty of translating the prefix "Beaver" into Japanese, they had been renamed *Maplecove* and *Mapledell*, but they reverted to *Beavercove* and *Beaverdell* when their stint on the Pacific ended.

The C.P.R. had plans for new passenger liners for both the Atlantic and Pacific in readiness in 1946, but delayed placing orders in the expectation that prices would fall, as they had done after the First World War. Since new ships would probably cost at least $15 million each, this seemed the prudent course, but it was based on a miscalculation; prices rose instead of declining. Any intention of restoring passenger service on the Pacific was soon abandoned. Grant McConachie was not alone in believing that for travel over its wide expanses, aircraft would soon supersede ships. On the Atlantic the situation seemed more promising. The *Empresses* were being booked to capacity, and cruising had been resumed in the winter season. There still appeared to be a future for the passenger liner. When in 1952 the Cunard Line, the Canadian Pacific's chief competitor in the Canadian passenger trade, ordered new ships, it became apparent that further delay on the part of the C.P.R. would be inadvisable. The first of three *Empresses* was ordered late in the year, but construction proceeded at a very deliberate pace. Her keel was not laid for a year and she did not enter service until the spring of 1956.

D. C. Coleman considered that his prime duty had been to guide the Canadian Pacific through the war and the immediate postwar years. This accomplished, he retired as chairman and president in February 1947. Sixty-eight years of age, he had served the railway for forty-seven of them and would continue to be a member of the board until his death in 1957.

His place was taken by William M. Neal, who had been with the railway since 1902. This was the third time he had succeeded Coleman; he had taken over the post of vice-president, western lines, from him in 1934 and that of vice-president of the system in 1942.

Neal's one-year tenure of the presidency is memorable chiefly because of his success in assuring a future for Canadian Pacific Air Lines. When the war ended, the government directive that the railway must divest itself of its air interests within a year still stood, and efforts to have it modified had met with no success. Neal had been attracted by Grant McConachie's unquenchable ambition and enthusiasm, and by 1946 had become sufficiently interested in the Air Lines to have himself appointed president. One of his early moves had been to bring McConachie to Montreal as assistant to the president. A year later, six days after Neal became president of the Canadian Pacific, McConachie succeeded him as president of Canadian Pacific Air Lines. He was thirty-eight at the time.

The government had not actually enforced the ban on air operations by railways when the one-year period ended; action had been limited to a prolonged review of all air licenses by the Air Transport Board. Neal and McConachie had mounted a spirited defense of the Canadian Pacific's air activities, and they now broadened it to include an effort to persuade the government to modify its earlier decision to make Trans-Canada Airlines the sole "chosen instrument" that would operate all Canadian international air services. McConachie had his sights set on the North Pacific; he wanted to see *Empresses* of the air succeed the famous *Empress* liners that had plied for half a century between Vancouver and Japan and China. This, surely, was a route to which the Canadian Pacific was entitled by inheritance.

In the end, Neal and McConachie won the day. Their first success came in 1947, when the Air Transport Board required the C.P.R. to give up all nonscheduled and charter licenses but gave it permission to operate a network of regional services in the West and one or two in Quebec. In 1948 the network was extended to the Yukon and the Arctic. The same year, the Canadian Pacific finally secured the concession that McConachie coveted—permission to fly across the Pacific. It is said that C. D. Howe, the minister of transport, granted it after consulting the president of the government-owned Trans-Canada Airlines, who took a dim view of the financial prospects of a service to the Orient and was not interested in providing it. Howe for his part attached two conditions to the concession: C.P. Air Lines must fly the route with Canadair Four aircraft, Canadian-built modifications of the Douglas DC-4, and in addition to a service to Japan and China they must provide one to Australia as well.

Howe could give authority for Canadian planes to take off across the Pacific; McConachie had to secure permission for them to land in the Orient and Australia. This involved negotiations with General Douglas MacArthur, head of the occupying forces in Japan, with Chiang Kai-shek in China, and with the governments in Hong Kong and Australia. These delicate missions McConachie accomplished successfully in personal negotiations that have been amusingly chronicled by his biographer, Ronald Keith.[2]

The Canadair Fours had been ordered for delivery in 1949. The first of them, christened *Empress of Sydney* in keeping with McConachie's conception of them as successors to the *Empress* liners, left Vancouver on a preinaugural flight to Honolulu, Fiji, and Australia on July 10. The first official departure was that of the *Empress of Vancouver*, three days later. On September 19 the first plane took off for the Orient by way of Alaska. As it happened, it was to be the only Canadian Pacific plane to touch down on mainland China for many years. The Communists were closing in on Shanghai as it arrived, and it was the last plane to leave the airport before the city was occupied.

Loss of the Chinese market was a serious blow to the new service's prospects, but the war in Korea brought it unexpected traffic. At the request of the government of Canada, planes were soon flying to and from Tokyo as often as four times a week. Over a period of fifty-six months, more than 39,000 United States military personnel flew from Vancouver on 703 Canadian Pacific flights.[3]

In 1949 the center of operations of the airlines was moved to Vancouver International Airport, where the company was able to acquire at a bargain price a vast hangar used by Boeing during the war as an aircraft factory. From it Canadian Pacific's domestic and international services now radiate on routes that total well over 50,000 miles.

McConachie's ambitions were far from satisfied by the permits to fly to the Orient and Australia. In 1953 his planes began to fly from Vancouver to Mexico and Peru, countries in which the Canadian Pacific had not been active previously; the service was later extended to Chile and the Argentine. He had long been fascinated by great circle routes, and he was eager to extend C.P. services to Europe and to reach it by a great circle polar route from Vancouver. This he was able to do in June 1955, when planes began to fly from Vancouver to Amsterdam by way of the pole. A few months later Toronto was linked by air with Mexico City, a route most people thought would never pay, but which was patronized heavily from the first flight.

Better and faster planes were as important as additional routes. By 1952, Convair aircraft offering the comfort of pressurized cabins had been introduced on domestic routes, and Douglas DC–6s were flying on the international services. As early as 1949, eager to pioneer jet aircraft on the Pacific, McConachie had somehow persuaded his hard-headed board of directors to order two de Havilland Comets, the first pure-jet airliners. Their great superiority in speed would have been particularly advantageous over the long Pacific routes. Unfortunately, Canadian Pacific shared in the tragedies that overwhelmed early planes of this type. Owing to an error on the pilot's part, the first of the two crashed at Karachi in March 1953, when bound from England to Australia on its delivery flight. Still jet-minded, McConachie and his board ordered three Mark II Comets, but the loss of other Comets pointed to structural defects, production was halted, and the orders lapsed. Jet service had to await the coming of the Bristol Britannia turbo-prop and the DC-8 pure jet. But by 1955 Canadian Pacific planes were already linking five continents over international routes totaling more than 22,000 miles, and the airlines had contrived to make a modest net profit each year since 1950.

On the sea and in the air the C.P.R. was making progress; on land the going had been tougher. The railway itself faced crucial decisions, and here the

Norris R. Crump, who piloted the Canadian Pacific through the tremendous transformation in its character and activities that took place after the Second World War. He was president from 1955 to 1964 and chairman from 1961 to 1972.

most important event was the arrival at the center of company authority of Norris R. Crump. In April 1948 he was appointed vice-president in charge of all rail lines and moved to Montreal.

Crump was the son of a railroader. His father had started as a section hand, had risen to be trainmaster in charge of the "Big Hill" at Field by 1896, and had ended his career as superintendent of the Canadian Pacific's Kettle Valley Division. Norris Crump's own service with the company began at his birthplace, Revelstoke, British Columbia, where he joined the motive power department when he was sixteen. He served his apprenticeship as a machinist and then began the long climb to positions of increasing responsibility that would lead eventually to the presidency. He took time off to secure a bachelor of science degree from Purdue University, an institution that took a special interest in railroads, and in the Depression years he managed to return and complete the degree of master of engineering, in 1936. Crump was then locomotive foreman at Moose Jaw, and it is significant that he chose as the subject of his research and thesis internal-combustion engines in the railroad field.

The thesis was no mere academic exercise; Crump was thirty-two when he completed it and had had fifteen years of practical experience in maintaining steam locomotives. Diesel-electric propulsion was attracting wide attention; the famous Burlington Zephyr had appeared in 1934, and the Santa Fe's equally famous Super Chief had made its first sensational thirty-nine-hour run from Chicago to Los Angeles shortly before Crump submitted his thesis. He found the new diesels fascinating, chronicled their history in considerable detail, and noted their many and varied advantages. Their thermal efficiency was much higher than that of steam locomotives and their fuel consumption much lower; they could average many more hours in service per day; their need for water was negligible and they could run long distances without refueling; parts could be replaced quickly and easily; routine servicing took much less time; track wear was reduced; some railroads were already operating diesel switchers without a fireman, and it seemed possible that multiple units could be operated by a single engine crew; safety was increased because the engineer, housed in a cab at the front of the locomotive instead of at the back, had a much better view of the track.

On the other hand, the diesel-electric was still so new that its durability had yet to be tested fully, and its first cost was very high; the two-unit locomotive of the Santa Fe Chief was said to have cost $350,000. What the railways insisted upon was "dependability along with minimum cost," and diesels could not yet provide this through the full spectrum of motive power needs. Though Crump considered that prediction was impossible at the existing stage of diesel development, he ventured the opinion that the old reliable "iron horse" would "hold the present important position for many decades to come." "In all probability," he added later, "Diesel services will overlap with steam power. Diesel switch engines, rail cars, articulated trains and locomotives will be used for various services. The Diesel electric for freight service is as yet an unexplored—but fertile, field."[4]

This was a more perceptive view of the future of the diesel than most people were taking at the time. The overall efficiency of the steam locomotive had doubled in the previous thirty years, and only later did it become evident that it had reached the peak of its development. All three of the major engine builders in the United States were convinced that the diesel-electric was suitable only for switching locomotives and some special services—a miscalculation that was eventually to drive them all out of engine building. General Motors, coming up from behind in the race with the lighter diesel engine that powered the Burlington Zephyr, went on to dominate the field and to find its only serious rival years later in General Electric.

In 1941, much sooner than Crump seems to have expected, the diesel-electric freight locomotive made its impressive first appearance when the Santa Fe acquired from General Motors a four-unit monster 193 feet in length that developed a total of 5,400 horsepower. Its success was immediate, and diesels by the hundred were soon being ordered by American railroads. In the interval Crump had moved to senior administration posts, but he remained an engineer at heart, deeply interested in the technicalities of diesel-electric power. When the war ended and costs began to skyrocket, he became convinced that only its wholesale adoption by the Canadian Pacific would enable the company to survive. Between 1945 and 1948, the ratio of operating expenses to rail revenues had risen from 81.75 to 92.33 percent; with freight rates lagging, only greater efficiency and economy could save the day. Crump was sure that conversion to diesel power would reduce costs in a spectacular way, for almost every advantage of the diesel that he had listed in his thesis could be translated into reductions in expenditure for labor, fuel, servicing, or maintenance of motive power or tracks.

W. M. Neal was succeeded as chairman in 1948 by G. A. Walker, K.C., formerly vice-president and general counsel. His successor as president was William A. Mather. Like Neal and Coleman before him, Mather had served as vice-president, western lines. He was a sound and capable railroader but cautious by nature. The difficult years he had spent in the West during the Depression had accentuated his conservatism, and to this his age—sixty-three—tended to contribute. He shared George Stephen's aversion to fixed charges and found particular satisfaction in seeing them decline, year by year. Now he was faced with Norris Crump, nearly twenty years his junior, who believed that the C.P.R. should have been buying diesel-electric locomotives a decade earlier and was convinced that the railway must spend many millions of dollars on diesel motive power or risk financial disaster. Crump made a convincing case and was quickly promoted to a level that enabled him to carry his plans into effect. In February 1949 he was elected a director, and in May he was appointed vice-president of the railway and a member of the executive committee.

Although it had acquired some seventy-five diesel switchers by 1948, the Canadian Pacific was still firmly committed to steam power. In 1944, with a view to postwar needs, it had built two experimental Pacific-type engines—the last of over a thousand locomotives to come from the railway's own shops. These were the first of the attractive and successful 1200 series, a hundred of which were purchased in the four years after the war. The old iron horse went out in a blaze of glory, for in addition to a dozen Mikados, the final orders for steam included six oil-burning 2–10–4 Selkirks, still the largest locomotives in the British Commonwealth. The last of the six, No. 5935, delivered in March 1949, was also the last standard-gauge steam locomotive built for a Canadian railway. Magnificent the Selkirks undoubtedly were, but these final examples were anachronisms. Designed for general service on the line through the mountains between Calgary and Revelstoke, their active life was to be no more than seven years; all Selkirks had been retired by the fall of 1956.

The *Canadian*, the Canadian Pacific's stainless steel "scenic dome" streamliner, leaving Montreal on its inaugural run to Vancouver on April 24, 1955.

Fortunately two have been preserved, No. 5934 in Metawa Park in Calgary and No. 5935, last of the breed, in the Canadian Railway Museum near Montreal.

The Canadian Pacific acquired its first road diesels just as it was taking over the last Selkirks. They were of two very different types, intended for service on opposite sides of the continent. The Esquimalt and Nanaimo Railway on Vancouver Island had been chosen as the first division to be dieselized; thirteen Baldwin-built 1,000-horsepower road-switchers took over there in 1949. Still in service, they are now among the oldest diesels in regular operation, and as such are of considerable interest to railway buffs. In the East, three 2,000-horsepower diesel locomotives received in 1949 operated with matching units of the Boston and Maine Railroad on the run between Montreal and Boston. Built by General Motors, they were notable because they were designed specifically for passenger service instead of the usual general purposes, and are said to have been the only diesel-electrics of the kind built for a Canadian railway. Like the last Selkirks, they soon became victims of changed circumstances. By 1956 passenger traffic to and from Boston by rail had declined to such an extent that dayliners took over and the locomotives were moved to other runs out of Montreal.

In response to Crump's urging, the pace of conversion to diesel power soon quickened. In 1950 diesels replaced steam on the Schreiber division of the main line north of Lake Superior. In 1951 they invaded the Calgary-Revelstoke division, upon which the Selkirks had reigned supreme. By 1954 all transcontinental passenger trains were diesel powered. Diesel units outnumbered steam by 944 to 776 in 1958, and conversion to diesel was deemed to have been completed in 1960, when 1,054 locomotives were on the roster. Some work equipment was still steam powered, but the surviving engines were phased out in the next few years. Apart from this, the last run by a Canadian Pacific steam locomotive was a special train from Montreal to St. Lin and return on November 6, 1960. Fittingly enough, the engine was a seventy-three-year-old veteran 4-4-0, built in the railway's Delorimier Avenue shops in 1887 and extensively rebuilt in 1913. It had been active on local lines in New Brunswick, where its crew and the roundhouse staff had kept it in such good condition that after the trip to St. Lin it went to the Canadian Railway Museum instead of to the scrappers.

The cost of the 1,054 diesel-electric units and the facilities required to service them was approximately $250 million. Crump estimated the savings that resulted from the change from steam to diesel power at $55 million a year.

The economies achieved were of many kinds. First came a major reduction in the sheer number of locomotives. In 1955, when the conversion program was well launched, the C.P.R. had 1,960 locomotives—556 diesel units and 1,404 steam engines. By 1960 diesel-electrics numbered 1,054, but 364 steam locomotives still survived in work and other services, a total of 1,418. By 1963 steam had disappeared and the 1,054 diesels were meeting the entire motive power needs of the railway. This they could do because they could operate more hours per day and their annual mileage was therefore much higher than that of the steam engines they replaced. For a diesel-electric road engine, the total could be about 200,000 miles; for a Hudson-type steam locomotive, it would be about 75,000 miles. The Hudson, moreover, would require a major overhaul about every 100,000 miles; the diesel might run nearly half a million miles between overhauls.

The diesel's ability to run long distances without refueling made it possible to reduce or eliminate service facilities at many points, so the water tanks that had long been a prominent feature in every railway landscape disappeared. Oil fuel could be supplied much more easily than coal. For fifty years the Canadian Pacific and the Pennsylvania Railroad had jointly operated a train ferry across Lake Erie to bring coal from mines in Ohio for the use of C.P.R. trains in Ontario; diesels made it possible to end this service. Other coaling facilities likewise disappeared at Jackfish, on the north shore of Lake Superior, where coal brought by ship had been stockpiled for use during the winter months when the lake was closed to navigation. A further economy

The *Canadian* dwarfed by the mountains as it runs through the spectacular scenery in the Rockies.

came from the diesel-electric's ability to reverse its electric motors and use them as a brake on downgrades. Normally this dynamic braking was sufficient to control a train on grades of up to 2 percent. Even on the famous "Big Hill" at Field, this braking power was an immense help. In the days of steam, heavy trains would arrive at the bottom with every wheel smoking, but diesels so reduced wear and tear on braking systems that the C.P.R. is said to have saved $100,000 a year on brake shoes alone.

Cars, tracks, and all manner of equipment had to be rebuilt or replaced after the Second World War. Rail renewal had fallen badly in arrears, millions of untreated ties had had to be used, and ballasting had been neglected. During the war the C.P.R. had built up a deferred maintenance fund to help make good these deficiencies, but shortages of labor and materials delayed the program. New rail needs were about 750 track miles per year, but for a time it was possible to renew an average of only about 500 miles each season. The tie problem was tackled promptly. Use of untreated ties decreased rapidly; 8.6 million treated ties were used for replacements in the first four postwar years, and by 1953, 87 percent of all ties in the principal lines were treated. Installation of automatic block signals was pushed forward, and by 1955 over 3,000 miles of track were so equipped. Rock ballast was extended to an equal mileage, most of it on the transcontinental line or between Quebec, Montreal, Toronto, and Windsor.

Much of the Canadian Pacific's rolling stock had become run down during the Depression; in 1943 alone, nearly 25,000 cars had needed heavy repairs. Orders for new freight cars in quantity were placed as soon as possible after the war, and as many as 5,000 were acquired in a single year. In nine years 31,402 new freight cars were added and over 22,000 old cars were retired. Of the 79,675 freight cars in service in 1955, nearly 40 percent were thus at most eight years old. Also, they were considerably larger than those they replaced and better adapted for existing traffic needs. The number of cars had risen by only 9 percent, but aggregate carrying capacity was up 21 percent.

The cost of rolling stock had begun the steep climb that has continued to the present day, partly as the result of inflation and partly due to the greater complexity of equipment. The total cost of the Canadian Pacific's rolling stock inventory in 1947 had been $413 million; President Mather estimated that the replacement cost would be $800 million.[5] A Mikado freight engine could be purchased for $22,000 in 1912; by 1947 the price had risen to $120,000. In 1974 the C.P.R. would be paying $532,000 for a 3,000-horsepower diesel-electric locomotive.

In the summer of 1950 the railway opened the 682-acre St. Luc marshaling yard on the western outskirts of Montreal, the first hump retarder yard in Canada and the first on the continent to be equipped with automatic switch control. From the hump, gravity takes the cars to a classification yard, where they are switched to one of forty-eight tracks, according to destination. They then move on to a forty-track departure yard, where trains are made up, and they are soon on their way; a major saving in time and costs results. The classification and departure yards have a capacity of about 2,000 cars each. In addition to the marshaling tracks, the yard has facilities for weighing, inspecting, and repairing cars. The major diesel maintenance shop for the region is also there; it services about a third of all of Canadian Pacific's locomotives.

For a dozen years and more after the war, the C.P.R. still took a lively interest in passenger traffic. During 1947–54, over 500 new passenger cars were purchased, and the interiors of many of the older sleeping, dining, and parlor cars were rebuilt, redecorated, and made more comfortable and attractive. Roomette cars were a popular innovation at this time, and all equipment assigned regularly to the principal routes was air-conditioned.

A recent photograph of the *Canadian* crossing Stoney Creek bridge as it runs down the eastern slope of the Selkirks, east of Rogers Pass and the Connaught Tunnel.

In the later 1920s, the Canadian Pacific had purchased forty-seven gas-electric passenger cars for use on branch lines. They attracted little attention but served the company faithfully and well for twenty years and more. In 1953 the C.P.R. acquired four diesel dayliners, their modern counterparts. Others followed, and by 1956 the number had risen to thirty-one, serving routes totaling 3,000 miles. In addition to branch lines, the routes included such important runs as those from Toronto to Detroit and from Montreal to Boston. Their success and smart appearance tended to obscure the fact that they were simply a cheaper means of handling dwindling passenger traffic that could no longer justify the operation of a full-fledged train.

In spite of this and other portents, Crump was hopeful that with new equipment of the highest standard the transcontinental service could be both a prestige operation and a paying proposition for a good many years to come.

Making what he now terms one of his misjudgments, in 1953 he persuaded the board to authorize the purchase of 173 streamlined stainless steel cars from the Budd Company. These would be sufficient to equip the *Canadian*, a new and faster transcontinental train that would take precedence over the existing *Dominion*, and in part reequip both the *Dominion* itself and the *Atlantic Limited*, operating between Montreal and Saint John. The order included thirty-six scenic dome cars, the first of the type ordered by a Canadian railway. Unlike the all-sleeping-car trains of the 1920s, the new *Canadian* and improved *Dominion* were to offer a very wide variety of accommodation, ranging from deluxe coaches to tourist and first-class sleepers, the latter offering sections, duplex roomettes, standard roomettes, single and double bedrooms, and drawing rooms. In addition to dining cars, one dome car in each train was to provide coffee shop service; another, at the rear of the train, would be the usual observation lounge.

Although in external appearance the cars looked much like hundreds of others built by the Budd Company, they were very different in detail. The run from Montreal and Toronto to Vancouver is exceptionally long and Canadian winters are unusually severe; many modifications had to be made to meet these conditions. Crump and two colleagues rode many of the famous name trains on the continent before the final specifications were settled, and Crump himself determined many of the details. The decorative themes were entirely Canadian, and every effort was made to create trains that would be outstandingly comfortable and attractive. The only concessions to cost were the tourist sleepers for the *Canadian*; these were existing cars rebuilt and sheathed with stainless steel in the C.P.R.'s own shops. Though a little taller than the Budd cars, they fitted into the new trains reasonably well.

The first *Canadians* left Montreal and Toronto on April 24, 1955. They offered the longest dome-train ride in the world and their schedule reduced the length of the journey from Montreal to Vancouver by more than sixteen hours. Travellers now spent only three nights on the train instead of four. Average train speed over the 2,881 miles was 40.72 miles per hour, as compared with 33.19 miles per hour for the *Dominion*, but this was attained largely by reducing the number and length of stops rather than by higher speeds.

It is worth glancing back at the *Dominion* of 1951, the last year in which it was powered by steam from coast to coast.

Every evening at 8:15 the year round, the long line of Tuscan red coaches left Windsor Station in Montreal, hauled by one of the famous Royal Hudson locomotives. This engine stayed with the train as far as Fort William (Thunder Bay), a distance of 990 miles. There another Royal Hudson took over for the still longer trip of 1,250 miles to Calgary—one of the longest sustained runs ever made by steam locomotives. In 1951 the great Selkirks still reigned over the 262 mountainous miles from Calgary to Revelstoke. There they handed over the train to a third Royal Hudson for the final 379 miles to Vancouver, where it arrived on the fourth morning.[6] Sixteen trains were needed to maintain the daily *Dominion* services from Montreal and Toronto. They represented the culmination of steam passenger service on the Canadian Pacific.

The *Canadian* and the reequipped *Dominion* were both popular, and for several seasons won an annual increase in patronage. But the same year the *Canadian* began to run, the C.P.R. discontinued thirty-nine passenger trains and reduced the frequency of twelve others. Crump's beautiful train had been introduced just as passenger traffic in general was beginning a long decline. In the next eight years, annual passenger train mileage would fall by 10 million miles, or nearly 50 percent.

In the spring of 1955, G. A. Walker retired as chairman of the Canadian Pacific and was succeeded by W. A. Mather. In his last presidential address to the shareholders, Mather reviewed some of the progress in modernization that had been made since 1947. The conversion of motive power to diesel was well advanced; the *Canadian* and a fleet of dayliners symbolized a transformation in passenger service; over 30,000 new cars had increased the efficiency of the freight services; new rail, 100-pound or heavier, had been laid on 2,000 miles of main line; mileage protected by automatic signals had been increased to 50 percent; the huge hump marshaling yard in Montreal had been completed; the first of the new *Empress* liners was about to be launched; and Canadian Pacific Air Lines were flying to the Orient, Australia, Mexico, and South America and were about to add Amsterdam to their destinations.

It had all cost hundreds of millions and had been financed, as we shall see, in spite of labor troubles, freight rate limitations, sharply increased competition from road transport and other competing forms of transportation, and a low overall return on capital that made it difficult to market securities.

Norris ("Buck") Crump succeeded Mather as president in May 1955. He had been the driving force behind much of this modernization, and the conversion to diesel power that he had championed had been the best investment in the entire program. Up to the end of 1955, $110 million would be spent on diesel locomotives and facilities to service them. By that time they were reducing costs by $24 million a year—$18 million by cutting transportation expenses and $6 million by a marked reduction in maintenance and repairs. Conversion reached the halfway point about the time Crump took over; it required no prophet to foretell that its tempo would be stepped up in the immediate future.

27

Wage Rates and Freight Rates

Modernization, which had begun in 1947 and under Crump's urging had been stepped up to an intensive five-year program in 1951, had cost $600 million by the time he assumed the presidency in the spring of 1955. About half of this sum had come from depreciation, deferred maintenance, and other reserve funds; $200 million came from new borrowing, and the rest from retained income that had been husbanded over the years. It had been a difficult period financially. Costs of every kind had risen rapidly with the lifting of wartime price restrictions; when freight rate increases were granted, they were largely offset by higher wage costs. Between 1947 and 1953 the annual payroll rose by $107 million.

The Canadian Pacific quickly discovered that it no longer had a relatively contented work force. For both the company and its employees, circumstances had changed drastically. Before the Second World War upper-bracket railwaymen had been regarded as the elite of Canadian labor. They were well paid in comparison with most industrial workers, and in spite of the tribulations and wage reductions that everyone had suffered during the Depression, the majority were still devoted to the company and took pride in its reputation and accomplishments. After the war this loyalty was subjected to severe strains. It became apparent that railwaymen had not only lost their favored position but were lagging behind other industrial workers, who were receiving substantial pay increases that were not being matched by the railways. The reason was evident: industries in general, many of which were expanding rapidly, were free to recoup higher costs of materials and wages by raising the prices of their products, whereas railway freight rates were still firmly controlled by the government through the Board of Transport Commissioners. It was clear, too, that the government hoped to keep freight rates at a low level, because any appreciable increase would be reflected quickly in higher prices for innumerable commodities all across the land.

From these circumstances arose the basic positions taken on the one hand by the company and on the other by the railway unions. When asked to increase wages, the Canadian Pacific pleaded inability to pay unless it was granted higher freight rates which would enable it to foot the bill. President Mather stated its case concisely to the shareholders in 1950: "There is no way open to your Company to satisfy demands which must result in higher operating costs, whether because of higher wage scales or easier working conditions, except to increase charges to the public for transportation services."[1]

The unions were unimpressed with this argument. They took the view that railwaymen were entitled to wages on a par with those paid for comparable work in other industries, and that wages at an appropriate level should be a first charge on railway revenues. Where the money came from to meet the added cost was not their affair.

Other circumstances complicated the situation. During the war years, labor had become accustomed to multi-union negotiations, and this continued to be the custom for railwaymen after 1945. The unions representing the numerous nonoperating personnel soon separated from the running trades, but the dividing of the front went no further. Multi-union action inevitably ended the personal relationships that had frequently existed in earlier years between company officials and many of the leaders of individual unions; professional labor negotiators appeared, on the American model, and bargaining sessions became elaborate and protracted trials of strength.

For this the strange and uncomfortable position of the Canadian Pacific itself was in part responsible. The C.P.R. and the Canadian National negotiated jointly, but it was the private corporation that really bore the heat of the day. The Canadian National had the comfortable knowledge that if wage concessions resulted in heavier deficits, the federal treasury would have to make them good. The Canadian Pacific had no such assurance. It could only expect, with reasonable confidence but not with certainty, that the Board of Transport Commissioners would grant rate increases that would compensate for the cost of higher wages. This made it essential to convince the transport commissioners that the railways had driven the best possible bargain, and that they had not yielded too easily to union demands. It is significant that twenty years passed before any wage agreement was concluded between the unions and the railways without the intervention of a board of conciliation. In many important instances, when one side or the other declined to accept a board's findings, the government itself had to step in and negotiate or impose a settlement. This was not unwelcome to the Canadian Pacific, for the government could scarcely decline to grant rate increases to meet the cost of a wage contract it had required the railway to accept.

There had been no general railway strike in Canada since Confederation, but between 1947 and 1954 the unions prepared for a nationwide stoppage on four occasions and carried the threat into effect once, in 1950.

A demand for holidays with pay, advanced in 1947, caused the first crisis. Workers in many other industries had won this concession, and the railway employees asked for comparable treatment. The companies were in the midst of their immediate postwar troubles and refused the demand. A board of conciliation not only supported the unions but held that inability to pay, the first-line argument of the railways, should not enter into the matter; "financial difficulties of railway management," it stated, "should not be permitted to obscure the force of the claims" put forward by the unions.[2] The railways nevertheless rejected the board's report, but the threat of a strike caused them to reconsider and accept its recommendations.

Rates of pay were the issue in the second dispute. The financial implications of the demand for holidays with pay were relatively minor; those of across-the-board wage increases were another matter. Late in 1947 the unions asked for a general raise of thirty-five cents per hour—a large demand for the time. The Canadian Pacific estimated that, if granted in full, it would increase the annual payroll by about $65 million, which was more than twice the company's net income from all sources after payment of fixed charges but before dividends. The unions contended that it was no more than was required to compensate for the rise in the cost of living and to make their pay comparable to that of other industrial workers in Canada. They also sought wage parity with railway workers in the United States—a claim that arose naturally, since all but one of the unions concerned were internationals with members in both countries.

Ability to pay weighed heavily with the board of conciliation, which concluded that the American situation was not relevant; freight rates there had risen by 50 percent since 1935, whereas there had been no increase at all in Canada. Comparable industrial rates of pay were hard to determine, since on this and later occasions it was found difficult to agree upon the precise group of workers whose pay should be used as a yardstick. Only the cost of living was a clear-cut issue, and the board recommended a wage increase of seven cents per hour. This the unions rejected, and preparations were made for a strike to take place in the middle of July 1948. The government then intervened and in effect imposed a settlement that gave the unions seventeen cents per hour. It can scarcely have been a coincidence that this award was made

A piggyback train. By May 1973 Canadian Pacific had carried two million trailers.

just three months after the Board of Transport Commissioners had at last authorized an increase of 21 percent in freight rates—the first general revision in twenty-six years.

Within a matter of months the railways were seeking further rate adjustments, and the unions were not far behind in presenting new demands. Hours of work were now the chief issue. Not long after the 1948 wage settlement, American railwaymen had secured a 40-hour week and a pay increase of seven cents per hour. The Canadian unions determined to press for the same concessions. Although the shorter workweek was their major objective, the only purely Canadian union involved increased its pay demand to ten cents per hour. This necessitated the appointment of two boards of conciliation, a complication minimized by giving the two a chairman in common.

Negotiations dragged on for months; not until May 1950 did the boards of conciliation recommend a pay increase of four cents per hour and a 44-hour workweek. The reports included a notable comment on the "inability to pay" contention: "railroaders must not be required to accept substandard wages or onerous working hours in order to underwrite railway deficits. If higher wages are deserved they must be paid, and the public must pay the cost." But it added: "This does not, however, imply that enlightened labour should proceed to extract what it can in the way of wage increases without regard to the condition of the business which employs it."[3]

The Canadian Pacific had let it be known that it had decided to "resist, temperately but firmly, any adjustments . . . in wage scales or conditions of employment that depart substantially from the findings of the Board of Conciliation. . . ."[4] The unions for their part considered that the award would require them to accept substandard wages and onerous working hours and announced that their members had voted to strike unless their demands were fully met. The railways were then persuaded to make a final offer in which, under official pressure, they acknowledged a moral obligation to introduce the 40-hour week "at the appropriate time," but limited their immediate offer to a 44-hour week with no reduction in pay or the existing hours and a wage increase of eight and a half cents per hour. Relations between the railways and the unions had been deteriorating, and presumably this accounts for the fact that these terms were presented arrogantly, in a letter signed by the president of the Canadian National, which described the offer as "the ultimate which can be expected" and went so far as to accuse the unions of bad faith. Predictably, this ended negotiations; the unions rejected both proposals, and on August 22 Canada experienced its first nationwide rail strike. A total of 125,700 workers left their jobs and an additional 46,300 had to be laid off. Rail operations came to a complete standstill.

It was obvious that the strike could not be permitted to continue for long. When renewed talks between the two parties failed to result in any prospect of a settlement, the government called a special session of Parliament and on August 30 passed the Maintenance of Railway Operation Act. This ordered the resumption of rail service within forty-eight hours, granted an interim wage increase of four cents an hour, and provided for the appointment of an arbitrator with power to settle unresolved issues. Granting of the shorter workweek was clearly anticipated, for the preamble to the act stated that the railways and their employees "appear to have agreed that existing wage rates should be increased, and the forty-hour week introduced";[5] the amount of the wage increases and the timing of the change in working hours remained to be settled. These were determined by the arbitrator, Mr. Justice R. L. Kellock, of the Supreme Court of Canada, who in December granted the unions both their original demands—the 40-hour week, which was to become effective by June 1, 1951, and a wage increase of seven cents per hour. It was a major victory for the railwaymen.

On paper, the Canadian Pacific seemed to have already received freight rate concessions that would absorb the impact of the Kellock awards. In March 1950 an increase of 16 percent was authorized by the Board of Transport Commissioners, and in June this was raised to 20 percent. But this could not be applied to all existing rates. The most important exception was grain, which usually accounted for between 30 and 40 percent of the C.P.R.'s total freight tonnage; it continued to move in accordance with the statutory Crow's Nest tariff. In many other instances competition from other carriers made it impracticable to apply the increases; to do so would simply divert traffic from the railway to highway or seaway. Thus, although the rate revisions granted up to the spring of 1950 had raised freight rates 40.4 percent above the 1939 level, the Canadian Pacific found that the average overall increase that could actually be carried into effect was only 27.6 percent.

In spite of its brevity, the strike cost the railways customers as well as revenue and demonstrated in a dramatic way the strength of the competition they were facing from alternative means of transportation. Air services were as yet at an early stage of development, but road transport was making off with important segments of the Canadian Pacific's traffic.

Long-distance truck services were still a thing of the future in Canada, but on shorter runs motor vehicle operations enjoyed many advantages. The roads they used were provided by the taxpayer; their services were highly flexible; they could move their vehicles about freely and easily to meet temporary or changing needs. Above all, they could offer a door-to-door service, whereas the railway was tied to its tracks and a freight depot unless the customer was sufficiently important to have a spur track to his premises.

The value of a commodity had always been a determining factor in setting freight rates. High-priced goods were seldom bulky, and it was upon these that the truckers set their sights, thereby taking from the C.P.R. much of its most lucrative business. Hampered by a multitude of regulations that had been necessary for the protection of the public in its monopoly days, the railway resented the freedom enjoyed by the truck operator. President Mather remarked upon this in 1951: "Trucks are not common carriers but operate on public highways as relatively free agents. They are permitted to select the most profitable traffic, to operate pretty much how they wish, where they wish, and charge what they wish."[6]

As early as 1934, highway competition was being felt sufficiently to prompt the Canadian Pacific to begin a pick-up and delivery service for less-than-carload freight. Limited at first to a few centers, within five years it had been extended throughout the system. But truck competition grew apace, especially in intercity transportation in eastern Canada.

It is interesting to note that even after the war the effective range of truck competition in Canada was considered to be no more than thirty-five miles; but major changes were in the offing. The capabilities of trucks were increasing rapidly, and there was great activity in highway improvement and construction. In cooperation with the provinces, the federal government decided to build the Trans-Canada Highway—a matter of particular concern to the Canadian Pacific, because the highway would parallel its transcontinental main line, often within sight of it, most of the way from Montreal to Vancouver.

To counter highway competition, the C.P.R. decided to go into the trucking business itself. If trucks and trains could be integrated, it hoped that the combined service would be more than a match for trucks alone. Immediately after the war ended, it began to establish truck services in western Canada that fanned out from such centers as Brandon, Lethbridge, and Red Deer. These were in areas served by branch lines, so doubtless the possibility that they might in time replace the branches was already in mind. By 1947 Canadian Pacific Transport Limited had come into existence and a number of established regional road transport companies had been acquired, including the OK Valley Freight Lines in the Okanagan valley in British Columbia and Island Freight Services on Vancouver Island. In 1954 Canadian Pacific's road services already had 280 units of equipment and were operating over routes totaling 3,500 miles.

Piggyback service—referred to at first as "trailer-on-flat-car service"—was the next development. This provided the basic convenience of trucks—transit from door to door—but avoided the long intercity highway haul by loading the trailer on a flatcar and moving it by rail. Service began between Montreal and Toronto on December 1, 1952, and was extended gradually, first to Hamilton and London and then to western centers. Six years later the C.P.R. offered a common carrier piggyback service between Montreal and Toronto, thus making it available to any road carrier who wished to take advantage of it.

The extent and capabilities of road transport had been demonstrated in a startling way by the national railway strike of 1950; the rail stoppage had much less impact than had been anticipated. True, no one doubted that railways were still and would continue to be an essential part of the Canadian economy; but highway carriers rose to the occasion so effectively that the railways suffered permanent damage. Some customers who had turned to trucks in the emergency did not return their patronage to the railways when the strike ended. Others, concerned about the future, decided to provide for eventualities by acquiring trucks of their own. Excluding rail employees, layoffs occasioned by the strike affected only a few thousand workers in the whole of Canada. Obviously the railroads were far from holding the near monopoly position that had been theirs in many parts of the country before the appearance of the highway carrier.

Freight rates have been a bone of contention in western Canada ever since the building of the Canadian Pacific. Any monopoly is suspect, and for a generation the C.P.R. offered the only means of transportation for most of the population. Manitoba's struggle against the monopoly clause of the Canadian

Pacific contract and the province's efforts to sponsor rival railways have been noted. Even such a major concession as the low rates on grain secured under the terms of the Crow's Nest Pass Agreement of 1897 did little to reduce the general feeling of hostility and suspicion toward the railway. Half a century later the prairies could see no injustice in the fact that in a vastly different price structure, the identical rates were still in effect.

Apart from grain, rates in general were indisputably lower in the East than in the West; and just as undeniably, the basic reason for this was that competition was much more prevalent there than it was in the West. After the Second World War, circumstances tended to perpetuate and to some extent to accentuate this discrimination. As we have seen, the railways found it impracticable to apply general freight-rate increases across the board; they could be applied in full only to commodities (such as ore and lumber) that were tied to the rails by their nature, and in areas where higher rates would not divert traffic to highways or waterways. By and large the prairies were such an area, and the impact of rate increases was felt most severely in western Canada.

Late in 1948 the federal government decided that some cognizance must be taken of this and other grievances relating to transportation. In December it appointed a Royal Commission that was instructed "to review and report upon the . . . disadvantages under which certain sections of Canada find themselves in relation to the various transportation services therein and to recommend what measures should be initiated in order that the national transportation policy may best serve the general well-being of Canada." From the point of view of the Canadian Pacific, this was essentially an inquiry into discontent over the level and incidence of its freight rates and a consideration of the revenues and profits that it should be entitled to earn.

It is significant that the two large central provinces, Ontario and Quebec, did not bother to present briefs to the commission. Their populations, representing 60 percent of the people of Canada, were concentrated mostly in a relatively small area that was well served by trucks and shipping as well as by railways. Competition kept rates at what was evidently regarded as an acceptable level.

The Prairie Provinces were heavily dependent upon export markets, and the cost of the long haul required to gain access to them was of vital concern. Moreover, as the commission noted, they were "bordered on both East and West by relatively barren areas . . . not locally productive of rail traffic," and they considered that the cost of operating trains through these areas was being levied unfairly on prairie traffic. In its brief, the province of Saskatchewan harked back to the circumstances under which the Canadian Pacific had followed an expensive all-Canadian route north of Lake Superior. This had been done, the brief asserted, for a national purpose. The railway had been "artificially located . . . through Canadian territory, when communication through the United States would have been more economical," and the penalty had been higher transportation costs.

This complaint displayed a curious blindness to history, for if railway communication with the Canadian West had been available only through the United States, it is unlikely that the West would today be part of Canada. W. A. Mackintosh has stressed the key role played by the all-Canadian route: "That portion of the railway which links Winnipeg with Lake Superior was and is the most essential part of Canada's transportation system. . . . Other parts of the railway system were important and essential, but none has had the significance of that section which overcomes the Laurentian barrier between the Great Lakes and the prairies."[7] The Royal Commission recognized that the route had been insisted upon in the national interest, and it recommended that "the cost of maintaining that portion of our transcontinental system which serves as a link or bridge between East and West [should] be charged upon the general revenues of the country."

The result was what became known as the "bridge subsidy." The cost of maintaining the Canadian Pacific's main line between Sudbury and Thunder Bay (551.5 miles) was to be refunded to the railway, and a like sum was to be paid to the Canadian National toward the cost of the upkeep of its lines through the same region. The railways were not to benefit financially; the subsidy, which was not to exceed $7 million per annum, was to be passed on to shippers in the form of reduced freight charges.

The position of the Maritime Provinces had changed little since the 1920s. The Intercolonial Railway (in the words of the preamble to the Maritime Freight Rates Act of 1927) had been intended "to afford the Maritime merchants, traders and manufacturers the larger market of the whole Canadian people instead of the restricted market of the Maritimes themselves." This it had failed to do because of the cost of the long haul to markets and sources of supply in central Canada. To decrease this handicap, the act of 1927 authorized a regional reduction in freight rates of 20 percent, later increased to 30 percent. Almost as important as the subsidy itself was the manner in which the cost was to be met. The railways were not to bear the cost of the subsidy; the government undertook to reimburse them for the reduction in rates they were to give to shippers. Both the Maritimes subsidy and the "bridge" subsidy embodied a principle of great significance: a railway service deemed to be in the national interest was being subsidized by the federal government.

In a series of notable "reservations and observations," one of the three commissioners, Henry F. Angus, dealt with several aspects of the financial predicament in which circumstances had placed the Canadian Pacific. Rising costs, he noted, are never popular: "Everyone accepts with equanimity and explains plausibly any changes in price which enlarge his income, and complains bitterly of any changes which increase his expenses." Freight rates could not be the only item to remain unchanged in a period of rising costs and inflation; "the increase in transportation costs must be accepted as a fact and dealt with by providing the carriers with revenue."[8] Amalgamation of the two great railway systems was not a practicable policy; the publicly and privately owned railways were going to continue to exist side by side, but their financial positions were very different. The deficits of the Canadian National were met by the taxpayer, and it had access to capital funds in the form of securities guaranteed by the government of Canada. The Canadian Pacific had to make its own way in the world, and "a sound transportation policy in Canada" required that it should "be able to raise the capital needed to maintain the quality of its services without recourse to measures which are financially unsound."[9] It must be able to attract new capital, and "to be forthcoming [this] must be assured of a fair return, and no such assurance is convincing unless the capital already invested is receiving a fair return. . . ."[10] Adequate revenues that would enable it to meet its fixed charges and pay dividends were therefore essential, and the relation of these needs to freight rates was obvious: "It follows that the general rate level must be set with the needs of the Canadian Pacific in mind. No other standard has been seriously suggested."[11]

The C.P.R. thus became the yardstick for the determination of rates, and the way in which this unintended role complicated its negotiations with the trade unions has already been noted. Repeatedly it was forced to agree to wage increases without any positive assurance that the higher freight rates that would be necessary to pay for them would be forthcoming. In theory this was supposed to encourage the railway to try to keep wage concessions to a minimum. Dr. Angus suggested that means should be found to "exonerate railway management from the invidious duty of satisfying the Board that no one could have driven a harder bargain."[12]

Canadian Pacific dividends, above all its surpluses, were often looked upon with disapproval and suspicion. For some years the Board of Transport Commissioners, when considering applications for rate increases, had taken into account an "earnings requirement" formula. This estimated the financial needs of the railways as the sum total of fixed charges, dividends (at a modest rate), and a surplus to provide for additions and improvements, after retirements. From the point of view of the C.P.R., the formula had serious defects. Among other things, it took no account of the very substantial capital expenditures that had been made from retained earnings, upon which no interest was paid. Its frailties were shown between 1947 and 1951, when the Canadian Pacific's net railway investment increased by $100 million, but its "requirement allowance," as determined by the formula, fell by $6.7 million.[13]

As an alternative, the C.P.R. suggested that the relevant section of the Railway Act should be amended to read as follows: "Rates shall not be deemed to be just and reasonable unless, taken as a whole, they are sufficient to provide a fair return upon the investment in the railway property of the Canadian Pacific Railway Company and the Board [of Transport Commissioners] may from time to time determine the investment in railway property upon which the return is to be calculated and the rate of such return."[14]

The board went so far as to determine the extent of the Canadian Pacific's investment in its railroad, which was found to be $1,175,791,000 as of December 31, 1952, but it declined to go further. The most interesting of its objections related to the circumstance, already noted, that the impact of a rate increase was not felt uniformly either through the economy or across the country: "The economic impact of freight rates is such that they should not be made the product of any automatic formula. This is particularly so where 100 percent of the cost, or the increase in cost, is sought to be automatically applied in general rate increases to a much lesser percentage of the revenue producing business and in particular to that narrowing section of the non-competitive and non-statutory rate structure where the economic leverage and consequences are the greatest."[15]

The Canadian Pacific had had 6½ percent in mind as an appropriate rate of return on its rail investment. This was far beyond the rate that its net income from rail operations represented at the time. In 1953 the figure was 2.40 percent; in 1954 it declined to 2.15 percent and in 1955 rose to 2.92 percent.

On the basic question of freight rates in general, the Royal Commission recommended the equalization of rates across Canada; the rate for a commodity should be the same, mile for mile, right across the country. But the transport commissioners encountered difficulties and were unable to apply the policy as extensively as the prairies in particular had hoped. Western discontent lived on, and the freight rates problem would persist for many a day.

28

Diversification

By the time Norris Crump became president of the Canadian Pacific in 1955, diversification was widely accepted as the path of prudence for large corporations. It was a policy Crump was to promote in a spectacular fashion, but it was one that had long been characteristic of the C.P.R. From the very beginning it had been more than just simply a railroad. Its original charter of 1881 empowered it among other things to own telegraph and telephone lines, to build wharves, docks, and grain elevators, and to operate shipping services. In addition a general clause granted it all "franchises and powers necessary or useful" to carry out its purposes—a provision so sweeping that it prompted the company's most formidable critic, Edward Blake, to remark that he did "not know of anything they are not authorized to do."[1]

Stephen and Van Horne soon added sleeping and dining cars, an express service, and hotels to the Canadian Pacific. In 1898 it acquired the smelter at Trail, and about the same time it became interested in coal mining. By the turn of the century, the large-scale irrigation project in southern Alberta was reaching the planning stage.

Specific legal authority for these and related activities was obviously desirable; therefore, in 1902 the Canadian Pacific secured important amendments to its charter. One of the new clauses stated that "in order to utilize its land grant and the land grants of other railway companies owned or controlled by the Company" it might "engage in general mining, smelting and reduction, the manufacture and sale of iron and steel, and lumber and timber manufacturing operations. . . ." Another clause empowered it to generate electricity and to dispose of power surplus to its needs; under a third it could excavate and operate ditches or canals on its lands and "generally exercise the powers of an irrigation company." Some doubt seems to have arisen about the railway's hotels, for the amendment included authority to "build, purchase, acquire or lease" buildings required for hotels and restaurants.

Perhaps the most interesting of many later charter amendments gave the company wide powers to acquire, construct, and operate aircraft. The petition for these rights may well have been prompted by a letter from Lord Shaughnessy to Sir Edmund Osler that was included in the first mail carried by air in Canada. The flight was from Montreal to Toronto; the date was June 24, 1918. "The opportunity to communicate with you by aeroplane, kindly furnished me to-day," Shaughnessy wrote, "suggests the thought that in all the discussion of public ownership of Canadian railways, the route through the air has been quite overlooked. Any scheme of Nationalization that left the land lines open to competition through the air where no rails, bridges and cross-ties . . . need be provided, would be defective and might bring financial disaster. Should the Government acquire the land transportation lines the route through the air should be corralled."[2] No doubt Shaughnessy wrote facetiously, but it can scarcely have been a coincidence that within a year the Canadian Pacific had asked for and had received authority to take to the air when it became so minded.

Though absorbed in the task of modernizing the railway, Crump considered that it was high time the Canadian Pacific looked into the possibility of developing its many other assets. With the shining exception of the Consolidated Mining and Smelting Company, in which it had a controlling interest, the C.P.R. had scarcely begun to exploit the immense resources that Crump realized were latent in its lands, urban real estate holdings, and timber limits.

The discovery of the Leduc field in 1947, which marked the beginning of a major oil industry in Alberta, had drawn attention to the company's mineral rights. These had been reserved in varying degrees over millions of acres in the Prairie Provinces. By 1952 the Canadian Pacific was receiving royalties from 450 oil wells, many of them in the Leduc field. Income from leases, from fees on land reserved for exploration, and from royalties on oil and gas, hitherto unimportant, began to rise steeply. In 1948 payments had totaled $1.3 million; by 1954 they had risen to $8.6 million. At the annual meeting in May 1955, a shareholder asked why the C.P.R. itself did not produce oil from its holdings. He was told that the directors considered the policy being followed to be in the best interests of the railway. Crump, who became president that same month, also had his doubts, and he soon set up a number of investigations intended to give the company a much better knowledge of the nature and potential of its properties. Within a year petroleum engineering consultants were busy surveying the more promising areas in which the C.P.R. held mineral rights. In January 1958 their findings resulted in the incorporation of Canadian Pacific Oil and Gas Limited, the first of a series of wholly owned or controlled subsidiaries that within a dozen years were to transform the Canadian Pacific into a vast conglomerate.

Of necessity, the new company began operations on a modest scale, for most of the Canadian Pacific's rights were either leased or under reservation; it took time to regain control of them. In spite of this, C.P. Oil and Gas lost no time in initiating its own drilling program. It brought in its first gas wells before the end of 1958 and its first oil wells in 1959. By 1963 it owned 123 gas and 73 oil wells. That same year, the Canadian Pacific, having repossessed its rights covering 11.9 million acres, sold them to its subsidiary.

This transaction had been made possible by the incorporation in 1962 of Canadian Pacific Investments Limited, the formation of which marked a great step forward in Crump's diversification plans. C.P.I. was intended to assume general supervision and control of companies carrying on the development of natural resources in which the Canadian Pacific had an interest. As a first step, the railway transferred to it, in return for capital stock, ownership of Canadian Pacific Oil and Gas and of a second wholly owned subsidiary, Pacific Logging Limited. The latter, dormant for some years, had just been reactivated to take charge of the company's timber lands. A further highly important transfer was made at the end of 1963, when the Canadian Pacific handed over to C.P.I. its controlling interest in the Consolidated Mining and Smelting Company, which centered upon the smelter at Trail. Meanwhile Canadian Pacific Investments itself had formed two subsidiaries, Canadian Pacific Hotels Limited and the Marathon Realty Company Limited. Means were thus created to detach the bulk of the railway's nontransportation interests and to place them under the care of a companion corporation.

There were two reasons for the reorganization. There was first the practical problem of good management. The Canadian Pacific's transportation interests were quite extensive and complicated enough to absorb the full time and attention of those responsible for them. If the railway's other assets and interests were to be developed on the scale Crump expected, they, too, would require full-time attention; there could be no thought of continuing to treat them as a sideline. Better results should be achieved by both aspects of the company's activities if each became the sole concern of its managers. Carrying this principle further, Crump adopted the profit center concept, which gave departments and subsidiaries as much autonomy as was practicable: "The method is to create manageable-sized units, to give managers authority to manage, and to hold them responsible for results. In this way the spirit of enterprise can be mobilized for maximum productive effort, and initiative and creative energies are given free rein."[3] There would, of course, be interlocking at the top: Crump was chairman and chief executive officer of Canadian Pacific Investments as long as he continued to be chairman of the Canadian Pacific, but only three directors served on the boards of both companies.

The second reason was a feeling that it would be wise as well as practical to establish a clear distinction between the transportation and other interests of the company. There had long been a tendency to do this. Shaughnessy had moved some distance toward it, and the segregation of most nonrail revenues in an "other income" item in the accounts was a practice of long standing.

In 1952 the matter had become involved in the never-ending controversy regarding freight rates. It will be remembered that H. F. Angus, a member of the Royal Commission on Transportation that reported in 1950, had suggested that the Board of Transport Commissioners should be asked to determine the Canadian Pacific's railroad investment. The intention was that the valuation should be the basis for calculating a "permissive income," which in turn would be a factor in setting the level of rates. The C.P.R. duly asked the board to establish the amount of investment, but clearly expected it to include only the railway proper. In the company's view, its other assets and income had nothing to do with rate-setting. This contention was promptly challenged by eight of the ten provincial governments, who united in presenting a brief to the transport commissioners. This denied emphatically that the Canadian Pacific had a "dual personality" and that the railway constituted "an entity distinct and separate from what they call the 'non-rail enterprises and investments' of the Company."[4] In an ably argued historical review by Vernon C. Fowke, it was contended that on every occasion upon which Parliament had granted the Canadian Pacific additional powers, it had been made clear that they were to be exercised only to further the purposes of the railway. Referring to the principal charter amendment of 1902, Fowke wrote: "The legislators did not contemplate in this section a company which would embark upon lumbering, mining, smelting and manufacturing in general or enter into the agricultural loan business, except for the better utilization of its land grants."[5]

The transport commissioners in effect dodged the issue by declining to set a permitted rate of return on railroad investment, but the point was raised again when another Royal Commission reviewed transportation matters in 1959. It considered carefully whether nonrail income and land grants and other subsidies received by the railways from governments should be a factor in determining freight rates, and its verdict was in the negative. It pointed out that so far as natural resources were concerned, the nation had "already instituted measures to recapture a portion of the return . . . through the media

The Cominco smelter at Trail, British Columbia, which has developed through the years from the tiny plant purchased from Augustus Heinze as part of a railway deal in 1898.

Canada Place, the first large project of Marathon Realty in Montreal, shown as it was nearing completion in 1967. It consists of a luxury hotel, the Château Champlain (center), and an office tower (still under construction, on the left). Windsor Station is on the right.

of income tax and royalties." As for "other income," the commission did "not recommend that assets and earnings of railway companies in businesses and investments other than railways be taken into account in setting freight rates."[6] Nevertheless, the question was bound to recur, and it could perhaps be countered more effectively if those businesses and investments passed into the possession of companies corporately distinct from the railway, though controlled by it.

Crump has contended that the Canadian Pacific was diversifying only within the resources that had come its way by subsidy or purchase, but both Canadian Pacific Investments and its subsidiaries soon ventured far beyond these limits. Canadian Pacific Oil and Gas was a case in point. Though its first preoccupation had been the rights in the railway's own lands, it soon took out reservations and leases on 400,000 additional acres in Alberta and Saskatchewan and later secured permits covering over 1.3 million acres in the Northwest Territories. To these it added an interest in Pan Arctic Oils Limited, which held petroleum and gas rights on a vast acreage in the Canadian Arctic Islands. Still farther afield it shared in the offshore searches for oil in the North Sea and on both coasts of Italy.

Early in its career, Canadian Pacific Investments had established an investment portfolio. Purchases included shares in Central-Del Rio Oils Limited, a firm with which Canadian Pacific Oil and Gas had had dealings. By early 1969 it had built up its holdings to a majority interest. C.P. Oil and Gas and Central-Del Rio were soon merged to form what was presently named Pan-Canadian Petroleum Limited. The combined concern held rights covering about 20 million acres in Canada and extended its overseas surveys to South America, Africa, and Indonesia. C.P.I. owned nearly 90 percent of the Pan-Canadian shares, the market value of which was over $363 million at the end of 1973.

Each of the major subsidiaries has had a comparable history of expansion. Canadian Pacific Hotels Limited was formed initially to undertake contracts for the management of hotels owned by outside interests, but it quickly became involved in the railway's own hotels, in which there had recently been important changes. The aging and badly located Royal Alexandra in Winnipeg had been closed. The arrangement with the Canadian National for the joint operation of Hotel Vancouver ended, leaving the C.P.R., after seventy-six years, without a hotel at its western terminus. On the credit side, the Royal York in Toronto had been enlarged from 1,200 to 1,600 rooms and had thereby regained its old status as the largest hotel in the British Commonwealth.

Part of one of Marathon Realty's housing developments in Vancouver.

Before long some of the most notable of the hotels, including the Royal York itself, the Empress in Victoria, and the Château Frontenac in Quebec, were sold to C.P. Hotels Limited, which soon assumed management of the whole C.P.R. chain. Thorough renovation programs were undertaken that modernized the older buildings yet preserved their distinctive character. Canadian Pacific Hotels itself built the luxurious 620-room Château Champlain in Montreal, which was completed in time to benefit from the rush of business occasioned by the world's fair in 1967. The Château Halifax, 50-percent owned, was opened in 1974.

First-class hotels added by management contracts have included the Château Lacombe in Edmonton and the Northstar Inn in Winnipeg. Motor hotels and lodges are operated in a number of smaller cities. A major departure came in 1973 when the hotel system became international; hotels are planned in Paris, Tel Aviv, and Mexico. Airways have replaced railways as the chief tourist travel routes, and it may be noted that all the cities in which large new hotels are projected, with the exception of Paris, are served by Canadian Pacific's airlines. In keeping with this trend, C.P. Hotels will build and operate the major hotel at the new Mirabel International Airport, near Montreal.

Marathon Realty fell heir to real estate problems of great complexity. The railway first sold to it 883,000 acres of agricultural land, all but a trifling fraction of it on the prairies. This was the residue of the famous land grants, some of them dating back to construction days. It was not an exciting acquisition; most of the good land had been sold long before, a fact reflected in the purchase price, which was slightly less than $6 an acre. Much more important was the transfer in 1965, for management and development, of all Canadian Pacific's nontransportation properties.

One problem Marathon faced was the difficult task of deciding the best alternative use for large downtown areas in major cities that had become redundant for railway purposes. Passenger traffic had declined to such a degree that imposing stations were no longer necessary, and trucking services had reduced the need for midtown freight yards. Their extensive sites offered interesting possibilities for profitable redevelopment, especially in Montreal, Toronto, Calgary, and Vancouver.

A number of the projects were too large for Marathon to finance alone; the first step, therefore, had to be the assembling of a consortium of firms willing to share in a development. Next came the preparation of a tentative plan that promised to meet their needs. The approval of public authorities had then to be sought, and this frequently involved three levels of government—civic, provincial, and federal. As likely as not, planning authorities would require changes in such basic specifications as the height of buildings, the proportion of the area to be devoted to open spaces, and the permissible density of population. Discussions, hearings, and the redrafting of plans would all take time and cause delay—and delay is perhaps the most serious hazard faced by such a project. Circumstances can change; costs can soar. Almost invariably there will be members of the consortium who cannot or will not wait, and in a measure the whole process has to begin over again.

Marathon's first important urban project was relatively uncomplicated. The Canadian Pacific had acquired property across the street from its famous Windsor Street Station in Montreal, and there Marathon built Place du Canada, a striking complex consisting of the thirty-eight-storey Château Champlain and an office tower. The hotel is wholly owned and Marathon has a substantial interest in the tower. Windsor Station was not involved; it was intended to figure in a second and much larger scheme.

In Calgary, too, things progressed more or less according to plan. On the site of the passenger depot and train sheds adjacent to Canadian Pacific's Hotel Palliser, Marathon built Palliser Square. Commercial and shopping facilities, an office tower, and an apartment building are dominated by the Husky Tower (a joint project with Husky Oil Limited), a 626-foot observation tower, complete with revolving restaurant.

Complications aplenty appeared in Vancouver. Here Marathon planned an ambitious Project 200 (so called because its total cost was roughly estimated at $200 million) on a twenty-three-acre waterfront plot encompassing the site of the passenger station, its train sheds, and some adjoining property. An artist's sketch suggested that it might consist of nine large towers and a number of lesser structures. Only one of the nine, Granville Square, a striking thirty-two-storey building occupied in great part by Canadian Pacific regional offices, has been completed. The popularity of its elevated plaza, which affords an unobstructed view of the harbor, bolstered the case for making greater provision in the overall plan for public access to the waterfront. Skyscraper redevelopment schemes are less well regarded locally than they were formerly, and Project 200 went back to the drawing boards.

In Toronto, Marathon and Canadian National are joint sponsors of Metro Centre, the largest redevelopment project of the kind in North America. The 190-acre site, close to the business center of the city, includes the Union Station and the adjoining railway yards, which parallel the shore of Lake Ontario. As in Project 200, the first plans for Metro Centre were overtaken by changes in circumstances and public attitudes, and major revisions were necessary to meet them. Matters were complicated by a demand for the preservation of the Union Station, the most imposing building of the kind in Canada. One project went ahead as planned: the Canadian National built an 1,800-foot communications tower that is the highest free-standing structure in the world.

Reevaluation and soaring costs are also delaying Marathon's large-scale redevelopment in Montreal, which is to include Windsor Station, the Canadian Pacific's head offices, and adjoining properties. As in Toronto, objections have been raised to the demolition of the station building, which has been a Montreal landmark for eighty years.

Marathon has thus encountered delays and difficulties with its most ambitious projects, which may well top the billion-dollar mark before they are completed, but it has carried out many lesser schemes with marked success. Industrial parks have been developed in Montreal, Toronto, Sudbury, Calgary, and Edmonton; more than a score of shopping centers have been built in as many cities across the country; housing has featured in its program. Marathon has not confined its activities to land acquired from the railway; industrial parks, shopping centers, and many of the housing developments have been built on property purchased for the purpose. Its largest residential projects have been in Vancouver, where the railway still held some 500 acres of its original land grant, including several substantial tracts in pleasant residential areas. The largest of Marathon's housing ventures covers ninety-four acres of the redundant False Creek railway yards; the projected population is nearly 8,000. Except for the transfer of several properties to the city of Vancouver, Marathon has sold very little of the railway's urban lands; it seems clear that the intention is to retain ownership. Arbutus Village, a residential development in Vancouver completed in 1973–74, was the first construction for sale that Marathon had undertaken, and even here the commercial and retail facilities built as part of the project were retained.

The Canadian Pacific's timber lands on Vancouver Island had not been included in the sales to Marathon Realty, nor had they been placed under its management. Totaling about 360,000 acres, they were the residue of the fabulously rich tract of 1.4 million acres of Esquimalt and Nanaimo Railway lands that had been bought by the C.P.R. at the same time it acquired the railway. The purchase may well have been the most profitable the Canadian Pacific ever made. In 1964 it sold 226,000 acres for $53.7 million, or roughly thirty-five times the cost of the whole tract in 1905.

In 1963–64 the remaining 134,000 acres had been sold to the Pacific Logging Company at a more modest price per acre. This company's main purpose, as its name implies, was to fell and sell logs. It purchased additional timber limits in 1967, enlarging its holdings on Vancouver Island to 290,000 acres, and the next year its log production totaled 242 million board feet. Inevitably its interests expanded to sawmills, not only on Vancouver Island but in Slocan, where a lumber company was purchased and a new mill built. Pacific Logging has devoted special attention to reforestation, and millions of seedlings have been planted on its logged-over areas.

Canadian Pacific Investments, looking farther afield, began to purchase shares of the Great Lakes Paper Company, one of the largest producers of newsprint in Canada. By 1971 it had acquired a controlling interest; Great Lakes Paper ceased to be an item in the investment portfolio and was added to the list of controlled companies.

C.P.I. has also acquired a substantial holding in MacMillan Bloedel Limited, the largest fully integrated forest company in Canada, which manufactures a wide variety of pulp, paper, and lumber products. At the end of 1975 it owned a 13.4-percent interest with a market value of $50.9 million. Relations between the Canadian Pacific and MacMillan Bloedel were becoming close; the latter had been one of the two purchasers of the Esquimalt and Nanaimo lands in 1964 and, as we shall see, a shipping subsidiary of the railway was carrying MacMillan Bloedel products overseas.

The 1975 balance sheet of Canadian Pacific Investments valued its properties relating to forest products, not including its MacMillan Bloedel stock, at 408.3 million. Substantial though this total was, it was less than half its stake in mines and minerals, which exceeded $873 million. Here, of course, the largest asset was a controlling interest in the Consolidated Mining and Smelting Company, renamed Cominco Limited in 1966.

The original smelter built at Trail by Augustus Heinze had been concerned primarily with copper. The Canadian Pacific added lead, which, as the copper mines declined, became Trail's chief product. It was joined by zinc during the First World War, when that metal was in critically short supply. This led to technical developments that had much to do with the Consolidated's later prosperity. The chief source of lead and zinc was the great Sullivan mine at Kimberley; the difficulty was that the two metals were usually found together and no satisfactory means of separating them was known. This meant that only pockets of ore rich in one metal or the other could be utilized. Separation by a flotation process had been developed in Australia, and in 1917 R. W. Diamond, who was familiar with it, was engaged and assigned the difficult task of adapting it to the complicated Sullivan ores. Success was attained in 1920, but it came at the lowest point in the company's financial fortunes. The metal market, which had boomed during the war, had collapsed, and the Consolidated was having the greatest difficulty in paying even its smallest bills. However, by 1923 a plant had been built that could process 3,000 tons of ore per day, and by degrees its capacity was increased to 11,000 tons. The results were dramatic. The whole of the Sullivan ore could now be processed, and costs were much reduced—a vital consideration to an industry that sells its products on world markets.

These developments had been guided by S. G. Blaylock, who had become general manager in 1918. The next important step was in the field of fertilizers. Great quantities of sulphur were going up the stacks of the Trail smelter, and a good deal of it drifted southward and across the American border, only seven miles away. Claims for damage to crops resulted, and the Consolidated decided to solve the problem profitably by recovering the sulphur and using it in the production of fertilizer. A large plant was completed at Warfield, near Trail, in 1931. This innovation, like the flotation breakthrough, came at an unfortunate time, for the Depression was at its worst and sales were slow in the first years.

By 1931 the Canadian Pacific had invested $15.2 million in the Consolidated. It held 51 percent of the shares and had received a cash return of $21.2 million in interest and dividends. In addition, revenue from the freight traffic arising from the operations at Trail and Kimberley had averaged $3.4 million over the previous ten years.[7]

As the Depression lifted, prosperity came to the Consolidated. In 1937 the C.P.R. received $5.88 million in dividends, and at the end of the year the market value of its shares exceeded $93 million. The peak in dividend payments came after the Second World War, when in the four years 1948–51 they averaged $17.4 million. In the decade previous to the sale of the shares to Canadian Pacific Investments in 1963, a fairer basis upon which to judge results, the railway received an average of $10.1 million.

In the last decade, Cominco has both diversified its activities and extended them to many parts of the world, but lead, zinc, and the silver found with them continue to be its basic interest. In the course of its history it has produced 7.9 million tons of zinc, 8.8 million tons of lead, and over 455 million ounces of silver.[8] Proven reserves indicate that the Sullivan mine still has a life expectancy of at least another thirty years, but an industry such as Cominco must always be looking far ahead. Its search for additional lead-zinc deposits has extended over many years and taken it to distant places. In 1927, promising indications were found at Pine Point, not far from Great Slave Lake, in the Northwest Territories, but the deposit was remote from transportation. In 1961 the government of Canada, as part of its program of northern development, undertook to build the Great Slave Lake Railway, which became part of the Canadian National system. In 1964 ore from Pine Point began to move to Trail, and by 1973 production there exceeded the output of the Sullivan mine. Recently a large deposit of high-quality lead-zinc ore has been found on Little Cornwallis Island, in the high Arctic; here again, a difficult transportation problem must be solved. Outside Canada, Cominco has developed a lead mine in Montana and lead-zinc mines in Greenland and Spain. It has a minority interest in smelters in Japan and India, both of which receive concentrate from the Pine Point mine. Its interests have extended to mercury in British Columbia, to tin and tungsten in Australia, and to diamonds in South Africa. It is producing extra-high-purity metals for the electronic industries and has added steel making to its activities.

After years of marginal profitability, the fertilizer branch, active in both Canada and the United States, is benefiting from the widespread demand for more foodstuffs. Potash mines have been developed in Saskatchewan, where huge deposits exist. The designed output is about a million tons a year, and proven reserves are sufficient to support full production for a century.

Cominco manages two subsidiaries of Canadian Pacific Investments, with which it shares ownership on a 60-40 basis. These are CanPac Minerals Limited and Fording Coal Limited. The former was incorporated in 1969, when PanCanadian Petroleum was coming into existence, to assume responsibility for the Canadian Pacific's mineral rights not related to oil and gas. Its greatest potential asset is coal, found in vast deposits, mostly in Alberta, believed to contain as much as 1,200 million tons. Fording Coal was formed to develop coal lands on the Fording River, in the Kootenay district of British Columbia. The railway had owned the field since 1909, but declining markets discouraged its exploitation. Conditions changed suddenly when deposits in the same area owned by Crows Nest Industries (successor to the Crow's Nest Pass Coal Company, in which James J. Hill and the Great Northern Railroad had held a major interest) were purchased by Kaiser Resources Limited. Kaiser had supplied the Japanese steel industry with iron ore, and now proposed to provide it with coking coal from the Kootenay mines. Transportation was the key problem, and as we shall see, the Canadian Pacific solved this with a unit train service over the 700 miles from the mines to Vancouver, the nearest seaport. Having solved this difficulty for Kaiser, the C.P.R. decided to develop its own coal field. In 1968 Fording Coal signed a contract with Japanese interests calling for the delivery of 45 million tons of coking coal over a fifteen-year period. The first shipments were made in April 1972. Development had been costly; by the end of 1972 capital expenditure had been about $90 million.

With an eye to the future, the railway, jointly with Shell Canada, formed a subsidiary to investigate the feasibility of moving coal in slurry form by pipeline. In 1970 visiting officials of Japanese steel companies saw the first coke-oven test using reconstituted slurry coal. The possibilities offered by pipelines are intriguing, and research soon broadened to include the practicability of moving a variety of other commodities by that means.

Reference has been made to the investment portfolio of Canadian Pacific Investments. This quickly became substantial, with the major holdings consisting of the common shares of a few corporations. At the end of 1975, stock in only four companies accounted for $184.4 of the total of $202.7 million invested in common shares. Three of them—MacMillan Bloedel, Rio Algom Mines, and TransCanada Pipe Lines—represented the forest industries, mining, and gas and oil, in all of which Canadian Pacific itself is active; this was less true of the fourth, the Algoma Steel Corporation. A further investment of $80 million in stock purchases in 1974 gave C.P. Investments a majority interest in Algoma, the second-largest steel producer in Canada. It has followed Central-Del Rio Oil and Great Lakes Paper in assuming the status of a controlled company.

In its early days Canadian Pacific Investments was financed by the railway, which transferred assets in return for C.P.I. shares or made cash purchases of shares. In 1966 its investment totaled $310.8 million. By that time a subsidiary, Canadian Pacific Securities Limited, had been formed to raise capital from outside sources. In November 1967, a $100 million issue of Canadian Pacific Investments convertible preferred shares was offered to the public —at the time the largest single stock issue in Canada's financial history. Since then loans, notes, and debentures issued by C.P.I. and individual subsidiaries and controlled companies have raised additional capital as required.

The sale of the preferred shares, it may be noted, had a negligible effect upon Canadian Pacific's control of the company, which rests securely upon the possession of 50 million common shares.

Norris Crump was the initial force behind this huge expansion of Canadian Pacific's nontransportation activities; he was in effect the creator of what has frequently been referred to as "the new company." But diversification must have gone much further than he anticipated. Two examples will suffice. Equipment leasing has now become a common practice, and in 1971 the Canadian Pacific incorporated CanPac Leasing Limited to secure a share of the business. At first it dealt chiefly in transportation and telecommunications equipment, but a much wider range of activities was planned, and no doubt for this reason this subsidiary was sold to Canadian Pacific Investments in 1973. Recently a need for more efficient waste disposal has become apparent; C.P. Investments has responded by forming CanPac Waste Disposal Systems Limited, to "serve as contractors to municipalities and industry in the collection, transportation, disposal and recycling of waste material," and in addition to "act as a research and consulting body, developing various methods for the treatment and handling of waste."

By the end of 1970, the assets of Canadian Pacific Investments had passed the billion-dollar mark; by the close of 1975 they were over 3.5 billion. In the interval it had been decided that the name Canadian Pacific Railway Company no longer reflected adequately the parent corporation's new and complicated character. On July 3, 1971, a few months after its ninetieth birthday, to the regret of traditionalists, the old name gave way to Canadian Pacific Limited. "The new name," the company insisted, "retains all the rich background of history associated with 'Canadian Pacific' at the same time as it accommodates the fact that varied transportation and natural resource activities have been added to the Company's original railway operation."[9]

29

On the Sea and in the Air

Prompt adaptation to changed conditions is essential to survival in today's transportation world. In this respect the ups and downs of Canadian Pacific's shipping operations since the Second World War form an interesting case history.

The Atlantic fleet assembled in the first postwar years was intended to restore the cargo services and to some extent the passenger services that had been available in 1939. There were no innovations except in matters of detail. The new *Beaver*-type freighters were similar in size and type to the original *Beaver* quintet that had entered service in 1927–28. The three *Empresses* were prewar liners, all twenty years old by the time they had been reconditioned. The most interesting thing about the passenger ships was the high proportion of the accommodation assigned to first class—a policy that paid off handsomely while space on the Atlantic was in short supply and ships were crowded.

The Canadian Pacific was anxious to build new *Empresses*, but delayed placing orders because it considered that prices were unreasonably high. But shipbuilding costs did not decline as expected, and increased competition forced the C.P.R. to act. In 1952 the Home Lines placed a ship on the Canadian run that in many respects outshone the *Empresses*, and the Cunard Line ordered new 22,000-ton liners for its Montreal service. Nevertheless, it was April 1956 before the 25,500-ton *Empress of Britain*, third ship of the name, made her maiden voyage. A sister ship, the *Empress of England*, followed a year later. The Home Lines had placed emphasis on attractive and extensive tourist-class accommodation, judging rightly that demand in the Canadian trade would be chiefly for comfortable quarters at moderate prices. In their new liners, both Cunard and Canadian Pacific followed this lead; the *Empresses* carried 148 in first class and 896 in tourist.

Though possessed of many good qualities, the new liners soon began to present problems in operation. It quickly became evident that they had arrived very late in the day. When they were ordered, sea passages were still in great demand. By the time the *Empress of England* entered service, airplanes were carrying as many passengers across the Atlantic as ships, and thereafter the number that crossed by sea declined rapidly.

Winter sailings were particularly hard hit; all the Atlantic lines turned to cruising, which offered some prospect of profitable off-season employment for their passenger ships. The Canadian Pacific had resumed cruising in 1950, and the new *Empresses* were intended from the first to cruise in winter, but they had difficulty in making their way in what soon became a highly competitive trade. Luxurious vessels designed exclusively for the purpose began to appear, and they made it painfully evident that the *Empresses* were essentially tourist-class ships in which the special requirements of cruising had not received sufficient attention. Some of their deficiencies were made good in a third and somewhat larger new liner, the *Empress of Canada*, completed in 1961. An extra deck, more space, and many more cabins with private facilities made her a considerably more attractive cruise ship.

The three new *Empresses* maintained the traditional weekly service between Montreal and Liverpool during a seven-month summer season, but this was destined to last only three years. Jet aircraft that crossed the Atlantic in little more than six hours and substantial reductions in air fares had a devastating effect on sea travel. The Home Lines, which had planned to place a new 40,000-ton superliner on the Canadian run in 1965, instead abandoned the route entirely in 1963. By that time the Canadian Pacific was convinced that its own *Empress* service was doomed, but it was hopeful that it might survive for another ten years. To reduce costs, the *Empress of Britain* was chartered to other operators for year-round cruising; when the venture failed to come up to expectations, she was sold. In 1967 the Cunard Line ended its Canadian service, but the *Empress of Canada* and *Empress of England* carried on until the autumn of 1970, when the *England* was withdrawn and sold.

Although fewer than 24,000 passengers had traveled by sea between Canada and Britain in 1970, as compared with 98,000 in 1960, the Canadian Pacific still hoped it could muster sufficient traffic to justify keeping one ship on the run. Its *Empresses* had sailed the seas for eighty years, and it was

The *Empress of Sydney*, the Canadair Four aircraft that inaugurated CP Air's transpacific services in 1949 with a flight to Australia.

The *Empress of Asia*, one of the first jumbo jets acquired by CP Air. Marking the progression in the Canadian Pacific services from sea to air, her name commemorates the liner built for the transpacific run in 1913 and destroyed by Japanese bombers off Singapore in 1942.

reluctant to give up. But a determined sales effort failed to produce results, and mounting deficits forced the retirement of the *Empress of Canada* in November 1971. She and her sisters had been the victims of four circumstances: frequent work stoppages by seamen and dockers, which played havoc with sailing schedules; rapidly rising operating costs; air competition, which both reduced patronage and made it impossible to raise fares to meet rising costs; and the difficulty, already mentioned, of competing in off-season cruising with glamorous ships built especially for the cruise trade.

It had been an expensive as well as a disappointing experience. The *Empress of Canada* had cost $22.6 million; the three new liners together had represented an investment of well over $50 million. They were sold for a fraction of this sum.

Vicissitudes suffered by the freighter services were almost as trying, but fortunately their story has a happier ending.

Reacting to changing trading conditions, the company rebuilt the Atlantic freighter fleet completely twice in a dozen years. By 1960 the Canadian Pacific had decided that smaller ships, more flexible in service and more economical to operate, were preferable to the 10,000-ton *Beavers* acquired just after the war. Over a three-year period, all seven were sold and replaced by chartered ships and four new *Beavers* averaging no more than 4,000 tons. But results were less satisfactory than anticipated for it was becoming more and more difficult for the old style break-bulk cargo carrier to operate profitably. In particular, crew and cargo handling costs were soaring. To counter crew costs, automation made its appearance on shipboard; to reduce handling, cargo was packaged in standard containers that made it possible for a ship to load or unload in a fraction of the usual time.

In 1965 the C.P.R. took delivery of a fifth and somewhat larger new freighter, the *Beaveroak*, equipped to enable the company to gain some experience in handling container traffic. Like all shipping lines that entered the trade, the Canadian Pacific had its troubles; nothing was as simple as it seemed. But by 1968 the C.P.R. had decided upon the complete containerization of its Atlantic cargo operations and had placed a $20 million order for three twenty-knot ships, each capable of carrying 779 standard containers. Over a year they could transport substantially more cargo than the existing eleven-ship fleet, consisting of the five *Beavers* and six chartered vessels. Pending their completion, the *Beaveroak* and two chartered ships inaugurated a regular container-ship service in 1969. The first of the new trio, the *CP Voyageur*, was delivered late in 1970. Her two sisters followed in 1971. Their speed enabled them to give a weekly service connecting Rotterdam, London, Le Havre, and Quebec.

Several aspects of the Canadian Pacific's container operation are noteworthy. To begin with, the ships were strengthened for navigation in ice, and sailed to Quebec in winter as well as in summer; the St. Lawrence was no longer regarded as being closed to shipping from late November until April. The C.P.R. had experimented with winter sailings as early as 1962 and found them to be practicable for suitably designed ships. This made it possible to handle container traffic through a single terminus—a marked economy, for the installations required in addition to the ships were costly. Millions were spent building the container terminal at Wolfe's Cove in Quebec, and within a few years millions more were spent enlarging it. An inland container terminal was developed at Lachine, and others have since become necessary across the country.

The Canadian Pacific reduced costs further by concentrating on a single service linking Rotterdam, London, Le Havre, and Quebec. For a time two reconstructed *Beavers* provided a second container service connecting Liverpool, the Clyde, and Quebec, but by agreement with Manchester Liners, the chief competitor in the Canadian trade, this was discontinued at the end of 1973. In return, Manchester Liners withdrew their service to Canada from Rotterdam and Felixstowe. In Britain, Canadian Pacific could thus concentrate on business from southern England, which it sought to attract to its ships at Tilbury, while Manchester Liners centered their efforts in the North. The agreement had one regrettable result, the closing of the Canadian Pacific offices in Liverpool, from which its ships had sailed since 1903, and in Glasgow, where the connection through the old Allan Line extended back a century and a half.

Even when the three new container ships were on the run, all was not smooth sailing. Strikes in both Canada and the United Kingdom disrupted schedules, as they had those of the *Empresses* before them. Moreover, because many shipowners had rushed into the container trade, the Atlantic suffered from overcapacity that kept rates at unremunerative levels. It was not until 1974 that the service turned the corner and became a profitable operation.

The fast new ships reduced the time that goods were in transit between Europe and points in eastern Canada from as much as seven weeks to as little as ten days. But most important, the company saw in the movement of containers an opportunity to develop a far-reaching intermodal transportation system. Ships, the railway, and highway transport could all become part of an integrated service.[1] By 1972 the railway had acquired 900 special "railtainer" flatcars to move containers from the Quebec terminal to distant points, and the C.P.R.'s trucking services had special trailers upon which to deliver them to nearer destinations. Canadian Pacific Steamships had con-

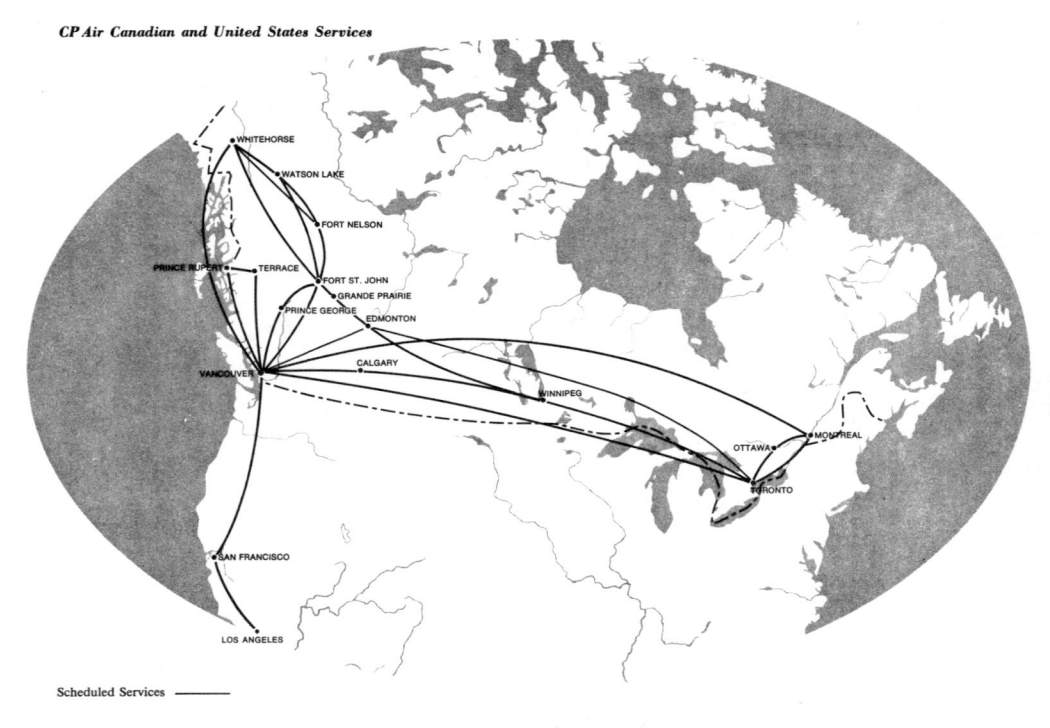

CP Air Canadian and United States services.

tainer trucking services on both sides of the Atlantic, based on Wolfe's Cove at Quebec and the Tilbury docks on the Thames. Containers could thus be picked up and delivered over a wide area in Britain, as well as at almost any point on Canadian Pacific's far-flung system in Canada.

The company did not entirely desert its old winter port of Saint John, New Brunswick. The railway serves the container terminal that has been established there by the National Harbours Board. Ships come to it from many parts of the world, including Australia, the Caribbean, and Europe, and C.P.R. "railtainer" cars carry their containers to inland destinations.

The decline in the C.P.R.'s traditional shipping services, already evident by 1963, prompted it to venture into a field that was completely new to it—the bulk carrier trade. This was undertaken by a wholly owned subsidiary, Canadian Pacific (Bermuda) Limited, incorporated in 1964. It marked the C.P.R.'s return to the Pacific, for it was the possibility of carrying lead concentrates, lumber, newsprint, and coal from British Columbia ports that first attracted its attention. It was also mindful of the high rates prevailing in the tanker charter market.

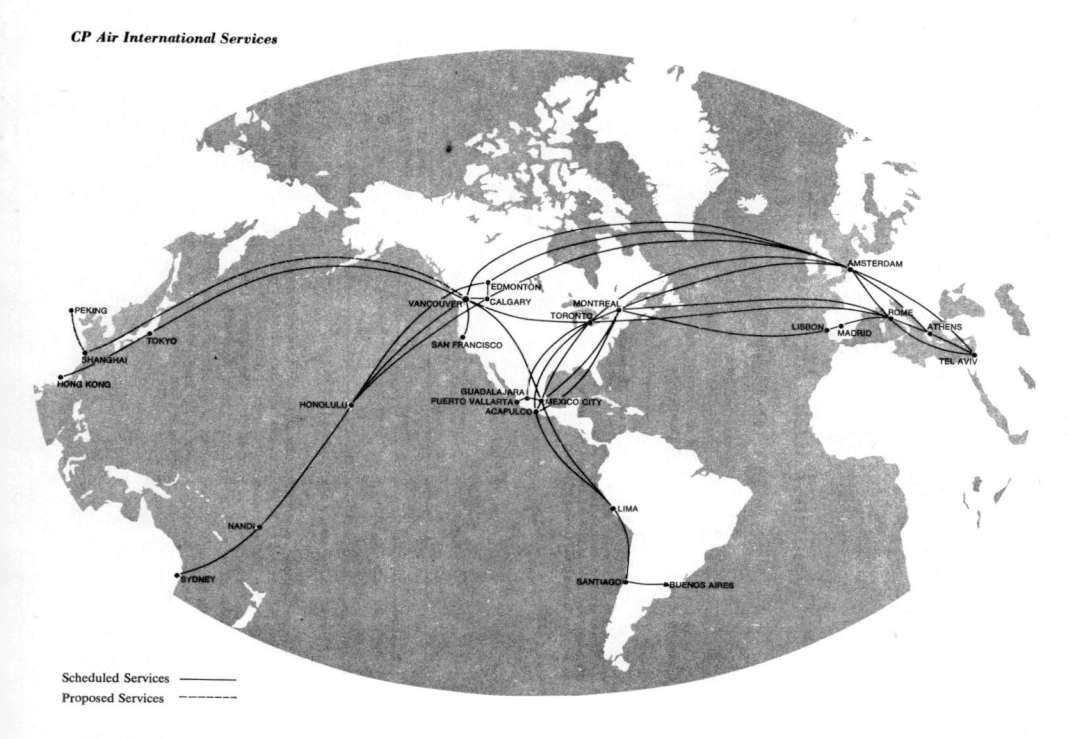

CP Air International services.

The new company began operations in 1965, when it purchased a 13,000-ton dry cargo vessel and placed her in service between British Columbia and Tokyo. The same year it ordered its first new ships—two 71,500-ton oil tankers. Both had been taken up on long-term charters before construction began, and this prudent policy of ordering a ship to fulfil a charter agreement was followed by the company in succeeding years.

It is doubtful if anyone concerned foresaw the scale upon which the CP (Bermuda) fleet would expand. The new tankers were followed by three 29,000-ton vessels specially designed to carry forest products; these were chartered by the shipping subsidiary of MacMillan Bloedel, in which the Canadian Pacific has a substantial interest. Two 58,000-ton bulk carriers suitable for cargoes of ore, grain, or coal were delivered next. Then came the largest ships in the fleet, two 253,000-ton crude oil tankers. These two ships alone represented an investment of $33 million. A third tanker of the same type has since been built. Other types in the fleet include 30,000-ton clean products tankers and two 122,000-ton bulk carriers. By the autumn of 1976, CP (Bermuda) will have twenty-five ships in service with a deadweight carrying capacity of over 1.8 million tons. All these ships have been built in Japan,

The Canadian Pacific's container dock at Wolfe's Cove, Quebec, with the container ship *CP Voyageur* alongside. The photograph illustrates the revolution that has taken place in transatlantic services, for the dock at this point was built originally in 1931 as the passenger terminal for the superliner *Empress of Britain*.

with the exception of the eight clean products tankers, which were built in the Netherlands. The latest, two-ship contract was placed in Denmark.

Financial returns have been substantial. In 1971 nonrecurring earnings from spot charters pushed net revenue to $11.1 million; the net return was $8.5 million in 1972. It declined to $6.6 million in 1973, due to "start-up" expenses in connection with new ships that were in service only part of the year, but increased again to $11.9 million in 1974, and to $13.2 million in 1975.

In the course of its ninety years of shipowning, the Canadian Pacific has followed many and varied schemes of nomenclature. *Empresses*, *Duchesses*, *Beavers*, and the *M* class liners are all a thing of the past, but *Princesses* still sail in the coastal services. The new Atlantic container ships, as the reference to the *CP Voyageur* has indicated, carry the *CP* prefix. The Bermuda fleet follows a more varied plan. Its first purchase (lost at sea in 1967, happily without loss of life) was named *R. B. Angus* in honor of the member of the original syndicate formed in 1880. The next two ships acquired were christened *Lord Mount Stephen* and *Lord Strathcona*. Later vessels have commemorated other notable figures, including all the presidents and chairmen of the Canadian Pacific. Marking still another departure, two of the ships delivered in 1974 were named *Fort Macleod* and *Fort Steele*, after two of the early posts of the Royal Canadian Mounted Police, who celebrated their centenary in 1973. Six more *Forts* were under construction.

The third *Empress of Canada*, last of the *Empress* liners. Retired when only ten years old, she made her final voyage for the Canadian Pacific in November 1971.

The *T. G. Shaughnessy*, one of the two largest units of the Canadian Pacific (Bermuda) fleet. Her carrying capacity is 253,000 tons.

Financially, the Canadian Pacific's stake in shipping is now greater than it has ever been. According to the consolidated balance sheet dated December 31, 1975, the cost of the existing fleet was $380.6 million. Having rebuilt its ocean fleet completely to meet radically altered conditions, Canadian Pacific ranks once again as one of the world's major shipowners.

The company's investment in its airline—$409.4 million—is now greater than its commitment to the sea. It has increased eightfold in only a dozen years.

In the 1950s Canadian Pacific Air Lines benefited substantially from the airlift to Tokyo occasioned by the struggle in Korea, from heavy immigrant traffic from Hong Kong, and from charter flights to the Canadian North, where chains of radar installations were under construction. In the same years, the company was concentrating its domestic services within British Columbia, Alberta, and the Yukon, an area conveniently near its maintenance base in Vancouver. The routes served in Quebec were turned over to Trans-Canada Airlines in 1955, in return for the right to fly from Toronto to Mexico, and two years later C.P.A. withdrew from Manitoba and Saskatchewan.

The long struggle to secure permission to fly Canadian Pacific planes across the continent, hitherto the exclusive preserve of Trans-Canada, met with some success in 1958. The concession was limited to one flight a day in each direction between Vancouver, Winnipeg, Toronto, and Montreal, but it was at least a beginning. The first transcontinental flights were made on May 4, 1959.

By that time the acquisition of Bristol Britannia turboprop aircraft had made considerably faster schedules possible on the international routes. They were poor substitutes for the much faster Comet pure jets that Grant McConachie had hoped to secure, but on the long overseas flights even a moderate increase in speed reduced flying time materially.

The years from 1958 to 1962 were a period of deficits for C.P.A.; it lost nearly $20 million in the five-year period. In the earlier years, it suffered from the competition of rival lines that were flying new jet aircraft half as fast again as its Britannias; when it secured jets of its own, it was faced at first with the problem of overcapacity. Canadian Pacific was still a relatively small airline: it carried only 381,000 passengers in 1961, the year it took delivery of its first DC-8 planes. But patronage increased steadily, and the nature of most of its services offered some compensations. The exceptionally long international flights over the Pacific helped to keep utilization of aircraft high; in 1966 it would average as much as 14.2 hours per day. And aircraft could be switched about to meet peak seasonal demands on different routes. Planes that flew extra flights on the North Atlantic from April to October could fly to Hawaii from December to March.

In June 1965 Grant McConachie, whose drive, enthusiasm, and salesmanship had virtually created the airline, died at the age of fifty-six, after a series of heart attacks. He had championed C.P.A. through many crises, not the least being a memorable occasion when its 1961 net loss of $7.6 million caused the Canadian Pacific directors to question the wisdom of carrying on. McConachie pointed out that the switch to jet aircraft had put airlines all over the world into the red, and contended that once the transition was accomplished all would be well. It was Crump's solid support at this critical time that carried the day, and events soon showed that McConachie's optimism was justified. The airline made a small profit in 1963, and in the five succeeding years net income totaled almost $25 million. Revenue passenger miles passed the billion mark in 1965, more than a million passengers were carried in 1968, and passenger revenue exceeded $100 million in 1969.

When McConachie died, his planes were spanning Canada and flying to five continents. Except for the domestic routes in British Columbia and Alberta, all services were being maintained by pure-jet aircraft. Just four weeks before McConachie's death, J. W. Pickersgill, the minister of transport, made a statement in Parliament on civil aviation policy that must have reminded McConachie of how far his airline had come since the anxious days just after the war. "It has now been decided," the minister said, "that Canadian Pacific Airlines will serve the whole Pacific area, the whole continent of Asia, Australia and New Zealand, southern and southeastern Europe and Latin America. Air Canada [as Trans-Canada Airlines had been renamed in 1964] will serve the United Kingdom, western, northern and eastern Europe, and the Caribbean. The only exception to the clearcut division is that Canadian Pacific Airlines will continue to serve the Netherlands." And a moment later he added: "The Government has undertaken to regard Air Canada and Canadian Pacific Airlines as its chosen instruments in the areas of the international operations allocated to each."[2]

The matter of increasing the frequency of transcontinental flights was left in abeyance, but an aviation consultant was to investigate and report. Here the essential thing was "that there must not be the kind of competition which would put Air Canada into the red,"[3] and the influence of the government's airline was sufficient to delay a concession for another three years. Air Canada was monopoly-minded and would have liked to absorb C.P.A., but when Crump was reasonably certain that the airline had a viable future, he was adamantly opposed to this. Once, when approached on the subject, he is reported to have replied: "How much do they want for TCA?"[4]

McConachie's mantle fell on John C. Gilmer, C.P.A.'s executive vice-president, who, owing to McConachie's illness, had for some time been carrying the chief burden of administration. Under his guidance the airline embarked upon a major expansion program in 1966 that included the purchase of "stretched" DC-8 and Boeing 737 aircraft and the construction of a large new overhaul and maintenance base in Vancouver. But overexpansion was avoided and the airline came through 1969 and 1970, a difficult time for the air industry, much more comfortably than most; too many aircraft, including the new wide-bodied jumbo jets, were chasing too few passengers.

Canadian Pacific's approach to the jumbos was more cautious than it might perhaps have been if McConachie had lived. Studies were made, but these always came up against the hard fact that the industry was suffering painfully from overcapacity. In theory, unit costs per seat decreased in the larger planes, but this was of significance only if the seats were occupied.

Air Canada acquired Boeing 747 jumbo jets in 1971, but the Canadian Pacific held off until 1973. By that time they had become essential if the company was to maintain its competitive position. This applied particularly to the service to the Orient and to the transcontinental route, for which some concessions had at last been forthcoming. A second daily flight was added in 1968, and the number increased gradually to seven. Canadian Pacific was authorized to offer 25 percent of total passenger capacity available between Vancouver and Montreal, which in effect meant one third of that being offered by Air Canada, the only other carrier. Even so the concession was still subject to conditions that complicated scheduling. In particular, all flights were required to terminate in Montreal or Vancouver, a stipulation that made it difficult, if not impossible, for an aircraft that made intermediate stops in Ottawa, Winnipeg, Edmonton, or Calgary to complete a round trip in twenty-four hours. This particular restriction was lifted for the benefit of the Boeing jumbo jets, which were permitted to operate between Vancouver and Toronto; but the shadow of conditions imposed for the benefit of Air Canada still hovered over Canadian Pacific's airline.

In 1973 CP Air, as Canadian Pacific Air Lines have been renamed for publicity purposes, were flying over unduplicated routes totaling 51,962 miles. As the map shows, the international routes formed a gigantic X centered on Vancouver. One arm reached Japan and China; a second extended to Hawaii and Australia; a third ran far southward to Mexico, Peru, Chili, and the Argentine; the fourth included polar and transcontinental routes leading to Amsterdam and to Portugal, Spain, Italy, Greece, and Israel.

Employees numbered 6,439. The number of passengers carried was 1,755,749, but because a high proportion of them were carried long distances, revenue passenger miles on scheduled flights totaled 2,890 million. Charter flights pushed the total beyond 3 billion miles. Gross operating revenues were $185.9 million, but mounting costs, particularly soaring fuel prices, limited net income to $4.2 million. By 1975, revenues had risen to $332.1 million, but a 22-percent increase in expenses resulted in a loss on the year's operations of $6.4 million—the first suffered in thirteen years.

At one time Grant McConachie hoped to head an airline that circled the globe, but this ambition no longer has a place in Canadian Pacific's plans. It would like to reach additional countries in South America and would be happy to see the service to the Orient extended from Hong Kong to Singapore. But the skies between Singapore and Tel Aviv are too crowded to make the prospect of competing there an inviting one. Even without this link, its network is so extensive that it recalls Canadian Pacific's old slogan "Spans the world."

30

The Sixties and Seventies

The Canadian Pacific has been accused at times of having lost interest in its railway. As recently as the 1974 annual meeting, Ian D. Sinclair, who succeeded Norris Crump as chairman, felt it necessary to make an explicit statement on the point: "Let me say here and now that it has never been our intention—and it is not our intention now—that we should cease to participate in the railway business or, for that matter, in any other branch of transportation in which we are currently engaged."

If the Canadian Pacific were becoming disenchanted with rails, its attitude would be understandable. The financial prospects of its nontransportation activities are much more exciting, and railway profits have represented a very low return on the vast sum invested. Net earnings in the 1960s were lower than they had been in the 1920s, though gross revenues had tripled by 1969. But the amount of money and effort that has been devoted to the modernization of the rail system in the last twenty years surely belies any lack of interest in its welfare by management.

Soon after Crump became president, steps were taken, in the interests of economy and efficiency, to simplify somewhat the company's complicated corporate structure and organization. As a first step, thirty-eight wholly owned, leased lines were absorbed. Next came a revision of the railway's territorial administration. Districts were abolished and four regions (Atlantic, Eastern, Prairie, and Pacific) were given direct control of the thirty-one operating divisions. At the beginning of 1961, the three subsidiaries in the United States—the St. Paul, Minneapolis and Sault Ste. Marie, the Duluth, South Shore and Atlantic, and the Wisconsin Central—were merged into a new Soo Line Railroad Company. All three had been victims of the Depression, and the last of the subsequent reorganizations had not been completed until 1954. Now they were being brought together and would form a substantial and profitable system totaling 4,716 miles.

Like Canadian Pacific Investments, the parent railway acquired and spawned subsidiaries. In 1958 it bought Smith Transport Limited, the largest trucking concern in Canada. Hitherto the emphasis of C.P.R. road services had been in the West; the Smith purchase gave the railway a solid position as a highway carrier in central Canada. In 1959 Canadian Pacific was operating 3,860 tractors, trailers, and other vehicles, and in a dozen years their number would virtually double. The important new shipping subsidiary, Canadian Pacific (Bermuda) Limited, was formed in 1964. In the past, C.P.R. ships had been confined to scheduled services on the Atlantic, on the Pacific, and in coastal waters; now its tankers and freighters would sail wherever business beckoned.

These additions reflected Crump's ambition to develop a system that would offer what came to be termed total transportation—services by rail, highway, sea, and air, fully integrated and tailored where necessary to fit the needs of individual industries. Trucks and trailers offered great flexibility of movement, since the latter could shift from road to piggyback rail; later, containers could move by road, rail, and sea. The cheap, all-purpose boxcars and flatcars, which for generations had been the mainstay of freight train consists, gave way to a great array of specialized and expensive rolling stock designed to meet specific transportation requirements.

Relatively early, the C.P.R. recognized the arrival of the computer age. An integrated data-processing program was started in 1955 and expanded steadily as successive computers gave place to more capable and sophisticated models. In addition to marshaling and analyzing a great mass of management information and operational data, the installation, one of the largest in Canada, was an invaluable aid to research. It could speed such investigations as an inquiry into train performance or the economic life of rolling stock. To the layman, perhaps its most comprehensible activity was keeping track of the precise whereabouts of Canadian Pacific's tens of thousands of freight cars, a task simplified by the railway's participation in the continentwide plan to label cars for automatic identification by trackside scanners.

In the midst of these changes and in spite of them, the C.P.R. became worried about its public image. It feared that to many it appeared "stodgy and tradition-encrusted."[1] In part this was doubtless a reaction to a comprehensive overhaul of outward appearance that had been undertaken by the Canadian National. The letters *CN* had been developed into a simple but striking trademark that soon became an identification on all the company's properties and equipment.

The Canadian Pacific's program was more elaborate. Its purpose, in the words of the official announcement, was "to match a new look with the Company's new performance and widened horizons." In addition to the neatly stylized initials *CP*, it included a symbol combining "a triangle, suggesting motion or direction, a segment of a circle suggesting global activities and a portion of a square suggesting stability."[2] All units of the transportation complex used the symbol, but each was distinguished by a shortened name and by a distinctive color—CP Rail by red, CP Air by orange, CP Ships by green, and CP Transport by blue. CP Rail carried the scheme a step farther by adopting a color code for different types of rolling stock. Red was chosen for the standard boxcar, but it was a brick red, not the familiar Tuscan red that had been used for many years.

The shortened names were highly effective and passed quickly into current use. The somewhat puzzling symbol made its way more slowly. No doubt for many it now identifies Canadian Pacific's services and properties, which is its prime purpose; but the pseudoheraldic significance of its design must be lost upon all but a handful of the millions who see it on all the company's possessions, from letterheads to locomotives.

In 1969, after the introduction of the new nomenclature and symbols, Crump applied the profit center concept to Canadian Pacific Limited. CP Rail—by far the largest of the centers—and CP Telecommunications operated as departments of CP Limited; CP Air, CP Ships, and CP Trucks (formerly CP Transport) were wholly owned subsidiary companies. Income was thus reported by function, and profits and losses showed up sharply in the accounts.

Throughout his seventeen years as president and chairman, Crump was seldom free from anxiety regarding the twin problems of wages and freight rates. Regularly every second year, when the agreements with the major unions were expiring, the long process of collective bargaining would begin. The initial positions of the two parties were almost always the same: the railway pleaded inability to pay unless it was assured of additional income that would meet the cost of wage increases, while the unions contended that wages at an appropriate level should be a first charge on railway revenues. As the years passed, each side had a further consideration to bear in mind. In theory, higher freight rates would pay for higher wages, but the railway knew that they would also divert traffic to rival carriers, unless by good fortune they, too, were faced with comparable rising costs. The new concern of the unions was with job security. In an effort to keep operating expenses as low as possible, the Canadian Pacific made a determined effort to reduce the number of its employees. By 1965 the hourly wage of the average railwayman was about the same as the daily rate in prewar days—an increase so great that labor-saving devices paid their way handsomely, even if the initial capital expenditure involved was substantial.

	NUMBER OF EMPLOYEES	PAYROLL IN MILLIONS	APPROXIMATE AVERAGE WAGE
1952	83,848	$ 269.3	$ 3,200
1957	77,142	285.7	3,700
1962	57,778	266.5	4,600
1967	51,956	317.4	6,100
1972	41,189	374.5	9,100

The table tells the story. The railway's work force reached its peak in 1952, when employees numbered nearly 84,000. Twenty years later the total had been reduced by more than 50 percent, to fewer than 42,000. True, the total payroll had risen by over $100 million in the last ten years and the average wage had nearly doubled; but so drastic a cut in the numbers employed raised problems and anxieties relating to tenure, terms of severance, and pensions that were of great moment to the unions. In recent years, intensified inflation has added to the worries of both the railway and its employees and has been a further counter in the bargaining process.

Each round of wage negotiations has had its own distinctive features. Those of 1958 were notable on two counts. Late in the year, faced with the prospect of a rail tie-up, the Board of Transport Commissioners in effect accepted the Canadian Pacific's plea of inability to pay and granted an interim increase in rates before a wage agreement had been reached with the unions. To this the government at once objected, and directed that it should not occur again. It went so far as to roll back the increased freight rates, but undertook to compensate the railways for the cutbacks. More important, it announced that a study would be made at once of "inequalities in the freight rate structure" and of measures to relieve them. This inquiry took the familiar form of a Royal Commission on Transportation, appointed in May 1959 and known as the MacPherson Commission, after its chairman, M. A. MacPherson, a Regina lawyer. Its findings were to be a landmark in Canadian transportation policy.

The Canadian Pacific soon let it be known that in its view the "only serious inequity" was that "arising from fixed statutory rates on grain and

Part of the huge Alyth freight classification yard at Calgary, showing the forty-eight classification tracks. When completed in 1971, it was the most fully automated operation of the kind on the continent.

grain products," the sixty-year-old legacy of the Crow's Nest Pass Agreement. These, the railway contended, fell "far short of just and reasonable remuneration for the handling of this traffic." It proposed that the rates should remain in effect, if this were deemed essential, but that they should be supplemented by a subsidy "to be assumed by the Government of Canada as necessary assistance from the people of Canada to Western grain growers."[3]

Within limits, this fell in with the thinking of the commission. The statutory grain rates were one of a number of "obsolete historical obligations" of which it felt the railways should be relieved. Railways and freight rates had been used as instruments of national policy on many occasions, and there was no objection to this so long as the railways were not required to foot the bill. If the government obliged them to provide services that were not remunerative, compensation should be forthcoming from the national treasury.

This point came to the fore at the end of 1960, when wage negotiations again reached an impasse. The government urged the railways to grant wage increases without a guarantee of reimbursement, but the railways refused. Moreover (doubtless with some foreknowledge of the attitude of the Royal Commission), they made it clear that they would make no wage concessions until there was a change in the government's policy regarding payment for services rendered in the national interest.

The result was a strike call for December 3 and the hurried passage of the Railway Operations Continuation Act on December 2, which outlawed strike action for six months. In this interval the first volume of the report of the MacPherson Commission set forth the thinking of the members on the point at issue and recommended a substantial interim payment to the railways. When it became clear that the latter would hold to their position and that the unions would take strike action, the government yielded and a $50 million interim payment was forthcoming.

The wage agreement of 1962 was hailed as "history making," because for the first time the report of a board of conciliation was unanimous and accepted by both parties. The railways may well have been influenced by the second volume of the Royal Commission's report, which held out the prospect of much greater freedom than they had enjoyed hitherto. It elaborated an opinion expressed in the earlier volume, that the regulation of transportation "should be minimized as much as possible . . . and such regulation as is retained should bear in a reasonably equitable fashion on all carriers."[4] At long last the railways were to be as free as their competitors. The chief limitations were to be a requirement that all rates should be compensatory, to prevent unfair competition, and provision of an adequate appeal procedure in areas where the railways still enjoyed a monopoly of transportation.

By 1964 the railways had become uneasy; the interim payments that had begun in 1960 had ceased, and no steps had been taken to introduce legislation that would implement the Royal Commission's recommendations. They stated their case to the prime minister, who replied that it was the government's "firm intention" to proceed with new railway legislation. As some delay was likely, the position of the railways would be reviewed in six months in order to see what temporary financial help should be given until the new law came into force.[5] With this assurance, the railways came to a settlement with the unions; but the National Transportation Act was not passed for nearly three years, and in 1966 Canada experienced its second nationwide railroad strike. As in 1950, Parliament promptly passed back-to-work legislation, and the wage dispute was settled finally by mediation and arbitration.

Job security was much to the fore in this series of settlements. In 1962 the Canadian Pacific recognized in principle that the employer had some responsibility to ensure employment for his workers. A job security fund was set up to assist with severance pay, retraining, and like measures. In 1965 the unions went so far as to demand a work stabilization agreement that would freeze the work force and require union agreement for any reduction. This was not granted, but the railways agreed to negotiate with the unions measures to minimize the effect of technological, operational, and organizational

The Diesel Movement Control Center in Windsor Station, Montreal. The location of every locomotive in the system is shown on the board.

An empty 88-car unit coal train rumbling along the shore of Columbia Lake on its way back from the Coast to the mines in East Kootenay.

changes that would have an adverse effect on employees. Eight years later, in 1973, when a third nationwide tie-up occurred, job security proved to be the most stubborn problem faced by the arbitrator appointed after the strike had been ended by legislation.

The issue was perhaps pointed up most sharply in a dispute with the firemen's union that arose about a year after Crump became president. The Canadian Pacific contended that firemen were unnecessary on diesel yard engines and opened negotiations to secure an agreement to that effect. But the firemen would have none of it and precipitated a strike that tied up train service for ten days in January 1957. The issue was then referred to a Royal Commissioner, who agreed with the railway that firemen were not needed on yarding locomotives. But in May 1958, when the C.P.R. gave notice that it would implement his findings, the firemen struck a second time. The compromise ultimately arrived at gave job security to any fireman with seniority prior to April 1, 1956; he would continue to fill his unnecessary job but would not be replaced when, for whatever reason, it became vacant. Even with this severe restriction, the saving brought about by the change soon became substantial; by 1963 it was already $900,000 a year.[6]

The Canadian Pacific's pension plan dates back to 1902, when Shaughnessy set aside the sum of $250,000 to form the nucleus of a pension fund. It was added to annually thereafter, and for thirty-five years was maintained entirely at the expense of the company. This original scheme was supplemented and replaced in 1937 by a contributory plan, to which all new employees were required to belong. Its terms were modified and the benefits increased many times thereafter. As from July 1, 1971, in accordance with new legislation, all pensions must now be paid from a single fund, including those formerly paid directly by the railway. In the last year under the older plan, there were 21,505 pensioners and the cost of pensions to the company was $36.6 million.

One of the provisions of the National Transportation Act of 1967 that was of special interest to the Canadian Pacific was the authority given to the Canadian Transport Commission to permit the discontinuance of unremunerative passenger services, or to subsidize them if they were deemed necessary in the public interest.

Like all major railways, the C.P.R. had suffered a rapid decline in the patronage of its passenger trains. In the hope and belief that first-class equipment would attract travelers, Crump had spent about $60 million on the finest stainless steel equipment for two of the transcontinental trains and some fifty diesel dayliners for secondary services. At first, revenues rose by about 7 percent, but thereafter they declined by 35 percent in only six years. Two of several reasons for this were clear: during the same period governments at all levels had spent $7 billion on roads (including $650 million for the Trans-Canada Highway, which paralleled the C.P.R. main line for most of its route) and the Department of Transport had expended about $900 million on air services, airports, and other air facilities. The railway stated the conclusion it had reached in its 1964 annual report to shareholders: "In view of the increased use of the private automobile over improved highways in short distance travel and the inherent advantages of the jet airliner over long distances, no prospect is envisaged by your Company of attracting rail passengers in sufficient numbers, on many segments of our lines, at prices they are willing to pay, to offset the expenses of providing this service."

In the eight-year period 1958–65, the C.P.R. estimated that its annual loss on passenger, mail, and express services averaged $25 million. It had reduced the number of transcontinental trains from three to two, and in 1965 it applied to the transport commissioners for permission to discontinue its second-line train, the *Dominion*. A considerable outcry followed, but the commissioners granted the request in 1966, on condition that the train would in effect be reinstated in the summer season of 1967 as the *Expo Limited*, to accommodate the crowds that would be flocking to the world's fair in Montreal.

In 1966 the Canadian National asked the Canadian Pacific to terminate the pooling arrangement, dating back to the Depression, under which the two railways jointly maintained services linking Toronto, Ottawa, and Montreal. The C.P.R. agreed, and for a short time operated trains of its own; but results were unpromising, and they were soon withdrawn. The Canadian Pacific's line from Montreal to Toronto is longer and slower than that of the C.N.R., and it was competing at a marked disadvantage. Nevertheless, the disappearance of a C.P.R. service between Canada's two largest cities came as a distinct shock.

Even more of a shock was the Canadian Pacific's application, submitted in 1970, for authority to discontinue the *Canadian* and thus end its transcontinental passenger service. It is doubtful if the railway actually wished or expected to receive the permission it requested.[7] What it was really seeking was the subsidy that would be forthcoming if the transport commissioners ruled (as they were virtually certain to do) that the train must be continued in the public interest. The application for cancellation was in fact the only way in which the railway could apply for the subsidy.

A considerable hue and cry and a series of hearings followed. A good deal of evidence was given to indicate that the train still met a definite trans-

Unloading continuous welded rail—a relatively recent development in Canada. The standard length of the sections is 1,440 feet, or more than a quarter of a mile.

The Canadian Pacific's road terminal at Lachine, a few miles up the St. Lawrence from Montreal.

portation need. Some contended that the obligation placed upon the company in its original charter to "forever efficiently maintain, work and run the Canadian Pacific Railway" clearly included the passenger service, regardless of changed times and circumstances. The railway claimed that the loss on the *Canadian* in 1968 had been $19.5 million; the commission's Railway Committee trimmed the estimate to $15.2 million, but it remained a very substantial sum. Moreover, the Canadian National Railways, after a vigorous and gallant attempt to build up passenger traffic, had also applied for permission to discontinue its *Super Continental*, which the committee found had incurred a deficit of $14 million. If continued, the trains would be entitled to a subsidy of up to 80 percent of these losses, and the bill facing the taxpayer would therefore be approximately $24 million a year. Incidentally, the accounts revealed that the main area of loss in operation had been the sleeping and dining car services, which add so much to the comfort and attractiveness of the trains. These had run up a deficit of $9.5 million on the *Canadian* and $10 million on the *Super Continental*.

The Transportation Commission took the unusual step of outlining its decisions and conclusions in advertisements in the press and of asking for suggestions from the public as to how some of the problems involved might be solved. It stated that it had "already made a firm decision that transcontinental passenger train service will be continued" and that it was "investigating various methods of integrating the services of the two transcontinental trains into a single, rationalized system." It was convinced that this could "reduce the heavy losses while maintaining a level of service that will meet the public need."

Both the *Canadian* and the *Super Continental* were to run as usual, pending the working out of the proposed integrated service. The advertisements appeared in April 1971, and the commission was hopeful that some scheme would be ready for implementation fairly soon. But the problem proved to be more complicated than expected; more than five years later no decision had been made. Only one point seemed reasonably certain: a joint service would have to use Canadian Pacific's Windsor Station in Montreal, since the dome cars in the *Canadian*, which presumably would be included in the train's consist, were too high to enter the Canadian National's Central Station.

Meanwhile the *Canadian* ran all summer long, with every berth and seat booked. Though service was simplified in some details, its standards were well maintained and the Canadian Pacific spent $900,000 reconditioning its equipment. During the summer months passengers had to reserve space months ahead or depend on last-minute cancellations. In the tourist season it was high costs, not lack of patronage, that presented the problem. Clearly, the train's future will depend upon the transport commission's concept of "public need."

All but two of the few passenger runs still operated by CP Rail have been reduced to coach services. Sleeping and dining cars are available only on the *Canadian* and on the overnight train between Montreal and Saint John. The half-dozen other services, the most important of which are between Montreal and Quebec and between Calgary and Edmonton, are all maintained by diesel rail cars, and the railway would like to get rid of most of them.

The future may be brighter than the immediate past suggests. The chairman of the Transport Commission's Railway Committee remarked recently that "there is now a realization that the steel wheel rolling on a steel rail represents a highly efficient way of moving people at a time when energy costs have risen and are certain to rise further."[8] Patronage on the Canadian National's services through the heavily populated corridor between Montreal and Windsor has increased. Both CP Rail and the C.N.R. (which already has advanced turbo-trains in service) have been looking at the latest experimental high-speed trains. Intercity train travel seems headed for a revival, but under whose auspices remains to be seen. Some version of the Amtrak scheme to operate all passenger services has been suggested for Canada.

Under the National Transportation Act, unremunerative branch lines as well as passenger services can be subsidized if the transport commission considers that they must remain open in the public interest. This is almost entirely a prairie problem, related to the marketing of grain. Trucks have siphoned off the miscellaneous traffic from most of the short branches built half a century and more ago to bring rails within teaming distance of the wheat farms, but many of the country elevators scattered along them still function. Traffic is scanty and seasonal, sometimes amounting to no more than half a dozen trains a year; but service must continue until alternative shipping arrangements for grain are available. These will likely be keyed to large gathering elevators along main lines and major branches, to which trucks will bring the grain. Meanwhile the old method is both very inefficient from the point of view of the railway and costly to the taxpayer. In 1972 CP Rail received $19.4 million in subsidies to maintain unremunerative branch lines totaling 4,438 miles—more than a quarter of the entire Canadian Pacific system.

Though highly important to the railways, grain traffic is a sore point with them. The National Transportation Act failed to deal with the "only serious inequity" about which the C.P.R. had made representations to the MacPherson Commission—the fixed statutory rates on grain and grain products that date back to the Crow's Nest Pass Agreement of 1897. After seventy-nine years, a rate of fourteen cents per 100 pounds between Winnipeg and Thunder Bay is still the basic yardstick by which rates on grain are determined.

The contrast between rates in Canada and the United States is startling. The distance from Winnipeg to Lake Superior is 420 miles; the rate, as just stated, is fourteen cents per hundredweight. South of the border the Canadian Pacific's own subsidiary, the Soo Line, is paid 61.5 cents to carry 100 pounds of grain the same distance, between Pleasant Lake, North Dakota, and Duluth. To quote a western example: CP Rail moves grain from Pincher Creek, Alberta, to Vancouver, 748 miles, for 22 cents per 100 pounds; the Burlington Northern receives 77 cents for carrying a comparable shipment 743 miles from Shelby, Montana, to Seattle.

At Canadian rates, revenue from grain shipments is half a cent per ton-mile. There have been endless discussions as to whether this covers the railways' expenses, let alone returning them a profit. The companies told the MacPherson Commission that they estimated the combined Canadian Pacific–Canadian National deficit on grain traffic to have been $70 million in 1958. Railroad expenses—constant and variable—are so complicated that the commission concluded, after much study, that it was impossible to segregate the actual cost of moving grain "within reasonable bounds of time and expense," but it was satisfied nevertheless that the loss had been greatly exaggerated. It hazarded the opinion that the shortfall of the Canadian Pacific was perhaps $2 million and that of the Canadian National $4 million.[9] Grain rates had to be such that the farmers could bear them, good years and bad; this was the reason Parliament kept control of them. Grain marketing was also of first importance to the railway, for it gave the West the purchasing power that resulted in much of their westbound traffic from central Canada. The commission added that Parliamentary control did not mean that there could never be an adjustment of rates; but the government was deaf to this suggestion.

Certainly the rate of return on grain traffic was not such as to encourage the railways to make large capital expenditures especially for its benefit. Grain was carried mostly in older boxcars that had been retired from first-line service, and with the advent of a wide variety of specialized rolling stock their numbers dwindled steadily. In 1963 the two national rail systems had 88,000 boxcars capable of carrying grain; ten years later they had only 48,000.

The pinch came in the late 1960s and succeeding years, when the world demand for wheat suddenly increased dramatically. Government officials who had been urging farmers to reduce the acreage sown in wheat were soon encouraging them to increase production. Large orders from China, Russia, and other countries generated rail traffic on an unprecedented scale. In the crop year 1966–67, the Canadian Pacific moved 220,310 cars of grain, each carrying an average of 2,000 bushels; in 1971–72 the total rose to 247,203 cars. About two thirds of them were delivered to Thunder Bay and one third to Vancouver. That year CP Rail carried 54 percent of all Canadian grain exported. In the calendar year 1971, grain constituted 27.5 percent of total freight tonnage of the two major railways, but owing to the statutory rates in force, it yielded only 10.1 percent of rail revenues.

By 1972 an acute shortage of grain cars had developed, in part due to the increase of traffic in other bulk commodities. Steel hopper cars, not the traditional boxcars, were clearly the best type for grain carrying, but they were expensive, and the railways were reluctant to purchase them for traffic that promised little if any return. On the advice of the Canadian Wheat Board, the official marketing agency, the government of Canada ordered 2,000 hopper cars, each with a capacity of 3,000 bushels. Of the total, 1,074 were leased to CP Rail. An additional 4,000 were purchased in 1975, thus providing 6,000 new cars in all, capable of moving 18 million bushels at a single loading.

To dwellers on the prairies, the statutory grain rates are sacrosanct. They decline to see any inconsistency in the maintenance of rates that were essential and satisfactory when wheat was priced at a dollar a bushel and railway operating expenses were low, but that are clearly far out of line seventy-five years later, when costs have soared and wheat is selling for as much as five dollars a bushel. In part their attitude is due to past history; the bad reputation the C.P.R. acquired in the West in its monopoly days at the turn of the century still lingers. And in spite of the major concession that the statutory rates constitute, prairie folk are still convinced that they are being discriminated against in the freight rate structure as a whole.[10]

That structure has changed radically since 1967, when the National Transportation Act gave the railways far greater freedom to set rates and to react quickly to competition. Tariffs had long been dominated by class rates, which set a rate for all commodities in all Canada; they placed major emphasis on the value of the item to be carried, which gave rise to the saying that the railways charged what the traffic would bear. Today most high-priced merchandise moves by air or by road; competition rules the tariff structure, and class rates account for a negligible proportion of the traffic. Apart from grain, virtually all freight moves under one of three types of rate. Agreed charges, as the name implies, are contractual rates agreed to by the railway and a shipper. For a period of not less than one year, the railway agrees to charge a specified rate and the shipper undertakes to give the railway all or a stated proportion of his business. What are known as competitive commodity rates are intended to meet competition from other carriers. Normal commodity rates are set with markets in mind. Their purpose is to enable Canadian producers to meet competition in Canada from imported goods and to help market Canadian products as widely as possible both within Canada and abroad.

Inevitably anomalies arise. Sometimes distance is not the determining factor when a rate is set with marketing considerations chiefly in mind. Thus the railway may charge more to carry a commodity from Toronto to Calgary than it does to carry it to Vancouver, 640 miles farther west. The reason may be that in Vancouver the commodity would be facing competition from imported Japanese goods, and unless it can be carried there cheaply, it will be priced out of the market. As long as the railway makes some profit, it is worth its while to quote the special low rate; otherwise the commodity would not move to the west coast, and both the railway and the manufacturer would suffer.

Recently F. S. Burbridge, president of the Canadian Pacific, summarized the considerations involved in constructing a freight tariff: "Our freight rates are really our prices. By and large, these rates simply reflect a number of factors—the distance the commodity is going to move, the nature of the commodity, and the nature of the competition for that commodity, whether it's carrier competition by truck or market competition. Freight rates simply reflect our assessment of these conditions in the light of the volume of the movement."[11]

Greater freedom to set rates has not resulted in higher charges. The ton-mile average revenue of Canadian railways dropped from 1.54 cents in 1967 to 1.36 cents in 1971. The decline was greater in the West than in the East, due to the marked increase in the tonnage of relatively low value bulk commodities that were carried. To a surprising degree, traffic in western Canada (by which is meant the region from Lake Superior to the west coast) originates and terminates within the area. In 1971 the proportion was 90 percent, or 76 million tons, of which 25 million tons were grain.

Under Crump's guidance, the Canadian Pacific faced competition with great vigor. It was thought at first that the St. Lawrence Seaway, opened in 1959, might compete for traffic that brought the railway an annual revenue of about $38 million, but the threat proved to be less serious than expected. Highway competition was countered by building up the Canadian Pacific's own road services, now the most extensive in Canada, and by the piggyback service that supplements them. The C.P.R. carried its millionth trailer in

November 1965 and the two-million mark was passed in May 1973. Pipelines placed oil beyond the railway's reach, but it is interesting to speculate about what might have happened if Crump had become president a few years earlier. The principal oil pipeline from the Alberta oil fields to central Canada was not completed until 1952, and it does not seem far-fetched to suppose that under more vigorous leadership the Canadian Pacific might have built pipelines as some American roads have done. It will be remembered that Canadian Pacific Investments now has a substantial interest in gas pipelines and that the railway, in partnership with Shell Canada, has set up ShelPac Research and Development Limited to investigate the possibility of moving coal in slurry form and other commodities by pipeline.

But Crump was at heart a railwayman, and his main effort was aimed at a major overhaul and upgrading of the rail system itself and its services, facilities, and rolling stock.

By 1961 Crump had attained his ambition to have all rail operations converted to diesel, but he soon set about further upgrading the Canadian Pacific's motive power. Beginning in 1963, a substantial number of older locomotives were rebuilt and their power was increased by as much as 40 percent. In 1964 the railway ordered twelve 2,500-horsepower locomotives, the most powerful units yet placed in service in Canada; they were regarded as the first of a "second generation" of diesels. In later engines, horsepower was increased to 3,000. New high-adhesion tracks giving better traction add to their efficiency. At the end of 1971, CP Rail's motive power consisted of 917 road engines and 271 yard switchers, a total of 1,188 units.

A system operations center in Montreal has improved engine utilization appreciably. A master indicator board records the whereabouts of all locomotives and of the 300 trains that are normally moving on CP Rail lines at any one time. This makes it possible to match locomotives to power needs much more quickly, and it is estimated that the center improved engine utilization in 1973 by 6 percent.

Mention has been made of specialized car equipment. Between the end of the Second World War and 1958, the Canadian Pacific spent approximately $300 million on 40,000 new freight cars. Many of these were of the old general-purpose types, but thereafter the trend was strongly toward highly specialized (and much more expensive) cars. They included covered hopper cars to move potash, cement, and minerals; hoppers with special linings to carry edible commodities; rack-type tri-level automobile cars and boxcars specially equipped to carry auto parts; boxcars with cushion underframes and with wide doors, to carry plywood; "Red Shield" boxcars designed with the special needs of pulp and paper in mind; insulated cars for heated service, and others insulated and equipped with mechanical refrigeration for the conveyance of meat and other perishable products. Over 2,000 special flatcars carry containers and trailers for the piggyback service.

Maintenance cost as well as the first cost of this specialized equipment is high; in 1971 car repairs cost CP Rail $41 million, which was 7 percent of all rail expenses. To counter this, great improvements have been made in the three major overhaul shops in Montreal, Winnipeg, and Calgary, and they are being supplemented by "one-spot" repair facilities in eight centers. The first shop of the kind was opened in Toronto in 1964. The purpose is to attend quickly to running repairs—wheel changes, brake checks, and other items that normally can be dealt with in not more than an hour. The Calgary "one-spot" shop, opened in 1974, consists of three tracks, each with its own crew and full equipment of jacks, hoists, and tools. Cars can be handled either loaded or empty, and about 100 can be dealt with daily.

In 1967 unit trains, with a consist made up of identical cars carrying a single commodity, appeared on the Canadian Pacific scene. They were made possible by the National Transportation Act, which authorized multiple-car freight rates. The first train of the kind carried sulphuric acid from Copper Cliff, near Sudbury, to southwestern Ontario. Later a thirty-car train moved coal from the mines at Coleman, Alberta, to Port Moody for export to Japan. The latter proved to be a portent of things to come, for it was in 1968 and 1969 that Kaiser Resources Limited and Canadian Pacific's own subsidiary, Fording Coal, undertook to ship millions of tons of coking coal to the steel industry in Japan.

The mines, near the Elk River in the Kootenay region of southeastern British Columbia, were 700 miles from the new deep-sea bulk terminal being developed at Roberts Bank, south of Vancouver. To solve the transportation problem this involved, CP Rail developed plans to operate unit trains that would make the 1,400-mile round trip in seventy-two hours. Each of the mile-long trains normally consisted of eighty-eight hopper cars and was hauled by four 3,000-horsepower locomotives. It was in these trains that CP Rail first used remote robot control. Two of the locomotives were positioned in the middle of the train and were controlled through a robot unit that could receive instructions from the lead locomotive by radio and decode them instantly into instructions to the mid-train engines. Robot control was used later in grain unit trains consisting of the hopper cars made available by the government of Canada, and it will likely soon be used in other heavy freights.

Part of the route from the Kootenay mines was over what had been formerly a lightly used connecting line. The upgrading required to make it capable of carrying the heavy coal trains included bridge replacements, and this reconstruction, together with the purchase of 578 hopper cars and 29 locomotives, cost the Canadian Pacific about $35 million. The Fording Coal contract required the purchase of an additional 410 hoppers and 24 diesels. But the efficiency of the unit-train service is impressive. Each hopper carries 105 tons of coal, and the cars can be turned over to unload without uncoupling. In 1965–67 Canadian Pacific required 1,200 cars to move a million tons of coal. Only 350 cars in the unit trains moved 3 million tons in a comparable period and did so at lower rates.

These coal developments on James J. Hill's old Kootenay stamping ground caused his ghost to walk. When the scale of the operation became evident, a Kaiser-controlled subsidiary, the Kootenay and Elk Railway, came into existence and sought permission to build a line south to the American border, where it would link up with the Burlington Northern Railroad, of which Hill's Great Northern is now a part. In keeping with the Hill tradition, its purpose was to siphon off the coal traffic, which the Burlington Northern would carry to the coast and then north into Canada to Roberts Bank. The Kootenay and Elk expected to claim running rights over forty miles of the Canadian Pacific's Crowsnest Pass line and to build fifty-five miles of new road. A few hundred yards of the new right-of-way were cleared in 1972, but CP Rail's strenuous objections have so far kept the project from progressing further.

The drive for improvement has extended, of course, to the track itself. High labor costs and efficiency alike dictated the adoption of mechanized means of track maintenance. Tie installation machines have replaced the old hand methods; a gang of twenty-three men can now install between 500 and 600 ties in a single day. The ties themselves are all treated, and their long life makes it possible to check them in sections, on a three- or five-year cycle. Spikes are no longer driven by hand; power has taken over. Ballasting is carried out by mechanical regulators that are equipped with powerful jacks that raise the rails to the desired height and are followed by tampers that force new rock ballast underneath the rails.

Since 1968 CP Rail has been laying welded rails, a practice of long standing in Europe. The standard rail length is 1,440 feet, but on curves exceeding 4 percent, short 72-foot lengths are used. Often, in the interests of economy, the latter are made up of two of the old standard 39-foot rails that are in good condition except for battered ends. The damaged ends are cut off and two of the old rails are welded together to form the new 72-foot length. Welded rails are now the standard replacement for all principal lines in Canada; in 1971 three quarters of the 201,000 tons of new rail laid in the country were continuous welded.

Time was when tracks were kept in good order with passenger trains chiefly in mind, but today's heavy, fast freights require just as good a track as the *Canadian*. This would apply especially to the grain and coal trains, and in particular to numbers 901 and 902, the top-line freights that began to shuttle back and forth between Toronto and Vancouver in July 1972. Limited to about seventy-five cars carrying high-priority commodities, they are usually made up of piggyback, container, and pool cars, and they operate on a schedule that is faster than that maintained by the *Dominion* when it was the Canadian Pacific's crack transcontinental. Train 901 leaves Toronto in the evening and delivers freight in Winnipeg the second morning, in Calgary the third, and in Vancouver the fourth.

Huge new automatic classification yards at Agincourt, near Toronto, and at Calgary, and expansions and improvements in many yards at other points have helped greatly to speed up freight handling. Once on their way, trains benefit from the centralized train control with which many of the busiest miles on the CP Rail system are now equipped. The Canadian Pacific had used automatic block signals extensively for many years, but centralized train control was first introduced on a few miles of the Montreal-Toronto line in 1958. Within a decade it had been applied to nearly 1,700 miles. Armed with complete details of the car capacity of all sidings and with remote control of signals and switches, its computer can schedule trains to the best advantage and use a line to maximum capacity.

Like all railways, Canadian Pacific has had its share of accidents, but on the whole the company's record has been a good one. It will be recalled that 30,000 passenger trains were brought down the Big Hill at Field safely before the famous spiral tunnels were completed. Yet every now and then something inexplicable happens; perhaps the most puzzling accident of all occurred at appropriately named Surprise Creek in 1929. The very high bridge there is one of a series on the line as it climbs westward to the Connaught Tunnel and Rogers Pass. A heavy train, pulled and pushed by three locomotives, had crossed the bridge without any hint of trouble, yet an hour later, when two engines were coming slowly down grade, it collapsed just as the first got clear and plunged the second into the gorge below.

Canada is a northern country whose railways have to contend with winter conditions that make keeping the lines open very literally a battle with the elements. The nature and severity of the weather vary from year to year, but snowplows and work gangs seldom have an easy time. The winter of 1942–43 is remembered as one of the worst, particularly because it was unusually severe in both East and West and came at a time when the Canadian Pacific was handling abnormally heavy wartime traffic. Storms were almost continuous from November to March, and snowplow mileage was eight times what it had been the previous year.[12]

Comparable with it, in the West at least, was the winter of 1971–72. Rogers Pass and the Fraser Canyon were the worst of many trouble spots. In spite of the great relief afforded by the Connaught Tunnel, there are still some eighty known slide paths in the pass upon which the railway's track men must keep a watchful eye. An artillery crew from the Canadian Armed Forces helps greatly by dislodging incipient slides with a well-placed shell before they become dangerous, but as at Surprise Creek, the unexpected can happen. In January slides held up traffic at seven different locations. One was 1,600 feet long and 16 feet deep, a second was 1,500 feet long and 10 feet deep, while a third, a thousand feet in length, had a depth of 30 feet. But the worst slide of this very difficult winter occurred at the Laurie tunnel and snowshed complex, some thirty miles east of Revelstoke, where the railway runs along the south side of the Illecillewaet River. The slide crashed 2,000 feet down the north side of the valley, bounced over the concrete sheds that protect the Trans-Canada Highway, and dropped to the river below. But instead of stopping there, its vast momentum propelled it on up the south side, where it destroyed 30 feet of the railway's snowshed and filled a further 300 feet with 5,000 cubic yards of tightly packed fine snow that became as hard as concrete. It was fifty-four hours before herculean efforts made it possible to reopen the line to traffic.

Fifteen miles farther east, a snowplow had a memorable encounter with another slide. Although pushed by three 3,000-horsepower locomotives, the plow was not only unable to make much impression on the slide, but became so firmly imbedded in it that the engines could not pull it free. In the end seven locomotives, mustering 21,000 horsepower, were required to break the slide's hold.[13]

The narrow gorge of the Fraser Canyon invites trouble when snowfall is heavy, but CP Rail usually fares better than the Canadian National, which runs along the opposite side of the river. Having had first choice, the Canadian Pacific location engineers naturally chose the side that seemed less likely to cause difficulties in winter. Thanks to much later construction, the C.N.R. has easier grades, but the C.P. line is the better of the two from the operational point of view.[14] From time to time one hears rumors that the Canadian Pacific is thinking of driving the world's longest railway tunnel, which would bypass many of the canyon's trouble spots. Its length would be more than twenty miles.

A shift is becoming perceptible in the Canadian economy, with greater emphasis on resources and the West and less on manufacturing and the East. In response, traffic on the western CP Rail lines has increased rapidly, and some forecast a rise of 50 percent or more within ten years. The strain on the single track in the mountains is already pronounced; through Rogers Pass and the Connaught Tunnel, it handles the heaviest tonnage of any single-track main line in North America. CP Rail is therefore planning ways and means of increasing its capacity. About 65 percent of traffic is westbound, so one immediate objective is to reduce the grades the heavily laden westbound trains now encounter. A total of forty miles of new track in four locations, estimated to cost $42 million, will lengthen the line sufficiently to enable grades at all those points to be reduced to 1 percent—a reduction that will increase locomotive capacity over some parts of the line by as much as one third. The heaviest existing grade, 2.2 percent, is up the eastern slope of the Selkirks to the Connaught Tunnel; a nineteen-mile diversion will be required there. The building of the Mica Dam on the Columbia River has made additional work necessary in the same subdivision. At present the track runs down the Columbia valley from Donald to Beavermouth, but the backwater from the dam will raise the water level at Beavermouth about eighty feet. The railway had therefore to take to the hills at Donald, and the replacement line called for the construction of four steel bridges and a 1,100-foot tunnel, and the removal of 4 million cubic yards of earth and a million cubic yards of rock.

Electrification of the mountain lines, tentatively planned by Shaughnessy sixty years ago, is again under active consideration. In 1971, CP Rail sent members of its operating and research departments to conduct performance tests in Norway and Switzerland, where electric locomotives are used extensively and winter conditions are comparable to those in Canada. The prospect is attractive: electric locomotives are easier to maintain, last two or three times as long as a diesel, have a much higher tractive level, and promise to cut operating costs substantially. But first cost will be high—perhaps $250 million for the 640-mile line between Calgary and Vancouver—and many technical matters remain to be settled. Power sources and costs must also be reconsidered in the light of the energy crisis. Meanwhile CP Rail has built a section of overhead wiring along its line near Ross Peak to test its resistance to the worst winter weather. Annual snowfall at the point chosen often exceeds 500 inches.

Norris Crump retired from the chairmanship on May 2, 1972. He had served the Canadian Pacific for almost fifty-two years, seventeen of them as its president or chairman. He had reshaped it and expanded it on a scale that earns him a place in its history in the select company of Stephen, Van Horne, Shaughnessy, and Beatty. He had encouraged it to spread its wings, had restored its fortunes at sea, and had given it a leading place on the highways. He had developed its nontransportation interests out of all recognition. From ties and rails to cars, motive power, and traffic control, he had transformed the railway itself.

Mileage changed little in the seventeen years; not including the Soo Line, the total was 16,997 in 1955 and 16,652 in 1972. Perhaps the most interesting addition was the thirty-one-mile branch that linked the Fording coal mines with the Crowsnest Pass line; millions of tons of coal were soon passing over it each year. The most notable deletion was at the western end of the Crowsnest route. In 1959 a mammoth washout near Jessica station, on the Kettle Valley line near Hope, led to the abandonment of fifty-two miles of track. They included the spectacular Coquihalla Pass, which it had been found almost impossible to keep open in winter, and the railway parted with the line without any great regret.[15]

A few statistics will summarize the changes in traffic that took place during Crump's seventeen years. The tonnage of revenue freight increased from 58.5 million in 1955 to 83.2 million in 1972. Revenue freight measured in ton-miles almost doubled, from 25,723 million to nearly 49,185 million. Rising costs (and the statutory grain rates) were reflected in a decline in revenue per ton-mile from 1.44 cents to 1.29 cents. Passenger traffic fell off sharply; the C.P.R. carried 9.5 million passengers in 1955, but the total had fallen to just over 5 million by 1972. Canadian Pacific's balance sheet placed its total assets at $2.1 billion in 1955; seventeen years later the figure was nearly $3.9 billion and would exceed 4 billion in another year.

Crump shared George Stephen's desire to see control of a majority of the Canadian Pacific's voting stock held in Canada. When he became president, less than 15 percent was in Canadian hands. Within ten years his objective had been attained; in 1965 Canadians owned 54.97 percent of the voting shares, and by 1972 the percentage had risen to 63.04.

Crump would be the last to claim exclusive credit for the progress made under his guidance. The transformation was a team effort; but his was the dominating personality. Though at first nominally subordinate to the chairman, W. A. Mather, Crump was from the beginning of his presidency the driving force in the company, and for three years after Mather's death early in 1961 he served as both president and chairman. Robert A. Emerson was then elected president. Emerson was a third-generation railwayman, whose grandfather had piloted wood-burning locomotives for the C.P.R. in early days; he had been born in the station house at Plum Coulee, Manitoba, where his father was agent. Emerson had risen rapidly from the ranks of the engineering staff, had served as chief engineer in Montreal, and had been vice-president since 1958. No doubt Crump saw in him a successor, but Emerson died suddenly in March 1966, less than eighteen months after becoming president.

His place was taken by Ian D. Sinclair, formerly the company's chief law officer, and it was Sinclair who succeeded Crump as chairman when he stepped down in May 1972. At the same time Frederick S. Burbridge was elected tenth president of the Canadian Pacific. Both Sinclair and Burbridge are Manitoba-born and both graduated in law from the University of Manitoba. Both also played a large part in preparing and presenting the Canadian Pacific's representations to the MacPherson Royal Commission on Transportation. Their appointments were in the Beatty tradition, and one suspects that Crump was probably the last man born and bred a railwayman who will rise to the top echelon of the company. The character of the corporation is changing; operations are now primarily the concern of the profit centers, and this is reflected in the recent reports of Canadian Pacific Limited. The last to include traffic statistics, even in summary, was that for the year 1968; the 1973 report was exclusively financial. For the operational record one must turn to the publications of Statistics Canada.

Two questions about the Canadian Pacific seem to be of perennial interest and an unfailing inspiration for controversy and elaborate calculation.

First, was the whole enterprise premature? Certainly it was, in the sense that no private interests would have dreamt of attempting to build the railway ninety-five years ago without a substantial subsidy. Sir John Macdonald was as acutely aware of this as anyone, but he perceived, as very few others did, that politically the railway was essential. If he had not found ways and means of constructing it when he did, Canada would almost certainly not extend today from sea to sea.

Secondly, was not the Canadian Pacific showered with money and land subsidies and did these not place the company under some sort of perpetual obligation to the people of Canada? This matter must be seen in perspective and proportion. The cash subsidy for the original main line was $25 million, which, to Stephen's surprise and discomfiture, turned out to be not a great deal more than a quarter of the cost of construction. As for the land grant, it was many years before land sales brought the company any return of real consequence. Much the most important contribution the grant made was the cancellation in 1886 of $10.2 million of the Canadian Pacific's debt to the government, in return for which the railway gave back 6.8 million of the subsidy acres.

These subsidies were not out of line. They were the least that it was thought would be sufficient to give the railway some prospect of an economically viable existence. As it turned out, the need was underestimated, and in all likelihood the Canadian Pacific would have foundered had it not been for

The seven corporate symbols that have been used by the Canadian Pacific over a span of ninety years. The first appeared on a timetable issued in July 1886, just after transcontinental train service had begun. By the end of the year it had been superseded by the second design, in which a beaver had been added. Why the beaver was chosen is a mystery, but it is an industrious animal and had been associated with Canada for centuries because of its importance in the fur trade. Later the design was simplified, and this third symbol was used for many years. In 1929 a completely new symbol was devised. It carried the slogan World's Greatest Transportation System and made provision for the identification of individual services. The words *Railway Lines* shown here could give way to *Hotels, Steamships,* or whatever was appropriate. In 1946 the beaver (this time a more active and attractive animal) was restored in a new design that also incorporated a new slogan: Spans the World. The words *Canadian Pacific* were in script. This symbol was common to all services. In 1960, in a further revision, the slogan disappeared and the corporate name was in sloping script. Finally, in 1968 came the present entirely new symbol, with pseudoheraldic significance. It is common to all services but is used in a variety of colors intended to identify them individually, and in association with the name of each—CR Rail, CP Ships, and so on.

the revenue from its eastern lines, to which the subsidies did not apply. The assistance given was very much less than the sums that twenty years later were poured into the lines now comprising the Canadian National Railways. Statistics Canada places the total of all cash subsidies given by the federal, provincial, and municipal governments to the Canadian Pacific and its numerous branch, acquired, and leased lines at $106.3 million. This includes the cost of the government-built lines that were handed over to the Canadian Pacific, which is given as $34 million. By contrast, cash grants and loan guarantees (all of which came home to roost) given by the federal and provincial governments to the Canadian Northern totaled $264 million, and the government of Canada spent $159 million building the National Transcontinental, which was intended to be the eastern connection of the Grand Trunk Pacific. These two items alone totaled $423 million, or almost four times the total assistance given to the C.P.R.

The Canadian Pacific's prospects have always been bound up with the prospects of Canada. Of necessity it has had to keep profits in mind, but it has always been acutely aware that it could prosper only if Canada prospered. No large organization in the business world is more sensitive to the ups and downs of economic activity than a major railroad. It has shared Canada's good times and her bad times. Though enterprising, its management has been shrewd, cautious, and conservative. Under Shaughnessy, it built up a structure of immense financial strength that brought it safely through wars and depressions. It has never failed to earn its working expenses, even at the worst of times, and has paid its shareholders sufficient in dividends to make it possible to attract the new capital essential for modernization and expansion. It has been able to do this, of course, because of the implicit recognition by the powers that be that revenues must be allowed to reach a level at which the Canadian Pacific can survive; but it is noteworthy that the same level has been insufficient to enable the Canadian National Railways to make a profit. True, the comparison is not a fair one; the national system is largely a political creation, burdened with many unproductive lines and services that it cannot abandon; but the management of the Canadian Pacific cannot help remarking that in effect the C.P.R. has been meeting the deficits of its great and respected rival. In the six years 1966–71, Canadian Pacific Limited paid $181.1 million in income taxes. In the same period, the government of Canada made "contributions for deficits" to the C.N.R. that totaled $161.7 million.

Canada was as generous to the Canadian Pacific as it could afford to be when the railway was starting out in life. In return, no single organization has contributed more to the country's development in the ninety years since the vital line linking East and West was completed.

Appendix

FINANCIAL AND TRAFFIC STATISTICS: 1881–1885

The statistics given in the earliest reports of the company are incomplete and to some extent contradictory, but from them the following table can be compiled:

YEAR ENDING DECEMBER 31	EARNINGS	EXPENSES	NET INCOME
1881	$ 961,492	$ —	$ —
1882	3,326,920	—	—
1883	5,423,696	4,862,553	561,143
1884	5,750,521	4,558,631	1,191,890

In 1883 earnings as stated included $1,274,000 for carrying "construction materials." This did not affect the figure for net income, as materials were carried at cost and this cost was included in expenses. In 1884 the corresponding figure was $623,193.

From the reports submitted by the Canadian Pacific and printed by the government in the official *Sessional Papers*, the following more complete table can be compiled:

YEAR ENDING JUNE 30	EARNINGS	EXPENSES	NET INCOME	TONS OF FREIGHT CARRIED
1882	$1,546,214	$1,148,299	$ 397,915	634,153
1883	4,490,352	3,953,468	537,884	1,065,272
1884	5,177,016	4,747,777	429,239	1,244,476
1885	6,928,869	4,557,520	2,371,349	1,653,969

From the beginning, the Canadian Pacific paid dividends on its capital stock. By the end of 1883 payments had totaled $2,128,000. Thereafter 3 percent per annum ($1,950,000) was paid from the dividend guarantee fund deposited with the government of Canada, and the company supplemented this with a 2-percent payment ($1,300,000) to make the annual return to shareholders 5 percent. In February 1885, when the company was in financial difficulties, George Stephen and Donald Smith personally provided the $650,000 required to pay the semi-annual supplementary dividend, but such payments then lapsed and were not resumed until August 1890.

FINANCIAL AND TRAFFIC STATISTICS: 1886–1972

For many years Statistics Canada (formerly the Dominion Bureau of Statistics) published an annual bulletin (catalog 52-202) giving financial and operating statistics for the Canadian Pacific from 1923 to date. A corresponding bulletin gave data relating to the Canadian National Railways. As the tables were becoming cumbersome, these two publications were replaced in 1974 by a combined bulletin (catalog 52-203) which gives statistics for both systems for the preceding five years.

Many of the financial figures given in the government bulletins do not correspond with those found in the Canadian Pacific's own reports, as the latter were compiled on a different basis. To cite one important example, there are wide variations in the items included under the heading "Rail revenues." But the discrepancies are essentially a matter of accounting practice; thus the figures given by the company and Statistics Canada for that key item, net income before fixed charges and dividends, were identical after 1934, and variations in the 1923–1934 returns were relatively small.

Naturally the reports and comments of the company's officials, often referred to or quoted in the text, are based on Canadian Pacific's own statistics, and it has therefore seemed preferable to make them the basic source for the financial tables that follow, particularly as they extend back many years before the official bulletins began to appear.

(IN THOUSANDS OF DOLLARS)

YEAR	MILES OPERATED	RAILWAY REVENUES	RAILWAY EXPENSES	NET EARNINGS	OPERATING RATIO
1886	4,464	$ 10,082	$ 6,378	$ 3,703	63.3%
1887	4,960	11,606	8,102	3,504	69.8
1888	5,074	13,196	9,325	3,871	70.7
1889	5,186	15,369	9,211	6,128	60.0
1890	5,564	16,553	10,253	6,210	61.9
1891	5,766	20,241	12,231	8,010	60.4
1892	6,015	21,409	12,989	8,420	60.4
1893	6,327	20,962	13,221	7,741	63.1
1894	6,344	18,752	12,329	6,423	65.7
1895	6,444	18,941	11,460	7,481	60.5
1896	6,476	20,682	12,574	8,108	60.8
1897	6,568	24,050	13,746	10,304	57.2
1898	6,681	26,139	15,664	10,475	59.9
1899	7,000	29,230	17,000	12,230	58.2

APPENDIX

(IN THOUSANDS OF DOLLARS)

YEAR	MILES OPERATED	RAILWAY REVENUES	RAILWAY EXPENSES	NET EARNINGS	OPERATING RATIO
1900*	—	14,168	8,890	5,278	—
1901	7,563	30,855	17,850	13,005	60.7
1902	7,587	37,503	23,417	14,086	62.4
1903	7,748	43,957	28,121	15,837	64.0
1904	8,332	46,469	32,256	14,213	69.4
1905	8,568	50,482	35,007	15,475	69.3
1906	8,777	61,670	38,696	22,973	62.7
1907	9,154	72,218	46,914	25,303	65.0
1908	9,420	71,384	49,592	21,792	69.5
1909	9,878	76,313	53,358	22,956	69.9
1910	10,078	94,989	61,150	33,840	64.4
1911	10,342	104,168	67,468	36,700	64.8
1912	10,767	123,320	80,021	43,298	64.9
1913	11,366	139,396	93,150	46,246	66.8
1914	11,825	129,815	87,389	42,426	67.3
1915	12,368	99,865	65,291	33,575	66.0
1916	12,917	129,482	80,256	49,226	59.7
1916†	12,955	76,718	45,843	30,875	—
1917	12,990	152,389	105,843	46,546	69.5
1918	12,993	157,533	123,035	34,502	78.1
1919	13,389	176,929	143,997	32,933	81.4
1920	13,402	216,641	183,488	33,153	84.7
1921	14,357	193,022	158,820	34,202	82.3

(IN THOUSANDS OF DOLLARS)

YEAR	MILES OPERATED	RAILWAY REVENUES	RAILWAY EXPENSES	NET EARNINGS	RATIO NET TO REVENUES	OPERATING RATIO
1922	13,093	$186,675	$150,373	$36,302	19.4%	80.6%
1923	13,123	195,837	158,358	37,479	19.1	80.9
1924	13,355	182,502	145,275	37,227	20.4	79.6
1925	13,678	183,356	143,201	40,155	21.9	78.1
1926	13,863	198,026	153,080	44,945	22.7	77.3
1927	14,074	201,146	161,630	39,516	19.6	80.4
1928	14,293	229,039	177,345	51,694	22.6	77.4
1929	14,563	209,731	166,586	43,145	20.6	79.4
1930	14,889	180,901	142,652	38,249	21.1	78.9

* Six months ending June 30, 1900; figures thereafter for fiscal year ending June 30.

† Six months ending Dec. 31, 1916; calendar year thereafter.

(IN THOUSANDS OF DOLLARS)

YEAR	MILES OPERATED	RAILWAY REVENUES	RAILWAY EXPENSES	NET EARNINGS	RATIO NET TO REVENUES	OPERATING RATIO
1931	15,636	142,338	116,655	25,683	18.0	82.0
1932	16,888	123,937	103,847	20,090	16.2	83.8
1933	17,030	114,270	93,408	20,862	18.3	81.7
1934	17,015	125,543	101,159	24,384	19.4	80.6
1935	17,221	129,679	107,281	22,398	17.3	82.7
1936	17,241	138,563	115,252	23,311	16.8	83.2
1937	17,223	145,086	121,343	23,742	16.4	83.6
1938	17,186	142,259	121,507	20,752	14.6	85.4
1939	17,176	151,281	122,757	28,524	18.9	81.1
1940	17,159	170,965	135,325	35,639	20.8	79.2
1941	17,150	221,446	175,489	45,958	20.8	79.2
1942	17,077	256,864	208,676	48,188	18.8	81.2
1943	17,034	297,108	247,896	49,212	16.6	83.4
1944	17,030	318,871	275,711	43,160	13.5	86.5
1945	17,029	316,109	280,055	36,054	11.4	88.6
1946	17,037	292,496	271,653	20,843	7.1	92.9
1947	17,035	318,586	295,694	22,892	7.2	92.8
1948	17,033	355,250	336,831	18,419	5.2	94.8
1949	17,031	363,252	342,620	20,632	5.7	94.3
1950	17,018	378,577	340,556	38,020	10.0	90.0
1951	17,009	428,912	402,099	26,813	6.3	93.7
1952	17,017	457,809	428,878	28,931	6.3	93.7
1953	17,018	470,572	441,687	28,885	6.1	93.9
1954	17,002	422,642	395,609	27,033	6.4	93.6
1955	16,997	448,599	411,272	37,327	8.3	91.7
1956	17,126	505,262	463,926	41,336	8.2	91.8
1957	17,111	487,565	449,319	38,246	7.8	92.2
1958	17,096	467,411	430,919	36,492	7.8	92.2
1959	17,096	477,806	441,760	36,046	7.5	92.5
1960	17,094	457,106	423,431	33,675	7.4	92.6
1961	17,033	465,490	427,839	37,651	8.1	91.9
1962	16,823	453,169	424,191	28,978	6.4	93.6
1963	16,742	477,198	441,936	35,262	7.4	92.6
1964	16,685	510,145	466,680	43,465	8.5	91.5
1965	16,667	518,035	477,795	40,240	7.8	92.2
1966	16,650	553,830	503,610	50,220	9.1	90.9
1967	16,641	560,695	521,059	39,636	7.1	92.9
1968	16,652	562,345	521,085	41,260	7.3	92.7
1969	16,598	580,018	545,383	34,635	6.0	94.0
1970	16,601	616,020	577,628	38,392	6.2	93.8
1971	16,608	658,820	613,064	45,756	6.9	93.0
1972	16,652	709,814	652,189	57,625	8.1	91.9

APPENDIX

(IN THOUSANDS OF DOLLARS)

YEAR	OTHER INCOME	INCOME BEFORE FIXED CHARGES	FIXED CHARGES	INCOME BEFORE DIVIDENDS	DIVIDENDS PREFERENCE	ORDINARY	TOTAL
1886	$ —	$ 3,703	$ 3,068	$ 635	(3% or $1,950,000 paid on ordinary shares from guarantee fund until August 1893.)		
1887	—	3,504	3,250	254			
1888	—	3,871	3,544	327			
1889	—	6,128	3,779	2,349			
1890	—	6,120	4,247	1,873	—	1,300	1,300
1891	—	8,010	4,664	3,346	—	1,300	1,300
1892	204	8,624	5,102	3,522	—	1,300	1,300
1893	210	7,951	5,338	2,613	—	1,300	1,300
1894	334	6,757	6,581	176	257	3,250	3,507
1895	553	8,034	6,659	1,375	128	1,232	1,360
1896	511	8,659	6,708	1,951	281	1,625	1,906
1897	341	10,645	6,783	3,862	327	1,625	1,952
1898	423	12,653	6,774	5,879	432	2,925	3,357
1899	1,150	13,380	6,817	6,563	656	2,600	3,256
1900*	1,011	6,289	3,434	2,855	599	1,625	2,224
1901	933	13,938	7,306	6,632	173	5,200	5,373
1902	959	15,045	7,335	7,710	1,247	3,250	4,497
1903	1,287	17,124	7,052	10,072	1,273	3,737	5,010
1904	1,691	15,904	7,586	8,318	1,303	5,070	6,373
1905	1,585	17,060	7,954	7,954	1,456	5,070	6,526
1906	1,317	24,290	8,350	15,940	1,563	6,084	7,647
1907	1,641	26,944	8,512	18,432	1,712	7,301	9,013
1908	1,542	23,334	8,770	14,564	1,819	8,518	10,337
1909	1,906	24,862	9,427	15,435	2,030	10,500	12,530
1910	2,426	36,266	9,917	26,349	2,156	18,600	20,756
1911	5,047	41,747	10,011	31,736	2,225	18,000	20,225
1912	5,158	48,456	10,525	37,931	2,400	19,000	21,400
1913	6,598	52,844	10,876	41,968	2,807	23,000	25,807
1914	8,588	51,014	10,227	40,787	3,032	26,000	29,032
1915	10,969	44,544	10,446	34,098	3,170	26,000	29,170
1916†	9,941	59,167	10,306	48,861	3,227	26,000	29,227
1916‡	6,415	37,290	5,132	32,158	1,614	13,000	14,614
1917§	10,713	57,259	10,229	47,030	3,227	26,000	29,227
1918	8,129	42,631	10,177	32,454	3,227	26,000	29,227
1919	9,049	41,982	10,161	31,821	3,227	26,000	29,227
1920	10,966	44,119	10,177	33,942	3,227	26,000	29,227
1921	10,987	45,189	11,519	33,670	3,227	26,000	29,227
1922	11,092	47,394	13,349	34,045	3,227	26,000	29,227
1923	11,391	48,870	13,471	35,399	3,675	26,000	29,675
1924	9,971	47,198	14,070	33,128	3,993	26,000	29,993

(IN THOUSANDS OF DOLLARS)

YEAR	OTHER INCOME	INCOME BEFORE FIXED CHARGES	FIXED CHARGES	INCOME BEFORE DIVIDENDS	PREFERENCE	DIVIDENDS ORDINARY	TOTAL
1925	11,357	51,512	14,439	37,073	4,006	26,000	30,006
1926	11,056	56,001	14,676	41,325	4,006	26,000	30,006
1927	11,877	51,392	15,379	36,013	4,006	26,000	30,006
1928	12,678	64,372	15,309	49,064	4,068	29,354	33,422
1929	15,232	58,377	16,149	42,228	4,675	30,750	35,425
1930	20,043	58,292	19,160	39,132	5,006	33,243	38,249
1931	10,952	36,635	22,050	14,585	5,411	16,750	22,161
1932	4,537	24,627	23,620	1,007	2,745	—	2,745
1933	6,222	27,085	24,389	2,696	—	—	—
1934	6,664	31,048	24,578	6,470	—	—	—
1935	4,594	26,992	24,160	2,832	—	—	—
1936	6,631	29,942	23,913	6,029	1,373	—	1,373
1937	11,630	35,372	25,910	9,462	2,745	—	2,745
1938	7,364	28,116	26,854	1,262	—	—	—
1939	6,765	35,289	25,507	9,782	—	—	—
1940	10,692	46,332	26,187	20,145	5,043	—	5,043
1941	13,382	59,340	24,978	34,362	5,043	—	5,043
1942	15,861	64,049	23,694	40,355	5,043	—	5,043
1943	16,271	65,482	22,500	42,982	5,043	6,700	11,743
1944	12,371	55,531	20,831	34,700	5,043	16,750	21,793
1945	15,107	51,161	19,547	31,614	5,031	16,750	21,781
1946	22,780	43,623	18,488	25,135	4,558	16,750	21,338
1947	24,789	47,681	15,787	31,894	4,558	16,750	21,338
1948	24,865	43,284	15,890	27,394	4,558	16,750	21,338
1949	23,637	44,269	14,544	29,725	3,873	16,750	20,623
1950	23,237	61,257	13,390	47,867	3,389	20,100	23,489
1951	29,344	56,156	12,849	43,307	3,328	20,100	23,428
1952	22,652	51,583	12,504	39,079	3,102	20,664	23,766
1953	16,802	45,687	14,237	31,450	3,131	20,710	23,841
1954	17,835	44,868	15,042	29,826	3,091	20,714	23,805
1955	22,894	60,221	16,189	44,032	3,136	20,792	23,928
1956	30,034	71,370	15,752	55,618	3,080	24,379	27,459
1957	23,442	61,688	14,902	46,786	3,029	21,090	24,119
1958	13,409	49,901	16,998	32,903	3,068	21,218	24,286
1959	12,678	48,724	17,435	31,289	3,029	21,498	24,527
1960	12,402	46,077	17,106	28,971	3,096	21,499	24,595
1961	11,717	49,368	16,907	32,461	3,204	21,499	24,703
1962	20,460	49,438	17,080	32,358	3,429	21,499	24,928
1963	21,402	56,664	16,538	40,126	3,407	21,499	24,906

* Six months ending June 30, 1900; thereafter for fiscal year ending June 30.
† Fiscal year ending June 30.
‡ Six months ending December 31, 1916.
§ Calendar year.

INCOME AND DIVIDENDS 1964–1972
(Since dividends have been paid to Canadian Pacific
Limited by Canadian Pacific Investments)
(IN MILLIONS OF DOLLARS)

	1964	1965	1966	1967	1968	1969	1970	1971	1972
Rail revenues	$43.4	$45.1	$50.2	$39.6	$41.3	$34.6	$38.4	$45.8	$57.6
Other income	16.8	20.6	17.9	11.9	23.4	19.2	18.2	26.6	20.9
Total	60.2	65.7	68.1	51.5	64.7	53.8	56.6	72.4	78.5
Fixed charges	16.2	16.4	20.0	18.6	21.9	22.4	27.8	33.8	33.8
Net income: rail and miscellaneous	44.0	49.3	48.1	32.9	42.8	31.4	28.8	38.6	44.7
Dividends from:									
C.P.I.	14.3	20.1	20.1	20.1	21.5	23.0	23.6	23.6	23.6
CP Air	—	—	—	4.1	1.6	1.4	1.4	1.4	2.2
Total income*	58.3	69.4	68.2	57.1	65.9	55.8	53.8	63.6	70.5
Dividends paid to shareholders									
Preference 4%	3.4	3.4	3.4	3.4	3.3	3.3	3.3	3.3	1.5
Ordinary:									
From rail and miscellaneous	21.5	17.9	21.5	21.5	21.5	21.5	21.5	22.2	24.4
From C.P.I.	14.3	20.1	20.1	20.1	21.5	23.0	23.6	23.6	23.6
From CP Air	—	—	—	—	—	1.4	1.4	1.4	2.2
Total ordinary	35.8	38.0	41.6	41.6	43.0	45.9	46.5	47.2	50.2
Preferred stock 7¼%	—	—	—	—	—	—	—	1.5	3.3

* Before certain extraordinary items, and excluding equity in earnings retained by subsidiaries.
Changes in accounting practices make it impracticable to extend this table to 1975.

The striking feature of Canadian Pacific's finances in recent years has been the spectacular growth in the assets and income of Canadian Pacific Investments Limited, the subsidiary responsible for its non-transportation activities. The net income of CPI rose from $33.7 million in 1971 to $141.9 million in 1975. The total net income of the parent Canadian Pacific Limited in 1975 was $174.8 million, of which $120.5 million was derived from CPI.

In round numbers, transportation contributed only about 30 percent of the income of Canadian Pacific Limited; rail operations alone provided about 20 percent. The other 70 percent came from CPI, three-quarters of it from the company's interests in oil, gas, coal and Cominco Limited.

YEAR	REVENUE FREIGHT, TONS (THOUSANDS)	REVENUE FREIGHT, TON-MILES (MILLIONS)	FREIGHT REVENUE PER TON-MILE (CENTS)	REVENUE PASSENGERS (THOUSANDS)
1886*	2,046	555	1.10	1,791
1887	2,144	688		1,949
1888	2,497	785	1.02	2,136
1889	2,639	967	.91	2,457
1890	3,379	1,208	.84	2,793
1891	3,847	1,392	.91	3,166
1892	4,231	1,583	.84	3,258
1893	4,227	1,453	.87	3,311
1894	3,892	1,314	.87	3,009
1895	4,275	1,491	.80	2,984
1896	4,421	1,770	.75	3,030
1897	5,174	1,956	.78	3,180
1898	5,582	2,142	.76	3,674
1899	6,621	2,539	.74	3,819
1901†	7,156	2,384	.79	4,338
1902	8,770	3,248	.75	4,797
1903	10,181	3,862	.74	5,524
1904	11,136	3,810	.77	6,251
1905	11,892	4,155	.76	6,891
1906	13,934	5,342	.74	7,753
1907	15,733	5,947	.77	8,780
1908	15,040	5,865	.75	9,463
1909	16,550	6,372	.76	9,784
1910	20,551	7,772	.77	11,173
1911	22,536	8,062	.81	12,080
1912	25,940	10,392	.77	13,751
1913	29,472	11,470	.77	15,480
1914	27,801	10,822	.75	15,638
1915	21,491	7,940	.76	13,203
1916†	29,277	14,058	.65	13,834
1916‡	16,200	7,872	—	9,184
1917*	31,199	14,678	.70	15,462
1918	29,857	12,886	.85	14,397
1919	25,103	11,121	1.00	15,816
1920	30,160	13,094	1.04	16,925
1921	23,711	10,087	1.19	15,318
1922	27,744	12,785	.99	14,436
1923	32,939	14,567	.96	16,224

* Calendar year
† Fiscal year ending June 30.
‡ Six months ending December 31, 1916.

APPENDIX

YEAR	REVENUE FREIGHT, TONS (THOUSANDS)	REVENUE FREIGHT, TON-MILES (MILLIONS)	FREIGHT REVENUE PER TON-MILE (CENTS)	REVENUE PASSENGERS (THOUSANDS)
1924	30,621	12,717	1.01	15,602
1925	32,969	13,364	1.00	15,042
1926	35,963	14,188	1.04	15,075
1927	36,874	14,870	1.01	15,110
1928	42,977	18,423	.96	14,751
1929	40,977	14,951	1.07	14,054
1930	33,733	12,370	1.07	12,446
1931	27,187	10,793	.99	9,442
1932	22,613	10,067	.90	7,916
1933	22,020	9,353	.91	7,174
1934	25,606	10,026	.94	7,593
1935	26,094	10,522	.93	7,424
1936	27,985	11,424	.92	7,387
1937	29,843	11,602	.95	7,821
1938	30,471	12,135	.91	7,454
1939	33,030	14,037	.86	7,255
1940	36,746	16,028	.85	7,781
1941	44,710	22,376	.79	9,145
1942	47,972	22,600	.87	13,457
1943	52,552	24,951	.88	17,597
1944	55,679	27,376	.85	18,461
1945	54,822	27,252	.84	17,741
1946	51,401	23,480	.93	15,584
1947	59,035	26,202	.96	14,636
1948	60,037	25,218	1.14	13,629
1949	56,446	24,261	1.21	11,969
1950	53,916	22,941	1.35	10,541
1951	60,650	26,827	1.32	10,461
1952	61,505	28,943	1.31	9,868
1953	59,257	27,456	1.43	9,427
1954	54,206	23,668	1.47	9,529
1955	58,489	25,723	1.44	9,544
1956	65,838	30,433	1.39	8,906
1957	58,493	27,281	1.50	8,037
1958	54,367	26,873	1.46	7,746
1959	57,879	25,953	1.57	7,740
1960	56,924	25,733	1.52	7,059
1961	58,832	26,451	1.54	6,275
1962	57,641	26,060	1.51	6,440
1963	59,254	29,134	1.44	6,749
1964	66,362	33,930	1.32	6,997
1965	67,411	33,773	1.37	6,868

YEAR	REVENUE FREIGHT, TONS (THOUSANDS)	REVENUE FREIGHT, TON-MILES (MILLIONS)	FREIGHT REVENUE PER TON-MILE (CENTS)	REVENUE PASSENGERS (THOUSANDS)
1966	71,941	37,950	1.23	6,019
1967	69,062	35,381	1.31	6,139
1968	67,993	34,582	1.39	5,288
1969	67,240	36,176	1.39	5,076
1970	77,400	41,994	1.30	5,306
1971	78,844	45,625	1.31	5,210
1972	83,193	49,185	1.30	5,074

Notes

Abbreviations

MP   Macdonald Papers, Public Archives of Canada
CPPL   Canadian Pacific Presidents' Letterbooks
PAC   Public Archives of Canada

NOTE: Complete publication data are given in Notes only for those titles that do not appear in Bibliography.

Chapter 1

1. U.S. Senate, Committee on Interstate Commerce Commission, 51st Congress, 1st Session. Report #847, 1890, p. 237.
2. Mackenzie, Memorandum to Lord Hobart, December 1801. W. K. Lamb, ed., *The Journals and Letters of Alexander Mackenzie*, Cambridge, 1970, p. 501.
3. Sir E. W. Watkin, *Canada and the States*, p. 14.
4. J. W. Longley, *Joseph Howe*, Toronto, 1904, p. 135.
5. Toronto *Globe*, March 6, 1862.
6. Quoted in Glazebrook, *A History of Transportation in Canada*, vol. 2, p. 45.
7. Watkin, *op. cit.*, p. 451.
8. D'Arcy McGee, *Two Speeches on the Union of the Provinces*, Quebec, 1865, p. 20.
9. *Northern Pacific Railroad Co., Statement of its Resources and Merits*, 1868, p. 13.
10. U.S. Senate, *Report on Pacific Railroads*, 1869.
11. Cooke to a Winnipeg correspondent, 1870, quoted in Currie, *The Grand Trunk Railway of Canada*, p. 302.
12. Brydges to Macdonald, January 25, 1870, *MP*.
13. Macdonald to Brydges, January 28, 1870, *MP*.
14. British Columbia, Legislative Council, *Debate on the Subject of Confederation with Canada*, March 1870. Reprinted Victoria, 1912, p. 81.
15. M. W. T. Drake, *ibid.*, p. 85.
16. *Ibid.*, p. 163.
17. Helmcken, *Reminiscences*, MS. in B.C. Archives.
18. Helmcken's diary of the Confederation negotiations; *British Columbia Historical Quarterly*, April 1940, p. 120.

19. Macdonald had private doubts about the feasibility of completing the railway in ten years. A dozen years later he wrote to the Marquis of Lorne: "I must confess that the fixing a period for the completion of the road was unwise, and I am sure that had I been present I should have resisted the insertion of such a stipulation, but I was suddenly stricken down with an illness supposed to be a mortal one, and was unconscious of all that was going on. However poor Cartier did it for the best." (Macdonald to Lorne, July 11, 1883. Lorne Papers, *PAC*.) As we shall see, delays in construction were to cause much friction with British Columbia.
20. Canada, House of Commons, *Debates*, March 28, 1871, p. 681.
21. *Ibid.*, March 31, 1871, p. 745.
22. Trutch to Helmcken, April 17, 1871. Helmcken Papers, B.C. Archives.
23. House of Commons, *Debates*, March 31, 1871, p. 747.

Chapter 2

1. Callander (now Bonfield) was 17 miles east of North Bay. The present town of Callander, often mistaken for the intended C.P.R. terminus, is 7 miles southeast of North Bay, on the C.N.R. line.
2. A. D. De Celles, *Sir George Etienne Cartier*, p. 52.
3. Taylor to Davis, November 19, 1870. L. B. Irwin, *Pacific Railways and Nationalism in the Canadian-American Northwest, 1845–1873*, p. 92.
4. *Report of the Royal Commissioners, Appointed by Commission . . . bearing the date of the Fourteenth Day of August, 1873*. Ottawa, 1873, p. 154. These were the commissioners appointed to investigate the Pacific Scandal.
5. Macdonald to Allan, February 3, 1871, *MP*.
6. Henry Cooke to Jay Cooke, April 6, 1871. Irwin, *op. cit.*, p. 146.
7. *Ibid.*
8. Ogden to Cooke, June 17, 1871. *Ibid.*, p. 165.
9. *Report of the Royal Commissioners*, 1873, p. 106.
10. *Ibid.*, p. 19.
11. Smith to Macdonald, February 20, 1873, *MP*.
12. Jay Cooke to Henry Cooke, August 8, 1871. Irwin, *op. cit.*, p. 148.
13. Hincks to Macdonald, August 4, 1871, *MP*.
14. Passed on April 11, 1871.
15. Macdonald to S. Bellingham, October 10, 1871, *MP*.
16. *Report of the Royal Commissioners*, 1873, p. 108.
17. See Rose to Macdonald, November 10, 1871, *MP*.
18. Cooke to H. C. Fahnestock, January 16, 1872. Irwin, *op. cit.*, p. 172.
19. Northern Pacific circular issued in 1871.
20. The prospectus was dated January 9, 1872.
21. Macdonald to Rose, January 11, 1872, *MP*.
22. *Report of the Royal Commissioners*, 1873, p. 35.
23. Brydges to Macdonald, March 11, 1872, *MP*.
24. Smith to Cooke, March 14, 1872. Irwin, *op. cit.*, p. 175.
25. Macdonald to Rose, April 17, 1872, *MP*.
26. Brydges to Macpherson, March 11, 1872, *MP*.

27. Allan to McMullen, June 12, 1872. Toronto *Globe*, July 4, 1873.
28. Allan to Cass, July 1, 1872. *Report of the Royal Commissioners*, 1873, pp. 211–12.
29. Allan affidavit, published in the *Globe*, July 7, 1873.
30. The report was dated September 26, 1872. *MP*.
31. Allan to McMullen, August 6, 1872. Irwin, *op. cit.*, p. 184.
32. Allan to Cass, August 7, 1872. *Ibid.*, p. 185.
33. Allan to McMullen, August 6, 1872. *Ibid.*, p. 184.
34. Allan to McMullen, September 16, 1872. Toronto *Globe*, July 4, 1873.
35. Allan to McMullen, October 24, 1872. *Ibid.*, July 7, 1873.
36. Macdonald to Rose, October 18, 1872. *MP*.
37. Macdonald to Cartier, January 4, 1873, *MP*. Cartier died in London on May 20.

Chapter 3

1. Don W. Thomson, *Men and Meridians*, vol. 2, Ottawa, 1967, p. 85.
2. George Grant, *Ocean to Ocean*, p. 253.
3. Blake to Mackenzie, July 1, 1876. De Kiewiet and Underhill, eds., *Dufferin-Carnarvon Correspondence*, Toronto, 1955, p. 399.
4. Dufferin to Carnarvon, October 6, 1876. *Ibid.*, pp. 261–2.
5. Quoted in F. W. Howay and E. O. S. Scholefield, *British Columbia*, Vancouver, 1914, vol. 2, p. 368.
6. Winnipeg *Free Press*, September 21, 1874.
7. Mackenzie to Blake, April 12, 1875. Dale C. Thomson, *Alexander Mackenzie*, p. 234.
8. Report of the Privy Council to the Governor General on the entry of British Columbia, July 8, 1874. Canada, *Sessional Papers*, 1875, no. 19, p. 25.
9. See Canada, Senate, *Debates*, March 20, 1876, p. 153.
10. Mackenzie to Brown, January 18, 1876. Dale C. Thomson, *op. cit.*, p. 257.
11. Mackenzie described the interviews on November 16 and 18, 1876, in a memorandum. *Dufferin-Carnarvon Correspondence*. pp. 406–10.
12. *Report* of the Royal Commission on the Canadian Pacific Railway, 1882, p. 1784.
13. House of Commons, *Debates*, May 10, 1879, p. 1899.
14. Quoted in J. S. Willison, *Reminiscences*, p. 36.
15. Fleming, *Report*, 1877, p. 87.

Chapter 4

1. Douglas Mackay, *The Honourable Company*, Toronto, 1938, p. 290.
2. Stephen to Huntington, December 14, 1874, Mackenzie Papers, *PAC*.
3. The agreement was signed in Montreal on March 27, 1876. For the text see Joseph P. Pyle, *Life of James J. Hill*, vol. 1, pp. 427–31.

4. Stephen to Sir Arthur Bigge, October 16, 1908, Royal Archives, Windsor Castle; Stephen to Macdonald, November 13, 1880, *MP*.
5. For the complete evaluation see Pyle, *op. cit.*, vol. 1, pp. 415–22.
6. This valuation was dated October 8, 1877.
7. The final agreement, dated March 13, 1878, is printed in full in Pyle, *op. cit.*, vol. 1, pp. 432–43.
8. O. D. Skelton, *The Railway Builders*, p. 139.
9. Gustavus Myers, *History of Canadian Wealth*, p. 258.
10. The charge was made by John Charlton, M.P., in Parliament; see House of Commons, *Debates*, 1884, p. 390.

Chapter 5

1. Sir Charles Tupper, *Recollections of Sixty Years in Canada*, p. 136.
2. Tupper to Fleming, April 15, 1880. Fleming, *Report*, 1880, p. 353.
3. The original memorandum is in the Tupper Papers, *PAC*.
4. McIntyre to Macdonald, July 5, 1880, *MP*.
5. Stephen to Macdonald, July 9, 1880, *MP*. The complete text of this remarkable letter is printed in Heather Gilbert, *Awakening Continent*, pp. 63–5.
6. Tupper, *op. cit.*, p. 140. See also E. M. Saunders, ed., *Life and Letters of the Right Hon. Sir Charles Tupper*, vol. 1, p. 286.
7. Tyler to the Grand Trunk shareholders, April 14, 1891. A. W. Currie, *The Grand Trunk Railway of Canada*, p. 307.
8. Macdonald to Goldwyn Smith, July 7, 1880, *MP*.
9. Stephen to Macdonald, September 27, 1880, *MP*.
10. Stephen to Macdonald, December 16, 1880, *MP*.
11. The complete text is printed in Harold Innis, *A History of the Canadian Pacific Railway*, pp. 296–324.
12. Stephen to Macdonald, October 18, 1880, *MP*.
13. Memorial of the Toronto Board of Trade, December 21, 1880, *MP*.
14. Macdonald to Galt, February 25, 1881, *MP*.

Chapter 6

1. McIntyre to Macdonald, August 12, 1880, *MP*.
2. I am indebted for this information to Dr. Muriel Hidy, who has had access to the Hill Papers.
3. James Murray Gibbon, *Steel of Empire*, pp. 214–15.
4. See Abbott to Macdonald, December 20, 1881, *MP*; also Drinkwater to Tupper, September 15, 1882, in which the C.P.R. asks specifically for approval of the route "by way of the Kicking Horse Creek and across the Selkirk Range via Beaver Creek." Canada, *Sessional Papers*, 1883, #27, p. 25.
5. Hill to Angus, July 1880. Joseph Pyle, *Life of James J. Hill*, vol. 1, pp. 315, 316, 318.
6. Stephen to Macdonald, September 12, 1882, *MP*.
7. Stephen to Macdonald, August 27, 1881, *MP*.

8. Stephen to Macdonald, October 15, November 5, 1881, *MP*.
9. Walter Vaughan, *The Life and Work of Sir William Van Horne*, p. 74.
10. As late as 1884 Macdonald was complaining to Stephen about Egan and his attitude: "I have it from every possible N West source that Egan has made the CPR so unpopular that the feeling amounts to hatred. Much of this is political, but he is described as an open and foul mouthed Fenian—speaking of Canada and England as Fenians only can speak—that the Irish-American rose is seen all along the line and that no Canadians need apply." Macdonald to Stephen, July 30, 1884, *MP*.
11. D. C. Coleman, *Canadian Pacific History*, p. 19.
12. Secretan, *Recollections*, MS. in Katherine Hughes Papers, *PAC*.
13. Van Horne to E. T. Talbot, manager, *Railway Age*, Chicago, November 26, 1883. A lengthy letter in which Van Horne gives a great many details about the construction of the line across the prairies. *CPPL*.
14. *Ibid.*
15. *Engineering*, London, April 24, 1884, p. 352. The magazine published a series of 20 articles between March 21 and September 19, 1884, describing the C.P.R. and its construction.
16. Van Horne to Irvine, NWMP *Report*, 1882, p. 14.
17. Vaughan, *op. cit.*, p. 134.
18. Stephen to W. E. Forster. Heather Gilbert, *Awakening Continent*, p. 81.
19. From Stephen's speech at Aberdeen in 1901, when he was given the freedom of the city. Pierre Berton, *The National Dream*, p. 319.
20. Stephen to Macdonald, September 7, 1882, *MP*.
21. Stephen to Macdonald, August 27, 1882, *MP*.
22. Stephen to Macdonald, September 7, 1882, *MP*.
23. Stephen to Macdonald, November 18, 1882, *MP*.
24. Stephen to Macdonald, December 13, 1882, *MP*.
25. Stephen to Arthur —— (almost certainly Sir Arthur Lawley), August 18, 1909. I am indebted to Mr. Eric Reford, of Montreal, for this reference. In the summer of 1883 J. L. Pierson, who over 40 years later wrote a book on Van Horne and the Canadian Pacific, visited Canada and traveled over the C.P.R. line as far as Medicine Hat. He was hard hit by the subsequent sharp decline in C.P.R. shares: "Although it all ended well," he wrote in some reminiscences, "nothing can make up for the misery I went through on the Exchange, when the shares fell to 36% and we were showered with criticism and reproaches." Mr. Allard Jiskoot kindly provided this translation.

Chapter 7

1. Stephen to Macdonald, April 23, 1888, *MP*.
2. Macdonald to Allan, May 2, 1873, *MP*.
3. Hickson to Macdonald, October 30, 1880, *MP*.
4. Hickson to Macdonald, December 24, 1880, *MP*.
5. E. B. Osler, leaflet entitled *Grand Trunk Railway versus Canadian Pacific Railway Monopoly*, February 1884.

6. Hickson to Rose, October 9, 1882, *MP*.
7. The copy of the prospectus in the Macdonald Papers is a "Fifth Proof" dated April 3, 1883.
8. Stephen to Macdonald, March 22, 1883, *MP*.
9. Rose to Macdonald, April 11, 1883 (first letter), *MP*.
10. Tyler spoke on March 29, 1883. Heather Gilbert, *Awakening Continent*, p. 122.
11. Stephen's letter to the G.T.R. shareholders was dated April 5, 1883. It is printed in full in Gilbert, *op. cit.*, pp. 274–77.
12. Rose to Macdonald, April 11, 1883 (first letter), *MP*.
13. Rose to Macdonald, April 11, 1883 (second letter of this date), *MP*.
14. Van Horne to Mount Stephen, July 27, 1894, *CPPL*.
15. Stephen to Tyler, April 16, 1883, *MP*.
16. G. R. Stevens, *Canadian National Railways*, vol. 1, pp. 347–8.
17. Van Horne to Stephen, October 31, 1884, *CPPL*.
18. Grand Trunk directors to Macdonald, February 5, 1884; quoted in Hickson to Macdonald, February 7, 1884, *MP*.
19. Van Horne to Macdonald, February 14, 1884, *CPPL*.
20. C.P.R. *Report*, 1884.
21. *Ibid.*

Chapter 8

1. Winnipeg *Free Press*, December 12, 1883, quotes from Van Horne's circular, dated April 14, 1882, that announced the bonus.
2. The progress of the strike is recorded in detail in the *Free Press*, December 12 to 27, 1883. For an account highly critical of the C.P.R. see Lorne and Caroline Brown, *An Unauthorized History of the RCMP*, Toronto, 1973, pp. 28–31.
3. Van Horne to G. F. Talbot, August 21, 1883, *CPPL*.
4. Van Horne to G. H. Middleton, September 10, 1883, *CPPL*.
5. Van Horne to C. B. Gold, July 10, 1883, *CPPL*.
6. Stephen to Macdonald, April 20, 1887, *MP*.
7. U.S. Senate, Committee on Interstate Commerce Commission, 51st Congress, 1st Session, Report #847, 1890, p. 167.
8. *Ibid.*, p. 168.
9. James Murray Gibbon, *Steel of Empire*, p. 249.
10. D. C. Masters, "Financing the C.P.R., 1880–5," *Canadian Historical Review*, XXIV no. 4 (December 1943), p. 356.
11. Merrill Denison, *Canada's First Bank*, vol. 2, p. 214.
12. Macdonald to Tupper, November 22, 1883, *MP*.
13. O. D. Skelton, *Life and Letters of Sir Wilfrid Laurier*, vol. 1, p. 273.
14. Stephen to Macdonald, December 15, 1883, *MP*.
15. Stephen to Macdonald, January 22, 1884, *MP*.
16. Stephen to Tupper, January 24, 1884. E. M. Saunders, *Life and Letters of the Right Hon. Sir Charles Tupper*, vol. 2, p. 26.

17. Stephen to Arthur —— [Sir Arthur Lawley], August 18, 1909.
18. I am indebted to the secretary of the Canadian Pacific for these details. Unfortunately some of the early transfer books were destroyed in a flood many years ago.
19. Stephen to Macdonald, February 10, 1884, *MP*.
20. Van Horne to the minister of railways, May 3, 1884, *MP*.
21. Van Horne to John Ross, April 15, 1884, *CPPL*.
22. Van Horne to John Ross, October 19, 1884, *CPPL*.
23. Van Horne to John Ross, October 31, 1884, *CPPL*.

Chapter 9

1. Stephen to Macdonald, August 27, 1882, *MP*.
2. Stephen to Macdonald, September 20, 1882, *MP*.
3. J. H. E. Secretan, *Canada's Great Highway*, p. 187.
4. Van Horne to Rogers, February 6, 1883, *CPPL*.
5. Van Horne to J. W. Sterling, January 30, 1883, *CPPL*.
6. Van Horne to minister of railways, May 19, 1884, *CPPL*.
7. G. G. Ramsay, "Over the Rocky Mountains by the Canadian Pacific Line in 1884," p. 126.
8. Henry Cambie, who was in charge of construction in the Fraser Canyon, recalled that among other things "we had to increase the curvature beyond anything we had ever seen up to that time on a main line of railway. . . ." (In Noel Robinson, *Blazing the Trail through the Rockies*, p. 110.)
9. W. H. Holmes, *Some Memories of the Construction of the C.P.R. in the Fraser Canyon*. Typescript in B.C. Archives.
10. Onderdonk to Stephen, August 15, 1884. James Murray Gibbon, *Steel of Empire*, p. 273.
11. Stephen to Macdonald, September 10, 1883, *CPPL*.
12. Van Horne to William Smithe, premier of B.C., September 9, 1884, *CPPL*.
13. Van Horne to A. W. Ross, November 21, 1884, *CPPL*.
14. Van Horne to the directors of the C.P.R., September 16, 1884, *CPPL*.
15. Van Horne to Onderdonk, September 10, 1884, *CPPL*.
16. Van Horne to the directors of the C.P.R., September 16, 1884, *CPPL*.
17. Van Horne to John Ross, August 28, 1884, *CPPL*.
18. Van Horne to John Ross, October 19, 1884, *CPPL*.
19. Macdonald to Stephen, July 18, 1884. Merrill Denison, *Canada's First Bank*, vol. 2, p. 220.
20. Macdonald to Tupper, January 24, 1885. Sir Joseph Pope (ed.), *Correspondence of Sir John Macdonald*, p. 332.
21. Tupper to Macdonald, February 25, 1885. *Ibid.*, p. 337.
22. Stephen to Macdonald, February 9, 1885. *Ibid.*, p. 333.
23. Stephen to Macdonald, March 26, 1885. *Ibid.*, p. 339.
24. Macdonald to Tupper, March 17, 1885, Tupper Papers, *PAC*.
25. Stephen to Macdonald, June 18, 1885. Pope, *op. cit.*, p. 346.
26. The oldest charter in the Canadian Pacific's corporate family tree is that of

the St. Andrews and Quebec Rail Road Company, incorporated in New Brunswick in 1836. Surveys began but were halted by the unsettled Maine boundary dispute. Construction did not begin until the charter was taken over by the New Brunswick and Canada Rail Road and Land Company in 1856.
27. Gibbon, *op. cit.*, p. 295, prints a facsimile of the poster.
28. Van Horne to Ramsay; quoted in Ramsay, *loc. cit.*, p. 129.
29. See the introduction by R. A. Billington to the narrative of one of the German guests, Nicholaus Mohr, *Excursion through America*, Chicago, 1973, p. lii.
30. Walter Vaughan, *Life and Work of Sir William Van Horne*, p. 131.
31. Van Horne did not forget the debt the C.P.R. owed Macdonald, to whom he sent the following telegram: "Thanks to your far seeing policy and unwavering support the Canadian Pacific Railway is completed the last rail was laid this (Saturday) morning at 9.22." *MP*.
32. A. O. Wheeler, *The Selkirk Range*, vol. 1, p. 173.

Chapter 10

1. U.S. Senate, Committee on Interstate Commerce Commission, 51st Congress, 1st Session, Report #847, 1890, p. 234.
2. Stephen to Macdonald, February 9, 1885, *MP*.
3. C.P.R. *Report*, 1884. Stephen spoke on June 13, 1885.
4. House of Commons, *Debates*, February 23, 1885, p. 204.
5. Van Horne to Macdonald, May 16, 1887, *MP*.
6. Van Horne to Stephen, July 24, 1888, *MP*.
7. "Both Pope and Tupper testify that this is the kind of road they *meant* to hand over to the Compy. I will not do either of them the injustice to believe that this was their intention at the time." Stephen to Macdonald, June 25, 1889, *MP*.
8. *The Canadian Pacific: The New Highway to the Orient*, 1893 edition, p. 48.
9. His diary is quoted in E. W. Watkin, *Canada and the States*, pp. 41–8.
10. Van Horne to Egan, December 1, 1883, *CPPL*.
11. Thomas Keefer, "The Canadian Pacific Railway," p. 79.
12. Blackwell to Fleming, July 5, 1879. Fleming, *Report on the C.P.R.*, 1880, pp. 307–8.
13. Lavallée, *Delorimier and Angus*, p. 9.
14. *Official Memorandum respecting the position and prospects of the Canadian Pacific Railway*, November 21, 1881, p. 4.
15. *Memorandum. The Trans-Pacific Connections of the Canadian Pacific Railway*. Private. February 1886. 47 pp.
16. Anderson, Anderson and Co. to Macdonald, October 11, 1889, *MP*.
17. M. McD. Duff wrote to Van Horne on April 26, 1913, inquiring about the house flag, and Van Horne returned the letter after adding the marginal note just quoted.

Chapter 11

1. Stephen to Macdonald, January 10, 1882, *MP*.
2. Brydges to Macdonald, October 23, 1880, *MP*.
3. Norquay to Macdonald, December 2, 1880, *MP*.
4. Morris to Macdonald, December 21, 1880, *MP*.
5. Macdonald stressed this point in a letter to Stephen dated July 2, 1887: "The Dominion disallows the Provincial Acts not out of regard to the CPR, but because it thinks those acts divert our Trade into foreign channels and is injurious to Canada. Such being the case Canada would not give up the power of disallowance even at the request of the CPR." *MP*.
6. Stephen to Macdonald, September 27, 1883, *MP*.
7. Van Horne to Stephen, January 14, 1884, *CPPL*.
8. Van Horne, memorandum for Stephen, December 6, 1883, *CPPL*.
9. Van Horne to Brydges, February 23, 1884, *CPPL*.
10. Van Horne to Egan, July 6, 1883, *CPPL*.
11. Stephen to Macdonald, May 15, 1887, *MP*.
12. The telegram was published in the Winnipeg *Morning Call*, May 21, 1887. The major portion of it is quoted in Heather Gilbert, *Awakening Continent*, p. 211.
13. Stephen to C.P.R. shareholders, September 12, 1887. The complete text is printed in Gilbert, *op. cit.*, pp. 280–5.
14. Stephen to Macdonald, October 19, 1887, *MP*.
15. The name of the pass was formerly spelled "Crow's Nest" and it was so spelled in 1897 when, as we shall see, the Canadian Pacific concluded the famous Crow's Nest Pass Agreement with the government of Canada, which determined freight rates on grain. The old spelling has been retained in references to the agreement, but those to the pass itself use the modern spelling.

Chapter 12

1. C.P.R. *Report*, 1888; Van Horne's remarks at the shareholders' meeting held on May 8, 1889.
2. *Ibid*.
3. Stephen to Macdonald, January 26, 1888, *MP*.
4. Stephen to Macdonald, April 22, 1888, *MP*.
5. McIntyre to Macdonald, December 27, 1881, *MP*.
6. Like the purchase of the International, this acquisition had political overtones. The Hon. J. G. Ross was deeply involved in the affairs of the Waterloo and Magog, and on April 21, 1886, Macdonald wrote to Stephen telling him that he had received a deputation headed by Ross "to ask the Govt to intercede for him with you to take his Railway . . . Pope and I desire you to stretch a point—nay a good many points in favour of our old friend and much oblige John Henry [Pope]." *MP*.

7. Canadian Northern Railway, Arbitration Proceedings, evidence, p. 2666.
8. Van Horne, memorandum for Stephen, August 14, 1889, *MP*.
9. Stephen to Macdonald, November 18, 1888, *MP*.
10. Stephen to Macdonald, September 3, 1889, *MP*.
11. Stephen to Macdonald, August 8, 1888, *MP*.
12. Stephen to Macdonald, June 4, 1889, *MP*.
13. Stephen to Macdonald, August 14, 1889, *MP*.
14. Macdonald to Stephen, September 17, 1889, *MP*.

Chapter 13

1. C.P.R. *Report*, 1889, p. 18.
2. George Ham, *Reminiscences of a Raconteur between the '40s and the '20s*, p. 325. See also Walter Vaughan, *The Life and Work of Sir William Van Horne*, pp. 209–11.
3. Van Horne to Egan, September 13, 1883, *CPPL*.
4. When the station was first built, the main office corridor had a length of 75 feet; this expanded eventually to 1,020 feet. At first there were only three telephones in the building, and the president had no private line!
5. James Murray Gibbon, *Steel of Empire*, p. 336.
6. Stephen to Macdonald, October 21, 1890, *MP*.
7. Stephen to Macdonald, April 23, 1887, *MP*.
8. Stephen to Macdonald, February 13, 1889, *MP*.
9. Van Horne is said to have so stated. See the draft letter from Katherine Hughes to R. M. Horne-Payne, April 25, 1917. Hughes Papers, *PAC*.
10. Van Horne to Mount Stephen, November 27, 1894, *CPPL*.
11. Van Horne to Adolph Boissevain, October 6, 1895, Van Horne Papers.
12. Van Horne to Mount Stephen. Vaughan, *op. cit.*, p. 222.
13. *Ibid.*, p. 224.
14. Van Horne to Seargeant, September 9, 1883, *CPPL*.
15. Van Horne to Beatty, July 5, 1884, *CPPL*.
16. Van Horne to Egan, August 4, 1884, *CPPL*.
17. Van Horne to Shaughnessy, September 7, 1904, Van Horne Papers.
18. Van Horne to Drummond, February 21, 1891. Vaughan, *op. cit.*, p. 203.
19. Van Horne to Laurier, 1896. *Ibid.*, p. 270.
20. Van Horne to Mount Stephen, 1896. *Ibid.*

Chapter 14

1. Van Horne to Stephen, 1888. Quoted in Walter Vaughan, *The Life and Work of Sir William Van Horne*, p. 214.

2. Van Horne to Stephen, 1890. *Ibid.*, p. 221.
3. Stephen to Macdonald, October 5, 1887, *MP*.
4. Van Horne to Macdonald, May 8, 1891, *MP*.
5. Van Horne to Stephen, May 15, 1891, *MP*.
6. Van Horne to Stephen, early 1891. James Murray Gibbon, *Steel of Empire*, pp. 338–9.
7. Van Horne to Mount Stephen, June 20, 1894, *CPPL*.
8. Van Horne to A. Manuel, November 2, 1894, *CPPL*.
9. Van Horne to Mount Stephen, July 27, 1894, *CPPL*.
10. R. M. Horne-Payne, who knew Van Horne well, believed that the difficulties between Van Horne and Mount Stephen and the latter's declining confidence in the C.P.R. arose from Mount Stephen's involvement in the Great Northern. He wrote in 1917: "The impression left on my mind after a lapse of over 20 years is that Mount Stephen had drifted away from the C.P.R. into the toils of the Great Northern, in connection with which he was involved in heavy financial responsibility both personally and towards a large number of his aristocratic friends in London." Van Horne "felt that Mount Stephen and Skinner [a C.P.R. director resident in London] found it unnecessarily difficult to find money for extensions or acquiring interests if they were distasteful to the Great Northern. . . . I do not think I ever heard him say a severe word of Mount Stephen, but he impressed me as being very cruelly disappointed with him." Horne-Payne to Katherine Hughes, July 24, 1917, Hughes Papers, *PAC*.
11. Mount Stephen to Hill, 1894?. Vaughan, *op. cit.*, pp. 233–4.
12. Van Horne to Skinner, April 17, 1896, *CPPL*.
13. Lance Whittaker, *Rossland*, pp. 40–1.
14. John Fahey, *Inland Empire*, p. 181; also Whittaker, *op. cit.*, p. 55.
15. Fahey, *op. cit.*, p. 188.
16. C.P.R. *Report*, 1896.
17. Quoted in the *Report* of the Royal Commission on Transportation, 1959, vol. 1, p. 80.
18. The description of the construction of the line is derived largely from L. H. Brown's unpublished study.
19. Report of Inspector Sanders, NWMP *Report*, 1898.

Chapter 15

1. Canada, Senate, *Debates*, February 3, 1881, p. 117.
2. Stephen to Forster, February 22, 1881, *MP*.
3. Land grants from state governments added another 51 million acres to the total. As of June 30, 1933, American railroads had been given title to a total of 182, 363, 978 acres. Federal Coordinator of Transportation, *Public Aids to Transportation*, Part I, Washington, 1938, p. 29.
4. Stephen to Macdonald, May 8, 1881, *MP*.
5. Stephen to Macdonald, June 20, 1883, *MP*.
6. Macdonald to Tupper, July 25, 1883, *MP*.

7. Any account of the Canadian Pacific's land activities must lean heavily on the detailed study by J. B. Hedges, *Building the Canadian West*.
8. Winnipeg *Free Press*, January 2, 1882.
9. P. Turner Bone, *When the Steel Went Through*, p. 63.
10. *Vancouver Historical Journal*, no. 3, 1960, p. 18.
11. Van Horne to Macdonald, January 4, 1890, *MP*.
12. Hedges, *op. cit.*, p. 116.

Chapter 16

1. At the meeting of shareholders held on October 5, 1910.
2. D. C. Coleman, "Rt. Hon. Lord Shaughnessy," in *Canadian Pacific History: Four Addresses*, p. 19.
3. Oscar Skelton, *The Railway Builders*, p. 177.
4. Coleman, *loc. cit.*, p. 26.
5. But Van Horne was not a stranger to the game of solitaire. "He had a keen sense of humour," Secretan recalled, "and I remember an incident when one of his guests who pranced gaily in where 'angels fear to tread' showed him a new game of 'solitaire,' which after carefully studying he proceeded to show the gentle stranger *forty eight* varieties of the same game." Secretan, in his MS. *Reminiscences*, *PAC*.
6. C.P.R. *Report*, 1897. Van Horne spoke at the meeting of shareholders held on April 6, 1898.
7. *Prairie Settlement: The Geographical Setting*, Toronto, 1934. p. 46. (Frontiers of Settlement Series)
8. *Ibid.*, p. 57.
9. See Coleman, *loc cit.*, pp. 21–2.
10. House of Commons, *Debates*, August 18, 1903, p. 9002.
11. Actually the D.A.R. line extended only to Windsor Junction, but it had running rights over the Intercolonial (now part of the Canadian National) to Halifax.

Chapter 17

1. Van Horne to Macdonald, October 28, 1890, *MP*.
2. For a detailed history of the service from Canada to Australia, see J. H. Hamilton, "The 'All-Red' Route," pp. 1–126.
3. For a detailed history of the coast service, see N. R. Hacking and W. K. Lamb, *The 'Princess' Story*, Vancouver, 1974.
4. C.P.R. *Report*, 1902; Shaughnessy to the shareholders, October 1, 1902.
5. James Murray Gibbon, *Steel of Empire*, p. 358.
6. Shaughnessy to E. B. Osler, February 23, 1903, *CPPL*.
7. George Musk, *Canadian Pacific Afloat*, p. 8.
8. C.P.R. *Report*, 1913; Shaughnessy to the shareholders, October 1, 1913.
9. Shaughnessy to Maitland Kersey, November 30, 1914, *CPPL*.

10. Shaughnessy to the shareholders, October 1, 1913.
11. Gibbon, *op. cit.*, pp. 369–70.

Chapter 18

1. Shaughnessy to the shareholders, May 1, 1918.
2. See J. B. Hedges, *Building the Canadian West*, p. 189.
3. *Ibid.*, p. 194.
4. Quoted in Hedges, p. 226.
5. Circular issued by Osler, Hammond and Nanton, quoted by Hedges, p. 155.
6. Shaughnessy to the shareholders, October 1, 1913.
7. Shaughnessy to J. S. Dennis, April 2, 1912, *CPPL*.
8. Shaughnessy to the shareholders, October 1, 1913.
9. J. Lorne McDougall, *Canadian Pacific*, p. 145.
10. Shaughnessy to Dennis, April 3, 1914, *CPPL*.

Chapter 19

1. Shaughnessy to Egan, July 27, 1903, *CPPL*.
2. Edmond Pugsley, *The Great Kicking Horse Blunder*, p. 54.
3. Shaughnessy to H. H. Blanchet, June 16, 1913, *CPPL*.
4. C.P.R. *Report*, 1913.
5. Shaughnessy to the shareholders, October 3, 1906.
6. See C.P.R., *Factors in Railway and Steamship Operation*, pp. 13–18.
7. In the 1886 *Memorandum* on transpacific connections, Stephen noted that the C.P.R. had "invented and supplied itself with a modification of the Pullman car system, applied to emigrant carriages, by which clean and comfortable slat beds are available for the use of passengers. . . ." He believed they would also "exactly meet the requirements" for transporting troops. The first dozen cars of the type were ordered in 1883.
8. Shaughnessy to the U.S. Consul, Montreal, October 17, 1912, *CPPL*.
9. Shaughnessy to Senator Choquette, August 30, 1912, *CPPL*.
10. Shaughnessy to David McNicoll, October 21, 1913, *CPPL*.
11. Shaughnessy to E. Pennington, February 17, 1913, *CPPL*.
12. Shaughnessy to E. Flagg, April 6, 1914, *CPPL*.
13. E. S. Cox, *World Steam in the Twentieth Century*, p. 49.
14. Lavallée, "CP Bygones," *Collectors' Items*, no. 5.
15. Shaughnessy memorandum, March 30, 1912, *CPPL*.
16. In his *History of the Canadian Pacific Railway*, p. 284, Innis tabulates the price range of C.P.R. shares, year by year, from 1890 to 1921.
17. Shaughnessy to the shareholders, October 5, 1910.

Chapter 20

1. Shaughnessy to W. R. Baker, August 11, 1914, *CPPL*.
2. Shaughnessy to Dunsmuir, March 22, 1915, *CPPL*.
3. Shaughnessy to the acting minister of the interior, August 10, 1914, *CPPL*.
4. Shaughnessy to E. Pennington, president of the Soo Line, January 30, 1918, *CPPL*.
5. Shaughnessy to Borden, October 22, 1914, *CPPL*.
6. Shaughnessy to the shareholders, May 1, 1918.

Chapter 21

1. Shaughnessy to Senator J. N. Kirchoffer, August 18, 1903, *CPPL*.
2. Shaughnessy to Robert Marpole, March 9, 1912, *CPPL*.
3. Borden to Shaughnessy, May 24, 1915, Borden Papers, *PAC*.
4. Flavelle to Borden, June 18, 1915, Borden Papers, *PAC*.
5. Shaughnessy's memorandum, sent to Borden. The covering letter is dated May 16, 1916. Borden Papers, *PAC*.
6. *Grain Growers' Guide*, May 10, 1916. Quoted in J. A. Eagle's unpublished paper *Lord Shaughnessy and the Railway Policies of Sir Robert Borden, 1903–1917*.
7. Borden diary, May 17, 1916. Quoted in Eagle, *op. cit.*
8. *Report* of the Royal Commission to inquire into Railways and Transportation in Canada, 1917, p. xx.
9. *Ibid.*, p. li.
10. *Ibid.*, p. xlviii.
11. *Ibid.*, p. lii.
12. *Ibid.*, p. cii.
13. Shaughnessy's memorandum on the Canadian Northern. It was sent to Borden with a note dated June 24, 1917, but was drafted much earlier, probably before the *Report* of the Royal Commission was released in April.
14. These details, cited by Eagle, *op. cit.*, are from the Flavelle Papers at Queen's University.
15. Borden to Dafoe, July 19, 1917, Dafoe Papers, University of Manitoba.
16. The proposal was issued in pamphlet form: *The Shaughnessy Plan. A proposal for the settlement of Canada's railway problem*. Addressed to the Government April 16, 1921 by Rt. Hon. Lord Shaughnessy, K.C.V.O.
17. Beatty's statement was printed in House of Commons *Debates*, November 4, 1919, p. 1730.
18. Roger Graham, *Arthur Meighen*, vol. 1, pp. 312–13. Meighen spoke in Montreal on November 5, 1919.
19. Shaughnessy to the shareholders, May 7, 1919.

Chapter 22

1. *Report* of the Royal Commission on Transportation, 1951, p. 241.
2. Beatty to the shareholders, May 7, 1924.
3. Shaughnessy to Sir George Foster, October 29, 1913, *CPPL*.
4. Beatty to the shareholders, May 4, 1927.
5. Beatty to the shareholders, May 4, 1932.
6. C.P.R., *Factors in Railway and Steamship Operation*, pp. 14, 16.
7. Norman Thompson and J. H. Edgar, *Canadian Railroad Development from the Earliest Times*, p. 199.

Chapter 23

1. When giving evidence before the Royal Commission on Railways and Transportation, on January 5, 1932.
2. The *Report* of the Royal Commission to inquire into Railways and Transportation in Canada, 1931–32, gives a detailed analysis of the expansion of the rival transcontinental rail systems in the period 1923–31.
3. D. H. Miller-Barstow, *Beatty of the C.P.R.*, p. 73.
4. *Report* of the 1931–32 Royal Commission, pp. 19–23, reviews branch line expenditures and policies.
5. E. W. Beatty, "The Canadian Transportation Problem," 1934, p. 114–15.
6. H. D. Kalman, *The Railway Hotels and the Development of the Château Style in Canada*, p. 22.
7. Shaughnessy to H. D. Reid, June 20, 1918, *CPPL*.
8. James Murray Gibbon, *Steel of Empire*, p. 365.
9. Beatty to the shareholders, May 7, 1930.
10. J. L. McDougall, in the *Canadian Forum*, May 1925, pp. 232–3.

Chapter 24

1. *Report* of the Royal Commission to inquire into Railways and Transportation in Canada, 1931–32, p. 5.
2. *Ibid.*, p. 43.
3. *Ibid.*, p. 25.
4. *Ibid.*, p. 13.
5. *Ibid.*, p. 62.
6. Beatty to Prime Minister Bennett, October 24, 1932. Printed in full in Beatty's *Statement . . . to the Standing Committee on Railways . . . of the Senate of Canada*, November 17, 1932, pp. 13–14.
7. Beatty, *Canada's Railway Problem and Its Solution*, address to the Canadian Club of Toronto, January 16, 1933, p. 15.
8. *Ibid.*, p. 12.
9. D. H. Miller-Barstow, *Beatty of the C.P.R.*, p. 122.

10. The report of the Senate committee is printed in Beatty's address to the Canadian Club of Toronto, pp. 6–8.
11. Beatty to the shareholders, May 4, 1938.
12. Beatty to the shareholders, May 2, 1934.
13. C.P.R. *Report*, 1934.
14. James Hedges, *Building the Canadian West*, p. 389 gives full details.
15. Employment and payroll figures are from official publications of Statistics Canada, *Canadian Pacific Limited, 1923–1971* and *Canadian National Railways, 1923–1971*.
16. Beatty to the shareholders, May 4, 1938. His remarks on this occasion included a review of the physical property of the railway.
17. Lavallée, *Delorimier and Angus*, p. 13.

Chapter 25

1. C.P.R. *Report*, 1943.
2. *Canadian Pacific Facts and Figures*, 1946 ed., p. 275.
3. Quoted in C.P.R. *Report*, 1944.
4. For a full account of this remarkable salvage feat, see James Taylor, *Gold From the Sea: The Epic Story of the "Niagara's" Bullion*, London, 1943.
5. George Musk, *Canadian Pacific Afloat*, p. 61.
6. Ronald Keith, *Bush Pilot with a Briefcase*, p. 241.
7. *Ibid.*, p. 248.

Chapter 26

1. D. H. Miller-Barstow, *Beatty of the C.P.R.*, p. 176.
2. Ronald Keith, *Bush Pilot with a Briefcase*, pp. 254–7, 261–6.
3. *Ibid.*, p. 278.
4. Crump's thesis, entitled *Internal Combustion Engines in the Railroad Field*, was submitted in June 1936.
5. Mather to the shareholders, May 5, 1948.
6. See the description of the *Dominion* in the article by Tom Earle entitled "The Big Train," *Spanner*, July–August 1951, pp. 16–18. It is interesting to note that in 1937, before the advent of the Hudsons and Selkirks, nine changes in engine were made between Montreal and Vancouver, much the longest continuous run being from Winnipeg to Medicine Hat, 656.8 miles.

Chapter 27

1. Mather to the shareholders, May 3, 1950.
2. Stephen Peitchinis, *Labour-Management Relations in the Railway Industry*, p. 175.
3. *Ibid.*, p. 196.

4. Mather to the shareholders, May 3, 1950.
5. For the text of the Maintenance of Railway Operation Act (1950), see Peitchinis, *op. cit.*, pp. 337–43.
6. Mather to the shareholders, May 2, 1951.
7. "Economic Factors in Canadian History," *Canadian Historical Review*, March 1923, p. 24.
8. *Report* of the Royal Commission on Transportation, 1951, p. 288.
9. *Ibid.*, p. 292.
10. *Ibid.*, p. 288.
11. *Ibid.*, p. 289.
12. *Ibid.*, p. 284.
13. See the proceedings of the annual meeting held May 2, 1951, p. 5.
14. Quoted in H. L. Purdy, *Transport Competition and Public Policy in Canada*, p. 215.
15. *Ibid.*, p. 219.

Chapter 28

1. House of Commons, *Debates*, December 15, 1880, p. 96.
2. Shaughnessy to Osler, June 22, 1918, *CPPL*.
3. Crump to the shareholders, May 7, 1969.
4. V. C. Fowke, *Evidence* tendered before the Board of Transport Commissioners, January 5, 1953, p. 5.
5. *Ibid.*, p. 31.
6. *Report* of the Royal Commission on Transportation, 1959, vol. 2, p. 75.
7. Beatty to the shareholders, May 4, 1932.
8. Cominco Limited, *Report*, 1973.
9. C.P.R. *Report*, 1971, p. 3.

Chapter 29

1. A further step toward this end was taken in the fall of 1974, when the piggyback and rail container services were consolidated to form CP Rail Intermodal Services.
2. House of Commons, *Debates*, June 1, 1965, p. 1814.
3. *Ibid.*, p. 1815.
4. Ronald Keith, *Bush Pilot with a Briefcase*, p. 308.

Chapter 30

1. *Spanner*, July–August, 1968, p. 4.
2. C.P.R. *Report*, 1968, p. 3.
3. C.P.R. *Report*, 1959, p. 5.
4. *Report* of the Royal Commission on Transportation, 1959, vol. 1, p. 29.
5. Prime Minister L. B. Pearson to N. R. Crump and Donald Gordon (president

of the C.N.R.), June 30, 1964. Stephen Peitchinis, *Labour-Management Relations in the Railway Industry*, p. 222. For the letter sent to the prime minister by Crump and Gordon on June 22, see pp. 219–22.
6. Crump to the shareholders, May 5, 1964.
7. This was probably Crump's personal view, but it was not shared by some of the young and unsentimental C.P.R. legal staff. Hearings on the discontinuance of the *Canadian* were held in Vancouver in August 1970. In the Vancouver *Sun*, August 31, 1970, Neale Adams reported an interview with Tom Mathews, a 32-year old C.P.R. lawyer. While he agreed that the *Canadian* was a "damn good train," he continued: "Somebody has to pay for that train. If it made money we would run it, believe me. . . . Okay, we're the young sharp knives. It's a piece of stainless steel to us. If it loses money, get rid of it."
8. David Jones, interviewed in Vancouver in April 1974.
9. *Report* of the Royal Commission on Transportation, 1959, vol. 1, p. 64.
10. Half a century ago, T. A. (later Senator) Crerar expressed the opinion that still prevails today: "Rightly or wrongly the view exists in the Prairie Provinces that Eastern rates have always been governed by water competition, and that if there is not some governing maximum in the Prairies, the railways will do what they have always done, put on all the traffic will bear on this part of the Dominion." Crerar to A. K. Cameron, December 22, 1924, Cameron Papers, *PAC*.
11. *CP Rail News*, February 14, 1973.
12. For an account of some of the difficulties encountered in the winter of 1942–43, see Marc McNeil, "Men against the Storm," in *Canadian Pacific Facts and Figures*, rev. ed. 1946, pp. 91–8.
13. *CP Rail News*, February 16, 1972, describes these and other battles with record storms in the winter of 1971–72.
14. The C.P.R. and C.N.R. make free use of each other's lines through the canyon if slides occur. Occasionally both lines are blocked at the same time, but of late double stoppages have averaged no more than seven hours a year.
15. Fifteen years earlier, in December 1944, the C.P.R. had secured complete ownership of the Crowsnest Pass–Kettle Valley line by purchasing the track between Princeton and Brookmere from the Great Northern. The Kettle Valley still has a western outlet to the C.P.R. main line through Spences Bridge.

Selected Bibliography

MANUSCRIPT SOURCES

PUBLIC ARCHIVES OF CANADA

John A. Macdonald Papers.
These include an extraordinary file of some 800 personal letters from George Stephen.

Alexander Mackenzie Papers.
Originals and microfilms of additional papers at Queen's University, Kingston.

Sir Charles Tupper Papers.

Sir Wilfrid Laurier Papers.

Sir Robert Borden Papers.

Katherine Hughes Papers.
These include a draft biography of Van Horne, a project taken over later by Walter Vaughan. The papers also include material gathered for use in writing the biography.

CANADIAN PACIFIC LIMITED

Presidents' Letterbooks.
The Canadian Pacific is only beginning to take a serious interest in assembling and arranging its noncurrent records of historical interest, but apparently no letterbooks of its first president, George Stephen, are in its possession. One short letterbook consists of copies of letters written by Van Horne to Stephen after the latter took up residence in England. At one time more must have been available, as Walter Vaughan, author of the biography of Van Horne,

states that they corresponded frequently and he quotes from letters the originals or copies of which cannot now be traced. Unfortunately Vaughan never dates with any precision the letters from which he quotes.

The Van Horne letterbooks are complete from the time he joined the company at the beginning of 1882 until 1901, and the Shaughnessy series is also complete from the time he became president in 1899 until his retirement in 1918.

Inevitably the letterbooks, which consist in all of over 150,000 pages, include a high proportion of routine correspondence, but they also include a large number of informative letters of great historical interest.

The correspondence of the later presidents is not yet available for research.

Van Horne Papers

This substantial collection is in the possession of Mrs. William Van Horne, widow of Sir William's grandson, who very kindly gave me access to it. It includes three letterbooks dating back to Van Horne's service with the Southern Minnesota in 1875–79, and an incomplete set of letterbooks and letter files running from 1893 to 1915. The correspondence is essentially personal, and is concerned primarily with Van Horne's numerous interests that lay outside the Canadian Pacific, especially after 1899. References to the affairs of the railway are relatively few.

Shaughnessy Papers

These are not available, but the present Lord Shaughnessy (the 3rd Baron) lent me a number of letters and documents in his possession that were most useful, particularly with regard to the proposed unification of railway management, and Lord Shaughnessy's relations with Sir Robert Borden.

Provincial Archives of British Columbia

W. H. Holmes Papers.

Vancouver City Archives

Walter Moberly Papers.

McGill University Archives

Walter Vaughan Papers.
These include the original manuscript of his biography of Van Horne. It was slightly abridged for publication, but the uncut text gives no additional information about the Van Horne and Stephen letters from which he quotes.

Unpublished Studies

Brown, Leslie H. *West of the Pass*. A study of the Crowsnest Pass region, including coal mining activities and the construction of the Canadian Pacific's line from Lethbridge to Kootenay Lake.

Bush, Edward Forbes. *The Canadian "Fast Line" on the North Atlantic, 1886–1915*. M.A. thesis, Carleton University, Ottawa, 1969.

Crump, Norris R. *Internal Combustion Engines in the Railroad Field*. M.E. thesis, Purdue University, 1936.

Eagle, John A. *Lord Shaughnessy and the Railway Policies of Sir Robert Borden, 1903–1917*. Paper read before the Canadian Historical Association, May 1972.

Young, Brian J. *Railway Politics in Montreal, 1867–1878*. Paper read before the Canadian Historical Association, May 1972.

OFFICIAL REPORTS AND DOCUMENTS

Debates of the Senate and House of Commons of the Parliament of Canada. In addition, the reports and proceedings of Standing and Select Committees concerned with transportation matters provide much information.

Sessional Papers. Until 1925 this cumulation of departmental reports, returns to Parliament, and additional papers submitted in Parliament was published in a set of bound volumes at the end of each session.

Reports of the Department of Railways and Canals, created in 1879, and of the Department of Transport, which succeeded it in 1936.

Fleming, Sandford. *Progress Report on the Canadian Pacific Exploratory Survey*. Ottawa, 1872.

———. *Canadian Pacific Railway. A Report of Progress on the Explorations and Surveys to January 1874*. Ottawa, 1874.

———. *Reports on Surveys and Preliminary Operations of the Canadian Pacific Railway up to January 1877*. Ottawa, 1877.

———. *Reports and Documents in Reference to the Location of the Line and a Western Terminal Harbour*. Ottawa, 1878.

———. *Reports and Documents in Reference to the Canadian Pacific Railway*. Ottawa, 1880.

Report of the Royal Commissioners, Appointed by Commission . . . bearing the date the Fourteenth Day of August, 1873. Ottawa, 1873. (The commissioners appointed to investigate the Pacific Scandal.)

Report of the Canadian Pacific Railway Royal Commission. 3 vols. Ottawa, 1882.

Report of the Royal Commission to inquire into Railways and Transportation in Canada. Ottawa, 1917.

Report of the Royal Commission to inquire into Railways and Transportation in Canada, 1931–32. Ottawa, 1932.

Report of the Royal Commission on Transportation, 1948. Ottawa, 1951.

Report of the Royal Commission on Transportation, 1959. 3 vols. Ottawa, 1961–62.

Royal Commissions, especially those of later date, in addition to taking evidence received submissions, frequently of great interest. Several of them also commissioned research studies.

Canadian Northern Arbitration. Proceedings. Ottawa, 1918.
See in particular the evidence of Sir Donald Mann, D. B. Hanna, and Z. A. Lash.

Publications of the *Dominion Bureau of Statistics* and of its successor, *Statistics Canada*. The latter's Transportation and Communications Division issues a series of periodical and annual publications that give a great amount of statistical data on railway transport in Canada, including financial, operational, and traffic statistics and information on such varied subjects as accidents, equipment, tracks, fuel, and employment.

Hearings, submissions, studies, and rulings of the *Board of Railway Commissioners*, first appointed in 1903, and its successor, the *Board of Transport Commissioners*, dating from 1938.

Dorman, Robert. *A Statutory History of the Steam and Electric Railways of Canada, 1836–1937.* Ottawa, 1938.

Peitchinis, Stephen G. *Labour-Management Relations in the Railway Industry.* Ottawa, 1971.

British Columbia. Legislative Council. *Debate on the Subject of Confederation with Canada.* March 1870. Reprinted, Victoria, 1912.

BOOKS

Abdill, George B. *Pacific Slope Railroads from 1854 to 1900.* Seattle, 1959.
Appleton, Thomas E. *Ravenscrag: The Allan Royal Mail Line.* Toronto, 1974.
Berton, Pierre. *The National Dream: The Great Railway 1871–1881.* Toronto, 1970.
———. *The Last Spike: The Great Railway 1881–1885.* Toronto, 1971.
Bone, P. Turner. *When the Steel Went Through: Reminiscences of a Railroad Pioneer.* Toronto, 1947.
Borden, Henry, ed. *Robert Laird Borden: His Memoirs.* Toronto, 1938.
Bowen, Frank C. *History of the Canadian Pacific Line.* London, 1928.
Bowesfield, Hartwell, ed. *The James Wickes Taylor Correspondence, 1859–1870.* Publications, Manitoba Record Society. Winnipeg, 1968.
Boyd, John. *Sir George Etienne Cartier, Bart.: His Life and Times.* Toronto, 1914.
Brown, Robert Craig, and Cook, Ramsay. *Canada 1896–1921: A Nation Transformed.* Canadian Centenary Series. Toronto, 1974.
Burpee, Lawrence J. *Sandford Fleming, Empire Builder.* London, 1915.
Cartwright, Sir Richard. *Reminiscences.* Toronto, 1912.
Chodos, Robert. *The CPR: A Century of Corporate Welfare.* Toronto, 1973.
Cox, E. S. *World Steam in the Twentieth Century.* London, 1969.
Creighton, Donald. *John A. Macdonald: The Young Politician.* Toronto, 1952.
———. *John A. Macdonald: The Old Chieftain.* Toronto, 1955.
Currie, A. W. *Economics of Canadian Transportation.* Toronto, 1954.
———. *The Grand Trunk Railway of Canada.* Toronto, 1957.

SELECTED BIBLIOGRAPHY

De Celles, A. D. *Sir George Etienne Cartier.* Toronto, 1910.
Denison, Merrill. *Canada's First Bank: A History of the Bank of Montreal.* Toronto, 1966–67.
Dorin, Patrick. *Canadian Pacific Railway: Motive Power. Rolling Stock. Capsule History.* Seattle, 1974.
Fahey, John. *Inland Empire: D. C. Corbin and Spokane.* Seattle, 1965.
Fournier, Leslie T. *Railway Nationalization in Canada: The Problem of the Canadian National Railways.* Toronto, 1935.
Gibbon, James Murray. *Steel of Empire: The Romantic History of the Canadian Pacific, the Northwest Passage of Today.* Toronto, 1935.
Gilbert, Heather. *Awakening Continent: The Life of Lord Mount Stephen.* Vol. 1, 1829–91. Aberdeen, 1965. [All published.]
Glazebrook, G. P. de T. *A History of Transportation in Canada.* Carleton Library ed. Toronto, 1967.
Gluck, Alvin C., Jr. *Minnesota and the Manifest Destiny of the Canadian Northwest.* Toronto, 1965.
Goodrich, Carter. *Government Promotion of American Canals and Railroads 1800–1890.* New York, 1960.
Graham, Roger. *Arthur Meighen. Vol. 1. The Door of Opportunity.* Toronto, 1960.
Grant, George Munro. *Ocean to Ocean: Sandford Fleming's Expedition through Canada in 1872.* Toronto, 1873. Facsimile ed. of revised and enlarged ed., Rutland, Vermont, 1967.
Grodinsky, Julius. *Transcontinental Railway Strategy, 1869–1893.* Philadelphia, 1962.
Hacking, Norman R., and Lamb, W. Kaye, *The Princess Story: A Century and a Half of West Coast Shipping.* Vancouver, 1975.
Ham, George H. *Reminiscences of a Raconteur between the '40s and the '20s.* Toronto, 1921.
Hanna, David B. *Trains of Recollection.* Toronto, 1924.
Harkin, W. A., ed. *Political Reminiscences of the Right Honourable Sir Charles Tupper, Bart.* London, 1914.
Hedges, James B. *Building the Canadian West: The Land and Colonization Policies of the Canadian Pacific Railway.* New York, 1939.
———. *The Federal Railway Land Subsidy Policy of Canada.* Cambridge, Mass., 1934.
Holbrook, Stewart H. *The Story of American Railroads.* New York, 1947.
Howay, F. W.; Sage, W. N.; and Angus, H. F. *British Columbia and the United States.* Relations of Canada and the United States Series. New Haven and Toronto, 1942.
Innis, Harold A. *A History of the Canadian Pacific Railway.* Toronto, 1923. Facsimile reprint with foreword by Peter George, Toronto, 1970.
———. *Settlement and the Mining Frontier.* Frontiers of Settlement Series. Toronto, 1936.
Irwin, Leonard B. *Pacific Railways and Nationalism in the Canadian-American Northwest, 1845–1873.* New York, 1968.
Keith, Ronald A. *Bush Pilot with a Briefcase: The Happy-go-lucky Story of Grant McConachie.* Toronto, 1972.

Larson, Henrietta M. *Jay Cooke, Private Banker.* Reprint ed. New York, 1968.
Lavallée, Omer. *Narrow Gauge Railways of Canada.* Montreal, 1972.
———. *Van Horne's Road.* Montreal, 1975.
Legget, Robert F. *Railroads of Canada.* Vancouver, 1973.
Lovett, H. A. *Canada and the Grand Trunk, 1829–1924.* Montreal, 1924.
MacBeth, R. G. *The Romance of the Canadian Pacific Railway.* Toronto, 1924.
McDougall, J. Lorne. *Canadian Pacific: A Brief History.* Montreal, 1968.
MacEwan, Grant. *Harvest of Bread.* Saskatoon, 1969.
MacGibbon, D. A. *The Canadian Grain Trade.* Toronto, 1932.
———. *Railway Rates and the Canadian Railway Commission.* Boston and New York, 1917.
Mackintosh, W. A. *Prairie Settlement: The Geographical Setting.* Frontiers of Settlement Series. Toronto, 1934.
Macnaughton, John. *Lord Strathcona.* Makers of Canada, Anniversary Edition. Toronto, 1926.
Manion, R. J. *Life is an Adventure.* Toronto, 1936.
Marsh, D'Arcy. *The Tragedy of Henry Thornton.* Toronto, 1935.
Mika, Nick and Helma. *Railways of Canada: A Pictorial History.* Toronto, 1972.
Miller-Barstow, D. H. *Beatty of the C.P.R.* Toronto, 1951.
Moir, George T. *Saints and Sinners: A True Story of . . . the Farthest West . . . Being the Dramatic Story of the Rivalry of the Canadian Pacific and the Great Northern Railways.* Victoria, 1947.
Morris, Keith. *The Story of the Canadian Pacific Railway.* London, 1920.
Myers, Gustavus. *A History of Canadian Wealth.* First Canadian edition, with introduction by Stanley Ryerson. Toronto, 1972.
Oberholtzer, Ellis P. *Jay Cooke, Financier of the Civil War.* Philadelphia, 1907.
Pierson, J. L. *Sir William Van Horne en de Canadian Pacific Spoorweg.* 3rd edition. Amersfoort, 1929.
Pope, Sir Joseph, ed. *Correspondence of Sir John Macdonald.* Toronto, 1921.
———. *Memoirs of the Rt. Hon. Sir John A. Macdonald.* Toronto, 1895.
Pope, Maurice, ed. *Public Servant: The Memoirs of Sir Joseph Pope.* Toronto, 1960.
Preston, W. T. R. *Life and Times of Lord Strathcona.* London, 1914.
Pugsley, Edmond E. *The Great Kicking Horse Blunder.* Vancouver, 1973.
Purdy, H. L. *Transport Competition and Public Policy in Canada.* Vancouver, 1972.
Pyle, Joseph P. *The Life of James J. Hill.* Garden City, 1917.
Roberts, Morley. *The Western Avernus, or Toil and Travel in Further North America.* London, 1896.
Saunders, E. M., ed. *The Life and Letters of the Rt. Hon. Sir Charles Tupper, Bart.* London, 1916.
Schull, Joseph. *Laurier: The First Canadian.* Toronto, 1965.
Secretan, J. H. E. *Canada's Great Highway: From the First Stake to the Last Spike.* London, 1924.
Shaw, Charles Aeneas. *Tales of a Pioneer Surveyor.* Toronto, 1970.
Skelton, Oscar D. *Life and Letters of Sir Wilfrid Laurier.* Toronto, 1921.
———. *The Railway Builders.* Chronicles of Canada Series. Toronto, 1916.

Smalley, E .V. *History of the Northern Pacific Railroad.* New York, 1883.
Stevens, G. R. *Canadian National Railways. Vol. 1. Sixty Years of Trial and Error (1826–1896).* Toronto, 1960.
———. *Canadian National Railways. Vol. 2 Towards the Inevitable (1896–1922).* Toronto, 1962.
———. *History of the Canadian National Railways.* Railroads of America Series. New York, 1973.
Stevens, John F. *An Engineer's Recollections.* New York, 1936.
Stover, John F. *The Life and Decline of the American Railroad.* New York, 1970.
Talbot, Frederick A. *The Making of a Great Canadian Railway: The Story of the . . . Grand Trunk Pacific Railway,* Toronto, 1912.
Thompson, Norman, and Edgar, J. H. *Canadian Railroad Development from the Earliest Times.* Toronto, 1933.
Thomson, Dale C. *Alexander Mackenzie, Clear Grit.* Toronto, 1960.
Thomson, Leslie R. *The Canadian Railway Problem.* Toronto, 1938.
Trout, J. M. and Trout, Edward. *The Railways of Canada for 1870–1, Shewing the Progress, Mileage, Cost of Construction, etc.* Toronto, 1871. Facsimile reprint, Toronto, 1970.
Tupper, Sir Charles. *Recollections of Sixty Years in Canada.* London, 1914.
Turner, Robert D. *Vancouver Island Railroads.* San Marino, 1973.
Underhill, F. H. and de Kiewiet, C. W., eds. *Dufferin-Carnarvon Correspondence 1874–1878.* Publications of the Champlain Society. Toronto, 1955.
Vaughan, Walter. *The Life and Work of Sir William Van Horne.* New York, 1920.
Waite, Peter B. *Canada 1874–1896: Arduous Destiny.* Canadian Centenary Series. Toronto, 1971.
Wassermann, Charles. *CPR—Das Weltreich des Bibers.* n.p., n.d.
Watkin, Sir E. W. *Canada and the States: Recollections, 1851–86.* London, 1887.
Wheeler, A. O. *The Selkirk Range.* Ottawa, 1905.
Wilgus, William J. *The Railway Interrelations of the United States and Canada.* Relations of Canada and the United States Series. New Haven and Toronto, 1937.
Willison, J. S. *Reminiscences, Political and Personal.* Toronto, 1919.
Willson, Henry Beckles. *Life of Lord Strathcona and Mount Royal.* London, 1915.
Woodworth, Marguerite. *History of the Dominion Atlantic Railway.* Kentville, N.S., 1936.

PAMPHLETS AND ARTICLES

An Account of the Working and Results of the Canadian Railway Company's Experimental Farms. The Wise Policy of Selecting the Southern Route for the C.P.R. endorsed by Facts. Winnipeg, 1884.
Beatty, E. W. "The Canadian Transportation Problem." *Papers and Proceedings of the Canadian Political Science Association,* Sixth Annual Meeting, Montreal, 1934.

Bladen, M. L. "Construction of Railways in Canada to the Year 1885." *Contributions to Canadian Economics*, V (1932).
———. "Construction of Railways in Canada. Part II. From 1885 to 1931." *Contributions to Canadian Economics*, VII (1943).
Coleman, D'Alton C. *Lord Mount Stephen (1829–1921) and the Canadian Pacific Railway*. Address to the Newcomen Society of England, American Branch. New York, 1945.
Engineering, London. Series of articles on the Canadian Pacific Railway, March 21 to September 19, 1884.
Fair, L. M. *The Transportation of Canadian Wheat to the Sea*. McGill University Economic Studies. Toronto, 1925.
Fleming, Sandford. *Practical Observations on the Construction of a Continuous Line of Railway from Canada to the Pacific Ocean on British Territory*. (Appendix to H. H. Youle, *A Sketch of an Overland Route to British Columbia*.) Toronto, 1862.
George, Peter J. "Rates of Return in Railway Investment and Implications for Government Subsidization of the Canadian Pacific Railway: Some Preliminary Results." *Canadian Journal of Economics*, I (1968).
Gilbert, Heather. "The Unaccountable Fifth: Solution of a Great Northern Enigma." *Minnesota History*, XLII (1971).
Greenberg, Delores. "A Study of Capital Alliances: The St. Paul and Pacific." *Canadian Historical Review*, LVII (1976).
Hamilton, J. H. "The 'All-Red Route' 1893–1953. A History of the Trans-Pacific Mail Service between British Columbia, Australia and New Zealand." *British Columbia Historical Quarterly*, XX (1956).
Kalman, Harold D. *The Railway Hotels and the Development of the Château Style in Canada*. University of Victoria Studies in Architectural History. Victoria, 1968.
Keefer, Thomas C. "The Canadian Pacific Railway." *Transactions*, American Society of Civil Engineers, no. 394, August 1888.
Lamb, W. Kaye. "The Pioneer Days of the Trans-Pacific Service, 1887–1891." *British Columbia Historical Quarterly*, I (1937).
———. "Empress to the Orient." *Ibid.*, IV (1940).
———. "Empress Odyssey." *Ibid.*, XII (1948).
Lavallée, Omer. *Delorimier and Angus. The Story in Pictures, Diagrams and Text of More Than Sixty Years of Steam Locomotive Building by the Canadian Pacific Railway Company*. 3rd edition. Montreal, 1963.
———. *Locomotives of the Canadian Pacific Railway*. Railway and Locomotive Historical Society, *Bulletin*, no. 83. Boston, 1951.
McDougall, J. Lorne. "The Relative Level of Crow's Nest Pass Grain Rates in 1899 and 1965." *Canadian Journal of Economics and Political Science*, XXXII (1966).
Mackintosh, W. A. "Economic Factors in Canadian History." *Canadian Historical Review*, IV (1923).
Martin, Chester. "Our 'Kingdom for a Horse': The Railway Land Grant System in Western Canada." *Report*, Canadian Historical Association, 1934.
Masters, D. C. "Financing the C.P.R., 1880–5." *Canadian Historical Review*, XXIV (1943).

Millar, J. S. *Canadian Pacific Railway. Correspondence and Papers shewing the Efforts the Company has made to secure Portland for its Winter Port.* n.p., 1884.
Osler, E. B. *Grand Trunk Railway versus the Canadian Pacific Monopoly.* n.p., 1884.
Ramsay, G. G. "Over the Rocky Mountains by the Canadian Pacific Line in 1884." *Macmillan's Magazine,* December 1884.
Reid, Robie L. "Alfred Waddington." *Transactions,* Royal Society of Canada, Section II, 1932.
Robinson, Noel. *Blazing the Trail Through the Rockies: The Story of Walter Moberly.* Vancouver, 1913.
Roe, F. G. "An Unsolved Problem of Canadian History." *Report,* Canadian Historical Association, 1936. (On reasons for the shift of the C.P.R. to a southern route; see comment by Harold Innis, *Canadian Historical Review,* XVIII [1937] pp. 87–9.)
Turnbull, Elsie G. *Topping's Trail.* Vancouver, 1964.
Waddington, Alfred. *Sketch of Proposed Railroad Line Overland through British North America.* Ottawa, 1871.
Whittaker, Lance H. *Rossland: The Golden City.* Rossland, 1949.
Youle, Henry Hind. *A Sketch of an Overland Route to British Columbia.* Toronto, 1962.

SOME PUBLICATIONS OF THE CANADIAN PACIFIC

Annual Reports

Two preliminary reports were issued, each entitled *Official Memorandum respecting the Position and Prospects of the Canadian Pacific Railway.* The first was dated November 21, 1881, the second December 12, 1882. Both were signed by George Stephen.

The first *Report,* so titled, was for the year ending December 31, 1883. For a dozen years and more the annual report also included some account of the proceedings of the company's annual meeting. Beginning with the sixteenth annual meeting (April 7, 1897), the proceedings were printed separately.

Staff Publications

Much interesting and useful information, some of which supplements the annual reports, appears in bulletins that have been issued over the years for the information of the railway's staff. The succession begins with the *Canadian Pacific Staff Bulletin,* which first appeared in 1934. In October 1947 it was succeeded by *Spanner,* which in turn gave way in September 1971 to *CP Rail News.*

Beatty, Sir Edward. *Statement . . . to the Standing Committee on Railways, Telegraphs and Harbours of the Senate of Canada, on Bill A, to Provide for Co-*

operation between the Canadian National Railway Company and the Canadian Pacific Railway Company. November 17, 1932.

———. *Canada's Railway Problem and Its Solution.* An address before the Canadian Club of Toronto, January 16, 1933. Montreal, 1933.

The first of some fifteen addresses delivered by Beatty in most of the major cities of Canada in the years 1933-38 in an effort to gain support for railway unification. They were printed in pamphlet form and widely distributed.

———. *Submission to the Senate of Canada Special Committee appointed to inquire into and report upon the best means of relieving the country from its extremely serious railway condition and financial burden consequent thereto.* Montreal, 1938.

Bonar, James C., comp. *The Canadian Pacific Railway Company.* Montreal [1951?].

Historical notes and a very useful chronology. Set in type but not published.

Canadian Pacific Foundation Library. *Canadian Pacific Facts and Figures.* Montreal, 1937. Revised and enlarged edition, Montreal, 1946.

———. *Factors in Railway and Steamship Operation.* Montreal, 1937.

Canadian Pacific History: Four Addresses delivered before the Canadian Pacific Officers' Luncheon Club, Montreal, during the 1935–36 Season. Montreal, 1936.

Of special interest are the addresses on Van Horne by George Hodge and on Lord Shaughnessy by D. C. Coleman.

Musk, George. *Canadian Pacific Afloat, 1883–1968. A Short History and Fleet List.* Revised edition. London, 1968.

Shaughnessy, 1st Baron. *The Shaughnessy Plan. A Proposal for the Settlement of Canada's Railway Problem.* Addressed to the Government April 16, 1921. Montreal, 1921.

Smith, J. Harry. *The Canadian Pacific. A National Institution, 1885–1935.* Montreal, 1935.

[Stephen, George.] *Memorandum. The Trans-Pacific Connections of the Canadian Pacific Railway.* Private. February 1886.

For many years railway companies with federal charters were required to submit annually to the secretary of state of Canada a return "showing the conditions of the Capital and Revenue Account, &., &." A large collection of these reports, most of them now very rare, is in the Public Archives of Canada. They include reports from many of the early C.P.R. subsidiaries, such as the Credit Valley and the Ontario and Quebec.

Index

Abbott, J. J. C., 28, 34, 72–73, 77, 178
Accident record, C.P.R., 117–119, 432
Ackworth, W. M., 294–295
Admiral Scheer, 354–355
Adolph Boissevain and Company, 93
Air brakes, 180
Air Canada, 411. *See also* Trans-Canada Airlines
Air-conditioned cars, C. P. R., 342
Aircraft rights, C.P.R., 388
Air Transport Board, 364
Alaska, 190, 241, 358
Albany, N.Y., 2
Alberta (province), 228; C.P.R. irrigation project, 252–254, 255, 339; oil industry, 388
Alberta, 106
Alberta Railway and Coal Company, 253
Alberta Railway and Irrigation Co., 257, 259
Aldridge, Walter H., 207, 259
Algoma, 106, 239
Allan, Henry, 245
Allan, Sir Hugh, 20, 24, 35, 51; and Cartier, 29–30; gathers Canadians to his project, 27; and Northern Colonization Railway, 21–22; position on trans-Canada railway, 30–31; quoted, 23, 29–30; role in "Pacific Scandal," 30–35; and trans-Canada railway contract, 25–26; vs. Macpherson and Interoceanic Railway Co., 30
Allan Line liners, 240, 246, 247–249, 301, 325, 338
Alsatian, 338
Americans, influex of to C.P.R., 83–85

Amsterdam money market: and the St. Paul and Pacific, 59, 60–61; and C.P.R., 93
Anderson, Anderson and Company, 149–150, 240
Angus, Henry F., quoted, 384–385
Angus, R. B., 61, 62, 77, 79, 107, 108, 113, 182; and C.P.R. "syndicate," 71–72; death of, 299; and St. Paul, Minneapolis and Manitoba, 196
Angus shops (Montreal), 272–273, 281, 307–308, 342; in Second World War, 354
Arbutus Village (Vancouver), 395
Archibald, Hon. Adams G., 19
Architecture, C.P.R. buildings, and Van Horne, 180–183
Argentine, air services to, 365
Athabasca, 106
Athenian, 242
Atlantic and North-West Railway, 97, 98, 99, 101, 168–169, 171–172
Atlantic Express, 143
Australia: air service to, 364; C.P.R. and ship service to, 241
Austria, C.P.R. and, 250

Baker, Colonel James, 198–200, 211
Baldwin Locomotive Works, 50, 270
Ballast, rock, 308–309, 372
Banff, 143, 273
Banff Springs Hotel, 182, 320
Bankhead mine, 258, 259
Bank of Montreal, 58, 61, 63, 89, 110–111, 128; C.P.R. borrows from, 1882, 91

Baring Brothers, 71, 132, 163
"Battle of Fort Whyte," 164
Beatty, Edward Wentworth (later Sir Edward), 291, 326, 327; and air service, 357–358; becomes C.P.R. president, 298–300; on Canadian National policy, 316–317; and C.P.N. shipping lines, 323; and C.P.R. branch building program, 313–316; and C.P.R. shipping services, 300–301, 361; and *Empress of Britain*, 325; and freight rates, 302–304, 306; on immigration, 315–316; quoted, 311; retirement and death, 346; and rolling stock, 307–308; and unification of C.P.R. and Canadian Northern, 329; and unification of C.P.R. with C.N.R., 330–332
Beatty, Henry, 105–106
Beatty Line. See North-West Transportation Company
Beaty, James, 23, 24
Beaverford, 354–355
Beaver Line service, 245
Beaver-type freighters, 361, 401, 404–405
Begg, Alexander, 218
Bellingham Bay and British Columbia Railway, 197
Bender, E. N., quoted, 84
Bennett, R. B., 327
"Big Hill," 117–119, 263
Blackfoot Indians, 87–88
Blackwell, Charles, 145
Blair, A. G., 209–232
Blake, Edward (Liberal leader), 15, 17, 39, 42, 49, 75, 132, 139, 154, 155 387; and Alexander Mackenzie, 46–48; and Confederation, 16
Blaylock, S. G., 397
Board of Railway Commissioners, 282, 284, 304, 305, 306, 333
Board of Transport Commissioners, 360, 377, 378–380, 385, 417
Bonds, C.P.R.: first-mortgage issued, 128–132; first-mortgage retired, 276; land grant, 163, 217–218, 251–252, 256
Bonfield, 19
Bootlegging, 88
Borden, Sir Robert L., 232, 281, 289–290, 291–297
Bowen, H. B., 319, 343
Bow River, 253
Branch lines, C.N.R., 313–314
Branch lines, C.P.R., 162, 311–312, 313; added, 1899–1913, 233–236, 237; building policy, 288; construction costs compared with CN.R., 314; construction financing, 158, 256; problems of building, 155; unremunerative, subsidized, 425

"Bridge subsidy," 384
British Columbia, 25, 46, 65; controversy over delay in railway construction, 44–45; floods (1894), 188; Great Northern in, 236–238; politics and projected trans-Canada railroad, 13–17; reaction to Burrard Inlet decision, 52–53; shipping, C.P.R., 241–244. See also Mining
British Columbia Coast Service, C.P.R., 243
British Columbia Southern Railway, 208, 210–211
British Columbia Steamer Service, C.P.R.–C.N.R. rivalry, 322–323
British Commonwealth Air Training Plan, 358
British North America Act, 8
Broad-guage lines, 96
Brotherhood of Locomotive Engineers, strike of 1883, 104–105
Brown, Francis R. F., 146–147
Brown, George (editor of the Toronto *Globe*), 5, 15, 27
Brydges, C. J., 12–13, 27, 28, 155–156
Budd Company, 374
Bulk carrier ships, C. P., 406–407
Bulwer-Lytton, Sir Edward, 5–6
Burbridge, Frederick S., 428, 436
Burlington Northern Railroad, 431
Burlington *Zephyrs*, 342, 366, 367
Burrard Inlet, 52, 64, 65. See also Port Moody
Bute Inlet, 18–19, 65
Bytown and Prescott Railway, 134

Cabin-class liners, 249, 301
Calgarian, 286
Calgary, 254, 258
Calgary and Edmonton Railway, 177, 234, 256, 257
Callander-Thunder Bay Line: as Eastern terminus, 77–78; slow construction on, 91. See also Bonfield
Campbell, Sir Alexander, 214
Campbellford, Lake Ontario and Western Railway, 234–235
Canada: Dominion of, created, 8–9; emigration from, 5; population distribution in 1881, 94
Canada, unification of. See Confederation
Canada Central Railway, 21–22, 46, 51, 67, 74, 95–96; acquisition by C.P.R., 77–78; reconstruction of, 139
Canada Northwest Land Company, 92, 217, 219–220
Canada Pacific Railway Company, 30–33
Canadian Southern Railroad, 97, 166

INDEX 479

Canadian, 374–375, 422
Canadian Airways Limited, 356
Canadian Australasian Line Limited, 338
Canadian-Australian Line, 241
"Canadianisation": and CP, 435; and C.P.R., 186
Canadian National-Canadian Pacific Railway Act, 332
Canadian National Railways (C.N.R.), 297, 310, 319, 320; branch line costs, 314; C.P.R. rivalry, 311, 312, 326–327; government support for, 311; passenger service, 422, 424; and Royal Commission (1932), 328–330
Canadian Northern Railway, 191, 229, 230–231, 234, 236, 285, 288–295, 310; attempted purchase by C.P.R., 295–297; becomes part of C.N.R., 297; and transcontinental line, 231–233; and unification, 329–332
Canadian Pacific Air Lines Limited, 356, 357–359, 363–365, 410–413; and trans-Pacific air service, 364–365. *See also* CP Air
Canadian Pacific Air Services Department, 358
Canadian Pacific (Bermuda) Limited, 406, 415
Canadian Pacific Hotels Limited, 389, 392–393
Canadian Pacific Investments Limited, 399, 400, 429; C.P.R. organizes, 389–392; expansion, 392; holdings, 392–399, 400
Canadian Pacific Irrigation Colonization Company, 254, 256–258
Canadian Pacific Limited (CP), new name for C.P.R. (1971), 400
Canadian Pacific Navigation Company (C.P.N.), 196, 241, 242, 243
Canadian Pacific Ocean Services. *See* Canadian Pacific Steamships Limited
Canadian Pacific Oil and Gas Limited, 389, 392. *See also* Pan-Canadian Petroleum Limited
Canadian Pacific Railway, Allan's proposal for described by Jay Cooke, 26–27
Canadian Pacific Railway (1881–), capital increased, 92; contract summarized, 72–75; incorporation approved, 76; renamed, 400
Canadian Pacific Railway Act of 1874, 43–44
Canadian Pacific Railway Company (1873), 33–35
Canadian Pacific Securities Limited, 399
Canadian Pacific Steamships Limited, 301
Canadian Pacific Transport Limited, 382

Canadian Smelting Works, 207
Canadian Transport Commission, 421, 422–425. *See also* Board of Transport Commissioners
Canadian Wheat Board, 427
Canals, 2–3
CanPac Leasing Limited, 400
CanPac Minerals Limited, 398
CanPac Waste Disposal Systems Limited, 400
Capital expenditures, C.P.R.–C.N. compared (1923–1931), 320
Cariboo, 18
Carnarvon, Lord, 45
"Carnarvon Terms," 45, 46, 48
Carp, Johan, 59, 60
Carrall, W. W., 13
Cartier, Sir George Etienne, 13, 14, 16, 17; and "Pacific Scandal," 29–33; quoted, 19
Cartwright, Richard, 39
Cass, General G. W., 23, 26
Central-Del Rio Oil Limited, 392
Centralized train control, 432
Central Vermont Railroad, 11
Champion No. 2 (side-wheeler), 106
Charter of C.P.R. amended, 387–388
Château Champlain, 393
Château Frontenac, 182–183, 188, 273, 274, 320, 393
Château Frontenac Company, 182
Château Halifax, 393
Château Lake Louise, 320
Chicago, 3, 6, 97, 235
Chicago Award, 286
Chile, air service to, 365
China, air service to, 364
Chinese laborers, 122
Clan Grant, 134
Climate. *See* Weather conditions
Coal, 398–399; in Crowsnest region, 210
Coal mines, C.P.R., 258–259
Coal-mining. *See* Mining
Cochrane, Francis, 289, 291
Coleman, D'Alton C., 225, 226, 346, 363
Colonization. *See* Immigration
Columbia and Kootenay Navigation Company, 208
Columbia and Kootenay Railway, 200, 222
Columbia and Red Mountain Railway, 206
Columbia and Western Railway, 206, 213, 222
Cominco Limited, 396. *See also* Consolidated Mining and Smelting Company
Competition, C.P.R. and, from other forms of transportation, 361
"Compulsory cooperation," C.P.R. and C.N.R., 331, 332–333
Computer age, and C.P.R., 415

Confederation, 8, 13–17, 19
Connaught Tunnel, 265–266, 434
Conservative Party, 15–16, 71–72, 107, 109, 192, 230, 232, 329; and C.P.R. relief bill, 111–112; C.P.R. support of (1891), 192; and 1885 crisis, 130; majority (1882), 90–93; and "Pacific Scandal," 30–35; and Thornton, 327; trans-Canada railway identified with, 17
Consolidated Mining and Smelting Company, 207, 259–260, 388, 389, 396–399; dividends, 338. See also Cominco Limited
Construction, C.P.R.: branch lines, financing, 158; costs of improvements, 138–139, 140; Columbia and Western line, 213; Crowsnest line, 211–213; lines contracted to Onderdonk, 122–123; main line, 77–80, 82, 85–87, 88, 89–91, 96, 104–105, 108, 116–118, 119–121, 123, 134, 138–139; Monashee Mountains tunnel, 213; Nipissing line, 105, 113–115; Ontario and Quebec line, 101–102; problems in Selkirk Range, 119–120; problems on Selkirk-Fort William line, 50; Yale-Kamloops line, 121–122.
Construction, of trans-Canada railway, 43–44, 51–52
Containers, as basis of intermodal transport system, C.P.R., 405–406, 415
Container ships, C.P., 404–406
Contract with government, fulfilled by C.P.R., 136
Cooke, Henry, quoted, 22
Cooke, Jay, 12, 20; Canadian dealings, 23; quoted, 24–25, 26–27. See also Jay Cooke and Company
Corbin, D. C., 200, 206, 207–208, 237
Countess of Dufferin, 50
Couplers, automatic, 180
Cox, E. X., quoted, 270
CP Air, 412, 416. See also Canadian Pacific Air Lines
CP Limited, 416. See also Canadian Pacific Limited
CP Rail, 416
CP Ships, 416. See also Shipping, C.P.R.
CP Trucks, 416. See also Trucking
Craigellachie, 134, 135
Credit Valley Railway, 95, 98, 99, 101, 102
Crow's Nest and Kootenay Lake Railway, 200
Crows Nest Industries, 398
Crowsnest Pass, 177, 201; coal deposits in, 198
Crow's Nest Pass Agreement, 193, 209–210, 285–286, 350, 383, 417–418, 425–426; rates made law (1905), 304, 306; reinstated, 303–304; suspended, 286
Crow's Nest Pass Coal Company, 236, 398. See also Kootenay Coal Company
Crowsnest Pass line, 211–213, 263–265, 435
Cruises, CP ships, 302, 402–404
Crump, Norris ("Buck"), 399–400; becomes C.P.R. president, 375; and competition, 428; contributions to C.P.R., 435–436; and C.P.R. passenger services, 373–374, 421; and diesel-electric locomotives, 366–368, 369–370; and diversification, 387, 389–390; and modernization of C.P.R., 414–415; retires as chairman, 434; support of CP Air Lines, 411
Cunard Line, 363, 401–402

Dawson Route, 10
Debenture stock, C.P.R., 276, 281–282
de Cosmos, Amor, 44
Dennis, J. S., Jr., 253
Department of Natural Resources, C.P.R., 256–258, 261
Depression: (1885–1896), 219–224; (1921–1922), 300, 309; (1930s), 311, 313, 326–327, 329, 333–343
de Reinach, Baron J., 112
Detroit, 3, 97
Diamond, R. W., 397
Dickins, C. H. ("Punch"), 357–358, 359
Digby–Saint John steamer service, 235
Dining cars, C.P.R., 142, 425
Diversification, C.P.R., 387–400
Dividends, C.P.R., 276–277, 285, 333–334, 352–353, 361
Dodwell, G. E., 151–152
Dome cars, 374
Dominion, 374–375, 422
Dominion Atlantic Railway, 235
Dominion Express Company, 141–142
Dominion Line, 240, 248
Double-track line, C.P.R., 262, 264–265
Draper, W. H., quoted, 5
Drayton, Sir Henry, 282, 294–295
Drexel, Morgan and Company, 93
Drinkwater, Charles, 77
Duchess liners, C.P.R., 325, 361–362
Duck Lake, 130
Duff, Lyman P., 328
Dufferin, Lady, 49–50
Dufferin, Lord, 48–50; quoted, 44
Duluth and Winnipeg Railway, 177, 202–204
Duluth, South Shore and Atlantic Railway, 167–168, 188, 202, 334, 414
Dunmore-Lethbridge line, 164

INDEX

Dunning, C. A., 327
Dunsmuir, James, 235
Dunsmuir, Robert, 235
Dutch investors. See Amsterdam money market

Eagle Pass line, 123, 134. See also Kicking Horse Pass Route
Earnings picture, C.P.R.: (1883–1884), 107; (1887–1889), 137; (1888–1892), 183–184; (1893), 186; (1894–1895), 188–189; (1896–1899), 189–190; (1902–1913), 274; (1912–1916), 280; (1916–1919), 285; (1918–1922), 300; (1923–1924), 309; (1924–1931), 326; (1932–1938), 333; (1938–1945), 348*t*; (1943–1944), 352; (1945–1949), 360–361; (1953–1955), 386
"Earnings requirement" formula of Board of Transport Commissioners, 385–386
Eastern network, C.P.R., 96–98, 101; financing independent lines, 98, 100, 103; need for, 94–95; profitability of, 103
Edgar, J. D., 44–45
Egan, John, 83, 104, 135
Elder Dempster Company, 245
Elections, 15, 30–31, 32, 53, 90. See also "Pacific Scandal"
Electrification of mountain lines, proposed by C.P.R., 266, 434
Elizabeth II (Queen of England), 345
Emerson, Robert A., 435
Employees, C.P.R.: 340, 350, 376, 417*t*. See also Job security; Laborers; Strikes; Unions; Wages
Employment program, Depression, of government, 341
Empress air service, 364
Empress Hotel (Victoria), 273–274, 393
Empress liners, 239–240, 247, 249; introduced, 152–154; Pacific, profit, 188; transatlantic, 246, 301–302, 362, 363, 401–404
Empress of Asia, 286
Empress of Australia, 301, 323
Empress of Britain, 287, 337, 346, 354
Empress of Britain (II), 325
Empress of China, 248
Empress of France, 325
Empress of India, 153–154, 286
Empress of Ireland, 250
Empress of Japan, 356
Empress of Russia, 286–287
Empress of Scotland. See *Empress of Japan*
Erie Canal, 2–3
Esquimalt, 44, 52, 65
Esquimalt and Nanaimo Railway, 235, 257–258, 369, 396

Europe, CP air services to, 365
Expo Limited, 422
Export trade, Canadian, Second World War, 346
Express service, C.P.R., 141–142

Farley, Jesse P., 59, 62
Farmers, 229–231
Farmers' cooperatives, 230
Farmers' Protective Union, 159
"Fertile Belt," 29
Fertilizers, 397–398
Financing, Canadian Northern, 289
Financing, C.P.R., 88–93, 125, 127–129, 162–163, 183–186, 216–218, 222, 275–278, 333–334; of Crowsnest Pass line, 209; in 1883, 107–108; government assistance for (1885), 129–132; by government loan, 109–111; of modernization, 377; settlement with government, 136; Stephen on, 185–186; through 1883, summarized, 112
Financing, government, of lines competing with C.P.R., 288. See also Canadian National Railways; Canadian Northern; Grand Trunk Pacific; National Transcontinental Railway
Fires, danger of, on C.P.R. mountain lines, 139
First-class cars, Van Horne appointments, 142–143
First-class service, on shipping lines, 325
First World War, and C.P.R. shipping, 279–280, 286–287; effects on C.P.R. rail traffic, 280–281; freight rates and wages, Canadian, during, 282–286; role of C.P.R. staff in, 281–282
Fish, Hamilton, 12, 20
Fixed charges, C.P.R., 276, 334, 353
Flavelle, Sir Joseph, 296, 328; quoted, 291–292
Fleming, Sandford (later Sir Sandford), 7, 19, 64, 118, 135; dies, 238; endorses Rogers Pass route, 117; surveys, 36, 37, 38, 50, 81
Floods, in British Columbia, 188
"Flying Wing," 86
Fording Coal Limited, 398–399
Fort Garry. See Winnipeg
Fort William, 46
Foster, Senator Asa B., 28, 51
Fowke, Vernon C., 390
Freight cars, C.P.R., 267, 308, 317–318, 343, 344; bought after Second World War, 372; grain, 426–427; 1901 shortage, 230; since Second World War, 429–431

Freighters, C.P.R. transatlantic, 324, 361, 401, 404–406. *See also* Shipping; CP Ships
Freight rates, 302–304, 305–306, 360, 376–377, 378–381, 419; Canadian, East vs. West, 382–384; Canadian, equalization, 386; Canadian, subsidies granted to equalize, 384; changed since 1967, 427–428; C.P.R., and diversification, 390–392; C.P.R., during Second World War, 350, 352; C.P.R. as yardstick in setting, 384–386; effects of increased, 416; First World War period, 282–286; grain, 158, 159, 425–427; Manitoba, 156, 158–159, 164; reduction in, 231; under Crow's Nest Pass Agreement, 209–210. *See also* Crow's Nest Pass Agreement
Freight service, Van Horne on, 240–241
Freight traffic, C.P.R.: (1894), 188; increased by Second World War, 347–348; (1902–1913), 274*t*; (1912–1918), 280; (1923–1924), 309; (1938–1945), 348*t*
French Canadians, 13, 29–30, 71
French River, 46

Galt family, 164
Gas wells. *See* Canadian Pacific Oil and Gas Limited
General Motors, 367
George VI (king of England), 345
German liners, purchased by C.P., 301
Gibbon, Murray, quoted, 80, 125–126, 226
Gilmer, John C., 412
Glasgow, 405
Glass, David, 51
Globe (Toronto), 5, 15, 16, 34, 89
Glyn Mills, 71
Government-built rail lines, C.P.R., 136
Government, Canadian: air transport policy of, 359; guarantees C.P.R. land grant bonds, 163; loan to C.P.R., 109–111; and Short Line agreement, 169–170
Gradients, C.P.R., 117–18, 262–264
Grain crop (1939), 346
Grain-elevator policy, of C.P.R., 229–230
Grain elevators, 159–160
Grain freight rate. *See* Crow's Nest Pass Agreement; Freight rates, grain
Grain Growers' Guide, 293
Grain shipments: via C.P.R. (1882–1886), 159; via C.P.R. (1928), 318; via C.P.R., 1925–1937, summarized; via C.P.R. (1966–1967) and CP Rail (1971–1972), 427
Grain trade, importance of, 303–305
"Grain watershed," 305
Granby Company, 236
Grand Trunk Pacific, 232, 288–296, 297

Grand Trunk Railway, 2, 3–4, 6, 96–97, 109, 132, 288; buys Montreal-Quebec North Shore Line, 101; and C.P.R., 28, 90, 95, 98, 99–101, 102, 132–133, 165–167, 190–191; and nationalization, 290–295, 297; projects transcontinental line, 231–232; Stephen on, 185–186; and transatlantic shipping lines, 240; and trans-Canada railway, 68–70. *See also* Canadian National Railways
Grant, G. M., quoted, 37
Grant, General U.S., 12
Great Central of Canada Company, 98, 99–101
Great Eastern Railway, 310
Great Lakes fleet, C.P.R., 105–106
Great Lakes Paper Company, 396
Great Northern Railroad, 106–107, 177, 205, 236–238; and Spokane Falls and Northern Railway, 208. *See also* Burlington Northern Railroad; Hill, James J.; St. Paul, Minneapolis and Manitoba
Great North West Central Railway, 234, 257
Great Western Railway, 96–97
Greenway, Thomas, 163
Grenfell, Pasco du P., 71
"Grits." *See* Liberal party
Guaranteed-dividend plan, for C.P.R., 107–109
Guarantee fund, for C.P.R., 184–185

Halifax, 150, 169, 172–173, 320
Hamilton, Lauchlan A., 220, 221
Haney, Michael, 212
Hanna, D. B., 310–311
Harris, Sir Arthur, 279
Hays, Charles M., 193, 231
Hedges, James, 224; quoted, 253
Heinze, Augustus F., 205–207, 259
Helmcken, Dr. J. S., 13–14
Herald (Montreal), 34
Hickson, Joseph, 95, 97, 102, 166, 190; and C.P.R. "surrender" to Grand Trunk, 99
Hill, James J., 55–56, 78, 79, 91, 156, 161, 431; conflict with Van Horne, 202–204; and C.P.R. "syndicate," 71–72; dies, 238; and early stages of C.P.R., 77–83; "invades" British Columbia, 205, 208; and purchase of St. Paul and Pacific, 59–63; relations with C.P.R., 195–197, 201–206, 236–238; sells C.P.R. stock, 112; and Soo Line, 167; valuation of St. Paul and Pacific, 59; and Van Horne's retirement, 225; withdrawal from C.P.R., 106–107
Hincks, Sir Francis, 23, 24, 25, 34–35

INDEX

Hind, Henry Youle, 6–7
Holidays, paid, won by Canadian railway workers, 378
Holmes, W. H., quoted, 122
Holt, Herbert S., 120–121, 177
Home lines, 401–402
Homestead Act, 216–217
Horetzky, Charles, 38
Horsey, A. W., 270–271
Hosmer, B. C., mine, 258–259
Hotels, C. N., 322
Hotels, C. P. R., 143, 180–183, 273–274, 322, 337, 392–393; in Second World War, 354. *See also* Canadian Pacific Hotels Limited; Empress Hotel; Hotel Vancouver; Royal York; names beginning Château
Hotel Vancouver, 182, 222, 273, 333, 392
Howe, Hon. C. D., 356, 359, 364
Howe, Joseph, quoted, 4
Huddart, James, 241
Huddart, Parker and Company, 241
Hudson Bay, 4
Hudson Bay railway, 161
Hudson locomotives, 345, 348–349
Hudson River, 2
Hudson's Bay Company, 2, 4, 6, 9–10, 11, 253; and Red River Transportation Company, 56; and settlement in West, 55; trading rights, 5
Huntington, Lucius C., 34, 58

Image, C. P. R., 415–416
Immigration, 251, 324; from Britain, 254; Canadian, after First World War, 315–316; from Ireland, 218–219; from U.S., 252, 254
Imperial Limited, 180
Indebtedness, bonded, of C. P. R., 353
Indians, 87–88
Intercolonial Railway, 42, 169, 173, 177–178, 292, 297, 384. *See also* Canadian National Railways
International Mercantile Marine, 248
International Railway Company of Canada, 169–172
International Railway of Maine, 172
Interoceanic Railway Company, 28, 30–33
Interprovincial and James Bay line, 257
Investment, C. P. R. return on, 386
Irrigation project, C. P. R., in Alberta, 252–254, 255, 339
Island Freight Services, 382

Japan, C. P. air service to, 364
Jason C. Pierce, 146
Jay Cooke and Company, 26, 33, 35. *See also* Cooke, Jay

Jervis Bay, 354, 355
Jet aircraft, 365, 410–412
Jiskoot, Allard, 93
Job security, and C. P. R., 417, 419–420
Johnson, John, 323, 361
Jones, Sir Alfred, 245
J. S. Kennedy and Company, 108. *See also* Kennedy, John S.

Kaiser Resources Limited, 398
Kamloops. *See* Kicking Horse Pass route; Yale-Kamloops line
Kamloops Lake, 65
Kaslo and Slocan Railway, 205, 238
Kellock, R. L., 380
Kennedy, John S., 59, 60, 62, 71, 72, 93, 100; sells C. P. R. stock, 112. *See also* J. S. Kennedy and Company
Kettle Valley Railway, 207–208, 237
Kicking Horse Pass route, 79–81, 87, 116, 266
King, W. L. Mackenzie, 327
Kittson, Norman, 55, 56, 71, 156; and purchase of St. Paul and Pacific, 59–61, 62
Klondike gold rush, 190, 241
Kohn, Reinach and Company, 71
Kootenay and Elk Railway, 431
Kootenay Central Railway, 237
Kootenay Coal Company, 210–211
Kootenay region, 198–200, 205–208, 210–212, 259–260, 398–399, 430–431; land grants, 257–258
Kuhn, Loeb and Company, 93

Laborers, mistreatment of, Crowsnest line construction, 212
Lachine Bridge, 97, 98, 99
Lacombe (Oblate missionary), 87–88
La Compagnie du Chemin à Rails du Saint-Laurent et du village d'Industrie, 134
Laidlaw, George, 95, 96, 97
Lake Louise, 143, 273
Lake Manitoba Railway and Canal Company, 194
Lake Nipissing, 22, 46, 66, 76
Lake steamers, 245, 246
Lake Superior and Winnipeg Railway, 57
Land companies, 217–218, 224
Land dealings, C.P.R., 257*t*
Land grant acquired by C.P.R., with Manitoba South Western Colonization Railway, 157–158
Land-grant bonds, C.P.R., offered, 89
Land grants: in British Columbia, 210–211; Columbia and Western Railway, 213
Land grants, C.P.R., 70, 73–74, 393, 257*t*–

Land grants, C.P.R. (cont'd)
258; final settlement, 251; original purpose of, 216; reduced and supplemented, 222; selection of, 215–216, 218, 223
Land grants: to U.S. railways, 215; in Vancouver, 182
Land sales, C.P.R., 216–218, 219–222, 251–252, 253–255, 256, 258, 339; cancellations, 255; improvement in (1897–1899), 224
Lansdowne, Lord, 135
Last-spike ceremony, 134–135
Laurentian Shield, 4, 5, 36, 50
Laurentian Shield line. *See* Thunder Bay Line
Laurier, Sir Wilfrid, 193, 209, 230, 231–232, 296
Lavallée, Omer, quoted, 147, 270, 344
Leduc field, 388
Lefroy, Lieutenant Colonel, 6
Lethbridge Collieries Limited, 259
Lethbridge-Dunmore line, 164
Liberal party, 15–16, 30, 39, 192, 193, 320; counteroffer to Stephen's, 76; debate on C.P.R. contract, 75–76; hostile to C.P.R., 90; and "Pacific Scandal," 33; and Thornton, 327; and Yale-Kamloops controversy, 140
Litchfield, E. B., 59
Liverpool (England), 246–247, 405
Livestock shipments, 228
Locomotives, C.P.R., 145–146, 147, 270–272, 307–308, 317, 319–320, 342, 343, 349; compound, 179; consolidation-type, 118; diesel electric, 342, 349, 367–370, 375; last steam, 368–369; steam and diesel electric compared, 367, 370–371; upgrading since 1963, 429
London (England) Hotel Project, C.P.R., 321
London money market: and C.P.R., 35, 71, 93; and C.P.R.-Grand Trunk feud, 99; and 1885 crisis, 132; and 1888 land-grant bonds, 163; and Great Central proposal, 100; and Northern Pacific, 23; and trans-Canada railway, 65
"Loop," 120

Macdonald, Sir John A., 8, 12, 13, 15, 16, 19, 51, 55, 169, 178; and American capital for trans-Canada railway, 22–24; and C.P.R. contract, 75–76; and C.P.R. crisis of 1885, 128, 131, 132; financing construction of trans-Canada railway, 64–70; government loan for C.P.R., 109–112; and monopoly clause, 162–163; and Northwest Rebellion, 131; political rebirth of, 53; quoted, 27; and Railway Act of 1872, 28; reconciliation with Donald Smith, 112–113; role in "Pacific Scandal," 31–35; and Stephen, 174–175; and Treaty of Washington, 25; and uniform franchise bill, 131–132; vs. Allan on trans-Canada railway, 26; and Yale-Kamloops line controversy, 140
Mackenzie, Alexander, 15–16, 17, 36, 192; assumptions on trans-Canada railway project, 42–43; awards Pembina branch contracts, 45; construction and survey costs under, 51–52; and Edward Blake, 46–48; and 1878 election, 53; and Lord Dufferin, 48–49; as minister of public works, 39; quoted, 2, 51
Mackenzie (Sir William) and Mann (Donald), 121, 172, 177, 193–194, 248, 289–291; line to Thunder Bay, 230–231
Mackenzie, Sir William. *See* Mackenzie and Mann
Mackintosh, W. A., quoted, 384
Macmillan Bloedel Limited, 396, 399, 407
MacNab, Sir Allan quoted, 15
Macoun, John, 79, 223
MacPherson Commission, 417–419, 426
Macpherson, Senator David L., 26, 27, 35, and trans-Canada railway, 28; vs. Allan, 30
MacPherson, M. A., 417
Maine Central Railway, 172
Main line, C.P.R.: construction completed, 134; substandard condition of, 137–138; Van Horne inspects, 126–127. *See also* Construction; Surveys
Maintenance, C.P.R.: deferred during Second World War, 371–372; mechanized, 431
Maintenance of Railway Operation Act, 380
Manchester Liners, 405
Manion, R. J., 327
Manitoba, 19–20, 162; agitation against C.P.R., 158–159, 161–164; government aids Canadian Northern, 230–231; and independent rail lines, 157; seeks competition for C.P.R., 230–231
Manitoba and North Western Railway, 158, 257
Manitoba Grain Act, 229
Manitoba Junction Railway, 57
Manitoba North Western Railway, 234
Manitoba South Eastern Railway, 231
Manitoba South Western Colonization Railway, 157, 164, 257; land grant, 222
Mann, Donald. *See* Mackenzie and Mann
Marathon Realty Company Limited, 389, 393–396

INDEX

Maritime Provinces, 111, 131, 169–170, 384; freight rates, 305; freight subsidy, 384
Martin, Joseph, 163–164
Martinson, R. V., 93
Mather, William A., 368, 375, 435; quoted, 377, 381
"McAdoo Award," 283–285, 302
McAdoo, William G., 282
McConachie, Grant, 357–359, 363–365, 410, 411
McEwen, Grant and Company, 35
McGee, Thomas D'Arcy, quoted, 8
McIntyre, Duncan, 67, 77, 79, 96; and Atlantic line, 168; and formation of C.P.R., 70–72; withdraws from C.P.R., 112
McMullen, George W., 23, 26, 51; and "Pacific Scandal," 32–34
McTavish, John, 218
McVittie, A. W., 230
Meighen, Arthur, 297
Metal mining, 396–398
Métis, 10, 12, 130
Metro Centre (Toronto), 395
Mexico, air service to, 365
Michel Loop, 211
Michigan Central Railway, 101, 235–236
Michipicoten River, 113
Midland group of short lines, 97
Mineral rights, C.P.R. land, 260–261
Mining: in British Columbia, 198; Hill's participation in, 236–237
Minneapolis, St. Paul and Sault Ste. Marie. See Soo Line; Soo Line Railroad Company
Minnesota Southern, Van Horne on, quoted, 159
Miowera ("Weary Mary"), 241
Missanabie, 286
Moberly, Walter, 38, 134
Mohawk River, 2
"Monopoly clause," of C.P.R. contract, 74, 75–76, 156–157; ended, 163; Manitoban resentment against, 158–159, 160–161, 163–164; Macdonald on, 162–163
Monopoly in transportation, fear of in Manitoba, 156
Montreal, 19, 22, 107; C.P.R. buildings, 180, 183; C.P.R. gains entry into, 90; C.P.R. shops in, 272; as trade center, 2
Montreal-Ottawa line, C.P.R., 177
Montreal-Toronto line, C.P.R., 165
Montrose, 355
"Morgan Combine," 248
Morin, A. N., 6
Morris, Alexander, quoted, 156
Mortgage bonds: and C.P.R., 89; C.P.R. issue (1885), 132; Stephen proposes for C.P.R., 128. *See also* Bonds
Morton, Bliss and Company, 71
Morton, Rose and Company, 71, 100, 102
Mountains, named for C.P.R. builders, 137
Mount Stephen, Lord. *See* Stephen, George
Munitions, made by C.P.R., 281, 354
Musk, George, quoted, 355
Muskegs, 50
Myers, Gustavus, 62, 63

Nakusp and Slocan Railway, 205, 238
Narrow gauge lines, 16, 177, 198, 206, 238. *See also* North Western Coal and Navigation Co.
National Harbours Board, 406
Nationalization of railways, becomes government policy, 288–293, 296; C.P.R. proposed for inclusion, 292–294; reports on by Royal Commission, 294–295. *See also* Canadian National Railways; Canadian Northern; Grand Trunk Railway; Grand Trunk Pacific; Intercolonial Railway; National Transcontinental Railway
National Labour Board, 352
National Policy, 53
National Transcontinental Railway, 232, 289–290, 297. *See also* Canadian National Railways
National Transportation Act (1967), 419, 425–426, 427, 430; Canadian government subsidies, 421, 422–424
Neal, William M., 357, 363–364, 368
Nelson, B. C., 200, 201, 205, 208, 209, 212
Nelson and Fort Sheppard Railway, 201
New Brunswick, 231–232
New Brunswick Railways, 172
Newcastle, Duke of, 5–6
New Westminster Southern, 197
New Whatcom, 197
Nipissing line, C.P.R., 127, 167; construction of, 105, 113–115. *See also* Thunder Bay line
Norquay, John, 156–157
North American Railway Contracting Company, 92–93, 108
Northern Alberta Railways, 313
Northern and Pacific Junction Railway, 166
Northern Colonization Railway, 21–22, 257
Northern, Northwestern and Sault Ste. Marie. *See* Northern and Pacific Junction Railway
Northern Pacific and Manitoba Railway, 163–164, 231
Northern Pacific Railroad, 13, 20, 24–25, 32–33, 60, 90, 157, 163–164; bankruptcy (1873), 35; forced into receivership

Northern Pacific Railroad (*cont'd*) (1893), 201; founded, 11; and "international" transcontinental route, 26–27; Jay Cooke becomes agent for, 12; and London money market, 23; prospectus of issue of land grant bonds, 27; and St. Paul and Pacific receivership, 56; and Sir Hugh Allan, 22, 26; and Spokane Falls and Northern Railway, 208
Northern Pacific Railway Company (Canada), 6
North Shore Line, 102, 132–133. *See also* Quebec, Montreal, Ottawa and Occidental Railway
North Shore Railway, 182
North West Air Staging Route, 358
Northwest Colonization Company, 252
North West Company, 2, 4
North Western Coal and Navigation Company, 164, 204–205
North-West Irrigation Act, 223
North-West Mounted Police, 87–88, 105, 132, 212
Northwest Rebellion, 130, 131
North-West Transportation Company, 105
Nova Scotia, 235
No. 8000 (steam engine), 343–344
Nos. 901 and 902 (freight trains), 432

Oblate mission, 87–88
Observation cars, 180
Ogden, W. B., 23, 26
Ogden shops (Calgary), 272–273, 354
Oil wells. *See* Canadian Pacific Oil and Gas Limited
OK Valley Freight Lines, 382
Oldman River, 211, 263–264
Onderdonk, Andrew, 65, 70, 121–123, 134, 212
Ontario, 26, 166, 234
Ontario and Pacific Junction Railway, 76
Ontario and Quebec Railway, 96, 98, 99, 100, 101; joint lease, 102–103
Operating ratio, C.P.R., 274, 285, 368
Orient service, CP, 149, 151, 152, 153
Osler, E. B., 92, 96, 97
Osler, Hammond and Nanton, 256
Ottawa, 22, 78
Owen Sound, 106
Owen Sound and Port Arthur shipping service, C.P.R., 239

Pacific Express, 143
Pacific Logging Company Limited, 389, 396
Pacific railway. *See* Trans-Canada railway
"Pacific Scandal," 29–35
Palliser, Captain John, 5

Palliser Square (Calgary), 394
Panama Canal, 304–305
Pan Arctic Oils Limited, 392
Pan-Canadian Petroleum Limited, 392
P & O Line, 149
Paris money market, and C.P.R., 71
Parliament, and C.P.R., 111, 128, 131–132. *See also* Conservative party; Government; Liberal party; Politics
Passenger cars, C.P.R., 267–270, 319, 342, 372–373, 374–375
Passenger service, C.P.R.: rail, 143, 373–375, 421–425; transatlantic, 324–325, 361–363, 401–404
Passenger traffic profits, C.P.R., 274
Passenger traffic, rail, 318, 349–350
Payments, Canadian government, to railways for "national interest" operations, 418–419, 425
Pearce, Sir William, 151–152
Pembina branch, 45–46, 48, 58, 61, 73, 236; unpopularity with Manitobans, 155–156
Pembina Mountain branch, 157
Pension plan, C.P.R., 421
Peru, air service to, 365
Petroleum, C.P.R. resources, 260–261
Pickersgill, J. W., 411
Pierson, J. L., 93
Piggyback service, 382, 430
Pine Point, 398
Pipelines, 399, 429
Place du Canada (Montreal), 394
Place Viger (Montreal), 183
Political patronage, 29–33, 51
Politics: and Canadian railways, 15–17; C.P.R. and public involvement in, 192–193
Pope, John Henry, 67, 109, 128, 140, 169, 170; quoted, 63; on Yale-Kamloops line, 139–140
Port Arthur, 105, 160, 231
Port Arthur and Owen Sound shipping service, C.P.R., 239
Portland, Maine, 168–169
Port Moody (B.C.), 124, 125
Potter, Richard, quoted, 95
Prairie Provinces, 311–314, 383, 427. *See also* Grain; Western Canada
Preferred shares, C.P.I., 399
Press attacks on C.P.R., 89, 90
Price, Bruce, 180, 182–183
Prince Rupert, 242
Princess steamers, 243, 286, 322, 408
Private enterprise, and trans-Canada railway construction, 66
Profit center concept, 389, 416
Profit centers, 436

INDEX

Project 200 (Vancouver), 394–395
"Provision magazines," 145
Puleston, Brown and Company, 70

Qu'Appelle, Long Lake and Saskatchewan Railroad and Steamboat Company, 177
Quebec City, 111, 131, 133, 231–232. *See also* Château Frontenac
Quebec Conferences of 1943 and 1944, 354
Quebec, Montreal, Ottawa and Occidental Railway, 90, 101

Rail, weight of, C.P.R., 308
Rail networks, in Canada, 1–2, 3
Rails, welded, 431
"Railtainer" cars, 405, 406
Railway Act (Canada), 386
Railway Act of 1872, 28
"Railway belt" (B.C.), 124
Railway charters, 18
Railway Labor Board (U.S.), 306
Railway Operations Continuation Act, 419
Ramsay, Prof. G. G., on runaway trains, 118–119
Red Mountain Railway, 206
Red River, 5, 6
Red River settlement, 10
Red River Transportation Company, 56, 156
Red River Valley Railway, 161, 163
Reed, S. B., 127
Regina (Saskatchewan), 86, 177, 320
Revenues: Canadian Pacific (Bermuda) Limited, 408; of C.P.R. shipping lines, 325. *See also:* Earnings picture, C.P.R.
Richardson, James, 356
Riel, Louis, 10, 130
Riel resistance, 19, 20, 30, 55
Rio Algom Mines, 399
Roadbed improvement, C.P.R., 177–178
Roberts Bank (deep-sea bulk terminal), 430–431
Robot control, 430
Rogers, Major A. B., 79–80, 116–117, 127, 135
Rogers Pass, 265–266
Rogers Pass riot, 132
Rogers Pass route, 117, 119
Rolling stock, C.P.R., 159, 272–273, 307–308, 311–318, 341–344, 372; (1881 and 1889), 148; increase in (1888–1889), 179–180; and Shaughnessy, 267–268. *See also* Freight cars; Locomotives; Passenger cars; Sleeping cars
Rose, Sir John, 27, 49, 71, 97, 99–100
Ross, James, 120, 135, 177
Ross, John, 114, 127
Rosser, General, 219

Rosser, Thomas L., 78, 82, 83
Royal Commission on Railways and Transportation (1931–1932), and C.P.R., 328–330
Royal York Hotel (Toronto), 321, 337, 392–393
Running rights, 165, 166–167
Rupert's Land, 4, 9–10, 13, 55

Safety devices, 180
St. Boniface, 49
Saint John (New Brunswick), 406
St. Lawrence and Ottawa Railway, 134
Saint Lawrence Seaway, 428
St. Lawrence waterway, 2, 3
St. Luc marshaling yard, 372
St. Paul (Minn.), 5, 10, 202
St. Paul and Pacific Railroad, 20, 54, 55; Hill's valuation of, 60; and Northern Pacific receivership, 56; physical and financial condition of (1874), 58–59; purchase of, 59–63. *See also* St. Paul, Minneapolis and Manitoba Railroad Company
St. Paul, Minneapolis and Manitoba Railroad Company, 62, 66–67, 106–107, 156, 177, 196, 201; organized, 61–62. *See also* Great Northern Railroad
Saint Paul, Minneapolis and Sault Ste. Marie, 414. *See also* Soo Line; Soo Line Railroad Company
St. Paul-Winnipeg railway proposed, 6, 20, 43. *See also* Pembina branch
St. Paul-Winnipeg steamers, 56
Salaries, of C.P.R. directors and officers (1883), 107
Sandon, C.P.R. depot dumped by rivals at, 205
Sante Fe *Chief* and *Super Chief*, 366–367
Saskatchewan, 228
Saskatchewan and Western line, 257
Sault-Ste. Marie, line to, 24–25, 165, 166–167
Sault Ste. Marie Railway and Bridge Company, 23
Schreiber, Collingwood, 114
Schwitzer, John E., 264–265
Scott, Thomas, 10
Seargeant, Lewis, 190
Second World War, 346–361; and CP Air facilities, 356–359; and C.P.R. facilities, 354; and C.P.R. finances, 352–353; and C.P.R. shipping losses, 354–356; and ocean shipping, 346–347; and railway employment, 350–352; and railway traffic, 347–350
Secretan, J. H. E., quoted, 84, 117
Selkirk (Manitoba), 39, 49, 65

Selkirk Range, 116–117; problems of, 119–120; Van Horne traverses, 127
Selkirks (locomotives), 368–369
Settlement. *See* Immigration
Shaughnessy, Thomas George (later Lord Shaughnessy), 83–84, 132, 172, 176, 182, 191, 258, 259, 325; and Allan Line, 248; becomes C.P.R. president, 225; and C.P.R. financing, 275–278; and C.P.R. irrigation project, 253; and C.P.R. rolling stock, 267–268; and CP steamer service, 243–246; death of, 299; and expansion of CP rail system, 227–228, 233–236, 237; and First World War, 279–281; and improvements to C.P.R. rail lines, 262–263, 264–265; miscalculations on Panama Canal, 305; and nationalization of competing lines, 290–299; on National Transcontinental Railway, 290; quoted, 321–322, 388; retirement, 277, 298; and sleeping cars, 268–270; temperament of, 226; valedictory address, 255–256
Shell Canada, 428
ShelPac Research and Development Limited, 429
Shepard, D. C., 85–87
Shipping connections, Atlantic, sought for C.P.R., 149–150, 154, 168, 169
Shipping, C.P.R., 239–251, 300–302, 323–325, 337–338, 401–405, 410; Atlantic, 149, 150, 168, 337; cruise business, 337–338; during First World War, 279–280, 286–287; losses in Second World War, 354–356; role in Second World War, 346; transatlantic, 323–325, 361–363, 402–404; transpacific, dropped, 362–363. *See also* Canadian Pacific (Bermuda) Limited; Great Lakes fleet, C.P.R.; Orient service; Shipping; CP Ships
Shipping: CP Ships, 405–406; Pacific, 406–407; projected British Europe-Orient route and C.P.R., 148–154
Shops, C.P.R. *See* Angus shops; Ogden shops; Weston shops; Winnipeg shops
"Short Line," 168, 169–173, 235
Shuswap and Okanagan Railway, 200
Sifton and Ward, 46
Sifton, Sir Clifford, 209, 210, 212, 228, 232
Sifton, J. W., 51
Signals, automatic block, 372
Simpson, Sir George, quoted, 140
Sinclair, Ian D., 414, 436
Skelton, O. D., quoted, 226
Sleeping cars, 101, 142–143, 268–270, 425
Smelters, 205
Smith, A. H., 294–295

Smith, Charles M., 23, 24, 26, 34
Smith, Donald A. (later Lord Strathcona), 27, 28, 54–55, 56–57, 60, 108, 127, 134, 135, 150, 156, 182; and C.P.R. contract, 71–72; and C.P.R. "syndicate," 70–72; dies, 238; and 1885 crisis, 128; holdings in Hill roads, 107; and Kicking Horse Pass route, 80; official honors, 137; and "Pacific Scandal," 33–34; and purchase of St. Paul and Pacific, 61, 62; relations with Stephen, 112–113; and St. Paul, Minneapolis and Manitoba, 196; and Soo Line, 167
Smith, Senator Frank, 130
Smith, J. Gregory, 11, 28
Smith, Marcus, 38, 52
Smithe, William, 124
Smithers, C. F., quoted, 109
Smith Transport Limited, 415
Soo Line, 167–168, 188, 202, 235, 334–336
Soo Line Railroad Company, 415
Souris branch, 158, 222, 257
South Eastern Railway, 97, 99, 101, 169, 171–172
Southern route to West Coast, completed by C.P.R., 237. *See also* Crowsnest Pass line
Speculation, in C.P.R. land, 219, 254–255
"Spite line," 236
Spokane (Wash.), 198–200
Spokane Falls and Northern Railway, 200, 206, 208
Spokane International Railway, 237, 334
Steamers. *See* Shipping
Steerage passengers. *See* Third-class steamer passengers
Stephen, George (later Baron Mount Stephen), 58, 79, 94–103, 108, 134, 172; assesses condition of main line, 137; and associates put up money to help C.P.R., 91–92; and Atlantic line, 168–170, 172–173; authority of, in C.P.R., 195–196; conflict with Van Horne, 203–204; contracts to build C.P.R., 70–72, 74–77; and C.P.R. crisis of 1885, 127, 128–130, 131–132; and C.P.R. expansion in East, 165–166; on C.P.R. financial history, 185–186; death of, 299; and Donald Smith, 112–113; doubts about Port Moody, 124; and Duluth and Winnipeg, 202–204; and early financing of C.P.R., 88–93; efforts to interest Britain in emigration scheme, 214–215, 218–219; and 1884 crisis, 110–111; and Grand Trunk difficulties, 191; and guaranteed dividend plan, 107–109; holdings in Hill roads, 107; joint cable with Tyler on

INDEX

Grand Trunk "surrender," 99; and land grants, 216–219; letter to Grand Trunk shareholders, 99; loses faith in C.P.R., 189; loses original C.P.R. "team," 112–113; and Macdonald, 174–175; and "monopoly clause," 156, 161–163; and negotiations on building C.P.R., 66, 67–68; official honors, 137; and purchase of St. Paul and Pacific, 60–61, 62–63; quoted, 81–82, 101, 106; resigns, 173; retirement, 175; seeks government loan (1883), 109–111; and St. Paul, Minneapolis and Manitoba, 196; and Sault Ste. Marie connections, 167; and steamship service, 148–150, 152, 154, 239–240; and Van Horne, 183, 225; and Yale-Kamloops line, 140
Stevens, G. R., quoted, 101
Stickney, Alpheus B., 78, 82, 83, 219
Stock, C.P.R., 18, 183–184, 276; reaches low in 1895, 189
Strathcona, Lord. *See* Smith, Donald A.
Strikes: Brotherhood of Locomotive Engineers (1893), 104–105; Canadian railway workers (1926), 307, (1950), 379–381, 382, (1973), 421; C.P.R. (1966), 419; C.P.R. fireman (1957–1958), 421; and C.P.R. shipping services, 404, 405
Strike threats, railway (1947–1954), 378
Subsidiaries, C.P.R., 389–400
Subsidies, 436–437, 438
Sullivan Mine, 260, 397, 398
Super Continental, 424
Superheaters, 343; Schmidt, 271
Surprise Creek, accident at, 432
Surveys, 116–118, 211; costs under Mackenzie, 52; for C.P.R., 79, 80–81, 123; expenditures on, 49; Fleming's, 36, 37, 38, 50, 81; for trans-Canada railway, 25
"Syndicate," C.P.R., defined, 70–72

Tankers, 407
Tartar, 242
Taxation, C.P.R., 285
Taylor, James W., 19–20
Telecommunications, CP, 416
Telegraph service, C.P.R., 141
Territorial Grain Growers' Association, 230
Third-class steamer passengers, 247, 324–325
Thompson, Sir John, 178
Thomson, Don W., quoted, 36
Thornton, Sir Henry, 310, 326–327, 329; and CN, 311; resigns, 330; rivalry with C.P.R., 317; and unification with C.P.R., 329
Thunder Bay-Canadian Northern line, 230

Thunder Bay line, C.P.R., 81–82, 262, 384; sale to government proposed, 232. *See also* Nipissing line
Ties, treated, 309
Tilbury, England, 405, 406
Tilley, Sir Leonard, 91–92, 128
Timber lands, C.P.R., 389, 395–396. *See also* Pacific Logging Company Limited
Toronto, 5, 19, 321; and C.P.R. "syndicate," 76. *See also* Metro Centre, Royal York
Toronto Board of Trade, quoted, 76
Toronto-Callander line, 166
Toronto, Grey and Bruce Railway, 96, 101, 105
Tourist-class steamer service, C.P.R., 324–325, 401–402
Townsites, C.P.R., and land speculation, 219
Tracks, summer and winter, C.P.R., 139
Traffic, C.P.R., 148, 267, 435
Trail smelter, 259. *See also* Consolidated Mining and Smelting Company
Trans-Canada Airlines, 356–357, 359, 364, 410, 411. *See also* Air Canada
Trans-Canada Highway, 361, 381, 422
TransCanada Pipe Lines, 399
Trans-Canada railway: financing of, 25–28, 35, 65, 66–71; private enterprise sought for construction, 43–44; surveys for, 36–39; U.S. capital and, 19, 23–24, 26–28, 30–33
Trans-Canada railway project, 4–7, 11, 13–19, 25–28, 30–31
Trans-Canada telegraph line, 45, 49
Trans-Canada wagon road, 13–14, 42, 45
Transcontinental lines, sought by Canadian Northern and Grand Trunk, 231
Transcontinental railway, proposed, "international route," 6, 11–12, 22–25, 26–27, 75–76, 81
Transportation, competing forms of, 380–382
Treaty of Washington, 25, 30
Troup, Captain J. W., 243–244
Trucking, 381, 382, 425
Trutch, J. W., 13, 48; quoted, 16–17
Truth, quoted, 89
Tunnels, spiral, 263
Tupper, Sir Charles, 64–68, 71, 100, 133, 169; and C.P.R. crises, 110–111, 128
Turboprop aircraft, 410
Tyler, Sir Henry, 68, 95, 97, 109, 132, 190–191, 193; attack on C.P.R., 98–99; and Great Central proposal, 100

Unger and Company, 108
Unions, 340, 377–380, 416–417

Union Steam Ship Company, 241, 338
United States: capital and trans-Canada railway, 23–24, 26–28, 30–33; competition for transatlantic shipping, 240–241; expansionism, 7–8, 11–13, 14, 16, 19–20; subsidiaries and C.P.R., 334–336; wages in, 307
Unit trains, 430–431
Unwin, L. B., 357, 359

Vancouver, 322; C.P.R. and C.N.R. hotels in, 333; C.P.R. real estate in, 182, 183; C.P.R. steamer service inaugurated, 152; as grain shipping center, 305; headquarters of CP Air Lines, 365; most profitable C.P.R. townsite, 221–222; named by Van Horne, 125–126; and service to Orient, 149; as Western terminus of C.P.R., 124–125. *See also* Hotel Vancouver; Project 200
Vancouver, Captain George, 125–126
Vancouver-Granville fire, 221
Vancouver Island, 38, 44, 235, 395–396
Vancouver townsite, 257–258
Vancouver, Victoria and Eastern Railway and Navigation Company, 207
Vanderbilt interests, and Soo Line, 167
Van Horne, William Cornelius (later Sir William), 82–86, 88–89, 113, 117, 172, 174; advocates various C.P.R. services, 141; and "Battle of Fort Whyte," 164; and Columbia and Western Railway, 206–207; contribution to C.P.R., 191–192; and C.P.R. architecture, 180–183; and C.P.R. hotel system, 143; and C.P.R. "surrender" to Grand Trunk, 99; dies, 235; economy measures of, 127; and 1884 crisis, 104–107; and 1894 crisis, 188; on emergency provisions, 144–145; and *Empress* ships, 154; and expansion in East, 165–166; and food, 132; on freight service, 240; and grain elevator network, 159–160; and Great Central proposal, 100–101; on high costs of government-built lines, 136–137; inspects main line, 126–127; and Kettle Valley, 207–208; knighted, 190, 194; and last-spike ceremony, 134–135; and liquor sales to construction crews, 113–114; and locomotive building, 146; names Craigellachie, 134; negotiates for Vancouver terminus, 124–125; and Northwest Rebellion, 130; official honors, 137; personal attention to C.P.R. sleeping cars, 142–143; and politics, 192–193; proposed as Grand Trunk president, 191; quoted, 1, 102; relationship with Stephen, 195–196, 203–204; response to possible competition in British Columbia, 200–201; retires as president, 225; rivalry with Hill, 196–197, 201–206; seeks economy in C.P.R. construction, 114; temperament, 225–226; and transatlantic freight service, 245; on Yale-Kamloops line, 140
Vaughan, H. H., 270–271
Vickes Express Company, 142
Victoria, B. C., 44, 65. *See also* Empress Hotel

Wabash Railway, 235
Waddington, Alfred, 18–19, 23, 24
Wage cuts, C.P.R., 340
Wage negotiations, C.P.R. role in joint, 377, 385
Wage raise, won by Canadian railwaymen (1948), 378–379
Wages, Canadian railway, 416, 418; First World War period, 282–284, 286; relation to freight rates, 377–379; Second World War period, 350–352; (1920–1926), 306–307
Walkem, George A., 44–45, 48, 52, 261, 368, 375
Wall Street Daily News, quoted, 109
Waterloo and Magog Railway, 171–172
Watkin, Edward, quoted, 4, 6
Weather conditions: effects on C.P.R. lines, 138–139; and 1880s depression, 219; and grain traffic, 336; provisions for dealing with snow, 144–145; and Rogers Pass, 265; winter, effects of, 432–433
Western Canada, continuing hostility to C.P.R., 382–384
Western Lines, CP Rail, traffic increases, 433–434
West Kootenay Power and Light Company, 260
Weston shops (Winnipeg), 272–273, 287
Wheat: strains of, 228–229; world demand for, 426–427
Whitehead, Joseph, 45, 46, 49, 50, 51
White Star Line, 248
White, Thomas, 290, 291, 293
Whyte, William, 164, 230
Willingdon branch, 312
Wilson, Sir Charles Rivers, 193
Windsor Street Station (Montreal), 180, 183, 273, 395
Winnipeg, 20, 39, 258, 273; affected by trans-Canada route change, 65; concessions to C.P.R., 79; construction headquarters, 78; land sales center, 254; and the Métis, 10
Winnipeg, Great Northern Railway, 194